A Framework for Human Resource Management

A Framework for Human Resource Management

THIRD EDITION

Gary Dessler

Florida International University

PEARSON

Prentice
Hall

Upper Saddle River, New Jersey 07458

Library of Congress Cataloging-in-Publication Data

Dessler, Gary‑
    A framework for human resource management / Gary Dessler.—3rd ed.
        p. cm.
    A complete multimedia and Internet-based learning package is available to supplement
the text.
    Includes bibliographical references and index.
    ISBN 0-13-144092-6
        1. Personnel management.   I. Title: Human resource management.   II. Title.

HF5549.D43788 2003
658.3—dc21

                                                    2003056542

Senior Editor: Jennifer Simon
Editor-in-Chief: Jeff Shelstad
Assistant Editor: Christine Genneken
Marketing Manager: Anke Braun
Marketing Assistant: Patrick Danzuso
Managing Editor (Production): John Roberts
Production Editor: Kelly Warsak
Production Assistant: Joe DeProspero

Permissions Supervisor: Suzanne Grappi
Manufacturing Buyer: Indira Gutierrez
Cover Design: Bruce Kenselaar
Cover Illustration: Robin Jareaux/Getty Images, Inc.
Composition/Full-Service Project Management: Interactive
    Composition Corporation/Brittney Corrigan-McElroy
Printer/Binder: Phoenix Color Corporation
Cover Printer: Phoenix Color Corporation

Credits and acknowledgments borrowed from other sources and reproduced, with
permission, in this textbook appear on appropriate page within text.

Pearson Education LTD.
Pearson Education Singapore, Pte. Ltd
Pearson Education, Canada, Ltd
Pearson Education–Japan

Pearson Education Australia PTY, Limited
Pearson Education North Asia Ltd
Pearson Educación de Mexico, S.A. de C.V.
Pearson Education Malaysia, Pte. Ltd

10 9 8 7 6
ISBN 0-13-144092-6

BRIEF CONTENTS

CONTENTS

PREFACE

A Framework for Human Resource Management provides students and practicing managers with a concise but thorough review of essential HR management concepts and techniques in a highly readable and understandable form. Adopters are using this book in many ways—as the textbook in introductory HR courses (as in intensive study abroad programs), in conjunction with exercises in applied HR courses, with complementary textbooks in courses blending several topics (such as HR and organization behavior), in specialized courses (such as "HR for high-tech companies"), and by practicing HR and line managers to update their HR-related skills. I am grateful to the professors, students, managers, and Prentice Hall sales associates who have helped make this a top-selling book, not only in English but also in several languages including Chinese.

Given this gratifying acceptance, you will find this new edition similar in most respects to edition 2. All managers have personnel-related responsibilities, so I've again aimed this book at all students of management, not just those who are or will be HR managers. The basic theme—to provide a concise but thorough review of core HR concepts and techniques—is unchanged. The table of contents and topic coverage is about the same.

However, in the interests of continuous improvement I have made several changes. The research and topics throughout all the chapters have, of course, been updated to reflect the latest findings and thinking in the HR field. In addition:

New *strategy openers* illustrate how that chapter's material relates to the company's strategic plan, and a new *HR framework* in each chapter summarizes the role of that chapter's material in the human resource management process.

A newly revised Chapter 9, *Ethics and Fair Treatment in Human Resource Management,* provides a comprehensive and practical explanation of how ethics and fair treatment underlie line and HR managers' HR-related decisions.

A revised Chapter 6, *Performance Management and Appraisal,* emphasizes the role of performance appraisal within the company's *performance management* efforts.

New and additional *end-of-chapter cases* provide additional opportunities for classroom analysis and discussions of HR management concepts and techniques.

A new *Managing HR Globally Module* provides an intense review of managing HR in a global enterprise.

No book like this ever reaches the light of day without the dedicated efforts of many people, and *Framework* is, of course, no exception. First, I want to acknowledge and thank the reviewers who took the time to make many very useful suggestions. The reviewers included Benjamin Bekhor, Pasadena City College; Rich Cober, Cleveland State University; Susan Gardner, California State University, Chico; Caren Goldberg, George Washington University; Kelly Anne Grace, Georgia Institute of Technology; MaryAnne Hyland, Adelphi University; Thomas Kanick, Broome Community College; Kathryn Lewis, California State University, Chico; Daniel O. Lybrook, Purdue University; Gwen Torkelson, Madison Area Technical College; Pamela R. Johnson, Ph.D., California State University, Chico; and Patrick McHugh, George Washington University.

I am very grateful to them all.

At Prentice Hall, I appreciate the efforts of all the professionals on the third edition team, including acquisitions editor Jennifer Simon, marketing manager Anka Braun, production editors Kelly Warsak and Brittney Corrigan-McElroy, and assistant editor Christine Genneken, and my debt continues to Natalie Anderson, who suggested I write what has become this very successful book. At home, I appreciate all my wife Claudia's support, and my son Derek's support, assistance, and practical suggestions.

Chapter 1

Managing Human Resources Today

- What Is Human Resource Management?
- The Changing Environment and Duties of HR Management
- HR's Strategic Challenges
- HR and Technology
- The Plan of This Book

When you finish studying this chapter, you should be able to:

- Answer *the question "What is human resource management?"*
- Discuss *the components of the changing environment of human resource management.*
- Describe *the nature of strategic planning.*
- Give *examples of human resource management's role as a strategic partner.*

INTRODUCTION

The first few years of the 21st century were rough for Dell Computer and the PC industry. To maintain its status as the world's number-one PC maker, Dell's average price per computer fell to about $2,000 in the first quarter of 2001, from about $2,300 the year before. Its profit margin fell from 21% to 18%. The only way it could keep that 18% margin intact while cutting prices was to find new ways to slash costs.[1] For a company that had always pursued a low-cost strategy, doing so wouldn't be easy. How could Dell cut costs from an already lean operation? The firm's HR managers had to find ways to support Dell's cost-cutting efforts.

1

WHAT IS HUMAN RESOURCE MANAGEMENT?

Human resource management refers to the practices and policies you need to carry out the personnel aspects of your management job, specifically, acquiring, training, appraising, rewarding, and providing a safe, ethical, and fair environment for your company's employees. These practices and policies include, for instance:

Conducting job analyses (determining the nature of each employee's job)
Planning labor needs and recruiting job candidates
Selecting job candidates
Orienting and training new employees
Managing wages and salaries (how to compensate employees)
Providing incentives and benefits
Appraising performance
Communicating (interviewing, counseling, disciplining)
Training and developing
Building employee commitment

And what a manager should know about:

Equal opportunity, ethics, and affirmative action
Employee health and safety and ethical treatment
Grievances and labor relations

Why Is HR Management Important to All Managers?

Why are these concepts and techniques important to all managers? Perhaps it's easier to answer this by listing some of the personnel mistakes you *don't* want to make while managing. For example, you don't want

To hire the wrong person for the job
To experience high turnover
To find employees not doing their best
To have your company taken to court because of your discriminatory actions
To have your company cited under federal occupational safety laws for unsafe practices
To allow a lack of training to undermine your department's effectiveness
To commit any unfair labor practices

Carefully studying this book can help you avoid mistakes like these. More important, it can help ensure that you get results—through others. Remember that you could do everything else right as a manager—lay brilliant plans, draw clear organization charts, set up modern assembly lines, and use sophisticated accounting controls—but still fail, for instance, by hiring the wrong people or by not motivating subordinates. On the other hand, many managers—from presidents to generals and supervisors—have been successful even without adequate plans, organizations, or controls. They were successful because they had the knack for hiring the right people for the right jobs and motivating, appraising, and developing them. Remember as you read this book that getting results is the bottom line of managing and that, as a manager, you will have to get these results through people. As one company president summed it up:

> For many years it has been said that capital is the bottleneck for a developing industry. I don't think this any longer holds true. I think it's the workforce and the company's inability to recruit and maintain a good workforce that does constitute the bottleneck for production. I don't know of any major project backed by good ideas, vigor, and enthusiasm that has been stopped by a shortage of cash. I do know of industries whose growth has been partly stopped or hampered because they can't maintain an efficient and enthusiastic labor force, and I think this will hold true even more in the future.[2]

Line and Staff Aspects of HRM

All managers are, in a sense, HR managers, because they all get involved in activities such as recruiting, interviewing, selecting, and training. Yet most firms also have a separate human resource department with its own human resource manager. How do the duties of this departmental HR manager and his or her staff relate to line managers' human resource duties? Let's answer this question by starting with short definitions of *line* versus *staff authority*.

Line Versus Staff Authority

Authority is the right to make decisions, to direct the work of others, and to give orders. In management, we usually distinguish between line authority and staff authority. **Line managers** are authorized to give orders. In addition, line managers are in charge of accomplishing the organization's basic goals. The managers for production and sales are generally line managers, for example. **Staff managers,** on the other hand, assist and advise line managers in accomplishing these goals. HR managers are generally staff managers. They have the authority and responsibility for advising line managers (such as those for production and sales) in areas such as recruiting, hiring, and compensation.

Managers may move from line to staff positions (and back) over the course of their careers. For example, line managers in areas like production and sales may well make unplanned career stopovers as staff HR managers. A survey by the Center for Effective Organizations at the University of Southern California found that about one-fourth of large U.S. businesses appointed managers with no HR experience as their top HR executives. Reasons given include the fact that these people may find it easier to give the firm's HR efforts a more strategic emphasis, and the possibility that they may sometimes be better equipped to integrate the firm's HR efforts with the rest of the business.[3]

In general, firms have an average of one HR employee for each 100 people in the workforce, although that ratio declines as total employment rises. HR and line managers generally share responsibility for most HR activities. For example, HR and line managers in about two-thirds of the firms in one survey shared responsibility for skills training.[4] (Thus, the supervisor might describe what training she thinks the new employee needs, HR might design the training, and the supervisor might then ensure that the training is having the desired effect.)

Line Managers' Human Resource Management Responsibilities

All supervisors thus spend much of their time on personnel-type tasks. As one expert says, "The direct handling of people is, and always has been, an integral part of every line manager's responsibility, from president down to the lowest-level supervisor."[5]

For example, one major company outlines its line supervisors' responsibilities for effective human resource management under the following general headings:

1. Placing the right person in the right job
2. Starting new employees in the organization (orientation)
3. Training employees for jobs that are new to them
4. Improving the job performance of each person
5. Gaining creative cooperation and developing smooth working relationships
6. Interpreting the company's policies and procedures
7. Controlling labor costs
8. Developing the abilities of each person
9. Creating and maintaining departmental morale
10. Protecting employees' health and physical conditions

In small organizations, line managers may carry out all these personnel duties unassisted. But as the organization grows, line managers need the assistance, specialized knowledge, and advice of a separate human resource staff.[6]

The Human Resource Department's HR Management Responsibilities

The human resource department provides the specialized assistance that the line managers need.[7] A summary of the HR positions you might find in a large company, along with their salaries, is presented in the organization chart in Figure 1.1. As you can see, HR positions include compensation and benefits manager, employment and recruiting supervisor, training specialist, employee relations executive, safety supervisor, and industrial nurse. Examples of job duties include:

Recruiters: Maintain contact within the community and perhaps travel extensively to search for qualified job applicants.
Equal employment opportunity (EEO) representatives or affirmative action coordinators: Investigate and resolve EEO grievances, examine organizational practices for potential violations, and compile and submit EEO reports.
Job analysts: Collect and examine detailed information about job duties to prepare job descriptions.
Compensation managers: Develop compensation plans and handle the employee benefits program.
Training specialists: Plan, organize, and direct training activities.
Labor relations specialists: Advise management on all aspects of union–management relations.[8]

THE CHANGING ENVIRONMENT AND DUTIES OF HR MANAGEMENT

HR's Changing Role

In actuality, employers' HR priorities and duties have evolved with changing times. In the early 1900s, "personnel" first took over hiring and firing from supervisors, ran the payroll department, and administered benefit plans. As technology in areas like testing and interviewing began to emerge, the personnel department began to play an expanded role in employee selection, training, and promotion.[9] Union legislation in the 1930s meant more HR emphasis on protecting the firm in its interaction with unions. The discrimination legislation of the 1960s and '70s meant large potential lawsuits and penalties to a company, and thus an expansion of HR's "protector" role.

Today, it's no secret to those reading this book that business is much more competitive than it's been in the past. The result is that employers like Dell increasingly want "personnel" to address strategic issues involving the competitiveness and performance of their firms. The metamorphosis of *personnel* into *human resource management* reflects the fact that in today's business environment, highly trained and committed employees, not machines, are often a firm's main real sustainable competitive advantage. Surveys, including one of over 1,000 North American companies, found that successful organizations do use many HR practices to help employees become more productive. These practices include leadership training, technical training, mentoring programs, and career workshops.[10]

A Changing Environment

Let's sum up some of the trends that are causing companies and their HR managers to increasingly focus on competitiveness and performance.

Globalization   Doing business internationally is big business today. For example, U.S. imports and exports jumped from $907 billion in 1991 to $2.5 trillion in 2000, and such trade now represents about 11% of what America produces.[11]

Globalization refers to the tendency of firms to extend their sales, ownership, and/or manufacturing to new markets abroad. Examples are all around us. Toyota produces the Camry in Kentucky, while Dell produces and sells PCs in China. Free trade areas—agreements that reduce tariffs and barriers among trading partners—further encourage international trade. NAFTA (the North American Free Trade Area) and the EU (European Union) are examples.

More globalization means more competition, and more competition means more pressure to be "world-class"—to lower costs, to make employees more productive, and to do things better and less expensively. As one expert puts it, "the bottom line is that the growing integration of the world economy into a single, huge marketplace is increasing the intensity of competition in a wide range of manufacturing and service industries."[12] From helping firms like Dell cut costs to formulating selection, training, and compensation policies for expatriate employees, managing globalization will be a major HR challenge in the next few years.

Figure 1.1 Typical Positions and Salaries Within a Large HR Department

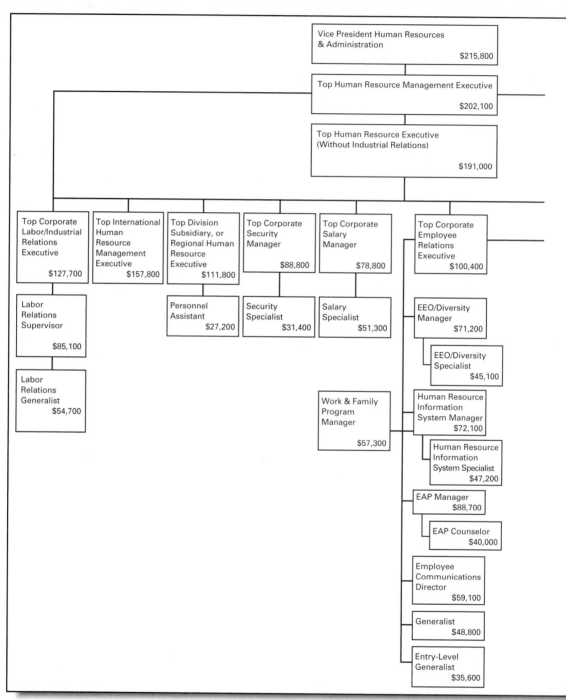

Source: Reprinted with permission from *Bulletin to Management (BNA Policy and Practice Series)* 48, no. 38 (September 18, 1997): 300–1. Copyright 1997 by The Bureau of National Affairs, Inc. (800-372-1033) <http://www.bna.com>.

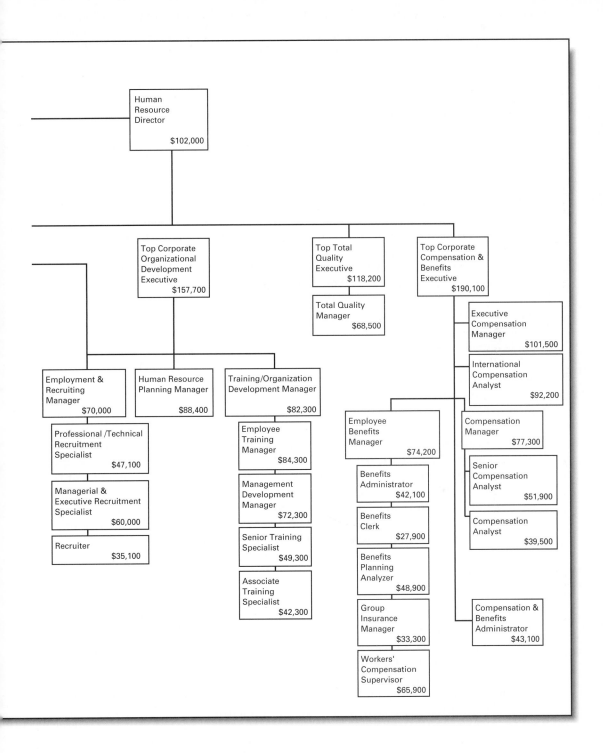

Human Resource Director
$102,000

Top Corporate Organizational Development Executive
$157,700

Top Total Quality Executive
$118,200

Top Corporate Compensation & Benefits Executive
$190,100

Total Quality Manager
$68,500

Executive Compensation Manager
$101,500

International Compensation Analyst
$92,200

Employment & Recruiting Manager
$70,000

Human Resource Planning Manager
$88,400

Training/Organization Development Manager
$82,300

Employee Benefits Manager
$74,200

Compensation Manager
$77,300

Professional /Technical Recruitment Specialist
$47,100

Employee Training Manager
$84,300

Senior Compensation Analyst
$51,900

Benefits Administrator
$42,100

Managerial & Executive Recruitment Specialist
$60,000

Management Development Manager
$72,300

Compensation Analyst
$39,500

Benefits Clerk
$27,900

Recruiter
$35,100

Senior Training Specialist
$49,300

Benefits Planning Analyzer
$48,900

Associate Training Specialist
$42,300

Group Insurance Manager
$33,300

Compensation & Benefits Administrator
$43,100

Workers' Compensation Supervisor
$65,900

Technological Advances   Many of these "world-class" improvements involve technology. For example, Carrier Corporation is the world's largest manufacturer of air conditioners and saves an estimated $100 million per year by using the Internet. In Brazil, for instance, Carrier handles all its transactions with its channel partners (its 550 dealers, retailers, and installers) over the Web. "The time required to get an order entered and confirmed by our channel partners has gone from six days to six minutes."[13] HR faces the challenge of quickly applying technology to the task of improving its own operations.

The Nature of Work   Technology is also changing the nature of work. Even factory jobs are more technologically demanding. For one thing, "knowledge-intensive high tech manufacturing in such industries as aerospace, computers, telecommunications, home electronics, pharmaceuticals, and medical instruments" are replacing factory jobs in steel, auto, rubber, and textiles.[14] Even traditional manufacturing jobs are going high tech. At Alcoa Aluminum's Davenport, Iowa plant, a computer stands at each workpost to help each employee control his or her machines. *Fortune* magazine says, "practically every package delivery, bank teller, retail clerk, telephone operator, and bill collector in America works with a computer [today]."[15] As Microsoft Corporation chairman Bill Gates put it: "In the new organization the worker is no longer a cog in a machine but is an intelligent part of the overall process. Welders at some steel jobs now have to know algebra and geometry to figure weld angles from computer-generated designs."[16]

Technology is not the only trend driving this change from "brawn to brains." Today over two-thirds of the U.S. workforce is employed in producing and delivering services, not products. Between 1998 and 2008, the number of jobs in goods-producing industries will stay almost unchanged, at about 25.5 million, while the number in service-producing industries will climb from 99 million to 118.8 million.[17]

For managers, this all means a growing emphasis on "knowledge workers" and human capital.[18] *Human capital* refers to the knowledge, education, training, skills, and expertise of a firm's workers.[19] Today, "the center of gravity in employment is moving fast from manual and clerical workers to knowledge workers, who resist the command and control model that business took from the military 100 years ago."[20] In this environment, managers can't just order employees around and closely monitor them. Managers need new world-class HR management systems and skills, to select, train, and motivate these employees and to get them to work more like committed partners.

The Workforce   At the same time, workforce demographics are changing. Most notably, the workforce is becoming more diverse as women, minority-group members, and older workers enter the workforce.[21] Between 1992 and 2005, workers classified as Asian and other will jump by just over 81%. Hispanics will represent 11% of the civilian labor force in 2005, up from 8% in 1992.[22] Women represented 46% of the workforce in 1994, and will represent an estimated 47.8% by 2005.[23] About two-thirds of all single mothers (separated, divorced, widowed, or never married) are in the labor force today, as are almost 45% of mothers with children under three years old.

The labor force is also getting older. The median age of the labor force in 1995 was 37.8 years and will rise to 40.5 years by 2005.[24] Employees will also likely remain in the workforce past the age at which their parents retired, due to Social Security and Medicare changes and the termination of traditional benefit plans by many employers.[25]

Creating unanimity and "human capital" from a diverse workforce is not easy. Most managers say they encourage diversity, but most management systems—how companies recruit, screen, and train and promote employees—". . . will not allow diversity, only similarity."[26] Establishing HR management programs that turn a diverse workforce into highly skilled knowledge workers can thus be a challenge.[27]

HR's Strategic Challenges

HR's priorities and tasks shift with changing times, because they need to "fit" or make sense in terms of the company's strategic direction. The central challenge facing HR is always to provide a set of services that make sense in terms of the company's strategy. A **strategy** is the company's plan for how it will match its internal strengths and weaknesses with external opportunities and threats in order to maintain a competitive advantage. For example, consider Dell's strategy to be a "low-cost leader," by using the Internet to sell PCs directly to end users at prices that competitors with intermediaries cannot match.

Strategy and HR   Dell's HR managers found a variety of ways to help top management execute the firm's low-cost leader strategy. For example, Dell now delivers most of its HR services via the Web. A Manager Tools section on its intranet contains about 30 automated Web applications (including executive search reports, hiring tools, and automated employee referrals). This allows managers to perform HR tasks that previously required costly participation by HR department personnel. The intranet also lets Dell employees administer their own 401(k) plans, check job postings, and monitor their total compensation statements. This dramatically reduces the number of HR people required to administer these activities, and thus the cost of doing so.[28]

Two things characterize the strategic challenges facing HR today. One (as at Dell) is the fact that most firms' strategies increasingly stress building organizational competitiveness and performance. This means that HR priorities at firms like Dell must increasingly focus on *boosting competitiveness* and managing employee performance—in other words on building high-performance work organizations.

Second, HR must therefore be more involved in *designing*—not just implementing—companies' strategies. Strategy formulation was traditionally a job for the company's operating (line) managers. The president and his or her staff might decide to enter new markets, drop product lines, or embark on a five-year cost-cutting plan. Then the president would more or less entrust the personnel implications of that plan (hiring or firing new workers, hiring outplacement firms for those fired, and so on) to HR management. Today's emphasis on gaining competitive advantage through people makes such an arrangement inadequate. In formulating its strategy, top management needs the input of the managers charged with hiring, training, and compensating the firm's employees. HR managers therefore need to understand at least the rudiments of strategic planning. Let's briefly discuss these.

Basics of Strategic Planning

Managers engage in three levels of strategic planning (see Figure 1.2).[29] At the first, companywide level, many firms consist of several businesses; for instance, PepsiCo includes Pepsi, Frito-Lay, and Pizza Hut. PepsiCo therefore needs a *corporate-level strategy.* A company's corporate-level strategy identifies the portfolio of businesses that, in total, comprise the company and the ways in which these businesses relate to each other. For example, a *diversification* strategy implies that the firm will expand by adding new product lines. A *vertical integration* strategy means the firm expands by, perhaps, producing its own raw materials, or selling its products direct. *Consolidation*—reducing the company's size—and *geographic expansion*—for instance, taking the business abroad—are some other corporate strategy possibilities.

At the next level down, each of these businesses (such as Pizza Hut) needs a *business-level/competitive strategy.* A competitive strategy identifies how to build and strengthen the business's long-term competitive position in the marketplace.[30] It identifies, for instance, how Pizza Hut will compete with Papa John's or how Wal-Mart competes with Target.

Companies try to achieve competitive advantages for each business they are in. We can define **competitive advantage** as any factors that allow an organization to differentiate its product or service from those of its competitors to increase market share.[31]

There are several competitive strategies companies use to achieve competitive advantage. One, *cost leadership,* means the enterprise aims to become the low-cost leader in an industry. Wal-Mart is a typical industry cost leader: It maintains its competitive advantage through its satellite-based distribution system, and (in its early days) by keeping store location costs to a minimum by placing stores on low-cost land outside small- to medium-sized towns.

Differentiation is a second example of a competitive strategy. In a differentiation strategy, a firm seeks to be unique in its industry along dimensions that are widely valued by buyers.[32] Thus, Volvo stresses the safety of its cars, Papa John's Pizza stresses fresh ingredients, Target sells somewhat more upscale brands than Wal-Mart, and Mercedes Benz emphasizes reliability and quality. Like Mercedes

Figure 1.2
Relationships Among Strategies in Multiple-Business Firms

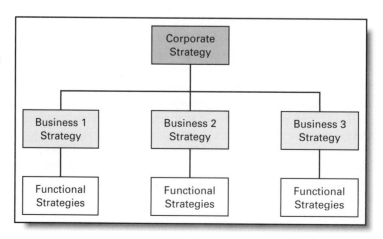

Benz, firms can usually charge a premium price if they successfully stake their claim to being substantially different from their competitors in some coveted way. Still other firms choose to compete as *focusers.* They carve out a market niche (as for Ferrari), and compete by providing a product or service their customers can get in no other way.

Finally, each individual business is composed of departments, such as manufacturing, sales, and HR management. *Functional strategies* identify the basic courses of action that each of the business's departments will pursue in order to help the business attain its competitive goals. The firm's functional strategies should make sense in terms of its business/competitive strategy. Dell's HR strategy of putting its activities on the Web to support the parent firm's low-cost competitive strategy is one example.

HR and Competitive Advantage   As noted above, *competitive advantage* means "any factors that allow an organization to differentiate its product or service from those of its competitors to increase market share," and committed, highly trained employees are often what set companies apart today. Low-cost, high-quality cars like Saturns aren't just a product of modern automated machines. In fact, all car companies have access to these machines. The thing that sets Saturn apart—its competitive advantage—is its people. They have highly committed employees all working hard and with self-discipline to produce the best cars that they can at the lowest possible cost.

It's clear that technology alone is no longer enough to set a company apart. Consider this example. An operations expert at Harvard University studied manufacturing facilities that had installed computer-integrated manufacturing systems.[33] The idea of computer-integrated manufacturing is to use computers to integrate product design, manufacturing, and storage to give a firm a competitive edge.

Surprisingly, the expert discovered that computer integration was not in itself associated with either producing a wider range of products or improved changeover times. Instead, what he found was that:

> The flexibility of the plants depended much more on people than on any technical factor. Although high levels of computer integration can provide critically needed advantages in quality and cost competitiveness, all the data in my study point to one conclusion: operational flexibility is determined primarily by a plant's operators and the extent to which managers cultivate, measure, and communicate with them. Equipment and computer integration are secondary.[34]

Or, as another writer concludes:

> In a growing number of organizations human resources are now viewed as a source of competitive advantage. There is greater recognition that distinctive competencies are obtained through highly developed employee skills, distinctive organizational cultures, management processes, and systems. This is in contrast to the traditional emphasis on transferable resources such as equipment. . . . Increasingly, it is being recognized that competitive advantage can be obtained with a high quality workforce that enables organizations to compete on the basis of market responsiveness, product and service quality, differentiated products, and technological innovation.[35]

Strategic Human Resource Management

The fact that employees today are central to achieving competitive advantage has led firms to focus more on **strategic human resource management.**[36] This is "the linking of HRM with strategic goals and objectives in order to improve business performance and develop organizational cultures that foster innovation and flexibility."[37] Put another way, it is "the pattern of planned human resource deployments and activities intended to enable an organization to achieve its goals."[38]

The term *HR strategies* refers to the specific HR courses of action the company pursues to achieve its aims. Thus, one of FedEx's strategic aims is to achieve superior levels of customer service and high profitability through a highly committed workforce. The overriding aim of its HR strategy is thus to build a committed workforce, preferably in a nonunion environment.[39] FedEx's specific HR strategies stem from this aim. They include: using various methods to build two-way communications; screening out potential managers whose values are not people oriented; guaranteeing to the greatest extent possible fair treatment and employee security for all employees; and instituting various promotion-from-within activities aimed at giving employees every opportunity to fully realize their potential at work. Figure 1.3 illustrates the interplay between HR strategy and the company's strategic plans and results.

Figure 1.3 Linking Corporate and HR Strategies

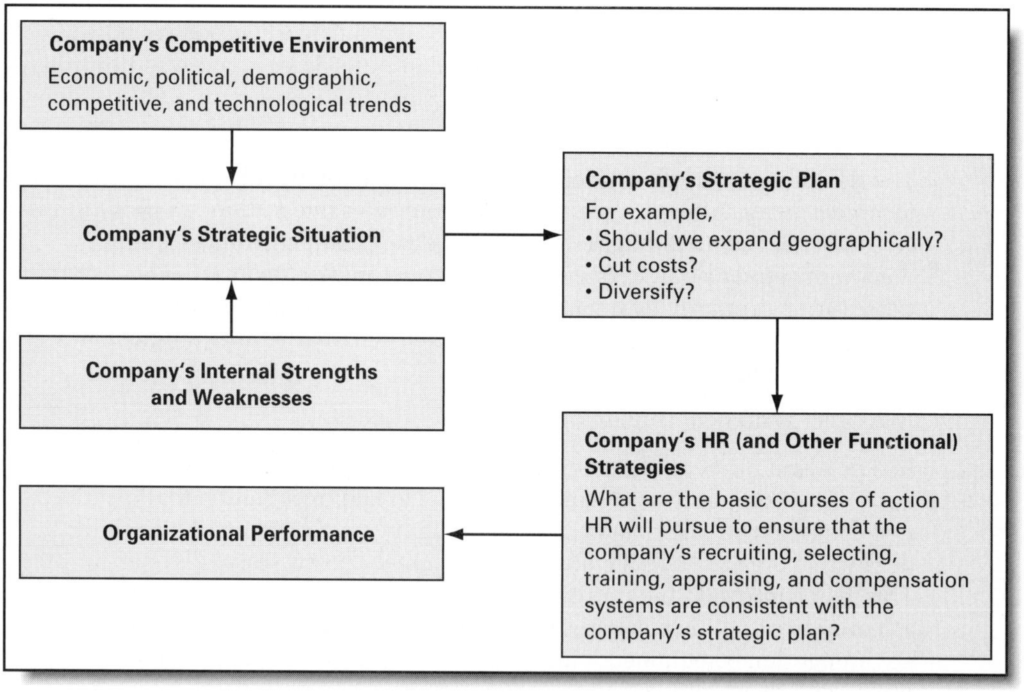

Source: © 2003 Gary Dessler, Ph.D.

HR's Roles as a Strategic Partner

Managers understandably differ in their views of just how strategic HR should be. Some doubt that HR needs to be strategic at all.[40] By this line of reasoning, HR activities simply "involve putting out small fires—ensuring that people are paid on the right day; the job advertisement meets the newspaper deadline; a suitable supervisor is recruited for the night shift by the time it goes ahead; and the sales manager remembers to observe due process before sacking the new rep who didn't work out."[41]

A more strategic view of HR is that its role is simply to "fit" and to help execute the company's strategy. In this view, top management crafts a corporate strategy, such as to purchase another company. HR's role is then to create the HR programs required to successfully implement that corporate strategy.[42] As two strategic planning experts have argued, "the human resources management system must be tailored to the demands of the business strategy."[43] The idea here is that "for any particular organizational strategy, there is purportedly a matching human resource strategy."[44]

A third, even more strategic view of HR is that it is an equal partner in the strategic planning process. Here, HR management's role is not just to tailor its activities to the demands of business strategy, nor, certainly, just to carry out operational day-to-day tasks such as ensuring that employees get paid. Instead, the need to forge a company's workforce into a competitive advantage gives HR a more strategic role. That role is to actively participate, as an equal partner, in both formulating and executing the company's strategic plan.[45] Let's look first at this strategy formulation role.

HR's Role in Formulating Strategy   Formulating a company's strategic plan requires identifying, analyzing, and balancing the company's *external opportunities and threats* on the one hand and its *internal strengths and weaknesses* on the other. Hopefully, the resulting strategic plans capitalize on the firm's strengths and opportunities, and minimize or neutralize its threats and weaknesses.

The HR function can play several roles here. For example, HR management is in a unique position to supply competitive intelligence that may be useful in the strategic planning process. Details regarding competitors' incentive plans, opinion survey data from employees that elicit information about customer complaints, and information about pending legislation such as labor laws and mandatory health insurance are some examples. Furthermore:

> From public information and legitimate recruiting and interview activities, you ought to be able to construct organization charts, staffing levels, and group missions for the various organizational components of each of your major competitors. Your knowledge of how brands are sorted among sales divisions and who reports to whom can give important clues as to a competitor's strategic priorities. You may even know the track record and characteristic behavior of the executives.[46]

HR also participates in the strategy formulation process by supplying information regarding the company's internal human strengths and weaknesses. For example, IBM's decision in the 1990s to buy Lotus Software was prompted in part by IBM's conclusion that its own human resources were insufficient to enable the firm to reposition itself as an industry leader in networking systems, or at least to do so fast enough.

Other firms build new strategies around human resource strengths. For example, in the process of automating its factories, farm equipment manufacturer John Deere developed a workforce that was exceptionally talented and expert in factory automation. This in turn prompted the firm to establish a new-technology division to offer automation services to other companies.[47]

One study illustrates the role that HR can play in implementing effective mergers and acquisitions. It found a direct correlation between HR involvement and the firm's success with the merger and/or acquisition. This study concluded that HR can and should be involved in quickly assessing and providing advice regarding employee attitudes, motivating and retaining talent, and helping plan and lead the integration of the workforces (for instance, in terms of merging the firm's compensation and benefits plans).[48]

HR's Role in Executing Strategy   We've seen that HR management also plays an essential role in executing a company's strategic plan. Dell's human resource strategies help the firm better execute Dell's low-cost strategy. FedEx's HR strategies help FedEx differentiate itself from its competitors by offering superior customer service and guaranteed on-time deliveries. HR management supports strategic implementation in other, familiar ways. For example, HR is heavily involved in the execution of most firms' downsizing and restructuring strategies, through outplacing employees, instituting pay-for-performance plans, reducing health care costs, and retraining employees. Thus, when Wells Fargo acquired First Interstate Bancorp, HR played a strategic role in the implementation—for instance, in merging two "wildly divergent" cultures and in dealing with the uncertainty and initial shock that rippled through the organizations when the merger was announced.[49]

To illustrate HR's strategic role, we will start each chapter with an introduction describing a company's strategic challenge, and then show in the chapter how it used HR to meet that challenge.

The Strategic Future of the HR Department   Ironically, the future of the HR department itself sometimes seems in doubt. Human resource departments will face further downsizing and "reengineering," says one expert, "as they face pressure from senior management to add value to the organization or have their functions contracted out."[50]

The belt-tightening in HR reflects two related causes: downsizing and outsourcing. At Sears Roebuck and Company, for instance, downsizing/reorganizing of the HR department resulted in slashing the corporate HR department from 700 to about 200 employees. HR responsibilities that had previously been dispersed at 32 U.S. locations were consolidated in one Atlanta office as part of this downsizing.[51] Outsourcing is having an impact, too. For example, in one survey, about 71% of respondents said they were outsourcing one or more[52] HR activities such as temporary staffing, recruiting, benefits administration, payroll, or training.[53] Cost reduction was the most commonly cited explanation.[54]

What can HR departments do to avoid getting outsourced out of existence? Certainly not just focus on traditional maintenance and administrative functions such as recruiting, testing, and payroll. To paraphrase one HR consultant, if an

HR department focuses only on maintenance and administration, it's going to become an endangered species, because outsourcing firms can do a better job of handling such tasks. Today, says this expert, the HR department needs to focus more on activities that add value to the firm's bottom line—activities such as strategic planning, change management, corporate culture transition, and the development of human capital.[55]

HR AND TECHNOLOGY

The HR function is therefore changing. Perhaps most notably, technology is dramatically altering how HR departments do business. Figure 1.4 provides a summary of this.[56] Thus, many firms are installing intranet portals to facilitate "self-service HR." At Dell, for instance, a section of the firm's intranet contains "manager tools." Here, about 30 automated Web applications (including executive search reports, hiring tools, and automated employee referrals) let managers unilaterally perform HR tasks that previously required direct participation by HR. The intranet also allows Dell employees to administer their own 401(k) plans, check job postings, and monitor their total compensation statements, for instance.[57]

Data warehouses are another example. A data warehouse is a large repository of information gleaned from various databases throughout an organization. In one state agency, for example, state managers can, from their desktop computers, easily find the average salary for each occupation, the agencies doing the most or least hiring, and who pays the highest salaries.[58]

HR is also becoming even more of a profession. For example, certification exams administered twice a year for the Society of Human Resource Management test knowledge of HR practices (such as staffing and appraisal), knowledge of business including financial analysis, and knowledge of change management techniques including problem solving and organizational transformation.[59]

THE PLAN OF THIS BOOK

The Integrated Nature of HR Management

This section presents a brief overview of the chapters to come, but do not think of these as independent, unrelated chapters and topics. Instead, each interacts with and affects the others, and all should fit with the employer's strategic plan. Figure 1.5 (which also introduces each chapter) summarizes this idea. For example, how you test and interview job candidates (Chapter 4) and train and appraise job incumbents (Chapters 5 and 6) depends on the job's specific duties and responsibilities (Chapter 3). How good a job you are doing selecting (Chapter 4) and training (Chapter 5) employees will affect how safely they do their jobs (Chapter 10). An employee's performance and thus his or her appraisal (Chapter 6) depends not just on the person's motivation, but on how well you identified the job's duties (Chapter 3), and screened and trained the employee (Chapters 4 and 5). And, as we've seen, each of your HR policies in each area—for instance, how you recruit,

Figure 1.4 How Technology Is Changing How HR Operates

Technology	How Used by HR
Application Service Providers (ASPs) and technology outsourcing	ASPs provide software applications, for instance, for processing employment applications. The ASPs host and manage the services for the employer from their own remote computers.
Web portals	Employers use these, for instance, to enable employees to sign up for and manage their own benefits packages and to update their personal information.
PCs and high-speed access	Make it easier for employees to take advantage of the employer's Web–assisted HR activities
Streaming desktop video	Used, for instance, to facilitate distance learning and training or to provide corporate information to employees quickly and inexpensively
The mobile Web and wireless net access	Used to facilitate employees' access to the company's Web–based HR activities
E-procurement	Used for ordering work materials more efficiently online
Internet and network monitoring software	Used to track employees' Internet and e-mail activities or to monitor their performance
Bluetooth	A special wireless technology used to synchronize various electronic tools like cellular phones and PCs, and thus facilitate employees' access to the employer's online HR services
Electronic signatures	Legally valid e-signatures that the employer can use to more expeditiously obtain signatures for applications and record-keeping
Electronic bill presentment and payment	Used, for instance, to eliminate paper checks and to facilitate payments to employees and suppliers
Data warehouses and computerized analytical programs	Help HR managers monitor their HR systems. For example, they make it easier to assess things like cost per hire, and to compare current employees' skills with the firm's projected strategic needs.

Source: Adapted from Samuel Greengard, "10 HR Technology Trends for 2001," *Workforce, HR Trends and Tools for Business Results* 80, no. 1 (January 2001): 20–22; Jim Meade, "Analytical Tools Give Meaning to Data," *HR Magazine* 46, no. 11 (November 2001): 97 ff.

Figure 1.5   Strategy and the Basic HR Process

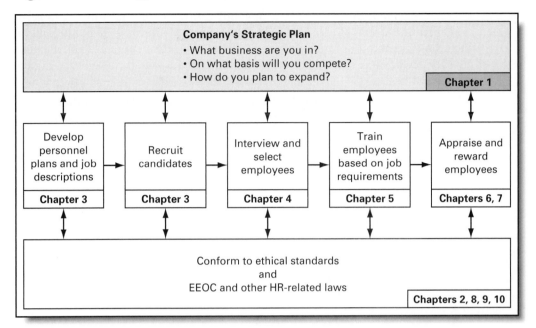

select, train, appraise, and compensate employees—should make sense in terms of the company's strategic plan.

Here's an outline of the chapters to come:

Chapter 2: Managing Equal Opportunity and Diversity.   What you'll need to know about equal opportunity laws as they relate to human resource management activities such as interviewing, selecting employees, and evaluating performance appraisals

Part I: Recruiting and Placing Employees

Chapter 3: Personnel Planning and Recruiting.   How to analyze a job and how to determine the job's requirements, specific duties, and responsibilities, as well as what sorts of people need to be hired and how to recruit them

Chapter 4: Testing and Selecting Employees.   Techniques such as testing that you can use to ensure that you're hiring the right people

Chapter 5: Training and Developing Employees.   Providing the training and development necessary to ensure that your employees have the knowledge and skills required to accomplish their tasks

Part II: Appraising and Compensating Employees

Chapter 6: Performance Management and Appraisal.   Techniques for managing and appraising performance

Chapter 7: Compensating Employees.   How to develop equitable pay plans, including incentives and benefits, for your employees

Part III: Employee Rights and Safety

Chapter 8: Managing Labor Relations and Collective Bargaining. Concepts and techniques concerning the relations between unions and management, including the union-organizing campaign; negotiating and agreeing on a collective bargaining agreement between unions and management; and managing the agreement

Chapter 9: Ethics and Fair Treatment in Human Resource Management. Ensuring ethical and fair treatment through discipline, grievance, and career management processes

Chapter 10: Protecting Safety and Health. The causes of accidents, how to make the workplace safe, and laws governing your responsibilities in regard to employee safety and health

REVIEW

Summary

1. Staffing, personnel management, or human resource management includes activities such as recruiting, selecting, training, compensating, appraising, and developing.

2. HR management is a part of every line manager's responsibilities. These HR responsibilities include placing the right person in the right job and then orienting, training, and compensating the person to improve his or her job performance.

3. The HR manager and his or her department provide various staff services to line management; for example, the HR manager or department assists in the hiring, training, evaluating, rewarding, promoting, and disciplining of employees at all levels.

4. Changes in the environment of HR management are requiring HR to play a more strategic role in organizations. These changes include growing work-force diversity, rapid technological change, globalization, and changes in the nature of work, such as the movement toward a service society and a growing emphasis on education and human capital.

5. One consequence of changes in the work environment is that HR management must be involved in both the formulation and the implementation of a company's strategies, given the need for the firm to use its employees as a competitive advantage.

6. *Strategic human resource management* may be defined as "the linking of HRM with strategic goals and objectives in order to improve business performance and develop organizational cultures that foster innovation and flexibility." HR is a strategic partner in that HR management works with other top managers to formulate the company's strategy as well as to execute it.

KEY TERMS

- human resource management
- authority
- line manager
- staff manager
- strategy
- competitive advantage
- strategic human resource management

DISCUSSION QUESTIONS AND EXERCISES

1. Explain what HR management is and how it relates to line management.
2. Give several examples of how HR management concepts and techniques can be of use to all managers.
3. Compare the work of line and staff managers. Give examples of each.
4. Working individually or in groups, develop a list showing how trends such as workforce diversity, technological trends, globalization, and changes in the nature of work have affected the college or university you are now attending or the organization for which you work.
5. Working individually or in groups, develop several examples showing how the new HR management practices mentioned in this chapter have or have not been implemented to some extent in the college or university you are now attending or in the organization for which you work.
6. Working individually or in groups, interview an HR manager. Based on that interview, write a short presentation regarding HR's role today in building a more responsive organization.
7. Why is it important for a company to make its human resources into a competitive advantage? How can HR contribute to doing so?
8. What is meant by *strategic human resource management,* and what exactly is HR's role in the strategic planning process?

APPLICATION EXERCISES

Case Incident   *Jack Nelson's Problem*

As a new member of the board of directors for a local bank, Jack Nelson was being introduced to all the employees in the home office. When he was introduced to Ruth Johnson, he was curious about her work and asked her what her machine did. Johnson replied that she really did not know what the machine was called or what it did. She explained that she had been working there for only two months. She did, however, know precisely how to operate the machine. According to her supervisor, she was an excellent employee.

At one of the branch offices, the supervisor in charge spoke to Nelson confidentially, telling him that "something was wrong," but she didn't know what. For one thing, she explained, employee turnover was too high, and no sooner had one employee been put on the job than another one resigned. With customers to see and loans to be made, she explained, she had little time to work with the new employees as they came and went.

All branch supervisors hired their own employees without communication with the home office or other branches. When an opening developed, the supervisor tried to find a suitable employee to replace the worker who had quit.

After touring the 22 branches and finding similar problems in many of them, Nelson wondered what the home office should do or what action he should take. The banking firm was generally regarded as a well-run institution that had grown from 27 to 191 employees during the past eight years. The more he thought about the matter, the more puzzled Nelson became. He couldn't quite put his finger on the problem, and he didn't know whether to report his findings to the president. ■

QUESTIONS

1. What do you think is causing some of the problems in the bank's home office and branches?
2. Do you think setting up an HR unit in the main office would help?
3. What specific functions should an HR unit carry out? What HR functions would then be carried out by supervisors and other line managers?

Source: From *Supervision in Action,* 4/e, by Claude S. George © 1985. Adapted by permission of Prentice Hall, Inc., Upper Saddle River, NJ.

Continuing Case

LearnInMotion.com: Introduction

The main theme of this book is that HR management—activities like recruiting, selecting, training, and rewarding employees—is not just the job of some central HR group, but rather one in which every manager must engage. Perhaps nowhere is this more apparent than in the typical small service business. Here the owner–manager usually has no personnel staff to rely on. However, the success of his or her enterprise (not to mention his or her family's peace of mind) often depends largely on the effectiveness with which workers are recruited, hired, trained, evaluated, and rewarded.

To help illustrate and emphasize the front-line manager's HR role, throughout this book we will use a continuing ("running") case, based on an actual small business in the northeastern United States. Each segment will illustrate how the case's main players—owner–managers Jennifer Mendez and Mel Hudson—confront and solve personnel problems each day by applying the concepts and techniques presented in that particular chapter. The names of the company and principals have been changed, as have a few of the details, but the company, people, dates, and HR and other problems are otherwise real. Here's some background information you'll need to answer questions that arise in subsequent chapters.

LearnInMotion.com: A Profile. Jennifer and Mel graduated from State University as business majors in June 1999, and got the idea for LearnInMotion.com as a result of a project they worked on together their last semester in their entrepreneurship class. The professor had divided the students into two- or three-person teams, and given them the assignment "create a business plan for a dot-com company."

The idea the two came up with was LearnInMotion.com. The basic idea of the Web site was to list a vast array of Web–based, CD-ROM-based, or textbook-based business-related continuing-education-type courses for "free agent learners"—in other words, for working people who wanted to take a course in business from the comfort of their own homes. The idea was that users could come to the Web site to find and then take a course in one of several ways. Some courses could be completed interactively on the Web via the site; others were in a form that was downloadable directly to the user's computer; others (which were either textbook or CD-ROM-based) could be ordered and delivered (in several major metropolitan areas) by independent contractor delivery people

using bicycles or motorized scooters. Their business mission was "to provide work-related learning when, where, and how you need it."

Based on their research, they knew the market for work-related learning like this was booming. The $63-billion U.S. corporate training market was (and is) growing at 10% annually, for instance, with no firm controlling more than 2%. In 1999, when they created their plan, 76 million adult U.S. learners participated in at least one education activity. Over 100,000 U.S. training and consulting firms offered seminars, courses, and other forms of training. They estimated that worldwide markets were at least two or three times the U.S. market.

At the same time, professional development activities like these were increasingly Internet-based. Thirteen percent of training was delivered via the Internet when they did their class project in 1999, and projections were for the e-learning/distance learning market to grow over 90% annually for the following three years. Tens of thousands of on- and off-line training firms, universities, associations, and other content providers were trying to reach their target customers via the Internet. Jennifer and Mel understandably thought they were in the right place at the right time. And perhaps they were.

Their business plan contained about 25 pages, including financial projection tables, and covered the usual array of topics: company summary; management; market trends and opportunities; competition; marketing plan; financial plan; and appendices. The one-page executive summary contained a synopsis of the plan and covered "the business," "the market," "strategies," "competition," "value proposition," "the revenue drivers," "the management," and "financials and funding." Most of this is self-descriptive. Revenue drivers referred to how the company would generate revenues (in this case, online banner ads and sponsorships, content providers' listing fees, and fees for courses actually taken). Financials and funding included basic financial projections as well as likely "exit strategies," which in this case included the possibility of a public offering, a merger with related sites, or sale of the site, perhaps to one of the superportals that were aggregating specialized sites as part of their strategies. They got an A for the business plan, an A for the course, and a standing ovation from the businesspeople the professor had invited to help evaluate the presentations.

When the two graduated in June 1999, it looked like the Internet boom would go on forever. It was not unusual for entrepreneurs still in their teens to create and sell Web sites. Some were selling their Web sites for literally hundreds of millions of dollars. Jennifer's father had some unused loft space in the SoHo area of New York, so with about $45,000 of accumulated savings, Jennifer and Mel incorporated and were in business. They retained the services of an independent contractor programmer and hired two people—a Web designer to create the graphics for the site (which would then be programmed by the programmer), and a content manager whose job was basically to keypunch information onto the site as it came in from content providers. By the end of 1999, they also completed upgrading their business plan into a form they could show to prospective venture capitalists. They sent the first version to three New York area venture capitalists. Then they waited.

And then they waited some more. They never heard back from the first three venture capitalists, so they sent their plan to five more. By now it was March 2000, and a dramatic event occurred: The values of a wide range of Internet and Internet-related sites dropped precipitously on the stock market. In some cases, entrepreneurs who had been worth $1 billion in February 1999 were worth $20 million or less by April. "Well, $20 million isn't bad," Mel said, so they pressed on. By day they called

customers to get people to place ads on their site, to get content providers to list their available courses, and to get someone—anyone—to deliver textbook- and CD-ROM-based courses, as needed, in the New York area.

By May 2000, they had about 300 content providers offering courses and content through LearnInMotion.com. In the summer, they got their first serious nibble from a venture capital firm. They negotiated with this company through much of the summer, came to terms in the early fall, and closed the deal—getting just over $1 million in venture funding—in November 2000.

After a stunning total of $75,000 in legal fees (they had to pay both their firm's and the venture capital firm's lawyers to navigate the voluminous disclosure documents and agreements), they had just over $900,000 to spend. The funding, according to the business plan, was to go toward accomplishing five main goals: redesigning and expanding the Web site; hiring about seven more employees; moving to larger office space; designing and implementing a personal information manager (PIM)/calendar (users and content providers could use the calendar to interactively keep track of their personal and business schedules); and, last but not least, driving up sales. LearnInMotion.com was off and running. ∎

QUESTIONS AND ASSIGNMENTS

1. Would a company like this with just a few employees and independent contractors have any HR tasks to address? What do you think those might be?
2. Based on your review of the online catalogs of firms such as Office Max, Staples, and HRNext.com, what basic HR systems would you recommend to Jennifer and Mel?

TAKE IT TO THE WEB

 For Internet exercises, updates to chapter material, and more, visit the Dessler Web site at

www.prenhall.com/dessler

1. "Dell Computer Vows to Persist with Price Strategy," *Knight Ridder/Tribune Business News* (May 18, 2001): item 01138000.
2. Quoted in Fred K. Foulkes, "The Expanding Role of the Personnel Function," *Harvard Business Review* (March/April 1975): 71–84. See also Warren Wilhelm, "HR Can Make the U.S. a Global Leader," *Personnel Journal* (May 1993): 280.
3. Steve Bates, "No Experience Necessary? Many Companies are Putting non-HR Executives in Charge of HR with Mixed Results," *HR Magazine* 46, no. 11 (November 2001): 34–41.
4. "Human Resource Activities, Budgets & Staffs, 1999–2000," *BNA Bulletin to Management* 51, no. 25 (June 29, 2000): S1–S6.
5. See Robert Saltonstall, "Who's Who in Personnel Administration," *Harvard Business Review* 33 (July/August 1955): 75–83, reprinted in Paul Pigors, Charles Meyers, and F. P. Malm, *Management of Human Resources* (New York: McGraw-Hill, 1969), pp. 61–73. See also Milorad Novicevic and Michael Harvey, "The Changing Role of the Corporate HR Function in Global Organizations of the Twenty-First Century," *International Journal of Human Resource Management* (December 2001): 1251–68.
6. Saltonstall, "Who's Who in Personnel Administration," 63.
7. For a detailed discussion of the responsibilities and duties of the human resource department, see Mary Zippo, "Personnel Activities: Where the Dollars Went in 1979," *Personnel* 57 (March/April 1980): 61–67; and "SHRM-BNA Survey No. 66, Human Resource Activities, Budgets, and Staffs: 2000–2001," *BNA Bulletin to Management* (June 28, 2001): 1–42.
8. U.S. Department of Labor, Bureau of Labor Statistics, *Occupational Outlook Handbook*, Bulletin 2250, 1986–1987 Edition, pp. 45–47.
9. "Immigrants in the Workforce," *BNA Bulletin to Management Datagraph* (August 15, 1996): 260–61. See also Tanuja Agarwala, "Human Resource Management: The Emerging Trends," *Indian Journal of Industrial Relations* (January 2002): 315–31; and Shani Caudron et al., "80 People, Events and Trends that Shaped HR," *Workforce* (January 2002): 26–56.
10. "Human Capital Critical to Success," *Management Review* (November 1998): 9.
11. *The World Almanac and Book of Facts, 1998* (Mahwah, NJ: K-III Reference Corporation, 1998), p. 207.
12. Ibid., 9. See also "The Impact of Globalization on HR," *Workplace Visions,* Society for Human Resource Management, no. 5 (2000): 1–8.
13. Paul Judge, "How I Saved $100 Million on the Web," *Fast Company* (February 2001): 174–81.
14. Richard Crawford, *In the Era of Human Capital* (New York: Harper Business, 1991), p. 10.
15. Bryan O'Reilly, "Your New Global Workforce," *Fortune* 14 (December 1992): 63.
16. This discussion is based on Gary Dessler, *Management: Principles and Practices for Tomorrow's Leaders* (Upper Saddle River, NJ: Prentice Hall, 2004): 15–22.
17. Roger Moncarz and Azure Reasor, "The 2000–10 Job Outlook in Brief," *Occupational Outlook Quarterly* (spring 2002): 9–44.
18. Ibid.
19. Crawford, *In the Era,* 26.
20. Peter Drucker, "The Coming of the New Organization," *Harvard Business Review* (January–February 1988): 45. See also James Guthime et al., "Correlates and Consequences of High Involvement Work Practices: The Role of Competitive Strategy," *International Journal of Human Resource Management* (February 2002): 183–97.
21. Gerald Ferris, Dwight Frank, and M. Carmen Galang, "Diversity in the Workplace: The Human Resources Management Challenge," *Human Resource Planning* 16, no. 1 (1993): 41–51. See also

"Charting the Projections: 2000–10," *Occupational Outlook Quarterly* (winter 2001–02): 36–41.

22. "Immigrants in the Workforce."

23. Moncarz and Azure, "The 2000–10 Job Outlook."

24. Ibid.

25. Ibid.

26. Ferris et al., "Diversity in the Workplace."

27. For related discussions, see, for example, Felice Schwartz, "Women in American Business: The Demographic Imperative," *Business and the Contemporary World* (summer 1993): 10–19; and also Karen Stephenson and Valdis Krebs, "A More Accurate Way to Measure Diversity," *Personnel Journal* (October 1993): 66–74.

28. "Human Resource Goes High-Tech: The 1999 HR Technology Conference and Exposition," *BNA Bulletin to Management* (October 14, 1999): S1–S4.

29. Patrick Gunnigle and Sara Moore, "Linking Business Strategy and Human Resource Management: Issues and Implications," *Personnel Review* 23, no. 1 (1994): 63–84. See also Joseph Martocchio, *Strategic Compensation* (Upper Saddle River, NJ: Prentice Hall, 2001), pp. 9–15.

30. Arthur Thompson and A. J. Strickland, *Strategic Management* (Homewood, IL: Irwin, 1992), p. 38. See also Paul Nutt, "Making Strategic Choices," *Journal of Management Studies* (January 2002): 67–96.

31. Gunnigle and Moore, "Linking Business Strategy," 64.

32. Michael Porter, *Competitive Strategy* (New York: The Free Press, 1980), p. 14.

33. David Upton, "What Really Makes Factories Flexible?" *Harvard Business Review* (July/August 1995): 74–86.

34. Ibid., 75.

35. Greer, *Strategy and Human Resources*, 105.

36. For a discussion, see, for example, Jay Galbraith, "Positioning Human Resource as a Value-Adding Function: The Case of Rockwell International," *Human Resources Management* 31, no. 4 (winter 1992): 287–300; and Felix Yip Wai-kwong et al., "The Performance Effects of Human Resource Managers' and Other Middle Managers' Involvement in Strategy Making under Different Business-Level Strategies: The Case in Hong Kong," *International Journal of Human Resource Management* (December 2001): 1325–46.

37. Catherine Truss and Lynda Gratton, "Strategic Human Resource Management: A Conceptual Approach," *The International Journal of Human Resource Management* 5, no. 3 (September 1994): 663.

38. P. Wright and G. McMahan, "Theoretical Perspectives for Strategic Human Resource Management," *Journal of Management* 18, no. 2 (1992): 292; and Mark Huselid et al., "Technical and Strategic Human Resource Management Effectiveness as Determinants of Firm Performance," *Academy of Management Journal* 40, no. 1 (1997): 171–88.

39. Although still largely nonunionized, FedEx's pilots did vote to join the Airline Pilots Union in 1995.

40. For a discussion, see Peter Boxall, "Placing HR Strategy at the Heart of Business Success," *Personnel Management* 26, no. 7 (July 1994): 32–34.

41. Ibid., 32.

42. Randall Schuler, "Human Resource Management Choices and Organizational Strategy," in Randall Schuler, S. A. Youngblood, and V. L. Huber (eds.), *Readings in Personnel and Human Resource Management*, 3rd ed. (St. Paul, MN: West, 1988).

43. For a discussion, see Truss and Gratton, "Strategic Human Resource Management," 660–71.

44. Ibid., 670.

45. For a discussion, see, for example, Randall Schuler, Peter Dowling, and Helen DeCieri, "An Integrative Framework of Strategic International Human Resource Management," *Journal of Management* 19, no. 2 (1993): 419–59; Vida Scarpello, "New Paradigm Approaches in Strategic Human Resource Management," *Group and Organization Management* 19, no. 2 (June 1994): 160–64; Sharon Peck, "Exploring the Link Between Organizational Strategy and the Employment Relationship: The Role of Human Resources Policies," *Journal of*

Management Studies 31, no. 5 (September 1994): 715–36; and Mark Youndt et al., "Human Resource Management, Manufacturing Strategy, and Firm Performance," *Academy of Management Journal* 39, no. 4 (1996): 836–66.

46. William Henn, "What the Strategist Asks from Human Resources," *Human Resource Planning* 8, no. 4 (1985): 195; quoted in Greer, *Strategy and Human Resources*, 117–18.

47. Greer, *Strategy and Human Resources*, 105.

48. Jeffrey Schmidt, "The Correct Spelling of M & A Begins with HR," *HR Magazine* 46, no. 6 (June 2001): 102–8.

49. Samuel Greengard, "You're Next! There's No Escaping Merger Mania!" *Workforce* (April 1997): 52–62.

50. "Human Resource Departments Fight for Their Future," *BNA Bulletin to Management* (January 25, 1996): 25.

51. Ibid.

52. "Core HR Functions Are Being Given Away as More Employers Join Outsourcing Trend," *BNA Bulletin to Management* (June 8, 2000): 177.

53. "Outsourcing Gains Attention," *BNA Bulletin to Management* (June 5, 1997): 180–81.

54. Ibid.

55. "The Shifting Role of HR Departments," *BNA Bulletin to Management* (May 16, 1996): 1. See also "HR Department Benchmarks and Analysis 2002," Washington, D.C., Bureau of National Affairs (2002).

56. Samuel Greengard, "10 HR Technology Trends for 2001," *Workforce, HR Trends and Tools for Business Results* 80, no. 1 (January 2001): 20–22; and Jim Meade, "Analytical Tools Give Meaning to Data," *HR Magazine* 46, no. 11 (November 2001): 97 ff.

57. "Human Resource Goes High-Tech: The 1999 HR Technology Conference and Exposition," *BNA Bulletin to Management* (October 14, 1999): S1–S4.

58. Bill Roberts, "HR Is Linked to Corporate Big Picture," *HR Magazine* (April 1999): 103–10.

59. Brenda Sunoo, "Certification Enhances HR's Credibility," *Workforce* (May 1999): 71–80.

Chapter 2

Managing Equal Opportunity and Diversity

- Selected Equal Employment Opportunity Laws
- Defenses Against Discrimination Allegations
- Illustrative Discriminatory Employment Practices
- The EEOC Enforcement Process
- Diversity Management and Affirmative Action Programs

When you finish studying this chapter, you should be able to:

- Summarize *the basic equal employment opportunity laws regarding age, race, sex, national origin, religion, and handicap discrimination.*

- Explain *the basic defenses against discrimination allegations.*

- Present *a summary of what employers can and cannot do with respect to illegal recruitment, selection, and promotion and layoff practices.*

- Explain *the Equal Employment Opportunity Commission enforcement process.*

INTRODUCTION

S ome experts claim that diversity creates conflicts and rising costs.[1] But that argument is lost on the owners of Longo Toyota in El Monte, California.[2] Longo supports its strategy of catering to a highly diverse customer base by hiring and developing salespeople who speak everything from Spanish and Korean to Mandarin and Tagalog. And by following that strategy, Longo may now be one of America's top-grossing auto dealers.

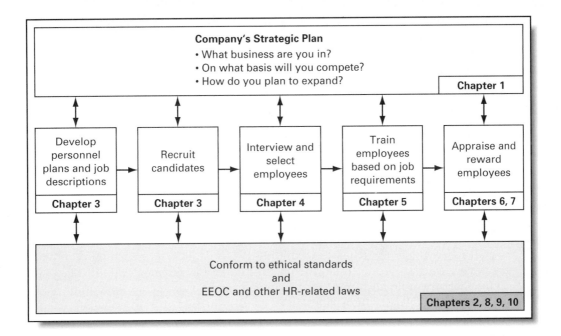

Company's Strategic Plan
- What business are you in?
- On what basis will you compete?
- How do you plan to expand?

Chapter 1

Develop personnel plans and job descriptions	Recruit candidates	Interview and select employees	Train employees based on job requirements	Appraise and reward employees
Chapter 3	Chapter 3	Chapter 4	Chapter 5	Chapters 6, 7

Conform to ethical standards
and
EEOC and other HR-related laws

Chapters 2, 8, 9, 10

SELECTED EQUAL EMPLOYMENT OPPORTUNITY LAWS

Hardly a day goes by without news reports of equal opportunity–related lawsuits at work. Thus, American Express Financial Advisers Inc. recently paid $31 million to settle a sex discrimination lawsuit. Female professional employees had alleged that Amex paid them less and provided them with fewer job opportunities than their male counterparts received.[3] Coca-Cola settled a race bias suit brought by thousands of its employees.[4] Even the federal government recently paid $508 million to over 1,100 women. The women alleged that the Voice of America and the U.S. Information Agency had denied them jobs because of their gender.[5] Understanding and managing equal opportunity and diversity at work is a crucial management job. In this chapter, we'll discuss the equal employment opportunity laws with which employers must comply. You cannot effectively perform day-to-day supervisory responsibilities like screening and appraising employees without understanding these laws. Let's start at the beginning.

Background

Legislation barring discrimination against minorities in the United States is nothing new. For example, the Fifth Amendment to the U.S. Constitution (ratified in 1791) states that "no person shall . . . be deprived of life, liberty, or property, without due process of the law."[6] Other laws as well as various court decisions made discrimination against minorities illegal by the early 1900s, at least in theory.[7] But as a practical matter, Congress and various presidents were reluctant to take dramatic action on equal employment issues until the early 1960s. At that point, "they were finally prompted to act primarily as a result of civil unrest among the minorities and women" who eventually became protected by the new equal rights legislation and the agencies created to implement and enforce it.[8]

Equal Pay Act of 1963

The **Equal Pay Act of 1963** (amended in 1972) was one of the first new laws passed. It made it unlawful to discriminate in pay on the basis of sex when jobs involve equal work—equivalent skills, effort, and responsibility—and are performed under similar working conditions. However, differences in pay do not violate the act if the difference is based on a seniority system, a merit system, a system that measures earnings by quantity or quality of production, or a differential based on any factor other than sex.

Title VII of the 1964 Civil Rights Act

What the Law Says   **Title VII of the 1964 Civil Rights Act** was another of these new laws. Title VII (as amended by the 1972 Equal Employment Opportunity Act) states that an employer cannot discriminate based on race, color, religion, sex, or national origin. Specifically, it states that it shall be an unlawful employment practice for an employer:[9]

1. *To fail or refuse to hire or to discharge an individual* or otherwise to discriminate against any individual with respect to his or her compensation, terms, conditions, or privileges of employment, because of such individual's race, color, religion, sex, or national origin.
2. *To limit, segregate, or classify his or her employees or applicants for employment* in any way that would deprive or tend to deprive any individual of employment opportunities or otherwise adversely affect his or her status as an employee, because of such individual's race, color, religion, sex, or national origin.[10]

The EEOC   The **Equal Employment Opportunity Commission (EEOC)** was instituted by Title VII; it consists of five members, appointed by the president with the advice and consent of the senate. Each member of the EEOC serves a term of five years. The EEOC of course has a staff of thousands to assist it in administering the Civil Rights law in employment settings.

Establishing the EEOC greatly enhanced the federal government's ability to enforce equal employment opportunity laws. The EEOC receives and investigates job discrimination complaints from aggrieved individuals. When it finds reasonable cause that the charges are justified, it attempts (through conciliation) to reach an agreement eliminating all aspects of the discrimination. If this conciliation fails, the EEOC has the power to go directly to court to enforce the law. Under the Equal Employment Opportunity Act of 1972, discrimination charges may be filed by the EEOC on behalf of an aggrieved individual, as well as by the individuals themselves. We explain this procedure in more detail later in this chapter.

Executive Orders

Under executive orders issued in the Johnson administration, most employers who do business with the U.S. government have an obligation beyond that imposed by

Title VII to refrain from employment discrimination. Executive Orders 11246 and 11375 don't just ban discrimination; they require that contractors take **affirmative action** to ensure equal employment opportunity (we will explain affirmative action later in this chapter). The orders also state a policy against employment discrimination based on age or physical handicap, in addition to race, color, religion, sex, or national origin. These orders also established the **Office of Federal Contract Compliance Programs (OFCCP),** which is responsible for implementing the executive orders and ensuring the compliance of federal contracts.

Age Discrimination in Employment Act of 1967

The **Age Discrimination in Employment Act (ADEA) of 1967,** as amended, makes it unlawful to discriminate against employees or applicants for employment who are 40 years of age or older, effectively ending most mandatory retirement. One-fifth of the court actions filed by the EEOC recently have been ADEA cases. (Another 30% have been sex discrimination cases.) This act is a *favored statute* among employees and lawyers because it allows jury trials and double damages to those proving "willful" discrimination.[11]

Vocational Rehabilitation Act of 1973

The **Vocational Rehabilitation Act of 1973** requires employers with federal contracts over $2,500 to take affirmative action for the employment of handicapped persons. The act does not require that an unqualified person be hired. It does require that an employer take steps to accommodate a handicapped worker unless doing so imposes an undue hardship on the employer.[12]

Pregnancy Discrimination Act of 1978

Congress passed the **Pregnancy Discrimination Act (PDA)** in 1978 as an amendment to Title VII. The act broadened the definition of sex discrimination to encompass pregnancy, childbirth, or related medical conditions. It prohibits using these for discrimination in hiring, promotion, suspension or discharge, or any other term or condition of employment.[13] Basically, the act says that if an employer offers its employees disability coverage, then pregnancy and childbirth must be treated like any other disability and must be included in the plan as a covered condition.[14] The U.S. Supreme Court ruled in *California Federal Savings and Loan Association* v. *Guerra* that if an employer offers no disability leave to any of its employees, it can (but need not necessarily) grant pregnancy leave to a woman who requests it when disabled for pregnancy, childbirth, or a related medical condition, although men get no comparable benefits.[15]

Federal Agency Guidelines

The federal agencies charged with ensuring compliance with the aforementioned laws and executive orders issue their own implementing guidelines. The overall purpose of these **federal agency guidelines** is to specify the procedures these agencies recommend employers follow in complying with the equal opportunity laws.

Uniform Guidelines on Employee Selection Procedures   Detailed guidelines to be used by employers have been approved by the EEOC, Civil Service Commission, Department of Labor, and Department of Justice.[16] These uniform guidelines supersede earlier guidelines developed by the EEOC alone. They set forth "highly recommended" procedures regarding such matters as employee selection, record keeping, preemployment inquiries, and affirmative action programs. As an example, the guidelines specify that any employment selection devices (including but not limited to written tests) that screen out disproportionate numbers of women or minorities must be *validated*. The guidelines also explain in detail *how* an employer can validate a selection device. (We explain this procedure in Chapter 4.) The OFCCP has its own *Manual of Guidelines*.[17] The American Psychological Association has published its own *Standards for Educational and Psychological Testing.*

Historically, these guidelines have fleshed out the procedures to use in complying with equal employment laws. For example, recall that the ADEA prohibited employers from discriminating against persons over 40 years old because of age. Subsequent EEOC guidelines stated that it was unlawful to discriminate in hiring (or in any way) by giving preference because of age to individuals within the 40-plus age bracket. Thus, if two people apply for the same job, and one is 45 and the other is 55, you may not lawfully turn down the 55-year-old candidate because of his or her age and expect to defend yourself by saying that you hired someone over 40.[18] (Hiring, say, a 53-year-old may be defensible, however.)

Sexual Harassment

Harassment on the basis of sex is a violation of Title VII when such conduct has the purpose or effect of substantially interfering with a person's work performance or creating an intimidating, hostile, or offensive work environment. The EEOC's guidelines further assert that employers have an affirmative duty to maintain workplaces free of sexual harassment and intimidation.[19] The Civil Rights Act of 1991 added teeth to this by permitting victims of intentional discrimination, including sexual harassment, to have jury trials and to collect compensatory damages for pain and suffering and punitive damages in cases in which the employer acted with "malice or reckless indifference" to the individual's rights.[20] Sexual harassment complaints rose about 10 percent per year in the late 1990s.[21]

The **Federal Violence Against Women Act of 1994** provides another avenue women can use to seek relief for violent sexual harassment. It provides that a person "who commits a crime of violence motivated by gender and thus deprives another" of her rights shall be liable to the party injured. Furthermore, employees can file discrimination suits claiming sexual harassment by people of their own sex.[22] (In one case, a worker on an offshore oil rig claimed that his male supervisors restrained him several times while another worker harassed him and that he ultimately had to quit out of fear of being raped.)

The EEOC guidelines define sexual harassment as unwelcome sexual advances, requests for sexual favors, and other verbal or physical conduct of a sexual nature that takes place under any of the following conditions:

1. Submission to such conduct is made either explicitly or implicitly a term or condition of an individual's employment.
2. Submission to or rejection of such conduct by an individual is used as the basis for employment decisions affecting such individual.
3. Such conduct has the purpose or effect of unreasonably interfering with an individual's work performance or creating an intimidating, hostile, or offensive work environment.[23]

Proving Sexual Harassment

There are three main ways an employee can prove sexual harassment.

Quid Pro Quo   The most direct way an employee can prove sexual harassment is to prove that rejecting a supervisor's advances adversely affected the employee's tangible benefits, such as raises or promotions. For example, in one case the employee was able to show that continued job success and advancement were dependent on her agreeing to the sexual demands of her supervisors. She showed that after an initial complaint to her employer she was subjected to adverse performance evaluations, disciplinary layoffs, and other adverse actions.[24]

Hostile Environment Created by Supervisors   It is not always necessary to show that the harassment had tangible consequences such as a demotion or termination. For example, in one case the court found that a male supervisor's sexual harassment had substantially affected a female employee's emotional and psychological ability to the point that she felt she had to quit her job. Therefore, even though no direct threats or promises were made in exchange for sexual advances, the fact that the advances interfered with the woman's performance and created an offensive work environment were enough to prove that sexual harassment had occurred. On the other hand, the courts do not interpret as sexual harassment any sexual relationships that arise during the course of employment but that do not have a substantial effect on that employment.[25] In one decision, for instance, the U.S. Supreme Court held that sexual harassment law doesn't cover ordinary "intersexual flirtation." In his ruling, Justice Antonin Scalia said courts must carefully distinguish between "simple teasing" and truly abusive behavior.[26]

Hostile Environment Created by Co-Workers or Nonemployees   Advances do not have to be made by the person's supervisor to qualify as sexual harassment: An employee's co-workers (or even the employer's customers) can cause the employer to be held responsible for sexual harassment. In one case, the court held that a sexually provocative uniform the employer required led to lewd comments and innuendos by customers toward the employee. When she complained that she would no longer wear the uniform, she was fired. Because the employer could not show that there was a job-related necessity for requiring such a uniform and because the uniform was required only for female employees, the court ruled that the employer, in effect, was responsible for the sexually harassing behavior. EEOC guidelines also state that an employer is liable for the sexually harassing acts of its nonsupervisor employees if the employer knew or should have known of the harassing conduct.

Court Decisions

The U.S. Supreme Court used the *Meritor Savings Bank, FSB* v. *Vinson* case to broadly endorse the EEOC's guidelines on sexual harassment. Two more recent U.S. Supreme Court decisions further clarified the law on sexual harassment.

In the first case, *Burlington Industries* v. *Ellerth*, the employee accused her supervisor of *quid pro quo* harassment. She said her boss propositioned and threatened her with demotion if she did not respond. The threats were not carried out, and she was in fact promoted. In the second case, *Faragher* v. *City of Boca Raton*, the employee accused the employer of condoning a hostile work environment: She said she quit her lifeguard job after repeated taunts from other lifeguards. The Court ruled in favor of the employees in both cases.

The Court's decisions have several important implications for employers. First, they make it clear that in a *quid pro quo* case it is *not* necessary for the employee to have suffered a tangible job action (such as being demoted) to win the case. Second, the Court spelled out an important defense against harassment suits. It said the employer must show that it took "reasonable care" to prevent and promptly correct any sexually harassing behavior and that the employee unreasonably failed to take advantage of the employer's policy.

In particular, the Court said that an employer could defend itself against sexual harassment liability by showing two things. First, it had to show "that the employer exercised reasonable care to prevent and correct promptly any sexually harassing behavior." Second, it had to demonstrate that the plaintiff "unreasonably failed to take advantage of any preventive or corrective opportunities provided by the employer." The Supreme Court specifically said that the employee's failing to use formal organizational reporting systems would satisfy the second component.

Many employers promptly took steps to ensure that they could show they did take reasonable care. For example, they promulgated strong sexual harassment policies, trained managers and employees regarding their responsibilities for complying with these policies, instituted reporting processes, investigated charges promptly, and then took corrective actions promptly, as required.[27] However, such steps, while laudable, may not be enough. Let's look at what managers and employers can do, in more detail.

What the Manager/Employer Should Do   As summarized in the *HR in Practice* box, employers can take steps (such as issuing a strong policy statement) to minimize liability if a sexual harassment claim is filed against the organization and to prevent such claims from arising in the first place. In general, employers (1) should take steps to ensure that harassment does not take place, and (2) should take immediate corrective action, even if the offending party is a nonemployee, once it knows (or should know) of harassing conduct.[28]

The manager, however, needs to keep in mind that steps like these are usually not, by themselves, enough. There are several issues to consider here. First, studies show that there are significant gender differences in perceptions of sexual harassment. Specifically, "women perceive a broader range of socio-sexual behaviors as harassing," particularly when those behaviors involve "hostile work environment harassment, derogatory attitudes toward women, dating pressure, or physical sexual contact."[29] In other words, what is harassment to a woman may be innocent to a man.

1. Take all complaints about harassment seriously. As one sexual harassment manual for managers and supervisors advises, "When confronted with sexual harassment complaints or when sexual conduct is observed in the workplace, the best reaction is to address the complaint or stop the conduct."[30] If complaints are not taken seriously, or it's risky to complain, or perpetrators are unlikely to be punished, then the firm's employees are likely to experience considerably higher levels of harassment.[31]

2. Issue a strong policy statement condemning such behavior. The EEOC's standards state that an effective anti-harassment policy should contain a clear explanation of the prohibited conduct; assurance of protection against retaliation for employees who make complaints or provide information related to such complaints; a clearly described complaint process that provides confidentiality and accessible avenues of complaint as well as prompt, thorough, and impartial investigations; and clear assurance that the employer will take immediate and appropriate corrective action where harassment has occurred.[32] An example, presented in Figure 2.1, states that "such behavior may result in . . . dismissal."

3. Inform all employees about the policy prohibiting sexual harassment and of their rights under the policy.

4. Develop and implement a complaint procedure.

5. Establish a management response system that includes an immediate reaction and investigation by senior management. The likelihood of employer liability is lessened considerably when the employer's response is "adequate" and "reasonably calculated to prevent future harassment."[33]

6. Begin management training sessions with supervisors and managers to increase their awareness of the issues. As with all training, it is advisable to make sure that the sexual harassment training programs are having the desired effect. In one study, researchers compared about 200 people who participated in a sexual harassment program with about 350 people who did not. In this study male participants in the sexual harassment program were actually *less* (not more) likely than other groups to perceive an action as sexual

Figure 2.1 Sample Sexual Harassment Policy

The company's position is that sexual harassment is a form of misconduct that undermines the integrity of the employment relationship. No employee—either male or female—should be subject to unsolicited and unwelcome sexual overtures or conduct, either verbal or physical. Sexual harassment does not refer to occasional compliments of a socially accepted nature. It refers to behavior that is not welcome, that is personally offensive, that debilitates morale, and that, therefore, interferes with work effectiveness. Such behavior may result in disciplinary action up to and including dismissal.

Source: © 1991 by CCH Incorporated. All Rights Reserved. Reprinted with permission from *Sexual Harassment Manual for Managers and Supervisors.*

harassment, less willing to report sexual harassment, and more likely to blame the victim![34]

7. Discipline managers and employees involved in sexual harassment.

8. Keep thorough records of complaints, investigations, and actions taken.

9. Conduct exit interviews that uncover any complaints and that acknowledge by signature the reasons for leaving.

10. Re-publish the sexual harassment policy periodically.

11. Encourage upward communication through periodic written attitude surveys, hotlines, suggestion boxes, and other feedback procedures to discover employees' feelings concerning any evidence of sexual harassment and to keep management informed.[35]

A second reason why even apparently "reasonable" precautions may be insufficient is that employees may be reluctant to use them. This is because a sexual harassment compliance procedure may be reasonable in the legal sense, but not so reasonable to the employees who must use it. In one study, researchers surveyed about 6,000 employees in the U.S. military. Their findings made it clear that reporting incidents of harassment often triggered retaliation and could harm the victim "in terms of lower job satisfaction and greater psychological distress." Under such conditions, it's no wonder that for many of these employees, the most "reasonable" thing to do was nothing, and avoid reporting. (Disclosures of such harassment at the U.S. Air Force Academy may illustrate just such a problem.) Managers who take preventing sexual harassment seriously therefore must ensure that the organization's climate (including management's real willingness to eradicate harassment), and not just its written rules and procedures, support employees who feel harassed.[36]

Contributing to the problem is the fact that most victims of sexual harassment don't sue or complain. Instead, they quit or try to avoid their harassers. The harassers themselves sometimes don't even realize that their abominable behavior is harassing or offending others. Sexual harassment training and policies can reduce these problems.[37]

What the Employee Can Do   An employee who believes he or she has been sexually harassed can also take several steps to address the problem.

The steps to take are based in part on how courts define sexual harassment. For example, "hostile environment" sexual harassment generally means that the discriminatory intimidation, insults, and ridicule that permeated the workplace were sufficiently severe or pervasive to alter the conditions of employment. Courts in these cases look at several things. These include whether the discriminatory conduct is frequent or severe; whether it is physically threatening or humiliating, or a mere offensive utterance; and whether it unreasonably interferes with an employee's work performance.[38] In turn, whether an employee subjectively perceives the work environment as abusive is related to such things as whether the employee welcomed the conduct or immediately made it clear that the conduct was unwelcome, undesirable, or offensive.[39] The steps an employee can take include:

1. File a verbal contemporaneous complaint or protest with the harasser and the harasser's boss stating that the unwanted overtures should cease because the conduct is unwelcome.

2. Write a letter to the accused. This may be a polite, low-key letter that does three things: provides a detailed statement of the facts as the writer sees them; describes his or her feelings and what damage the writer thinks has been done; and states that he or she would like to request that the future relationship be on a purely professional basis. Deliver this letter in person, with a witness if necessary.
3. If the unwelcome conduct does not cease, file verbal and written reports regarding the unwelcome conduct and unsuccessful efforts to get it to stop with the harasser's manager and/or the human resource director.
4. If the letters and appeals to the employer do not suffice, the accuser should turn to the local office of the EEOC to file the necessary claim.
5. If the harassment is of a serious nature, the employee can also consult an attorney about suing the harasser for assault and battery, intentional infliction of emotional distress, and injunctive relief and to recover compensatory and punitive damages.

Selected Court Decisions Regarding Equal Employment Opportunity (EEO)

Several early court decisions helped to form the interpretive foundation for EEO laws such as those involving sexual harassment. We summarize some important decisions in this section.

Griggs* v. *Duke Power Company   *Griggs* (1971) was a landmark case because the Supreme Court used it to define unfair discrimination. In this case, a suit was brought against the Duke Power Company on behalf of Willie Griggs, an applicant for a job as a coal handler. The company required its coal handlers to be high school graduates. Griggs claimed that this requirement was illegally discriminatory because it wasn't related to success on the job and because it resulted in more blacks than whites being rejected for these jobs.

Griggs won the case. The decision of the Court was unanimous, and in his written opinion Chief Justice Burger laid out three crucial guidelines affecting equal employment legislation. First, the court ruled that discrimination on the part of the employer need not be overt; in other words, the employer does not have to be shown to have intentionally discriminated against the employee or applicant—it need only be shown that discrimination took place. Second, the court held that an employment practice (in this case requiring the high school diploma) must be shown to be *job related* if it has an unequal impact on members of a **protected class.** In the words of Justice Burger:

> The act proscribes not only overt discrimination but also practices that are fair in form, but discriminatory in operation. The touchstone is business necessity. If an employment practice which operates to exclude Negroes cannot be shown to be related to job performance the practice is prohibited.[40]

Third, Burger's opinion clearly placed the burden of proof on the employer to show that the hiring practice is job related. Thus, the *employer* must show that the employment practice (in this case, requiring a high school diploma) is needed to perform the job satisfactorily if it has a disparate impact on (unintentionally discriminates against) members of a protected class.

Albemarle Paper Company* v. *Moody   In the *Griggs* case, the Supreme Court decided that a screening tool (such as a test) had to be job related or valid—that is, performance on the test must be related to performance on the job. The 1975 *Albemarle* case is important because here the Court provided more details regarding how an employer should validate its screening tools. In other words, it helped to clarify what the employer had to do to prove that the test or other screening tools are related to or predict performance on the job.[41] For example, the Court ruled that before using a test to screen job candidates, the employer must analyze and document the job's specific duties and responsibilities. The Court also ruled that the performance standards for employees on the job in question should be clear and unambiguous, so the employer could identify which employees were performing better than others (and thus whether the screening tools were effective).

In arriving at its decision, the Court also cited the EEOC guidelines concerning acceptable selection procedures and made these guidelines the "law of the land."[42] The court's ruling had the effect of establishing the detailed EEOC (now federal) guidelines on validation as the procedures for validating employment practices.[43]

The Civil Rights Act of 1991

Subsequent Supreme Court rulings in the 1980s actually had the effect of limiting the protection of women and minority groups under equal employment laws; this prompted congress to pass a new Civil Rights Act. President George Bush signed the **Civil Rights Act of 1991 (CRA 1991)** into law in November 1991. The effect of CRA 1991 was to roll back the clock to where it stood before the 1980s decisions, and in some respects to place even more responsibility on employers.

First, CRA 1991 addressed the issue of *burden of proof.* Today, after CRA 1991, the process of filing and responding to a discrimination charge goes something like this. The plaintiff (say, a rejected applicant) demonstrates that an employment practice (such as a test) has a disparate (or "adverse") impact on a particular group. (*Disparate impact* "means that an employer engages in an employment practice or policy that has a greater adverse impact [effect] on the members of a protected group under Title VII than on other employees, regardless of intent."[44]) Requiring a college degree for a job would have an adverse impact on some minority groups, for instance. Disparate impact claims do *not* require proof of discriminatory intent. Instead, the plaintiff must show two things. First, he or she must show that a significant disparity exists between the proportion of (say) women in the available labor pool and the proportion hired. Second, he or she must show that an apparently neutral employment practice, such as word-of-mouth advertising or a requirement that the job holder "be able to lift 100 pounds," is causing the disparity.[45]

Then, once the plaintiff shows such disparate impact, the *employer* has the *burden of proving* that the challenged practice is job related for the position in question. For example, the employer has to show that lifting 100 pounds is actually required for the position in question, and that the business could not run efficiently without the requirement—that it is a business necessity.

The 1991 Civil Rights Act marked a substantial change in the geographic applicability of equal rights legislation. Congressional legislation generally only applies within U.S. territorial borders unless specifically stated otherwise.[46] However, CRA 1991 specifically expanded coverage by amending the definition of *employee* in Title VII to mean a U.S. citizen employed in a foreign country by a U.S.-owned or -controlled company.[47] At least theoretically, therefore, U.S. citizens now working overseas for U.S. companies enjoy the same equal employment opportunity protection as those working within U.S. borders.[48]

Two factors limit the wholesale application of CRA 1991 to U.S. employees abroad, however. First, the civil rights protections are not universal or automatic because there are numerous exclusions. For example, an employer need not comply with Title VII if compliance would cause the employer to violate the law of the host country. (For instance, some foreign countries have statutes prohibiting the employment of women in management positions.)

A more vexing problem is the practical difficulty of enforcing CRA 1991 abroad. For example, the EEOC investigator's first duty in an extraterritorial case is to analyze the finances and organizational structure of the respondent, but in practice few, if any, investigators are trained for this duty and no precise standards exist for such investigations.[49] Similarly, one expert has argued that U.S. courts are "little help in overseas investigations, because few foreign nations cooperate with the intrusive enforcement of U.S. civil law."[50] It is possible, therefore, that in this case CRA 1991's bark will be considerably worse than its bite and that, as one expert says, "Congress' well-meaning effort to leave no American uncovered by U.S. antidiscrimination law will not have its intended effect."[51]

CRA 1991 also makes it easier to sue for *money damages* in certain cases. It provides that an employee who is claiming *intentional discrimination* (which is called *disparate treatment*) can ask for (1) compensatory damages and (2) punitive damages, if it can be shown the employer engaged in discrimination "with malice or reckless indifference to the federally protected rights of an aggrieved individual."[52] This is a marked change from what prevailed until 1991. Victims of intentional discrimination who had not suffered financial loss and who sued under Title VII could not then sue for compensatory or punitive damages. All they could expect was to have their jobs reinstated (or be awarded a particular job). They were also eligible for back pay, attorney's fees, and court costs. (See also the *Global Issues in HR* box.)

Finally, CRA 1991 also states:

> An unlawful employment practice is established when the complaining party demonstrates that race, color, religion, sex, or national origin was a motivating factor for any employment practice, even though other factors also motivated the practice.[53]

In other words, an employer cannot avoid liability by proving it would have taken the same action—such as terminating someone—even without the discriminatory motive.[54] If there is any such motive, the practice may be unlawful.

The Americans with Disabilities Act

What is the ADA?   The **Americans with Disabilities Act (ADA)** aims to reduce or eliminate serious problems of discrimination against disabled individuals. The act prohibits employers from discriminating against qualified disabled individuals. It also says employers must make "reasonable accommodations" for physical or mental limitations unless doing so imposes an "undue hardship" on the business.

The ADA's pivotal terms are important in understanding its impact. For example, specific disabilities aren't listed; instead, the EEOC's implementing regulations provide that an individual is disabled if he or she has a physical or mental impairment that substantially limits one or more major life activities. They also provide that an impairment includes any physiological disorder or condition, cosmetic disfigurement, or anatomical loss affecting one or more of several body systems, or any mental or psychological disorder.[55] On the other hand, the act does set forth certain conditions that are not to be regarded as disabilities, including homosexuality, bisexuality, voyeurism, compulsive gambling, pyromania, and certain disorders resulting from the person's currently using illegal drugs.[56]

Simply being disabled does not qualify someone for a job, of course. Instead, the act prohibits discrimination against qualified individuals—those who, with (or without) a reasonable accommodation, can carry out the essential functions of the job. This means that the individual must have the requisite skills, educational background, and experience to do the essential functions of the position. A job function is essential when, for instance, it is the reason the position exists, or because the function is so highly specialized that the person doing the job is hired for his or her expertise or ability to perform that particular function.[57]

If the individual can't perform the job as currently structured, the employer is required to make a reasonable accommodation unless doing so would present an undue hardship. *Reasonable accommodation* might include redesigning the job, modifying work schedules, or modifying or acquiring equipment or other devices to assist the person in performing the job. Court cases illustrate what "reasonable accommodation" means. For example, a Wal-Mart door greeter was diagnosed with and treated for back problems. When she returned to work she asked her employer if she could sit on a stool while on duty. The employer rejected her request, contending that standing was an essential part of the greeter's job. She sued, but the federal district court agreed with the employer that the door greeters must act in an "aggressively hospitable manner," which can't be done sitting on a stool.[58]

The ADA in Practice   ADA complaints are flooding the EEOC and the courts. However, the chances of prevailing in ADA cases are against the plaintiff; employers prevailed in about 96% of federal circuit court decisions in one recent year. A main reason is that employees are failing to show that they are disabled and qualified to do the job.[59] Unlike Title VII of the Civil Rights Act, there's a heavy burden on the employee to establish that he or she is protected by the ADA. The employee has to establish that he or she has a disability that fits under the ADA's definition. Doing so is more complicated than proving that one is a particular age, race, or gender. The types of disabilities alleged in ADA charges have been somewhat surprising. Mental disabilities now account for the greatest number of claims brought under the ADA.[60]

A recent U.S. Supreme Court decision typifies what plaintiffs face. An assembly line worker sued Toyota, arguing that carpal tunnel syndrome and tendonitis prevented her from doing her job (*Toyota Motor Manufacturing of Kentucky, Inc.* v. *Williams*). The U.S. Supreme Court ruled that the ADA covers carpal tunnel syndrome and tendonitis only if her impairments affect not just her job performance, but her daily living activities too. Here, the employee admitted that she could perform personal tasks and chores such as washing her face, brushing her teeth, tending her flower garden, and fixing breakfast and doing laundry. The court said the disability must be central to the employee's daily living (not just job) to qualify under the ADA. The court will therefore look at each case (for instance, of carpal tunnel syndrome) individually.[61]

Many other cases similarly denied the plaintiff's claim. In one, the court held that the employer did not discriminate against a blind bartender by requiring her to transfer to another job because she was unable to spot underage or intoxicated customers.[62] In another (*Murphy* v. *United Parcel Service*), the U.S. Supreme Court decided that a person whose disability was mitigated by medication could not claim a disability as a limitation if he had not taken his medication.[63] On the other hand, one U.S. Circuit Court of Appeals held that punctuality was not an essential job function for a laboratory assistant who was habitually tardy. (The court decided he could perform the job's 7 1/2 hours of data entry even if he arrived late.[64]) And, Wal-Mart recently had to reinstate hearing-impaired workers and pay a $750,000 fine for discrimination under the ADA.[65]

Implications for Managers   The ADA imposes numerous legal obligations on employers. These include (but are not limited to) the following:

- Employers may not make preemployment inquiries about a person's disability, although employers may ask questions about the person's ability to perform specific job functions.
- Employers should review job application forms, interview procedures, and job descriptions for potentially discriminatory items, and identify the essential functions of the jobs in question.
- Employers must make a reasonable accommodation unless doing so would result in undue hardship.

However, given ADA court decisions like those discussed, there are, additionally, several practical implications to keep in mind when dealing with ADA-related matters.[66] First, courts will tend to define "disabilities" quite narrowly. Employers may therefore require that the employee provide documentation of the disorder, and assess what effect that disorder has on the employee's job performance. A disability is not necessarily covered by ADA. Employers should therefore ask questions such as: Does the employee have a disability that substantially limits a major life activity? Is the employee qualified to do the job? Can the employee perform the essential functions of the job? Can any reasonable accommodation be provided without creating an undue hardship on the employer?[67] Second, it's clear from these decisions that employers "do not need to allow *misconduct or erratic performance* (including absences and tardiness), even if that behavior is linked to the disability."[68] Third, the employer does not have to *create a new job* for the disabled worker nor reassign that person to a light-duty position for indefinite period, unless such a position exists.[69] Fourth, one

Table 2.1 Summary of Important Equal Employment Opportunity Actions

ACTION	WHAT IT DOES
Title VII of 1964 Civil Rights Act, as amended	Bars discrimination because of race, color, religion, sex, or national origin; instituted EEOC
Executive orders	Prohibit employment discrimination by employers with federal contracts of more than $10,000 (and their subcontractors); established office of federal compliance; require affirmative action programs
Federal agency guidelines	Indicate policy covering discrimination based on sex, national origin, and religion, as well as employee selection procedures; for example, require validation of tests
Supreme Court decisions: *Griggs* v. *Duke Power Company, Albemarle Paper Company* v. *Moody*	Ruled that job requirements must be related to job success; that discrimination need not be overt to be proved; that the burden of proof is on the employer to prove the qualification is valid
Equal Pay Act of 1963	Requires equal pay for men and women for performing similar work
Age Discrimination in Employment Act of 1967	Prohibits discriminating against a person 40 or over in any area of employment because of age
State and local laws	Often cover organizations too small to be covered by federal laws
Vocational Rehabilitation Act of 1973	Requires affirmative action to employ and promote qualified handicapped persons and prohibits discrimination against handicapped persons
Pregnancy Discrimination Act of 1978	Prohibits discrimination in employment against pregnant women, or related conditions
Vietnam Era Veterans' Readjustment Assistance Act of 1974	Requires affirmative action in employment for veterans of the Vietnam War era
Wards Cove v. *Atonio, Patterson* v. *McLean Credit Union*	Made it more difficult to prove a case of unlawful discrimination against an employer
Martin v. *Wilks*	Allowed consent degrees to be attacked and could have had a chilling effect on certain affirmative action programs
Americans with Disabilities Act of 1990	Strengthens the need for most employers to make reasonable accommodations for disabled employees at work; prohibits discrimination
Civil Rights Act of 1991	Reverses *Wards Cove, Patterson,* and *Martin* decisions; places burden of proof back on employer and permits compensatory and punitive money damages for discrimination

expert advises, "*don't treat employees* as if they are disabled." If they can control their conditions (for instance, through medication), they usually won't be considered disabled. However, if they are treated as disabled by their employers (for instance, with respect to the jobs they're assigned), they'll normally be "regarded as" disabled and protected under the ADA.[70]

State and Local Equal Employment Opportunity Laws

In addition to the federal laws, all states and many local governments also prohibit employment discrimination.

In most cases, the effect of the state and local laws is to further restrict employers regarding their treatment of job applicants and employees. In many cases, state equal employment opportunity laws cover employers that are not covered by federal legislation (such as those with fewer than 15 employees).[71] Similarly, some local governments extend the protection of age discrimination laws to young people as well, barring discrimination not only of those over 40, but also of those over 17. For instance, it would be illegal to advertise for "mature" applicants because that might discourage some teenagers from applying. The point is that many actions that might be legal under federal laws are illegal under state and local laws.[72]

State and local equal employment opportunity agencies (often called *human resources commissions, commissions on human relations,* or *fair employment commissions*) play a role in the equal employment compliance process. When the EEOC receives a discrimination charge, it usually defers it for a limited time to the state and local agencies that have comparable jurisdiction. Then, if satisfactory remedies are not achieved, the charges are referred back to the EEOC for resolution.

Summary

Table 2.1. summarizes these and selected other equal employment opportunity legislation, executive orders, and agency guidelines.

DEFENSES AGAINST DISCRIMINATION ALLEGATIONS

What Is Adverse Impact?

To understand how employers defend themselves against employment discrimination claims, we should first briefly review some basic legal theory.

Adverse impact plays a central role in discriminatory practice allegations. Under the Civil Rights Act of 1991, a person who believes he or she has been unintentionally discriminated against need only establish a prima facie case of discrimination; this means showing that the employer's selection procedures had an adverse impact on a protected minority group. *Adverse impact* "refers to the total employment process that results in a significantly higher percentage of a protected group in the candidate population being rejected for employment, placement, or promotion."[73] "Employers may not institute an employment practice that causes a disparate impact on a particular class of people unless they can show that the practice is job related and necessary."[74]

What does this mean? If a minority or other protected group applicant for the job feels he or she has been discriminated against, the applicant need only show that the selection procedures resulted in an adverse impact on his or her minority group. (There are several ways to do this, for example, by showing that 80% of the white applicants passed the test, but only 20% of the black applicants passed; if this is the case, a black applicant has a prima facie case proving adverse impact.) Then, once the employee has proved his or her point, the burden of proof shifts to the employer. It becomes the employer's task to prove that its test, application blank, interview, or the like, is a valid predictor of performance on the job (and that it was applied fairly and equitably to both minorities and nonminorities).

Discrimination law distinguishes between disparate *treatment* and disparate *impact*. **Disparate treatment** "exists where an employer treats an individual differently because that individual is a member of a particular race, religion, gender, or ethnic group."[75] For example, it ". . . requires no more than a finding that women (or protected minority group members) were intentionally treated differently . . . because of their gender (or minority status)," according to one appeals court decision. Disparate treatment means intentional discrimination. *Disparate impact* claims do not require proof of discriminatory intentions. Instead, the plaintiff must show that there is a significant disparity between the proportion of (say) women in the available labor pool and the proportion hired, and that there's an apparently neutral employment practice (such as word-of-mouth advertising) causing the disparity.[76] Proving that there was a business necessity for the practice is the defense.

Bringing a Case of Discrimination: Summary   Assume that an employer turns down a member of a protected group for a job based on a test score (or some other employment practice, such as interview questions or application blank responses). Further assume that the person believes that he or she was discriminated against due to being in a protected class and decides to sue the employer.

All he or she has to do is show (to the court's satisfaction) that the employer's test had an adverse impact on members of his or her minority group. Then, the burden of proof shifts to the employer, which then has the burden of defending itself against the charges of discrimination.

There are then two defenses that the employer can use: the **bona fide occupational qualification** (BFOQ) defense and the business necessity defense. Either can be used to justify an employment practice that has been shown to have an adverse impact on the members of a minority group.[77] (A third defense is that the decision was made on the basis of legitimate nondiscriminatory reasons, such as poor performance, having nothing to do with the alleged prohibited discrimination.)

Bona Fide Occupational Qualification

One approach an employer can use to defend against charges of discrimination is to claim that the employment practice is a bona fide occupational qualification for performing the job. Specifically, Title VII provides that

> it should not be an unlawful employment practice for an employer to hire an employee . . . on the basis of religion, sex, or national origin in those certain instances where religion, sex, or national origin is a bona fide occupational qualification reasonably necessary to the normal operation of that particular business or enterprise.

For example, an employer can use age as a BFOQ to defend itself against a disparate treatment (intentional discrimination) charge when federal requirements impose a compulsory age limit, such as when the Federal Aviation Agency sets a ceiling of age 64 for pilots. Actors required for youthful or elderly roles or persons used to advertise or promote the sales of products designed for youthful or elderly consumers suggest other instances when age may be a BFOQ, although the courts set the bar high: the reason for the discrimination must go to the essence of the business. As another example, courts held a bus line's maximum-age hiring policy for bus drivers to be a BFOQ. The court said that the essence of the business is safe transportation of passengers, and given that, the employer should strive to employ the most qualified persons available.[78] Yet Supreme Court decisions such as *Western Airlines, Inc.* v. *Criswell* seem to be narrowing BFOQ exceptions under ADEA. In this case the Court held that the airline could not impose a mandatory retirement age (of 60) for flight engineers, even though they could for pilots. (In March 2001, over objections by the FAA and the two major commercial pilots' unions, Congress passed new legislation allowing commercial airline pilots to fly up to age 65, if in good health—a five-year increase.[79]) The BFOQ defense is not explicitly allowed for race or color.

Business Necessity

The **business necessity** defense requires showing that there is an overriding business purpose for the discriminatory practice and that the practice is therefore acceptable.

It's not easy to prove that a practice is a business necessity.[80] The Supreme Court has made it clear that business necessity does not encompass such matters as avoiding inconvenience, annoyance, or expense to the employer. The Second Circuit Court of Appeals held that *business necessity* means an "irresistible demand" and that to be retained the practice "must not only directly foster safety and efficiency," but also be essential to these goals.[81] Similarly, another court held that

> the test is whether there exists an overriding legitimate business purpose such that the practice is necessary to the safe and efficient operation of a business; thus, the business purpose must be sufficiently compelling to override any racial impact; and the challenged practice must effectively carry out the business purpose it is alleged to serve.[82]

Thus, it is not easy to prove that a practice is required for business necessity. For example, an employer cannot generally discharge employees whose wages have been garnished merely because garnishment (requiring the employer to divert part of the person's wages to pay his or her debts) creates an inconvenience for the employer. On the other hand, many employers have used this defense successfully. Thus, in *Spurlock* v. *United Airlines,* a minority candidate sued United Airlines, stating that its requirements that a pilot candidate have 500 flight hours and a college degree were unfairly discriminatory. The Court agreed that these requirements did have an adverse impact on members of the person's minority group. However, the Court held that in light of the cost of the training program and the tremendous human and economic risks involved in hiring unqualified candidates, the selection standards were required by business necessity and were job related.[83]

Attempts by employers to show that their selection tests or other employment practices are valid represent one example of the business necessity defense. The employer is required to show that the test or other practice is job related—in other words, that it is a valid predictor of performance on the job. Where such validity can be established, the courts have often supported the use of the test or other employment practice as a business necessity. Used in this context, the word *validity* means the degree to which the test or other employment practice is related to or predicts performance on the job. We discuss validation in Chapter 4.

ILLUSTRATIVE DISCRIMINATORY EMPLOYMENT PRACTICES

A Note on What You Can and Cannot Do

In this section, we present several illustrations of what managers can and cannot do under equal employment laws. But before proceeding, keep in mind that most federal laws, such as Title VII, do not expressly ban preemployment questions about an applicant's race, color, religion, sex, age, or national origin. Similarly:

> With the exception of personnel policies calling for outright discrimination against the members of some protected group, it is not really the intrinsic nature of an employer's personnel policies or practices that the courts object to. Instead, it is the result of applying a policy or practice in a particular way or in a particular context that leads to an adverse impact on some protected group.[84]

For example, it is not illegal to ask a job candidate about her marital status (although at first glance such a question might seem discriminatory). You can ask such a question as long as you can show either that you do not discriminate or that the practice can be defended as a BFOQ or business necessity.

In other words, illustrative inquiries and practices such as those summarized on the next few pages are not illegal per se. But, in practice, there are two good reasons most employers avoid such questionable practices. First, although federal law may not bar asking such questions, many state and local laws do. Second, the EEOC has said that it disapproves of such practices as asking women their marital status or applicants their age. Therefore, simply asking such questions may draw the attention of the EEOC and other regulatory agencies. Employers who use such practices thus increase their chances of having to defend themselves against charges of discriminatory employment practices.

Recruitment

Word of Mouth   You cannot rely on word-of-mouth dissemination of information about job opportunities when your workforce is all (or substantially all) white or all members of some other class such as all female, all Hispanic, and so on. Doing so might reduce the likelihood that others will become aware of the jobs and thus apply for them.

Misleading Information   It is unlawful to give false or misleading information to members of any group or to fail to refuse to advise them of work opportunities and the procedures for obtaining them.

Help Wanted Ads   "Help wanted—male" and "Help wanted—female" advertising classifieds are violations of laws forbidding sex discrimination in employment unless sex is a BFOQ for the job advertised.[85] Also, you cannot advertise in any way that suggests that applicants are being discriminated against because of their age. For example, you cannot advertise for a "young" man or woman.

Selection Standards

Educational Requirements   An educational requirement may be held illegal when (1) it can be shown that minority groups are less likely to possess the educational qualifications (such as a high school diploma), and (2) such qualifications are also not job related. For example, in the *Griggs* v. *Duke Power Company* case, a high school diploma was found both unnecessary for job performance and discriminatory against blacks. Unnecessary prerequisites (such as requiring a high school diploma where one is not required to perform the job) reportedly remains a problem today.[86] (There may be jobs for which it is a necessity, though.)

Tests   According to former Chief Justice Burger:

> Nothing in the [Title VII] act precludes the use of testing or measuring procedures; obviously they are useful. What Congress has forbidden is giving these devices and mechanisms controlling force *unless they are demonstrating a reasonable measure of job performance.*

Tests that disproportionately screen out minorities or women and are not job related are deemed unlawful by the courts. But remember that a test or other selection standard that screens out a disproportionate number of minorities or women is not *by itself* sufficient to prove that the test *unfairly* discriminates. It must also be shown that the tests or other screening devices are not job related.

Preference to Relatives   You cannot give preference to relatives of your current employees with respect to employment opportunities if your current employees are substantially nonminority.

Height, Weight, and Physical Characteristics   Maximum weight rules for employees don't usually trigger adverse legal rulings. However, some minority groups have a higher incidence of obesity, so employers must ensure that their weight rules aren't adversely impacting those groups. Similarly, "few applicants or employees will be able to demonstrate an actual weight-based disability" (in other words, that they are 100% above their ideal weight or there is a physiological cause for their disability). Few are thus entitled to reasonable accommodations under the ADA. In practice, however, studies do suggest that employers may treat overweight female applicants and employees to their disadvantage, and this needs to be closely monitored.[87]

Health Questions   The EEOC sued American Airlines, alleging that it asked an applicant questions about his medical history and medical condition before he was hired. Under the ADA, "employers are generally prohibited from asking questions about applicants' medical history or requiring preemployment physical examinations." However, such questions and exams can be used once the job offer has been extended to determine that the applicant can safely perform the job.[88]

Arrest Records   You cannot ask about or use a person's arrest record to disqualify him or her automatically for a position because there is always a presumption of innocence until proof of guilt. In addition, arrest records in general have not been shown valid for predicting job performance, and a higher percentage of minorities than nonminorities have been arrested.

Application Forms   Employment applications generally shouldn't contain questions pertaining, for instance, to applicants' disabilities, workers' compensation history, age, arrest record, or U.S. citizenship. Personal information required for legitimate tax or benefit reasons (such as who to contact in case of emergency) are best collected after the person has been hired.[89] Note that while equal employment laws discourage employers from asking for such information, no such laws prohibit the applicants from providing such information. One study examined 107 resumes from Australian managerial applicants. It found that many provided this sort of information, such as regarding marital status, ethnicity, age, and gender.[90]

Sample Discriminatory Promotion, Transfer, and Layoff Procedures

Fair employment laws protect not just job applicants but current employees as well.[91] Therefore, any employment practices regarding pay, promotion, termination, discipline, or benefits that (1) are applied differently to different classes of persons; (2) have the effect of adversely affecting members of a protected group; and (3) cannot be shown to be required as a BFOQ or business necessity may be held to be illegally discriminatory. For example, the EEOC recently issued a new enforcement guidance making it clear that employers may not discriminate against employees in connection with their benefits plans.[92]

Uniforms. When it comes to discriminatory uniforms and suggestive attire, courts have frequently sided with the employee. For example, a bank's dress policy requiring female employees to wear prescribed uniforms consisting of five basic color-coordinated items but requiring male employees only to wear "appropriate business attire" is an example of a discriminatory policy. And requiring female employees (such as waitresses) to wear sexually suggestive attire as a condition of employment has also been ruled as violating Title VII in many cases.[93]

THE EEOC ENFORCEMENT PROCESS

Processing a Charge

What happens if a person decides to file an EEOC complaint? There are several steps involved.[94] Under CRA 1991, the charge must generally be filed within 180 days after the alleged unlawful practice took place. This charge must be filed in writing and under oath, by (or on behalf of) either the person claiming to be aggrieved or a member of the EEOC who has reasonable cause to believe that a violation occurred. In practice, though, a person's charge to the EEOC is often first deferred to the relevant state or local regulatory agency; if the latter waives jurisdiction or cannot obtain a satisfactory solution to the charge, it is referred back to the EEOC.

After a charge has been filed (or the state or local deferral period has ended), the EEOC has 10 days to serve notice of the charge on the employer. The EEOC then investigates the charge to determine whether there is reasonable cause to believe it is true; it is expected to make this determination within 120 days. If no reasonable cause is found, the EEOC must dismiss the charge, in which case the person who filed the charge has 90 days to file a suit on his or her own behalf. If reasonable cause for the charge is found, the EEOC must attempt to conciliate. If this conciliation is not satisfactory, the EEOC may bring a civil suit in a federal district court or issue a notice of right to sue to the person who filed the charge. Figure 2.2 summarizes important questions an employer should ask after receiving notice from the EEOC that a bias complaint has been filed.

The EEOC now refers about 10% of its charges to a voluntary mediation mechanism. If the plaintiff agrees to mediation, the employer is asked to participate.

Figure 2.2 Questions to Ask When an Employer Receives Notice That EEOC Has Filed a Bias Claim

---

1. Exactly what is the charge and is your company covered by the relevant statutes? (For example, Title VII and the Americans with Disabilities Act generally apply only to employers with 15 or more employees. The Age Discrimination in Employment Act applies to employers with 20 or more employees, but the Equal Pay Act applies to virtually all employers with one or more employees.) Did the employee file his or her charge on time, and was it processed in a timely manner by the EEOC?

2. What protected group does the employee belong to? Is the EEOC claiming disparate impact or disparate treatment?

3. Are there any obvious bases upon which you can challenge and/or rebut the claim? For example, would the employer have taken the action if the person did not belong to a protected group? Does the person's personnel file support the action taken by the employer? Conversely, does it suggest the possibility of unjustified discriminatory treatment?

4. If it is a sexual harassment claim, are there offensive comments, calendars, posters, or screensavers on display in the company?

5. In terms of the practicality of defending your company against this claim, who are the supervisors that actually took the allegedly discriminatory actions and how effective will they be as potential witnesses? Have you received an opinion from legal counsel regarding the chances of prevailing? Even if you do prevail, what do you estimate will be the out-of-pocket costs of taking the charge through the judicial process? Would you be better off settling the case, and what are the prospects of doing so in a way that will satisfy all parties?

Sources: From *Fair Employment Practices Summary of Latest Developments* (January 7, 1988), p. 3. Copyright 1988 by The Bureau of National Affairs, Inc. (800-372-1033) www.bna.com; Kenneth Sovereign, *Personnel Law* (Upper Saddle River, NJ: Prentice Hall, 1994), pp. 36–37; "EEOC Investigations: What an Employer Should Know," Equal Employment Opportunity Commission (July 18, 2003) www.eoc.gov/small/investigations.html.

A mediation session usually lasts up to four hours. If no agreement is reached or one of the parties rejects participation, the charge is then processed through the EEOC's usual mechanisms.[95]

The new mediation program seems to be successful. Since its implementation, about 11,600 private sector charges have been resolved through the program; charging parties have obtained more than $150 million through the program. Nine out of ten participants say they would participate again.[96] The EEOC seems to be getting more efficient. In one recent year its backlog of pending cases dropped from about 81,000 to about 65,000. And in 2000, the EEOC won a record $307.3 million in benefits for discrimination victims.[97] It obtains much of this money without suing, during the preliminary, administrative, and conciliation processes. In one year, the EEOC obtained about $178 million for plaintiffs that way. This underscores the need to understand how to respond to a discrimination charge and deal with the EEOC.[98]

Faced with an offer to mediate, three responses are generally possible: agree to mediate the charge; make a settlement offer without participating in mediation; or prepare a "position statement" for the EEOC. If the employer does not mediate or make an offer, the position statement is required. It should include information relating to the company's business and the charging party's position; a description of any rules or policies and procedures that are applicable; and the chronology of the offense that led to the adverse action.[99]

How to Respond to Employment Discrimination Charges

There are several things to keep in mind when confronted by a charge of illegal employment discrimination; some of the more important can be summarized as follows:[100]

1. Be methodical. One expert notes that when you get official correspondence from the EEOC, "Odds are you won't be opening a love letter." Therefore, proceed methodically: Is the charge signed and dated and notarized by the person who filed it? Was it filed within the time allowed? Does the charge name the proper employer? Is it filed against a company that is subject to federal antidiscrimination statutes (for instance, only companies with 15 or more employees are subject to Title VII and the ADA)? Company records and persons with first-hand knowledge of the facts then should be scoured.[101]
2. Remember that EEOC investigators are not judges and aren't empowered to act as courts; they cannot make findings of discrimination on their own but can merely make recommendations. If the EEOC eventually determines that an employer may be in violation of a law, its only recourse is to file a suit or issue a notice of right to sue to the person who filed the charge.
3. Some experts advise meeting with the employee who made the complaint to determine all relevant issues. For example, ask: *What happened? Who was involved? When did the incident take place? Was the employee's ability to work affected? Were there any witnesses?* Then prepare a written statement summarizing the complaints, facts, dates, and issues involved and request that the employee sign and date this.[102]

4. Give the EEOC a position statement based on your own investigation of the matter. According to one management attorney, employers' position statements should contain words to the following effect: "We understand that a charge of discrimination has been filed against this establishment and this statement is to inform the agency that the company has a policy against discrimination and would not discriminate in the manner charged in the complaint." The statement should be supported by some statistical analysis of the workforce, copies of any documents that support the employer's position, or an explanation of any legitimate business justification for the employment decision that is the subject of the complaint.[103]

5. Ensure that there is information in the EEOC's file demonstrating lack of merit of the charge; often the best way to do that is not by answering the EEOC's questionnaire but by providing a detailed statement describing the firm's defense in its best and most persuasive light.

6. Limit the information supplied as narrowly as possible to only those issues raised in the charge itself. For example, if the charge only alleges sex discrimination, the firm should not respond unwittingly to the EEOC's request for a breakdown of employees by age and sex. Releasing too much information invites more probing by the EEOC, says one expert.[104]

7. Seek as much information as possible about the charging party's claim in order to ensure that you understand the claim and its ramifications.

8. Prepare for the EEOC's *fact-finding conferences,* which are supposed to be informal meetings held early in the investigatory process aimed at defining issues and determining whether there is a basis for negotiation. According to one expert, however, the EEOC's emphasis is often on settlement. Its investigators therefore use the conferences to find weak spots in each party's respective position so that they can use this information as leverage to push for a settlement. Therefore, thoroughly prepare witnesses who are going to testify at a fact-finding conference, especially supervisors, because their statements can be considered admissions against the employer's interest.

Mandatory Arbitration of Employment Discrimination Claims

Given the fact that even winning a discrimination lawsuit can cost an employer more than $100,000 in attorneys' fees and defense costs, it's not surprising that more employers are switching to compulsory mandatory arbitration.[105] For example, after a long and expensive equal employment lawsuit, Rockwell International implemented a grievance procedure that provides for binding arbitration at the last step. Initially, Rockwell's 970 executives had to sign a mutual agreement to arbitrate employment disputes as a condition of participation in an executive stock plan. The program (called, as is traditional, an *alternative dispute resolution,* or ADR, program) was later extended to cover all nonunion employees at some locations. New hires at Rockwell must also sign the agreement to arbitrate as a condition of employment, and current employees must sign it to be promoted or transferred.[106] ADR plans appear to be becoming more popular, although the EEOC has reasserted its long-standing opposition to such mandatory arbitration of workplace bias claims.[107]

Diversity Management and Affirmative Action Programs

To some extent the goals of equitable and fair treatment driving equal employment legislation are being rendered moot by demographic changes and globalization. Employers, in other words, have little choice but to willingly push for more diversity. Today, as we've seen, white males no longer dominate the labor force, and women and minorities will represent the lion's share of labor force growth over the foreseeable future. Furthermore, globalization increasingly requires employers to hire minority members with the cultural and language skills to deal with customers abroad. As a result, companies like Longo Toyota are increasingly striving for racial, ethnic, and sexual workforce balance, "not because of legal imperatives, but as a matter of enlightened economic self-interest."[108] At least one study suggests that cultural diversity contributes to improved productivity, return on equity, and market performance.[109]

Although there's no unanimity about what *diversity* means, there's considerable agreement about the components of diversity. For example, in one study a majority of the respondents listed race, sex, culture, national origin, handicap, age, and religion as diversity components. In other words, these comprise the demographic building blocks that represent diversity at work and what people often think of when asked what employers mean by diversity.[110]

Managing Diversity

Managing diversity means maximizing diversity's potential advantages while minimizing the potential barriers—such as prejudices and bias—that can undermine the functioning of a diverse workforce. In practice, diversity management involves both compulsory and voluntary management actions. We've seen that there are many legally mandated actions employers must take to minimize employment discrimination.

However, while such compulsory actions can reduce the more blatant diversity barriers, blending a diverse workforce into a close-knit and thriving community also requires employers to take other steps. Based on one review of research studies, one diversity expert concluded that five sets of voluntary organizational activities are at the heart of any diversity management program. We can summarize these as follows:

Provide strong leadership.   Companies with exemplary reputations in managing diversity typically have CEOs who champion the cause of diversity. Leadership means, for instance, taking a strong stand on the need for change and becoming a role model for the behaviors required for the change.

Assess the situation.   The company must assess the current state of affairs with respect to diversity management. One study found that the most common tools for measuring diversity include equal employment hiring and retention metrics, employee attitude surveys, management and employee evaluations, and focus groups.[111]

Provide diversity training and education.   One expert says that "the most commonly utilized starting point for . . . managing diversity is some type of employee education program."[112] (Yet some argue that generalized diversity training is actually backfiring, for instance, by diminishing participants' specific attention to racial relations.[113])

Change culture and management systems. Ideally, education programs should be combined with other concrete steps aimed at changing the organization's culture and management systems—for example, change the performance appraisal procedure to emphasize that supervisors will henceforth be appraised based partly on their success in reducing intergroup conflicts.

Evaluate the diversity management program. For example, do employee attitude surveys now indicate any improvement in employees' attitudes toward diversity?

Boosting Workforce Diversity

Employers use various means to increase workforce diversity. Many companies, such as Baxter Healthcare Corporation, start by adopting strong company policies advocating the benefits of a culturally, racially, and sexually diverse workforce: "Baxter International believes that a multi-cultural employee population is essential to the company's leadership in healthcare around the world." Baxter then publicizes this philosophy throughout the company.

Next, Baxter takes concrete steps to foster diversity at work. These steps include evaluating diversity program efforts, recruiting minority members to the board of directors, and interacting with representative minority groups and networks. Diversity training is another concrete activity. It aims at sensitizing all employees about the need to value differences, build self-esteem, and generally create a more smoothly functioning and hospitable environment for the firm's diverse workforce.

Strategy and HR   Workforce diversity makes strategic sense: "as firms reach out to a broader customer base, they need employees who understand particular customer preferences and requirements."[114]

Longo Toyota built its competitive strategy on that idea. With a 60-person salesforce that speaks more than 20 languages, Longo's staff provides a powerful competitive advantage for catering to an increasingly diverse customer base. The HR department has thereby contributed to Longo's success. While other dealerships lose half their salespeople every year, Longo retains 90% of its staff, in part by emphasizing a promotion-from-within policy that's made more than two-thirds of its minorities managers. It has also taken steps to attract more women, for instance by adding a sales management staff to spend time providing the training inexperienced salespeople usually need. In a business in which competitors can easily imitate products, showrooms, and most services, Longo has built a competitive advantage based on employee diversity.

Equal Employment Opportunity Versus Affirmative Action

Equal employment opportunity aims to ensure that anyone, regardless of race, color, disability, sex, religion, national origin, or age, has an equal chance for a job based on his or her qualifications. *Affirmative action* goes beyond equal employment opportunity by requiring the employer to make an extra effort to hire and promote those in a protected group. Affirmative action thus includes specific actions (in recruitment, hiring, promotions, and compensation) to eliminate the present effects of past discrimination. According to the EEOC, an affirmative action program should result in "measurable, yearly improvements in hiring, training, and promotion of minorities and females" in all parts of the organization.

Steps in an Affirmative Action Program

According to the EEOC, in an affirmative action program the employer ideally takes eight steps:

1. Issues a written equal employment policy indicating that it is an equal employment opportunity employer, as well as a statement indicating the employer's commitment to affirmative action.
2. Appoints a top official with responsibility and authority to direct and implement the program.
3. Publicizes the equal employment policy and affirmative action commitment.
4. Surveys present minority and female employment by department and job classification to determine locations where affirmative action programs are especially desirable.[115]
5. Develops goals and timetables to improve utilization of minorities, males, and females in each area where utilization has been identified.
6. Develops and implements specific programs to achieve these goals. According to the EEOC, this is the heart of the affirmative action program. Here the employer has to review its entire human resource management system (including recruitment, selection, promotion, compensation, and disciplining) to identify barriers to equal employment opportunity and to make needed changes.
7. Establishes an internal audit and reporting system to monitor and evaluate progress in each aspect of the program.
8. Develops support for the affirmative action program, both inside the company (among supervisors, for instance) and outside the company in the community.[116]

When designing an affirmative action program, the **good faith effort strategy** emphasizes identifying and eliminating the obstacles to hiring and promoting women and minorities on the assumption that eliminating these obstacles will result in increased utilization of women and minorities. It may include setting goals (although strict quotas would not be advisable).

Some employers have also attempted to better manage diversity through voluntary affirmative action programs, which means employers voluntarily make an extra effort to hire and promote those in protected (such as female or minority) groups. This is in contrast to the involuntary affirmative action programs a number of courts have imposed on some employers since enactment of the 1964 Civil Rights Act.

Employers should know that voluntary affirmative action programs may conflict with the Civil Rights Act of 1991.[117] Two experts have written that "read literally, this new statutory restriction appears to bar employers from giving any consideration whatsoever to an individual's status as a racial or ethnic minority or as a woman when making an employment decision."[118] At the present time, this does not seem to be much of a problem, as long as employers emphasize the external recruitment and internal development of better-qualified minority and female employees, "while basing employment decisions on legitimate criteria."[119] However, employers have to take care that in achieving the desired goal of workforce diversity they do not inadvertently, "step over the line of permissible diversity management into the realm of unlawful affirmative action (i.e., reverse discrimination)."[120]

Corporate affirmative action programs would not seem to be significantly affected by the U.S. Supreme Court's June 2003 affirmative action decision. That decision outlawed the University of Michigan's quota-based admissions program. Since few employers set such quotas for minority hiring, the court's "narrow opinion" should have little effect in the workplace.[121]

REVIEW

Summary

1. Legislation barring discrimination is not new. For example, the Fifth Amendment to the U.S. Constitution (ratified in 1791) states that no person shall be deprived of life, liberty, or property without due process of law.

2. Legislation barring employment discrimination includes Title VII of the 1964 Civil Rights Act (as amended), which bars discrimination because of race, color, religion, sex, or national origin; various executive orders; federal guidelines (covering procedures for validating employee selection tools, etc.); the Equal Pay Act of 1963; and the Age Discrimination in Employment Act of 1967. In addition, various Court decisions (such as *Griggs* v. *Duke Power Company*) and state and local laws bar various aspects of discrimination.

3. The EEOC was created by Title VII of the Civil Rights Act. It is empowered to try conciliating discrimination complaints, but if this fails, the EEOC has the power to go directly to court to enforce the law.

4. The Civil Rights Act of 1991 had the effect of revising several Supreme Court equal employment decisions and "rolling back the clock." For example, it placed the burden of proof back on employers and held that a nondiscriminatory reason was insufficient to let an employer avoid liability for an action that also had a discriminatory motive.

5. The Americans with Disabilities Act prohibits employment discrimination against the disabled. Specifically, qualified persons cannot be discriminated against if the firm can make reasonable accommodations without undue hardship on the business.

6. A person who believes he or she has been discriminated against by a personnel procedure or decision must prove either that he or she was subjected to unlawful disparate treatment (intentional discrimination) or that the procedure in question has a disparate impact (unintentional discrimination) on members of his or her protected class. Once a prima facie case of disparate treatment is established, an employer must produce evidence that its decision was based on legitimate reasons (such as BFOQ). If the employer does that, the person claiming discrimination must prove that the employer's reasons are only a pretext for letting the company discriminate. Once a prima facie case of disparate impact has been established, the employer must produce evidence that

the allegedly discriminatory practice or procedure is job related and is based on a substantial business reason.

7. An employer should avoid various specific discriminatory human resource management practices:

   a. *In recruitment.* An employer usually should not rely on word-of-mouth advertising or give false or misleading information to minority group members. Also (usually), an employer should not specify the desired sex in advertising or in any way suggest that applicants might be discriminated against.

   b. *In selection.* An employer should avoid using any educational or other requirements where (1) it can be shown that minority-group members are less likely to possess the qualification and (2) such requirement is also not job related. Tests that disproportionately screen out minorities and women and that are not job related are deemed unlawful. Remember that you can use various tests and standards, but you must prove that they are job related or show that they are not used to discriminate against protected groups.

8. In practice, a person's charge to the EEOC is often first referred to a local agency. When the EEOC finds reasonable cause to believe that discrimination occurred, it has 30 days to try to work out a conciliation. Important points for the employer to remember include (1) EEOC investigators can only make recommendations, (2) you cannot be compelled to submit documents without a court order, and (3) you may limit the information you do submit. Also, make sure you clearly document your position (as the employer).

9. An employer can use three basic defenses in the event of a discriminatory practice allegation. One is *business necessity.* Attempts to show that tests or other selection standards are valid is one example of this defense. *Bona fide occupational qualification* is the second defense. This is applied when, for example, religion, national origin, or sex is a bona fide requirement of the job (such as for actors or actresses). A third is that the decision was made on the basis of legitimate nondiscriminatory reasons (such as poor performance) having nothing to do with the prohibited discrimination alleged.

10. Eight steps in an affirmative action program (based on suggestions from the EEOC) are (1) issue a written equal employment policy, (2) appoint a top official, (3) publicize the policy, (4) survey present minority and female employment, (5) develop goals and timetables, (6) develop and implement specific programs to achieve goals, (7) establish an internal audit and reporting system, and (8) develop support of in-house and community programs.

11. Recruitment is one of the first activities to which EEOC laws and procedures are applied. We turn to this in the following chapter.

KEY TERMS

- Title VII of the 1964 Civil Rights Act
- Equal Employment Opportunity Commission (EEOC)
- affirmative action
- Office of Federal Contract Compliance Programs (OFCCP)
- Equal Pay Act of 1963
- Age Discrimination in Employment Act (ADEA) of 1967
- Vocational Rehabilitation Act of 1973

- Vietnam Era Veterans' Readjustment Act of 1974
- Pregnancy Discrimination Act (PDA)
- federal agency guidelines
- sexual harassment
- Federal Violence Against Women Act of 1994
- *Griggs* v. *Duke Power Company*
- protected class
- *Albemarle Paper Company* v. *Moody*
- *Wards Cove Packing Company* v. *Atonio*
- Civil Rights Act of 1991 (CRA 1991)
- Americans with Disabilities Act (ADA)
- adverse impact
- bona fide occupational qualification (BFOQ)
- business necessity
- good faith effort strategy

DISCUSSION QUESTIONS AND EXERCISES

1. What is Title VII? What does it state?
2. What important precedents were set by the *Griggs* v. *Duke Power Company* case? The *Albemarle* v. *Moody* case?
3. What is adverse impact? How can it be proven?
4. Assume that you are a supervisor on an assembly line; you are responsible for hiring subordinates, supervising them, and recommending them for promotion. Compile a list of discriminatory management practices you should avoid.
5. Explain the defenses and exceptions to discriminatory practice allegations.
6. What is the difference between affirmative action and equal employment opportunity?
7. Explain how you would set up an affirmative action program.

APPLICATION EXERCISES

Case Incident   *A Case of Racial Discrimination?*

John Peters was a 44-year-old cardiologist on the staff of a teaching hospital in a large city in the southeastern United States. Happily married with two teenage children, he had served with distinction for many years at this same hospital, and in fact served his residency there after graduating from Columbia University's medical school.

Alana Anderson was an attractive African-American registered nurse on the staff at the same hospital with Peters. Unmarried and without children, she lived in a hospital-owned apartment on the hospital grounds and diligently devoted almost all her time to her work at the hospital or to taking additional coursework to further improve her already excellent nursing skills.

The hospital's chief administrator, Gary Chapman, took enormous pride in what he called the extraordinary professionalism of the doctors, nurses, and other staff members at his hospital. Although he took a number of rudimentary steps to guard against blatant violations of equal employment opportunity laws, he believed that most of the professionals on his staff were so highly trained and committed to the highest professional standards that "they would always do the right thing," as he put it.

Chapman was therefore upset to receive a phone call from Peters, informing him that Anderson had (in Peters's eyes) "developed an unwholesome personal attraction" to him and was bombarding the doctor with Valentine's Day cards, affectionate personal notes, and phone calls—often to the doctor's home.

Concerned about hospital decorum and the possibility that Peters was being sexually harassed, Chapman met privately with Anderson, explained that Peters was very uncomfortable with the personal attention she was showing to him, and asked that she please not continue to exhibit her show of affection for the doctor.

Chapman assumed that the matter was over. Several weeks later, when Anderson resigned her position at the hospital, Chapman didn't think much of it. He was therefore shocked and dismayed to receive a registered letter from a local attorney, informing him that both the hospital and Peters and Chapman personally were being sued by Anderson for racial discrimination. Her claim was that Chapman, in their private meeting, had told her, "We don't think it's right for people of different races to pursue each other romantically at this hospital." According to the lawyer, his preliminary research had unearthed several other alleged incidents at the hospital that apparently supported the idea that racial discrimination at the hospital was widespread. ■

QUESTIONS

1. What do you think of the way Chapman handled the accusations from Peters and his conversation with Anderson? How would you have handled them?
2. Do you think Peters had the basis for a sexual harassment claim against Anderson? Why or why not?
3. What would you do now if you were Chapman to avoid further incidents of this type?

Continuing Case

LearnInMotion.com: A Question of Discrimination

One of the problems LearnInMotion's Jennifer and Mel faced concerned the inadequacies of the firm's current personnel management practices and procedures. The previous year had been a swirl of activity—creating and testing the business model, launching the site, writing and rewriting the business plan, and finally getting venture funding. And, it would be accurate to say that in all that time, they put absolutely no time into employee manuals, personnel policies, or HR-related matters. Even the 25-page business plan was of no help in this regard. The plan provided considerable detail regarding budgetary projections, competition, market growth, and business strategy. However, it was silent when it came to HR, except for containing short bios of the current employees, and projections of the types of positions that would have to be staffed in the first two years.

Almost from the beginning, it was apparent to both of them that they were "out of our depth" (as Mel put it) when it came to the letter and spirit of equal employment opportunity laws. Having both been through business school, they were familiar with the general requirements, such as not asking applicants their ages. However, those general guidelines weren't always easy to translate into practice during the actual applicant interviews. Two incidents particularly concerned them. One of the applicants for a sales position was in his 50s, which made him about twice as old as any other applicant. While Mel didn't mean to be discriminatory, he found himself asking this candidate questions such as "Do you think you'll be able to get up to speed selling an Internet product?" and "You know, we'll be working very long hours here; are you up to that?"—questions that he did not ask of other, younger candidates.

There was also a problem with a candidate for the other position (content manager). This person had been incarcerated for a substance abuse problem several years before. Mel asked him several questions about this, as well as whether he was now "clean" or "under any sort of treatment." Jennifer thought questions like these were probably O.K., but she wasn't sure.

There was also a disturbing incident in the office. There were already two content management employees, Ruth and Dan, whose job was to actually place the courses and other educational content on the Web site. Dan, along with Alex the Web surfer, occasionally used vulgarity—for instance, when referring to the problems the firm was having getting the computer supplier to come to the office and repair a chronic problem with the firm's server. Mel's attitude was that "boys will be boys." However, Jennifer saw Ruth cringe several times when "the boys" were having one of these exchanges, and felt strongly that this behavior had to stop. However, she was not sure language like this constituted "a hostile environment" under the law, although she did feel that at a minimum it was uncivil. The two owners decided it was time to institute and implement some HR policies that would ensure that their company and its employees adhere to the letter and the spirit of the equal employment opportunity laws. Now they want you, their management consultants, to help them actually do it. Here's what they want you to do for them. ■

QUESTIONS AND ASSIGNMENTS

1. Our company is in New York City. We now have only about five employees, and are only planning on hiring about three or four more. Is our company in fact even covered

by equal rights legislation? (Hint: Does the government's Web site provide any clues?)

2. Were we within our legal rights to ask the possibly age-related and substance-abuse-related questions? Why or why not?

3. Did Dan and Alex create a hostile environment for Ruth? Why or why not? How should we have handled this matter?

4. What have we been doing wrong up to now with respect to EEO-related matters, and how do you suggest we rectify the situation in the future?

Experiential Exercise
Too Informal?

Dan Jones had run his textile plant in a midsize southern town for many years without a whiff of trouble with the EEOC. He did not take formal steps to avoid making EEO-type mistakes; just the opposite. In fact, a professor from a local college had once told him to be more careful about how applicants were recruited and screened and employees were treated. However, Jones's philosophy was "if it ain't broke, don't fix it," and because he'd never had any complaints, he assumed that his screening process wasn't "broke."

For many years Jones had no problems. If he needed a new employee, he simply asked his current employees (most of whom were Hispanic) if they had any friends who were looking for jobs. Sometimes, he would also ask the local state employment office to list the open jobs and send over some candidates. He then had his sewing supervisor and plant manager (both also Hispanic) interview the applicants. No tests or other background checks were carried out, in part, said Jones, because "most of these applicants are friends and relatives of my current employees, and they wouldn't send me any lemons."

Now Jones is being served with a formal notice from the county's Equal Rights Commission. It seems that of the 20 or so non-Hispanic applicants sent to Jones's firm last year from the state employment office, none had received a job offer. In fact, Jones's supervisor had not even returned the follow-up card to the employment office to verify that each applicant had shown up and been interviewed. Jones was starting to wonder if his HR process was too informal.

Purpose: The purpose of this exercise is to provide practice in analyzing and applying knowledge of equal opportunity legislation to a realistic problem.

Required Understanding: Be thoroughly familiar with the material presented in this chapter. In addition, read "Too Informal?" the case on which this experiential exercise is based.

How to Set up the Exercise/Instructions:

1. Divide the class into groups of four or five students.

2. Each group should develop answers to the following:
   a. How could the EEOC prove *adverse impact?*
   b. Cite specific discriminatory personnel practices at Dan Jones's company.
   c. How could Jones's company defend itself against the allegations of discriminatory practice?

3. If time permits, a spokesperson from each group can present his or her group's findings. Would it make sense for this company to try to defend itself against the discrimination allegations?

TAKE IT TO THE WEB

 For Internet exercises, updates to chapter material, and more, visit the Dessler Web site at

www.prenhall.com/dessler

ENDNOTES

1. Orlando Richard, "Racial Diversity, Business Strategy, and Firm Performance: A Resource Based View," *Academy of Management Journal* 43, no. 2 (April 2000): 164–75.

2. Kevin Wallsten, "Diversity Pays Off in Big Sales for Toyota Dealership," *Workforce* 77, no. 9 (September 1998): 91–93.

3. "American Express Financial Advisers Reach $31 Million Agreement on Sex Bias Charges," *BNA Fair Employment Practices* (February 28, 2002): 26.

4. "Coca-Cola Agrees to Settle Race Bias Suit; Proceeds Expected to Be Shared by 2,000," *BNA Fair Employment Practices* (June 22, 2000): 75.

5. "Federal Government Settles for $508 Million Bias Case Involving U.S. Information Agency," *BNA Fair Employment Practices* (March 30, 2000): 39.

6. Note that private employers are *not* bound by the U.S. Constitution.

7. Based on or quoted from *Principles of Employment Discrimination Law,* International Association of Official Human Rights Agencies, Washington, D.C. In addition, see W. Clay Hamner and Frank Schmidt, *Contemporary Problems in Personnel,* rev. ed. (Chicago: St. Clair Press, 1977), Chapter 3. See also Bruce Feldacker, *Labor Guide to Labor Law* (Upper Saddle River, NJ: Prentice Hall, 2000); and www.eeoc.gov Web site. Employment discrimination law is a changing field, and the appropriateness of the rules, guidelines, and conclusions in this chapter and book may also be affected by factors unique to the employer's operation. They should be reviewed by the employer's attorney before implementation.

8. James Higgins, "A Manager's Guide to the Equal Employment Opportunity Laws," *Personnel Journal* 55, no. 8 (August 1976): 406.

9. The Equal Employment Opportunity Act of 1972, Subcommittee on Labor or the Committee of Labor and Public Welfare, United States Senate, March 1972, p. 3. In general, it is not discrimination but unfair discrimination against a person merely because of that person's race, age, sex, national origin, or religion that is forbidden by federal statutes. In the federal government's *Uniform Employee Selection Guidelines, unfair* discrimination is defined as follows: "unfairness is demonstrated through a showing that members of a particular interest group perform better or poorer on the job than their scores on the selection procedure (test, etc.) would indicate through comparison with how members of the other groups performed." For a discussion of the meaning of fairness, see James Ledvinka, "The Statistical Definition of Fairness in the Federal Selection Guidelines and Its Implications for Minority Employment," *Personnel Psychology* 32 (August 1979): 551–62. In summary, a selection device (such as a test) may discriminate—for example, between low and high performers. However, unfair discrimination—discrimination that is based solely on the person's race, age, sex, national origin, or religion—is illegal.

10. Initially, attempts to assert that discrimination based on sexual orientation was illegal were unsuccessful, and even the EEOC was unsympathetic. However, a relevant case (*Watkins* v. *U.S. Army*, F.2d 1428, 1429, 9th Cir. 1988) involving an army sergeant

forced to resign after 14 years of notable service raised the possibility of successful suits by identifying homosexuals as a "suspect class that deserves special protection against discrimination." Sabrina Wrenn, "Gay Rights and Workplace Discrimination," *Personnel Journal* 67, no. 10 (October 1988): 94; "Proposed Bill Would Ban Workplace Discrimination Based on Sexual Orientation," *HR Focus* (October 1994): 1, 8.

11. Bureau of National Affairs, *Fair Employment Practices* (October 8, 1992): 117.

12. Note that under the Vocational Rehabilitation Act, the law strictly speaking applied only to a particular "program" of the employer. In March 1988 Congress passed the Civil Rights Restoration Act of 1987, overturning this interpretation. Then, with few exceptions, any institution, organization, corporation, state agency, or municipality using federal funding in any of its programs had to abide by the section of the act prohibiting discriminating against handicapped individuals. See "Federal Law Mandates Affirmative Action for Handicapped," *BNA Fair Employment Practices* (March 30, 1989): 42.

13. Ann Harriman, *Women/Men Management* (New York: Praeger, 1985), pp. 66–68.

14. Commerce Clearing House, "Pregnancy Leave," *Ideas and Trends* (January 23, 1987): 10.

15. "High Court Upholds Pregnancy Law," *BNA Fair Employment Practices* (January 22, 1987): 7; Betty Sonthard Murphy, Wayne E. Barlow, and D. Diane Hatch, "Manager's Newsfront: U.S. Supreme Court Approves Preferential Treatment for Pregnancy," *Personnel Journal* 66, no. 3 (March 1987): 18.

16. Thomas Dhanens, "Implications of the New EEOC Guidelines," *Personnel* 56 (September/October): 32–39.

17. "First Two Chapters of Long-Awaited Manual Released by OFCCP," *BNA Fair Employment Practices* (January 5, 1989): 6.

18. 29 CFR 1625.2(a), quoted in Paul Greenlaw and John Kohl, "Age Discrimination and Employment Guidelines," *Personnel*

Journal 61, no. 3 (March 1982): 224–28. See also Gillian Flynn, "The Maturing of the ADEA," *Workforce* (October 2002): 86–87.

19. Patricia Linenberger and Timothy Keaveny, "Sexual Harassment: The Employer's Legal Obligations," *Personnel* 58 (November/December 1981): 60–68.

20. Larry Drake and Rachel Moskowitz, "Your Rights in the Workplace," *Occupational Outlook Quarterly* (summer 1997): 19–20.

21. Timothy Bland and Sue Stalcup, "Managing Harassment," *Human Resource Management* 40, no. 1 (spring 2001): 51–62.

22. Edward Felsenthal, "Justice's Ruling Further Defines Sexual Harassment," *Wall Street Journal* (March 5, 1998): B1, B5.

23. Mary Rowe, "Dealing with Sexual Harassment," *Harvard Business Review* 61 (May/June 1981): 42–46.

24. Robert H. Faley, "Sexual Harassment: Critical Review of Legal Cases with General Principles and Preventive Measures," *Personnel Psychology* 35, no. 3 (autumn 1982): 590–91; "In Terms of Sexual Harassment, What Makes an Environment 'Hostile'?" *BNA Fair Employment Practices* (June 1988): 78.

25. Linenberger and Keaveny, "Sexual Harassment," 64.

26. Felsenthal, "Justice's Ruling Further Defines Sexual Harassment," B5.

27. See Mindy D. Bergman et al., "The (Un)reasonableness of Reporting: Antecedents and Consequences of Reporting Sexual Harassment," *Journal of Applied Psychology* 87, no. 2 (2002): 230–42; see also W. Kirk Turner and Christopher Thrutchley, "Employment Law and Practices Training: No Longer the Exception—It's the Rule," *Society for Human Resource Management Legal Report* (July–August 2002): 1–2.

28. See the discussion in "Examining Unwelcome Conduct in a Sexual Harassment Claim," *BNA Fair Employment Practices* (October 19, 1995): 124. See also Molly Bowers et al., "Just Cause in the Arbitration of Sexual Harassment Cases," *Dispute Resolution Journal* 55, no. 4 (November 2000): 40–55.

29. Maria Rotundo et al., "A Meta-Analytic Review of Gender Differences in Perceptions of Sexual Harassment," *Journal of Applied Psychology* 86, no. 5 (2001): 914–22.

30. Commerce Clearing House, *Sexual Harassment Manual,* for managers and supervisors (Chicago: Commerce Clearing House, 1991) p. 8.

31. Louise Fitzgerald et al., "Antecedents and Consequences of Sexual Harassment in Organizations: A Test of an Integrated Model," *Journal of Applied Psychology* 82, no. 4 (1997): 577–89.

32. "New EEOC Guidance Explains Standards of Liability for Harassment by Supervisors," *BNA Fair Employment Practices* (June 24, 1999): 75.

33. "Adequate Response Bars Liability," *BNA Fair Employment Practices* (June 26, 1997): 74.

34. Shereen Bingham and Lisa Scherer, "The Unexpected Effects of a Sexual Harassment Educational Program," *Journal of Applied Behavioral Science* 37, no. 2 (June 2001): 125–53.

35. Federick L. Sullivan, "Sexual Harassment: The Supreme Court Ruling," *Personnel* 65, no. 12 (December 1986): 42–44. See also Gillian Flynn, "A Pioneer Program Nurtures a Harassment Free Workplace," *Workforce* (October 1997): 38–43; and Michael Marmu and Hervé Quenoau, "Sexual Harassment: Different Standards for Different Racial and Ethnic Groups?" *Journal of Individual Employment Rights* 9, no. 4 (2001): 309–21.

36. Bergman et al., "The Un(reasonableness) of Reporting," 237.

37. Jason Janov, "Sexual Harassment and the Three Big Surprises," *HR Magazine* 46, no. 11 (November 2001): 123 ff.

38. See the discussion in "Examining Unwelcome Conduct in a Sexual Harassment Claim," *BNA Fair Employment Practices* (October 19, 1995): 124.

39. Ibid., 124.

40. *Griggs* v. *Duke Power Company,* 3FEP cases 175.

41. James Ledvinka, *Federal Regulation of Personnel and Human Resource Management* (Boston: Kent, 1982), p. 41.

42. IOFEP cases 1181.

43. James Ledvinka and Lyle Schoenfeldt, "Legal Developments in Employment Testing: Albemarle and Beyond," *Personnel Psychology* 31, no. 1 (spring 1978): 1–13. It should be noted that in its *Albemarle* opinion, the Court made one important modification regarding the EEOC guidelines. The guidelines required employers using tests that screened out disproportionate numbers of minorities or women to validate those tests—prove that they did in fact predict performance on the job—and further to prove that there was no other alternative screening device the employer could use that did not screen out disproportionate numbers of minorities and women. This second requirement proved a virtually impossible burden for employers. Up through the *Griggs* decision, it was not enough to just validate the test; instead, the employer also had to show that some other tests or screening tools were not available that were also valid but that did not screen out a disproportionate numbers of minorities or women. In the *Albemarle* case, the Court held that the burden of proof was no longer on the employer to show that there was no suitable alternative screening device available. Instead, the burden for that was now on the charging party (the person allegedly discriminated against) to show that a suitable alternative is available. Ledvinka and Schoenfeldt, "Legal Developments," 4; Gary Lubben, Dwayne Thompson, and Charles Klasson, "Performance Appraisal: The Legal Implications of Title VII," *Personnel* (May/June 1980): 11–21.

44. Bruce Feldacker, *Labor Guide to Labor Law* (Upper Saddle River, NJ: Prentice Hall, 2000), p. 513.

45. "The Eleventh Circuit Explains Disparate Impact, Disparate Treatment," *BNA Fair Employment Practices* (August 17, 2000): 102. See also Kenneth York, "Disparate Results in Adverse Impact Tests: The 4/5ths Rule and the Chi Square Test," *Public Personnel Management* 31, no. 2 (summer 2002): 253–62.

46. Patricia Feltes, Robert Robinson, and Ross Fink, "American Female Expatriates and the Civil Rights Act of 1991: Balancing Legal and Business Interests," *Business Horizons* (March/April 1993): 82–85.

47. Ibid., 84.

48. Title VII does not apply to foreign operations not owned or controlled by a U.S. employer, however.

49. Based on Gregory Baxter, "Over There: Enforcing the 1991 Civil Rights Act Abroad," *Employee Relations Law Journal* 19, no. 2 (autumn 1993): 257–66.

50. Ibid., 265.

51. Ibid.

52. Commerce Clearing House, "House and Senate Pass Civil Rights Compromise by Wide Margin," *Ideas and Trends in Personnel* (November 13, 1991): 179.

53. Ibid., 182.

54. Mark Kobata, "The Civil Rights Act of 1991," *Personnel Journal* (March 1992): 48.

55. Elliot H. Shaller and Dean Rosen, "A Guide to the EEOC's Final Regulations on the Americans with Disabilities Act," *Employee Relations Law Journal* 17, no. 3 (winter 1991–1992): 408. See also Jonathon Mook, "Supreme Court Addresses Reasonable Accommodation, but Uncertainty Remains," *Employee Relations Law Journal* (fall 2002): 7–27.

56. Ibid., 409.

57. See, for example, Paul Starkman, "The ADA's 'Essential Job Function' Requirements: Just How Essential Does an Essential Job Function Have to Be?" *Employee Relations Law Journal* 26, no. 4 (spring 2001): 43–102.

58. "No Sitting for Store Greeter," *BNA Fair Employment Practices* (December 14, 1995): 150.

59. "Odds Against Getting Even Are Long in ADA Cases," *BNA Bulletin to Management* (August 20, 2000): 229; "Determining Employers' Responsibilities Under ADA," *BNA Fair Employment Practices* (May 16, 1996): 57. See also Barbara Lee, "The Implications of ADA Litigation for Employers: A Review of Federal Appellate Court Decisions," *Human Resource Management* 40, no. 1 (spring 2001): 35–50.

60. James McDonald, Jr., "The Americans with Difficult Personalities Act," *Employee Relations Law Journal* 25, no. 4 (spring 2000): 93–107.

61. "Supreme Court Says Manual Task Limitation Needs Both Daily Living, Workplace Impact," *BNA Fair Employment Practices* (January 17, 2002): 8.

62. "Blind Bartender Not Qualified for Job, Court Says in Dismissing Americans with Disabilities Act Claim," *BNA Fair Employment Practices* (February 4, 1999): 17.

63. "Mitigating Measures and ADA," *BNA Fair Employment Practices* (September 2, 1999): 108.

64. "Differing Views: Punctuality as Essential Job Function," *BNA Fair Employment Practices* (April 27, 2000): 56.

65. www.eeoc.gov/press/6-14-01.html.

66. Lee, "Implications of ADA Litigation for Employers."

67. "Determining Employers' Responsibilities Under ADA," 57.

68. Lee, "Implications of ADA Litigation for Employers."

69. Ibid.

70. Timothy Bland, "The Supreme Court Focuses on the ADA," *HR Magazine* (September 1999): 42–46. See also James Hall and Diane Hatch, "Supreme Court Decisions Require ADA Revision," *Workforce* (August 1999): 60–66.

71. James Ledvinka and Robert Gatewood, "EEO Issues with Preemployment Inquiries," *Personnel Administrator* 22, no. 2 (February 1977): 22–26.

72. Based on "A Wrap-up of State Legislation: 1988 Anti-bias Laws Focus on AIDS," *BNA Fair Employment Practices* (January 5, 1988): 3–4.

73. John Klinefelter and James Thompkins, "Adverse Impact in Employment Selection," *Public Personnel Management* (May/June 1976): 199–204.

74. John Moran, *Employment Law* (Upper Saddle River, NJ: Prentice Hall, 1997), p. 168.

75. Ibid., 166.

76. "Eleventh Circuit Explains Disparate Impact, Disparate Treatment," 102.

77. International Association of Official Human Rights Agencies, *Principles of Employment Discrimination Law* (Washington, D.C.); James M. Higgins, "A Manager's Guide to the Equal Opportunity Laws," *Personnel* 55 (August 1976); Ledvinka, *Federal Regulation of Personnel and Human Resource Management.*

78. *Usery* v. *Tamiami Trail Tours,* 12FEP cases 1233.

79. "Congress Legislates to Increase Commercial Pilot Age," *Airline Industry Information* (March 15, 2001).

80. Howard Anderson and Michael Levin-Epstein, *Primer of Equal Employment Opportunity* (Washington, D.C.: Bureau of National Affairs, 1982), pp. 13–14.

81. *U.S.* v. *Bethlehem Steel Company,* 3FEP cases 589.

82. *Robinson* v. *Lorillard Corporation,* 3FEP cases 653.

83. *Spurlock* v. *United Airlines,* 5FEP cases 17.

84. Ledvinka and Gatewood, "EEO Issues with Preemployment Inquiries," 22–26.

85. Anderson and Levin-Epstein, *Primer of Equal Opportunity,* 28.

86. "Many Well-Intentioned HR Policies Hold Legal Headaches, Consultant Says," *BNA Bulletin to Management* (February 17, 2000): 47.

87. Mark Roehling, "Weight-Based Discrimination in Employment: Psychological and Legal Aspects," *Personnel Psychology* 52 (1999): 969–1016.

88. "American Airlines, Worldwide Flight Sued by EEOC Over Questioning of Applicants," *BNA Fair Employment Practices* (October 12, 2000): 125.

89. Richard Connors, "Law at Work," lawatwork.com/news/applicat.html.

90. Lynn Bennington and Ruth Wein, "Aiding and Abetting Employer Discrimination: The Job Applicant's Role," *Employee Responsibilities and Rights* 14, no. 1 (March 2002): 3–16.

91. This is based on Anderson and Levin-Epstein, *Primer of Equal Opportunity,* 93–97.

92. "EEOC Issues New Enforcement Guidance on Discrimination in Employee Benefits," *BNA Fair Employment Practices* (October 12, 2000): 123.

93. Eric Matusewitch, "Tailor Your Dress Codes," *Personnel Journal* 68, no. 2 (February 1989): 86–91; Matthew Miklaue, "Sorting Our a Claim of Bias," *Workforce* 80, no. 6 (June 2001): 102–3.

94. Even during President Reagan's administration—often viewed as a not particularly supportive period for equal rights enforcement in the United States—an EEOC press release dated June 13, 1988 said it filed 527 court actions during fiscal year 1987, "setting an agency record for legal activity and maintaining its high level of enforcement on behalf of persons discriminated against in the work place." Quoted in Commerce Clearing House, *Ideas and Trends in Personnel* (June 28, 1988): 101–2.

95. "EEOC's New Nationwide Mediation Plan Offers Option of Informal Settlements," *BNA Fair Employment Practices* (February 18, 1999): 21.

96. "Independent Report Shows High Satisfaction for Participants," *BNA Fair Employment Practices* (October 12, 2000): 127.

97. "EEOC Reached Record Monetary Benefits, Continued Cutting Inventory of Last Year," *BNA Fair Employment Practices* (February 3, 2000): 15.

98. "EEOC Reaps Record Benefits," *BNA Fair Employment Practices* (April 2, 1998): 37. The proliferation of employment class-action suits (Coca-Cola recently paid $192.5 million to settle one such suit) has understandably increased the need for concern. Deborah Sudberry et al., "Keeping the Monster in the Closet: Avoiding Employment Class-Action," *Employee Relations Law Journal* 26, no. 2 (fall 2000): 5–33; "Coca-Cola Agrees to Pay $192.5 Million, Makes HR Policy Changes to Settle Lawsuit," *BNA Fair Employment Practices* 36, no. 9 (November 23, 2000): 141–42.

99. Timothy Bland, "Sealed Without a Kiss," *HR Magazine* (October 2000): 85–92.

100. Robert H. Sheahan, "Responding to Employment Discrimination Charges," *Personnel Journal* 60, no. 3 (March 1981): 217–20; Wayne Baham, "Learn to

Deal with Agency Investigations," *Personnel Journal* 67, no. 9 (September 1988): 104–7.

101. Bland, "Sealed Without a Kiss," 85–92.
102. "Conducting Effective Investigations of Employee Bias Complaints," *BNA Fair Employment Practices* (July 13, 1995): 81.
103. Based on Commerce Clearing House, *Ideas and Trends in Personnel* (January 23, 1987): 14–15.
104. "Tips for Employers on Dealing with EEOC Investigations," *BNA Fair Employment Practices* (October 31, 1996): 130.
105. "Preventing Costly Employment Discrimination Lawsuits," *BNA Fair Employment Practices* (September 9, 1994): 105.
106. David Nye, "When the Fired Fight Back," *Across-the-Board* (June 1995): 31–34.
107. "EEOC Opposes Mandatory Arbitration," *BNA Fair Employment Practices* (July 24, 1997): 85.
108. James Coil, III, and Charles Rice, "Managing Work-Force Diversity in the 90s: The Impact of the Civil Rights Act of 1991," *Employee Relations Law Journal* 18, no. 4 (spring 1993): 547–65. See also Stephanie Mehta, "What Minority Employees Really Want," *Fortune* (July 10, 2000): 81–188.
109. Orlando Richard, "Racial Diversity, Business Strategy, and Firm Performance: A Resource Based View," *Academy of Management Journal* 43, no. 2 (2000): 164–77.
110. Michael Carrell and Everett Mann, "Defining Work-Force Diversity in Public Sector Organizations," *Public Personnel Management* 24, no. 1 (spring 1995): 99–111. See also Richard Koonce,

"Redefining Diversity," *Training and Development Journal* (December 2001): 22–33.
111. Patricia Digh, "Creating a New Balance Sheet: The Need for Better Diversity Metrics," *Mosaics,* Society for Human Resource Management (September/October 1999): 1.
112. Taylor Cox, Jr., *Cultural Diversity in Organizations: Theory, Research and Practice* (San Francisco: Berrett-Koehler, 1993), p. 236.
113. Robert Grossman, "Is Diversity Working?" *HR Magazine* (March 2000): 47–50.
114. Richard Orlando, "Racial Diversity, Business Strategy, and Firm Performance: A Resource Based View," *Public Personnel Management* 24, no. 1 (spring 1995): 99–111.
115. Frank Jossi, "Reporting Race," *HR Magazine* (September 2000): 87–94.
116. U.S. Equal Employment Opportunity Commission, *Affirmative Action and Equal Employment* (Washington, DC: January 1974); Antonio Handler Chayes, "Make Your Equal Opportunity Program Court Proof," *Harvard Business Review* (September 1974): 81–89. See also David Kravitz and Steven Klineberg, "Reactions to Two Versions of Affirmative-Action Among Whites, Blacks, and Hispanics," *Journal of Applied Psychology* 85, no. 4 (2000): 597–611.
117. Coil and Rice, "Managing Work-Force Diversity in the 90s," 548.
118. Ibid., 560.
119. Ibid., 562–63.
120. Ibid., 563.
121. "Lawyers, Scholars Differ on Likely Impact of Affirmative Action Rulings on Workplace," *BNA Fair Employment Practices* (July 3, 2003): 79–80.

Chapter 3

Personnel Planning and Recruitment

- What Is Job Analysis?
- The Recruitment and Selection Process
- Workforce Planning and Forecasting
- Recruiting Job Candidates
- Developing and Using Application Forms

When you finish studying this chapter, you should be able to:

- Describe *the basic methods of collecting job analysis information.*
- Conduct *a job analysis.*
- Explain *the process of forecasting personnel requirements.*
- Compare *eight methods for recruiting job candidates.*
- Explain *how to use application forms to predict job performance.*

INTRODUCTION

Sutter Health, a nonprofit health care network in Sacramento, California, knew its expansion strategy would fail if it couldn't fill its 10,000 job openings. The company's future depended on attracting many more recruits, but how should it do so? Sutter Health decided to move its job postings online, only to find that this alone was not the solution. Project manager Keith Vencel had to help Sutter devise a new recruiting program.[1]

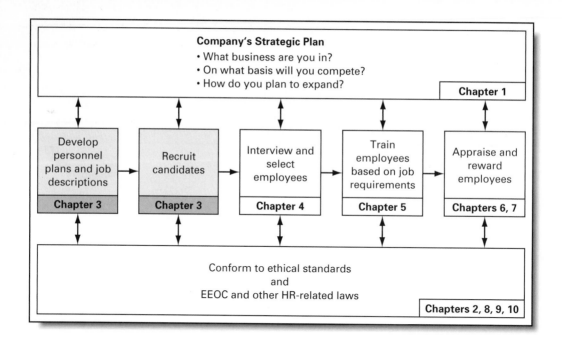

Company's Strategic Plan
• What business are you in?
• On what basis will you compete?
• How do you plan to expand?

Chapter 1

Develop personnel plans and job descriptions	Recruit candidates	Interview and select employees	Train employees based on job requirements	Appraise and reward employees
Chapter 3	Chapter 3	Chapter 4	Chapter 5	Chapters 6, 7

Conform to ethical standards
and
EEOC and other HR-related laws

Chapters 2, 8, 9, 10

WHAT IS JOB ANALYSIS?

Job Analysis Defined

Organizations consist of jobs that have to be staffed. **Job analysis** is the procedure through which you determine the duties of these jobs and the characteristics of the people who should be hired for them. The analysis produces information on the job's activities and requirements. This information is then used for developing **job descriptions** (what the job entails) and **job specifications** (what kind of people to hire for the job).[2]

A supervisor or HR specialist normally does the job analysis,[3] perhaps using a questionnaire like the one in the chapter Appendix (Figure A3.3, pages 110–111). The information collected typically includes information on the work activities performed (such as cleaning, selling, teaching, or painting), and information about such matters as physical working conditions and work schedule.

Job analysis information is the basis for several interrelated HR management activities. For example, information regarding the job's duties may be the basis for creating training programs, and information about the human traits required to do the job are used to decide what sort of people to recruit and hire. Job analysis therefore plays a central role in HR management. The U.S. Federal Agencies Uniform Guidelines on Employee Selection ". . . . stipulate that job analysis is a crucial step in validating all major personnel activities."[4]

Job Analysis and Equal Employment Opportunity   Job analysis therefore plays a central role in equal employment compliance. We discussed EEO issues in Chapter 2. Employers must be able to show that their screening tools and appraisals are related to performance on the job in question. To do this, of course, the manager must know what the job entails—which in turn requires a competent job analysis.

Methods of Collecting Job Analysis Information

In practice, employers usually collect job analysis data from multiple job incumbents, using questionnaires and interviews. They then average data from these employees from different departments to determine how much time a typical employee (say, a sales assistant) spends on each of several specific tasks (such as interviewing). However, even with the same job title, there tend to be differences in what people do from department to department. It's therefore important to understand the departmental context of the job. Do not assume that the way someone with a particular job title spends his or her time is necessarily the same from department to department.[5]

Various techniques are used to do a job analysis (in other words, to collect information on the duties, responsibilities, and activities of the job). Some of the more popular techniques are as follows.

Interviews   Job analysis interviews may involve interviewing job incumbents or one or more supervisors who are thoroughly knowledgeable about the job. Typical interview questions might include: "What is the job being performed?" "What are the major duties of your position?" "What exactly do you do?" "What activities do you participate in?"

Interviews are probably the most widely used method for determining a job's duties and responsibilities, and their wide use reflects their advantages. Most important, interviewing allows the worker to report activities and behavior that might not otherwise surface. For example, a skilled interviewer could unearth important activities that occur only occasionally, or informal communication (between, say, a production supervisor and the sales manager) that would not be obvious from the organization chart.

Interviewing's major problem is distortion of information, whether due to outright falsification or honest misunderstandings.[6] A job analysis is often used as a prelude to changing a job's pay rate. Employees, therefore, sometimes legitimately view them as efficiency evaluations that may affect their pay. Employees thus tend to exaggerate certain responsibilities and minimize others. Obtaining valid information can thus be a slow process.

Questionnaires   Employees can also be asked to fill out questionnaires to describe their job-related duties and responsibilities. Here it is important to decide how structured the questionnaire should be and what questions to include. Some questionnaires are very structured checklists. Each employee is presented with an inventory of perhaps hundreds of specific duties or tasks (such as "change and splice wire"). Each is asked to indicate whether he or she performs each task and, if so, how much time is normally spent on each. At the other extreme, the questionnaire can be open-ended and simply ask the employee to "describe the major duties of your job." In practice, the best questionnaire often falls between these two extremes. As illustrated in Figure A3.3 (see Appendix, pages 110–111), a typical job analysis questionnaire might have several open-ended questions (such as "Is the incumbent performing duties he/she considers unnecessary?") as well as structured questions (concerning, for instance, previous experience required).

Observation   Direct observation is especially useful when jobs consist mainly of observable physical activity. Jobs such as janitor, assembly-line worker, and accounting clerk are examples. On the other hand, observation is usually not appropriate when the job entails a lot of unmeasurable mental activity (lawyer, design engineer). Nor is it useful if the employee engages in important activities that might occur only occasionally, such as a nurse who handles emergencies.

Participant Diary/Logs   Another approach is to ask workers to keep a diary/log or list of what they do during the day. For every activity the employee engages in, he or she records the activity (along with the time) in a log. This can produce a very complete picture of the job, especially when supplemented with subsequent interviews with the worker and his or her supervisor. Some employees may try to exaggerate some activities and underplay others. However, the detailed, chronological nature of the log tends to mediate against this. Some employees may compile their logs by periodically dictating what they're doing into a handheld dictating machine.

Other Job Analysis Methods   You may encounter several other job analysis methods, most notably those in the chapter Appendix.

Writing Job Descriptions

The job analysis should provide the basis for writing a job description. A job description is a written statement of *what* the jobholder does, *how* he or she does it, and under *what conditions* the job is performed. The manager in turn uses this information to write a job specification that lists the knowledge, abilities, and skills needed to perform the job satisfactorily. Figure 3.1 presents a typical job description. As is usual, it contains several types of information.

Job Identification   As in Figure 3.1, the job identification section contains the job title, which specifies the title of the job, such as marketing manager, sales manager, or inventory control clerk.[7]

Job Summary   The job summary should describe the general nature of the job, listing only its major functions or activities.

Relationships   A relationships statement may show the jobholder's relationships with others inside and outside the organization, and might look like this for a human resource manager:[8]

> *Reports to:* Vice-president of employee relations
> *Supervises:* Human resource clerk, test administrator, labor relations director, and one secretary
> *Works with:* All department managers and executive management
> *Outside the company:* Employment agencies, executive recruiting firms, union representatives, state and federal employment offices, and various vendors[9]

Responsibilities and Duties   This section is the heart of the job description, and presents a detailed list of the job's responsibilities and duties. Here, list and describe in several sentences each of the job's major duties. For instance, you might further

Figure 3.1 Sample Job Description

OLEC CORP.
Job Description

Job Title:	Marketing Manager
Department:	Marketing
Reports To:	President
FLSA Status:	Non Exempt
Prepared By:	Michael George
Prepared Date:	April 1, 2002
Approved By:	Ian Alexander
Approved Date:	April 15, 2002

JOB SUMMARY

Plans, directs, and coordinates the marketing of the organization's products and/or services by performing the following duties personally or through subordinate supervisors.

ESSENTIAL DUTIES AND RESPONSIBILITIES include the following. Other duties may be assigned.

Establishes marketing goals to ensure share of market and profitability of products and/or services.

Develops and executes marketing plans and programs, both short and long range, to ensure the profit growth and expansion of company products and/or services.

Researches, analyzes, and monitors financial, technological, and demographic factors so that market opportunities may be capitalized on and the effects of competitive activity may be minimized.

Plans and oversees the organization's advertising and promotion activities including print, electronic, and direct mail outlets.

Communicates with outside advertising agencies on ongoing campaigns.

Works with writers and artists and oversees copywriting, design, layout, pasteup, and production of promotional materials.

Develops and recommends pricing strategy for the organization which will result in the greatest share of the market over the long run.

Achieves satisfactory profit/loss ratio and share of market performance in relation to pre-set standards and to general and specific trends within the industry and the economy.

Ensures effective control of marketing results and that corrective action takes place to be certain that the achievement of marketing objectives are within designated budgets.

Evaluates market reactions to advertising programs, merchandising policy, and product packaging and formulation to ensure the timely adjustment of marketing strategy and plans to meet changing market and competitive conditions.

Recommends changes in basic structure and organization of marketing group to ensure the effective fulfillment of objectives assigned to it and provide the flexibility to move swiftly in relation to marketing problems and opportunities.

Conducts marketing surveys on current and new product concepts.

Prepares marketing activity reports.

(Continued)

What Is Job Analysis? **69**

SUPERVISORY RESPONSIBILITIES

Manages three subordinate supervisors who supervise a total of five employees in the Marketing Department. Is responsible for the overall direction, coordination, and evaluation of this unit. Also directly supervises two non-supervisory employees. Carries out supervisory responsibilities in accordance with the organization's policies and applicable laws. Responsibilities include interviewing, hiring, and training employees; planning, assigning, and directing work; appraising performance; rewarding and disciplining employees; addressing complaints and resolving problems.

QUALIFICATIONS

To perform this job successfully, an individual must be able to perform each essential duty satisfactorily. The requirements listed below are representative of the knowledge, skill, and/or ability required. Reasonable accommodations may be made to enable individuals with disabilities to perform the essential functions.

EDUCATION and/or EXPERIENCE

Master's degree (M.A.) or equivalent; or four to ten years related experience and/or training; or equivalent combination of education and experience.

LANGUAGE SKILLS

Ability to read, analyze, and interpret common scientific and technical journals, financial reports, and legal documents. Ability to respond to common inquiries or complaints from customers, regulatory agencies, or members of the business community. Ability to write speeches and articles for publication that conform to prescribed style and format. Ability to effectively present information to top management, public groups, and/or boards of directors.

MATHEMATICAL SKILLS

Ability to apply advanced mathematical concepts such as exponents, logarithms, quadratic equations, and permutations. Ability to apply mathematical operations to such tasks as frequency distribution, determination of test reliability and validity, analysis of variance, correlation techniques, sampling theory, and factor analysis.

REASONING ABILITY

Ability to define problems, collect data, establish facts, and draw valid conclusions. Ability to interpret an extensive variety of technical instructions in mathematical or diagram form.

define the duty "selects, trains, and develops subordinate personnel" as follows: "develops spirit of cooperation and understanding," "ensures that work group members receive specialized training as necessary," and "directs training involving teaching, demonstrating, and/or advising."

The Department of Labor's *Dictionary of Occupational Titles* can be used to itemize the job's duties and responsibilities. An illustrative description is shown in Figure 3.2. The dictionary lists a human resource manager's specific duties and responsibilities, including "plans and carries out policies relating to all phases of personnel activity," "recruits, interviews, and selects employees to fill vacant positions," and "conducts wage survey within labor market to determine competitive wage rate."

The *Dictionary of Occupational Titles* is being replaced as a source of occupational information by the U.S. Department of Labor's *Occupational Information Network,* or O*NET (www.doleta.gov/programs/onet). As of today, O*NET contains data adapted from preexisting sources such as the *Dictionary of Occupational Titles.* However, it is growing fast, and adding new data about jobs in today's increasingly

Figure 3.2 "Personnel Manager" Description from *Dictionary of Occupational Titles*

166.117–018 MANAGER, PERSONNEL (profess. & kin.) alternate titles: manager, human resources

Plans and carries out policies relating to all phases of personnel activity: Recruits, interviews, and selects employees to fill vacant positions. Plans and conducts new employee orientation to foster positive attitude toward company goals. Keeps record of insurance coverage, pension plan, and personnel transactions, such as hires, promotions, transfers, and terminations. Investigates accidents and prepares reports for insurance carrier. Conducts wage survey within labor market to determine competitive wage rate. Prepares budget of personnel operations. Meets with shop stewards and supervisors to resolve grievances. Writes separation notices for employees separating with cause and conducts exit interviews to determine reasons behind separations. Prepares reports and recommends procedures to reduce absenteeism and turnover. Represents company at personnel-related hearings and investigations. Contracts with outside suppliers to provide employee services, such as canteen, transportation, or relocation service. May prepare budget of personnel operations, using computer terminal. May administer manual and dexterity tests to applicants. May supervise clerical workers. May keep records of hired employee characteristics for governmental reporting purposes. May negotiate collective bargaining agreement with BUSINESS REPRESENTATIVE, LABOR UNION (profess. & kin.) *187.167–018. GOE: 11.05.02 STRENGTH: S GED: R5 M5 L5 SVP: 8 DLU: 88*

Source: Dictionary of Occupational Titles, 4th ed. (Washington, DC: U.S. Department of Labor, Employment Training Administration, U.S. Employment Service, 1991).

information-based economy. Built-in software allows users to see the most important characteristics of an occupation, as well as the training, experience, and education and knowledge that are required to do the job well.[10]

Authority   This section defines the limits of the jobholder's authority. For example, the jobholder might have authority to approve purchase requests up to $5,000, grant time off or leaves of absence, discipline department personnel, recommend salary increases, and interview and hire new employees.[11]

Standards of Performance   Some job descriptions also contain a standards-of-performance section. This states the standards the employee is expected to achieve in each of the job description's main duties and responsibilities.

Working Conditions and Physical Environment   The job description also lists the general working conditions involved in the job. These might include noise level, hazardous conditions, heat, and other conditions.

Writing Job Descriptions That Comply with the ADA   As explained in Chapter 2, the Americans with Disabilities Act (ADA) does not require employers to have job descriptions. However, almost all ADA lawsuits revolve around the question, What are the essential functions of the job? Without a job description listing these functions, it is difficult to convince a court that the functions were in fact essential to the job.[12] The corollary is that the essential functions can't just be listed on the description, but should also be clearly identified as "essential."[13] Essential job functions are those job duties that employees must be able to perform, with or without reasonable accommodation.[14]

Using the Internet   Most employers probably still write their own job descriptions, but more and more are turning to the Internet. One site, www.jobdescription. com, illustrates why. The process is simple. Search by alphabetical title, keyword, category, or industry to find the desired job title. This leads you to a generic job description for that title—say, "computers & EDP systems sales representative." You can then use the wizard to customize the generic description for this position. For example, you can add specific information about your organization, such as job title, job codes, department, and preparation date. And you can indicate whether the job has supervisory abilities, and choose from a number of possible desirable competencies and experience levels.[15]

Writing Job Specifications

The job specification starts with the job description and then answers the question, What human traits and experience are required to do this job well?[16] It shows what kind of person to recruit and for what qualities that person should be tested. The job specification may be a separate section on the job description or a separate document entirely.

Writing job specifications for trained employees is relatively straightforward. For example, suppose you want to fill a position for a trained bookkeeper (or trained counselor or programmer). In cases like these, your job specifications might focus mostly on traits such as length of previous service, quality of relevant training, and previous job performance. Thus, it's usually not too difficult to determine the human requirements for placing already trained people on a job.

But the problems are more complex when you're seeking to fill jobs with untrained people (probably with the intention of training them on the job). Here you need to specify qualities such as physical traits, personality, interests, or sensory skills that imply some potential for performing the job or for having the ability to be trained for the job. For example, suppose the job requires detailed manipulation on a circuit board assembly line. You might want to ensure that the person scores high on a test of finger dexterity. Your goal, in other words, is to identify those personal traits—or human requirements—that predict which candidate would do well on the job and which would not. Identifying these human requirements for a job is accomplished either through a subjective, judgmental approach or through statistical analysis.

Common sense needs to be applied when compiling a list of the job's human requirements. Certainly job-specific human traits such as manual dexterity and educational level are important. However, it's important not to ignore the fact that there are also work behaviors (such as industriousness, thoroughness, good attendance, and honesty) that seem to apply to almost any job, but might not normally be unearthed through a job analysis.[17]

Job Analysis in a "Jobless" World

A job is a set of closely related activities carried out for pay, but over the past few years, the concept of job has been changing quite dramatically. As one observer put it:

> The modern world is on the verge of another huge leap in creativity and productivity, but the job is not going to be part of tomorrow's economic reality. There still is and will always be enormous amounts of work to do,

but it is not going to be contained in the familiar envelopes we call jobs. In fact, many organizations are today well along the path toward being "de-jobbed."[18]

"De-jobbing" is a product of the changes taking place in business today. There is accelerating product and technological change and globalized competition. The intensity of both competition and uncertainty are higher. Firms therefore need to be responsive, flexible, and more competitive. They are thus instituting high-performance workplace policies and practices. These include management systems based on flexible, multi-skilled job assignments, and on high-involvement practices like teamwork and participative decision making. In team environments, workers must be multi-skilled, since one's assignment may change hourly or daily. With organizational hierarchies flatter, each manager's span of control expands, and subordinates often get more leeway—and broader jobs. All this has helped to blur the meaning of *job* as "a set of well-defined and clearly delineated responsibilities." Employers often want their employees to define their jobs much more broadly and flexibly then they have in the past.

The Future of Job Descriptions   Most firms today continue to use job descriptions and to rely on jobs as traditionally defined. However, it's clear that more firms are moving toward new organizational configurations, ones built around jobs that are broad and that may change every day. Some feel that "job descriptions, although they include the ubiquitous phrase, 'and all other duties as assigned,' are still relatively rigid and limiting."[19] Another writer has said, "In such a situation people no longer take their cues from a job description or a supervisor's instructions. Signals come from the changing demands of the project. Workers learn to focus their individual efforts and collective resources on the work that needs doing, changing as that changes. Managers lose their 'jobs,' too."[20] There is some evidence from related research that firms that try to combine such high-performance workplace practices with more structured jobs may actually perform worse—not better—than their peers.[21]

THE RECRUITMENT AND SELECTION PROCESS

Employers use job analysis and job descriptions for several things—for example, as the basis for developing training programs or for determining how much to pay for various jobs. But the most familiar use for job descriptions is probably as the basis for deciding what types of people to recruit and then select for the company's jobs.

This recruiting and selecting process is a series of steps, as follows:

1. Do workforce planning and forecasting to determine the positions to be filled.
2. Build a pool of candidates for these jobs by recruiting internal or external candidates.
3. Have the applicants fill out application forms and perhaps undergo an initial screening interview.
4. Utilize various selection techniques such as tests, background investigations, and physical exams to identify viable job candidates.

5. Send one or more viable job candidates to the supervisor responsible for the job.
6. Have the candidate(s) go through one or more selection interviews with the supervisor and other relevant parties for the purpose of finally determining to which candidate(s) an offer should be made.

Workforce planning and recruiting are the subjects of the remainder of this chapter. Chapter 4 then focuses on employee selection techniques including tests, background checks, and physical exams.

WORKFORCE PLANNING AND FORECASTING

Workforce (or personnel, or employment) planning is the process of formulating plans to fill the employer's future openings, based on projecting (1) the positions that are expected to be open and (2) whether these will be filled by inside or outside candidates. Therefore, it refers to planning to fill any or all of the firm's future positions, from maintenance clerk to CEO. However, most firms use the term *succession planning* to refer to the process of planning how to fill the company's most important top executive positions.

Personnel planning is (or should be) an integral part of a firm's strategic and HR planning processes. Thus, a firm's plan to expand abroad should prompt its management to formulate revenue, organizational, and personnel plans to support the new expansion strategy. When JDS Uniphase, which designs, develops, and manufactures and markets products for the fiber optics market, decided to expand its Melbourne, Florida, operations, it expanded its employment there from 140 people to almost 750. The firm needed to make fairly specific plans showing how many of what sorts of people to hire, and where these new employees should come from. One big question is always whether to fill projected openings from within or from outside the firm. In other words, should you plan to fill them with current employees or by recruiting from outside?

Each option produces its own set of HR plans. Current employees may require training, development, and coaching before they're ready to fill new jobs—and, thus, development plans. Going outside requires deciding what recruiting sources to use, among other things.

How does the manager decide how many employees he or she needs over the next few years? Like all good plans, management builds personnel plans on *premises*—basic assumptions about the future. Forecasting generates these premises. Again, if you're planning for employment requirements, you'll usually need to forecast three things: personnel needs; the supply of inside candidates; and the supply of outside candidates. We'll start with personnel needs.

How to Forecast Personnel Needs

The expected demand for your product or service is paramount when forecasting personnel needs. The usual process is therefore to forecast revenues first. Then estimate the size of the staff required to achieve this volume. In addition to expected demand, staffing plans may reflect:

1. Projected turnover (as a result of resignations or terminations)
2. Quality and skills of your employees (in relation to what you see as the changing needs of your organization)
3. Strategic decisions to upgrade the quality of products or services or enter into new markets
4. Technological and other changes resulting in increased productivity
5. The financial resources available to your department

While some firms use sophisticated computerized personnel forecasting tools, there are several simple ways for a manager to estimate future personnel needs.[22] **Trend analysis** involves studying your firm's employment levels over the past five years or so to predict future needs. Thus, you might compute the number of employees in your firm at the end of each of the past five years, or perhaps the number in each subgroup (such as salespeople, production people, secretarial, and administrative) at the end of each of those years. The purpose is to identify employment trends you think might continue into the future.

Another approach, **ratio analysis,** means making forecasts based on the ratio between some causal factor (such as sales volume) and the number of employees required (for instance, number of salespeople). For example, suppose you find that a salesperson traditionally generates $500,000 in sales. Then, if the sales revenue-to-salespeople ratio remains the same, you would require six new salespeople next year (each of whom produces an extra $500,000 in sales) to produce, say, the desired extra $3 million in sales.

The **scatter plot** is another method. It shows graphically how two variables (such as a measure of business activity and your firm's staffing levels) are related. If they are, then if you can forecast the level of business activity, you should also be able to estimate your personnel requirements.

For example, assume a 500-bed hospital expects to expand to 1,200 beds over the next five years. The director of nursing and the human resource director want to forecast the requirement for registered nurses. The human resource director decides to determine the relationship between size of hospital (in terms of number of beds) and number of nurses required. She calls five hospitals of various sizes and gets the following figures:

Size of Hospital (Number of Beds)	Number of Registered Nurses
200	240
300	260
400	470
500	500
600	620
700	660
800	820
900	860

Figure 3.3
Determining the
Relationship
Between Hospital
Size and Number
of Nurses

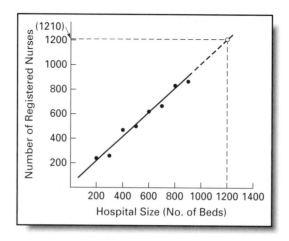

Note: After fitting the line, you can extrapolate—project—
how many employees you'll need, given your projected
volume.

Figure 3.3 shows hospital size on the horizontal axis. Number of nurses is shown on the vertical axis. If the two factors are related, then the points will tend to fall along a straight line, as they do here. If you carefully draw in a line to minimize the distances between the line and each one of the plotted points, you will be able to estimate (forecast) the number of nurses needed for each given hospital size. Thus, for a 1,200-bed hospital, the human resource director would assume she needs about 1,210 nurses.[23]

Managerial judgment always plays a big role in employment planning. It's rare that any historical trend, ratio, or relationship will continue unchanged into the future. Judgment is thus required to adjust the forecast based on factors you believe will change in the future. Important factors that may influence your forecast include, for instance, decisions to upgrade the quality of products or services or enter into new markets, technological and administrative changes resulting in increased productivity, and the financial resources you plan to have available.

Forecasting the Supply of Inside Candidates

The preceding forecast provides only half the staffing equation, by answering the question, How many employees will we need? Next, the manager has to try to assess the projected *supply* of both internal and external candidates.

A qualifications inventory can facilitate forecasting the supply of internal candidates. **Qualifications inventories** contain summary data such as each current employee's performance record, educational background, and promotability, compiled either manually or in a computerized system. **Personnel replacement charts** (see Figure 3.4) show the present performance and promotability for each potential replacement for important positions. As an alternative, you can develop a *position replacement card* for each position, showing possible replacements as well as present performance, promotion potential, and training required by each possible candidate.

Computerized Information Systems   Qualifications inventories on hundreds or thousands of employees cannot be adequately maintained manually. Many firms

Figure 3.4 Management Personnel Replacement Chart

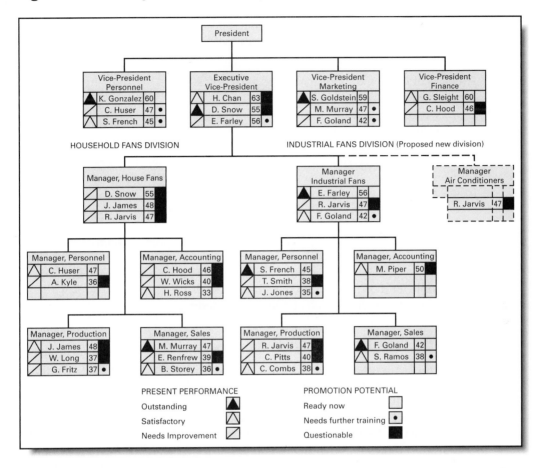

computerize this information, and a number of packaged systems are available for accomplishing this task.[24]

In one such system, employees fill out a Web–based survey in which they describe their background and experience. When a manager needs a qualified person to fill a position, he or she describes the position (for instance, in terms of the education and skills it entails) and then enters this information into the computer. After scanning its bank of possible candidates, the program presents the manager with a listing of qualified candidates.

Succession Planning Forecasting the availability of inside candidates is particularly important in succession planning. In a nutshell, succession planning refers to the plans a company makes to fill its most important executive positions. In practice, the process often involves a fairly complicated and integrated series of steps. For example, potential successors for top management might be routed through the top jobs at several key divisions as well as overseas, and might then be sent through the Harvard Business School's Advanced Management Program. As a result, a more comprehensive definition of *succession planning* is "the process of ensuring a suitable supply of successors for current and future key jobs arising from business strategy, so that the careers of individuals can be planned and managed to optimize the organization's needs and the individuals' aspirations."[25] Succession planning includes these activities:

- Analysis of the demand for managers and professionals by company level, function, and skill
- Audit of existing executives and projection of likely future supply from internal and external sources
- Planning of individual career paths based on objective estimates of future needs and drawing on performance appraisals and assessments of potential
- Career counseling undertaken in the context of a realistic understanding of the future needs of the firm, as well as those of the individual
- Accelerated promotions, with development targeted against the future needs of the business
- Performance-related training and development to prepare individuals for future roles as well as current responsibilities
- Planned strategic recruitment not only to fill short-term needs but also to provide people for development to meet future needs
- The actual activities by which openings are filled[26]

Forecasting the Supply of Outside Candidates

If there are not enough qualified inside candidates to fill anticipated openings, employers focus next on projecting supplies of outside candidates—those not currently employed by your organization. This may require forecasting general economic conditions, local market conditions, and occupational market conditions.

The first step is to forecast general economic conditions and, for instance, the expected prevailing rate of unemployment. Usually, the lower the rate of unemployment, the lower the labor supply and the more difficult it is to recruit personnel.

Local labor market conditions are also important. For example, in the 1990s, the growth of computer and semiconductor firms prompted low unemployment in cities like Seattle, quite aside from general economic conditions in the country (a situation that reversed in the early 2000s).

Finally, you may want to forecast the availability of potential job candidates in specific occupations (engineers, drill press operators, accountants, and so on) for which you will be recruiting. Recently, for instance, there has been an oversupply of computer systems specialists. Sources such as *Occupational Outlook Quarterly* from the U.S. Labor Department can be useful here.

RECRUITING JOB CANDIDATES

Once authorized to fill a position, the next step is to develop an applicant pool, either from internal sources of applicants or external ones. Recruiting is important because the more applicants you have, the more selective you can be in your hiring.

Recruiting is (or should be) a more complex activity than most managers think it is. It does not just involve placing ads or calling employment agencies. For one thing, your recruitment efforts should make sense in terms of your company's strategic and other plans. For example (as noted earlier), decisions to expand abroad or to fill a large number of anticipated openings implies that you've carefully thought through when and how you will do your recruiting—the sources you will use, for instance. Second (and related to this), some recruiting methods are superior to others, depending on who you are recruiting for and what your resources are. Third, the success you have with your recruiting actually depends to a great extent on non-recruitment HR issues and policies. For example, deciding to pay a 10% higher salary and better benefits than most firms in your locale should, other things equal, help you build a bigger applicant pool faster.[27] The bottom line is that your recruiting plans (and HR plans in general) must be internally consistent, and must make sense in terms of your company's strategy. With that in mind, let us look at the basic sources of outside recruits.

Internal Sources of Candidates

Although *recruiting* may bring to mind employment agencies and classified ads, filling open jobs with current employees (internal recruiting) is often an employer's best source of recruits. To be effective, this approach requires using job posting, personnel records, and skill banks.[28] **Job posting** means "posting the open job—on company bulletin boards and/or on the Web—and listing its attributes, such as qualifications, supervisor, working schedule, and pay rate" (as in Figure 3.5). Some union contracts require such postings to ensure that union members get first choice of better positions. Yet posting is also good practice in nonunion firms, if it facilitates the transfer and promotion of qualified inside candidates. *Personnel records* are also useful here. An examination of personnel records (including application forms) may uncover employees who are working in jobs below their educational or skill levels. It may also reveal persons who have potential for further training or those who already have the right background for the open jobs in question. Computerized skills banks (as discussed previously) can help ensure you identify and consider qualified inside candidates for the openings.

Advertising as a Source of Candidates

Internal candidates may not be sufficient to fill your recruiting needs. In that case, the manager turns to outside sources, often starting with placing ads.

To use help wanted ads successfully, you need to address two issues: the media and the ad's construction. The selection of the best medium (be it your local paper, the *Wall Street Journal*, or a technical journal) depends on the type of positions for which you're recruiting. Your local newspaper is usually the best source of blue-collar help, clerical employees, and lower-level administrative employees. For specialized employees, you can advertise in trade and professional journals such as the *American Psychologist, Sales Management, Chemical Engineering*, and *Electronic News*. In publications such as *Travel Trade, Women's Wear Daily, American Banker, Hospital Administration*, and the *Chronicle of Higher Education*, you would most likely place

Figure 3.5 Job Posting Form for Hard Copy or Web Submissions

JOB POSTING FORM

Please complete all applicable areas and return via e-mail (JobForm@bigCo.com) or FAX (123-456-7890)

Date Posted _____

Reply no later than _____

Type of Employment   Summer _____   Part-Time _____   Full Time _____

Job Title of Open Position _____

Employer _____ Department _____

Location Address _____

Web Site _____

Pay Scale _____ Shifts/Hours _____ # of Vacancies _____

Brief Job
Description _____
_____
_____
_____
_____

Qualifications: Required Skills and
Abilities _____
_____
_____
_____

Desired Skills and
Abilities _____
_____
_____
_____

How to Apply: By FAX or e-mail as above, no later than _____ . Please ensure
HR has updated copy of your résumé. Selections will be made by _____ .

Figure 3.6

General Sales Manager

A leading manufacturer with multi-state locations is looking for a General Sales Manager with Vice Presidential potential for our East Coast Region. This proven leader will manage a sixteen (16) member sales team of outside salesmen and sales managers. Assist in the development and implementation of sales/marketing strategies, sales tools, and promotional material. Direct the introduction, promotion, and sales of new products.

Develop additional channels of distribution for our ever expanding product line. Continually train and further develop the sales and marketing team. You will have an M.B.A. with over ten (10) years of proven progressive sales experience and five (5) years successful sales management experience. You will need to have a familiarity with CRM systems and hands-on working knowledge of Word, Excel, and Power Point programs. You will report directly to the Vice President of Sales and Marketing in our southern Putnam county New York regional office. Send resume, salary history, and references in confidence to: **T8065**

---

your ads for professionals such as bankers, hospital administrators, or educators. One drawback to such trade paper advertising is that there may be a month or more between insertion of the ad and publication of the journal, for instance. Yet ads remain good sources, and ads such as Figure 3.6 continue to appear.

Help wanted ads in papers such as the *Wall Street Journal* can be good sources of middle- or senior-management personnel. For instance, the *Wall Street Journal* has several regional editions so that you can target the entire country or the appropriate geographic area for coverage. Most print media also let employers place their ads on the magazine's or newspaper's help wanted Web sites.

Employment Agencies as a Source of Candidates

There are three basic types of employment agencies: (1) those operated by federal, state, or local governments; (2) those associated with nonprofit organizations; and (3) privately owned agencies.[29]

Public, state employment service agencies exist in every state. They are aided and coordinated by the U.S. Department of Labor. The latter also maintains a nationwide computerized job bank to which state employment offices are connected. Public agencies are a major source of blue-collar and often white-collar workers.

Today, these agencies' usefulness is on the rise. Beyond just filling jobs, counselors will visit an employer's work site, review the employer's job requirements, and even assist the employer in writing job descriptions. And some states, like Illinois and Wisconsin, are turning their local state employment service agencies into "one-stop" shops. Under this concept, "employers and jobseekers now access, under a single roof, a broader array of employment security, workforce-development, and business-support programs. Services available to employers include recruitment services, tax credit information, employee training programs and access to the latest local and national labor market information."[30]

Other employment agencies are associated with nonprofit organizations. For example, most professional and technical societies have units that help their members find jobs. Similarly, many public welfare agencies try to place people who are in special categories, such as those who are physically disabled or who are war veterans.

Private employment agencies are important sources of clerical, white-collar, and managerial personnel. Such agencies charge a fee for each applicant they place. These fees are usually set by state law and are posted in their offices. The trend is toward "fee-paid jobs," in which the employer pays the fees.

Some specific reasons you might want to turn to an agency include the following:

- Your firm does not have its own HR department and is not geared to do recruiting and screening.
- Your firm has found it difficult in the past to generate a pool of qualified applicants.
- A particular opening must be filled quickly.
- There is a perceived need to attract a greater number of minority or female applicants.
- The recruitment effort is aimed at reaching individuals who are currently employed and who might feel more comfortable dealing with employment agencies than with competing companies.

On the other hand, employment agencies are no panacea. For example, the employment agency's screening may let poor applicants bypass the preliminary stages of your own selection process.[31] Unqualified applicants may thus go directly to the supervisors responsible for the hiring, who may in turn naïvely hire them.

Temporary Workers   Many employers supplement their permanent employee base by hiring contingent or temporary workers, often through temporary help agencies. Also called *part-time* or *just-in-time* workers, the *contingent workforce* is big and growing and is broadly defined as "workers who don't have permanent jobs."[32]

Contingent staffing owes its growing popularity to several things. First, corporate downsizing seems to be driving up the number of temporary workers firms employ. For example, although Du Pont says it cut its workforce by 47,000 in the past few years, it also estimates that only 70% of those workers actually stopped working for the company: "The remaining 30%—about 14,000 workers—returned as vendors or contractors."[33] Historically, employers have also used "temps" to fill in for the days or weeks that permanent employees were out sick or on vacation. Today's desire for ever-higher productivity also contributes to temp workers' growing popularity. In general, as one expert puts it, "productivity is measured in terms of output per hour paid for," and "if employees are paid only when they're working, as contingent workers are, overall productivity increases."[34] Contingent workers also usually aren't paid any benefits, which is another saving for the employer. Temp workers also let employers readily expand and contract with changes in demand.

Some firms today employ so many temp workers that they hire special agencies to manage their temporary workforces. New York–based MasterCard, for instance, has a temporary workforce of 200 to 400 workers on any given day, and retained Manpower, Inc., a large temporary staffing agency, to coordinate the hiring, training, and paperwork of temporary workers. In such a situation, the temporary employment agency may even assign on-site supervisors to the employer to manage the duties involved in managing the temporary employees.[35]

The contingent workforce is no longer limited to clerical or maintenance staff. Thus, in one recent year, almost 100,000 people found temporary work in engineering, science, or management support occupations.[36] In fact, growing numbers of firms use temporary workers as short-term chief financial officers, or even chief executive officers. Perhaps 60% of the total U.S. temporary payroll is nonclerical, and includes "CEOs, human resources directors, computer systems analysts, accountants, doctors, and nurses."[37]

Executive Recruiters as a Source of Candidates

Executive recruiters (also called *headhunters*) are special employment agencies retained by employers to seek out top-management talent for their clients. They fill jobs in the $60,000 and up category, although $80,000 is often the lower limit. The percentage of your firm's positions filled by these services might be small. However, these jobs include the most crucial executive and technical positions. For executive positions, headhunters may be your *only* source. The employer pays their fees.

Headhunting firms can be useful. They have many contacts and are especially adept at contacting qualified candidates who are employed and not actively looking to change jobs. They can also keep your firm's name confidential until late into the search process. The recruiter can save top management time by doing the preliminary work of advertising for the position, and screening what could turn out to be hundreds of applicants. The recruiter's fee might actually turn out to be insignificant compared to the cost of the executive time saved.

But there are pitfalls. As an employer, you must explain completely what sort of candidate is required and why. Some recruiters are also more salespeople than professionals. They may be more interested in persuading you to hire a candidate than in finding one who will do the job you want. Recruiters also claim that what their clients say or think they want is often not really what they need. Therefore, be prepared for some in-depth dissecting of your request. Also make sure to meet the person who will be handling your search, and nail down exactly what the charges will be.[38]

As in most industries, technology is changing the executive search business. Top firms traditionally took up to seven months to complete a big search. Much of that time went into shuffling chores between headhunters and the researchers who develop the initial "long list" of candidates; this often took too long in today's fast-moving environment.[39] Most of these firms are therefore establishing Internet-linked computerized databases, the aim of which, according to one senior recruiter, is "to create a long list by pushing a button."[40] Recruiter Korn/Ferry launched an Internet service called Futurestep to draw more managerial applicants into its files;

in turn, it has teamed up with the *Wall Street Journal*, which runs a career Web site of its own.[41]

As a job candidate, keep several things in mind when dealing with executive search firms. Many of these firms pay little heed to unsolicited résumés, preferring instead to find their own candidates. Some firms may also present an unpromising candidate to a client simply to make their other one or two proposed candidates look better. Some eager clients may also jump the gun, checking your references and undermining your present position prematurely. Also remember that executive recruiters and their clients are usually more impressed with candidates who are obviously "not looking" for a job, and that overeagerness to take a job can be a candidate's downfall.[42] Finally, do not confuse executive search firms with the many executive assistance firms that help out-of-work executives find jobs. The latter charge the jobseekers handsome fees to assist with things like résumé preparation and interview skills. They rarely actually reach out to prospective employers to find their clients jobs.

College Recruiting and Interns as a Source of Candidates

Many promotable candidates originally get hired through college recruiting. Such recruiting is thus an important source of management trainees, as well as of professional and technical employees.

There are two main problems with on-campus recruiting. First, it is relatively expensive and time consuming for the recruiters. Schedules must be set well in advance, company brochures printed, records of interviews kept, and much recruiting time spent on campus. Second, recruiters themselves are sometimes ineffective. Some recruiters are unprepared, show little interest in candidates, and act superior. Many recruiters also don't effectively screen their student candidates. For example, students' physical attractiveness often outweighs other more valid traits and skills.[43] Some recruiters also tend to assign females to "female type" jobs and males to "male type" jobs.[44] Such findings underscore the need to train recruiters before sending them to a campus.[45]

Campus recruiters should have two goals. The main goal is screening, which means determining whether a candidate is worthy of further consideration. Exactly which traits you look for depend on your specific recruiting needs. However, the checklist presented in Figure 3.7 is typical. Traits to assess include motivation, communication skills, education, appearance, and attitude.[46]

Although the main goal is to find and screen good candidates, the other aim is to attract them to your firm. A sincere and informal attitude, respect for the applicant, and prompt follow-up letters can help you to sell the employer to the interviewee.

Jobseekers should know that recruiters are usually coy when it comes to revealing the full amount they're willing to pay. For example, one researcher found that 9 out of 10 recruiters say they do not reveal, during hiring interviews, the full amount they're willing to pay to hire good employees for the job. Thus, there's often more flexibility at the top than applicants may realize.[47]

Internships   Many college students get their jobs through college internships, a recruiting approach that has grown dramatically in recent years. Today, it's

Figure 3.7 Campus Applicant Interview Review

CAMPUS INTERVIEW REPORT

Name_____ Anticipated Graduation Date _____

Current Address _____
If different than placement form

Position Applied For_____

If Applicable (Use Comment Section if necessary)

      Drivers License   Yes _____ No _____

      Any special considerations affecting your availability for relocation?

      _____

      _____

      Are you willing to travel? _____ If so, what % of time _____

EVALUATION	Outstanding	Above Average	Average	Below Average
Education: Courses relevant to job? Does performance in class indicate good potential for work?	_____	_____	_____	_____
Appearance: Was applicant neat and dressed appropriately?	_____	_____	_____	_____
Communication Skills: Was applicant mentally alert? Did he or she express ideas clearly?	_____	_____	_____	_____
Motivation: Does applicant have high energy level? Are his or her interests compatible with job?	_____	_____	_____	_____
Attitude: Did applicant appear to be pleasant, people-oriented?	_____	_____	_____	_____

COMMENTS: (Use back of sheet if necessary)

      _____

      _____

      _____

Given Application   Yes _____ No _____ Received Transcript Release Authorization _____

Recommendations   Invite _____ Reject _____

Interviewed by: _____ Date: _____

Campus _____

Source: From *Handbook of Personnel Forms, Records, and Reports* by Joseph J. Famularo. Copyright © 1982 McGraw-Hill Book Company. Reprinted by permission of The McGraw-Hill Companies.

estimated that almost three-quarters of all college students take part in an internship before they graduate.[48]

Internships can be win-win situations for both students and employers. For students, an internship may mean being able to hone business skills, check out potential employers, and learn more about their likes (and dislikes) when it comes to choosing careers. Employers can use the interns to make useful contributions while they're being evaluated as possible full-time employees.

Referrals and Walk-ins as a Source of Candidates

Employee referrals campaigns are another option. Here announcements of openings and requests for referrals are made on the organization's Intranet and posted on walls. Prizes may be offered for referrals that culminate in hirings.

Employee referral programs have their pros and cons. Current employees can and usually do provide accurate information about the job applicants they are referring, especially because they're often putting their reputations on the line by recommending them.[49] The new employees may also come with a more realistic picture of what working in the firm is really like after speaking with their friends who are currently employed there. Referral programs may also result in higher-quality candidates, insofar as employees are reluctant to refer less-qualified candidates. But the success of the campaign depends a lot on your employees' morale.[50] And the campaign can backfire if an employee's referral is rejected and the employee becomes dissatisfied. Using referrals exclusively may also turn out to be discriminatory if most of your current employees (and their referrals) are male or white.

Employee referral programs are increasingly popular. Of the firms responding to one survey, 40% said they use an employee referral system and hire about 15% of their employees through such referrals. A cash award for referring candidates who are hired is the most common referral incentive. Large firms reportedly spent about $34,000 annually on their referral programs (including cash payments for candidates), medium companies spent about $17,000, and small ones with fewer than 500 employees spent about $3,600. The cost per hire, however, was uniformly low: Average per hire expenses were only $388, far below the cost of an employment service.[51] Employee referrals have been the source of almost half of all hires at AmeriCredit since the firm kicked off its "you've got friends, we want to meet them" employee referrals program. Employees making a referral receive $1,000 awards, with the payments spread over a year. As the head of recruiting says, "Quality people know quality people. If you give employees the opportunity to make referrals, they automatically suggest high-caliber people because they are stakeholders. . . . "[52]

Particularly for hourly workers, *walk-ins*—direct applications made at your office—are a major source of applicants, and you can even encourage them by posting "for hire" signs on your property. Treat all walk-ins courteously and diplomatically, both out of common decency and to support your firm's community reputation. Many employers thus give every walk-in a brief interview with someone in the HR office, even if it is only to get information on the applicant in case a position should open in the future. Good business practice also requires answering all letters of inquiry from applicants promptly and courteously.

Don't underestimate the importance of employee referrals or in-house job postings. One review of recruitment sources concluded, for instance, that "referrals by current personnel, in-house job postings, and the rehiring of former employees are the most effective [recruiting] sources. Walk-ins have been slightly less effective, and the least effective sources are newspaper ads, school placement services, and employment agencies (government/private)."[53]

Former Employees

It is increasingly common to welcome back employees who previously left "for greener pastures." For example, many former employees are finding that the life of a start-up entrepreneur is not all they'd hoped it would be. Will McPherson, who leads a sales team for Phoenix, Arizona–based Brill Pharmaceutical Corporation, recently faced such a situation. A salesperson who had left about a year earlier to pursue a start-up venture returned when it didn't work out. McPherson decided to rehire him. "I felt a little used (and I told him that) but when you've got someone who you know will do well asking for a job, it's hard to turn him down. You can't just not hire somebody [out of] principle."[54]

Recruiting via the Internet

Virtually all large firms and many smaller ones use the Internet for recruiting. For example, www.gepowercareers.com (part of General Electric's home Web site) not only provides useful information about working for the company, but includes numerous useful jobseeker aids, such as separate category buttons titled "experienced professionals," "entry-level," and "military officer."[55] Many firms do more than list jobs on their sites.[56] NEC Electronics, Unisys Corp., and LSI Logicorp all posted Internet-based "cyber fairs" to recruit for applicants.[57] Cisco Systems offers links to such things as "hot jobs"—job descriptions for hard-to-fill positions and Cisco culture—a look at Cisco work life.[58] About 71% of the Standard & Poor's 500 companies make employment information just one click away from their home pages.[59]

Internet recruiting has several advantages. Newspapers may charge employers from $50 to $100 to several thousand dollars for print ads, while job listings on the Internet may cost as little as $10 each.[60] Newspaper ads might have a life span of perhaps 10 days, whereas the Internet ad may attract applications for 30 days or more.[61] Internet recruiting can also be fast, since responses to electronic job listings may start coming in at once. Employers increasingly use Internet support tools such as Recruiter Toolbox of Oakbrook Terrace, Illinois, to help them develop online ads that include prescreening tests to further automate the recruiting process.[62]

Some firms have been phenomenally successful generating applications through Web–based recruiting.[63] Yet some employers cite just such a flood of responses as a possible downside of Internet recruiting. The problem is that the relative ease of responding to Internet ads may encourage unqualified jobseekers to apply; furthermore, the nature of the Internet is that applications may arrive from geographic areas that are unrealistically far away. On the whole, though, more applicants are usually better than fewer, and more companies are using their computers to scan, digitize,

Online recruiting Web sites like monster.com represent just the tip of the iceberg for employers seeking good résumés. For example, one online recruiter points out that "while monster and its competitors have about 5 million unique résumés in their databases, you can find double or triple that number on the open Internet." These résumés are hidden away at the Web sites of virtual communities such as GeoCities and Tripod, and at the Web sites of archived newsgroup postings and several message boards.

Suppose, for example, you want to find résumés of programmers in Florida who are comfortable on the UNIX platform. On GeoCities, www.GeoCities.com, in the text field under "explore our neighborhoods," type:

resume *and* programmer *and* UNIX *and* Florida Then, click "search" and start reviewing résumés.

You can get even better results on sites like Angelfire or Tripod. These allow you to use Boolean operators (such as *and, or, not,* and *near*), and even to focus specifically on telephone area codes for your search. So, for your programmer search, on Angelfire, type:

resume *and* programmer *and* UNIX *and* (Florida *near* 305 or 954) Then click the "go get it" button for personal Web sites and résumés of possible candidates.

Source: Glenn Gutmacher, "Secrets of Online Recruiter's Exposed!" *Workforce* (October 2000): 44–50.

and process applicant résumés automatically.[64] More firms also install *applicant tracking systems* to support their on- and off-line recruiting efforts. Well-known applicant tracking systems (such as recruitsoft.com and Itrack-IT solutions) help employers keep track of their applicants. They also help the employers perform searches (such as by skill or college degree) and to match candidates with positions. Systems like these also help employers compile reports, such as "EEO applicant summary" and "applicants by reject reason."[65] While many employers use their own Web sites and software to attract and process applications, others farm out that work to application service providers (ASPs), as just noted. Others let job boards like careerbuilder.com, hire.com, and monster.com post their open jobs and compile the online applications. A sample list of recruiting Web sites is presented in Figure 3.8.[66] Also see the *HR in Practice* box.

H&R Block Financial Advisers (part of H&R Block) used to compile and process their own online applications. The company also used newspaper ads and their HR staff to manually review applications. Now the company uses www.hire.com. Hire.com collects and compiles résumés through a specialized H&R Block Financial Advisers recruiting Web site, and then segments the résumés and applications based on type of job. H&R Block also uses the Web to search for keywords on résumés that jobseekers have posted at various sites, and then invites selected individuals to apply for positions. (H&R Block searches for keywords such as *insurance license,* and *certified financial planner.*)[67]

E-recruiting has some potential legal pitfalls. For example, if more young people or fewer minorities use the Internet, then automated online application gathering and screening might mean the employer inadvertently excludes higher numbers of

Figure 3.8 Sample List of Recruiting Web Sites

America's Job Bank   **www.ajb.dni.us**
On this site candidates can search for jobs by occupation, location, education and experience levels, and salary. Those with a military background can search for civilian jobs that match their areas of expertise. Employers can cull a pool of nearly two million jobseekers.

CareerBuilder   **www.careerbuilder.com**
CareerBuilder, which recently merged with careerpath.com, offers information about career advancement and workplace trends, including tips and news for students and recent grads. Users can search more than 50 leading job sites that are part of the CareerBuilder network, with access to more than three million job postings.

CareerIndex.com   **www.careerindex.com**
This lets you search several recruiting sites simultaneously. For example, you can choose from Monster.com and CareerWeb.com and others. You can find both U.S. and international jobs here, as well as post your résumé and test your skills.

CareerMosaic   **www.careermosaic.com**
CareerMosaic offers insider profiles on such companies as Microsoft and Canon. Jobseekers can search for openings by geographical area, job description, or company name. CareerMosaic has links to more than a dozen countries in North America, Europe, and the Pacific Rim.

CareerShop.com   **www.careershop.com**
In addition to providing easy searches for jobseekers and a pool of nearly 300,000 résumés for employers, CareerShop offers a marketplace for freelancers and employers, guidance for employers on human resources issues, and myriad counseling services.

ComputerJobs.com   **www.computerjobs.com**
ComputerJobs.com is the leading information technology employment site, with job opportunities organized by specific skills and regional markets. As part of its virtual recruiting service for employers, ComputerJobs.com will do online behavioral testing and credit checks of candidates.

Dice.com   **www.dice.com**
This is the first place to look for many IT professionals. This site lists over 150,000 job openings, both permanent and contractual.

Employment911.com   **www.employment911.com**
A Meta-site: It can speed your search by quickly scanning its own listings and those of 35 other sites.

JobOptions   **www.joboptions.com**
Contemplating a move? On the JobOptions site users can compute comparable salaries for different cities based on housing and other factors, and they can search by job classification, location, and qualifications. Employers can search more than 250,000 résumés.

Jobs.com   **www.jobs.com**
Get the inside scoop on working for major companies with Jobs.com's Testify section. Jobs.com offers free software that simplifies the process of writing and delivering a résumé via the Internet. The site features interactive career fairs (with chat and video Webcasts) with employers.

(Continued)

Recruiting Job Candidates

older applicants or minority applicants. Furthermore, the U.S. government's Office of Federal Contract Compliance Programs requires certain employers to track "applicant flow data." To do so, the employer needs detailed information regarding applicants—information the screening software might not provide.[68]

Strategy and HR   With 10,000 job openings per year, Sutter Health had to generate a lot more recruits to continue its fast-growth strategy. However, moving its job postings online not only didn't help, but actually complicated the process.[69]

Moving the postings online did generate many more applications—300,000 a year, to be exact—but it didn't speed up the hiring process. Sutter Health was hit by so many résumés coming in by e-mail and through its Web site that the applications ended up in a huge pile, waiting for Sutter affiliates' HR departments to get to them. It was obvious that if the company wanted to grow and to provide the value-added services to its affiliates it had built its reputation on, it needed a new recruiting approach.

Sutter Health's solution was to sign on with a company called Recruitsoft, Inc., of San Francisco. Recruitsoft is an e-recruiting applications service provider (ASP), and it now does all the work of hosting Sutter Health's job site. As an applications service provider, Recruitsoft doesn't just post Sutter Health job openings and collect its résumés. Recruitsoft also gives Sutter Health "an automated way to evaluate, rank and match IT and other job candidates with specific openings." For example, Recruitsoft's system automatically screens incoming résumés, compares them with Sutter's job requirements, and flags high-priority applicants. And this, says Keith Vencel, the project manager who came up with this solution, helped Sutter cut its recruiting process from weeks to days—and thereby helped ensure that Sutter's expansion strategy stays on track.

Recruiting a More Diverse Workforce

Recruiting a diverse workforce is not just socially responsible; it's a necessity. As noted earlier, the composition of the U.S. workforce is changing dramatically: The white labor force is projected to increase less than 15%, whereas the black labor force is expected to grow by nearly 29% and the Hispanic labor force by more than 74% by the end of 2005. Women will account for about 64% of the net increase in the labor force in these years. Related to this, about two-thirds of all single mothers are in the labor force today, as are almost 45% of mothers with children under three.

Therefore, smart employers have to actively recruit a more diverse workforce. This means taking special steps to recruit older workers, minorities, and women.

Older Workers as a Source of Candidates   More employers are looking to older workers as a source of recruits, for several reasons. Because of buyouts and early retirements, many workers have retired early and are ready and willing to reenter the job market.[70] Furthermore, over the next 10 or so years the number of annual retirees will double to approximately 4 million, and, according to a demographer, "there will be, I guarantee it, many millions of boomers who will have to work beyond age 65 because they simply haven't saved enough money to retire."[71] (A survey by the American Association of Retired Persons concluded that about 80% of the baby boomers expect to work after retirement.[72]) Furthermore, fewer 18- to 25-year-olds are entering the workforce.[73]

Is it practical in terms of productivity to keep older workers? The answer seems to be yes.[74] Age-related changes in physical ability, cognitive performance, and personality have little effect on a worker's output except in the most physically demanding tasks.[75] Similarly, creative and intellectual achievements do not decline with age, and absenteeism drops as age increases. Older workers also usually display more company loyalty than youthful workers, tend to be more satisfied with their jobs and supervision, and can be trained or retrained as effectively as anyone.

Recruiting and attracting older workers involves any or all of the sources described earlier (advertising, employment agencies, and so forth), but with one big difference. Recruiting and attracting older workers generally requires a comprehensive HR retiree effort before the recruiting begins, in part because older workers may have some special preferences.[76] The aim is to make the company an attractive place in which the older worker can work. For example:

- *Develop flexible work options.* At Wrigley Company, workers over 65 can progressively shorten their work schedules; another company uses "minishifts" to accommodate those interested in working less than full time.[77]
- *Create or redesign suitable jobs.* At Xerox, unionized hourly workers over 55 with 15 years of service and those over 50 with 20 years of service can bid on jobs at lower stress and lower pay levels if they so desire.
- *Offer flexible benefit plans.* Older employees often put more emphasis on longer vacations or on continued accrual of pension credits than do younger workers.

Recruiting Single Parents   About two-thirds of all single parents are in the workforce today, and this group thus represents an important source of candidates.

Formulating an intelligent program for attracting single parents should begin with understanding the considerable problems that they often encounter in balancing work and family life.[78] In one recent survey, working single parents (the majority are single mothers) stated that their work responsibilities interfered significantly with their family life. They described as a no-win situation the challenge of having to do a good job at work and being a good parent, and many expressed disappointment at feeling like failures in both endeavors.

The respondents generally viewed themselves as having "less support, less personal time, more stress and greater difficulty balancing job and home life" than other working parents.[79] However, most were hesitant to dwell on their single-parent status at work for fear that such a disclosure would affect their jobs adversely.

Thirty-five percent of the single mothers reported feeling that it was more difficult for them to achieve a proper work-family balance, compared with 10% of the dual-earner mothers.[80]

Given such concerns, the first step in attracting (and keeping) single parents is to make the workplace as user friendly for single mothers as practical. Organizing regular, ongoing support groups and other forums at which single parents can share their concerns is a good way to provide the support that may be otherwise lacking. Furthermore, although many firms have instituted programs aimed at becoming more family friendly, they may not be extensive enough, particularly for single parents. For example, *flextime* programs provide employees some flexibility (such as one-hour windows at the beginning or end of the day) around which to build their workdays. The problem is that "for some single mothers, this flexibility can help but it may not be sufficient to really make a difference in their ability to juggle work and family schedules."[81] In addition to providing increased flexibility, employers can and should train their supervisors to have an increased awareness of and sensitivity to the sorts of challenges single parents face. As two researchers concluded:

> Very often, the relationships which the single mother has with her supervisor and co-workers is a significant factor influencing whether the single-parent employee perceives the work environment to be supportive.[82]

Single parents reentering the workforce can turn to various agencies for support. For example, *displaced homemakers*—individuals who reenter the workforce after a long period out of the workforce, or who are forced to work due to hardship—can call the Displaced Homemakers Network (202–628–6767) for advice on obtaining training and placement.[83] Women entering or reentering the workforce can also call *Women Work! The National Network for Women's Employment* (1–800–235–2732) in Washington, D.C., for referrals to local training programs and information about financial aid options, child support, and health insurance.

Recruiting Minorities and Women   The same prescriptions that apply to recruiting single parents apply to recruiting minorities and women. In other words, employers have to formulate comprehensive plans for attracting minorities and women, plans that may include reevaluating personnel policies, developing flexible work options, redesigning jobs, and offering flexible benefit plans.

An employer can do many specific things to become more attractive to minorities. To the extent that many minority applicants may not meet the educational or experience standards for a job, many companies (including Aetna Life & Casualty) offer remedial training in basic arithmetic and writing.[84] Diversity data banks or nonspecialized minority-focused recruiting publications are another option. For example, Hispan Data provides recruiters at companies such as McDonald's access to a computerized data bank; it costs a candidate $5 to be included.[85] Checking with your own minority employees can also be useful. In one study, about 32% of jobseekers of Hispanic origin cited "check with friends or relatives" as a strategy when looking for jobs.[86] The *Global Issues* box provides an additional perspective.

Welfare-to-Work   Employers are also implementing various "welfare-to-work" programs for attracting and assimilating as new employees former welfare recipients. In 1996 President Clinton signed the Personal Responsibility and Welfare

As companies expand across national borders, they must increasingly tap overseas recruiting sources.[87] For example, Gillette International has an international graduate training program aimed at identifying and developing foreign nationals. Gillette subsidiaries overseas hire outstanding business students from top local universities. These foreign nationals are then trained for six months at the Gillette facility in their home countries. Some are selected to then spend 18 months being trained at the firm's Boston headquarters in areas such as finance and marketing. Those who pass muster are offered entry-level management positions at Gillette facilities in their home countries. However, you don't have to be a multinational to have to recruit abroad. Desperate for qualified nurses, many hospitals (such as Sinai and Northwest hospitals in the Baltimore, Maryland, area) are recruiting in countries like the Philippines, India, and China.[88]

Furthermore, when employers hire "global" employees, they're not just hiring employees who will be sent to work abroad. Although it's true that for many corporations "international recruitment is synonymous with expatriate selection,"[89] HR professionals recognize today that with business increasingly being multinational, "every employee needs to have a certain level of global awareness."[90]

As a result, many employers want their recruiters to look for evidence of global awareness early in the interview process. For example, at the U.S. headquarters of Tetra PAK, Inc., the personnel manager reportedly looks for expatriate potential every time she makes a hire: "We don't often go out and search for someone to go abroad next year . . . but when we recruit, we always look for candidates who have global potential. We're interested in people who eventually could relocate internationally and handle that adjustment well."[91] International experience (including internships and considerable travel abroad) as well as language proficiency are two of the things employers such as these often look for.

In any case, technology has made the task of recruiting abroad somewhat easier. For example, the Internet, fax, and videoconferencing can make the recruiting process easier by enabling you to place ads more easily and then do at least your initial screening while the candidate is still abroad.[92]

Reconciliation Act, an act that prompted many employers to implement these types of programs. (The act required 25% of people receiving welfare assistance to be either working or involved in a work-training program by September 30, 1997, with the percentage rising each year to 50% by September 30, 2002.[93])

The key to welfare-to-work programs' success seems to be the employer's pre-training assimilation and socialization program, during which participants receive counseling and basic skills training spread over several weeks.[94] For example, Marriott hired 600 welfare recipients under its Pathways to Independence program. The heart of the program is a six-week preemployment training program. This teaches work and life skills and is designed to rebuild workers' self-esteem and instill positive attitudes about work.[95] Programs such as Marriott's have reportedly been successful. For instance, 77% of the welfare recipients hired by the company are reportedly still employed there.[96] On the other hand, other companies report difficulty in hiring and assimilating people off welfare, in part because they sometimes lack basic work skills such as reporting for work on time, working in teams, and "taking orders without losing their temper."[97]

DEVELOPING AND USING APPLICATION FORMS

Purpose of Application Forms

Once you have a pool of applicants, the selection process can begin, and for most employers the **application form** is the first step in this process. (Some firms first require a brief, prescreening interview.) The application form is a good way to quickly collect verifiable and therefore fairly accurate historical data from the candidate. It usually includes information about such areas as education, prior work history, and hobbies.

A filled-in form provides at least four types of information.[98] First, you can make judgments on substantive matters, such as Does the applicant have the education and experience to do the job? Second, you can draw conclusions about the applicant's previous progress and growth, a trait that is especially important for management candidates. Third, you can draw tentative conclusions regarding the applicant's stability based on previous work record. (However, be careful not to assume that an unusual number of job changes necessarily reflects on the applicant's stability; for example, the person's two most recent employers may have had to lay off large numbers of employees.) Fourth, you can use the data to check references and to assess the veracity of the applicant's answers.

In practice, most organizations need several application forms. For technical and managerial personnel, for example, the form may require detailed answers to questions concerning such areas as the applicant's education. The form for hourly factory workers might focus on such areas as the tools and equipment the applicant has used.

Equal Opportunity and Application Forms

Employers should carefully review their application forms to ensure that they comply with equal employment laws. Questions concerning race, religion, age, sex, or national origin are generally not illegal per se under federal laws, but are illegal under certain state laws. However, the EEOC views them with disfavor. If the applicant shows that a disproportionate number of protected group applicants gets screened out, then the burden of proof will be on the employer to prove that the potentially discriminatory items are both related to success or failure on the job and not unfairly discriminatory. Perhaps due to their proliferation, online application forms may be particularly susceptible to illegal or inadvisable questions. One survey of 41 Internet-based applications found that over 97% contained at least one inadvisable question. There were an average of just over four inappropriate questions per form. Questions regarding the applicant's past salary, age, and driver's license information led the list.[99]

Figure 3.9 presents the approach one employer—the FBI—uses to collect application form information. The Employment History section requests detailed

Figure 3.9 Employment Application

FEDERAL BUREAU OF INVESTIGATION

**Preliminary Application for
Special Agent Position
(Please Type or Print in Black Ink)**

Date: _____

<table>
<tr><td colspan="2">FIELD OFFICE USE ONLY
Right Thumb Print</td></tr>
<tr><td>Div:</td><td>Program:</td></tr>
</table>

I. PERSONAL HISTORY

Name in Full   (Last, First, Middle)

List College Degree(s) Already Received or Pursuing, Major, School, and Month/Year:

Marital Status: ☐ Single   ☐ Engaged   ☐ Married   ☐ Separated   ☐ Legally Separated   ☐ Widowed   ☐ Divorced

Birth Date (Month, Day, Year)

Birth Place:

Social Security Number: (Optional)

Do you understand FBI employment requires availability for assignment anywhere in the U.S.?

Current Address

Street   Apt. No.

City   State   Zip Code

Home Phone _____

Area Code   Number

Work Phone _____

Area Code   Number

Are you: CPA ☐ Yes ☐ No   Licensed Driver ☐ Yes ☐ No   U. S. Citizen ☐ Yes ☐ No

Have you served on active duty in the U. S. Military? ☐ Yes ☐ No If yes, indicate branch of service and dates (month/year) of active duty. Include military school attendance (month/year):

How did you learn or become interested in FBI employment as a Special Agent?

Have you previously applied for FBI employment? ☐ Yes ☐ No
If yes, location and date:

Do you have a foreign language background? ☐ Yes ☐ No   List proficiency for each language on reverse side.

Have you ever been arrested for any crime (include major traffic violations such as Driving Under the Influence or While Intoxicated, etc.)? ☐ Yes ☐ No If so, list all such matters on a continuation sheet, even if not formally charged, or no court appearance or found not guilty, or matter settled by payment of fine or forfeiture of collateral. Include date, place, charge, disposition, details, and police agency on reverse side.

II. EMPLOYMENT HISTORY

Identify your most recent three years FULL-TIME work experience, after high school (excluding summer, part-time and temporary employment).

From Month/Year	To Month/Year	Title of Position and Description of Work	# of hrs. Per week	Name/Location of Employer

III. PERSONAL DECLARATIONS

Persons with a disability who require an accommodation to complete the application process are required to notify the FBI of their need for the accommodation.

Have you used marijuana during the last three years or more than 15 times? ☐ Yes ☐ No

Have you used any illegal drug(s) or combination of illegal drugs, other than marijuana, more than 5 times or during the last 10 years? ☐ Yes ☐ No

All information provided by applicants concerning their drug history will be subject to verification by a preemployment polygraph examination.

Do you understand all prospective FBI employees will be required to submit to an urinalysis for drug abuse prior to employment? ☐ Yes ☐ No

Please do not write below this line.

I am aware that willfully withholding information or making false statements on this application constitutes a violation of Section 1001. Title 18, U.S. Code and if appointed, will be the basis for dismissal from the Federal Bureau of Investigation. I agree to these conditions and I hereby certify that all statements made by me on this application are true and complete, to the best of my knowledge.

Signature of applicant as usually written (**Do Not Use Nickname**)

information on each prior employer, including job title, duties, name of supervisor, and whether the employment was involuntarily terminated. Also note that in signing the application, the applicant certifies his or her understanding of several things: that falsified statements may be cause for dismissal; that investigation of credit, employment, and driving records is authorized; that a medical examination may be required; that drug screening tests may be required; and that employment is for no definite period of time.

Mandatory Dispute Resolution   Although the EEOC is generally opposed to the idea, more employers are requiring applicants to sign *mandatory alternative dispute resolution forms* as part of the application process. For example, the employment application package for Circuit City requires applicants to agree to arbitrate certain legal disputes related to their application for employment or employment with the company (including, for instance, those relating to the Age Discrimination in Employment Act).[100]

While mandatory arbitration is on the rise, it is also under attack.[101] Courts, federal agencies, and even the organizations providing arbitrators are concerned that binding arbitration strips away too many employees' rights (*voluntary* arbitration is not under attack). A Maryland federal district court ruled that Circuit City could not force its arbitration program on a job applicant in a case there. A recent U.S. Supreme Court decision allows workers with employment disputes to go to court even though they signed pre-hire arbitration agreements.[102]

REVIEW

Summary

1. Developing an organization structure results in jobs that have to be staffed. Job analysis is the procedure through which you find out (1) what the job entails and (2) what kinds of people should be hired for the job. It involves six steps: (1) Determine the use of the job analysis information, (2) collect background information, (3) select the positions to be analyzed, (4) collect job analysis data, (5) review information with participants, and (6) develop a job description and job specification.

2. The job description should portray the work of the position so well that the duties are clear without reference to other job descriptions. Always ask yourself: Will the new employee understand the job if he or she reads the job description?

3. The job specification supplements the job description to answer the question What human traits and experience are necessary to do this job well? It tells what kind of person to recruit and for what qualities that person should be tested. Job specifications are usually based on the educated guesses of managers; however, a more accurate statistical approach to developing job specifications can also be used.

4. De-jobbing is a product of the rapid changes taking place in business today. As firms try to speed decision making by taking steps such as flattening their chains of command, individual jobs are becoming broader and much less specialized. Increasingly, firms don't want employees to feel limited by a specific set of responsibilities such as those listed in a job description. As a

result, more employees are deemphasizing detailed job descriptions, often substituting brief job summaries, perhaps combined with summaries of the skills required for the position.

5. Developing personnel plans requires three forecasts: one for personnel requirements, one for the supply of outside candidates, and one for the supply of inside candidates. To predict the need for personnel, first project the demand for the product or service. Next project the volume of production required to meet these estimates. Finally, relate personnel needs to these production estimates.

6. Once personnel needs are projected, the next step is to build up a pool of qualified applicants. We discussed several sources of candidates, including internal sources (or promotion from within), advertising, employment agencies, executive recruiters, college recruiting, the Internet, and referrals and walk-ins. Remember that it is unlawful to discriminate against any individual with respect to employment because of race, color, religion, sex, national origin, or age (unless these are bona fide occupational qualifications).

7. Once you have a pool of applicants, the work of selecting the best can begin. We turn to employee selection in the following chapter.

KEY TERMS

- job analysis
- job description
- job specification
- trend analysis
- ratio analysis
- qualifications inventories
- personnel replacement charts
- job posting
- application form

DISCUSSION QUESTIONS AND EXERCISES

1. What items are typically included in a job description? What items are not shown?
2. What is job analysis? How can you make use of the information it provides?
3. We discussed several methods for collecting job analysis data. Compare these methods, explain what each is useful for, and list the pros and cons of each.
4. Explain how you would conduct a job analysis.
5. Working individually or in groups, obtain copies of job descriptions for clerical positions at the college or university you attend or the firm where you work. What types of information do they contain? Do they give you enough information to explain what the job involves and how to do it? How would you improve the descriptions?
6. Compare five sources of job candidates.
7. What types of information can an application form provide?
8. Working individually or in groups, bring to class several classified and display ads from this Sunday's help wanted ads. Analyze the effectiveness of these ads.
9. Working individually or in groups, obtain a recent copy of the *Monthly Labor Review* or *Occupational Outlook Quarterly*, both published by the U.S. Bureau of Labor Statistics. Based on information in either of these publications, develop a forecast for the next five years of occupational market conditions for various occupations, such as accountant, nurse, and engineer.

10. Working individually or in groups, visit your local office of your state employment agency. Come back to class prepared to discuss the following questions: What types of jobs seemed to be available through this agency, predominantly? To what extent do you think this particular agency would be a good source of professional, technical, and/or managerial applicants? What sort of paperwork are applicants to the state agency required to complete before their applications are processed by the agency? What other opinions did you form about the state agency?

11. Working individually or in groups, review help wanted ads placed over the past few Sundays by local employment agencies. Do some employment agencies seem to specialize in some types of jobs? If you were an HR manager seeking a relationship with an employment agency for each of the following types of jobs, which local agencies would you turn to first, based on their help wanted ad history: engineers, secretaries, data processing clerks, accountants, and factory workers?

APPLICATION EXERCISES

Case Incident   A Tight Labor Market for Cleaners

While most of the publicity about "tight" labor markets usually revolves around systems engineers, nurses, and chemical engineers, some of the tightest markets are often found in some surprising places. For example, if you were to ask Mary Carter, the head of her family's six-store chain of dry-cleaning stores, what the main problem was in running their firm, the answer would be quick and short: hiring good people. The typical dry-cleaning store is heavily dependent on hiring good managers, cleaner-spotters, and pressers. Employees generally have no more than a high school education (many have less), and the market is very competitive. Over a typical weekend, literally dozens of want ads for cleaner-spotters or pressers can be found in area newspapers. These people are generally paid about $8 an hour, and they change jobs frequently.

Why so much difficulty finding good help? The work is hot and uncomfortable; the hours are often long; the pay is often the same or less than the typical applicant could earn working in an air-conditioned environment, and the fringe benefits are usually nonexistent, unless you count getting your clothes cleaned for free.

Complicating the problem is the fact that Mary and other cleaners are usually faced with the continuing task of recruiting and hiring qualified workers out of a pool of individuals who are almost nomadic in their propensity to move around. The turnover in her stores and the stores of many of their competitors is often 400% per year. The problem, Mary says, is maddening: "On the one hand, the quality of our service depends on the skills of the cleaner-spotters, pressers, and counter staff. People come to us for our ability to return their clothes to them spotless and crisply pressed. On the other hand, profit margins are thin and we've got to keep our stores running, so I'm happy just to be able to round up enough live applicants to be able to keep my stores fully manned." ■

QUESTIONS

1. Provide a detailed list of recommendations concerning how Mary should go about increasing the number of acceptable job applicants, so that her company need no longer hire just about anyone who walks in the door. Specifically, your recommendations should include:
   a. Completely worded classified ads
   b. Recommendations concerning any other recruiting strategies you would suggest she use
2. What practical suggestions could you make that might help reduce turnover and make the stores an attractive place in which to work, thereby reducing recruiting problems?

Continuing Case

LearnInMotion.com:
Who Do We Have to Hire?

As the excitement surrounding the move into their new offices wound down, the two principal owners of LearnInMotion.com, Mel and Jennifer, turned to the task of hiring new employees. In their business plan they'd specified several basic aims for the venture capital funds they'd just received, and hiring a team topped the list. They knew their other goals—boosting sales and expanding the Web site, for instance—would be unreachable without the right team.

They were just about to place their ads when Mel asked a question that brought them to a stop: "What kind of people do we want to hire?" It seemed they hadn't really considered this. They knew the answer in general terms, of course. For example, they knew they needed at least two salespeople, plus a programmer, a Web designer, and several content management people to transform the incoming material into content they could post on their site. But it was obvious that job titles alone really didn't provide enough guidance. For example, if they couldn't specify the exact duties of these positions, how could they decide whether they needed experienced employees? How could they decide exactly what sorts of experiences and skills they had to look for in their candidates if they didn't know exactly what these candidates would have to do? They wouldn't even know what questions to ask.

And that wasn't all. For example, there were obviously other tasks to do, and these weren't necessarily included in the sorts of things that salespeople, programmers, Web designers, or content management people typically do. Who was going to answer the phones? (Jennifer and Mel had originally assumed they'd put in one of those fancy automated call directory and voice-mail systems until they found out it would cost close to $10,000.) As a practical matter, they knew they had to have someone answering the phones and directing callers to the proper extension. Who was going to keep track of the monthly expenses and compile them for the accountants, who'd then produce monthly reports for the venture capitalist? Would the salespeople generate their own leads? Or would LearnInMotion.com have to hire Web surfers to search and find the names of people for the sales staff to call or e-mail? What would happen when the company had to purchase supplies, such as fax paper or computer disks? Would the owners have to do this themselves, or should they have someone in-house do it for them? The list, it seemed, went on and on.

It was obvious, in other words, that the owners had to get their managerial act together and draw up the sorts of documents they'd read about as business majors—job descriptions, job specifications, and so forth. The trouble is, it all seemed a lot easier when they read the textbook. Now they want you, their management consultants, to help them actually do it. Here's what they want you to do for them. ■

QUESTIONS AND ASSIGNMENTS

1. Draw up a set of job descriptions for each of the positions in the case: salesperson, Web designer, programmer, and content manager. You may use whatever sources you want, but preferably search the Internet and relevant Web sites, since you want job descriptions and lists of duties that apply specifically to dot-com firms.
2. Next, using sources similar to those in Question 1 (and whatever other sources you can think of), draw up specifications for each of these jobs, including things such as desirable work habits, skills, education, and experience.

3. Next, keeping in mind that this company is on a tight budget, write a short proposal explaining how it should accomplish the other activities it needs done, such as answering the phones, compiling sales leads, producing monthly reports, and purchasing supplies.

Experiential Exercise

Purpose: The purpose of this exercise is to give you experience in developing a job description, by developing one for your instructor.

Required Understanding: You should understand the mechanics of job analysis and be thoroughly familiar with the job analysis questionnaire (see Figure A3.3 in the chapter Appendix) and with finding job descriptions on the Internet.

How to Set up the Exercise/Instructions: Set up groups of four to six students for this exercise. As in all exercises in this book, the groups should be separated and should not converse with each other. Half the groups in the class will develop the job description using the job analysis questionnaire, and the other half of the groups will develop it using an Internet source such as www.jobdescription.com. Each student should review the questionnaire before joining his or her group.

1. Each group should do a job analysis of the instructor's job; half the groups (to repeat) will use the job analysis questionnaire for this purpose, and half will use the one from the Internet Web site.

2. Based on this information, each group will develop its own job description and job specification for the instructor.

3. Next, each group should choose a partner group, one that developed the job description and job specification using the alternate method. (A group that used the job analysis questionnaire should be paired with a group that used the Internet.)

4. Finally, within each of these new combined groups, compare and criticize each of the two sets of job descriptions and job specifications. Did each job analysis method provide different types of information? Which seems superior? Does one seem more advantageous for some types of jobs than others?

TAKE IT TO THE WEB

For Internet exercises, updates to chapter material, and more, visit the Dessler Web site at

www.prenhall.com/dessler

ENDNOTES

1. Maria Seminerio, "E-Recruiting Takes Next Step—Tools Help High-Techs Spot the Best IT People," *The Week* (April 23, 2001): 49–51.
2. Frederick Morgenson and Michael Campion, "Accuracy in Job Analysis: Toward an Inference Based Model," *Journal of Organizational Behavior* 21, no. 7 (November 2000): 819–27.
3. Ernest J. McCormick, "Job and Task Analysis," in Marvin D. Dunnette (ed.), *Handbook of Industrial and Organizational Psychology* (Chicago: Rand McNally, 1976), pp. 651–96.

4. The quote is from James Clifford, "Manage Work Better to Better Manage Human Resources: A Comparative Study of Two Approaches to Job Analysis," *Public Personnel Management* (spring 1996): 89–102.

5. Michael K. Lindel et al., "Relationship Between Organizational Context and Job Analysis Task Ratings," *Journal of Applied Psychology* 83, no. 5 (1998): 769–76.

6. Wayne Cascio, *Applied Psychology in Personnel Management* (Reston, VA: Reston, 1978), p. 140.

7. James Evened, "How to Write a Good Job Description," *Supervisory Management* (April 1981): 14–19.

8. Ibid., 16.

9. Ibid., 17.

10. Matthew Mariani, "Replaced with a Database: O*NET Replaces the *Dictionary of Occupational Titles*," *Occupational Outlook Quarterly* (spring 1999): 3–9.

11. Ibid., 18.

12. Deborah Kearney, *Reasonable Accommodations: Job Descriptions in the Age of ADA, OSHA, and Workers Comp* (New York: Van Nostrand Reinhold, 1994), p. 9.

13. Ibid.

14. Michael Esposito, "There's More to Writing Job Descriptions Than Complying with the ADA," *Employee Relations Today* (Autumn 1992): 279.

15. Gary Dessler, *Human Resource Management*, 9th ed. (Upper Saddle River, NJ: Prentice Hall, 2002), pp. 64–76.

16. See Ernest J. McCormick and Joseph Tiffin, *Industrial Psychology* (Englewood Cliffs, NJ: Prentice Hall, 1974), pp. 56–61.

17. Steven Hunt, "Generic Work Behavior: An Investigation into the Dimensions of Entry-Level, Hourly Job Performance," *Personnel Psychology* 49 (1996): 51–83.

18. William Bridges, "The End of the Job," *Fortune* (September 19, 1994): 64.

19. Sharon Leonard, "The Demise of Job Descriptions," *HR Magazine* (August 2000): 184.

20. Bridges, "End of the Job," 68.

21. Robert McNabb and Keith Whitfield, "Job Evaluation and High-Performance Practices: Compatible or Conflictual?" *Journal of Management Studies* 30, no. 2, (March 2001): 293–312.

22. Richard B. Frantzreb, "Human Resource Planning: Forecasting Manpower Needs," *Personnel Journal* 60, no. 11 (November 1981): 850–57. See also John Gridley, "Who Will Be There When? Forecast the Easy Way," *Personnel Journal* 65 (May 1986): 50–58.

23. Based on an idea in Elmer H. Burack and Robert D. Smith, *Personnel Management: A Human Resource Systems Approach* (St. Paul, MN: West, 1997), pp. 134–35.

24. For a discussion of qualifications inventories, see, for example, John Lawrie, "Skill Inventories: Pack for the Future," *Personnel Journal* (March 1987): 127–30; John Lawrie, "Skill Inventories: A Developmental Process," *Personnel Journal* (October 1987): 108–10.

25. This is a modification of a definition found in Peter Wallum, "A Broader View of Succession Planning," *Personnel Management* (September 1993): 45.

26. Ibid., 43–44.

27. Tom Porter, "Effective Techniques to Attract, Hire, and Retain 'Top Notch' Employees for Your Company," *San Diego Business Journal* 21, no. 13 (March 27, 2000): B36.

28. Arthur R. Pell, *Recruiting and Selecting Personnel* (New York: Regents, 1969), pp. 10–12.

29. Ibid., 34–42.

30. Lynn Doherty and E. Norman Sims, "Quick, Easy Recruitment Help—From a State?" *Workforce* (May 1998): 36.

31. Ibid., 40.

32. Allison Thompson, "The Contingent Work Force," *Occupational Outlook Quarterly* (spring 1995): 45.

33. Amy Kover, "Manufacturing's Hidden Asset: Temp Workers," *Fortune* (November 10, 1997): 28–29.

34. One Bureau of Labor Statistics study suggests that temporary employees produce the equivalent of two or more hours of work per day more than their permanent counterparts. For a discussion, see Shari Caudron, "Contingent Workforce Spurs

HR Planning," *Personnel Journal* (July 1994): 54.

35. "Temps Get a Boss of Their Own," *BNA Bulletin to Management* (November 7, 1996): 360.

36. Ibid., 47.

37. Brenda Paik Sunoo, "From Santa to CEO—Temps Play All Roles," *Personnel Journal* (April 1996): 34–44.

38. John Wareham, *Secrets of a Corporate Headhunter* (New York: Playboy Press, 1981), pp. 213–25.

39. "Search and Destroy," *The Economist* (June 27, 1998): 63.

40. Ibid.

41. Ibid.

42. Allen J. Cox, *Confessions of a Corporate Headhunter* (New York: Trident Press, 1973).

43. Robert Dipboye, Howard Fronkin, and Ken Wiback, "Relative Importance of Applicant Sex, Attractiveness, and Scholastic Standing in Evaluation of Job Applicant Resumes," *Journal of Applied Psychology* 61 (1975): 39–48. See also Laura M. Graves, "College Recruitment: Removing the Personal Bias from Selection Decisions," *Personnel* (March 1989): 48–52.

44. Dipboye et al., "Relative Importance," 39–48. See also "A Measure of the HR Recruitment Function: The 1994 College Relations and Recruitment Survey," *Journal of Career Planning and Employment* 53, no. 3 (spring 1995): 37–48.

45. See "College Recruiting," in *Personnel* (May/June 1980). For a study of how applicant sex can impact recruiters' evaluations, see, for example, Laura Graves and Gary Powell, "The Effect of Sex Similarity on Recruiters' Evaluations of Actual Applicants: A Test of the Similarity–Attraction Paradigm," *Personnel Psychology* 48, no. 1 (spring 1995): 85–98.

46. See, for example, Richard Becker, "Ten Common Mistakes in College Recruiting—Or How to Try Without Really Succeeding," *Personnel* 52, no. 2 (March/April 1975): 19–28. See also Sara Rynes and John Boudreau, "College Recruiting in Large Organizations: Practice, Evaluation, and Research

Implications," *Personnel Psychology* 39 (winter 1986): 729–57.

47. "In Negotiating Game, Most Recruiters Hold Back, Knowing Few Candidates Hold Out for Better Offer," *BNA Bulletin to Management* (2000): 291.

48. "Internships Provide Workplace Snapshot," *BNA Bulletin to Management* (May 22, 1997): 168.

49. "Employee Referrals Improve Hiring," *BNA Bulletin to Management* (March 13, 1997): 88.

50. Ibid., 13.

51. The study on employment referrals was published by Bernard Hodes Advertising, Dept. 100, 555 Madison Avenue, New York, NY 10022. See also Allan Halcrow, "Employees Are Your Best Recruiters," *Personnel Journal* (November 1988): 43–49; Andy Bargerstock and Hank Engel, "Six Ways to Boost Employee Referral Programs," *HR Magazine* 39, no. 12 (December 1994): 72 ff.

52. Michelle Martinez, "The Headhunter Within," *HR Magazine* (August 2001): 48–56.

53. A. Zottoli and John Wanous, "Recruitment Source Research: Current Status and Future Directions," *Human Resource Management Review* 10 (November 4, 2000): 353–82.

54. "Hiring Workers the Second Time Around," *BNA Bulletin to Management* (January 30, 1997): 40.

55. Michelle Neely Martinez, "Get Job Seekers to Come to You," *HR Magazine* (August 2000): 45–52.

56. Elaine Appleton, "Recruiting on the Internet," *Datamation* (August 1995): 39.

57. Julia King, "Job Networking," *Enterprise Networking* (January 26, 1995).

58. Flynn, "Cisco Turns the Internet Inside (and) Out," 28–34.

59. "Does Your Company's Website Click with Job Seekers?" *Workforce* (August 2000): 26. See also Daniel Feldman and Brian Iccaas, "Internet Job Hunting: A Field Study of Applicant Experiences with On-line Recruiting," *Human Resource Management* (summer 2002): 175–92.

60. "Internet Recruiting Holds Promise," *BNA Bulletin to Management* (July 17, 1997): 232.

61. Ibid.

62. "Online Filtering of Applicants Let Key Skills Shine Through," *BNA Bulletin to Management* (June 29, 2000): 206.

63. "Internet Recruiting Takes Off," *BNA Bulletin to Management* (February 20, 1997): 64. See also Gillian Flynn, "E-recruiting Ushers in Legal Dangers," *Workforce* (April 2002): 70–75.

64. Laura Romei, "Human Resource Management Systems Keep Computers Humming," *Managing Office Technology* (November 1994): 45.

65. Jim Meade, "Where Did They Go?" *HR Magazine* (September 2000): 81–84.

66. *Fortune,* Tech Guide (2000): 102. See also Joanne Charles, "Finding a Job on the Web," *Black Enterprise* (March 2000): 90; "Browse, Click, Career: Online Sites for Job Recruiting and Searching are Blooming on the Web," *Fortune* (December 1, 2000): 223.

67. Samuel Greengard, "Smarter Screening Takes Technology and HR Save," *Workforce* (June 2002): 57–60.

68. Gillian Flynn, "E-recruiting Ushers in Legal Dangers," 70.

69. Seminerio, "E-Recruiting Takes Next Step," 49–51.

70. "Retirees Increasingly Reentering the Workforce," *BNA Bulletin to Management* (January 16, 1997): 17.

71. Diane Cyr, "Lost and Found—Retired Employees," *Personnel Journal* (November 1996): 41.

72. Dayton Fandray, "Gray Matters," *Workforce* (July 2000): 28.

73. Harold E. Johnson, "Older Workers Help Meet Employment Needs," *Personnel Journal* (May 1988): 100–105.

74. Glenn McEvoy and Wayne Cascio, "Cumulative Evidence of the Relationship Between Employee Age and Job Performance," *Journal of Applied Psychology* 74, no. 1 (February 1989): 11–17.

75. Goddard, "How to Harness America's Gray Power," 33.

76. "Older Workers Valued but Hard to Find, Employers Say," *BNA Bulletin to Management* (April 30, 1998): 129–34.

77. For this and other examples here, see Goddard, "How to Harness America's Gray Power."

78. Unless otherwise noted, this section is based on Judith Casey and Marcie Pitt-Catsouphes, "Employed Single Mothers: Balancing Job and Home Life," *Employee Assistance Quarterly* 9, no. 3/4 (1994): 37–53.

79. Ibid., 44.

80. Ibid., 45.

81. Ibid., 48.

82. Ibid.

83. See Robert W. Wendover, "Smart Hiring," *B & E Review* (July/September 1990): 6–15.

84. Elizabeth Blacharczyk, "Recruiters Challenged by Economy, Shortages," *HR News* (February 1990): B4. Diversity management programs may also make a firm more attractive to job candidates. See, for example, Margaret Williams and Talya Bauer, "The Effect of Managing Diversity Policy on Organizational Attractiveness," *Group and Organization Management* 19, no. 3 (September 1994): 295–308.

85. Jennifer Koch, "Finding Qualified Hispanic Candidates," *Recruitment Today* 3, no. 2 (spring 1990): 35.

86. This compares with 21.5% for black jobseekers and 23.9% for white jobseekers. Michelle Harrison Ports, "Trends in Job Search Methods, 1990–92," *Monthly Labor Review* (October 1993): 64.

87. This is based on Jennifer Laabs, "The Global Talent Search," *Personnel Journal* (August 1991): 38–42.

88. Scott Graham, "Hospitals Recruiting Overseas," *Baltimore Business Journal* (June 1, 2001): 1.

89. Jennifer Laabs, "Recruiting in the Global Village," *Workforce* (spring 1998): 30–33.

90. Ibid., 10.

91. Ibid., 11.

92. Ibid.

93. Bill Leonard, "Welfare Reform: A New Deal for HR," *HR Magazine* (March 1997): 78–86.

94. Herbert Greenberg, "A Hidden Source of Talent," *HR Magazine* (March 1997): 88–91.

95. "Welfare-to-Work: No Easy Chore," *BNA Bulletin to Management* (February 13, 1997): 56.

96. Ibid.

97. Ibid.

98. Pell, *Recruiting and Selecting Personnel,* 96–98. See also Wayne Cascio, "Accuracy of Verifiable Biographical Information Blank Responses," *Journal of Applied Psychology* 60 (December 1975) for a discussion of accuracy of bio data.

99. J. Craig Wallace et al., "Applying for Jobs Online: Examining the Legality of Internet-based Application Forms," *Public Personnel Management* 20, no. 4 (winter 2000): 497–504.

100. Circuit City Stores, Inc., Employment Packet, January 1997.

101. De'Ann Weimer and Stephanie Anderson Forest, "Forced into Arbitration? Not Anymore," *Business Week* (March 16, 1998): 66, 68.

102. *Ryan's Family Steakhouse Inc.* v. *Floss,* "Supreme Court Let Stand Decision Finding Prehire Arbitration Agreements Unenforceable," *BNA Bulletin to Management* (January 11, 2001): 11.

Appendix

Enrichment Topics in Job Analysis

Additional Job Analysis Methods

Job Analysis Record Sheet   You may encounter several other job analysis methods. For example, the U.S. Civil Service Commission has a standardized procedure for comparing and classifying jobs. Information here is compiled on a *job analysis record sheet* (see Figure A3.1). Identifying information (such as job title) and a brief summary of the job are listed first. Next the job's specific tasks are listed in order of importance. Then, for each task, the analyst specifies such things as the knowledge required (for example, the facts or principles the worker must be acquainted with to do his or her job); skills required (for example, the skills needed to operate machines or vehicles); and abilities required (for example, mathematical, reasoning, problem-solving, or interpersonal abilities).

Position Analysis Questionnaire   The *position analysis questionnaire* (PAQ) is a very structured job analysis questionnaire.[1] The PAQ is filled in by a job analyst, a person who should be acquainted with the particular job to be analyzed. The PAQ contains 194 items, each of which (such as "written materials") represents a basic element that may or may not play an important role in the job. The job analyst decides whether each item plays a role on the job and, if so, to what extent. In Figure A3.2, for example, "Written materials" received a rating of 4, indicating that written materials (such as books, reports, and office notes) play a considerable role in this job.

The advantage of the PAQ is that it provides a quantitative score or profile of any job in terms of how that job rates on five basic job traits such as "having decision-making/communications/social responsibilities." The PAQ lets you assign a single quantitative score or value to each job. You can therefore use the PAQ results to compare jobs relative to one another; this information can then be used to assign pay levels for each job.

U.S. Department of Labor Procedure
The U.S. Department of Labor (DOL) procedure also aims to provide a standardized method by which different jobs can be quantitatively rated, classified, and compared. The heart of this analysis is a rating of each job in terms of an employee's specific functions with respect to *data, people,* and *things.* As illustrated in Table A3.1, a set of basic activities called *worker functions* describes what a worker can do with respect to data, people, and things. With respect to *data,* for instance, the basic functions include synthesizing, coordinating, and copying. Note also that each worker function has been assigned an importance level. Thus, "coordinating" is 1, and "copying" is 5. If you were analyzing the job of a receptionist/clerk, for example, you might label the job 5, 6, 7, which would represent copying data, speaking-signaling people, and handling things.

A Practical Job Analysis Method
Without their own job analysts or (in many cases) HR managers, many small-business owners and managers face two hurdles when doing job analyses and job descriptions. First, they often need a more streamlined approach than those provided by questionnaires like the one shown in Figure A3.3. Second, there is always

Figure A3.1 Portion of a Completed Civil Service Job Analysis Record Sheet

---

JOB ANALYSIS RECORD SHEET

IDENTIFYING INFORMATION

Name of Incumbent:	A. Adler
Organization/Unit:	Welfare Services
Title:	Welfare Eligibility Examiner
Date:	11/12/02
Interviewer:	E. Jones

BRIEF SUMMARY OF JOB

Conducts interviews, completes applications, determines eligibility, provides information to community sources regarding food stamp program; refers noneligible food stamp applicants to other applicable community resource agencies.

TASKS*

1. Decide (determine) eligibility of applicant in order to complete client's application for food stamps using regulatory policies as guide.

   Knowledge Required
   —Knowledge of contents and meaning of items on standard application form
   —Knowledge of Social-Health Services food stamp regulatory policies
   —Knowledge of statutes relating to Social-Health Services food stamp program

   Skills Required
   —None

   Abilities Required
   —Ability to read and understand complex instructions such as regulatory policies
   —Ability to read and understand a variety of procedural instructions, written and oral, and convert these to proper actions
   —Ability to use simple arithmetic: addition and subtraction
   —Ability to translate requirements into language appropriate to laymen

   Physical Activities
   —Sedentary

   Environmental Conditions
   —None

   Typical Work Incidents
   —Working with people beyond giving and receiving instructions

   Interest Areas
   —Communication of data
   —Business contact with people
   —Working for the presumed good of people

2. Decides upon, describes, and explains other agencies available for client to contact in order to assist and refer client to appropriate community resource using worker's knowledge of resources available and knowledge of client's needs.

(Continued)

Knowledge Required

—Knowledge of functions of various assistance agencies
—Knowledge of community resources available and their locations
—Knowledge of referral procedures

Skills Required

—None

Abilities Required

—Ability to extract (discern) persons' needs from oral discussion
—Ability to give simple oral and written instructions to persons

Physical Activities

—Sedentary

Environmental Conditions

—None

Typical Work Incidents

—Working with people beyond giving and receiving instructions

Interest Areas

—Communication of data
—Business contact with people
—Abstract and creative problem solving
—Working for the presumed good of people

Source: This job might typically involve five or six tasks. For *each* task, list the knowledge, skill abilities, physical activities, environmental conditions, typical work incidents, and interest areas.

Table A3.1   Basic Department of Labor Worker Functions

	DATA	PEOPLE	THINGS
Basic Activities	0 Synthesizing 1 Coordinating 2 Analyzing 3 Compiling 4 Computing 5 Copying 6 Comparing	0 Mentoring 1 Negotiating 2 Instructing 3 Supervising 4 Diverting 5 Persuading 6 Speaking/signaling 7 Serving 8 Taking instructions/helping	0 Setting up 1 Precision working 2 Operating/controlling 3 Driving/operating 4 Manipulating 5 Tending 6 Feeding/offbearing 7 Handling

Note: Determine employee's job "score" on data, people, and things by observing his or her job and determining, for each of the three categories, which of the basic functions illustrates the person's job. "0" is high; "6," "8," and "7" are lows in each column.

Figure A3.2 Portions of a Completed Page from the Position Analysis Questionnaire

1 INFORMATION INPUT

	Extent of Use (U)
NA	Does not apply
1	Nominal/very infrequent
2	Occasional
3	Moderate
4	Considerable
5	Very substantial

1.1 Sources of Job Information

Rate each of the following items in terms of the extent to which it is used by the worker as a source of information in performing his job.

1.1.1 Visual Sources of Job Information

1 | 4   Written materials (books, reports, office notes, articles, job instructions, signs, etc.)

2 | 2   Quantitative materials (materials which deal with quantities or amounts, such as graphs, accounts, specifications, tables of numbers, etc.)

3 | 1   Pictorial materials (pictures or picturelike materials used as *sources* of information, for example, drawings, blueprints, diagrams, maps, tracings, photographic films, x-ray films, TV pictures, etc.)

4 | 1   Patterns/related devices (templates, stencils, patterns, etc., used as *sources* of information when *observed* during use; do *not* include here materials described in item 3 above)

5 | 2   Visual displays (dials, gauges, signal lights, radarscopes, speedometers, clocks, etc.)

6 | 5   Measuring devices (rulers, calipers, tire pressure gauges, scales, thickness gauges, pipettes, thermometers, protractors, etc., used to obtain visual information about physical measurements; do *not* include here devices described in item 5 above)

7 | 4   Mechanical devices (tools, equipment, machinery, and other mechanical devices which are *sources* of information when *observed* during use or operation)

8 | 3   Materials in process (parts, materials, objects, etc., which are *sources* of information when being modified, worked on, or otherwise processed, such as bread dough being mixed, workpiece being turned in a lathe, fabric being cut, shoe being resoled, etc.)

9 | 4   Materials *not* in process (parts, materials, objects, etc., not in the process of being changed or modified, which are *sources* of information when being inspected, handled, packaged, distributed, or selected, etc., such as items or materials in inventory, storage, or distribution channels, items being inspected, etc.)

10 | 3   Features of nature (landscapes, fields, geological samples, vegetation, cloud formations, and other features of nature which are observed or inspected to provide information)

11 | 2   Man-made features of environment (structures, buildings, dams, highways, bridges, docks, railroads, and other "man-made" or altered aspects of the indoor or outdoor environment which are *observed* or *inspected* to provide job information; do not consider equipment, machines, etc., that an individual uses in his work, as covered by item 7)

Note: The 194 PAQ elements are grouped into six dimensions. This exhibits 11 of the "Information Input" questions or elements. Other PAQ pages contain questions regarding mental processes, work output, relationships with others, job context, and other job characteristics.

Source: E. J. McCormick, P. R. Jeanneret, and R. D. Mecham, *Position Analysis Questionnaire.* Copyright 1989 by Purdue Research Foundation, West Lafayette, IN. Reprinted with permission.

Figure A3.3 Job Analysis Questionnaire for Developing Job Descriptions
Use a questionnaire like this to interview job incumbents, or have them fill it out.

Job Analysis Information Sheet

Job Title _____ Date _____

Job Code _____ Dept. _____

Superior's Title _____

Hours worked _____ AM to _____ PM

Job Analyst's Name _____

1. **What is the job's overall purpose?**
   _____

2. **If the incumbent supervises others,** list them by job title; if there is more than one employee with the same title, put the number in parentheses following the title.
   _____

3. **Check those activities** that are part of the incumbent's supervisory duties.
   ❏ Training
   ❏ Performance appraisal
   ❏ Inspecting work
   ❏ Budgeting
   ❏ Coaching and/or counseling
   ❏ Others (please specify) _____

4. **Describe the type and extent of supervision** received by the incumbent.
   _____

5. **JOB DUTIES:** Describe briefly WHAT the incumbent does and, if possible, HOW he/she does it. Include duties in the following categories:
   a. Daily duties (those performed on a regular basis every day or almost every day)
   _____

   b. Periodic duties (those performed weekly, monthly, quarterly, or at other regular intervals)
   _____

   c. Duties performed at irregular intervals
   _____

6. Is the incumbent performing duties he/she considers unnecessary? If so, describe.
   _____

7. Is the incumbent performing duties not presently included in the job description? If so, describe.
   _____

8. **EDUCATION:** Check the box that indicates the educational requirements for the job (not the educational background of the incumbent).

   ❏ No formal education   ❏ Eighth grade education

   ❏ High school diploma (or equivalent)   ❏ 2-year college degree (or equivalent)

   ❏ 4-year college degree (or equivalent) ❏ Graduate work or advanced degree
   (specify)

   ❏ Professional license (specify)

(Continued)

9. **EXPERIENCE:** Check the amount of experience needed to perform the job.

❏ None	❏ Less than one month
❏ One to six months	❏ Six months to one year
❏ One to three years	❏ Three to five years
❏ Five to ten years	❏ More than ten years

10. **LOCATION:** Check location of job and, if necessary or appropriate, describe briefly.

❏ Outdoor	❏ Indoor
❏ Underground	❏ Pit
❏ Scaffold	❏ Other (specify)

11. **ENVIRONMENTAL CONDITIONS:** Check any objectionable conditions found on the job and note afterward how frequently each is encountered (rarely, occasionally, constantly, etc.).

❏ Dirt	❏ Dust
❏ Heat	❏ Cold
❏ Noise	❏ Fumes
❏ Odors	❏ Wetness/humidity
❏ Vibration	❏ Sudden temperature changes
❏ Darkness or poor lighting	❏ Other (specify)

12. **HEALTH AND SAFETY:** Check any undesirable health and safety conditions under which the incumbent must perform and note how often they are encountered.

❏ Elevated workplace	❏ Mechanical hazards
❏ Explosives	❏ Electrical hazards
❏ Fire hazards	❏ Radiation
❏ Other (specify)	

13. **MACHINES, TOOLS, EQUIPMENT, AND WORK AIDS:** Describe briefly what machines, tools, equipment, or work aids the incumbent works with on a regular basis.

_____

14. Have concrete work standards been established (errors allowed, time taken for a particular task, etc.)? If so, what are they?

_____

15. Are there any personal attributes (special aptitudes, physical characteristics, personality traits, etc.) required by the job?

_____

16. Are there any exceptional problems the incumbent might be expected to encounter in performing the job under normal conditions? If so, describe.

_____

17. Describe the successful completion and/or end results of the job.

_____

18. What is the seriousness of error on this job? Who or what is affected by errors the incumbent makes?

_____

19. To what job would a successful incumbent expect to be promoted?

[**_Note:_** This form is obviously slanted toward a manufacturing environment, but it can be adapted quite easily to fit a number of different types of jobs.]

Source: www.hrnext.com, accessed July 28, 2001.

the reasonable fear that in writing their job descriptions, they will overlook duties that subordinates should be assigned, or assign duties not usually associated with such positions. What they need is an encyclopedia listing all or most positions they might encounter, including a detailed listing of the duties normally assigned to these positions.

Help is at hand: The small-business owner has at least three options. The *Dictionary of Occupational Titles*, mentioned earlier, provides detailed descriptions of thousands of jobs and their human requirements. Web sites like www.jobdescription.com provide customizable descriptions by title and industry. And the Department of Labor's O*NET is a third alternative. We'll focus on using O*NET for creating job descriptions in this section.

Step 1. Decide on a Plan
Start by developing at least the broad outline of a corporate plan. What do you expect your sales revenue to be next year, and in the next few years? What products do you intend to emphasize? What areas or departments in your company do you think will have to be expanded, reduced, or consolidated, given where you plan to go with your firm over the next few years? What kinds of new positions do you think you'll need in order to accomplish your strategic goals?

Step 2. Develop an Organization Chart
Next, develop an organization chart for the firm. Show who reports to the president and to each of his or her subordinates. Complete the chart by showing who reports to each of the other managers and supervisors in the firm. Start by drawing up the organization chart as it is now. Then, depending upon how far in advance you're planning, produce a chart showing how you'd like your chart to look in the immediate future (say, in two months) and perhaps two or three other charts showing how you'd like your organization to evolve over the next two or three years.

You can use several tools here. For example, MSWord includes an organization charting function: On the Insert menu, click Object, then Create New. In the Object type box, click MS Organization Chart, and then OK. Software packages such as OrgPublisher for Intranet 3.0 from TimeVision of Irving, Texas, are another option.[2]

Step 3. Use a Job Analysis/Description Questionnaire
Next, use a job analysis questionnaire to determine what each job entails. You can use one of the more comprehensive questionnaires (see Figure A3.3); however, the job description questionnaire in Figure A3.4 is a simpler and often satisfactory alternative. Fill in the required information, then ask the supervisors and/or employees to list the job's duties (on the bottom of the page), breaking them into daily duties, periodic duties, and duties performed at irregular intervals. You can distribute a sample of one of these duties (see Figure A3.5) to supervisors and/or employees to facilitate the process.

Step 4: Obtain Lists of Job Duties from O*NET
The list of job duties you uncovered in the previous step may or may not be complete. We'll therefore use O*NET to compile a more comprehensive list. (Refer to Figure A3.6 for a visual example as you read along.) Start by going to online.onetcenter.org (top). Here, click on Find Occupations. Assume you want to create job descriptions for retail salespeople. Type in Retail Sales for the occupational titles, and Sales and Related from the job families drop-down box. Click Find Occupations to continue, which brings you to the Find Occupations Search Result (middle). Clicking on Retail Salespersons—snapshots—produces the job summary and specific occupational duties for retail salespersons (bottom). For a small operation, you might want to combine the duties of the retail salesperson with those of first-line supervisors/managers of retail salespeople.

Step 5: Compile the Job's specification from O*NET
Next, return to the Snapshot for Retail Salesperson (bottom). Here, instead of choosing

Figure A3.4 Job Description Questionnaire

**Background Data
for Job Description**

Job Title _____   Department _____

Job Number _____   Written By _____

Today's Date _____   Applicable DOT Codes _____

I. **Applicable DOT Definition(s):**

II. **Job Summary:**
   (List the more important or regularly performed tasks)

III. **Reports To:**

IV. **Supervises:** _____

V. **Job Duties:** _____
   *(Briefly describe, for each duty, what employee does and, if possible, how
   employee does it. Show in parentheses at end of each duty the approximate
   percentage of time devoted to duty.)*

   A. Daily Duties:

   B. Periodic Duties:
      (Indicate whether weekly, monthly, quarterly, etc.)

   C. Duties Performed at Irregular Intervals:

Figure A3.5   Background Data for Examples

Example of Job Title: Customer Service Clerk

Example of Job Summary: Answers inquiries and gives directions to customers, authorizes cashing of customers' checks, records and returns lost charge cards, sorts and reviews new credit applications, works at customer-service desk in department store.

Example of One Job Duty: Authorizes cashing of checks: authorizes cashing of personal or payroll checks (up to a specified amount) by customers desiring to make payment by check. Requests identification, such as driver's license, from customers, and examines check to verify date, amount, signature, and endorsement. Initials check and sends customer to cashier.

Figure A3.6 Shown in the Three Screen Captures, O*NET Easily Allows the User to Develop Job Descriptions.
http://online.onetcenter.org

(Continued)

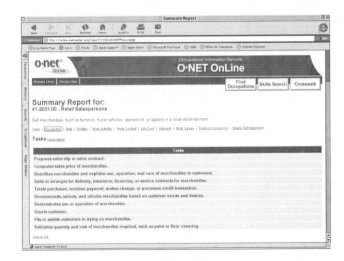

occupation-specific information, choose, for example, Worker Experiences, Occupational Requirements, and Worker Characteristics. You can use this information to develop a job specification for recruiting, selecting, and training the employees.

Step 6: Complete Your Job Description
Finally, using Figure A3.4, write an appropriate job summary for the job. Then use the information obtained in Steps 4 and 5 to create a complete listing of the tasks, duties, and human requirements of each of the jobs you will need to fill.

ENDNOTES

1. Note that the PAQ (and other quantitative techniques) can also be used for job evaluation, which is explained in Chapter 7.

2. David Shair, "Wizardry Makes Charts Relevant," *HR Magazine* (April 2000): 127.

Chapter 4

Testing and Selecting Employees

- The Basics of Testing and Selecting Employees
- Using Tests at Work
- Interviewing Prospective Employees
- Using Other Selection Techniques

When you finish studying this chapter, you should be able to:

- Define *basic testing concepts, including validity and reliability.*

- Discuss *at least four basic types of personnel tests.*

- Explain *the pros and cons of background investigations, reference checks, and preemployment information services.*

- Explain *the factors and problems that can undermine an interview's usefulness, and techniques for eliminating them.*

INTRODUCTION

*C*ity Garage, a 200-employee chain of 25 auto service and repair shops in Dallas–Fort Worth, had expanded rapidly since its founding in 1993. However, its growth strategy was hampered by the problems it had hiring and keeping good employees.[1] "Because we grew so quickly, there were certain aspects we didn't concentrate on as much as we did others. One was hiring," said training director Rusty Reinoehl. One thing it discovered was that not all its managers had the same level of interviewing and hiring skills. The result was more employee turnover, and too few managers to staff new stores. For a firm planning to

116

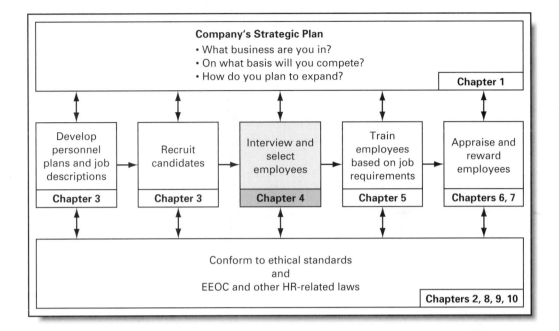

Company's Strategic Plan
- What business are you in?
- On what basis will you compete?
- How do you plan to expand?

Chapter 1

Develop personnel plans and job descriptions	Recruit candidates	Interview and select employees	Train employees based on job requirements	Appraise and reward employees
Chapter 3	Chapter 3	Chapter 4	Chapter 5	Chapters 6, 7

Conform to ethical standards
and
EEOC and other HR-related laws

Chapters 2, 8, 9, 10

expand to 50 or 60 shops throughout Texas in the next few years, City Garage needed a new approach to employee testing and selection if it wanted to implement its growth strategy.

THE BASICS OF TESTING AND SELECTING EMPLOYEES

With a pool of completed applications, your next step is to select the best person for the job. This usually means whittling down the applicant pool by using the screening tools explained in this chapter, including tests, background and reference checks, and interviews.

Why Careful Selection Is Important

Selecting the right employees is important for several reasons. First, your own performance always depends in part on your subordinates. Employees with the right skills and attributes will do a better job for you and the company. Employees without these skills or who are abrasive or obstructionist won't perform effectively, and your own performance and the firm's will suffer.

Underperformance is not the sole problem. By some estimates, 75% of employees have stolen from their employers at least once; 33% to 75% have engaged in behaviors such as theft, vandalism, and voluntary absenteeism; almost 25% say they've had knowledge of illicit drug use among co-workers; and 7% of a sample of employees reported being victims of coworkers' physical threats.[2] The time to screen out such undesirables is before they are in the door, not after.

Effective screening is also important because it's costly to recruit and hire employees. Hiring and training even a clerk can cost $5,000 or more in fees and supervisory time. The total cost of hiring a manager could easily be 10 times as high, after search fees, interviewing time, reference checking, and travel and moving expenses are tallied.

Legal Implications and Negligent Hiring   Careful selection is also important because of the legal implications of incompetent selection. For one thing (as we saw in Chapter 2), EEO legislation and court decisions require you to systematically evaluate your selection procedure's effectiveness to ensure that you're not unfairly discriminating against any protected group. Furthermore, courts are increasingly finding employers liable when employees with criminal records or other problems use their access to customers' homes or other similar opportunities to commit crimes. Hiring workers with such backgrounds without proper safeguards is called *negligent hiring*.[3]

Validity

Generally speaking, you should ensure that the test (or interview questions, or other screening tools you use) are *valid,* or measure what they are supposed to measure. Sometimes what you're measuring is fairly obvious, but sometimes it's not. A test is a sample of a person's behavior, but some tests more clearly reflect the behavior being sampled than do others. A typing test, for instance, clearly corresponds to an on-the-job behavior—typing. At the other extreme, there may be no apparent relationship between the items on the test and the behavior. For example, in the Thematic Apperception Test illustrated in Figure 4.1, the person is asked to explain how he or she interprets the blurred picture. Is the young woman day dreaming of her affectionate mother, or hoping that a rival will grow old before her time? That interpretation is then used to draw conclusions about the person's personality and behavior. In such tests, it is harder to "prove" that the tests are measuring what they are purported to measure—that they are *valid.*

Figure 4.1 Sample Picture from Thematic Apperception Test

Source: Reprinted by permission of the publishers from Henry A. Murray, *Thematic Apperception Test,* Cambridge, MA: Harvard University Press, Copyright © 1943 by the President and Fellows of Harvard College, © 1971 by Henry A. Murray.

Test validity answers the question Does this test measure what it's supposed to measure?[4] Stated differently, "validity refers to the confidence one has in the meaning attached to the scores."[5] With respect to employee selection tests, the term *validity* often refers to evidence that the test is job related, in other words, that performance on the test is a *valid predictor* of subsequent performance on the job. A selection test must be valid because, without proof of its validity, there is no logical or legally permissible reason to continue using it to screen job applicants.

In employment testing, there are two main ways to demonstrate a test's validity: **criterion validity** and **content validity.** Demonstrating criterion validity means demonstrating that those who do well on the test also do well on the job, and that those who do poorly on the test do poorly on the job. In psychological measurement, a predictor is the measurement (in this case, the test score) that you are trying to relate to a criterion, such as performance on the job. In criterion validity, the two should be closely related. The term *criterion validity* comes from that terminology.

The employer demonstrates the *content validity* of a test by showing that the test constitutes a fair sample of the content of a job. A typing test used to hire a typist is an example. If the content of the typing test is a representative sample of the typist's job, then the test is probably content valid.

Reliability

Reliability is a test's second important characteristic and refers to its consistency. It is "the consistency of scores obtained by the same person when retested with the identical tests or with an equivalent form of a test."[6] A test's reliability is very important: If a person scored 90 on an intelligence test on Monday and 130 when retested on Tuesday, you probably wouldn't have much faith in the test.

There are several ways to estimate a test's consistency or reliability. You could administer the same test to the same people at two different points in time, comparing their test scores at time two with their scores at time one; this would be a retest estimate. Or you could administer a test and then administer what experts believe to be an equivalent test at a later date; this would be an equivalent-form estimate. The Scholastic Aptitude Test is an example of the latter.

A test's internal consistency is another measure of its reliability. For example, assume you have 10 items on a test of vocational interest. These items are supposed to measure in various ways the person's interest in working outdoors. You administer the test and then statistically analyze the degree to which responses to these items vary together. This would provide a measure of the internal reliability of the test and is referred to as an *internal comparison estimate*. Internal consistency is one reason you often find questions that apparently are repetitive on some test questionnaires.

How to Validate a Test

What makes a test such as the Graduate Record Examination (GRE) useful for college admissions directors? What makes a mechanical comprehension test useful for managers trying to hire machinists?

The answer to both questions is usually that people's scores on these tests have been shown to be predictive of how people perform. Thus, other things equal,

Figure 4.2 How to Validate a Test

Step 1: Analyze the Job. First, analyze the job and write job descriptions and job specifications. Specify the human traits and skills you believe are required for adequate job performance. For example, must an applicant be aggressive? Must the person be able to assemble small, detailed components? These requirements become your predictors. They are the human traits and skills you believe to be predictive of success on the job.

In this first step, you must also define what you mean by "success on the job" because it is this success for which you want predictors. The standards of success are called *criteria*. You could focus on production-related criteria (quantity, quality, and so on), personnel data (absenteeism, length of service, and so on), or judgments (of worker performance by persons such as supervisors). For an assembler's job, predictors for which to test applicants might include manual dexterity and patience. Criteria that you would hope to predict with your test might then include quantity produced per hour and number of rejects produced per hour.

Step 2: Choose the Tests. Next, choose tests that you think measure the attributes (predictors) important for job success. This choice is usually based on experience, previous research, and best guesses, and you usually won't start off with just one test. Instead, you choose several tests, combining them into a test battery aimed at measuring a variety of possible predictors, such as aggressiveness, extroversion, and numeric ability.

Step 3: Administer Tests. Administer the selected test(s) to employees. Predictive validation is the most dependable way to validate a test. The test is administered to applicants before they are hired. Then these applicants are hired using only existing selection techniques, not the results of the new test you are developing. After they have been on the job for some time, you measure their performance and compare it to their performance on the earlier test. You can then determine whether their performance on the test could have been used to predict their subsequent job performance.

Step 4: Relate Test Scores and Criteria. Next, determine whether there is a significant relationship between scores (the predictor) and performance (the criterion). The usual way to do this is to determine the statistical relationship between scores on the test and performance through correlation analysis, which shows the degree of statistical relationship.

Step 5: Cross-Validate and Revalidate. Before putting the test into use, you may want to check it by cross-validating, by again performing steps 3 and 4 on a new sample of employees. At a minimum, an expert should validate the test periodically.

---

students who score high on the GRE also do better in graduate school. Applicants who score higher on a mechanical comprehension test perform better as machinists.

Strictly speaking, an employer should be fairly sure that scores on the tests are related in a predictable way to performance on the job before using that test to screen employees. In other words, it is important that you validate the test before using it. You do this by ensuring that test scores are a good predictor of some criterion such as job performance. In other words, you should demonstrate the test's criterion validity. This validation process usually requires the expertise of an industrial psychologist, and is summarized in Figure 4.2.

Ethical and Legal Questions in Testing

Equal Employment Opportunity Aspects of Testing   We've seen that various federal and state laws bar discrimination on the basis of race, color, age, religion, sex, disability, and national origin. With respect to testing, these laws boil down to two things: (1) You must be able to prove that your tests were related to success or failure on the job; and (2) you must prove that your tests don't unfairly discriminate against either minority or nonminority subgroups. If confronted by a legitimate discrimination charge, the burden of proof rests with you. Once the plaintiff shows that one of your selection procedures has a *disparate impact* on his or her protected class, you must demonstrate the validity and selection fairness of the allegedly discriminatory test or item. Disparate impact means there is a significant discrepancy between rates of rejection of members of the protected groups and others.

You can't avoid EEO laws by not using tests, by the way. EEO guidelines and laws apply to any and all screening or selection devices, including interviews, applications, and references. In other words, the same burden of proving job relatedness falls on interviews and other techniques (including performance appraisals) that falls on tests.

Individual Rights of Test Takers and Test Security   Test takers have various privacy and information rights. Under the American Psychological Association's standard for educational and psychology tests (which guide professional psychologists but are not legally enforceable), they have the right to the confidentiality of the test results and the right to informed consent regarding the use of these results. They have the right to expect that only people qualified to interpret the scores will have access to them or that sufficient information will accompany the scores to ensure their appropriate interpretation. They have the right to expect that the test is secure; no person taking the test should have prior information concerning the questions or answers.

Using Tests as Supplements   Do not use tests as your only selection technique; instead, use them to supplement other techniques such as interviews and background checks. Tests are not infallible. Even in the best cases, the test score usually accounts for only about 25% of the variation in the measure of performance. In addition, tests are often better at telling you which candidates will fail than which will succeed.

USING TESTS AT WORK

Tests have long been used to predict behavior and performance, and they can be effective. For example, researchers administered an aggression questionnaire to high school hockey players prior to the season. Preseason aggressiveness as measured by the questionnaire predicted the amount of minutes they subsequently spent in the penalty box for penalties such as fighting, slashing, and tripping.[7]

Want to see what such tests are like? Try the short test in Figure 4.3 to see how prone you might be to on-the-job accidents.

How Are Tests Used at Work?

Employers use tests to measure a wide range of candidate attributes, including cognitive (mental) abilities, motor and physical abilities, personality and interests, and achievement. Many firms such as Kinko's have applicants take online or off-line computerized tests—sometimes by phone, using the touchtone keypad—to quickly

Figure 4.3 Sample Selection Test

CHECK YES OR NO	YES	NO
1. You like a lot of excitement in your life.		
2. An employee who takes it easy at work is cheating on the employer.		
3. You are a cautious person.		
4. In the past three years you have found yourself in a shouting match at school or work.		
5. You like to drive fast just for fun.		

Analysis: According to John Kamp, an industrial psychologist, applicants who answered no, yes, yes, no, no to questions 1, 2, 3, 4, and 5 are statistically likely to be absent less often, to have fewer on-the-job injuries, and, if the job involves driving, to have fewer on-the-job driving accidents. Actual scores on the test are based on answers to 130 questions.

Source: Courtesy of NYT Permissions.

prescreen applicants prior to more in-depth interviews and background checks.[8] And, firms don't just use tests for lower-level workers. For example, consultants McKinsey & Co. flew 54 MIT MBA students to Miami for two days of multiple-choice business knowledge tests, case-oriented case studies, and interviews. Barclays Capital gives graduate and undergraduate job candidates aptitude tests instead of first-round interviews.[9]

Employee testing is not just for large employers. For example, Outback Steakhouse (which now has 45,000 employees) has used preemployment testing since 1991, just two years after the company started. The testing is apparently quite successful. While turnover rates for hourly employees may reach 200% in the restaurant industry, Outback's turnover ranges from 40% to 60% per year. Outback does this by using a test to screen out applicants who don't fit the unique Outback culture. Outback is looking for employees who are highly social, meticulous, sympathetic, and adaptable. They use a special personality assessment test as part of a three-step preemployment interview process. Applicants take the test, and the company then compares the candidate's results to the profile for Outback Steakhouse employees. Those who score low on certain traits (like compassion) don't move to the next step. Those who do get interviewed by two managers. The latter focus on asking "behavioral" questions, such as What would you do if a customer asked for a side dish we don't have on the menu?[10] The basic types of tests are as follows.

Tests of Cognitive Abilities   Employers often want to assess a candidate's cognitive or mental abilities. For example, you may be interested in determining whether

Figure 4.4 Two Problems from the Test of Mechanical Comprehension

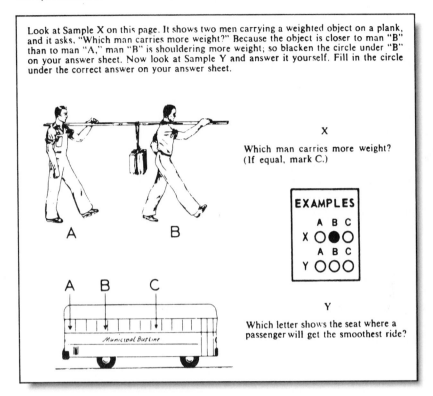

Look at Sample X on this page. It shows two men carrying a weighted object on a plank, and it asks, "Which man carries more weight?" Because the object is closer to man "B" than to man "A," man "B" is shouldering more weight; so blacken the circle under "B" on your answer sheet. Now look at Sample Y and answer it yourself. Fill in the circle under the correct answer on your answer sheet.

X

Which man carries more weight? (If equal, mark C.)

EXAMPLES

A B C
X ○ ● ○
A B C
Y ○ ○ ○

Y

Which letter shows the seat where a passenger will get the smoothest ride?

Municipal Bus Line

Source: From the Bennett Mechanical Comprehension Test. Copyright © 1942, 1967–1970, 1980 by The Psychological Corporation. Reproduced by permission. All rights reserved. "Bennett Mechanical Comprehension Test" and "BMCT" are registered trademarks of The Psychological Corporation.

a supervisory candidate has the intelligence to do the paperwork required of the job or whether a bookkeeper candidate has the required numeric aptitude.

Intelligence tests, such as IQ tests, are tests of general intellectual abilities. They measure not a single intelligence trait, but rather a range of abilities, including memory, vocabulary, verbal fluency, and numeric ability. Today, psychologists often measure intelligence with individually administered tests such as the Stanford-Binet or the Wechsler test. Employers use other IQ tests such as the Wonderlic to provide quick measures of IQ for both individuals and groups of people.

There are also measures of specific mental abilities. Tests in this category are often called "aptitude tests" because they aim to measure the applicant's aptitudes for the job in question. For example, consider the Test of Mechanical Comprehension illustrated in Figure 4.4. It tests the applicant's understanding of basic mechanical principles. It may therefore reflect a person's aptitude for jobs—such as engineer—that require mechanical comprehension.

Tests of Motor and Physical Abilities   There are many motor or physical abilities you might want to measure, such as finger dexterity, strength, manual dexterity, and reaction time (for instance, for machine operators or police candidates). The Stromberg Dexterity Test is one example. It measures the speed and accuracy of simple judgment as well as the speed of finger, hand, and arm movements.

Measuring Personality and Interests   A person's mental and physical abilities alone seldom explain his or her job performance. Other factors, such as motivation and interpersonal skills, are important, too. Personality and interests inventories are sometimes used as predictors of such intangibles. As a consultant recently put it, most people are hired based on qualifications, but most are fired for nonperformance. And nonperformance (or performance) "is usually the result of personal characteristics, such as attitude, motivation, and especially, temperament."[11]

Employers use personality and interests inventories to measure and predict such intangibles. Firms including Dell Computer, Motorola, and GE increasingly use personality tests to help screen even top-level candidates. As part of its selection process for CEO candidates, Hewlett-Packard put its eventual choice Carly Fiorina and other finalists through a two-hour 900-question personality test. Candidates had to indicate whether statements like "When I bump into a piece of furniture, I usually get angry" were true or false.[12]

Personality tests measure basic aspects of an applicant's personality, such as introversion, stability, and motivation. Many of these tests are projective, meaning that an ambiguous stimulus such as an inkblot or clouded picture is presented to the person taking the test and he or she is then asked to interpret or react to it. Because the pictures are ambiguous, the person's interpretation must come from within. He or she supposedly projects into the picture his or her own emotional attitudes about life. Thus, a security-oriented person might describe the woman in Figure 4.1 as "Me worrying about my mother worrying about what I'll do if I lose my job."

Personality tests—particularly the projective type—are the most difficult to evaluate and use. An expert must analyze the test taker's interpretations and reactions and infer from them his or her personality. The usefulness of such tests for selection then assumes that you find a relationship between a measurable personality trait (such as introversion) and success on the job.

The difficulties notwithstanding, studies confirm that personality tests can help companies hire more effective workers. Industrial psychologists often emphasize the "big five" personality dimensions as they apply to personnel testing: extroversion, emotional stability, agreeableness, conscientiousness, and openness to experience.[13] One study focused on the extent to which these five personality dimensions predicted performance (for instance, in terms of job and training proficiency) for professionals, police officers, managers, sales workers, and skilled/semi-skilled workers. Conscientiousness showed a consistent relationship with all job performance criteria for all the occupations. Extroversion was a valid predictor of performance for managers and sales employees—two of the occupations involving the most social interaction. Openness to experience and extroversion predicted training proficiency for all occupations.[14]

There are many other examples. The responsibility, socialization, and self-control scales of the California Psychological Inventory were used to successfully predict dysfunctional job behaviors among law-enforcement officers.[15] Emotional stability, extroversion, and agreeableness were found to be negatively related to whether expatriates of multinational companies want to leave their assignments early.[16]

Employee theft is another aspect of employee behavior that has proven amenable to employee personality testing.[17] See also the *Global Issues* box on page 138.

Because they are personal in nature, employers should always use personality tests with caution, particularly where the focus is on aberrant behavior. Rejected candidates may (validly) claim that the results are false, or that they violate the Americans with Disabilities Act or employees' privacy.[18]

Interest inventories compare one's interests with those of people in various occupations. Thus, if a person takes the Strong-Campbell Interest Inventory, he or she receives a report comparing his or her interests to those of people already in occupations such as accounting, engineering, management, and medical technology.

Achievement Tests   An achievement test is basically a measure of what a person has learned. Most of the tests you take in school are achievement tests. They measure your knowledge in areas such as economics, marketing, or personnel. In addition to job knowledge, achievement tests can measure applicants' abilities; a typing test is one example.[19]

Computerized Testing   Computerized tests are increasingly replacing conventional paper-and-pencil and manual tests. For example, a computerized testing procedure was developed for the selection of clerical personnel in a large manufacturing company.[20] In this case, eight test components were constructed to represent actual work performed by secretarial personnel, such as maintaining and developing databases and spreadsheets, answering the telephone and filing, and handling travel arrangements. For example, for the word processing test, applicants were given three minutes (monitored by the computer) to type as much of a letter as possible; the computer recorded and corrected the manuscript.[21]

Management Assessment Centers

In a **management assessment center,** management candidates take tests and make decisions in simulated situations, and are scored on their performance. The time at the assessment center is usually two or three days and involves 10 to 12 management candidates performing realistic management tasks (such as making presentations) under the observation of expert appraisers. The center may be a plain conference room, but often it is a special room with a one-way mirror to facilitate unobtrusive observations. Examples of the simulated but realistic exercises included in a typical assessment center are as follows:

- *The in-basket.* In this exercise, the candidate is faced with an accumulation of reports, memos, notes of incoming phone calls, letters, and other materials collected in the in-basket of the simulated job he or she is to take over. The candidate takes appropriate action on each of these materials.
- *The leaderless group discussion.* A leaderless group is given a discussion question and told to arrive at a group decision. The raters then evaluate each group member's interpersonal skills, acceptance by the group, leadership ability, and individual influence.
- *Individual presentations.* A participant's communication skills and persuasiveness are evaluated by having the person make an oral presentation on an assigned topic.

Most studies suggest that assessment centers are useful for predicting success in management jobs.[22] On the other hand, the cost of organizing and running such a center can be quite high. Some, therefore, suggest that a straightforward review of participants' personnel files can often do as good a job as assessment center evaluations of predicting which participants would succeed.[23]

An analysis of more than 200 assessment centers provides a snapshot of typical assessment center practices. Supervisor recommendations play a big role in who is invited to participate. Center candidates typically get little information about the assessment center before it begins. Specially trained line or staff managers serve as assessors to observe the multiple exercises. Candidates generally get about a hour's worth of oral feedback and a written report following the center. Promotion is the most popular reason for bringing candidates to assessment centers. In-basket and leaderless group exercises are among the assessment tools used most often.[24]

Testing on the Web

Firms are increasingly using the Web to test and screen applicants. For example, the financial firm Capital One previously used three paper-and-pencil tests for preemployment screening: a cognitive skills test, a math test, and a "biodata" job history test (which the firm used to predict job stability).[25] The process was reportedly time consuming and inefficient: "In Tampa, we were having to process several thousand people a month just to hire 100," says a company officer. The company's new online system eliminates the paper-and-pencil process. Applicants for call center jobs complete an online application and online math and biodata tests. They also take an online role-playing call simulation. For the latter, they put on a headset, and the CD-ROM program plays seven different customer situations. Applicants (playing the role of operators) answer multiple-choice questions online regarding how they would respond.

Strategy and HR   City Garage's top managers knew they'd never be able to implement their growth strategy without a dramatic change in how they tested and hired employees.[26] Their old hiring process consisted of a paper-and-pencil application and one interview, immediately followed by a hire/don't hire decision. While that might work for a slow-growth operation, it was unsatisfactory for a fast-growing operation like City Garage. For one thing, local shop managers didn't have the time to evaluate every applicant, so "if they had been shorthanded too long, we would hire pretty much anybody who had experience," said training director Rusty Reinoehl. There was also inconsistency: Some managers had better interviewing and hiring skills than others. Complicating the problem was that City Garage's competitive strategy didn't rely just on finding talented mechanics with toolboxes. City Garage competitively differentiates itself with an "open garage" arrangement, where customers interact directly with technicians. Therefore, finding mechanics who not only tolerate but react positively to customer inquiries is essential.

City Garage's solution was to purchase the Personality Profile Analysis (PPA) online test from Dallas-based Thomas International USA. Doing so added a third step to the application and interview process. After a quick application and background check, likely candidates take the 10-minute, 24-question PPA. City Garage staff then enter the answers into the PPA Software system, and receive test results in less than two minutes. These show whether the applicant is high or low in four personality characteristics. It also produces follow-up questions about areas that might cause problems. For example, applicants might be asked how they've handled possible weaknesses such as lack of patience. If candidates answer those questions satisfactorily, they're asked back for extensive, all-day interviews, after which hiring decisions are made.

INTERVIEWING PROSPECTIVE EMPLOYEES

Although not all companies use tests or assessment centers, it is very unusual for a manager not to interview a prospective employee; interviewing is thus an indispensable management tool. An **interview** is a procedure designed to solicit information from a person's oral responses to oral inquiries. A *selection interview,* which we'll focus on in this chapter, is "a selection procedure designed to predict future job performance on the basis of applicants' oral responses to oral inquiries."[27]

Types of Selection Interviews

As you probably know from your own experience, there are several types of selection interviews. For example, there are *nonstructured* and *structured interviews.* In the former, you ask questions as they come to mind, and there is generally no set format to follow. In a more structured or directive interview, such as the one in Figure 4.5, the questions and perhaps even acceptable responses are specified in advance and the responses may be rated for appropriateness of content.

Structured interviews are generally more valid. With structured interviews, all applicants get all required questions from all the interviewers with whom they meet. This can build consistency and fairness into the process. Structured interviews can also help inexperienced interviewers to ask questions and conduct useful interviews. On the other hand, structured interviews don't always leave the flexibility to pursue points of interest as they develop.

We can also classify interviews according to the type of questions they emphasize. In *situational interviews,* questions focus on the candidate's ability to project what his or her behavior would be in a given situation.[28] For example, you might ask a candidate for a supervisor position how he or she would respond to a subordinate coming to work late three days in a row. A *behavioral interview* is another type of interview. Here you ask interviewees how they behaved in the past in some situation. Thus, an interviewer might ask, "Did you ever have a situation in which a subordinate came in late? If so, how did you handle the situation?" For example, when Citizen's Banking Corporation in Flint, Michigan, found that 31 of the 50 people in its call center quit in one year, Cynthia Wilson, the center's head, switched to behavioral interviews. Many of those who left did so because they didn't enjoy fielding questions from occasionally irate clients. So Wilson no longer tries to predict how candidates will act based on asking them if they want to work with angry clients. Instead, she asks behavioral questions like, "Tell me about a time you were speaking with an irate person, and how you turned the situation around." Wilson says this makes it much harder to fool the interviewer, and, indeed, only four people left her center in the following year.[29]

Figure 4.5 Structured Interview Form for College Applicants

CANDIDATE RECORD NAP 100 (10/77)

CANDIDATE NUMBER | NAME (LAST NAME FIRST) | COLLEGE NAME | COLLEGE CODE

I | U 921 (1-7) | (8-27) | (28-30)

INTERVIEWER NUMBER
0 (33-40)
INTERVIEWER NAME

SOURCE (41)
Campus ☐ C
Walk-In ☐ W
Intern ☐ I
Agency ☐ A

RACE (42)
White ☐ W
Black ☐ B
Asian ☐ A
Hispanic ☐ H
Native Am. ☐ NA

SEX (43)
Male ☐ M
Female ☐ F
Init.
Cont.
Date (46-51)

DEGREE (53)
Bachelors ☐ B
Masters ☐ M
Law ☐ L
Majors

AVERAGE (A = 4.0)
Overall (54-55)
Acct'g. (56-57)

CLASS STANDING (58-59)
Top 10% ☐ 10
Top 25% ☐ 25
Top Half ☐ 50
Bottom Half ☐ 75

CAMPUS INTERVIEW EVALUATIONS

ATTITUDE – MOTIVATION – GOALS
POOR ☐ AVERAGE ☐ GOOD ☐ OUTSTANDING ☐
(POSITIVE, COOPERATIVE, ENERGETIC, MOTIVATED, SUCCESSFUL, GOAL ORIENTED)
COMMENTS:

COMMUNICATIONS SKILLS-PERSONALITY-SALES ABILITY
POOR ☐ AVERAGE ☐ GOOD ☐ OUTSTANDING ☐
(ARTICULATE, LISTENS, ENTHUSIASTIC, LIKEABLE, POISED, TACTFUL, ACCEPTED, CONVINCING)
COMMENTS:

EXECUTIVE PRESENCE – DEAL WITH TOP PEOPLE
POOR ☐ AVERAGE ☐ GOOD ☐ OUTSTANDING ☐
(IMPRESSIVE, STANDS OUT, A WINNER, REMEMBERED, LEVEL HEADED, AT EASE, AWARE)
COMMENTS:

INTELLECTUAL ABILITIES
POOR ☐ AVERAGE ☐ GOOD ☐ OUTSTANDING ☐
(INSIGHTFUL, CREATIVE, CURIOUS, IMAGINATIVE, UNDERSTANDS, REASONS, INTELLIGENT, SCHOLARLY)
COMMENTS:

JUDGMENT – DECISION-MAKING ABILITY
POOR ☐ AVERAGE ☐ GOOD ☐ OUTSTANDING ☐
(MATURE, SEASONED, INDEPENDENT, COMMON SENSE, CERTAIN, DETERMINED, LOGICAL)
COMMENTS:

LEADERSHIP
POOR ☐ AVERAGE ☐ GOOD ☐ OUTSTANDING ☐
(SELF-CONFIDENT, TAKES CHARGE, EFFECTIVE, RESPECTED, MANAGEMENT MINDED, GRASPS AUTHORITY)
COMMENTS:

CAMPUS INTERVIEW SUMMARY

INVITE (Circle) YES NO
DATE AVAILABLE

AREA OF INTEREST (Circle)
AUDIT   TAX
MCS   ABC
OTHER

SEMESTER HRS.
Acct'g. _____
Audit _____
Tax _____

OFFICES PREFERRED:
No. 1 _____
No. 2 _____
No. 3 _____

SUMMARY COMMENTS: _____

We can also classify interviews based on how we administer them. For example, most interviews are administered *one-on-one;* two people meet alone and one interviews the other by seeking oral responses to oral inquiries. Most selection processes are also sequential. In a *sequential interview* several people interview the applicant in sequence before a selection decision is made. In a *panel interview* the candidate is interviewed simultaneously by a group (or panel) of interviewers, rather than sequentially.

Some interviews are done entirely by *phone*. These interviews can actually be more accurate than face-to-face ones for judging an applicant's conscientiousness, intelligence, and interpersonal skills. Since neither side has to worry about things like clothing or handshakes, the telephone interviews may let both focus more on substantive answers. Or perhaps candidates—somewhat surprised by unexpected calls from the recruiter—simply give more spontaneous answers.[30] In a typical study, interviewers tended to evaluate applicants more favorably in telephone versus face-to-face interviews, particularly where the interviewees were less physically attractive. The interviewers came to about the same conclusions regarding the interviewees whether the interview was face-to-face or by videoconference. The applicants themselves preferred the face-to-face interviews.[31]

How Useful Are Interviews?

While virtually all employers use interviews, the statistical evidence regarding their validity is quite mixed. Much of the early research gave selection interviews low marks for reliability and validity.[32] However, today studies confirm that the "validity of the interview is greater than previously believed."[33] The key is that the interview's usefulness depends on how you administer it. Specifically, we can make the following generalizations, based on one study of interview validity:

- With respect to predicting job performance, situational interviews yield a higher mean (average) validity than do behavioral interviews.
- Structured interviews, regardless of content, are more valid than unstructured interviews for predicting job performance.
- Both when they are structured and when they are unstructured, individual interviews tend to be more valid than are panel interviews, in which multiple interviewers provide ratings in one setting.[34]

In summary, structured situational interviews (in which you ask the candidates what they would do in a particular situation) conducted one-on-one seem to be the most useful for predicting job performance. However, whether you are an effective interviewer depends in part on avoiding common interviewing mistakes, a subject to which we now turn.

How to Avoid Common Interviewing Mistakes

Several common interviewing mistakes can undermine an interview's usefulness. Some of these common mistakes—and suggestions for avoiding them—are described in this section.

Snap Judgments   One of the most consistent findings is that interviewers tend to jump to conclusions—make snap judgments—about candidates during the first few minutes of the interview. In fact, this often occurs even before the interview begins, based on test scores or résumé data.[35] One London-based psychologist interviewed the chief executives of 80 top companies. She came to this conclusion about snap judgments in selection interviews: "Really, to make a good impression, you don't even get time to open your mouth. . . . An interviewer's response to you will generally be preverbal—how you walk through the door, what your posture is like, whether you smile, whether you have a captivating aura, whether you have a firm, confident handshake. You've got about half a minute to make an impact and after that all you are doing is building on a good or bad first impression. . . . It's a very emotional response."[36]

For interviewees, such findings underscore why it's important to start off on the right foot with the interviewer. Interviewers usually make up their minds about you during the first few minutes of the interview, and prolonging the interview past this point usually adds little to change their decisions. From the interviewer's point of view, the findings underscore the importance of consciously delaying a decision and keeping an open mind until the interview is over.

Negative Emphasis   Jumping to conclusions is especially troublesome given the fact that interviewers also tend to have a consistent negative bias. They are generally more influenced by unfavorable than favorable information about the candidate. Furthermore, their impressions are much more likely to change from favorable to unfavorable than from unfavorable to favorable. Often, in fact, interviews are mostly searches for negative information.

What are the implications? As an interviewer, remember to keep an open mind and consciously work against being preoccupied with negative impressions. As an interviewee, remember the old saying that "You only have one chance to make a good first impression." If you start with a poor initial impression, you'll find it almost impossible to overcome that first, bad impression during the interview.

Not Knowing the Job   Interviewers who don't know precisely what the job entails and what sort of candidate is best suited for it usually make decisions based on incorrect stereotypes about what makes a good applicant. They then erroneously match interviewees against these incorrect stereotypes. Studies therefore indicate that more job knowledge on the part of interviewers translates into better interviews.[37] Interviewers should know as much as possible about the nature of the position for which they're interviewing, and about the human requirements (e.g., interpersonal skills, job knowledge) that the job requires.

Pressure to Hire   Being under pressure to hire undermines an interview's usefulness. In one study a group of managers were told to assume that they were behind in their recruiting quota. A second group was told that they were ahead of their quota. Those behind evaluated the same recruits much more highly than did those ahead.[38]

Candidate Order (Contrast) Error   Candidate order (or contrast) error means that the order in which you see applicants affects how you rate them. In one study, managers were asked to evaluate a candidate who was "just average" after first evaluating several "unfavorable" candidates. The average candidate was evaluated more favorably than he might otherwise have been, because in contrast to the unfavorable candidates the average one looked better than he actually was.[39]

Influence of Nonverbal Behavior   Not just what the candidate says but how he or she looks and behaves can influence the interviewer's ratings. For example, studies show that interviewers rate applicants who demonstrate more eye contact, head moving, smiling, and similar nonverbal behaviors higher. Such behaviors often account for over 80% of the applicant's rating.[40] In another study, vocal cues (such as the interviewee's pitch, speech rates, and pauses) and visual cues (such as physical attractiveness, smile, and body orientation) correlated with the evaluator's judgments of whether or not the interviewees could be liked and trusted, and were credible.[41]

A candidate's nonverbal behavior seems to send signals about his or her personality and thus whether to make a job offer. In one study of 99 graduating college seniors, the interviewee's apparent level of extroversion influenced whether he or she received follow-up interviews and job offers. In part, this seems to be because "interviewers draw inferences about the applicant's personality based on the applicant's behavior during the interview."[42] Extroverted applicants seem particularly prone to self-promotion, and self-promotion is strongly related to the interviewer's perceptions of candidate-job fit.[43]

An applicant's attractiveness and sex also play a role.[44] In general, studies of attractiveness find that individuals ascribe more favorable traits and more successful life outcomes to attractive people.[45] A gender study reportedly found that "even when female managers exhibited the same career-advancing behaviors as male managers, they still earned less money and were offered fewer career-progressing transfer opportunities."[46] In another study, researchers asked subjects to evaluate candidates for promotability based on photographs. Men were perceived to be more suitable for hire and more likely to advance to the next executive level than were equally qualified women, and more attractive candidates, especially men, were preferred over less attractive ones.[47] Yet another study suggested that in some cases more attractive women may actually be less likely to be offered managerial positions than are less attractive women, possibly because the interviewers erroneously equate attractiveness with femininity and femininity with nonmanagerial jobs.[48]

Race also plays a role. One study examined racial differences in ratings of black and white interviewees when the interviewees appeared before three interview panels: panels in which the racial composition was primarily black (75% black, 25% white), racially balanced (50% black, 50% white), and primarily white (75% white, 25% black).[49] On the primarily black panels, black and white raters judged black and white candidates similarly. On the other hand, in the primarily white panels or in those in which black and white interviewers were equally represented, white candidates were rated higher by white interviewers, and black candidates were rated higher by black interviewers.

The structure of the interview may influence the extent to which race plays a role. One review of 31 studies concluded that structured interviews produced less of a difference between minority and white interviewees on average than did unstructured interviews.[50] However such findings don't necessarily apply to other EEOC-protected classes. In another study of structured interviews, candidates evidencing a wide range of specific disabilities (such as childcare demands, HIV-positive status, and being wheelchair-bound) had less chance of obtaining a positive decision, even when the person performed superior in the structured interview.[51]

Evidence like this suggests several implications. With respect to nonverbal behavior (such as eye contact), it seems apparent that otherwise inferior candidates who are trained to "act right" in interviews are often appraised more highly than are more competent applicants without the right nonverbal interviewing skills. Interviewers should thus endeavor to look beyond the behavior to who the person is and what he or she is saying. Second, demographic and physical attributes, such as attractiveness, sex, or race, may influence your decisions as an interviewer. Because such attributes are generally irrelevant to job performance, interviewers should anticipate the potential impact of such biases and guard against letting them influence their ratings.

Guidelines for Conducting an Interview

You can generally conduct the interview more effectively if you follow the guidelines outlined in this section.

Plan the Interview   Begin by reviewing the candidate's application and résumé, and note any areas that are vague or that may indicate strengths or weaknesses. Review the job specification and plan to start the interview with a clear picture of the traits of an ideal candidate. In one study, about 39% of the 191 applicants said interviewers were unprepared or unfocused.[52]

Structure the Interview   Few steps are as important as structuring the interview. Doing so not only assures greater consistency, but also helps ensure that you are asking questions that provide real insight into how the person will perform on the job—and that, of course, is the main point of the interview. There are several things you can do to increase the standardization of the interview or otherwise assist the interviewer to ask more consistent and job-relevant questions.[53] They include:[54]

1. Base questions on actual job duties. This will minimize irrelevant questions based on beliefs about the job's requirements. It may also reduce the likelihood of bias, because there's less opportunity to "read" things into the answer.
2. Use job knowledge, situational or behavioral questions, and use objective criteria to evaluate the interviewee's responses. Questions that ask for opinions and attitudes, goals and aspirations, and self-descriptions and self-evaluations encourage self-promotion and allow candidates to avoid revealing weaknesses. Examples of structured questions include: (1) *situational or behavioral questions* like "Suppose you were giving a sales presentation and a difficult technical question arose that you could not answer. What would you do?"; (2) *past behavior questions* like "Can you provide an example of a specific instance where you developed a sales presentation that was highly effective?"; (3) *background questions* like "What work experiences, training, or other qualifications do you have for working in a teamwork environment?"; (4) *job knowledge* questions like "What factors should you consider when developing a TV advertising campaign?"
3. Train interviewers. For example, review EEO laws with prospective interviewers and train them to avoid irrelevant or potentially discriminatory questions.
4. Use the same questions with all candidates. Using the same questions with all candidates can also reduce bias by giving all the candidates the exact same opportunity.
5. Use rating scales to rate answers, if possible. For each question, provide a range of sample ideal answers, and a quantitative score for each. Then rate each candidate's answers against this scale.
6. Use multiple interviewers or panel interviews. Doing so can reduce bias by diminishing the importance of one interviewer's idiosyncratic opinions, and by bringing in more points of view.
7. If possible, use a structured interview form. Interviews based on structured guides, like the one in Figure 4.6, usually result in the best interviews.[55] At the very least, list your questions before the interview.

Figure 4.6 Structured Interview Guide

APPLICANT INTERVIEW GUIDE

To the interviewer: This Applicant Interview Guide is intended to assist in employee selection and placement. If it is used for all applicants for a position, it will help you to compare them, and it will provide more objective information than you will obtain from unstructured interviews.

Because this is a general guide, all of the items may not apply in every instance. Skip those that are not applicable and add questions appropriate to the specific position. Space for additional questions will be found at the end of the form.

Federal law prohibits discrimination in employment on the basis of sex, race, color, national origin, religion, disability, and in most instances, age. The law of most states also ban some or all of the above types of discrimination in employment as well as discrimination based on marital status or ancestry. Interviewers should take care to avoid any questions that suggest that an employment decision will be made on the basis of any such factors.

Job Interest

Name _____ Position applied for _____

What do you think the job (position) involves? _____

Why do you want the job (position)? _____

Why are you qualified for it? _____

What would your salary requirements be? _____

What do you know about our company? _____

Why do you want to work for us? _____

Current Work Status

Are you now employed? _____ Yes _____ No. If not, how long have you been unemployed? _____

Why are you unemployed? _____

If you are working, why are you applying for this position? _____

When would you be available to start work with us? _____

Work Experience

(Start with the applicant's current or last position and work back. All periods of time should be accounted for. Go back at least 12 years, depending upon the applicant's age. Military service should be treated as a job.)

Current or last
employer _____ Address _____

Dates of employment: from _____ to _____

Current or last job title _____

What are (were) your duties? _____

Have you held the same job throughout your employment with that company? _____ Yes _____ No. If not, describe the

various jobs you have had with that employer, how long you held each of them, and the main duties of each. _____

What was your starting salary? _____ What are you earning now? _____ Comments _____

Name of your last or current supervisor _____

What did you like most about that job? _____

What did you like least about it? _____

Why are you thinking of leaving? _____

Why are you leaving right now? _____

Interviewer's comments or observations _____

(Continued)

What did you do before you took your last job? _____

Where were you employed? _____

Location _____ Job title _____

Duties _____

Did you hold the same job throughout your employment with that company? _____ Yes _____ No. If not,

describe the jobs you held, when you held them, and the duties of each. _____

_____

What was your starting salary? _____ What was your final salary? _____

Name of your last supervisor _____

May we contact that company? _____ Yes _____ No

What did you like most about that job? _____

What did you like least about that job? _____

Why did you leave that job? _____

Would you consider working there again? _____

Interviewer: If there is any gap between the various periods of employment, the applicant should be asked about them. _____

_____

Interviewer's comments or observations _____

_____

What did you do prior to the job with that company? _____

What other jobs or experience have you had? Describe them briefly and explain the general duties of each. _____

_____

Have you been unemployed at any time in the last five years? _____ Yes _____ No. What efforts did you make to find work?

_____

What other experience or training do you have that would help qualify you for the job applied for? Explain how and where you

obtained this experience or training. _____

Educational Background

What education or training do you have that would help you in the job for which you have applied? _____

_____

Describe any formal education you have had. (Interviewer may substitute technical training, if relevant.) _____

_____

Off-Job Activities

What do you do in your off-hours? _____ Part-time job _____ Athletics _____ Spectator sports _____ Clubs _____ Other

Please explain. _____

Interviewer's Specific Questions

Interviewer: Add any questions to the particular job for which you are interviewing, leaving space for brief answers.
(Be careful to avoid questions which may be viewed as discriminatory.)

_____

_____

_____

Personal

Would you be willing to relocate? _____ Yes _____ No

Are you willing to travel? _____ Yes _____ No

What is the maximum amount of time you would consider traveling? _____

_____

(Continued)

Are you able to work overtime? _____

What about working on weekends? _____

Self-Assessment

What do you feel are your strong points? _____

_____

What do you feel are your weak points? _____

_____

Interviewer: Compare the applicant's responses with the information furnished on the application for employment. Clear up any

discrepancies. _____

_____

Before the applicant leaves, the interviewer should provide basic information about the organization and the job opening, if this has not already been done. The applicant should be given information on the work location, work hours, the wage or salary, type of remuneration (salary or salary plus bonus, etc.), and other factors that may affect the applicant's interest in the job.

Interviewer's Impressions

Rate each characteristic from 1 to 4, with 1 being the highest rating and 4 being the lowest.

Personal Characteristics	1	2	3	4	Comments
Personal appearance					
Poise, manner					
Speech					
Cooperation with interviewer					
Job-Related Characteristics					
Experience for this job					
Knowledge of job					
Interpersonal relationships					
Effectiveness					

Overall Rating for Job

1	2	3	4	5
_____ Superior	_____ Above average	_____ Average	_____ Marginal	_____ Unsatisfactory
	(well qualified)	(qualified)	(barely qualified)	

Comments or remarks _____

_____

_____

Interviewer _____ Date _____

Source: Copyright 1992 The Dartnell Corporation, Chicago, IL. Adapted with permission.

8. Take brief notes during the interview. Doing so may help to overcome "the recency effect" (in other words, putting too much weight on the last few minutes of the interview). It may also help the interviewer keep an open mind rather than making a snap judgment based on inadequate information early into the interview, and may also help the interviewer jog his or her memory once the

- **Don't** ask questions that can be answered yes or no.
- **Don't** put words in the applicant's mouth or telegraph the desired answer, for instance, by nodding or smiling when the right answer is given.
- **Don't** interrogate the applicant as if the person is a criminal, and don't be patronizing, sarcastic, or inattentive.
- **Don't** monopolize the interview by rambling, nor let the applicant dominate the interview so you can't ask all your questions.

- **Do** ask open-ended questions.
- **Do** listen to the candidate to encourage him or her to express thoughts fully.
- **Do** draw out the applicant's opinions and feelings by repeating the person's last comment as a question (for example, "You didn't like your last job?").
- **Do** ask for examples.[56] For instance, if the candidate lists specific strengths or weaknesses, follow up with, "What are specific examples that demonstrate each of your strengths?"

interview is complete. The research suggests that the interviewer should take notes, but not copious ones, instead noting just the key points of what the interviewee says.[57]

The interview should take place in a private room where telephone calls are not accepted and you can minimize interruptions.

Establish Rapport   The main reason for the interview is to find out about the applicant. To do this, start by putting the person at ease. Greet the candidate and start the interview by asking a noncontroversial question, perhaps about the weather or the traffic conditions that day. As a rule, all applicants—even unsolicited dropins—should receive friendly, courteous treatment, not only on humanitarian grounds but because your reputation is on the line.

Be aware of the applicant's status. For example, if you are interviewing someone who is unemployed, he or she may be exceptionally nervous and you may want to take additional steps to relax the person.[58]

Ask Questions   Try to follow your structured interview guide or the questions you wrote out ahead of time. You'll find a menu of questions to choose from (such as "What best qualifies you for the available position?") in Figure 4.7.

One way to get more candid answers is to make it clear you're going to conduct reference checks. Ask, "If I were to arrange for an interview with your boss, and if the boss were very candid with me, what's your best guess as to what he or she would say are your strengths, weaker points, and overall performance?"[59]

Some dos and don'ts for asking questions are summarized in the *HR in Practice* box.

Close the Interview   Toward the close of the interview, leave time to answer any questions the candidate may have and, if appropriate, to advocate your firm to the candidate.

Figure 4.7   Interview Questions to Expect

1. Did you bring a résumé?
2. What salary do you expect to receive?
3. What was your salary in your last job?
4. Why do you want to change jobs or why did you leave your last job?
5. What do you identify as your most significant accomplishment in your last job?
6. How many hours do you normally work per week?
7. What did you like and dislike about your last job?
8. How did you get along with your superiors and subordinates?
9. Can you be demanding of your subordinates?
10. How would you evaluate the company you were with last?
11. What were its competitive strengths and weaknesses?
12. What best qualifies you for the available position?
13. How long will it take you to start making a significant contribution?
14. How do you feel about our company—its size, industry, and competitive position?
15. What interests you most about the available position?
16. How would you structure this job or organize your department?
17. What control or financial data would you want and why?
18. How would you establish your primary inside and outside lines of communication?
19. What would you like to tell me about yourself?
20. Were you a good student?
21. Have you kept up in your field? How?
22. What do you do in your spare time?
23. What are your career goals for the next five years?
24. What are your greatest strengths and weaknesses?
25. What is your job potential?
26. What steps are you taking to help achieve your goals?
27. Do you want to own your own business?
28. How long will you stay with us?
29. What did your father do? Your mother?
30. What do your brothers and sisters do?
31. Have you ever worked on a group project and, if so, what role did you play?
32. Do you participate in civic affairs?
33. What professional associations do you belong to?
34. What is your credit standing?
35. What are your personal likes and dislikes?
36. How do you spend a typical day?
37. Would you describe your family as a close one?
38. How aggressive are you?
39. What motivates you to work?
40. Is money a strong incentive for you?
41. Do you prefer line or staff work?
42. Would you rather work alone or in a team?
43. What do you look for when hiring people?
44. Have you ever fired anyone?
45. Can you get along with union members and their leaders?
46. What do you think of the current economic and political situation?
47. How will government policy affect our industry or your job?
48. Will you sign a noncompete agreement or employment contract?
49. Why should we hire you?
50. Do you want the job?

Source: Reprinted from *Jobsearch: The Complete Manual for Job Seekers.* Copyright © 1990 H. Lee Rust. Used with permission of the publisher, AMACOM, a division of American Management Association International, New York, NY. All rights reserved. www.amanet.org.

With many firms going global these days, there's a high likelihood you'll be interviewed for an assignment that involves some time abroad. What do companies look for when trying to identify international executives, and do you think you might have what it takes? If you'd like to know, read on.

A recent study by behavioral scientists at the University of Southern California provides some insights into these questions. The behavioral scientists studied 838 lower-, middle-, and senior-level managers from six international firms and 21 countries, focusing particularly on the manager's personal characteristics. Specifically, the researchers studied the extent to which personal characteristics such as "sensitivity to cultural differences" could be used to distinguish between managers who

Figure 4.8 Traits Distinguishing Successful International Executives

SCALE	SAMPLE ITEM
Sensitive to Cultural Differences	When working with people from other cultures, works hard to understand their perspectives.
Business Knowledge	Has a solid understanding of our products and services.
Courage to Take a Stand	Is willing to take a stand on issues.
Brings Out the Best in People	Has a special talent for dealing with people.
Acts with Integrity	Can be depended on to tell the truth regardless of circumstances.
Is Insightful	Is good at identifying the most important part of a complex problem or issue.
Is Committed to Success	Clearly demonstrates commitment to seeing the organization succeed.
Takes Risks	Takes personal as well as business risks.
Uses Feedback	Has changed as a result of feedback.
Is Culturally Adventurous	Enjoys the challenge of working in countries other than his/her own.
Seeks Opportunities to Learn	Takes advantage of opportunities to do new things.
Is Open to Criticism	Appears brittle—as if criticism might cause him/her to break.*
Seeks Feedback	Pursues feedback even when others are reluctant to give it.
Is Flexible	Doesn't get so invested in things that he/she cannot change when something doesn't work.

*Reverse scored.

Source: From "Early Identification of International Executive Potential," by Gretchen Spreitzer, Morgan McCall Jr., and Joan Mahoney, *Journal of Applied Psychology* 82, no. 1 (February 1997). Copyright © 1997 by the American Psychological Association. Adapted with permission.

had high potential as international executives and those whose potential was not so high.

Fourteen personal characteristics successfully distinguished the managers identified by their companies as high potential from those identified as not high potential in 72% of the cases. To get an initial, tentative impression of how you would rate, review the 14 characteristics (along with some sample items), which are listed in Figure 4.8. For each, indicate (by placing a number in the space provided) whether you strongly agree (7), strong disagree (1), or fall somewhere in between.[60] The average would be about 50.

Generally speaking, the higher you score on these 14 characteristics, the more likely it is that you might have been identified as a high-potential international executive in this study.

Try to end all interviews on a positive note. Tell the applicant whether there is an interest and, if so, what the next step will be. Similarly, make rejections diplomatically (for instance, with a statement such as "Although your background is impressive, there are other candidates whose experience is closer to our requirements"). If the applicant is still being considered but a decision can't be reached at once, say so. If your policy is to inform candidates of their status in writing, do so within a few days of the interview.

Review the Interview   After the candidate leaves, review your interview notes, fill in the structured interview guide (if this was not done during the interview), and review the interview while it's fresh in your mind.

USING OTHER SELECTION TECHNIQUES

Background Investigations and Reference Checks

Most employers try to check the background and references of job applicants, and there are two key reasons for doing so. One is to verify the accuracy of factual information previously provided by the applicant; the other is to uncover damaging background information such as criminal records and suspended drivers' licenses.[61] In Chicago, for instance, a major pharmaceutical firm discovered that it had hired gang members in mail delivery and computer repair. The gang members were stealing close to a million dollars per year in computer parts and then using the mail department to ship them to a nearby computer store they owned.[62]

The most commonly verified background areas are legal eligibility for employment (to comply with immigration laws), dates of prior employment, military service (including discharge status), education, and identification (including date of birth and address).[63] Other items should include county criminal records (current residence, last residence), motor vehicle record; credit; licensing verification; Social Security number; and reference checks.[64] The position determines how deeply you search. For example, a credit and education check would be more important for hiring an accountant than a groundskeeper. In any case, do not limit your background checks only to new hires. For example, also periodically check, say, the credit ratings of employees who have easy access to company assets, and the driving records of employees who routinely use company cars.

There are several ways to collect background information. Most employers at least try to verify an applicant's current position and salary with his or her current employer by phone (assuming that doing so was cleared with the candidate). Others call the applicant's current and previous supervisors to try to discover more about the person's motivation, technical competence, and ability to work with others. As we'll see in a moment, some employers get background reports from commercial credit rating companies or employment screening services. These can provide information about an applicant's credit standing, indebtedness, reputation, character, lifestyle, and the truthfulness of the person's application data. There are thousands of databases and sources for obtaining background information, including sex offender registries, workers compensation histories, nurses aid registries, and sources for criminal, employment, and educational histories.[65]

Reference Check Effectiveness   Handled correctly, background checks are an inexpensive and straightforward way of verifying factual information (such as current and previous job titles) about applicants. However, reference checking can also backfire. For one thing, it is not easy for the reference to prove that the bad reference he or she gave an applicant was warranted. The rejected applicant thus has various legal remedies, including suing the reference for defamation of character, a fact that can understandably inhibit former employers and supervisors from giving candid references.[66] In one case, for instance, a man was awarded $56,000 after being turned down for a job because, among other things, he was called a "character" by a former employer.

It is not just the fear of legal reprisal that can lead to a useless or misleading reference. Many supervisors don't want to diminish a former employee's chances for a job. Others might rather give an incompetent employee good reviews if it will get rid of him or her. Even when checking references via the phone, therefore, you have to be careful to ask the right questions, and to judge whether the reference's answers are evasive and, if so, why.

Making Reference Checks More Productive   You can do several things to make your reference checking more productive. First, use a structured form as in Figure 4.9. The form helps ensure that you don't overlook important questions. Second, use the references offered by the applicant as merely a source for other references who may know of the applicant's performance. Thus, you might ask each of the applicant's references, "Could you please give me the name of another person who might be familiar with the applicant's performance?" In that way, you begin getting information from references who may be more objective because they weren't referred directly by the applicant. Some experts suggest contacting at least two superiors, two peers, and two subordinates from each job previously held by the candidate to form a reliable picture of the candidate.[67] Also, ask open-ended questions, such as "How much structure does the applicant need in his or her work?" in order to get the references to talk more about the candidate.[68]

Companies fielding requests for references should ensure that only authorized managers give them. Employees have taken legal action for defamatory references. There are even companies that, for a small fee, will call former employers on behalf of former employees who believe they're getting bad references from their former

Figure 4.9 Telephone or Personal Interview Form

TELEPHONE OR PERSONAL INTERVIEW

☐ FORMER EMPLOYER
☐ CHARACTER REFERENCE

COMPANY _____ ADDRESS _____ PHONE _____

NAME OF PERSON
CONTACTED _____ POSITION
OR TITLE _____

1. I WISH TO VERIFY SOME FACTS GIVEN BY
   (MISS, MRS., MS., MR.) _____

   WHO IS APPLYING FOR EMPLOYMENT WITH OUR FIRM.
   WHAT WERE THE DATES OF HIS/HER EMPLOYMENT BY
   YOUR COMPANY?   FROM _____ TO _____

2. WHAT WAS THE NATURE OF HIS/HER JOB?   AT START _____

   AT LEAVING _____

3. HE/SHE STATES THAT HE/SHE WAS EARNING $
   WHEN HE/SHE LEFT. IS THAT CORRECT?   YES   NO $ _____

4. WHAT DID HIS/HER SUPERIORS THINK OF HIM/HER? _____

   WHAT DID HIS/HER SUBORDINATES THINK OF HIM/HER? _____

5. DID HE/SHE HAVE SUPERVISORY RESPONSIBILITY?   YES   NO _____

   (IF YES) HOW DID HE/SHE CARRY IT OUT? _____

6. HOW HARD DID HE/SHE WORK? _____

7. HOW DID HE/SHE GET ALONG WITH OTHERS? _____

8. HOW WAS HIS/HER ATTENDANCE RECORD?   PUNCTUALITY? _____

9. WHAT WERE HIS/HER REASONS FOR LEAVING? _____

10. WOULD YOU REHIRE HIM/HER? (IF NO) WHY?   YES   NO _____

11. DID HE/SHE HAVE ANY DOMESTIC, FINANCIAL, OR
    PERSONAL TROUBLE WHICH INTERFERED WITH
    HIS/HER WORK?   YES   NO _____

12. DID HE/SHE DRINK OR GAMBLE TO EXCESS?   YES   NO _____

13. WHAT ARE HIS/HER STRONG POINTS? _____

14. WHAT ARE HIS/HER WEAK POINTS? _____

REMARKS: _____

Source: Adapted by permission of the publisher from *Book of Employment Forms,* American Management Association.

employers. One supervisor, describing a former city employee, reportedly "used swear words, said he was incompetent and said that he almost brought the city down on its knees."[69] There are reportedly now "dozens" of reference checking firms like Allison & Taylor Reference Checking Inc. in Jamestown, New York, doing this sort of work.[70] Some suggested reference checking questions are summarized in Figure 4.10.

Figure 4.10
Reference
Checking
Questions

Reference Checking Questions

Just the facts
What were the candidate's dates of employment?
What was the candidate's title?
What were the candidate's general responsibilities?
What is your relationship to the candidate (peer, subordinate, superior)?
How long have you known the candidate?

On the job
How would you describe the overall quality of the candidate's work? Can you give me some examples?
(For superiors) What areas of performance did you have to work on?
What would you say are the candidate's strengths?
What would you say are the candidate's weaknesses?
How would you compare the candidate's work to the work of others who performed the same job?
What kind of environment did the candidate work in?
How much of a contribution do you think the candidate made to your company or department?
How would you describe the candidate's ability to communicate?
How does the candidate handle pressure/deadlines?
How well does the candidate get along with co-workers?
How well does the candidate get along with managers?
How well does the candidate supervise others? Can you give me your impressions of his/her management style? Describe the candidate's success in motivating subordinates.
How does the candidate handle conflict situations?
Based on the candidate's performance with your company, do you think he/she would be good in the type of position we're considering him/her for?
What motivates the candidate? How ambitious is he/she?

The bottom line
Why did the candidate leave your company?
Would you rehire this person?
Would you recommend this candidate for this type of position?
What type of work is the candidate ideally suited for?
Were there any serious problems with the candidate that we need to be aware of before making a hiring decision?
Do you have any additional information to share with us about the candidate?

Source: Reprinted with the permission of *HR Magazine,* published by the Society for Human Resource Management, Alexandria, VA.

There are several other things you can do to screen out undesirables. Always get at least two forms of identification and always require applicants to fill out a job application. Always compare the application to the résumé (people tend to be more creative on their résumés than on their application forms, where they must certify the information).[71]

Using Preemployment Information Services   Computer databases have made it easier to check background information about candidates. As a result, numerous employment screening services such as Hirecheck (see www.hirecheck.com) now use databases to conduct background checks for employers. They access dozens of databases, by county, to quickly compile background information for employers.

Although they are valuable, use such services with caution. Perhaps most importantly the manager should make sure the screening service does not ensnare it by taking any actions that run afoul of EEO laws. As discussed in Chapter 2, numerous equal employment laws discourage or prohibit using unfairly discriminatory information in employee hiring. For example, under the Americans with Disabilities Act, employers should avoid preemployment inquiries into the existence, nature, or severity of a disability. In choosing a screening firm to use, the employer should make sure the firm requires an applicant-signed release authorizing the background check, complies with relevant laws such as the Fair Credit Reporting Act, and uses only legal data sources. A basic criminal check might cost $25, while a comprehensive background check costs about $200.[72]

Honesty Testing

Polygraph Tests   The polygraph (or "lie detector") machine is a device that measures physiological changes such as increased perspiration. The assumption is that such changes reflect changes in the emotional stress that accompanies lying. The usual procedure is for an applicant or current employee to be attached to the machine with painless electronic probes. He or she is then asked a series of neutral questions by the polygraph expert. Once the person's emotional reactions to giving truthful answers to neutral questions has been ascertained, questions such as "Have you ever taken anything without paying for it?" can be asked. In theory, the expert can determine with some accuracy whether the applicant is lying.

Complaints about offensiveness as well as grave doubts about the polygraph's accuracy culminated in signing the Employee Polygraph Protection Act into law in 1988. With few exceptions, the law prohibits most employers from conducting polygraph examinations of all applicants and most employees. Even in the case of ongoing investigations of theft, the employer's right to use polygraphs is quite limited under the act.[73]

Paper-and-Pencil Honesty Tests   The virtual elimination of the polygraph as a screening device triggered a burgeoning market for other types of honesty testing devices. Paper-and-pencil honesty tests are psychological tests designed to predict job applicants' proneness to dishonesty and other forms of counterproductivity.[74] Most of these tests measure attitudes regarding things such as tolerance of others

Ask blunt questions.[75] Within the bounds of legality, you can ask very direct questions in the face-to-face interview. For example, says one expert, there is nothing wrong with asking the applicant, "Have you ever stolen anything from an employer?" Other questions to ask include "Have you recently held jobs other than those listed on your application?" "Have you ever been fired or asked to leave a job?" "What reasons would past supervisors give if they were asked why they let you go?" "Have past employers ever disciplined you or warned you about absences or lateness?" "Is any information on your application misrepresented or falsified?"

Listen, rather than talk. Allow the applicant to do the talking so you can learn as much as possible about the person.

Ask for a credit check. Include a clause in your application form that gives you the right to certain background checks on the applicant, including credit checks and motor vehicle reports.

Check all references. Rigorously pursue employment and personal references.

Consider using a paper-and-pencil test. Consider utilizing paper-and-pencil honesty tests and psychological tests as part of your honesty screening.

Test for drugs. Devise a drug testing program and give each applicant a copy of the policy.

Conduct searches. Establish a search-and-seizure policy. Give each applicant a copy of the policy and require each to return a signed copy. The policy should state that all lockers, desks, and similar property remain the property of the company and may be inspected routinely.

Use caution. Being rejected for dishonesty carries with it more stigma than does being rejected for, say, poor mechanical comprehension. Furthermore, some states, including Massachusetts and Rhode Island, limit the use of paper-and-pencil honesty tests. Therefore, ensure that you are protecting your candidates' and employees' rights to privacy and that you are adhering to the law in using honesty tests.

who steal, acceptance of rationalizations for theft, and admission of theft-related activities.

Psychologists initially raised concerns about the proliferation of paper-and-pencil honesty tests, but studies do tend to support these tests' validity.[76] One study focused on 111 employees hired by a major retail convenience store chain to work at convenience store or gas station outlet counters.[77] "Shrinkage" was estimated to equal 3% of sales, and internal theft was believed to account for much of this. The researchers found that scores on an honesty test successfully predicted theft, as measured by termination for theft. One large-scale review of the use of such tests for measuring honesty, integrity, conscientiousness, dependability, trustworthiness, and reliability recently concluded that the "pattern of findings" regarding the usefulness of such tests "continues to be consistently positive."[78]

In practice, detecting dishonest candidates involves not just paper-and-pencil tests but also a comprehensive screening procedure including reference checking and interviews. One expert suggests the steps presented in the *HR in Practice* box.

Graphology

The use of graphology (handwriting analysis) is based on the assumption that the writer's basic personality traits will be expressed in his or her handwriting. Handwriting analysis thus has some resemblance to projective personality tests.

Although some writers estimate that more than 1,000 U.S. companies use handwriting analysis to assess applicants for certain strategic positions, the validity of handwriting analysis is questionable, to say the least.[79] In general, the evidence suggests that graphology does not predict job performance.[80]

Physical Examinations

Physical examinations are often the next step in the selection process, and there are several reasons for requiring them. Such exams can confirm that the applicant qualifies for the physical requirements of the position and can unearth any medical limitations that should be taken into account in placing the applicant. The examination can also detect communicable diseases that may be unknown to the applicant. Under the ADA, a person with a disability can't be rejected for the job if he or she is otherwise qualified and if the person could perform the essential job functions with reasonable accommodation. According to the ADA, a medical exam is permitted during the period between the job offer and commencement of work, but only if such exams are standard practice for all applicants for that job category.[81]

Drug Screening

Drug abuse is a serious problem at work.[82] The U.S. Chamber of Commerce estimates that employee drug and alcohol use costs U.S. employers more than $60 billion each year in reduced productivity, increased accidents, increased sick benefits, and higher workers' compensation claims.[83]

Employers are therefore increasingly conducting drug tests. The most common practice is to test new applicants just before they are formally hired. Many firms also test current employees when there is reason to believe an employee has been using drugs after a work accident, or in the face of obvious behavioral symptoms or of chronic lateness or high absenteeism. Some firms administer drug tests on a random or periodic basis, while others do so only when transferring or promoting an employee.[84] Virtually all (96%) employers that conduct such tests use urine sampling.[85] Unfortunately, drug testing in general doesn't always correlate very closely with actual impairment levels.[86] Although Breathalyzers and blood tests for alcohol such as those given at the roadside to inebriated drivers correlate closely with impairment levels, urine and blood tests for other drugs only indicate whether the drug residues are present. They cannot measure impairment or, for that matter, habituation or addiction.[87]

Drug testing therefore raises several issues. Without strong evidence linking blood or urine drug levels to impairment, some argue that drug testing violates citizens' rights to privacy and due process, and that the procedures themselves are degrading and intrusive. Others argue that workplace drug testing might identify one's use of drugs during leisure hours, but have little or no relevance to the job itself.[88] Furthermore, as one attorney writes, "It is not uncommon for employees to claim that drug tests violate their rights to privacy under common law or, in some states, a state statutory or constitutional provision."[89]

In fact, it is not clear that drug testing improves either safety or performance. At least one study, reported by a committee of the National Academy of Sciences, concluded that other than alcohol, there is no clear evidence that drugs diminish safety or job performance.[90] Another study, conducted in three hotels, concluded that preemployment drug testing seemed to have little or no effect on workplace accidents. However, a combination of preemployment and random ongoing testing was associated with a significant reduction in workplace accidents.[91]

Several federal laws have direct relevance for workplace drug testing. Under the ADA, courts might well view a former drug user (one who no longer uses illegal drugs and successfully completed or is participating in a rehabilitation program) as a qualified applicant with a disability.[92] U.S. Department of Transportation workplace regulations require firms with more than 50 eligible employees in transportation industries to conduct alcohol testing on workers with sensitive or safety-related jobs. These include mass-transit workers, air traffic controllers, train crews, and school bus drivers.[93]

What should you do when a candidate tests positive? Most companies do not hire such candidates, and a few immediately fire current employees whose test results are positive.[94] However, current employees have more legal recourse if dismissed and must therefore be told the reason for their dismissal if they are dismissed for a positive drug test.[95] But, particularly where safety-sensitive jobs are concerned, courts appear to side with employers. In one case, for instance, the U.S. Court of Appeals for the First Circuit (which includes Maine, Massachusetts, New Hampshire, Rhode Island, and Puerto Rico) ruled that Exxon acted properly in firing a truck driver who failed a drug test. Exxon Corporation's drug-free workplace program included random testing of employees in safety-sensitive jobs. In this case, the employee drove a tractor trailer carrying 12,000 gallons of flammable motor fuel and tested positive for cocaine; Exxon discharged him. The union representing the employee challenged the firing, an arbitrator reduced the penalty to a two-month suspension, and the appeals court reversed the arbitrator's decision and ruled that the employer acted properly in firing the truck driver, given the safety-sensitiveness of the job.[96]

Complying with the Immigration Law

Under the Immigration Reform and Control Act of 1986, people hired in the United States must prove that they are eligible to be employed in the United States. A person does not have to be a U.S. citizen to be employed under this act. However, employers should ask a candidate who is about to be hired whether he or she is a U.S. citizen or an alien lawfully authorized to work in the United States.

There are two basic ways prospective employees can show their eligibility for employment. One is to show a document such as a U.S. passport or alien registration card with photograph that proves both identity and employment eligibility. However, many prospective employees do not have either of these documents. Therefore, the other way to verify employment eligibility is to see a document that proves the person's identity, along with a separate document showing the person's employment eligibility, such as a work permit.

Employers run the risk of accepting fraudulent documents, and here they can protect themselves in several ways. Systematic background checks are the most obvious. Preemployment screening should include employment verification, criminal record checks, drug screens, and reference checks. You can verify Social Security cards by calling the Social Security Administration. Employers can avoid accusations of discrimination by verifying the documents of all applicants, not just those they think may be suspicious.[97]

Employers cannot and should not use the I-9 Employment Eligibility Verification form required to document eligibility to discriminate in any way based on race or country of national origin. For example, the requirement to verify eligibility does not provide any basis to reject an applicant just because he or she is a foreigner, or not a U.S. citizen, or an alien residing in the United States, as long as that person can prove his or her identity and employment eligibility.

REVIEW

Summary

1. In this chapter we discuss several techniques for screening and selecting job candidates: The first is testing.

2. Test validity answers the question What does this test measure? Criterion validity means demonstrating that those who do well on the test do well on the job. Content validity is demonstrated by showing that the test constitutes a fair sample of the content of the job.

3. As used by psychologists, the term *reliability* always means "consistency." One way to measure reliability is to administer the same (or equivalent) tests to the same people at two different points in time. Or you could focus on internal consistency, comparing the responses to roughly equivalent items on the same test.

4. There are many types of personnel tests in use, including intelligence tests, tests of physical skills, tests of achievement, aptitude tests, interest inventories, and personality tests.

5. Under equal opportunity legislation, an employer may have to prove that his or her tests are predictive of success or failure on the job. This usually requires a predictive validation study, although other means of validation are often acceptable.

6. Management assessment centers are screening devices that expose applicants to a series of real-life exercises. Performance is observed and assessed by experts, who then check their assessments by observing the participants when they are back at their jobs. Examples of such real-life exercises include a simulated business game, an in-basket exercise, and group discussions.

7. Several factors and problems can undermine the usefulness of an interview: making premature decisions, letting unfavorable information predominate, not knowing the requirements of the job, being under pressure to hire, not allowing for the candidate order effect, and nonverbal behavior.

8. The five steps in the interview include plan, establish rapport, question the candidate, close the interview, and review the data.

9. Once you've selected and hired your new employees, they must be trained. We turn to training in the following chapter.

KEY TERMS

- test validity
- criterion validity
- content validity
- reliability
- management assessment centers
- interview

DISCUSSION QUESTIONS AND EXERCISES

1. Explain what is meant by *reliability* and *validity*. What is the difference between them? In what respects are they similar?
2. Write a short essay discussing some of the ethical and legal considerations in testing.
3. Working individually or in groups, contact the publisher of a standardized test such as the SAT and obtain written information regarding the test's validity and reliability. Present a short report in class discussing what the test is supposed to measure and the degree to which you think the test does what it is supposed to do, based on the reported validity and reliability scores.
4. Give some examples of how interest inventories could be used to improve employee selection. In doing so, suggest several examples of occupational interests that you believe might predict success in various occupations, including college professor, accountant, and computer programmer.
5. Why is it important to conduct preemployment background investigations? How would you go about doing so?
6. For what sorts of jobs do you think computerized interviews are most appropriate? Why?
7. Give a short presentation titled "How to Be Effective as an Interviewer."
8. Briefly discuss and give examples of at least five common interviewing mistakes. What recommendations would you give for avoiding these interviewing mistakes?

APPLICATION EXERCISES

Case Incident   The Tough Screener

Everyone who knows Mark Rosen knows he is a very tough owner when it comes to screening applicants for jobs in his firm. His company, located in a large northeastern city, provides financial planning advice to wealthy clients and sells insurance and sets up pension plans for individuals and businesses. His firm's clients range from professionals such as doctors and lawyers to business owners, who are fairly sophisticated in financial matters and very busy people. They expect accurate advice provided in a clear and expeditious manner.

Rosen has always been described as somewhat autocratic. The need to be very selective in whom he hires has led him to be extraordinarily careful about how he screens his job applicants. Some of his methods are probably beyond reproach. For example, he requires every applicant to provide a list of names and phone numbers for at least five people he or she worked with at each previous employer to be used as references. The resulting reference check is time consuming but effective.

On the other hand, given legislation including the Civil Rights Act of 1991 and the ADA, some of his other "tough" screening methods could be problematic. For example, Rosen requires that all applicants take a purported honesty test, which he found in the catalog of an office supply store. He also believes it is extremely important to check every viable applicant's credit history and workers' compensation history in order to screen out what he refers to as "potential undesirables." Unknown to his applicants, he runs a credit check on each of them and also retains the services of a firm that checks workers' compensation and driving violation histories. ■

QUESTIONS

1. What specific legal problems do you think Rosen might run into as a result of his firm's current screening methods? What steps would you suggest he take to eliminate these problems?
2. Given what you know about Rosen's business, write a two-page proposal describing an employee testing and selection program that you would recommend for his firm. Say a few words about the sorts of tests, if any, you would recommend and the application form questions you would ask, as well as other methods, including drug screening and reference checking.

Continuing Case

LearnInMotion.com: Do You Have Sales Potential?

Of all the positions LearnInMotion had to fill, none were more pressing—or problematic—than those of the company's salespeople. The job was pressing because the clock was already ticking on the uses of the company's funds. The firm was already paying over $5,000 a month in rent and had signed obligations for a wide range of other expenses, including monthly computer payments to Compaq ($2,000 a month), a phone system ($800 a month), a burglar alarm ($200 a month), advertising (required by their venture capital fund, and equal to $4,000 a month), their own salaries ($10,000 a month), high-speed DSL lines ($600 a month), phones ($400 a month), and the services of a consulting programmer ($4,000 a month). As a result, even "doing nothing" they were burning through almost $40,000 per month. They had to have a sales force.

However, hiring good salespeople was becoming increasingly difficult. Hiring people like this should have been fairly straightforward: LearnInMotion's salespeople have to sell to basically two types of customers. They have to try to get potential customers to purchase banner space or button space on LearnInMotion's various Web site pages. To make this easier, Jennifer and Mel had prepared an online media kit. It describes the Web site metrics—for instance, in terms of monthly page views, and in terms of typical user metrics such as reported age and income level. In addition to selling banner ads, salespeople also have to try to get the companies that actually produce and make available educational CD-ROMs and courses to make those courses and programs available through LearnInMotion.com. None of these are "big-ticket" sales: Because the site is new and small, they can't really charge advertisers based on the number of users who click on their ads, so they simply charge a quarterly fee of $1,500 to list courses, or place ads. Content providers also have to agree to split any sales 50–50 with LearnInMotion. The Web surfer and office manager spend part of their time scouring the Web to identify specific people as potential customers. The salespeople then contact these people, "take them through" the Web site to show its advantages and functions, and answer the potential customer's questions.

This sales job, in other words, was fairly typical, so it shouldn't have been so difficult to fill, but difficult it was. Perhaps it was because it was a dot-com, or perhaps they just weren't offering enough compensation; whatever it was, the two owners were finding it extremely difficult to hire one, let alone two, good salesperson.

Perhaps the biggest problem here was deciding which of the personable candidates who showed up actually had sales potential. Jennifer and Mel did learn a couple of interesting things about interviewing sales candidates. For example, when they asked the first what his average monthly sales had been in the past six months at his former employer, he answered, "Oh, I got the award for highest sales last month." That seemed great to Mel, until later Jennifer pointed out to him that that answer really didn't answer their question. Things got even "weirder"—to use Mel's term—when five out of six of the next sales candidates gave more or less the same answer: "I was the top producer"; "I was one of the top three producers"; "They sent me to Las Vegas for being the top sales producer"; and so on. Getting applicants to actually divulge, specifically, what their average monthly sales had been in the past six months was, as they say, like pulling teeth. Given that fact, and the relatively few sales candidates they have had, it has become increasingly obvious to the owners that basing their hiring decision solely on the person's experience is not going to work. In other words, they have to have some way to ascertain whether the candidate has sales potential, and whether he or she has the cognitive aptitude to discuss LearnInMotion's services with what were, in fact, quite sophisticated customers. They want you, their management consultants, to help them. Here's what they want you to do for them. ■

QUESTIONS AND ASSIGNMENTS

1. What would be the advantages and disadvantages to our company of routinely administering a "sales potential" test to sales candidates? Which would you suggest?

2. Specifically, what other screening techniques should our company use to select high-potential sales candidates?
3. Tell us: What have we been doing wrong, and what should we do now?

4. Create a set of situational and behavioral questions you think we should ask candidates in our interviews with them.

Experiential Exercise

Purpose: The purposes of this exercise are:

1. To give you practice in developing a structured interview form, and
2. To give you practice in using this form

Required Understanding: The reader should be familiar with the interviewing problems discussed, and with the example of the structured interview form presented in Figure 4.6.

How to Set Up the Exercise/Instructions:

1. Set up groups of four or five students. One student will be the interviewee, and the other students in the group will develop the structured interview form and, as a group, interview the interviewee.
2. Instructions for the *interviewee:* Please do not read the exercise beyond this point (you can leave the room for a few minutes).
3. Instructions for the *interviewers:* You are a business owner who has to interview a candidate for marketing manager in about an hour. Each of you knows you'd do best to use a structured interview form to guide the interview, so you're now meeting for about half an hour to develop such a form, based in part on the job description presented in Figure 3.1 (p. 69). (*Hint:* Start by listing the most

relevant abilities and then rate these in importance on a five-point scale. Then use the high-rated abilities on your interview form.)

4. As soon as you have completed your structured interview form, call in your interviewee and explain that he or she is a candidate for the job and that you (to whom the candidate will report if hired) and perhaps one or more managers will interview him or her as a group. You may tell the interviewee what his or her job summary calls for.

Next, interview the candidate, with each interviewer separately keeping notes on his or her own copy of the group's structured interview form. Each interviewer can take turns asking questions.

After the interview, discuss the following questions in the group. Based on each interviewer's notes, how similar were your perceptions of the candidate's responses? Did you all agree on the candidate's potential for the job? Did the candidate ask good questions of his or her interviewers? Did any of the interviewers find themselves jumping to conclusions about the candidate?

TAKE IT TO THE WEB

 For Internet exercises, updates to chapter material, and more, visit the Dessler Web site at

www.prenhall.com/dessler

ENDNOTES

1. Gilbert Nicholson, "Automated Assessments for Better Hires," *Workforce* 29, no. 12 (December 2000): 102–4.
2. See Rebecca Bennett and Sandra Robinson, "Development of a Measure of Workplace Deviance," *Journal of Applied Psychology* 85, no. 3 (2000): 349.
3. See, for example, Ann Marie Ryan and Marja Lasek, "Negligent Hiring and Defamation: Areas of Liability Related to Pre-employment Inquiries," *Personnel Psychology* 44, no. 2 (summer 1991): 293–319.
4. Leona Tyler, *Tests and Measurements* (Upper Saddle, NJ: Prentice Hall, 1971), p. 25.
5. Robert M. Guion, "Changing Views for Personnel Selection Research," *Personnel Psychology* 40, no. 2 (summer 1987): 199–213.
6. Anne Anastasi, *Psychological Patterns* (New York: Macmillan, 1968), reprinted in W. Clay Hamner and Frank Schmidt, *Contemporary Problems in Personnel* (Chicago: St. Clair Press, 1974), pp. 102–9.
7. Brad Bushman and Gary Wells, "Trait Aggressiveness and Hockey Penalties: Predicting Hot Tempers on the Ice," *Journal of Applied Psychology* 83, no. 6 (1998): 969–74.
8. Scott Hayes, "Kinko's Dials into Automated Applicants Screening," *Workforce* 78, no. 11 (November 1999): 71–73; Gilbert Nicholson, "Automated Assessments," 102–7.
9. Rachel Emma Silverman, "Sharpen Your Pencil," *Wall Street Journal* (December 5, 2000).
10. Sarah Gale, "Three Companies Cut Turnover with Tests," *Workforce* (April 2002): 66–69.
11. William Wagner, "All Skill, No Finesse," *Workforce* (June 2000): 108–16.
12. Cora Daniels, "Does This Man Need a Shrink?" *Fortune* 143, no. 3 (February 5, 2001): 205–6.
13. See, for example, Douglas Cellar et al., "Comparison of Factor Structures and Criterion-Related Validity Coefficients for Two Measures of Personality Based on the Five Factor Model," *Journal of Applied Psychology* 81, no. 6 (1996): 694–704; Jesus Salgado, "The Five Factor Model of Personality and Job Performance in the European Community," *Journal of Applied Psychology* 82, no. 1 (1997): 30–43.
14. Murray Barrick and Michael Mount, "The Big Five Personality Dimensions and Job Performance: A Meta Analysis," *Personnel Psychology* 44, no. 1 (spring 1991): 1–26. See also Robert Schneider, Leatta Hough, and Marvin Dunnette, "Broad-Sided by Broad Traits: How to Sink Science in Five Dimensions or Less," *Journal of Organizational Behavior* 17, no. 6 (November 1996): 639–55.
15. Charles Sarchione et al., "Prediction of Dysfunctional Job Behaviors Among Law-Enforcement Officers," *Journal of Applied Psychology* 83, no. 6 (1998): 904–12.
16. Paula Caligiuri, "The Big Five Personality Characteristics as Predictors of Expatriate's Desire to Terminate the Assignment and Supervisor Rated Performance," *Personnel Psychology* 53 (2000): 67–68.
17. Brian Niehoff and Robert Paula, "Causes of Employee Theft and Strategies that HR Managers Can Use for Prevention," *Human Resource Management* 39, no. 1 (spring 2000): 51–64. See also Andrew Vinchur et al., "A Meta Analytic Review of Predictors of Job Performance for Salespeople," *Journal of Applied Psychology* 83, no. 4 (1998): 586–97. For a sample of the employment tests available, see, for example, "Introduction to 1999 Testing and the Employee Survey Matrix," *HR Magazine* (February 1999): 153–67.
18. "Can Testing Prevent Violence?" *BNA Bulletin to Management* (November 28, 1996): 384.
19. Kathryn Tyler, "Put Applicants' Skills to the Test," *HR Magazine* (January 2000): 75–79.
20. Neal Schmitt et al., "Computer-Based Testing Applied to Selection of Secretarial Candidates," *Personnel Psychology* 46 (1991): 149–65.
21. Randall Overton et al., "The Pen-Based Computer as an Alternative Platform for

Test Administration," *Personnel Psychology* 49 (1996): 455–64.

22. For example, see Ahron Tziner et al., "A Four Year Validation Study of an Assessment Center in a Financial Corporation," *Journal of Organizational Behavior* 14 (1993): 225–37.

23. Phillip Lowry, "Selection Methods: Comparison of Assessment Centers with Personnel Records' Evaluations," *Public Personnel Management* 23, no. 3 (fall 1994): 383–94.

24. Annette Spychalski et al., "A Survey of Assessment Center Practices in Organizations in the United States," *Personnel Psychology* 50 (1997): 83.

25. Gilbert Nicholson, "Automated Assessments," 102–7.

26. Ibid.

27. Michael McDaniel et al., "The Validity of Employment Interviews: A Comprehensive Review and Meta-Analysis," *Journal of Applied Psychology* 79, no. 4 (1994): 599. See also Richard Posthuma et al., "Beyond Employment Interview Validity: A Comprehensive Narrative Review of Recent Research and Trends over Time," *Personnel Psychology* 55 (2002): 1–81.

28. Ibid., 601. See also Steven Maurer, "The Potential of the Situational Interview: Existing Research and Unresolved Issues," *Human Resource Management Review* 7, no. 2 (summer 1997): 185–201; see also Allen Huffcutt et al., "Comparison of Situational and Behavior Description Interview Questions for Higher Level Positions," *Personnel Psychology* 54 (autumn 2001): 619–44; Stephen Maurer, "A Practitioner Based Analysis of Interviewer Job Expertise and Scale Format as Contextual Factors in Situational Interviews," *Personnel Psychology* 55 (2002): 307–27.

29. Bill Stoneman, "Matching Personalities with Jobs Made Easier with Behavioral Interviews," *American Banker* 165, no. 229 (November 30, 2000): 8a.

30. "Phone Interviews Might Be the Most Telling, Study Finds," *BNA Bulletin to Management* (September 1998): 273.

31. Susan Strauss et al., "The Effects of Videoconference, Telephone, and Face-to-Face Media on Interviewer and Applicant Judgments in Employment Interviews," *Journal of Management* 27, no. 3 (2001): 363–81.

32. See, for example, M. M. Harris, "Reconsidering the Employment Interview: A Review of Recent Literature and Suggestions for Future Research," *Personnel Psychology* 42 (1989): 691–726; Richard Posthuma et al., "Beyond Employment Interview Validity: A Comprehensive Narrative Review of Recent Research and Trends Over Time," *Personnel Psychology* 55, no. 1 (spring 2002): 1–81.

33. Timothy Judge et al., "The Employment Interview: A Review of Recent Research and Recommendations for Future Research," *Human Resource Management* 10, no. 4 (2000): 392. There is disagreement regarding the relative superiority of individual versus panel interviews. See, for example, Marlene Dixon et al., "The Panel Interview: A Review of Empirical Research and Guidelines for Practice," *Public Personnel Management* (fall 2002): 397–28.

34. The validity discussion and these findings are based on McDaniel et al., "Validity of Employment Interviews," 607–10. See also Robert Dipboye, et al., "The Validity of Unstructured Panel Interviews," *Journal of Business & Strategy* 16, no. 1 (fall 2001): 35–49, and Marlene Dixon et al., "The Panel Interview: A Review of Empirical Research and Guidance," *Public Personnel Management* 3, no. 3 (fall 2002): 397–428.

35. Ibid., 608.

36. Anita Chaudhuri, "Beat the Clock: Applying for a Job? A New Study Shows That Interviewers Will Make Up Their Minds about You Within a Minute," *The Guardian* (June 14, 2000): 2–6.

37. Don Langdale and Joseph Weitz, "Estimating the Influence of Job Information on Interviewer Agreement," *Journal of Applied Psychology* 57 (1973): 23–27.

38. R. E. Carlson, "Selection Interview Decisions: The Effects of Interviewer Experience, Relative Quota Situation, and Applicant Sample on Interview Decisions," *Personnel Psychology* 20 (1967): 259–80.

39. R. E. Carlson, "Effects of Applicant Sample on Ratings of Valid Information in an Employment Setting," *Journal of Applied Psychology* 54 (1970): 217–22.

40. See, for example, T. V. McGovern and H. E. Tinsley, "Interviewer Evaluations of Interviewees' Nonverbal Behavior," *Journal of Vocational Behavior* 13 (1978): 163–71. See also Scott Fleischmann, "The Messages of Body Language in Job Interviews," *Employee Relations* 18, no. 2 (summer 1991): 161–76.

41. Tim DeGroot and Stephen Motowidlo, "Why Visual and Vocal Interview Cues Can Affect Interviewer's Judgments and Predicted Job Performance," *Journal of Applied Psychology* (December 1999): 968–84.

42. David Caldwell and Jerry Burger, "Personality Characteristics of Job Applicants and Success in Screening Interviews," *Personnel Psychology* 51 (1998): 119–36.

43. Amy Kristof-Brown et al., "Applicant Impression Management: Dispositional Influences and Consequences for Recruiter Perceptions of Fit and Similarity," *Journal of Management* 28, no. 1 (2002): 27–46.

44. See, for example, Madelaine Heilmann and Lewis Saruwatari, "When Beauty Is Beastly: The Effects of Appearance and Sex on Evaluation of Job Applicants for Managerial and Nonmanagerial Jobs," *Organizational Behavior and Human Performance* 23 (June 1979): 360–70; Cynthia Marlowe, Sondra Schneider, and Carnot Nelson, "Gender and Attractiveness Biases in Hiring Decisions: Are More Experienced Managers Less Biased?" *Journal of Applied Psychology* 81, no. 1 (1996): 11–21; see also Shari Caudron, "Why Job Applicants Hate HR," *Workforce* (June 2002): 36.

45. Marlowe et al., "Gender and Attractiveness Biases in Hiring Decisions," 11.

46. Ibid.

47. Ibid., 18.

48. Heilmann and Saruwatari, "When Beauty Is Beastly," 360–72.

49. Amelia J. Prewett-Livingston et al., "Effects of Race on Interview Ratings in a Situational Panel Interview," *Journal of Applied Psychology* 81, no. 2 (1996): 178–86; see also Richard White Jr., "Ask Me No Questions, Tell Me know Lies: Examining the Uses and Misuses of the Polygraph," *Public Personnel Management* 30, no. 4 (winter 2001): 483–93.

50. Alan Huffcutt and Philip Roth, "Racial Group Differences in Employment Interview Evaluations," *Journal of Applied Psychology* 83, no. 2 (1998): 179–89.

51. Michael Miceli et al., "Potential Discrimination in Structured Employment Interviews," *Employee Responsibilities and Rights* 13, no. 1 (March 2001): 15–38.

52. "The Tables Have Turned," *American Management Association International* (September 1998): 6.

53. Williamson et al., "Employment Interview on Trial," 901; Michael Campion, David Palmer, and James Campion, "A Review of Structure in the Selection Interview," *Personnel Psychology* 50 (1997): 655–702.

54. Unless otherwise specified, the following are based on Williamson et al., "Employment Interview on Trial," 901–2.

55. Carlson, "Selection Interview Decisions," 259–80.

56. Panel Kaul, "Interviewing Is Your Business," *Association Management* (November 1992): 29. See also Nancy Woodward, "Asking for Salary Histories," *HR Magazine* (February 2000): 109–12. Gathering information about specific interview dimensions such as social ability, responsibility, and independence (as is often done with structured interviews) can improve interview accuracy, at least for more complicated jobs. See also Yoza Ganzach et al., "Making Decisions from an Interview: Expert Measurement and Mechanical Combination," *Personnel Psychology* 53 (2000): 1–20; Paul Falcone, "Five Questions," *HR Magazine* (February 2000): 129–35.

57. Catherine Middendorf and Therese Macan, "Note Taking in the Employment Interview: Effects on Recall and Judgment," *Journal of Applied Psychology* 87, no. 2 (2002): 293–303.

58. Edwin Walley, "Successful Interviewing Techniques," *The CPA Journal* (September 1993): 70.

59. "Looking to Hire the Very Best? Ask the Right Questions. Lots of Them," *Fortune* (June 21, 1999): 192–94.

60. Gretchen Spreitzner, Morgan McCall Jr., and John Mahoney, "Early Identification of International Executive Potential," *Journal of Applied Psychology* 82, no. 1 (February 1997): 6–29.

61. Seymour Adler, "Verifying a Job Candidate's Background: The State of Practice in a Vital Human Resources Activity," *Review of Business* 15, no. 2 (winter 1993): 3–8. See also James Burns Jr., "Employment References: Is There a Better Way?" *Employee Relations Law Journal* 23, no. 2 (fall 1997): 157–68.

62. Based on Samuel Greengard, "Have Gangs Invaded Your Workplace?" *Personnel Journal* (February 1996): 47–57; Carroll Lachnit, "Protecting People and Profits with Background Checks," *Workforce* (February 2002): 52.

63. Adler, "Verifying a Job Candidate's Background," 6.

64. Lachnit, "Protecting People and Profits with Background Checks," 52. See also Robert Howie and Lawrence Shapero, "Preemployment Criminal Background Checks: Why Employers Should Look Before They Leap," *Employee Relations Law Journal* (summer 2002): 63–77.

65. Ibid., 50ff.

66. For example, see Lawrence Dube Jr., "Employment References and the Law," *Personnel Journal* 65, no. 2 (February 1986): 87–91. See also Mickey Veich, "Uncover the Resume Ruse," *Security Management* (October 1994): 75–76; Mary Mayer, "Background Checks in Focus," *HR Magazine* (January 2002): 59–62.

67. Howard Fischer, "Select the Right Executive," *Personnel Journal* (April 1989): 110–14.

68. "Getting Applicant Information Difficult but Still Necessary," *BNA Bulletin to Management* (February 5, 1999): 63.

69. "Undercover Callers Tipoff Job Seekers to Former Employers' Negative References," *BNA Bulletin to Management* (May 27, 1999): 161.

70. Kris Maher, "Reference Checking Firms Flourish, but Complaints About Some Arise," *Wall Street Journal* (March 5, 2002): B8.

71. Lachnit "Protecting People and Profits," 54; Shari Caudron, "Who Are You Really Hiring?" *Workforce* (November 2002): 31.

72. Lachnit, "Protecting People," 52.

73. This is based on "When Can Workers Refuse Lie Detector Tests?" *BNA Bulletin to Management* (March 9, 1995): 73, and on the case *Lyle* v. *Mercy Hospital Anderson, DCS, Ohio*, 1995, 10 IER cases 401.

74. John Jones and William Terris, "Post-Polygraph Selection Techniques," *Recruitment Today* (May/June 1989): 25–31.

75. These are based on Commerce Clearing House, *Ideas and Trends* (December 29, 1988): 222–23. See also "Driving Integrity Through Interview," *BNA Bulletin to Management* (June 4, 1987): 184.

76. For a discussion of the earlier concerns see, for example, Kevin Murphy, "Detecting Infrequent Deception," *Journal of Applied Psychology* 72, no. 4 (November 1987): 611–14.

77. John Bernardin and Donna Cooke, "Validity of an Honesty Test in Predicting Theft Among Convenience Store Employees," *Academy of Management Journal* 36, no. 5 (1993): 1097–1108.

78. Paul Sackett and James Wanek, "New Developments in the Use of Measures of Honesty, Integrity, Conscientiousness, Dependability, Trustworthiness, and Reliability for Personnel Selection," *Personnel Psychology* 49 (1996): 821.

79. See, for example, Gershon Ben-Shakhar et al., "Can Graphology Predict Occupational Success? Two Empirical Studies and Some Methodological Ruminations," *Journal of Applied Psychology* 71, no. 4 (November 1986): 645–53.

80. Anthony Edwards, "An Experiment to Test the Discrimination Ability of Graphologists," *Personality and Individual Differences* B, no. 1 (January 1992): 69–74; George Langer, "Graphology in Personality Assessment: A Reliability and Validity Study," *Dissertation Abstracts*

International: Section B: The Sciences and Engineering 54, no. 7-B (1994): 3856.

81. Mick Haus, "Pre-Employment Physicals and the ADA," *Safety and Health* (February 1992): 64–65.

82. Discussed in Scott MacDonald, Samantha Wells, and Richard Fry, "The Limitations of Drug Screening in the Workplace," *International Labor Review* 132, no. 1 (1993): 99. See also Randall Kesselring and Jeffrey Pittman, "Drug Testing Laws and Employment Injuries," *Journal of Labor Research* (spring 2002): 293–301.

83. Ian Miners et al., "Put Drug Detection to the Test," *Personnel Journal* 66, no. 8 (August 1987): 191–97.

84. MacDonald et al., "Limitations of Drug Screening in the Workplace," 98.

85. Eric Greenberg, "Workplace Testing: Who's Testing Whom?" *Personnel* (May 1989): 39–45.

86. MacDonald et al., "The Limitations of Drug Screening in the Workplace," 102–4.

87. Ibid., 103.

88. Ibid., 105–6.

89. Ann O'Neill, "Legal Issues Presented by Hair Follicle Testing," *Employee Relations Today* (winter 1991–1992): 411–15.

90. Lewis Maltby, "Drug Testing: A Bad Investment," *Business Ethics* 15, no. 2 (March 2001): 7.

91. Frank Lockwood et al., "Drug Testing Programs and Their Impact on Workplace Accidents: A Time Series Analysis," *Journal of Individual Employment Rights* 8, no. 4 (2000): 295–306.

92. O'Neill, "Legal Issues Presented by Hair Follicle Testing," 411.

93. Richard Lisko, "A Manager's Guide to Drug Testing," *Security Management* 38, no. 8 (August 1994): 92.

94. Eric Greenberg, "Workplace Testing: Results of a New AMA Survey," *Personnel* (April 1988): 40.

95. Michael McDaniel, "Does Pre-employment Drug Use Predict On-the-Job Suitability?" *Personnel Psychology* 41, no. 4 (winter 1988): 717–29.

96. *Exxon Corp.* v. *Esso Workers Union, Inc.*, CA1#96–2241, July 8, 1997; discussed in *BNA Bulletin to Management* (August 7, 1997): 249.

97. Russell Gerbman, "License to Work," *HR Magazine* (June 2000): 151–60.

Chapter 5

Training and Developing Employees

- Orienting Employees
- The Training Process
- Training Techniques
- Managerial Development and Training
- Evaluating the Training and Development Effort

When you finish studying this chapter, you should be able to:

■ Describe *the basic training process.*

■ Discuss *at least two techniques used for assessing training needs.*

■ Explain *the pros and cons of at least five training techniques.*

■ Explain *what management development is and why it is important.*

■ Describe *the main development techniques.*

INTRODUCTION

*E*ngland's TV Channel 4 has two mandates—to serve minority interests, and to be on the cutting edge of TV broadcasting. Changes in TV broadcasting over the past few years—more privatization, for instance—meant big changes if it wanted to stay on the cutting edge. For one thing, its strategy had to change. Because of the new UK broadcasting act, Channel 4 had to start selling and transmitting its own commercial airtime, rather than having those duties handled by ITV, another large UK television network. In turn, this strategic change

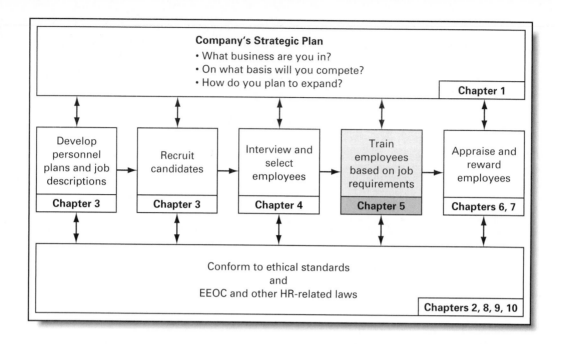

Company's Strategic Plan
- What business are you in?
- On what basis will you compete?
- How do you plan to expand?

Chapter 1

Develop personnel plans and job descriptions	Recruit candidates	Interview and select employees	Train employees based on job requirements	Appraise and reward employees
Chapter 3	Chapter 3	Chapter 4	Chapter 5	Chapters 6, 7

Conform to ethical standards
and
EEOC and other HR-related laws

Chapters 2, 8, 9, 10

meant Channel 4 had to expand its sales force and install a new high-tech control system for activities like program and commercial scheduling.[1] Strategic changes like these confronted Channel 4's management with another problem. It had to hire and train, almost overnight, all the necessary new employees—the new salespeople, information technology people, everyone. Management knew it wouldn't be able to implement its new strategy without a world-class training effort.

ORIENTING EMPLOYEES

After screening and selecting the new employees, management turns to the task of orienting and training them on their new jobs. **Employee orientation** provides new employees with the basic background information they need to perform their jobs satisfactorily, such as information about company rules. Orientation is one component of the employer's new-employee socialization process. Socialization is the ongoing process of instilling in all employees the prevailing attitudes, standards, values, and patterns of behavior that are expected by the organization and its departments.[2]

Orientation programs range from brief, informal introductions to lengthy, formal programs of a half a day or possibly more. In either, new employees usually get handbooks that cover matters such as working hours, performance reviews, getting on the payroll, and vacations, as well as a tour of the facilities. Other information might cover employee benefits, personnel policies, the employee's daily routine, company organization and operations, and safety measures and regulations.[3] (Because there is a possibility that courts will find that your employee handbook's contents represent a contract with the employee, disclaimers should be included.

These should make it clear that statements of company policies, benefits, and regulations do not constitute the terms and conditions of an employment contract, either express or implied.)

A successful orientation should accomplish four things. The new employee should feel welcome. He or she should understand the organization in a broad sense (its past, present, culture, and vision of the future), as well as key facts such as policies and procedures. The employee should be clear about what the firm expects in terms of work and behavior. And, hopefully, the person should begin the process of becoming socialized into the firm's preferred ways of acting and doing things.[4]

The HR specialist usually performs the first part of the orientation, and explains such matters as working hours and vacation. The employee then meets his or her new supervisor. The latter continues the orientation by explaining the exact nature of the job, introducing the person to his or her new colleagues, and familiarizing the new employee with the workplace.

THE TRAINING PROCESS

Training refers to the methods used to give new or present employees the skills they need to perform their jobs.

Training's focus has broadened in the past few years. Training used to focus on teaching technical skills, such as training assemblers to solder wires or training teachers to make up lesson plans.[5] Today, it might also mean remedial-education training, because quality improvement programs require employees to produce charts and graphs, and analyze data.[6] Similarly, employees today may require team-building, decision-making, and communication skills training. And, as firms become more technologically advanced, employees require training in technological and computer skills, such as computer-aided design and manufacturing.[7] This change from purely production process training helps explain why an average production worker receives about 37 hours of training per year.[8]

Training therefore plays an increasingly vital role in implementing the employer's strategic plans. As one trainer puts it: "We don't just concentrate on the traditional training objectives anymore . . . . We sit down with management and help them identify strategic goals and objectives and the skills and knowledge needed to achieve them. Then we work together to identify whether our staff has the skills and knowledge, and when they don't, that's when we discuss training needs."[9] Similarly, training today plays a key role in employers' *performance management* process. This is the process employers use to make sure employees are working toward organizational goals. It means taking an integrated, goal-oriented approach to assigning, training, assessing and rewarding employees' goal-oriented efforts.[10] Taking a performance management approach to training assumes that the training effort explicitly makes sense in terms of what the company wants each employee to contribute to achieving the company's goals.

Strategy and HR   In the UK, Channel 4's strategy has changed dramatically in the last few years. With the UK's new broadcasting act, Channel 4 had to start selling and transmitting its own air time. And that meant quickly instituting training programs to support an expanded sales force and new high-tech control system.

Management accomplished this in part by introducing a series of interactive, intranet-based e-learning training programs. Says the managing director of the company that created the programs for Channel 4, "By working closely with the HR, business affairs and ultimate rights departments at Channel 4, we have produced a series of learning programs that are high on visual impact and fit in with the culture of the channel." Employees access the training modules through Channel 4's intranet. The training programs include animated meetings that demonstrate the different scenarios employees might face on the job.[11]

The Training and Development Process

Training and development programs can be visualized as consisting of four steps, as summarized in Figure 5.1. Typically, the process results in a *training manual*. This might contain the person's job description, an outline of the training program, and a written description of what the trainee is expected to learn, as well as (possibly) several short self-tests.

Training Needs Analysis   The first step in training is to determine what training, if any, is required. Some call this the "skills gapping" process. Employers determine the skills each job requires, and the skills of the job's current or prospective employees. Training is then designed to eliminate the skills gap.[12] Assessing new employees' training needs usually involves *task analysis*—breaking the jobs into subtasks and teaching each to the new employee. Needs analysis for current employees is more

Figure 5.1   The Four Steps in the Training and Development Process

1. **NEEDS ANALYSIS**
   - Identify specific job performance skills needed to improve performance and productivity.
   - Analyze the audience to ensure that the program will be suited to their specific levels of education, experience, and skills, as well as their attitudes and personal motivations.
   - Set training objectives.

2. **INSTRUCTIONAL DESIGN**
   - Gather instructional objectives, methods, media, description and sequence of content, examples, exercises, and activities. Organize them into a curriculum.
   - Make sure all materials, such as video scripts, leaders' guides, and participants' workbooks, complement each other, are written clearly, and blend into unified training geared directly to the stated learning objectives.

3. **VALIDATION**
   - Introduce and validate the training before a representative audience. Base final revisions on pilot results to ensure program effectiveness.

4. **IMPLEMENTATION**
   - When applicable, boost success with a train-the-trainer workshop that focuses on presentation knowledge and skills in addition to training content. Then implement training program.

Source: Adapted from *HRFocus*, April 1993. Copyright © 1993 American Management Association International. Reprinted by permission of American Management Association International, New York, NY. All rights reserved. http://www.amanet.org.

complex: Is training the solution, or is performance down because the person is not motivated? Here *performance analysis* is required.

Task analysis is used for determining the new employees' training needs. Particularly with lower-echelon workers, it is common to hire inexperienced personnel and train them.[13] Your aim is to provide them with the skills and knowledge required for effective performance. How do you determine what skills and knowledge are required? Task analysis is a detailed study of the job to determine what specific skills—such as soldering (in the case of an assembly worker) or interviewing (in the case of a supervisor)—are required. The job description and job specification will provide useful information. They list the specific duties and skills required on the job and become the basic reference point in determining the training required for performing the job. Figure 5.2 summarizes methods for uncovering a job's training requirements.

For current employees whose performance is deficient, task analysis is usually not enough. **Performance analysis** means verifying that there is a significant performance deficiency and determining whether that deficiency should be rectified through training or through some other means (such as transferring the employee or changing the compensation plan).

Employers identify employees' performance deficiencies and training needs in several ways. A typical list would include:

- supervisor, peer, self-, and 360-degree performance reviews;
- job-related performance data (including productivity, absenteeism and tardiness, accidents, short-term sickness, grievances, waste, late deliveries, product quality, downtime, repairs, equipment utilization, and customer complaints);
- observation by supervisors or other specialists;
- interviews with the employee or his or her supervisor;
- tests of things like job knowledge, skills, and attendance;
- attitude surveys;
- individual employee daily diaries;
- devised situations such as role plays and case studies and other types of tests;
- assessment centers;
- and management-by-objective type evaluations.[14]

The first step is usually to appraise the employee's performance. Examples of specific performance deficiencies follow:

> "I expect each salesperson to make 10 new contracts per week, but John averages only six."
> "Other plants our size average no more than two serious accidents per month; we're averaging five."

Distinguishing between "can't do" and "won't do" problems is the heart of performance analysis. First, determine whether it's a "can't do" problem and, if so, its specific causes. For example, perhaps the employees don't know what to do or what your standards are, or there are obstacles in the system such as lack of tools or supplies. Perhaps job aids are needed, such as color-coded wires that show assemblers what wire goes where; or poor screening results in hiring people who haven't the skills to do the job; or training is inadequate. On the other hand, it might be a "won't do" problem, in which employees *could* do a good job if they wanted to. If

Figure 5.2 Tools for Uncovering a Job's Training Needs

Sources for Obtaining Job Data	Training Need Information
1. Job Descriptions	Outlines the job's typical duties and responsibilities but is not meant to be all-inclusive. Helps define performance discrepancies.
2. Job Specifications or Task Analysis	List specified tasks required for each job. More specific than job descriptions. Specifications may extend to judgments of knowledge and skills required of job incumbents.
3. Performance Standards	Objectives of the tasks of job, and standards by which they are judged. This may include baseline data as well.
4. Perform the Job	Most effective way of determining specific tasks, but has serious limitations in higher-level jobs because performance requirements typically have longer gaps between performance and resulting outcomes.
5. Observe Job-Work Sampling	Same as 4 above.

6. Review Literature Concerning the Job
  a. Research in other industries
  b. Professional journals
  c. Documents
  d. Government sources
  e. Ph.D. theses
	Possibly useful in comparison analyses of job structures, but far removed from either unique aspects of the job structure within any *specific* organization or specific performance requirements.

7. Ask Questions About the Job
  a. Of the job holder
  b. Of the supervisor
  c. Of higher management
	Inputs from several viewpoints can often reveal training needs or training desires.

8. Training Committees or Conferences	Same as 7 above.

9. Analysis of Operating Problems
  a. Downtime reports
  b. Waste
  c. Repairs
  d. Late deliveries
  e. Quality control
	Indications of task interference, environmental factors, etc.

Source: Adapted from P. Nick Blanchard and James Thacker, *Effective Training: Systems, Strategies and Practices* (Upper Saddle River, NJ: Prentice Hall, 1999), pp. 138–39.

this is the case, the manager may have to change the reward system, perhaps by implementing an incentive system.

Setting Training Objectives   After training needs have been uncovered, concrete, measurable training objectives should be set. Training, development, or (more generally) instructional objectives are "a description of a performance you want learners to be able to exhibit before you consider them competent."[15] For example:

> Given a tool kit and a service manual, the technical representative will be able to adjust the registration (black line along paper edges) on this Xerox duplicator within 20 minutes according to the specifications stated in the manual.[16]

Objectives specify what the trainee should be able to accomplish after successfully completing the training program. They thus provide a focus for the efforts of both the trainee and the trainer and a benchmark for evaluating the success of the training program. A helpful tactic is also to create, for the trainee, a perceived motivational training need, such as by illustrating with a filmed example what can go wrong if the training isn't taken seriously.[17]

TRAINING TECHNIQUES

After you have determined the employees' training needs, created a perceived need, and set training objectives, you can design, validate and implement a training program. Popular training techniques are described in this section.

On-the-Job Training

There are several types of **on-the-job training** (OJT). The most familiar is the coaching or understudy method. Here an experienced worker or the trainee's supervisor trains the employee, on the job. At lower levels, trainees may acquire skills for, say, running a machine by observing the supervisor. But this technique is also widely used at top-management levels. Some firms use the position of "assistant to" to train and develop the company's future top managers, for instance. Job rotation, in which an employee (usually a management trainee) moves from job to job at planned intervals, is another on-the-job technique. Special assignments similarly give lower-level executives first-hand experience in working on actual problems.

The Men's Wearhouse, with 455 stores nationwide, makes extensive use of on-the-job training. It has few full-time trainers. Instead, the Men's Wearhouse has a formal process of "cascading" responsibility for training: Every manager is formally accountable for the development of his or her direct subordinates.[18]

Apprenticeship Training

More employers are going "back to the future" by implementing apprenticeship training programs, an approach to training that began in the Middle Ages. Apprenticeship training is a structured process by which individuals become skilled workers through a combination of classroom instruction and on-the-job training. It is widely used to train individuals for many occupations, including electrician and plumber.[19]

Apprenticeship training involves having the learner/apprentice study under the tutelage of a master craftsman.[20] In Germany, for instance, students ages 15 to 18 often divide their time between classroom instruction in vocational schools and part-time work under the master craftsman. The apprenticeship lasts about three years and ends with a certification examination.

Several U.S. facilities of Siemens are successfully using such an approach. For example, the Siemens Stromberg-Carlson plant in Florida has apprenticeships for adults and high school students training for jobs as electronics technicians. Here, according to an observer,

> Adults work on the factory floor, receive classroom instruction at Seminole Community College, and also study at the plant's hands-on apprenticeship lab. Graduates receive Associates Degrees in telecommunications and electronics engineering. High school students spend two afternoons per week at the apprenticeship lab.[21]

Simulated Training

Simulated training is a technique in which trainees learn on the actual or simulated equipment they will use on the job but receive their training off the job. Therefore, it aims to obtain the advantages of on-the-job training without actually putting the trainee on the job. Such training is a necessity when it is too costly or dangerous to train employees on the job. Putting new assembly-line workers right to work could slow production, for instance, and when safety is a concern—as with pilots—simulated training may be the only practical alternative.

Simulated training may just take place in a separate room with the equipment the trainees will actually be using on the job. (Some therefore call it **vestibule training.**) However, it often involves the use of equipment simulators. In pilot training, for instance, the main advantages of flight simulators are[22]

- *Safety.* Crews can practice hazardous flight maneuvers in a safe, controlled environment.
- *Learning efficiency.* The absence of the conflicting air traffic and radio chatter that exists in real flight situations allows for total concentration on the business of learning how to fly the craft.
- *Money.* The cost of using a flight simulator is only a fraction of the cost of flying an aircraft. This includes savings on maintenance costs, pilot cost, fuel cost, and the cost of not having the aircraft in regular service.

Audiovisual and Distance Learning Techniques

Audiovisual techniques such as films, closed-circuit television, audiotapes, and videotapes or disks can be very effective and are widely used.[23] The Ford Motor Company uses videos in its dealer training sessions to simulate sample reactions to various customer complaints, for example.

Teletraining   Firms today also use various forms of distance learning methods for training. Distance learning techniques include the traditional paper-and-pencil correspondence courses, as well as teletraining, videoconferencing, and Internet-based classes.[24]

For example, companies today are using teletraining, through which a trainer in a central location can train groups of employees at remote locations via television hookups.[25] For example, AMP Incorporated (which makes electrical and electronic connection devices) uses satellites to train its engineers and technicians at 165 sites in the United States and 27 other countries. To reduce costs for one training program, AMP supplied the program content. PBS affiliate WITF, Channel 33 of Harrisburg, Pennsylvania, supplied the equipment and expertise required to broadcast the training program to 5 AMP facilities in North America.[26] Macy's, a New York–based retailer, has established the Macy's Satellite Network, in part to provide training to the firm's 59,000 employees around the country.[27]

In a low-tech twist to televised teletraining, some firms are successfully using the telephone. For example, Cadillac has what it calls the Craftsman's League, which is a training, testing, and motivational program for Cadillac dealers' mechanics. Employees receive Cadillac materials and service manuals regarding factory-approved service procedures and ongoing technical changes. Then, four times per year, technicians must take a phone exam on any one of eight categories, including, for instance, paint repair and electrical and mechanical systems.[28]

Videoconference Distance Learning   Videoconferencing is an increasingly popular way to train employees who are geographically separated from each other—or from the trainer. It is "a means of joining two or more distant groups using a combination of audio and visual equipment."[29] Videoconferencing allows people in one location to communicate live with people in another city or country or with groups in several other cities.[30] The communication links are established by sending specially compressed audio and video signals over telephone lines or via satellite. Keypad systems allow for audience interactivity. For instance, in a program at Texas Instruments, the keypad system lets instructors determine immediately whether trainees are learning.[31]

Given that videoconferencing is by nature visual, interactive, and remote, there are several things to keep in mind before getting up in front of the camera. For example, because the training is remote, it's particularly important to prepare a training guide ahead of time, specifically a manual the learners can use to keep track of the points that the trainer is making. Several other hints are to avoid bright, flashy jewelry or heavily patterned clothing;[32] arrive at least 20 minutes before the session is to begin, and test all equipment you will be using.

Computer-Based Training

In computer-based training (CBT), the trainee uses a computer-based system to interactively increase his or her knowledge or skills. Although simulated training doesn't necessarily have to rely on computerization, computer-based training almost always involves presenting trainees with computerized simulations, and using multimedia including videodiscs to help the trainee learn how to do the job.[33]

Consider this example of computer-assisted training, aimed at training employment interviewers to conduct correct and legally defensible interviews.[34] Trainees start with a computer screen that shows the "applicant's" employment application, as well as information about the job. The trainee then begins a simulated interview by typing in questions, which are answered by a videotaped model acting as the applicant and whose responses to a multitude of questions have been programmed into the computer. Some items require follow-up questions. As each question is answered, the trainee records his or her evaluation of the applicant's answer and makes a decision about the person's suitability for the position. At the end of the session the computer tells the trainee where he or she went wrong (perhaps in asking discriminatory questions, for instance) and offers further instructional material to correct these mistakes.

CBT programs can be very beneficial. Studies indicate that interactive technologies reduce learning time by an average of 50%.[35] They can also be very cost-effective once designed and produced: FedEx reportedly expects to save more than $100 million by using an interactive system for employee training.[36]

Training via CD-ROM, the Internet, and Learning Portals

Other types of technology-based learning are booming. Management Recruiters International (MRI) uses the firm's PC-based ConferView system (see Figure 5.3) to train hundreds of employees—each in their individual offices—simultaneously.[37] Instead of sending new rental sales agents to weeklong classroom-based training

Figure 5.3   Doug Donkin, an Instructor for Management Recruiters International (MRI), Uses the Firms ConferView System to Conduct MRI University Training. ConferView Is One Type of Videoconferencing Technology that Allows Companies to Train Hundreds of Employees Simultaneously.

Source: Courtesy of Management Recruiters International, Inc.

courses, Value Rent-a-Car now provides them with interactive, multimedia-based training programs utilizing CD-ROMs. These programs help the sales agents learn the car rental process. It does this by walking them through various procedures such as how to operate the rental computer system.[38] Polls suggest that such training technology will continue to grow in popularity. For example, one poll of 1,911 trainers found that almost 83% plan to increase their use of multimedia/CD-ROMs, 81% their use of the Internet, and 80% their use of computer-based training.[39] As another example, McDonald's developed about 11 different courses for its franchisees' employees and put the programs on CD-ROMs. The programs consist of graphics-supported lessons, and require trainees to make choices to show their understanding.[40]

Internet-based learning programs are another increasingly popular option. Many firms simply let their employees take online courses offered by online course providers such as Click2Learn.com. Others use their proprietary internal *intranets* to facilitate computer-based training. For example, Silicon Graphics transferred many of its training materials onto CD-ROMs. However, they were soon replacing the CD-ROM distribution method with distribution of training materials via its intranet. "Now employees can access the programs whenever they want. Distribution costs are zero, and if the company wants to make a change to the program, it can do so at a central location."[41]

Learning Portals   Many firms use business portals for various purposes today. Also called Enterprise Information Portals (EIPs), they are, like Yahoo!, windows to the Internet, but also much more. Through its business portal, categories of a firm's employees—secretaries, engineers, salespeople, and so on—are able to access all the corporate applications they need to use, and "get the tools you need to analyze data inside and outside your company, and see the customized content you need, like industry news and competitive data."[42]

Companies increasingly convey their employee training through such portals. Business to consumer (B2C) portals such as DigitalThink.com, Headlight.com, and Click2Learn.com contract with employers to deliver online training courses to the firms' employees. Some B2Cs are "vortals," or vertical industry learning portals; they target specific industries with relevant offerings. For example, KnowledgePlanet.com contracted with a firm called VerticalNet to create learning portals for specific industries. Other firms are creating their own learning portals for employees and customers. Called business to employee (B2E) portals, they let the company contract with specific training content providers, who offer their content to the firm's employees via the portal.[43]

Learning portals put more information into everyone's hands, when they want it. Instead of limiting training opportunities to teacher-led conventional classes or to periodic training sessions, training becomes available "24-7." Employees can learn at their own pace, when they want to.[44] The portals' built-in technology doesn't just let the employee take a course. It also often grades his or her work, tracks what courses he or she has completed, and even reminds the person what courses are scheduled when. Note, however, that while e-learning is beneficial, one study, by Michigan State University researchers, found that on-site employee education programs produced better results than online training, in terms of subsequent test results.[45] A survey by the American Society for Training and Development (ASTD) found that about 40% of responding firms devoted less than 10% of their training budgets to e-learning. Another 40% devote from 10% to 30% to it.[46]

Training for Special Purposes

Training today does more than just prepare employees to perform their jobs effectively. Training for special purposes—dealing with AIDS and adjusting to diversity, for instance—is required too. A sampling of such special-purpose training programs follows.

Literacy Training Techniques Functional illiteracy—the inability to handle basic reading, writing, and arithmetic—is a serious problem at work. By one estimate, 50% of the U.S. population reads below the eighth-grade level, and about 90 million adults are functionally illiterate.[47] One survey of 316 employers concluded that about 43% of all new hires required basic skill improvements, as did 37% of current employees.[48] This need reflects, in part, the changing nature of work. Today's emphasis on teamwork and quality requires employees to have a level of analytical skills that's impossible to attain without the ability to adequately read, write, and understand numbers.

Employers take various approaches to teaching literacy and other basic skills. The Life Skills program implemented at the Bellwood plant of Borg-Warner Automotive, Inc. is one example. Based on test scores, managers chose employee participants and placed them in three classes of 15 students each.

There were two trainers from a local training company. Each session was to run a maximum of 200 hours. However, employees could leave when they reached a predetermined skill level, so that some were in the program for only 40 hours and others stayed the entire course.[49] Classes were five days per week, two hours per day, with classes scheduled so that one hour was during the employee's personal time and the second was on company time. In this program, employees were paired so that they could help each other (for instance, someone good with decimals was paired with someone who was not). The students then helped each other through a series of timed exercises in math and reading.

Another simple approach is to have supervisors teach basic skills by giving employees writing and speaking exercises. After each exercise has been completed, the supervisor can provide personal feedback.[50] One way to do this is to convert materials used in the employees' jobs into instructional tools. For example, if an employee needs to use a manual to find out how to replace a certain machine part, teach that person how to use an index to locate the relevant section.[51] Another approach is to bring in outside professionals (such as teachers from a local high school) to teach, say, remedial reading or writing.[52] Having employees attend adult education or high school evening classes is another option.

Values Training Many training programs today are aimed at educating employees about the firm's most cherished values and at convincing employees that these should be their values as well.

The orientation program at Saturn Corporation illustrates this. The first two days are devoted to discussions of benefits, safety and security, and the company's production process—just-in-time delivery, materials management, and so forth.[53] On the third and fourth days, the focus shifts to values. Each new employee gets a copy of Saturn's mission card. Trainees and trainer then go through each of the Saturn values listed on the card—teamwork, trust and respect for the individual, and quality, for example—to illustrate its meaning. Short, illustrated exercises are used. The new employees might be asked, "If you saw a team member do this, what would you do?" or "If you saw a team member 'living' this value, what would you see?"

Diversity Training   With an increasingly diverse workforce, more firms have implemented diversity training programs. As a personnel officer for one firm put it, "We're trying to create a better sensitivity among our supervisors about the issues and challenges women and minorities face in pursuing their careers."[54] *Diversity training* refers to "techniques for creating better cross-cultural sensitivity among supervisors and nonsupervisors with the aim of creating more harmonious working relationships among a firm's employees." For example, Adams Mark Hotel & Resorts conducted a diversity training seminar for about 11,000 employees. It combined lectures, video, and employee role playing to emphasize sensitivity to race and religion.[55] After settling a huge lawsuit for race discrimination, Coca-Cola implemented an ongoing diversity training program. It includes "Leveraging the Power of People and Ideas," a new two-day diversity training course that all U.S. employees are required to attend annually. (The firm also took other steps, including appointing a diversity director, establishing a diversity advisory council, and tying management compensation to reaching diversity goals.[56])

Diversity training is no panacea, and a poorly conceived program can backfire. Potential negative outcomes include "the possibility of post-training participant discomfort, reinforcement of group stereotypes, perceived disenfranchisement or backlash by white males, and even lawsuits based on managers' exposure of stereotypical beliefs blurted out during 'awareness raising' sessions."[57]

Strictly speaking, it's probably more accurate to talk about diversity-oriented training programs than about diversity training. According to one survey of HR directors, there are several specific training programs aimed at counteracting potential problems associated with a diverse workforce. These include (from most used to least used) improving interpersonal skills, understanding/valuing cultural differences, improving technical skills, socializing into corporate culture, reducing stress, indoctrinating into U.S. work ethic, mentoring, improving English proficiency, improving basic math skills, and improving bilingual skills for English-speaking employees.[58]

Training for Teamwork and Empowerment   Many firms today use work teams and employee empowerment to improve their effectiveness. Both the team approach and worker employment are components of what many firms call **worker involvement programs** and performance improvement programs. These programs aim to boost organizational effectiveness by getting employees to participate in the planning, organizing, and general managing of their jobs.

Most employees must be trained to be good team members. For instance, Toyota devotes many hours to training new employees to listen to each other and to cooperate. Toyota's training process stresses dedication to teamwork. For example, the program uses short exercises to illustrate examples of good and bad teamwork, and to mold new employees' attitudes regarding good teamwork.

Some firms use outdoor training such as Outward Bound programs to build teamwork.[59] Outdoor training usually involves taking a firm's management team out into rugged, mountainous terrain. There they learn cooperation and team spirit, and the need to trust and rely on each other by overcoming physical obstacles. As one participant put it, "Every time I climbed over a rock, I needed someone's help."[60] An example of one activity is the trust fall, in which an employee has to slowly lean back and fall backward, perhaps from a height of 10 feet, into the waiting arms of five or 10 team members. The idea is to build trust, particularly in one's colleagues.[61]

MANAGERIAL DEVELOPMENT AND TRAINING

Management development is any attempt to improve managerial performance by imparting knowledge, changing attitudes, or increasing skills. It thus includes in-house programs such as courses, coaching, and rotational assignments, professional programs such as American Management Association (AMA) seminars; and university programs such as executive MBA programs.[62] It is estimated that well over one million U.S. managers participate in management development programs yearly[63] for a cost to industry of several billion dollars per year.[64]

The ultimate aim of such development programs is, of course, to enhance the future performance of the organization itself. For this reason, the general management development process consists of assessing the company's needs (for instance, to fill future executive openings, or to make the firm more responsive), appraising the managers' performance, and then developing the managers themselves.

Globalization and increased competitiveness mean it's more important today for leader development programs to be organizationally relevant and effective. The program should make sense in terms of the company's strategy and goals. There is typically much emphasis on clarifying a program's business purpose and desired outcomes, and linking the program more clearly to the company's mission. This means involving the top management team in formulating the program's aims, and also specifying concrete competencies and knowledge outcomes, rather than just attitudes. There is also today more emphasis on supplementing traditional development methods (such as lectures, case discussion groups, and simulations) with realistic methods like action learning projects where trainees solve actual company problems.[65] Several principles for designing leader development programs (such as "use practical, concrete content") are summarized in Figure 5.4.

Development methods (many equally useful for first-line supervisors, too) are described on the next few pages.

Managerial On-the-Job Training

On-the-job training is not just for non-supervisory employees. It is also a popular manager development method. Important techniques include **job rotation,** the **coaching/understudy** method, and **action learning.** *Job rotation* means moving management trainees from department to department to broaden their understanding of all parts of the business.[66] The trainee—often a recent college graduate—may spend several months in each department; this helps not only broaden his or her experience but also discover the jobs he or she prefers. The person may be just an observer in each department, but more commonly becomes fully involved in its operations. The trainee thus learns the department's business by actually doing it, whether it involves

Figure 5.4 The New Leadership Development

- Use practical, concrete content, not academic or theoretical.
- Structure job-related activities rather than those irrelevant to the real work of the organization.
- Use involving, emotionally engaging, action-oriented learning methods and activities.
- Create ongoing activities and short (3- to 5-day) sessions, rather than long, one-time events.
- Focus on implementation skills instead of stopping at problem-solving and decision-making skills.
- Emphasize learning that can be immediately applied instead of distant applications.
- Generate accountability on the part of participants.
- Use the most respected, talented executives of the organization. Let them coach the aspiring leaders.
- Organize groups from the same organizational level. They'll be more comfortable and will face similar issues.

Source: Jack Zenger, Dave Ulrich, and Norm Smallwood, "The New Leadership Development," *Training & Development* (March 2000): 26.

sales, production, finance, or some other function. With the *coaching/understudy* method, the new manager, of course, receives ongoing advice, often from the person he or she is scheduled to replace.

Action Learning

Action learning gives managers time to work full time on real projects, analyzing and solving problems in departments other than their own.[67] The trainees meet periodically within a four- or five-person project group to discuss their findings.

For example, several CIGNA International Property and Casualty Corporation managers spent four weeks in an action learning group.[68] The group was assigned the problem of analyzing the strategies of one of the insurance company's business units over the previous three years. Each of the four weeks was devoted to a different set of activities. In the first week, the group received training from business professors as well as a briefing from the division staff that had the business problem. In the second, they split into four teams and traveled the country interviewing about 100 of the division's employees, distributors, and customers on a one-to-one basis. In the third week, the group assimilated and analyzed the data, and in the fourth week, it formulated recommendations and wrote a 40-plus-page paper. The group presented its recommendations to the president and executive staff of the troubled division at the end of the fourth week and fielded questions from the executives.[69]

The Case Study Method

The **case study method** presents a trainee with a written description of an organizational problem. The person analyzes the case in private, diagnoses the problem, and presents his or her findings and solutions in a discussion with other trainees.[70]

The case study method has several aims. It aims, first, to give trainees realistic experience in identifying and analyzing complex problems in an environment in which their trained discussion leader can subtly guide their progress. Through the class discussion of the case, trainees also learn that there are usually many ways to approach and solve complex organizational problems. And, they learn that their own needs and values often influence the solutions they suggest.

The case study method ideally has five main features:[71] (1) the use of actual organizational problems; (2) the maximum possible involvement of participants in stating their views, inquiring into others' views, confronting different views, and making decisions; resulting in (3) a minimal degree of dependence on the faculty members; who, in turn, (4) hold the position that there are rarely any right or wrong answers, and that cases are incomplete and so is reality; and (5) who still strive to make the case study method as engaging as possible through creation of appropriate levels of drama.[72]

Integrated case scenarios expand the case analysis concept by creating long-term, comprehensive case situations. For example, the FBI Academy created an integrated case scenario. It starts "with a concerned citizen's telephone call and ends 14 weeks later with a simulated trial. In between is the stuff of a genuine investigation, including a healthy sampling of what can go wrong in an actual criminal inquiry." To create such scenarios, scriptwriters (often just creative employees in the firm's training group) create scripts. The scripts include themes, background stories, detailed personal histories, and role-play instructions. In the case of the FBI, the scenarios are aimed at developing specific training skills, such as interviewing witnesses and analyzing crime scenes.[73]

Management Games

In computerized **management games,** trainees split into five- or six-person companies, each of which has to compete with the others in a simulated marketplace. Each company sets a goal (such as "maximum sales") and can make several decisions. For example, the group may be allowed to decide how much to spend on advertising, how much to produce, how much inventory to maintain, and how many of which product to produce. Usually, the game compresses a two- or three-year period into days, weeks, or months. As in the real world, each company usually can't see what decisions the other firms have made, although these decisions do affect their own sales. For example, if a competitor decides to increase its advertising expenditures, that firm may end up increasing its sales at the expense of the others.[74]

Management games can be good development tools. People learn best by getting involved in the activity itself, and the games can be useful for gaining such involvement.

Outside Seminars

Many organizations offer seminars and conferences aimed at developing managers. The AMA, for instance, provides thousands of courses in areas such as general management, human resources, sales and marketing, and international management.

The courses cover topics such as how to sharpen business writing skills, strategic planning, and assertiveness training for managers.[75] Other organizations offering management development services include AMR International, Inc., the Conference Board, and Cornell University.

Many of these programs offer continuing education units (CEUs) for course completion. Earning CEUs provides a recognized measure of educational accomplishment, says the AMA, one that is today used by more than 1,000 colleges. CEUs generally can't be used to obtain degree-granting credit at most colleges or universities, but they provide a record of the fact that the trainee participated in and completed a conference or seminar.

University-Related Programs

Colleges and universities provide several types of management development activities. First, many schools provide continuing education programs in leadership, supervision, and the like. As with the AMA, these range from one- to four-day programs to executive development programs lasting one to four months.

Many also offer individual courses in areas such as business, management, and health care administration. Managers can take these as matriculated or nonmatriculated students to fill gaps in their backgrounds. Thus, a prospective division manager with a gap in experience with accounting controls might sign up for a two-course sequence in managerial accounting. Finally, schools offer degree programs such as the master of business administration (MBA).

Some companies have experimented with offering selected employees in-house degree programs in cooperation with colleges and universities. Many also offer a variety of in-house lectures and seminars by university staff. For example, Technicon, a high-tech medical instruments company, asked one university to offer an executive education program for its key middle managers. The coursework covered topics ranging from finance to executive communication.[76] Schools such as Duke University offer programs (like MBAs) online; some customize the programs for client companies.

Universities and corporations are also experimenting with videolinked classroom education. For example, the School of Business and Public Administration at California State University, Sacramento, and a Hewlett-Packard facility in Roseville, California, are videolinked. A videolink allows for classroom learning on campuses with simultaneous broadcasting to other locations via telephone communication lines.

Some global issues in manager development are discussed in the *Global Issues in HR* box on page 174.

Behavior Modeling

Behavior modeling involves showing trainees the right, or *model,* way of doing something, letting each person practice the right way to do it, and providing feedback regarding each trainee's performance.[77] It has been used, for example, to train middle managers to better handle interpersonal situations such as performance problems and undesirable work habits.

The basic behavior modeling procedure is as follows:

1. *Modeling.* First, trainees watch films or videotapes or disks that show model persons behaving effectively in a problem situation.
2. *Role playing.* Next, the trainees are given roles to play in a simulated situation; here, they practice and rehearse the effective behaviors demonstrated by the models.
3. *Social reinforcement.* The trainer provides reinforcement in the form of praise and constructive feedback based on how the trainee performs in the role-playing situation.

Selecting and developing executives to run the employer's overseas operations present management with a dilemma. One expert cites "an alarmingly high failure rate when executives are relocated overseas." This failure rate is usually caused by inappropriate selection and poor expatriate development.[78] Yet in an increasingly globalized economy, employers must develop managers for overseas assignments despite these difficulties.

A number of companies, including Dow and Ciba-Geigy, have developed and implemented international executive relocation programs that are successful. In addition to the general requirements for successful executive development programs previously listed, preparing and training executives for overseas assignments should also include the following considerations:

1. Choose for international assignments candidates whose educational backgrounds and experiences are appropriate for overseas assignments. For example, a person who has already accumulated a track record of successfully adapting to foreign cultures (perhaps through overseas college studies and summer internships) will more likely succeed as an international transferee.

2. Choose those whose personalities and family situations can withstand the cultural changes they will encounter in their new environments. When many of

these executives fail, it's not because the individuals couldn't adapt, but because their spouses or children were unhappy in the new foreign setting.

3. Brief candidates fully and clearly on all relocation policies. Transferees should be given a realistic preview of what the assignment will entail, including the company's policy regarding matters such as moving expenses and salary differentials.

4. Give executives and their families comprehensive training in their new country's culture and language.

5. Provide all relocating executives with a mentor to monitor their overseas careers and help them secure appropriate jobs with the company when they repatriate. (At Dow, for instance, this person is usually a high-level manager in the expatriate's functional area.) This helps to avoid the problem of having expatriates feel lost overseas, particularly in terms of career progress.

6. Establish a repatriation program that helps returning executives and their families readjust to their professional and personal lives in their home country. At Dow, for instance, the expatriate receives his or her new job assignment as much as a year before returning to the United States.[79]

4. *Transfer of training.* Finally, trainees are encouraged to apply their new skills when they are back on their jobs.

Studies suggest that behavior modeling can be very effective. For example, 160 novice computer users from the U.S. Naval Construction Battalion at Gulfport, Mississippi, were put through one of three types of training—Behavioral modeling, self-paced study, or lecturing. The researchers concluded, "Behavior modeling was clearly superior across all evaluation measures. Trainees in this condition learned more than other trainees, did best at demonstrating the skills taught in training in a hands-on test, and were most satisfied with the computer system four weeks after training."[80]

In-House Development Centers

Many firms have **in-house development centers,** which usually combine classroom learning (lectures and seminars, for instance) with other techniques such as assessment centers, in-basket exercises, and role playing to help develop employees and other managers. For example, *Fortune* magazine calls Crotonville, General Electric's (GE) Management Development Institute, the "Harvard of corporate America." The firm's management development courses range from entry-level programs in manufacturing and sales to a course for English majors called "Everything You Always Wanted to Know About Finance."[81]

For many firms, their learning portals are becoming their virtual corporate universities. While firms such as General Electric have long had their own bricks-and-mortar corporate universities, learning portals let even smaller firms have their own corporate universities, on the Web. Bain & Company, a management consulting firm, has such a Web–based virtual university for its employees. It provides a means not only for conveniently coordinating all the company's training efforts but also for delivering Web–based modules that cover topics from strategic management to mentoring.[82]

Many companies today try to avoid the "country club" atmospheres of earlier corporate universities. For example, at Boeing's Leadership Center, you won't find the golf course that often marks other such universities. And the training experience is described as "intense, but . . . one of the most useful intense experiences I've ever had."[83]

Organizational Development

Organizational development (OD) aims to change the attitudes, values, and beliefs of employees so that the employees can identify and implement changes (such as reorganizations), usually with the aid of an outside change agent, or consultant.

Action research is the foundation of most OD programs or interventions. It means gathering data about the organization and its operations and attitudes, with an eye toward solving a particular problem (for example, conflict between the sales and production departments); feeding back these data to the parties (employees) involved; and then having these parties team-plan solutions to the problems. In OD, the participants always get involved in gathering data about themselves and their organization, analyzing these data, and planning solutions based on these analyses.[84]

Specific examples of OD efforts include survey feedback, sensitivity training, and team building. **Survey feedback** uses questionnaires to survey employees' attitudes and to provide feedback. The aim here is usually to crystallize for the managers the fact that there is a problem that must be addressed. Then the department managers can use the results to turn to the job of discussing and solving it. Employee attitude surveys have been used since at least the 1930s to assess and document employee morale.[85] Their continuing wide use reflects the fact, as several researchers recently concluded, that:

> There is validity in employee reports of their experiences and these reports can be very useful as diagnoses of the degree to which a new strategy is

being implemented and the degree to which policies and practices are related to the achievement of strategic goals like customer satisfaction and customer attention.[86]

Sensitivity training aims to increase participants' insights into their behavior and the behavior of others by encouraging an open expression of feelings in the trainer-guided "T-group laboratory" (the "T" is for training).[87] Sensitivity training seeks to accomplish its aim of increasing interpersonal sensitivity by requiring frank, candid discussions in the T-group, discussions of participants' personal feelings, attitudes, and behavior. As a result, it is a controversial method surrounded by heated debate and is used much less today than in the past.[88]

Finally, **team building** refers to a group of OD techniques aimed at improving the effectiveness of teams at work. The typical team-building program begins with the consultant interviewing each of the group members prior to the group meeting. He or she asks them what their problems are, how they think the group functions, and what obstacles are in the way of the group's performing better.[89] The consultant usually categorizes the interview or attitude survey data into themes and presents the themes to the group at the beginning of the meeting. They might include, for example, "Not enough time to get my job done," or "I can't get any cooperation around here." The group then ranks the themes by importance. The most important ones form the agenda for the meeting. The group examines and discusses the issues, examines the underlying causes of the problem, and begins work on a solution to the problems.

Building High-Performance Learning Organizations

In a fast-changing world, the last thing a company needs is for new information—about competitors' actions, customers' preferences, or technological improvements—to be ignored or lost in a bureaucratic sinkhole. For years, for instance, General Motors seemed oblivious to the competitive and technological advances of its foreign competitors; it finally awoke when its board decided that too much market share had been lost. On the other hand, firms such as Microsoft and GE are traditionally quick on their feet, "adept at translating new knowledge into new ways of behaving."[90]

HR's Role in Building Learning Organizations   Firms such as GE have successfully made the leap into rebuilding themselves as learning organizations. A **learning organization** "is an organization skilled at creating, acquiring, and transferring knowledge, and at modifying its behavior to reflect new knowledge and insights."[91]

Training can help develop such skills. At Xerox, for instance, employees are trained to analyze and display data on special simple statistical charts and to plan the actions they will take to solve the problem using special planning charts.[92] GE has programs for building the skills required to perform and evaluate experiments, such as how to use statistical methods and design experiments.[93]

Providing Employees with Lifelong Learning   Employers can't build learning organizations just around managers. In today's empowered organizations, employers must also depend on first-line employees—the team members building the Saturn cars, or the Microsoft programmers—to recognize new opportunities, identify problems, and react quickly with analyses and recommendations. As a result, the need has arisen for encouraging lifelong learning, in other words, for providing extensive continuing training from basic remedial skills to advanced decision-making techniques throughout employees' careers.

One Canadian Honeywell manufacturing plant called its lifelong learning program the Honeywell Scarborough Learning for Life Initiative.[94] It was "a concerted effort to upgrade skill and education levels so that employees can meet workplace challenges with confidence."[95] It began with adult basic education. In partnership with the employees' union, the company offered courses in English as a second language, basic literacy, arithmetic, and computer literacy. Next the factory formed a partnership with a local community college. Honeywell provides in-house afterwork college-level courses to all factory employees—hourly, professional, and managerial—giving them the opportunity to earn college diplomas and certificates.[96] Employees also receive job-related training for two hours every other week. Sessions focus on skills specifically important to the job, "such as the principles of just-in-time inventory systems, team effectiveness, interpersonal communication skills, conflict resolution, problem solving and dealing with a diverse workforce."[97]

Organizational Change

Today, intense international competition means companies have to change fast, perhaps changing their strategies to enter new businesses, or their organization charts, or their employees' attitudes and values.

Major organizational changes like these are never easy, but perhaps the hardest part of leading a change is overcoming the resistance to it. Individuals, groups, and even entire organizations may resist the change, perhaps because they are accustomed to the usual way of doing things; or because of perceived threats to their power and influence; or because of the fear of the unknown; or because of what the employee sees as a violation of the unwritten "personal compact" or agreement he or she has with the company (for instance, in terms of what the employer expects from the employee and vice versa).[98]

Lewin's Process for Overcoming Resistance   Psychologist Kurt Lewin formulated a model of change to summarize what he believed was the basic process for implementing a change with minimal resistance. To Lewin, all behavior in organizations was a product of two kinds of forces: those striving to maintain the status quo and those pushing for change. Implementing change thus meant either reducing the forces for the status quo or building up the forces for change. Lewin's process consisted of three steps:

1. *Unfreezing,* which means reducing the forces that are striving to maintain the status quo, usually by presenting a provocative problem or event to get people to recognize the need for change and to search for new solutions.
2. *Moving,* which means developing new behaviors, values, and attitudes, sometimes through organizational structure changes and sometimes through the other management development techniques (such as team building).
3. *Refreezing,* which means building in the reinforcement to make sure the organization doesn't slide back into its former ways of doing things.

1. *Establish a sense of urgency.* For instance, create a crisis by exposing managers to major weaknesses relative to competitors.

2. *Mobilize commitment to change through joint diagnosis of business problems.* Next, create one or more task forces to diagnose the business problems. Such teams can produce a shared understanding of what can and must be improved and thereby mobilize the commitment of those who must actually implement the change.

3. *Create a guiding coalition.* No leader can accomplish any significant change alone. That's why most leaders create a guiding coalition of influential people who can be missionaries and implementers of change.

4. *Develop a shared vision.* Create a general statement of the organization's intended direction that evokes emotional feelings in organization members.

5. *Communicate the vision.* Use multiple forums, repetition, and leading by example to foster support for the new vision.

6. *Remove barriers to the change: Empower employees.* Accomplishing the change usually requires the assistance of the employees themselves, but sometimes this requires empowering them—in other words, removing barriers that stand in the way of their being able to actually assist in making the changes. For example, Sony's CEO removed the former studio executives and installed a new team when he set about fixing Sony's movie business.[99] Allied Signal CEO Lawrence Bossidy put all of his 80,000 employees through quality training within two years.[100]

7. *Generate short-term wins.* Maintain employees' motivation to stay involved in the change by ensuring that they have short-term goals to achieve from which they will receive positive feedback.

8. *Consolidate gains and produce more change.* As momentum builds and changes are made, the leader has to guard against renewed complacency. To do this, the leader and guiding coalition can use the increased credibility that comes from short-term wins to change all the systems, structures, and policies that don't fit well with the company's new vision.

9. *Anchor the new ways of doing things in the company's culture.* Few organizational changes survive without a corresponding change in employees' shared values. For example, if you want to emphasize more openness, camaraderie, and customer service, you as a leader must get the organization's employees to share those values. Do this by issuing a core value statement, by "walking the talk," and by using signs, symbols, rewards, and ceremonies to reinforce the values you want your employees to share.

10. *Monitor progress and adjust the vision as required.* For example, use regular surveys to monitor customer and employee attitudes.

Of course, the devil is in the details, and actually finding the right techniques that will help you accomplish each of those three steps and then using them is the difficult part. A 10-step process for leading organizational change is summarized in the *HR in Practice* box.[101]

Evaluating the Training and Development Effort

There are two basic issues to address when evaluating a training program. The first is the design of the evaluation study and, in particular, whether to use *controlled experimentation.* The second is what training effect to measure.

Controlled experimentation is the best method to use in evaluating a training program. In a controlled experiment, both a training group and a control group (which receives no training) are used. Data (for instance, on quantity of production or quality of soldered junctions) is obtained both before and after the training effort in the group exposed to training, and before and after a corresponding work period in the control group. In this way it is possible to determine the extent to which any change in performance in the training group resulted from the training itself rather than from some organizationwide change such as a raise in pay; we assume that the latter would have equally affected employees in both groups. This approach is feasible and is sometimes used.[102] In terms of current practices, however, one survey found that something less than half of the companies responding attempted to obtain before-and-after measures from trainees; the number of organizations using control groups was negligible.[103]

Training Effects to Measure

Four basic categories of training outcomes can be measured:

1. *Reaction.* First, evaluate trainees' reactions to the program. Did they like the program? Did they think it worthwhile?
2. *Learning.* Second, test the trainees to determine whether they learned the principles, skills, and facts they were supposed to learn.
3. *Behavior.* Next, ask whether the trainees' behavior on the job changed because of the training program. For example, are employees in the store's complaint department more courteous toward disgruntled customers than previously?
4. *Results.* Finally, but probably most importantly, ask What final results were achieved in terms of the training objectives previously set? Did the number of customer complaints about employees drop? Did the reject rate improve? Did scrappage cost decrease? Was turnover reduced?

Computerization is facilitating the evaluation process. For example, Bovis Land Lease in New York City offers its 625 employees numerous courses in construction and other subjects. The firm uses special learning management software to monitor which employees are taking which courses, and the extent to which employees are improving their skills.[104]

Review

Summary

1. The training process consists of five steps: needs analysis, instructional design, validation, and implementation and evaluation.

2. Vestibule training, or simulated training, combines the advantages of on- and off-the-job training.

3. On-the-job training is a third basic training technique. It might take the form of

the coaching/understudy method, job rotation, or special assignments and committees. Other training methods include audiovisual techniques, lectures, computer-aided instruction, apprenticeship training, simulated training, CD-ROM- and Internet-based training, learning portals, and special-purpose training.

4. Management development is aimed at preparing employees for future jobs with the organization, or at solving organizationwide problems concerning, for instance, inadequate interdepartmental communication.

5. On-the-job experience is the most popular form of management development.

6. Managerial on-the-job training methods include job rotation, coaching, and action learning. Case studies, management games, outside seminars, university-related programs, behavior modeling, and in-house development centers are other methods.

7. Organizational development is an approach to instituting change in which employees themselves play a major role in the change process by providing data, by obtaining feedback on problems, and by team-planning solutions. There are several OD methods, including sensitivity training, team development, and survey feedback.

8. Overcoming employee resistance is a crucial aspect of implementing organizational change. The *HR in Practice* box summarizes the organizational change process.

KEY TERMS

- employee orientation
- training
- task analysis
- performance analysis
- on-the-job training (OJT)
- vestibule or simulated training
- worker involvement programs
- management development

- job rotation
- coaching/understudy method
- action learning
- case study method
- management games
- behavior modeling
- in-house development centers

- organizational development (OD)
- survey feedback
- sensitivity training
- team building
- learning organization
- controlled experimentation

DISCUSSION QUESTIONS AND EXERCISES

1. A well-thought-out orientation program is especially important for employees (such as recent graduates) who have had little or no work experience. Explain why you agree or disagree with this statement.

2. You're the supervisor of a group of employees whose task is to assemble tuning devices that go into radios. You find that quality is not what it should be and that many of your group's tuning devices have to be brought back and reworked; your own boss says, "You better start doing a better job of training your workers."
   a. What are some of the staffing factors that could be contributing to this problem?
   b. Explain how you would go about assessing whether it is, in fact, a training problem.

3. Explain how you would go about developing a training program for teaching this course.

4. John Santos is an undergraduate business student majoring in accounting. He has just failed the first accounting course, Accounting 101, and is understandably upset. Explain how you would use performance analysis to identify what, if any, are Santos's training needs.

5. What are some typical on-the-job training techniques? What do you think are some of the main drawbacks of relying on informal on-the-job training for helping new employees become accustomed to their jobs?

6. Experts argue that one reason for implementing special global training programs is the need to avoid lost business "due to cultural insensitivity." What sort of cultural insensitivity do you think is referred to and how might that translate into lost business? What sort of training program would you recommend to avoid such cultural insensitivity?

7. Do you think job rotation is a good method to use for developing management trainees? Why or why not?

8. Working individually or in groups, contact a provider of management development seminars such as the American Management Association. Obtain copies of the provider's recent listings of seminar offerings. At what levels of managers do they aim their seminar offerings? What seems to be the most popular type of development program? Why do you think that's the case?

9. Working individually or in groups, use the definition of a *learning organization* from this chapter to discuss whether you think the college you are currently attending is or is not a learning organization. On what do you base your conclusion?

APPLICATION EXERCISES

Case Incident

Reinventing the Wheel at Apex Door Company

Jim Delaney, president of Apex Door Company, has a problem. No matter how often he tells his employees how to do their jobs, they invariably "decide to do things their way," as he puts it, and arguments ensue between Delaney, the employee, and the employee's supervisor. One example is in the door-design department; the designers are expected to work with the architects to design doors that meet the specifications. Although it's not "rocket science," as Delaney puts it, the designers often make mistakes— such as designing in too much steel—a problem that can cost Apex tens of thousands of wasted dollars, especially considering the number of doors in, say, a 30-story office tower.

The order processing department is another example. Although Jim has a specific, detailed way he wants each order written up, most of the order clerks don't understand how to use the multi-page order form, and they improvise when it comes to a question such as whether to classify a customer as "industrial" or "commercial."

The current training process is as follows. None of the jobs have training manuals per se,

although several have somewhat out-of-date job descriptions. The training for new employees is all on the job: Usually, the person leaving the company trains the new person during the one- or two-week overlap period, but if there's no overlap, the new person is trained as well as possible by other employees who have occasionally filled in on the job in the past. The training is basically the same throughout the company—for machinists, secretaries, assemblers, and accounting clerks, for example. ■

QUESTIONS

1. What do you think of Apex's training process? Could it help to explain why employees "do things their way," and if so, how?
2. What role do job descriptions play in training?
3. Explain in detail what you would do to improve the training process at Apex. Make sure to provide specific suggestions.

Continuing Case

LearnInMotion.com:
The New Training Program

"I just don't understand it," said Mel. "No one here seems to follow instructions, and no matter how many times I've told them how to do things, they seem to do them their own

way." At present, LearnInMotion.com has no formal orientation or training policies or procedures. Jennifer believes that is one reason why employees generally ignore the standards that she and Mel would like employees to adhere to.

Several examples illustrate this. One of the jobs of the Web designer (her name is Maureen) is to take customers' copy for banner ads and adapt it for placement on LearnInMotion.com. She has been told several times not to tinker in any way with a customer's logo: Most companies put considerable thought and resources into logo design, and, as Mel has said, "whether or not Maureen thinks the logo is perfect, it's the customer's logo, and she's to leave it as it is." Yet just a week ago, they almost lost a big customer when Maureen, to "clarify" the customer's logo, modified its design before posting it on LearnInMotion.

That is just the tip of the iceberg. As far as Jennifer and Mel are concerned, it is the sales effort that is completely out of control. For one thing, even after several months on the job, it still seems as if the salespeople don't know what they're talking about. For example, LearnInMotion has several co-brand arrangements with Web sites like Yahoo! This means if Yahoo! users are interested in ordering educational courses or CDs, other sites' users can easily click through to LearnInMotion. Jennifer has noticed that during conversations with customers, the two salespeople often have no idea of which sites co-brand with LearnInMotion, or how to get to the LearnInMotion site from the partner Web site.

The salespeople also need to know a lot more about the products themselves. For example, one salesperson was trying to sell someone who produces programs on managing call centers on the idea of listing its products under LearnInMotion's "communications" community. In fact, the "communications" community is for courses on topics like interpersonal communications and how to be a better listener; it has nothing to do with managing the sorts of call centers that, for instance, airlines use for handling customer inquiries. As another example, the Web surfer is supposed to get a specific e-mail address with a specific person's name for the salespeople to use; instead he often just comes back with an "information@xyz"-type e-mail address off a Web site. The list goes on and on.

Jennifer feels the company has had other problems because of the lack of adequate employee training and orientation. For example, a question came up recently when employees found they weren't paid for the July 4 holiday: They assumed they'd be paid, but they were not. Similarly, when a salesperson left after barely a month on the job, there was considerable debate about whether the person should receive severance pay and accumulated vacation pay. Other matters to cover during an orientation, says Jennifer, include company policy regarding lateness and absences, health and hospitalization benefits (there are none, other than workers' compensation), and matters like maintaining a safe and healthy workplace, personal appearance and cleanliness, personal telephone calls and e-mail, substance abuse, and eating or smoking on the job.

Jennifer believes that implementing orientation and training programs would help ensure that employees know how to do their jobs. She and Mel further believe that it is only when employees understand the right way to do their jobs that there is any hope those jobs will in fact be carried out in the way the owners want them to be. Now they want you, their management consultants, to help them. Here's what they want you to do for them. ■

QUESTIONS AND ASSIGNMENTS

1. Specifically, what should we cover in our new employee orientation program, and how should we convey this information?
2. In the HR course Jennifer took, the book suggested using task analysis to identify tasks performed by an employee. Should we use this for the salespeople? If so, what, roughly speaking, would be involved?
3. Which specific training techniques should we use to train our salespeople, Web designer, and Web surfer, and why?

Experiential Exercise

Purpose: The purpose of this exercise is to give you practice in developing a training program.

Required Understanding: You should be thoroughly familiar with the training methods discussed in this chapter, including computer-based training, vestibule training, and on-the-job training. Because you'll be developing a training program for directory assistance operators, you should read the following description of a directory assistance operator's duties.

Customers contact directory assistance operators to obtain the telephone numbers of persons whose numbers are not yet listed, whose listings have changed, or whose numbers are unknown to the customer. These operators check the requested number via a computerized video display, which then transmits the numbers to the customer. If more than one number is requested, the operator reports the first number, and the system then transmits the second to the caller. A number must be found quickly so that the customer is not kept waiting. It is often necessary to check various spellings of the same name because customers frequently give incorrect spellings.

Imagine that you are the supervisor of about 10 directory assistance operators in a small regional phone company that has no formal training program for new operators. Because you get one or two new operators every few months, you think it would raise efficiency for you to develop a new directory assistance operator's training program for your own use in your department. Consider what such a program would consist of before proceeding to your assigned group.

How to Set Up the Exercise/Instructions: Divide the class into groups of four or five students. In keeping with the procedure discussed for setting up a training program, your group should, at a minimum, go through the following steps:

1. List the duties and responsibilities of the job (of directory assistance operator) using the description provided.
2. List some assumed standards of work performance for the job.
3. Within your group, develop some assumptions about what parts of the job give new employees the most trouble (you'd normally be able to do this based on your experience as the operators' supervisor).
4. Determine what kind of training is needed to overcome these.
5. Develop a new directory assistance operators' training package that provides two things. First, provide a one-page outline showing the type(s) of training each new operator in your unit will go through. For example, you might indicate that the first two hours on the job will involve the new operator observing existing operators, four hours of lectures, etc.

   Second, in this package, expand on exactly what each training technique will involve. For example, if you are going to use computer-based training, show the content to be included. If you're going to use lectures, provide an outline of what you'll discuss.

If time permits, a spokesperson from each group can put his or her group's training program outline on the board, and the class can discuss the relative merits of each group's proposal.

TAKE IT TO THE WEB

 For Internet exercises, updates to chapter material, and more, visit the Dessler Web site at

www.prenhall.com/dessler

1. Cathy Cooper, "Connect Four," *People Management* 7, no. 3 (February 8, 2001): 42–45.

2. For a good discussion of socialization see, for example, George Chao et al., "Organizational Socialization: Its Content and Consequences," *Journal of Applied Psychology* 79, no. 5 (1994): 730–43; Blake Ashforth and Alan Saks, "Socialization Tactics: Longitudinal Effects on Newcomer Adjustment," *Academy of Management Journal* 39, no. 1 (1996): 149–78.

3. Joseph Famularo, *Handbook of Modern Personnel Administration* (New York: McGraw-Hill, 1972), pp. 23.7–23.8. See also Ronald Smith, "Employee Orientation: Ten Steps to Success," *Personnel Journal* 63, no. 12 (December 1984): 46–49.

4. Sabrina Hicks, "Successful Orientation Programs," *Training & Development* (April 2000): 59. See also Howard Klein and Natasha Weaver, "The Effectiveness of an Organizational Level Orientation Program in the Socialization of New Hires," *Personnel Psychology* 53 (2000): 47–66.

5. See, for example, Carolyn Wiley, "Training for the 90s: How Leading Companies Focus on Quality Improvement, Technological Change, and Customer Service," *Employment Relations Today* (spring 1993): 80.

6. Ibid., 81–82.

7. Harley Frazis, Diane Herz, and Michael Horrigan, "Employer-Provided Training: Results from a New Survey," *Monthly Labor Review* (May 1995): 3–17.

8. Wiley "Training for the 90s," 82. See also "Employee Training: Practices in 1995," *BNA Bulletin to Management* (November 2, 1995): 352; and "Employee Training," *BNA Bulletin to Management* (January 23, 1997): 28–29; Douglas Hotek, "Skills for the 21st Century Supervisor: What Factory Personnel Think," *Performance Improvement Quarterly* 15, no. 2 (2002): 61–83.

9. Christine Ellis and Sarah Gale, "A Seat at the Table," *Training* (March 2001): 90–96.

10. Peter Glendinning, "Performance Management: Pariah or Messiah?" *Public Personnel Management* 31, no. 2 (summer 2002): 161–78.

11. Cathy Cooper, "Connect Four," 42–45.

12. Marcia Jones, "Use Your Head When Identifying Skills Gaps," *Workforce* (March 2000): 118.

13. E. J. McCormick and J. Tiffin, *Industrial Psychology* (Upper Saddle River, NJ: Prentice Hall, 1974), p. 245. See also James C. Georges, "The Hard Realities of Soft Skills Training," *Personnel Journal* 68, no. 4 (April 1989): 40–45; Robert H. Buckham, "Applying Role Analysis in the Workplace," *Personnel* 64, no. 2 (February 1987): 63–65; J. Kevin Ford and Raymond Noe, "Self-Assessed Training Needs: The Effects of Attitudes Towards Training, Management Level, and Function," *Personnel Psychology* 40, no. 1 (spring 1987): 39–54; James Klein, "Empirical Research on Performance Improvement," *Performance Improvement Quarterly* (2002): 99–110.

14. P. Nick Blanchard and James Thacker, *Effective Training: Systems, Strategies, and Practices* (Upper Saddle River, NJ: Prentice Hall, 1999), pp. 154–56.

15. Richard Camp et al., *Toward a More Organizationally Effective Training Strategy and Practice* (Upper Saddle River, NJ: Prentice Hall, 1986), p. 100.

16. J. P. Cicero, "Behavioral Objectives for Technical Training Systems," *Training and Development Journal* 28 (1973): 14–17. See also Larry D. Hales, "Training: A Product of Business Planning," *Training and Development Journal* 40, no. 7 (July 1986): 87–92; Pamela Prewitt, "Army Job Standard vs. Training Standard," *Training and Development Journal* 51, no. 9 (September 1997): 52–53.

17. Erica Gordon Sorohan, "We Do; Therefore, We Learn," *Training & Development* (October 1993): 47–55; Melvin LeBlanc, "Learning Objectives Key to Quality Safety," *Occupational Hazards*

(January 1994): 127–28. See also Kimberly A. Smith-Jentsch et al., "Can Pre-Training Experiences Explain Individual Differences in Learning?" *Journal of Applied Psychology* 81, no. 1 (1996): 110–16.

18. Donna Goldwaser, "Me a Trainer?" *Training* (April 2001): 60–66.

19. Frazis et al., "Employer-Provided Training" 4.

20. "German Training Model Imported," *BNA Bulletin to Management* (December 19, 1996): 408. See also David Finegold and Karin Wagner, "Are Apprenticeships Still Relevant in the 21st Century? The Case Study of Changing Youth Training Arrangements in German Banks," *Industrial and Labor Relations Review* (July 2002): 667–85.

21. Ibid.

22. Kenneth Wexley and Gary Latham, *Developing and Training Human Resources in Organizations* (Glenview, IL: Scott Foresman, 1981), p. 141. See also Raymond Wlozkowski, "Simulation," *Training and Development Journal* 39, no. 6 (June 1985): 38–43.

23. Wexley and Latham, *Developing and Training Human Resources in Organizations,* 131–33. See also Teri O. Grady and Mike Matthews, "Video . . . Through the Eyes of the Trainee," *Training* 24, no. 7 (July 1987): 57–62. For a description of the use of computer-based multimedia training, see Erica Schroeder, "Training Takes Off, Using Multimedia," *PC Week* (August 29, 1994): 33–34.

24. Michael Blotzer, "Distance Learning," *Occupational Hazards* (March 2000): 53–54.

25. Mary Boone and Susan Schulman, "Teletraining: A High-Tech Alternative," *Personnel* 62, no. 5 (May 1985): 4–9. See also Ron Zemke, "The Rediscovery of Video Teleconferencing," *Training* 23, no. 9 (September 1986): 28–36; Paul Munger, "High-Tech Training Delivery Methods: When to Use Them," *Training and Development Journal* 51, no. 1 (January 1997): 46–47.

26. Joseph Giusti, David Baker, and Peter Braybash, "Satellites Dish Out Global Training," *Personnel Journal* (June 1991): 80–84.

27. "Macy's Goes 'On Air' to Inform Employees," *BNA Bulletin to Management* (May 15, 1997): 160.

28. "Cadillac Offers a Top-of-the-Line Training Program," *Personnel Journal* (February 1996): 25.

29. Michael Emery and Margaret Schubert, "A Trainer's Guide to Videoconferencing," *Training* (June 1993): 60. See also Mark Van Buren, "Learning Technologies: Can They or Can't They?" *Training & Development* (April 2000): 62.

30. Ibid., 60.

31. "Employer to Learn the Benefits of Distance Learning," *BNA Bulletin to Management* (April 25, 1996): 130.

32. These are based on or quoted from Emery and Schubert, "Trainer's Guide to Videoconferencing," 61.

33. See, for example, Tim Falconer, "No More Pencils, No More Books!" *Canadian Banker* (March/April 1994): 21–25.

34. Ralph E. Ganger, "Training: Computer-Based Training Works," *Personnel Journal* 73, no. 11 (November 1994): 51–52. See also Anat Arkin, "Computing: The Future Means of Training?" *Personnel Management* 26, no. 8 (August 1994): 36–40.

35. These are summarized in Rockley Miller, "New Training Looms," *Hotel and Motel Management* (April 4, 1994): 26, 30.

36. Ibid., 26.

37. Shari Caudron, "Your Learning Technology Primer," *Personnel Journal* (June 1996): 120–36.

38. Ibid., 130.

39. Ibid., 122.

40. Dina Berta, "Computer-Based Training Clicks with Both Franchisees and Their Employees," *Nation's Restaurant News* (July 9, 2001): 1, 18; see also Daniel Cable and Charles Parsons, "Socialization Tactics and Person-Organization Fit," *Personnel Psychology* 54 (2001): 1–23.

41. Larry Stevens, "The Intranet: Your Newest Training Tool?" *Personnel Journal* (July 1996): 27–31; see also Kenneth Brown, "Using Computers to Deliver Training: Which Employees Learn and Why?"

Personnel Psychology 54, no. 2 (summer 2001): 271–96; Jason Lewis and Dan Michaluk, "Four Steps to Building E-learning Success," *Workforce* (May 2002): 42.

42. David Kirkpatrick, "The Portal of the Future? Your Boss Will Run It," *Fortune* (August 2, 1999): 222–27. See also Cynthia Pantazis, "Maximizing E-learning to Train the 21st Century Workforce," *Public Personnel Management* (spring 2002): 21–26.

43. Tom Barron, "A Portrait of Learning Portals," www.learningcircuits.com/may2000/barron.html.

44. Eileen Garger, "Goodbye Training, Hello Learning," *Workforce* (November 1999): 35–42.

45. Brian O'Connell, "A Poor Grade for E-learning," *Workforce* 81, no. 7 (July 2002): 15.

46. Allyson Schafter, "An E-learning Survey," *Training & Development* (November 2001): 74–77.

47. Dannah Baynton, "America's $60 Billion Problem," *Training* 38, no. 5 (May 2001): 51.

48. "Skill Deficiencies Pose Increasing Problems," *BNA Bulletin to Management* (October 26, 1995): 337–38.

49. Valerie Frazee, "Workers Learn to Walk So They Can Run," *Personnel Journal* (May 1996): 115–20.

50. Ibid., 124.

51. *BNA Bulletin to Management* (December 17, 1987): 408.

52. Stephen Dolainski, "Partnering with the (School) Board," *Workforce* (May 1997): 28–37.

53. Adapted from Gary Dessler, *Winning Commitment* (New York: McGraw-Hill, 1993), Chapter 7.

54. See Joyce Santora, "Kinney Shoes Steps Into Diversity," *Personnel Journal* (September 1991): 74; see also Richard Koonce, "Redefining Diversity," *Training & Development* (December 2001): 22–32.

55. "Adams Mark Hotel & Resorts Launches Diversity Training Program," *Hotel and Motel Management* 216, no. 6 (April 2001): 15.

56. Henry Unger, "Coca-Cola Employees to Attend Diversity Training Annually," *Knight Ridder/Tribune Business News* (October 10, 2000), item 0028501d.

57. Sara Rynes and Benson Rosen, "What Makes Diversity Programs Work?" *HR Magazine* (October 1994): 64. See also Thomas Diamante and Leo Giglio, "Managing a Diverse Workforce: Training as a Cultural Intervention Strategy," *Leadership & Organization Development Journal* 15, no. 2 (1994): 13–17.

58. Willie Hopkins, Karen Sterkel-Powell, and Shirley Hopkins, "Training Priorities for a Diverse Workforce," *Public Personnel Management* 23, no. 3 (fall 1994): 433.

59. Based on Jennifer Laabs, "Team Training Goes Outdoors," *Personnel Journal* (June 1991): 56–63.

60. Ibid., 56. See also Shari Caudron, "Teamwork Takes Work," *Personnel Journal* (February 1994): 41–49.

61. Heidi Campbell, "Adventures in Teamland," *Personnel Journal* (May 1996): 56–62.

62. Lester A. Digman, "Management Development: Needs and Practices," *Personnel* 57 (July/August 1980): 45–57. See also James Cureton, Alfred Newton, and Dennis Tesolowski, "Finding Out What Managers Need," *Training and Development Journal* 40, no. 5 (May 1986): 106–7. Results of a 10-year survey show an increasingly important role for executive development in building and revitalizing corporate competitiveness. See Albert Vicere, Maria Taylor, and Virginia Freeman, "Executive Development in Major Corporations: A Ten-Year Study," *Journal of Management Development* 13, no. 1 (1994): 4–22.

63. William Kearney, "Management Development Programs Can Pay Off," *Business Horizons* 18 (April 1975): 81–88. See also Michael Hitt et al., "Human Capital and Strategic Competitiveness in the 1990s," *Journal of Management Development* 13, no. 1 (1994): 35–46.

64. According to a survey by Digman, the median percentage of executives receiving training during a typical year was 23%;

middle managers, 38%; and first-line supervisors, 20%. See also Vicere et al., "Executive Development in Major Corporations."

65. Jack Zenger, Dave Ulrich, and Norm Smallwood, "The New Leadership Development," *Training & Development* (March 2000): 22–27.

66. Dale Yoder et al., *Handbook of Personnel Management and Labor Relations* (New York: McGraw-Hill, 1958), pp. 10–27; for a review, see William Rothwell, H. C. Kazanas, and Darla Haines, "Issues and Practices in Management Job Rotation Programs as Perceived by HRD Professionals," *Performance Improvement Quarterly* 5, no. 1 (1992): 49–69.

67. Based on Nancy Fox, "Action Learning Comes to Industry," *Harvard Business Review* 56 (September/October 1977): 158–68.

68. Based on Paul Froiland, "Action Learning: Taming Real Problems in Real Time," *Training* (January 1994): 27–34. See also Gillian Cribbs, "Back in Fashion—Yet Again. Action Learning: The Perennial Attraction of Action Learning Is That Its Objective Is to Help Resolve Real-Life Situations," *The Financial Times* (May 23, 2000): 6.

69. For several other examples of action learning, see Barry Smith, "Building Managers from the Inside Out—Developing Managers Through Competency-Based Action Learning," *Journal of Management Development* 12, no. 1 (1993): 43–48; Thomas Downham, James Noel, and Albert Prendergast, "Executive Development," *Human Resource Management* 31, nos. 1 and 2 (spring/summer 1992): 95–107. See also Michael Gregory, "Accrediting Work-Based Learning: Action Learning, a Model for Empowerment," *Journal of Management Development* 13, no. 4 (1994): 41–52; Louise Keys, "Action Learning: Executive Development of Choice for the 1990s," *Journal of Management Development* 13, no. 8 (1994): 50–56; Allison Rossett, "Action Learning in Action: Transforming Problems and People for World-Class Organizational Learning," *Personnel Psychology* (winter 1999): 1100.

70. Wexley and Latham, *Developing and Training Human Resources in Organizations*, 193.

71. Chris Argyris, "Some Limitations of the Case Method: Experiences in a Management Development Program," *Academy of Management Review* 5, no. 2 (1980): 291–28. For a discussion of the advantages of case studies over traditional methods, see, for example, Eugene Andrews and James Noel, "Adding Life to the Case Study," *Training and Development Journal* 40, no. 2 (February 1986): 28–33. See also Gerald F. Smith, "Experience Is the Best Teacher: Avoiding the Pitfalls of Methodolotry," *National Productivity Review* (summer 1999): 57–65.

72. David Rogers, *Business Policy and Planning* (Upper Saddle River, NJ: Prentice Hall, 1977), pp. 532–33. See also Barra Cinneide, "The Role and Effectiveness of Case Studies: Student Performance in Case Study vs. 'Theory' Examinations," *Journal of European Industrial Training* (January 1997): 3–11.

73. Chris Whitcomb, "Scenario-Based Training at the FBI," *Training & Development* (June 1999): 42–46.

74. For a discussion of management games and other noncomputerized training and development simulations, see Charlene Marmer Solomon, "Simulation Training Builds Teams Through Experience," *Personnel Journal* (June 1993): 100–105; Kim Slack, "Training for the Real Thing," *Training and Development* (May 1993): 79–89; Bruce Lierman, "How to Develop a Training Simulation," *Training and Development* (February 1994): 50–52. Training games aren't limited to the computer-aided variety. See, for example, "Stop Playing Games," *Training & Development* (February 1999): 29–36.

75. Mona Pintkowski, "Evaluating the Seminar Marketplace," *Training and Development Journal* 40, no. 1 (January 1986): 74–77.

76. Lawrence G. Bridwell and Alvin B. Marcus, "Back to School—A High-Tech

Company Sent Its Managers to Business School—to Learn 'People' Skills," *Personnel Administrator* 32, no. 3 (March 1987): 86–91.

77. This section based on Allen Kraut, "Developing Managerial Skill via Modeling Techniques: Some Positive Research Findings—A Symposium," *Personnel Psychology* 29, no. 3 (autumn 1976): 325–61. See also Steven Simon and Jon Werner, "Computer Training Through Behavioral Modeling, Self-Paced and Instructional Approaches: A Field Experiment," *Journal of Applied Psychology* 81, no. 6 (1996): 648–59.

78. Paul Blocklyn, "Developing the International Executive," *Personnel* (March 1989): 44–47. See also T. S. Chan, "Developing International Managers: A Partnership Approach," *Journal of Management Development* 13, no. 3 (1994): 38–46.

79. This section based on Blocklyn. See also "Developing Global Executives," *BNA Bulletin to Management* 44, no. 10 (March 11, 1993): 73–74; D. Bradford Neary and Don O'Grady, "The Role of Training in Developing Global Leaders: A Case Study at TRW, Inc.," *Human Resource Management* 39, nos. 2 and 3 (summer/fall 2000): 185–93.

80. Simon and Warner, op. cit., 655

81. Thomas Stewart, "How GE Keeps Those Ideas Coming," *Fortune* (August 12, 1991): 43.

82. Russell Gerbman, "Corporate Universities 101," *HR Magazine* (February 2000): 101–6.

83. Carolyn Cole, "Boeing U," *Workforce* (October 2000): 63–68.

84. Mark Frohman, Marshall Sashkin, and Michael Kavanagh, "Action Research as Applied to Organization Development," *Organization and Administrative Science* 7 (spring/summer 1976): 129–42; Paul Shelbar, "The Seven Deadly Sins of Employee Attitude Surveys," *Personnel* 66, no. 6 (June 1989): 66–71. See also George Gallup, "A Surge in Surveys," *Personnel Journal* 67, no. 8 (August 1988): 42–43.

85. Benjamin Schneider, Steven Ashworth, A. Catherine Higgs, and Linda Carr, "Design, Validity, and Use of Strategically Focused Employee Attitude Surveys," *Personnel Psychology* 49 (1996): 695–705.

86. Ibid., 74.

87. Based on J. P. Campbell and M. D. Dunnette, "Effectiveness of T-Group Experiences in Managerial Training and Development," *Psychological Bulletin* 7 (1968): 73–104. See also Paul Sachdev, "Cultural Sensitivity Training Through Experiential Learning: A Participatory Demonstration Field Education Project," *International Social Work* 40, no. 1 (January 1997): 7–25.

88. Peter Smith, "Controlled Studies of the Outcome of Sensitivity Training," *Psychological Bulletin* 82 (1976): 597–622. See also Michael Blum and James Wall Jr., "HRM: Managing Conflicts in the Firm," *Business Horizons* 40, no. 3 (May 1997): 84–87.

89. Wendell French and Cecil Bell Jr., *Organization Development* (Englewood Cliffs, NJ: Prentice Hall, 1978). See also David M. Zakeski, "Reliable Assessments of Organizations," *Personnel Journal* 67, no. 12 (December 1988): 42–44.

90. David A. Garvin, "Building a Learning Organization," *Business Credit* (January 1994): 20.

91. David A. Garvin, "Building a Learning Organization," *Harvard Business Review* (July/August 1993): 80.

92. Garvin, "Building a Learning Organization," *Business Credit,* 21.

93. Ibid.

94. Based on Norman Nopper, "Reinventing the Factory with Lifelong Learning," *Training* (May 1993): 55–57.

95. Ibid., 56.

96. Ibid.

97. Ibid., 64. For another example, see Kevin Kelly and Peter Burrows, "Motorola: Training for the Millennium," *Business Week* (March 28, 1994): 158–60; "Some Nuts and Bolts of Lifelong Learning," *Training* (March 1994): 30.

98. Paul Strebel, "Why Do Employees Resist Change?" *Harvard Business Review* (May/June 1996): 86–92.

99. Kathryn Harris, "Mr. Sony Confronts Hollywood," *Fortune* (December 23, 1996): 36.

100. Noel Tichy and Ram Charan, "The CEO as Coach: An Interview with Allied Signal's Lawrence A. Bossidy," *Harvard Business Review* (March/April 1995): 77.

101. The 10 steps are based on Michael Beer et al., "Why Change Programs Don't Produce Change," *Harvard Business Review* (November/December 1990): 158–66; Thomas Cumings and Christopher Worley, *Organization Development and Change* (Minneapolis: West Publishing, 1993); John Kotter, *Leading Change* (Boston: Harvard Business School Press, 1966).

102. See, for example, Charlie Morrow, M. Quintin Jarrett, and Melvin Rupinski, "An Investigation of the Effect and Economic Utility of Corporate-Wide Training," *Personnel Psychology* 50 (1997): 91–119.

103. R. E. Catalano and D. L. Kirkpatrick, "Evaluating Training Programs—The State of the Art," *Training and Development Journal* 22, no. 5 (May 1968): 2–9. See also J. Kevin Ford and Steven Wroten, "Introducing New Methods for Conducting Training Evaluation and for Linking Training Evaluation to Program Redesign," *Personnel Psychology* 37, no. 4 (winter 1984): 651–66; Basil Paquet et al., "The Bottom Line," *Training and Development Journal* 41, no. 5 (May 1987): 27–33; Harold E. Fisher and Ronald Weinberg, "Make Training Accountable: Assess Its Impact," *Personnel Journal* 67, no. 1 (January 1988): 73–75; Timothy Baldwin and J. Kevin Ford, "Transfer of Training: A Review and Directions for Future Research," *Personnel Psychology* 41, no. 1 (spring 1988): 63–105; Anthony Montebello and Maurine Haga, "To Justify Training, Test, Test Again," *Personnel Journal* 73, no. 1 (January 1994): 83–87; Pamela Kidder and Janice Rouiller, "Evaluating the Success of a Large-Scale Training Effort," *National Productivity Review* 16, no. 2 (1997): 79–89.

104. Todd Raphel, "What Learning Management Reports Do for You," *Workforce* 80, no. 6 (June 2001): 56–58.

Chapter 6

Performance Management and Appraisal

- Basic Concepts in Performance Management
- An Introduction to Appraising Performance
- Basic Appraisal Methods
- The Appraisal Feedback Interview
- Toward More Effective Appraisals
- Performance and Career Management

When you finish studying this chapter, you should be able to:

- Explain *the purpose of performance appraisal.*
- Answer *the question Who should do the appraising?*
- Discuss *the pros and cons of at least eight performance appraisal methods.*
- Explain *how to conduct an appraisal feedback interview.*

INTRODUCTION

*W*hen Jacques Nasser began his short stint as CEO of Ford Motor Company some years ago, he didn't want to just make Ford the world's best car company; he wanted it to be one of the world's best companies of any kind. He pursued that strategy with enormous intensity. He reorganized Ford, eliminated layers of bureaucracy, promoted non-Americans to prominent positions, brought in new executives from outside the industry, and initiated dozens of quality improvement and similar programs. However, he knew that to make the firm world class he also had to make it clear to employees that he would not tolerate poor performance. He therefore needed a new, more intense way of

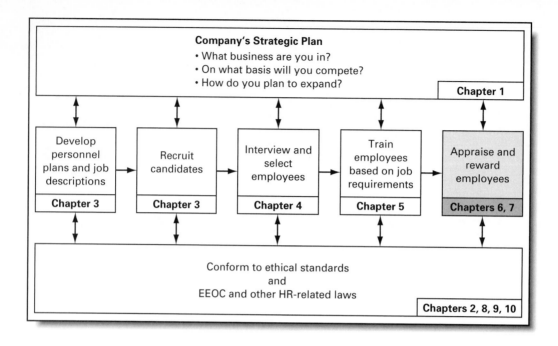

Company's Strategic Plan
• What business are you in?
• On what basis will you compete?
• How do you plan to expand?
Chapter 1

Develop personnel plans and job descriptions	Recruit candidates	Interview and select employees	Train employees based on job requirements	Appraise and reward employees
Chapter 3	Chapter 3	Chapter 4	Chapter 5	Chapters 6, 7

Conform to ethical standards and EEOC and other HR-related laws
Chapters 2, 8, 9, 10

evaluating Ford's 18,000 managers to help make his high performance strategy a reality. What appraisal method should he use?

BASIC CONCEPTS IN PERFORMANCE MANAGEMENT

Performance appraisal means evaluating an employee's current and/or past performance relative to his or her performance standards. Although "appraising performance" usually brings to mind specific appraisal tools such as the teaching appraisal form in Figure 6.1, the actual forms are only part of the appraisal process. Appraising performance also assumes that performance standards have been set, and also that you'll give the employee feedback and incentives to help him or her eliminate performance deficiencies or continue to perform above par.

The idea that appraisals are just one element in the process of improving employee performance is nothing new. However, managers generally take the integrated nature of that process—of setting goals, training employees, and then appraising and rewarding them—much more seriously today than they have in the past. They call the whole, integrated process **performance management.** This is the process through which companies ensure that employees are working toward organizational goals, and includes practices through which the manager defines the employee's goals and work, develops the employee's skills and capabilities, evaluates the person's goal-directed behavior, and then rewards him or her in a fashion that hopefully makes sense both in terms of the company's needs and the person's career aspirations.[1] The idea is to make sure that these elements are internally

Figure 6.1 Departmental
Teaching Appraisal Form

Evaluating Faculty for Promotion and Tenure

Classroom Teaching Appraisal by Students

Teacher_____ Course _____

Term _____ Academic Year_____

Thoughtful student appraisal can help improve teaching effectiveness. This questionnaire is designed for that purpose, and your assistance is appreciated. Please do not sign your name.

Use the back of this form for any further comments you might want to express; use numbers 10, 11, and 12 for any additional questions that you might like to add.

Directions: Rate your teacher on each item, giving the highest scores for exceptional performances and the lowest scores for very poor performances. Place in the blank space before each statement the rating that most closely expresses your view.

Excep- tional			Moder- ately Good			Very Poor	Don't Know
7	6	5	4	3	2	1	X

_____ 1. How do you rate the agreement between course objectives and lesson assignments?

_____ 2. How do you rate the planning, organization, and use of class periods?

_____ 3. Are the teaching methods and techniques employed by the teacher appropriate and effective?

_____ 4. How do you rate the competence of the instructor in the subject?

_____ 5. How do you rate the interest of the teacher in the subject?

_____ 6. Does the teacher stimulate and challenge you to think and to question?

_____ 7. Does he or she welcome differing points of view?

_____ 8. Does the teacher have a personal interest in helping you in and out of class?

_____ 9. How would you rate the fairness and effectiveness of the grading policies and procedures of the teacher?

_____ 10. Considering all the above items, what is your overall rating of this teacher?

_____ 11. How would you rate this teacher in comparison with all others you have had in the college or university?

Source: Reprinted with permission from *Evaluating Faculty for Promotion and Tenure,* by Richard I. Miller, pp. 164–65. Copyright © 1987 Jossey-Bass, Inc., Publishers. All rights reserved. This permission is used by permission of John Wiley & Sons, Inc.

consistent, and that they all make sense in terms of what the company wants to achieve.

The increasing popularity of taking a performance management approach reflects several things. It reflects, first, the popularity of the total quality management (TQM) concepts advocated several years ago by management experts like W. Edwards Deming. Basically, Deming argued that all the business's functions and processes including design, planning, production, distribution, and field service should focus on maximizing customer satisfaction through continuous improvement.[2] TQM proponents like Deming generally argued for eliminating performance appraisals.[3] They said that the organization is a system of interrelated parts, and that an employee's performance is more a function of things like training, communication, tools, and supervision than of his or her own motivation. Today's performance management approach reflects managers' attempts to more explicitly recognize the interrelated nature of the factors that influence employee performance. And, it reflects the emphasis managers necessarily place today on fostering high-performance goal-directed efforts in a globally competitive world.

Defining the Employee's Goals and Work Efforts

At the heart of performance management is the idea that the employee's efforts should be goal directed.[4] On the one hand, the manager should appraise the employee based on how that person did with respect to achieving the specific standards by which he or she expected to be measured. On the other hand, the manager should make sure that the employee's goals and performance standards make sense in terms of the company's broader goals. Ideally, in any company, there is a hierarchy of goals. Top management's goals—say, to double sales—imply subordinate goals for each manager and employee down the chain of command. If Nasser wanted to boost Ford's output by 40% in three years, his production managers might have to each boost output by 10 cars per employee-hour each year, to achieve that 40% output gain.

As you can see, clarifying what you expect from your employee is trickier than it may appear. Employers usually write job descriptions, but the descriptions rarely include specific goals. All sales managers in the firm might have the same job description, for instance. Your sales manager's job description may list duties such as "supervise sales force" and "be responsible for all phases of marketing the division's products," but you may also expect your sales manager to personally sell at least $600,000 worth of products per year by handling the division's two largest accounts; to keep the sales force happy; and to keep customers away from the executives (including you).[5] Unfortunately, some supervisors tend to be lax when it comes to setting specific goals for their employees. They then wonder why they have problems managing those employees' performance.

You therefore have to quantify your expectations. The most straightforward way to do this (for the sales manager job, for instance) is to set measurable standards for each expectation. You might measure the "personal selling" activity in terms of how many dollars of sales the manager is to generate personally. Perhaps measure "keeping the sales force happy" in terms of turnover (on the assumption that less than 10%

of the sales force will quit in any given year if morale is high). The point is that employees should always know ahead of time how and on what basis you're going to appraise them.[6] You can't expect them to manage their own performance if they don't know quantitatively how you expect them to perform.

Effective Goal Setting

Setting goals is one thing; setting effective goals is another. One way to think of this is to remember that the goals you set should be "SMART." They are *specific*, and clearly state the desired results. They are *measurable*, and answer the question How much? They are *attainable*. They are *relevant*, and clearly derive from what the manager and company want to achieve. And, they are *timely*, and reflect deadlines and milestones.[7]

To expand on this a bit, goals are only useful to the extent that employees are motivated to achieve them. Research known as "the goal-setting studies" provides useful insights into setting motivational goals. These studies suggest four things:

1. *Assign Specific Goals*   Employees who are given specific goals usually perform better than those who are not.
2. *Assign Measurable Goals*[8]   Put goals in quantitative terms and include target dates or deadlines. Goals set in absolute terms (such as "an average daily output of 300 units") are less confusing than goals set in relative terms (such as "improve production by 20%"). If measurable results will not be available, then "satisfactory completion"—such as "satisfactorily attended workshop" or "satisfactorily completed his or her degree"—is the next best thing. In any case, target dates or deadlines should always be set.
3. *Assign Challenging but Doable Goals*   Goals should be challenging, but not so difficult that they appear impossible or unrealistic.[9] When is a goal too difficult or too hard? One expert says:

   A goal is probably too easy if it calls for little or no improvement in performance when conditions are becoming more favorable, or if the targeted level of performance is well below that of most other employees in comparable positions. A goal is probably too difficult if it calls for a large improvement in performance when conditions are worsening, or if the targeted level of performance is well above that of people in comparable positions.[10]

4. *Encourage Participation*   Throughout your management career (and often several times a day) you'll be faced with this question: should I just tell my employees what their goals are, or should I let them participate with me in setting their goals? The evidence suggests that participatively set goals *do not* consistently result in higher performance than assigned goals, nor do assigned goals consistently result in higher performance than participatively set ones. *It is only when the participatively set goals are more difficult (are set higher) than the assigned ones that the participatively set goals produce higher performance.* It does tend to be easier to set higher standards when your employees can participate in the process, and to that extent participation can facilitate standards setting, and performance.[11]

An Introduction to Appraising Performance

Why Appraise Performance?

There are three main reasons to appraise subordinates' performance. First, appraisals provide important input on which promotion and salary raise decisions can be made. Second, the appraisal lets the boss and subordinate develop a plan for correcting any deficiencies the appraisal might have unearthed, and to reinforce the things the subordinate does correctly. Finally, appraisals can serve a useful career-planning purpose, by providing the opportunity to review the employee's career plans in light of his or her exhibited strengths and weaknesses.

Who Should Do the Appraising?

Appraisals by the immediate supervisor are still at the heart of most appraisal processes. Getting a supervisor's appraisal is relatively straightforward and also makes sense. The supervisor should be—and usually is—in the best position to observe and evaluate his or her subordinate's performance, and is also responsible for that person's performance. Most appraisals (92% in one survey) are made by the employee's immediate supervisor. These appraisals were in turn reviewed by the supervisor's own supervisor in 74% of the respondents in this survey.[12]

Yet although widely used, supervisors' ratings are no panacea and sole reliance on them is not always advisable.[13] For example, an employee's supervisor may not understand or appreciate how people such as customers and colleagues who depend on the employee rate the person's performance. Furthermore, it is conceivable that an immediate supervisor may be biased for or against the employee. One or more other options are therefore sometimes used to obtain appraisal data.

Peer Appraisals   With more firms using self-managing teams, appraisal of an employee by his or her peers—**peer appraisal**—is becoming more popular. At Digital Equipment Corporation, for example, an employee due for an annual appraisal chooses an appraisal chairperson. The latter then selects one supervisor and three peers to evaluate the employee's work.[14]

Research indicates that peer appraisals can be effective. One study involved undergraduates placed into self-managing work groups. The researchers found that peer appraisals had "an immediate positive impact on [improving] perception of open communication, task motivation, social loafing, group viability, cohesion, and satisfaction."[15]

Rating Committees   Some companies use rating committees. A rating committee is usually composed of the employee's immediate supervisor and three or four other supervisors.

Using multiple raters can be advantageous. It can help cancel out problems such as bias on the part of individual raters. It can also provide a way to include in the appraisal the different facets of an employee's performance observed by different appraisers. This is probably why composite ratings tend to be more reliable, fair, and valid than those done by individual supervisors.[16]

Self-Ratings   Employees' self-ratings of performance are also sometimes used, usually in conjunction with supervisors' ratings. The basic problem with self-ratings is that employees usually rate themselves higher than their supervisors or peers would rate them.[17] One study found that, when asked to rate their own job performances, 40% of employees in jobs of all types placed themselves in the top 10%, and virtually all remaining employees rated themselves at least in the top 50%. At least one recent study concluded that individuals do not necessarily always have such positive illusions about their own performance. However, in rating the performance of their groups, group members still consistently assigned their group unrealistically high performance ratings.[18]

Appraisal by Subordinates   Some firms let subordinates evaluate their supervisors' performance, a process many call **upward feedback.**[19] Such feedback can help top managers diagnose management styles, identify potential people problems, and take corrective action with individual managers, as required. Firms such as FedEx use upward feedback to help improve supervisory performance; for example, if a supervisor scores low on the item "I feel free to tell my manager what I think," FedEx managers are trained to ask their groups questions such as "What do I do that makes you feel that I'm not interested?"

Anonymity can have a big impact on the usefulness of upward feedback. Managers who get feedback from subordinates who identify themselves view the upward feedback process more positively than do managers who get anonymous feedback. However, subordinates are more comfortable giving anonymous responses, and those who must identify themselves tend to give inflated ratings.[20]

Research supports the idea that upward feedback can improve a manager's performance. One study focused on 252 managers during five annual administrations of an upward feedback program. Managers who were initially "rated poor or moderate showed significant improvements in [their] upward feedback ratings over the five-year period. . . ." Furthermore, managers who met with their subordinates to discuss their upward feedback improved more than the managers who did not.[21]

360-Degree Feedback   With 360-degree feedback, performance information is collected all around an employee, from his or her supervisors, subordinates, peers, and internal or external customers.[22] This is generally done for development rather than for pay raises. The usual process is to have the raters complete appraisal surveys on the ratee. Computerized systems then compile all this feedback into individualized reports that go to ratees. The person may then meet with his or her supervisor to develop a self-improvement plan.[23] Participants, at least, seem to prefer this approach. One study concluded that 360-degree program participants rated their experience of most aspects of training and development as significantly better than did non-program participants.[24]

However, some doubt 360-degree feedback's objectivity. Employees usually do these reviews anonymously, so those with an ax to grind can misuse the system. Office politics can prompt retaliatory assessments. A Dilbert cartoon strip, announcing that evaluations by co-workers will help decide raises, has one character asking, "If my co-workers got small raises, won't there be more available in the budget for me?"[25] More seriously, with multiple ratees and multiple raters, noncomputerized 360-degree assessments can be paperwork nightmares.

Thus, 360-degree appraisal systems are the subject of considerable debate. One study, by the HR consulting firm Watson Wyatt, found that companies using 360-degree-type feedback have lower market value (in terms of stock price). For example, those using peer review have a market value about 5% lower than similar companies that don't use peer reviews, and those that allow subordinates to evaluate the managers are valued almost 6% lower than similar firms that don't. These findings don't necessarily suggest a cause-and-effect relationship between nontraditional appraisal methods and market value, but they are a red flag. The findings suggest that any firm implementing 360-degree feedback should carefully assess the potential costs of the program, focus any feedback very clearly on concrete goals, carefully train the people who are giving and receiving the feedback, and not rely solely on 360-degree feedback for performance appraisal.[26]

There are also various ways to reduce the administrative costs associated with this approach. For example, Visual 360 from MindSolve Technologies of Gainesville, Florida, lets the rater log in, open a screen with a rating scale, and then rate the person along a series of competencies with ratings such as "top five percent."[27]

There are also several systems for accomplishing 360-degree assessments via the Internet. For example, in the Internet-based 360 system used at Farmington, Connecticut–based Otis Elevator Company, managers and others are evaluated by their peers, customers, teammates, supervisors, direct subordinates, suppliers, and themselves. The system is fully encrypted. Passwords ensure that only authorized persons can access the actual Internet-based evaluations.[28]

Even if you do not opt for a 360-degree approach, there is wisdom in having more than one supervisor appraise an employee. One of the most consistent findings in appraisal research is that the ratings obtained from different sources rarely match.[29] Multiple raters often do see different facets of an employee's performance. It's therefore advisable to obtain ratings from both the supervisor, his or her boss, and perhaps another manager who is familiar with the employee's work.

BASIC APPRAISAL METHODS

The manager usually conducts the appraisal using one or more of the formal methods described in this section.

Graphic Rating Scale Method

A **graphic rating scale** lists a number of traits and a range of performance for each. As in Figure 6.2, it lists traits (such as quality and reliability) and a range of performance values (in this case from unsatisfactory to outstanding) for each trait. The supervisor rates each subordinate by circling or checking the score that best describes the subordinate's performance for each trait, then totals the scores for all traits.

Alternation Ranking Method

Ranking employees from best to worst on a trait or traits is another popular appraisal method. Because it is usually easier to distinguish between the worst and best employees than to rank them, an **alternation ranking method** is useful. With this

Figure 6.2 Graphic Rating Scale

Performance Appraisal Form

Employee Name _____ Title _____

Department _____ Employee Payroll Number_____

Reason for Review: ☐ Annual   ☐ Promotion   ☐ Unsatisfactory Performance
                   ☐ Merit   ☐ End Probation Period   ☐ Other_____

Date employee began present position ____ / ____ / ____

Date of last appraisal ____ / ____ / ____   Scheduled appraisal date ____ / ____ / ____

Instructions : Carefully evaluate employee's work performance in relation to current job requirements. Check rating box to indicate the employee's performance.

RATING DEFINITIONS

O=**Outstanding**—Performance is exceptional in all areas and is recognizable as being far superior to others.
V=**Very Good**—Results clearly exceed most position requirements. Performance is of high quality and is achieved on a consistent basis.
G=**Good**—Competent and dependable level of performance. Meets performance standards of the job.

I=**Improvement Needed**—Performance is deficient in certain areas. Improvement is necessary.
U=**Unsatisfactory**—Results are generally unacceptable and require immediate improvement. No merit increase should be granted to individuals with this rating.
N=**Not Rated**—Not applicable or too soon to rate.

PERFORMANCE DIMENSIONS	RATINGS:	O	V	G	I	U	N
1. Quality—The accuracy, thoroughness, and acceptability of work performed							
2. Productivity—The quantity and efficiency of work produced in a specified period of time							
3. Job Knowledge—The practical/technical skills and information used on the job							
4. Reliability—The extent to which employee can be relied upon regarding task completion and follow-up							
5. Availability—The extent to which employee is punctual, observes prescribed work break/meal periods, and the overall attendance record							
6. Independence—The extent of work performed with little or no supervision							

Basic Appraisal Methods

Figure 6.3 Alternation Ranking Method

ALTERNATION RANKING SCALE

For the Trait: _____

For the trait you are measuring, list all the employees you want to rank. Put the highest-ranking employee's name on line 1. Put the lowest-ranking employee's name on line 20. Then list the next highest ranking on line 2, the next lowest ranking on line 19, and so on. Continue until all names are on the scale.

Highest-ranking employee

1. _____   11. _____
2. _____   12. _____
3. _____   13. _____
4. _____   14. _____
5. _____   15. _____
6. _____   16. _____
7. _____   17. _____
8. _____   18. _____
9. _____   19. _____
10. _____   20. _____

Lowest-ranking employee

---

method a form like that in Figure 6.3 is used to indicate the employee who is highest on the trait being measured and also the one who is the lowest, alternating between highest and lowest until all employees to be rated have been addressed.

Paired Comparison Method

With the **paired comparison method,** every subordinate to be rated is paired with and compared to every other subordinate on each trait.

For example, suppose there are five employees to be rated. With this method, a chart such as that in Figure 6.4 shows all possible pairs of employees for each trait. Then for each trait, the supervisor indicates (with a plus or minus) who is the better employee of the pair. Next, the number of times an employee is rated better is added up. In Figure 6.4, employee Maria ranked highest (has the most plus marks) for "quality of work," and Art ranked highest for "creativity."

Forced Distribution Method

With the **forced distribution method,** the manager places predetermined percentages of subordinates in performance categories, as when a professor "grades on a curve."

Figure 6.4 Paired Comparison Method

FOR THE TRAIT "QUALITY OF WORK"

Employee Rated:

As Compared to:	A Art	B Maria	C Chuck	D Diane	E José
A Art		+	+	−	−
B Maria	−		−	−	−
C Chuck	−	+		+	−
D Diane	+	+	−		+
E José	+	+	+	−	

Maria Ranks Highest Here

FOR THE TRAIT "CREATIVITY"

Employee Rated:

As Compared to:	A Art	B Maria	C Chuck	D Diane	E José
A Art		−	−	−	−
B Maria	+		−	+	+
C Chuck	+	+		−	+
D Diane	+	−	+		−
E José	+	−	−	+	

Art Ranks Highest Here

Note: + means "better than," − means "worse than." For each chart, add up the number of +'s in each column to get the highest-ranked employee.

More firms are adopting this practice. Sun Microsystems recently began forced ranking of all its 43,000 employees. Managers appraise employees in groups of about 30. There is a top 10%, a middle 70%, and a bottom 10%. The bottom 10% can either take a quick exit package or embark on a 90-day performance improvement action plan. If they're still in the bottom 10% in 90 days, they get a chance to resign and take severance pay. Some decide to stay, but "if it doesn't work out," the firm fires them without severance.[30]

Strategy and HR Ford CEO Jacques Nasser opted for just such an approach for his firm's 18,000 managers. His new corporate strategy aimed to make Ford one of the world's top-performing companies. He therefore wanted the new appraisal system to convey the fact that performance was paramount, and that underperformers had no place at the new world-class Ford.

He modeled the new management appraisal process on one used by firms like IBM, Sun, and GE. Under his program, managers received A, B, or C grades. Executives rated "C" risked losing their bonuses or raises. And C grades two years in a row meant that Ford may demote or fire the executive. Nasser initially wanted 10% of managers to be graded C, but quickly reduced that to 5% when the complaints began. He apparently imposed the new system with little warning or discussion.

His forced distribution approach immediately triggered a storm. Executives called it unfair, and several sued. Some claimed Ford was targeting middle-aged male executives as a way of clearing them out. Ford's initial response to the suits was that "the program is going to continue." Soon, though, they were saying, "there is always review going on of all of our processes."

Ford soon discontinued the program. Some say that what works at a firm like GE or Sun may not work at one where one family controls 40% of the votes, and where the apparent toughness may reflect badly on the Fords. Soon, Nick Scheele, chairman of Ford of Europe, was brought in to help Nasser run the firm and execute its strategy.[31] Nasser left the firm within a year. Some on the board may have felt that Nasser's high-performance strategy had diverted too much attention from the firm's core car business. Others probably felt that he could have handled imposing the new forced-choice appraisal system more diplomatically.

As most students know, forced distribution grading systems are more unforgiving than most other means of appraising performance. With a forced distribution system, you're either in the top 5% or 10% (and thus get that "A"), or you're not. And, if you're in the bottom 5% or 10%, you get an "F", no questions asked. Your professor hasn't the wiggle room to give everyone As, Bs, and Cs. Some students have to fail. Given this, employers need to be doubly careful to protect their appraisal plans from managerial abuse. Office politics and managerial bias can taint ratings. To protect against bias claims, employers should therefore take several steps.[32] Appoint a review committee to review any employee's low ranking. Train raters to be objective. And consider using 360-degree appraisals (or at least multiple raters) in conjunction with the forced distribution approach.

Critical Incident Method

The **critical incident method** entails keeping a record of uncommonly good or undesirable examples of an employee's work-related behavior and reviewing it with the employee at predetermined times.

Employers often use the critical incident method to supplement a rating or ranking method. This helps ensure that the supervisor thinks about the subordinate's appraisal all during the year, because the incidents must be accumulated; therefore, the rating does not just reflect the employee's most recent performance. Keeping a running list of critical incidents should also provide concrete examples of what specifically your subordinates can do to eliminate any performance deficiencies.

Behaviorally Anchored Rating Scales

A behaviorally anchored rating scale (BARS) is an appraisal method that combines the benefits of narrative critical incidents and quantitative ratings by anchoring a quantified scale with specific narrative examples of good and poor performance.

Figure 6.5 is an example that shows the behaviorally anchored rating scale for the trait "salesmanship skills" used for armed forces recruiters. Note how the various performance levels are anchored with specific behavioral examples such as "When a prospect states an objection to being in the Navy, the recruiter ends the conversation. . . ."

The Management by Objectives Method

The **management by objectives (MBO)** method requires the manager to set specific measurable goals with each employee and then periodically discuss the latter's progress toward these goals. The term *MBO* usually refers to an organizationwide

Figure 6.5
Behaviorally Anchored
Rating Scale

> **Salesmanship Skills**
>
> Skillfully persuading prospects to join the navy; using navy benefits and opportunities effectively to sell the navy; closing skills; adapting selling techniques appropriately to different prospects; effectively overcoming objections to joining the navy.
>
> 9 — A prospect stated he wanted the nuclear power program or he would not sign up. When he did not qualify, the recruiter did not give up; instead, he talked the young man into electronics by emphasizing the technical training he would receive.
>
> 8 —
> The recruiter treats objections to joining the navy seriously; he works hard to counter the objections with relevant, positive arguments for a navy career.
>
> 7 —
> When talking to a high school senior, the recruiter mentions names of other seniors from that school who have already enlisted.
>
> 6 —
> When an applicant qualifies for only one program, the recruiter tries to convey to the applicant that it is a desirable program.
>
> 5 —
> When a prospect is deciding on which service to enlist in, the recruiter tries to sell the navy by describing navy life at sea and adventures in port.
>
> 4 —
> During an interview, the recruiter said to the applicant, "I'll try to get you the school you want, but frankly it probably won't be open for another three months, so why don't you take your second choice and leave now."
>
> 3 —
> The recruiter insisted on showing more brochures and films even though the applicant told him he wanted to sign up right now.
>
> 2 —
> When a prospect states an objection to being in the navy, the recruiter ends the conversation because he thinks the prospect must not be interested.
>
> 1 —

Source: From "Behavior Based Rating Scales," by Walter C. Borman, *Performance Assessment: Methods & Applications,* edited by Ronald A. Berk. Reprinted by permission of the John Hopkins University Press.

goal-setting and appraisal program that consists of six steps:

1. *Set the organization's goals.* Establish an organizationwide plan for next year and set goals.
2. *Set departmental goals.* Department heads and their superiors jointly set goals for their departments.
3. *Discuss departmental goals.* Department heads discuss the department's goals with all subordinates in the department and ask them to develop their own

individual goals. In other words, how can each employee contribute to the department's attaining its goals?

4. *Define expected results (set individual goals).* Department heads and their subordinates set short-term performance targets.
5. *Conduct performance reviews and measure the results.* Department heads compare the actual performance of each employee with expected results.
6. *Provide feedback.* Department heads hold periodic performance review meetings with subordinates to discuss and evaluate the subordinates' progress in achieving expected results.

Computerized and Web–Based Performance Appraisals

Several relatively inexpensive performance appraisal software programs are on the market.[33] These generally enable managers to log notes on their subordinates during the year, and then to rate these subordinates on a series of computerized performance traits. The programs then generate written text to support each part of the appraisal.

For example, Employee Appraiser (developed by the Austin-Hayne Corporation, San Mateo, California) presents a menu of more than a dozen evaluation dimensions, including dependability, initiative, communication, decision making, leadership, judgment, and planning and productivity. Within each dimension are various performance factors, again presented in menu form. For example, under "Communication" are separate factors for writing, verbal communication, receptivity to feedback and criticism, listening skills, ability to focus on the desired results, keeping others informed, and openness.

When the user clicks on a performance factor, he or she is presented with a relatively sophisticated version of a graphic rating scale. However, instead of numbers, Employee Appraiser uses behaviorally anchored examples. For example, for verbal communication there are six choices, ranging from "presents ideas clearly" to "lacks structure." After the manager picks the phrase that most accurately describes the worker, Employee Appraiser generates an appraisal with sample text.

PerformanceNow, from KnowledgePoint of Petaluma, California, lets managers evaluate employees based on their competencies, goals, and development plans. Managers can choose from standard competencies such as "communications," or create their own. Clicking on the "rate" button in the dialog boxes then brings up ratings from 1 to 5.[34]

PerformancePro.net from the Exxceed Company of Chicago, Illinois, is an Internet-based performance review system. It helps the manager and his or her subordinates develop performance objectives for the employee, and to conduct the annual review.[35]

The Web site improvenow.com lets employees fill out a 60-question assessment online with or without their supervisor's approval, and then give the supervisor the team's feedback with an overall score.[36]

Electronic Performance Monitoring

With electronic performance monitoring (EPM), computer network technology is used to provide managers with access to their employees' computer terminals and telephones, thus "allowing managers to determine at any moment throughout the day the pace at which employees are working, their degree of accuracy, log-in and log-off times, and even the amount of time spent on bathroom breaks."[37] It appears that more than 10 million workers—more than 10% of the U.S. workforce—are subject to EPM.[38]

Research studies indicate that EPM can improve productivity under certain circumstances. For example, for more routine, less complex jobs, highly skilled and monitored subjects keyed in more data entries than did highly skilled unmonitored participants.[39] However, EPM can also backfire. In this same study, low-skilled but highly monitored participants did more poorly than did low-skilled, unmonitored participants. Empirical studies also provide strong evidence linking EPM with increased stress.[40]

THE APPRAISAL FEEDBACK INTERVIEW

An appraisal usually culminates in an **appraisal interview,** in which the supervisor and subordinate review the appraisal and make plans to remedy deficiencies and reinforce strengths. Interviews like these can be uncomfortable because few people like to receive—or give—negative feedback.[41] Adequate preparation and effective implementation are therefore essential.

Preparing for the Appraisal Interview

Adequate preparation involves three steps. First, give the subordinate at least a week's notice to review his or her work, and to read over his or her job description, analyze problems, and compile questions and comments. Next, study his or her job description, compare the employee's performance to his or her standards, and review the files of the person's previous appraisals. Finally, choose the right place for the interview and schedule enough time for it. The interview should be done in a private area where you won't be interrupted by phone calls or visitors. Find a mutually agreeable time for the interview and leave enough time—perhaps one-half hour for lower-level personnel such as clerical workers and maintenance staff, and an hour or so for management employees.

Conducting the Interview

There are several things to keep in mind when actually conducting appraisal interviews. First, the interview's main aim is to reinforce satisfactory performance or to diagnose and improve unsatisfactory performance. One way to help accomplish this is to be direct and specific. Talk in terms of objective work data, using examples such as absences, quality records, inspection reports, and tardiness. Second, get agreement before the subordinate leaves on how things will be improved and by when. An action plan showing steps and expected results (as in Figure 6.6) can be useful. Related to this, there are times when an employee's performance is so poor that a formal written warning is required. Such warnings should identify the standards under which the employee is judged, make it clear that the employee was aware of the standard, specify any violation of the standard, and show that the employee had an opportunity to correct his or her behavior.

Figure 6.6 An Example of an Action Plan

ACTION PLAN

Date: May 18, 2003

For: John, Assistant Plant Manager
Problem: Parts inventory too high
Objective: Reduce plant parts inventory by 10% in June

Action Steps	When	Expected Results
Determine average monthly parts inventory	6/2	Established a base from which to measure progress
Review ordering quantities and parts usage	6/15	Identify overstock items
Ship excess parts to regional warehouse and scrap obsolete parts	6/20	Clear stock space
Set new ordering quantities for all parts	6/25	Avoid future overstocking
Check records to measure where we are now	7/1	See how close we are to objective

---

The aim of the appraisal is often to get the employee to improve, and to that extent you should ensure that the process is fair. Letting the employee participate in the appraisal process by at least letting his or her opinions be heard is therefore essential.[42]

Supervisors may also have to deal with defensiveness. For example, when a person is accused of poor performance, the first reaction is usually denial. By denying the fault, the employee avoids having to question his or her own competence. Such defensiveness is normal. It is prudent not to attack the person's defenses (for instance, by trying to "explain someone to themselves" by saying things like, "You know the real reason you're using that excuse is that you can't bear to be blamed for anything"). Another tactic is to postpone action—for instance, by giving the person a five-minute breather to cool down after being informed of unsatisfactory performance.

TOWARD MORE EFFECTIVE APPRAISALS

Few of the manager's jobs are fraught with more peril than appraising subordinates' performance. Employees in general tend to be overly optimistic about what their ratings are, and also know that their raises, career progress, and peace of mind may hinge on how they are rated. This alone should make it somewhat difficult to rate performance. Even more problematic, however, are the numerous structural problems (discussed below) that can cast doubt on just how fair the process is.

Figure 6.7   A Graphic Rating Scale with Unclear Standards

	Excellent	Good	Fair	Poor
Quality of work				
Quantity of work				
Creativity				
Integrity				

Note: For example, what exactly is meant by "good," "quantity of work," and so forth?

Dealing with Common Appraisal Problems

Several chronic problems undermine appraisals and graphic rating scales in particular. Fortunately, as explained in this section, there are also ways to avoid or solve these problems.

Unclear Standards   The unclear standards appraisal problem means that an appraisal scale is too open to interpretation. As in Figure 6.7, the rating scale may seem objective, but would probably result in unfair appraisals because the traits and degrees of merit are open to interpretation. For example, different supervisors would probably define "good" performance differently. The same is true of traits such as "quality of work." The best way to rectify this problem is to develop and include descriptive phrases that define each trait and degree of merit.

Halo Effect   The **halo effect** means that the rating of a subordinate on one trait (such as "gets along with others") influences the way you rate the person on other traits (such as "quantity of work"). Thus, an unfriendly employee might be rated unsatisfactory for all traits rather than just for the trait "gets along with others." Being aware of this problem is a major step toward avoiding it.

Central Tendency   The **central tendency** problem refers to a tendency to rate all employees about average. For example, if the rating scale ranges from 1 to 7, a supervisor may tend to avoid the highs (6 and 7) and lows (1 and 2) and rate most of his or her employees between 3 and 5. Such a restriction can distort the evaluations, making them less useful for promotion, salary, and counseling purposes. Ranking employees instead of using a graphic rating scale can eliminate this problem because all employees must be ranked and thus can't all be rated average.

Leniency or Strictness   Conversely, some supervisors tend to rate all their subordinates consistently high or low, a problem referred to as the strictness/leniency problem. Again, one solution is to insist on ranking subordinates, because that forces the supervisor to distinguish between high and low performers.

The appraisal you do may, in fact, be less objective than you realize. One study focused on how personality influenced the peer evaluations students gave their peers. Raters who scored higher on "conscientiousness" tended to give their peers lower ratings; those scoring higher on "agreeableness" gave higher ratings.[43]

Bias Bias refers to the tendency to let individual differences like age, race, and sex affect the appraisal ratings employees receive. A study illustrates how bias can influence the way one person appraises another. In this study researchers sought to determine the extent to which pregnancy is a source of bias in performance appraisals.[44] The results suggest that pregnant women may face additional workplace discrimination above and beyond any gender bias that may already exist against women in general. Despite having been exposed to otherwise identical behavior by the same female "employee," the student raters of this study "with a remarkably high degree of consistency" assigned lower performance ratings to pregnant women than to nonpregnant women.[45] Furthermore, men raters seemed more susceptible to negative influence than did women. One implication is that raters must be forewarned of such problems and trained to use objectivity in rating subordinates. Table 6.1 summarizes the pros and cons of the most popular rating methods.

Table 6.1 Important Similarities and Differences, and Advantages and Disadvantages of Appraisal Tools

Tool	Similarities/Differences	Advantages	Disadvantages
Graphic rating scale	These are both absolute scales aimed at measuring an employee's *absolute* performance based on objective criteria as listed on the scales.	Simple to use; provides a quantitative rating for each employee.	Standards may be unclear; halo effect, central tendency, leniency, bias can also be problems.
BARS		Provides behavioral "anchors." BARS is very accurate.	Difficult to develop.
Alternation ranking	These are both methods for judging the *relative* performance of employees relative to each other, but still based on objective criteria.	Simple to use (but not as simple as graphic rating scales); avoids central tendency and other problems of rating scales.	Can cause disagreements among employees and may be unfair if all employees *are*, in fact, excellent.
Forced distribution method		End up with a predetermined number of people in each group.	Appraisal results depend on the adequacy of your original choice of cutoff points.
Critical incident method	These are both more subjective, narrative methods for appraising performance, generally based, however, on the employee's absolute performance.	Helps specify what is "right" and "wrong" about the employee's performance; forces supervisor to evaluate subordinates on an ongoing basis.	Difficult to rate or rank employees relative to one another.
MBO		Tied to jointly agreed-upon performance objectives.	Time consuming.

Steps to take to ensure your appraisals are legally defensible include:

- Develop appraisal criteria from documented job analyses. Specifically, a formal job analysis should be conducted as a prerequisite for the development of valid performance appraisal criteria.
- Communicate performance standards to employees in writing.
- Base appraisals on separate evaluations of each of the job's performance dimensions. In particular, use of a single overall rating of performance or ranking of employees on a similar global standard is not acceptable to the courts.[46] Such systems are often characterized as vague by the courts. Courts generally require that separate ratings along each performance dimension be combined through some formal weighting system to yield a summary score.
- Include an employee appeals process. Employees should have the opportunity to review and make comments, written or verbal, about their appraisals before they become final and should have a formal appeals process through which to appeal their ratings.
- One appraiser should never have absolute authority to determine a personnel action. This is one reason why multiple-raters procedures are becoming more popular.
- Document all information bearing on a personnel decision in writing. Three experts assert that "without exception, courts condemn informal performance evaluation practices that eschew documentation."[47]
- Train supervisors in the use of the appraisal instruments. If formal rater training is not possible, at least provide raters with written instructions for using the rating scale for evaluating personnel.

Legal Issues in Performance Appraisal[48]

Since passage of Title VII, courts have often found that inadequate employee appraisal systems lay at the root of illegal discriminatory actions (such as failure to promote an otherwise qualified minority candidate).[49] The courts' view is understandable. The performance appraisal affects raises, promotions, training opportunities, and other career-related HR actions. If the manager is inept or biased in the appraisals he or she does, how can the promotion decisions that stem from those appraisals be defended? The employer's appraisal process must therefore be legally defensible. You will find recommendations in the *HR in Practice* box for ensuring the legal defensibility of an employer's performance appraisal system.[50]

PERFORMANCE AND CAREER MANAGEMENT

We may define a *career* as the "occupational positions a person has had over many years." Many people look back on their careers with satisfaction, knowing that what they might have achieved they did achieve, and that their career hopes were satisfied. Others are less fortunate and feel that, at least in their careers, their lives and their potential went unfulfilled.

Employers, of course, have a significant impact on their employees' careers, and thereby on their career satisfaction and success. Recruiting, selecting, placing, training, appraising, rewarding, promoting, and separating the employee all affect the person's career, and therefore his or her career satisfaction and success. Some firms institute relatively formal *career management* processes. We can define **career management** as a process for enabling the employees to better understand and develop their career skills and interests, and to use these skills and interests most effectively both within the company and, if necessary, after they leave the firm. Other firms do relatively little.

Career-Oriented Appraisals

Ideally, the firm's career management processes should dovetail with its performance management system. In particular, performance appraisals should not just focus on telling someone how he or she has done. They also provide an ideal chance for the supervisor and employee to discuss and link the employee's performance, career interests, and developmental needs into a rational career plan. Thus, the career goals the employee sets, and the training and development he or she goes on to, should reflect the career plans that evolve from the appraisal process.

As an example, Figure 6.8 illustrates J. C. Penney's management appraisal form. It requires both a "promotability recommendation" and "projections for associate development." Before the annual appraisal, the associate and his or her manager review J. C. Penney's Management Career Grid (see Figure 6.9). The grid itemizes all supervisory positions at J. C. Penney (grouped by kind of job) and includes specific job titles such as "regional catalog sales manager," "cosmetic market coordinator," "regional training coordinator," and "project manager, public affairs." The firm also provides a "work activities scan sheet." This contains thumbnail job descriptions for all the grid's jobs.

The management career grid's instructions identify typical promotional routes. They also stipulate that, "When projecting the next assignment for a management

Figure 6.8 Portion of J. C. Penney's Appraisal Form

Date & trembles Midyear Follow Up
9/10/02 GPT / LLS

Management Characteristics and Strategic Directions: Fill in letter for each using ratings below. See reverse for definitions.
Ratings: O = Outstanding G = Good S = Satisfactory ND = Needs Development TN = Too New to Rate or Not Applicable

I. Leadership G II. Awareness ND III. Sense of Urgency ND IV. Judgement G V. Planning & Organizing G VI. Team Process Participation G VII. Fashion Credibility G VIII. EEO Management G

Additional Comments, Strengths and Opportunities Lee achieved very solid results in Men's -- nice sales, good team development and depth of lines. Shoes is a real opportunity for Lee. Many decisions must be made more quickly by Lee, using merchandise systems better.

OVERALL PERFORMANCE RATING 3
(See reverse for instructions)

Manager Signature	Date of Appraisal	Reviewer Signature	Date of Review	Associate Signature	Date of Appraisal	Is this associate willing to move residence? (Check One)
Garry D. Turner	4-15-96	Phil Adams	4-1-96	Lee Smith	4/15/96	[X] Yes [ ] Not Now

See Associate Career Grid for Instructions

Promotability Recommendation: Enter letter here → B

A This Year B Second or third year C Fourth or fifth year
D Can grow with job E Recommend lateral transfer F Is at responsibility level
G Recommend less responsibility H Promotable this store I Too New To Rate

High Potential: Check if this associate has exceptional growth potential top 5% in drive and ability [ ]

Projections for Associate Development	Year 19 97		Year 19 ___	
	Position Title	Position Code/Volume	Position Title	Position Code/Volume
First Choice Projection	Sr. Merch. Mgr.	4300		
Alternate Projection				

DP. 2036 (Rev. 2/90) T.O.C. # 008-7427-1000

Note: This is a career-oriented appraisal.

Figure 6.9 Portion of J. C. Penney's Management Career Grid

Instructions and Use of Grid for Making Associate Projections of Development

1) Promotability—Enter the appropriate Promotability letter in the box provided [see Figure 6.8]. If the answer to Promotability is D, F, or I, leave the "High Potential" and "Projections for Associate Development" sections blank.

2) High Potential—The High Potential box should be checked if this associate has exceptional growth potential—is within the top 5% in drive and ability. Please keep in mind that appraisal ratings and high potential ratings, while related reflect two distinct judgments—performance in current assignment versus exceptional potential for growth. A "1" rated associate is not necessarily high potential or vice versa.

		FIELD MANAGEMENT	
OPERATIONS		**MERCHANDISE**	
Position Title/Volume	Code	Position Title/Volume	Code
Regional Operations Manager	1002	Manager of Geographic Markets	1017
		Manager of Business Planning	1025
		District Manager	1121
		Store Manager 30+ D.S.	0109
		Entity Store Manager	0110
		Store Manager 22–30 D.S.	0108
		Store Manager 15–22 D.S.	0107
		Regional Business Planning Manager	1026
		Store Manager 10–15 D.S.	0106
		Store Manager Under 10 D.S.	0105
Regional Catalog Sales Center Manager	1150	Regional Merchandiser/Geographic Markets	1146
Regional Programs Manager	1100		
Regional Systems Manager	1027		
		Store Manager 5–10 S.L.	0104
Regional Catalog Sales Manager	1139	Business Planning Manager	**40()0
District Operations Manager	2290	District Special Events & Publicity Manager	2800
District Operations/Personnel Manager	2310	Store Merchandise & Marketing Manager	4260
Regional Loss Prevention Manager	4804		
Operations Manager 30+ D.S.	1329	Store Manager 3–5 S.L.	0103
District Merchandise Systems Coordinator	2330	General Merchandising Manager 30+ D.S.	4299

associate, you should consider not only merchandise positions but also operations and personnel positions as well as general management positions." Promotional plans can thus cross these four groups, as well as up one or two job levels. Thus, a senior merchandising manager might aim for promotion to assistant buyer (a general management job at J. C. Penney's) or general merchandise manager. The system helps managers to think through their career plan at the firm, and hopefully nurtures their commitment to J. C. Penney's and to its goals.

Managing the Early Career Management Stages

Ideally, the employer's support of the employee's career begins well before the appraisal, and often before the person is even hired. Before hiring, *realistic job previews* can help prospective employees more accurately gauge whether the job is for them, and particularly whether the job's requirements fit the candidate's interests and skills. Then, *the first job* can be crucial for building confidence and a more realistic picture of what he or she can and cannot do. Hopefully, the job and the new employee's expectation about what to expect will coincide. If not, *reality shock,* a phenomenon that occurs when a new employee's high expectations confront the reality of an unchallenging job, may set in.

Mentoring—having a senior person assist and help guide the protégé's career— can positively affect the younger person's career, including faster promotions and salary progression, and reduced anxiety. However, mentoring relationships can also backfire. For example, personality problems or an unrealistically high sense of entitlement on the part of the protégé (regarding access to the mentor's time and advice) can adversely affect the mentor and protégé.[51]

Mentors don't have to be formally assigned, and there's evidence that informal mentoring may actually be superior. In one study, protégés with informal mentors reported their mentors provided more career development and support than did those with formal mentors. Employees with histories of informal mentors also earned significantly more than did those with histories of formal mentors. Employees with both formal and informal mentors received more compensation and promotions than did those without mentors, however.[52] It would appear that, at a minimum, employees would do well to find themselves mentors.

Employers take various other steps to support their employees' career-related needs. As noted above, *career-oriented appraisals* can help ensure that the person's current position makes sense in terms of his or her skills, and that the person has a sensible career path. Similarly, providing periodic, planned *job rotation* can help the person develop a more realistic picture of what he or she is (and is not) good at, and thus the sort of future career moves that might be best. Many employers, such as Saturn Corporation, provide employees with *career planning workshops.* Here they use tests and similar exercises to learn more about what careers might be best for them.

Formal career development programs like these benefit the employer, too. For example, Sun Microsystems maintains a career development center staffed by seven certified counselors, for helping employees fill in the gaps in their development and to choose internal career opportunities at Sun. The firm believes its program helps explain why their average employee tenure of four years is more than twice what it is estimated to be at other Silicon Valley firms.[53]

Managing Promotions and Transfers

Promotions (either domestically or internationally, see the *Global Issues* box) are, of course, one of the more significant HR decisions to result from the performance appraisal. In developing promotion policies, employers need to address several issues.

One concerns seniority versus competence. Competence is normally the basis for promotions, although in many organizations civil service or union requirements and similar constraints still give an edge to more senior applicants.

Furthermore, if competence is to be the basis for promotion, how should we measure it? Defining past performance is usually straightforward. Managers use

Several factors complicate the task of appraising an expatriate's performance.[54] First, the question of who appraises the expatriate is a crucial issue. Obviously, local management must have some input into the appraisal, but the appraisals may then be distorted by cultural differences. Thus, a U.S. expatriate manager in India may be evaluated somewhat negatively by his host-country bosses who find his use of participative decision making inappropriate in their culture. On the other hand, home office managers may be so geographically distanced from the expatriate that they can't provide valid appraisals because they're not fully aware of the situation the manager faces. This can be problematic: The expatriate may be measured by objective criteria such as profits and market share, but local events such as political instability may undermine the manager's performance while remaining invisible to home office staff.[55]

Two experts make five suggestions for improving the expatriate appraisal process:

1. Stipulate the assignment's difficulty level. For example, being an expatriate manager in China is generally considered more difficult than working in England, and the appraisal should take into account such difficulty-level differences.

2. Weigh the evaluation more toward the on-site manager's appraisal than toward the home-site manager's distant perceptions of the employee's performance.

3. If, as is usually the case, the home-site manager does the written appraisal, have him or her ask a former expatriate from the same overseas location to provide background advice during the appraisal process. This can help ensure than unique local issues are considered during the appraisal process.

4. Modify the performance criteria normally used for that particular position to fit the overseas position and characteristics of that particular locale. For example, "maintaining positive labor relations" might be more important in Chile, where labor instability is more common, than it would be in the United States.

5. Attempt to give the expatriate manager credit for relevant insights into the functioning of the operation and specifically the interdependencies of the domestic and foreign operations. In other words, don't just appraise the expatriate manager in terms of quantifiable criteria such as profits or market share. His or her recommendations regarding how home office/foreign subsidiary communications might be enhanced and other useful insights should affect the appraisal, too.

performance appraisals for this. However, sizing up how even a high-performing employee will do in a new, more challenging job is not so easy. Innumerable great salespeople turn out to be awful managers, for instance. As we have discussed elsewhere in this book, many employers therefore choose to use formal selection devices like tests and assessment centers to supplement the performance appraisals.

With more firms downsizing and flattening their organizations, "promotions" today often mean lateral moves or transfers. In such situations, the promotional aspect is not so much a higher-level job or more pay, but the opportunity to assume new, same-level responsibilities (such as a salesperson moving into HR) or increased, enriched decision-making responsibilities within the same job.

Toward More Effective Appraisals

A *transfer* is a move from one job to another, usually with no change in salary or grade. Employees may seek transfers not just for advancement, but for noncareer reasons, such as better hours, location of work, and so on. One familiar question is whether transferring employees from locale to locale upsets the employee's family life. Studies suggest that "mobile" families are no less satisfied with their family lives than "stable" ones. However, approximately 50% of top managers are reluctant to relocate.[56]

Women and men face different challenges as they advance through their careers. Women report greater barriers (such as being excluded from informal networks) than do men, and report greater difficulty getting developmental assignments and geographic mobility opportunities. Men are more likely to get developmental opportunities. Women historically had to be more proactive to get such assignments. Because developmental experiences like these are so important, "organizations that are interested in helping female managers advance should focus on breaking down the barriers that interfere with women's access to development experiences."[57]

Retirement

For many employees, years of appraisals and career development may end with retirement. About 30% of the employers in one survey said they therefore offered formal **preretirement counseling** aimed at easing the passage of their employees into retirement. Among employers that did not have preretirement education programs, 64% believed that such programs were needed, and most of these said their firms had plans to develop them within two or three years. The most common preretirement practices were:

> Explanation of Social Security benefits (reported by 97% of those with preretirement education programs)
> Leisure-time counseling (86%)
> Financial and investment counseling (84%)
> Health counseling (82%)
> Psychological counseling (35%)
> Counseling for second careers outside the company (31%)
> Counseling for second careers inside the company (4%)

Many employees today are choosing not to fully retire, or, if they do retire, to take a full- or part-time position with the same or another company. This trend reflects two things: (1) Increased life expectancies, and the fact that retirees today often have many useful years ahead of them, and (2) the catastrophic effects that the stock market bust of the early 2000s had on many pension funds.

In any event, more firms are granting part-time employment to employees as an alternative to outright retirement. Several surveys of blue- and white-collar employees showed that about half of all employees over age 55 would like to continue working part time after they retire.[58]

Technology and Career Planning

Software programs are available for improving the employer's career planning process. For example, *workforce vision* from Criterion, Inc., in Irving, Texas, helps the company analyze an employee's training needs. Clicking on the employee's name launches his or her work history, competencies, career path, and other information. For each competency (such as leadership and customer focus), it shows a "gap analysis" graphically on a bar chart, to highlight the person's strengths and weaknesses. The supervisor and employee can then organize developmental activities around the person's needs.[59]

Many people use the Web to help analyze and advance their careers. Well-known Web–based career assessment tools include www.self-directed-search.com; www.review.com/birkman; www.keirsey.com; and www.careerdiscovery.com. Some firms have created their own internal career development Web sites. For example, Unisys's Web–based career center helps its employees identify their strengths and improve their career understanding and progress.[60]

A Final Word

In a sense, *performance management* starts at the end and works backward. Top management asks, What is our strategy and what do we want to achieve? Each manager in the chain of command then asks, What does this mean for the goals we set for our employees, and for how we train, appraise, promote, and reward them? The performance appraisal is just one link in that process. Poor performance does not always reflect low motivation. It may suggest inadequate training or ineffective goals, for instance. This is why managing performance requires looking beyond just the appraisal, and taking an integrated, performance management approach to improving performance.[61] One firm labeled the HR function responsible for appraisal, compensation, training, and management development "Performance Management and Rewards." It did so to reflect the firm's new focus on performance, and the fact that *managing performance* requires thinking through all the HR actions that can influence how the person performs.[62]

In terms of performance management's component elements, we discussed training in Chapter 5, and goal setting, appraisal, and career management here in Chapter 6. We'll turn, in the next few chapters, to how to reward high performers, or to discipline or dismiss those who underperform.

REVIEW

Summary

1. *Performance appraisal* means evaluating an employee's current or past performance relative to his or her performance standards.

2. Managers appraise their subordinates' performance to obtain input on which promotion and salary raise decisions can be made, to develop plans for correcting performance deficiencies, and for career planning purposes. Supervi-

sory ratings are still at the heart of most appraisal processes.

3. The appraisal is generally conducted using one or more popular appraisal methods or tools. These include graphic rating scales, alternation ranking, paired comparison, forced distribution, critical incidents, behaviorally anchored rating scales, MBO, computerized performance appraisals, and electronic performance monitoring.

4. An appraisal typically culminates in an appraisal interview. Adequate preparation, including giving the subordinate notice, reviewing his or her job description and past performance, choosing the right place for the interview, and leaving enough time for it are essential. In conducting the interview, the aim is to reinforce satisfactory performance or to diagnose and improve unsatisfactory performance. A concrete analysis of objective work data and development of an action plan are therefore advisable. Employee defensiveness is normal and needs to be dealt with.

5. Many experts argue that traditional appraisals may actually backfire by causing conflict between supervisors and subordinates and leading to dysfunctional behaviors. The appraisal process can be improved, first, by eliminating chronic problems that often undermine appraisals and graphic rating scales in particular. These common problems include unclear standards, halo effect, central tendency, leniency or strictness, and bias.

6. Care should also be taken to ensure that the performance appraisal is legally defensible. For example, appraisal criteria should be based on documented job analyses, employees should receive performance standards in writing, and multiple performance dimensions should be rated.

7. Some experts suggest taking a performance management approach to the performance appraisal. For example, measure results objectively, determine the cause of the performance deficiency, use 360-degree feedback, and conduct a thorough analysis of key external and internal customers' needs and expectations on which to base performance appraisal standards.

KEY TERMS

- performance management
- peer appraisal
- upward feedback
- graphic rating scale
- alternation ranking method
- paired comparison method
- forced distribution method
- critical incident method
- management by objectives
- appraisal interview
- halo effect
- central tendency
- career management
- mentoring

DISCUSSION QUESTIONS AND EXERCISES

1. Discuss the pros and cons of at least four performance appraisal tools.
2. Working individually or in groups, develop a graphic rating scale for the following jobs: secretary, engineer, and directory assistance operator.
3. Working individually or in groups, evaluate the rating scale in Figure 6.1. Discuss ways to improve it.
4. Explain how you would use the alternation ranking method, the paired comparison method, and the forced distribution method.
5. Working individually or in groups, develop, over the period of a week, a set of critical incidents covering the classroom performance of one of your instructors.
6. Explain the problems to be avoided in appraising performance.
7. Discuss the pros and cons of using various potential raters to appraise an employee's performance.
8. Explain how to conduct an appraisal interview.

APPLICATION EXERCISES

Case Incident   *Back with a Vengeance*

Conducting an effective appraisal is always important. However, an appraisal can have life-and-death implications when you're dealing with unstable employees, particularly those who must be dismissed. An employee of a U.S. Postal Service station was recently terminated. The employee came back and shot and killed several managers who had been instrumental in the former employee's dismissal. It turned out this person had a history as a troublemaker and that many clues regarding his unstable nature over many years had been ignored. ■

QUESTIONS

1. Could a company with an effective appraisal process have missed so many signals of instability over several years? Why? Why not?
2. What safeguards would you build into your appraisal process to avoid missing such potentially tragic signs of instability and danger?
3. What would you do if confronted during an appraisal interview by someone who began making threats regarding the use of firearms?

Continuing Case

LearnInMotion.com: The Performance Appraisal

Jennifer and Mel disagree over the importance of having performance appraisals. Mel says it's quite clear whether any particular LearnInMotion employee is doing his or her job. It's obvious, for instance, if the salespeople are selling, if the Web designer is designing, if the Web surfer is surfing, and if the content management people are managing to get the customers' content up on the Web site in a timely fashion. Mel's position, like that of many small-business managers, is that "we have 1,000 higher-priority things to attend to" such as boosting sales and creating the calendar. And in any case, he says, the employees already get plenty of day-to-day feedback from him or Jennifer regarding what they're doing right and what they're doing wrong.

This informal feedback notwithstanding, Jennifer believes that a more formal appraisal approach is required. For one thing, they're approaching the end of the 90-day introductory period for many of these employees, and the owners need to make decisions about whether they should go or stay. And from a practical point of view, Jennifer believes that sitting down and providing formal, written feedback is more likely to reinforce what employees are doing right, and to get them to modify what they may be doing wrong. "Maybe this is one reason we're not getting enough sales," she says. They've been debating this for about an hour. Now, they want you, their management consultants, to advise them on what to do. Here's what they want you to do for them. ■

1. Is Jennifer right about the need to evaluate the workers formally? Why or why not? If you think she's right, how do you counter Mel's arguments?

2. Develop a performance appraisal method for the salespeople, or Web designer, or Web surfer. Please make sure to include any form you want the owners to use.

Experiential Exercise

Purpose: The purpose of this exercise is to give you practice in developing and using a performance appraisal form.

Required Understanding: You are going to develop a performance appraisal form for an instructor and should therefore be thoroughly familiar with the discussion of performance appraisals in this chapter.

How to Set Up the Exercise/Instructions: Divide the class into groups of four or five students.

1. First, based on what you now know about performance appraisals, do you think Figure 6.1 is an effective scale for appraising instructors? Why or why not?

2. Next, your group should develop its own tool for appraising the performance of an instructor. Decide which of the appraisal tools (graphic rating scales, alternation ranking, and so on) you are going to use and then design the instrument itself.

3. Next, have a spokesperson from each group put his or her group's appraisal tool on the board. How similar are the tools? Do they all measure about the same factors? Which factor appears most often? Which do you think is the most effective tool on the board? Can you think of any way of combining the best points of several of the tools into a new performance appraisal tool?

ENDNOTES

1. Peter Glendinning, "Performance Management: Pariah or Messiah," *Public Personnel Management* 31, no. 2 (summer 2002): 161–78.

2. See, for example, Joel E. Ross, *Total Quality Management: Text, Cases, and Readings* (Delray Beach, FL: Saint Lucie Press, 1993), p. 1.

3. See, for example, Greg Boudreaux, "Response: What TQM Says About Performance Appraisal," *Compensation and Benefits Review* (May/June 1994): 20–24.

4. Vesa Suutari and Marja Tahbanainen, "The Antecedents of Performance Management Among Finnish Expatriates," *Journal of Human Resource Management* 13, no. 1 (February 2002): 53–75.

5. For a discussion, see Gary English, "Tuning Up for Performance Management," *Training and Development Journal* (April 1991): 56–60.

6. See, for example, Doug Cederblom and Dan Pemerl, "From Performance Appraisal to Performance Management: One Agency's Experience," *Personnel Management* 31, no. 2 (summer 2002): 131–40.

7. "Setting Department Goals You Can Actually Achieve," *Info-Tech Advisor Newsletter* 22 (January 2002).

8. Gary Yukl, *Skills for Managers and Leaders* (Upper Saddle River, NJ: Prentice Hall, 1991), pp. 132–33; see also Gary Latham, "Cognitive and Motivational Effects of Participation" *Journal of Organizational Behavior* (January 1994): 49–64.

9. Yukl, *Skills for Managers,* 133. See also Miriam Erez, Daniel Gopher, and Nira

Arzi, "Effects of Goal Difficulty, Self-Set Goals, and Monetary Rewards on Dual Task Performance," *Organizational Behavior and Human Decision Processes* (December 1990): 247–69; Thomas Lee, "Explaining the Assigned Goal-Incentive Interaction: The Role of Self-Efficacy and Personal Goals," *Journal of Management* (July–August 1997): 541–50.

10. Yukl, *Skills for Managers,* 133.

11. See, for example, Anthony Mento, Normal Cartledge, and Edwin Locke, "Maryland versus Michigan versus Minnesota: Another Look at the Relationship of Expectancy and Goal Difficulty to Task Performance," *Organizational Behavior and Human Performance* (June 1980): 419–40. See also Robert Renn, "Further Examination of the Measurement of Properties of Leifer & McGannon's 1996 Goal Acceptance and Goal Commitment Scales," *Journal of Occupational and Organizational Psychology* (March 1999): 107–14.

12. Allan Locher and Kenneth Teel, "Appraisal Trends," *Personnel Journal* (September 1988): 139–45. The survey included 324 responding companies. See also Gail Dutton, "Making Reviews More Efficient and Fair," *Workforce* (April 2001): 76–80; Carla Joinson, "Making Sure Employees Measure Up," *HR Magazine* (March 2001): 36–41.

13. For a discussion, see Keki Bhote, "Boss Performance Appraisal. A Metric Whose Time Has Gone," *Employment Relations Today* 21, no. 1 (spring 1994): 1–9.

14. Carol Norman and Robert Zawacki, "Team Appraisals—Team Approach," *Personnel Journal* (September 1991): 101–3.

15. Vanessa Druskat and Steven Wolf, "Effects and Timing of Developmental Peer Appraisals in Self-Managing Workgroups," *Journal of Applied Psychology* 84, no. 1 (1999): 58–74.

16. Robert Libby and Robert Blashfield, "Performance of a Composite as a Function of the Number of Judges," *Organizational Behavior and Human Performance* 21 (April 1978): 121–29; M. M. Harris and J. Schaubroeck, "A Meta-Analysis of Self-Supervisor, Self-Peer, and Peer-Supervisor Ratings," *Personnel Psychology* 41 (1988): 43–62.

17. See, for example, John Lawrie, "Your Performance: Appraise It Yourself!" *Personnel* 66, no. 1 (January 1989): 21–33.

18. Forest Jourden and Chip Heath, "The Evaluation Gap in Performance Perceptions: Illusory Perceptions of Groups and Individuals," *Journal of Applied Psychology* 81, no. 4 (August 1996): 369–79.

19. Manuel London and Arthur Wohlers, "Agreement Between Subordinate and Self-Ratings in Upward Feedback," *Personnel Psychology* 44 (1991): 375–90; Robert McGarvey and Scott Smith, "When Workers Rate the Boss," *Training Magazine* (March 1993). See also Todd Maurer et al., "Peer and Subordinate Performance Appraisal Measurement Equivalents," *Journal of Applied Psychology* 83, no. 5 (1998): 693–702.

20. David Antonioni, "The Effects of Feedback Accountability on Upward Appraisal Ratings," *Personnel Psychology* 47 (1994): 349–55.

21. Alan Walker and James Smither, "A Five-Year Study of Upward Feedback: What Managers Do With Their Results Matters," *Personnel Psychology* 52 (1999): 393–423.

22. Kenneth Nowack, "360-Degree Feedback: The Whole Story," *Training and Development* (January 1993): 69; Matthew Budman, "The Rating Game," *Across the Board* 31, no. 2 (February 1994): 35–38. See also "360-Degree Feedback on the Rise Survey Finds," *BNA Bulletin to Management* (January 23, 1997): 31.

23. For further discussion on this technique, see, for example, Manuel London and James Smither, "Can Multi-Source Feedback Change Perceptions of Goal Accomplishment, Self-Evaluations, and Performance-Related Outcomes? Theory Based Applications and Directions for Research," *Personnel Psychology* 48, no. 4 (winter 1995): 803–39.

24. Christopher Mabey, "Closing the Circle: Participant Views of a 360-Degree Feedback Program," *Human Resource Management Journal* 11, no. 1 (2001): 41–53.

25. Carol Hymowitz, "Do 360-Degree Job Reviews by Colleagues Promote Honesty or Insults?" *Wall Street Journal* (December 12, 2000): B1.

26. Bruce Pfau, "Does a 360-Degree Feedback Negatively Affect the Company Performance?" *HR Magazine* (June 2002): 55–59.

27. Jim Meade, "Visual 360: A Performance Appraisal System That's 'Fun,'" *HR Magazine* (July 1999): 118–19.

28. G. Douglas Huet-Cox, "Get the Most from 360-Degree Feedback: Put It on the Internet," *HR Magazine* (May 1999): 92–102. See also Keith Morical, "A Product Review: 360 Assessment," *Training and Development* (April 1999): 43–53.

29. Jeffrey Facteau and S. Bartholomew Craig, "Performance Appraisal Ratings from Different Rating Scores," *Journal of Applied Psychology* 86, no. 2 (2001): 215–27.

30. Del Jones, "More Firms Cut Workers Ranked at Bottom to Make Way for Talent," *USA Today* (May 30, 2001): B1; "Straight Talk About Grading on a Curve," *BNA Bulletin to Management* (November 1, 2001): 351.

31. Alex Taylor III, "Crunch Time for Jac: Can CEO Jacques Nasser Fix Ford's Quality and Sales Woes—and Save His Job?" *Fortune* 143, no. 13 (June 25, 2001): 34–37; "Basking in the Sunshine: Nasser and the Press," *Automotive News* 75, no. 5934 (June 11, 2001): 8; Diana Kurylko, "Ford Defends Reviews of Managers," *Automotive News* 75, no. 5937 (July 2, 2001): 8.

32. "Straight Talk About Grading Employees on a Curve," *BNA Bulletin to Management* (November 1, 2001): 351.

33. See, for example, Edward Baig, "So You Hate Rating Your Workers?" *Business Week* (August 22, 1994): 14.

34. Jim Meade, "Automated Performance Appraisal for the LAN and the Net," *HR Magazine* (October 1998): 42–43.

35. Gary Meyer, "Performance Reviews Made Easy, Paperless," *HR Magazine* (October 2000): 181–84.

36. Ann Harrington, "Workers of the World, Rate Your Boss!" *Fortune* 16 (2000): 340–42.

37. John Aiello and Kathryn Kolb, "Electronic Performance Monitoring and Social Context: Impact on Productivity and Stress," *Journal of Applied Psychology* 80, no. 3 (1995): 339.

38. *Stories of Mistrust and Manipulation: The Electronic Monitoring of the American Workforce* (Cleveland, OH: 9 to 5, Working Women Education Fund, 1990).

39. Aiello and Kolb, "Electronic Performance Monitoring and Social Context," 339–53.

40. See, for example, John Aiello and Y. Shao, "Computerized Performance Monitoring," paper presented at the Seventh Conference of the Society for Industrial and Organizational Psychology, Montreal, Quebec, Canada, May 1992.

41. Donald Fedor and Charles Parsons, "What Is Effective Performance Feedback?" in Gerald Ferris and M. Ronald Buckley, *Human Resources Management*, 3d ed. (Upper Saddle River, NJ: Prentice Hall, 1996), pp. 265–70.

42. Brian Cawley et al., "Participation in the Performance Appraisal Process and Employee Reactions: A Meta-Analytic Review of Field Investigations," *Journal of Applied Psychology* 83, no. 4 (1998): 615–33.

43. H. John Bernardin et al., "Conscientiousness and Agreeableness as Predictors of Rating Leniency," *Journal of Applied Psychology* 85, no. 2 (2000): 232–34.

44. Jane Halpert, Midge Wilson, and Julia Hickman, "Pregnancy as a Source of Bias in Performance Appraisals," *Journal of Organizational Behavior* 14 (1993): 649–63. See also Michael Mount et al., "Rater–Ratee Effects in Developmental Performance Ratings of Managers," *Personnel Psychology* 50 (1997): 51–69.

45. Ibid., 655.

46. James Austin, Peter Villanova, and Hugh Hindman, "Legal Requirements and Technical Guidelines Involved in Implementing Performance Appraisal Systems," in Gerald Ferris and M. Ronald Buckley, *Human Resources Management*, 3d ed. (Upper Saddle River, NJ: Prentice Hall, 1996), pp. 271–88.

47. Ibid., 282.

48. Wayne Cascio and H. John Bernardin, "Implications of Performance Appraisal Litigation for Personnel Decisions,"

Personnel Psychology, summer 1981, pp. 211–12; Gerald Barrett and Mary Kernan, "Performance Appraisal and Terminations: A Review of Court Decisions since *Brito v. Zia* with Implications for Personnel Practices," *Personnel Psychology* 40, no. 3 (autumn 1987), pp. 489–504.

49. Ibid.
50. Ibid.
51. Daniel Feldman, "Toxic Mentor or Toxic Protégés? A Crucial Reexamination of Dysfunctional Mentoring," *Human Resource Management Review* 9, no. 3 (1999): 247–78.
52. Belle Rose Ragins and John Cotton, "Mentor Functions and Outcomes: A Comparison of Men and Women in Formal and Informal Mentoring Relationships," *Journal of Applied Psychology* 84, no. 4 (1999): 529–50. This section is based on Gary Dessler, *Human Resource Management* (Upper Saddle River, NJ: Prentice Hall, 1997), pp. 392–401.
53. "Career Guidance Steers Workers Away from Early Exits," *BNA Bulletin to Management* (September 7, 2000): 287.
54. Except as noted, this is based on Gary Addou and Mark Mendenhall, "Expatriate Performance Appraisal: Problems and Solutions," in Mark Mendenhall and Gary Addou, *International Human Resource Management* (Boston: PWS-Kent Publishing, 1991), p. 30.
55. Ibid., 36. See also Maddy Janssens, "Evaluating International Managers'

Performance: Parent Company Standards as Control Mechanisms," *International Journal of Human Resource Management* 5, no. 4 (December 1994): 30.
56. Richard Chanick, "Career Growth for Baby Boomers," *Personnel Journal* 71, no. 1 (January 1992): 40–46.
57. Karen Lyness and Donna Thompson, "Climbing the Corporate Ladder: Do Female and Male Executives Follow the Same Route?" *Journal of Applied Psychology* 85, no. 1 (2000): 86–101.
58. "Preretirement Education Programs," *Personnel* 59 (May/June 1982): 47. For an example of a program aimed at training preretirees to prepare for the financial aspects of their retirement, see, for example, Maureen Minehan, "The Aging of America Will Increase Elder Care Responsibilities," *HR Magazine* 42, no. 7 (July 1997): 184.
59. Jim Meade, "Boost Careers and Succession Planning," *HR Magazine* (October 2000): 175–78.
60. Gina Imperato, "Get Your Career in Sight," *Fast Company* (March 2000): 318–34.
61. Allan Mohrman Jr. and Susan Albers-Mohrmon, "Performance Management is Running the Business," *Compensation and Benefits Review* (July–August 1995): 69.
62. Dick Grote, "The Secrets of Performance Appraisal," *Across the Board* 37, no. 5 (May 2000): 14–16.

Chapter 7

Compensating Employees

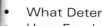

- What Determines How Much You Pay?
- How Employers Establish Pay Rates
- Current Trends in Compensation
- Incentive Plans
- Employee Benefits

When you finish studying this chapter, you should be able to:

- ■ Explain *each of the five basic steps in establishing pay rates.*

- ■ Discuss *four basic factors determining pay rates.*

- ■ Compare *and* contrast *piecework and team or group incentive plans.*

- ■ List *and* describe *each of the basic benefits most employers might be expected to offer.*

INTRODUCTION

*A*s IBM's CEO in the late 1990s, Louis Gerstner Jr. knew he needed a strategy to get his company moving. For years, employees had worked in a sort of cocoon, insulated from the market, paid not for performance but mainly for seniority. He had to refocus his employees' attention on a new set of values. He said winning must be an obsession; execution is built on speed and decisiveness; and IBMers must cultivate teamwork. One of his first steps was to order a total overhaul of IBM's whole compensation plan. The new plan had to make rewards contingent on performance, on the market, and on winning.[1]

Employee compensation refers to all forms of pay or rewards going to employees and arising from their employment,[2] and has two main

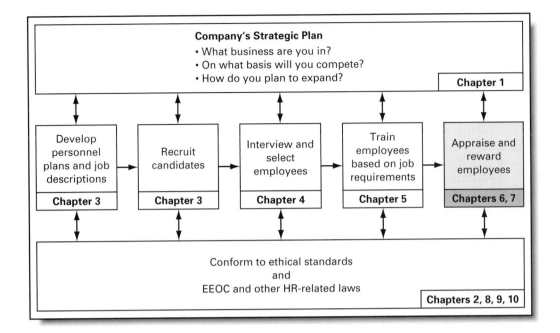

Company's Strategic Plan
• What business are you in?
• On what basis will you compete?
• How do you plan to expand?

Chapter 1

Develop personnel plans and job descriptions	Recruit candidates	Interview and select employees	Train employees based on job requirements	Appraise and reward employees
Chapter 3	Chapter 3	Chapter 4	Chapter 5	Chapters 6, 7

Conform to ethical standards
and
EEOC and other HR-related laws

Chapters 2, 8, 9, 10

components: *direct financial payments* (in the form of wages, salaries, incentives, commissions, and bonuses) *and indirect payments* (in the form of financial benefits like employer-paid insurance and vacations). We'll discuss both in this chapter.

WHAT DETERMINES HOW MUCH YOU PAY?

Four basic factors determine what people are paid: legal, union, policy, and equity factors. We'll look at each, starting with legal considerations.

Some Important Compensation Laws

Numerous laws stipulate what employers can or must pay in terms of minimum wages, overtime rates, and benefits. For example:[3]

1938 Fair Labor Standards Act   The **Fair Labor Standards Act,** originally passed in 1938 and since amended many times, contains minimum wage, maximum hours, overtime pay, equal pay, record-keeping, and child labor provisions covering the majority of U.S. workers—virtually all those engaged in the production and/or sale of goods for interstate and foreign commerce.

One important provision governs overtime pay. It states that employers must pay overtime at a rate of at least one and a half times normal pay for any hours worked over 40 in a workweek.

The act also sets a minimum wage. (The minimum wage in 2003 was $5.15 for the majority of those covered by the act, although a number of states have set their own minimum hourly rates above the federally mandated minimums.[4] For example, the minimum wage in California as of January 1, 2002, was $6.75.[5]) About 80 cities such as Boston and Chicago also require businesses that have contracts with the city to pay wages ranging from $6.25 to $12 an hour.[6] The act also contains child labor provisions. These prohibit employing minors between 16 and 18 years of age in hazardous occupations such as mining, and also carefully restricts employment of those under 16.

Some employees are *exempt* from the act or certain provisions of the act, and particularly from the act's overtime provisions. Whether you pay the employee hourly or based on a weekly, monthly, or yearly salary does not determine if he or she is exempt or nonexempt. The employee's responsibilities, duties, and salary level determines that. However, bona fide executive, administrative, and professional employees are generally exempt from the act's minimum wage and overtime requirements.[7] Figure 7.1 shows examples of exempt and nonexempt positions.[8]

Violating this act's provisions can be problematic. For example, several years ago a federal judge ordered the owners of a Colorado beef processing plant to pay nearly $2 million in back wages to 5,071 employees. He found that the firm had violated the Fair Labor Standards Act by not paying those employees "time-and-a-half" their regular rate of pay for hours worked in excess of 40 per week.[9] Some firms try to evade the letter of the law by claiming that employees who are doing, say, computer programming are not employees but "independent contractors" (who are more like consultants than employees); this tactic rarely works, when challenged.[10]

1963 Equal Pay Act   The **Equal Pay Act,** an amendment to the Fair Labor Standards Act, states that employees of one sex may not be paid wages at a rate lower than that paid to employees of the opposite sex for doing roughly equivalent work. Specifically, if the work requires equal skills, effort, and responsibility and is performed under similar working conditions, employees of both sexes must receive equal pay unless the differences in pay are based on a seniority system, a merit system, the quantity or quality of production, or any factor other than sex.

1964 Civil Rights Act   Title VII of the **Civil Rights Act** makes it an unlawful practice for an employer to discriminate against any individual with respect to hiring, compensation, terms, conditions, or privileges of employment because of race, color, religion, sex, or national origin.

Other Discrimination Laws   Various other discrimination laws influence compensation decisions. For example, the Age Discrimination in Employment Act prohibits age discrimination against employees who are 40 years of age and older in all aspects of employment, including compensation.[11] The Americans with Disabilities Act similarly prohibits discrimination against qualified persons with disabilities in all aspects of employment, including compensation. The Family and Medical Leave Act entitles eligible employees, both men and women, to take up to 12 weeks of unpaid, job-protected leave for the birth of a child or for the care of a child, spouse, or parent. Employers that are federal government contractors or subcontractors are required by various executive orders not to discriminate and to take affirmative action in various areas of employment, including compensation.

Figure 7.1
Who Is Exempt?
Who Is Not Exempt?

Exempt, Nonexempt Examples

Exempt Professionals

Attorneys
Physicians
Dentists
Pharmacists
Optometrists
Architects
Engineers
Teachers
Certified public accountants
Scientists
Computer systems analysts

Nonexempt

Paralegals
Nonlicensed accountants
Accounting clerks
Newspaper writers

Exempt Executives

Corporate officers
Department heads
Superintendents
General managers
Individual who is in sole charge of an
"independent establishment" or branch

Nonexempt

Working foreman/forewoman
Working supervisor
Lead worker
Management trainees

Exempt Administrators

Executive assistant to the president
Personnel directors
Credit managers
Purchasing agents

Nonexempt

Secretaries
Clerical employees
Inspectors
Statisticians

Note: These lists are general in nature, and exceptions exist. Any questionable allocation of exemption status should be reviewed by labor legal counsel.

How Unions Influence Compensation Decisions

For unionized companies, union-related issues of course also influence pay plan design. The National Labor Relations Act (NLRA) of 1935 granted employees the right to organize, to bargain collectively, and to engage in concerted activities for the purpose of collective bargaining or other mutual aid or protection. Historically, the wage rate has been the main issue in collective bargaining. However, other pay-related issues including time off with pay, income security (for those in industries with periodic layoffs), cost-of-living adjustments, and various benefits such as health care are also important.[12]

Compensation Policies

As at IBM, an employer's strategy and compensation policies significantly impact the wages and benefits it pays. At IBM, Gerstner wanted the company's new pay plan to focus employees' attention on performance and customer service. This meant new pay policies that emphasized pay for performance. Another consideration is whether you want to be a leader or a follower regarding pay. For example, a hospital might have a policy of starting nurses at a wage at least 20% above the prevailing market wage. Other important policies include the basis for salary increases, promotion and demotion policies, and overtime pay policy.[13] Locality also plays a role. For example, a job that pays $36,831 annually in New York might pay about $31,773 in California and $25,640 in Florida because of geography-based cost of living and other differentials.[14]

Equity and Its Impact on Pay Rates

Equity, specifically the need for external equity and internal equity, is a key factor in determining pay rates. Externally, pay must compare favorably with rates in other companies, or an employer will find it hard to attract and retain qualified employees. Pay must also be equitable internally: Each employee should view his or her pay as equitable given other employees' pay in the organization.

Salary inequities can trigger disappointment and conflict. Some firms therefore maintain secrecy over pay matters. However, online pay forums on sites like vault.com and Salary.com make it relatively easy today for employees to judge if they're being paid equitably.[15]

HOW EMPLOYERS ESTABLISH PAY RATES

In practice, setting pay rates while ensuring external and internal equity usually entails five steps:

1. Conduct a salary survey of what other employers are paying for comparable jobs (to help ensure external equity).
2. Employee committee determines the worth of each job in your organization through job evaluation (to ensure internal equity).
3. Group similar jobs into pay grades.
4. Price each pay grade by using wage curves.
5. Develop rate ranges.

We explain each of these steps in this section, starting with salary surveys.

Step 1: Conduct the Salary Survey

Salary (or compensation) surveys—formal or informal surveys of what other employers are paying for similar jobs—play a central role in pricing jobs. Virtually every employer therefore conducts such surveys for pricing one or more jobs.[16]

Employers use salary surveys in three ways. First, they use them to price *benchmark jobs*. These anchor the employer's pay scale. The manager slots other jobs around them, based on their relative worth to the firm. (*Job evaluation*, explained next, is the technique used to determine the relative worth of each job.) Second, employers usually price 20% or more of their positions directly in the marketplace (rather than relative to the firm's benchmark jobs), based on a formal or informal survey of what comparable firms are paying for comparable jobs. Finally, surveys also collect data on benefits such as insurance, sick leave, and vacation time.

Finding salary data and negotiating raises are not as mysterious as they used to be, thanks to the Internet. Figure 7.2 summarizes some popular salary survey Web sites. The Bureau of Labor Statistics recently organized its various pay surveys into a new National Compensation Survey, and began publishing this information on the Web. The Internet site is *//stats.bls.gov.*[17]

Figure 7.2   Some Pay-Data Web Sites

SPONSOR	INTERNET ADDRESS	WHAT IT PROVIDES	DOWNSIDE
Salary.com	Salary.com	Salary by job and zip code, plus job and description	Based on national averages adjusted by geographical differences
Wageweb	www.wageweb.com	Average salaries for more than 150 clerical, professional, and managerial jobs	Charges $100 for breakdowns by industry, geography, etc.
Exec-U-Net	www.execunet.com	Salary, bonus, and options for about 650 management posts	Charges an initial $125 for job details
PinPoint Salary Service	members.aol.com/ payraises	Individualized pay analyses, based on title, experience, desired industry, etc.	First job analysis costs $95
Futurestep*	www.futurestep.com	Pay analyses of people eligible for managerial posts paying $50,000 to $200,000 a year	Participants automatically subject to queries from Korn/Ferry recruiters

* An alliance between recruiters Korn/Ferry International and *The Wall Street Journal.*   Source: *WSJ Reports*

Source: Adapted from Joann S. Lublin, "Web Transforms Art of Negotiating Raises," *Wall Street Journal* (September 22, 1998): B1.

Step 2: Determine the Worth of Each Job: Job Evaluation

Purpose of Job Evaluation   **Job evaluation** is a formal and systematic comparison of jobs to determine the worth of one job relative to another. The basic job evaluation procedure is to compare the content of jobs in relation to one another, for example, in terms of their effort, responsibility, and skills. Suppose you know (based on your salary survey and compensation policies) how to price key benchmark jobs and can use job evaluation to determine the relative worth of all the other jobs in your firm relative to these key jobs. Then you are well on your way to being able to equitably price all the jobs in your organization.

Compensable Factors   There are two basic approaches to comparing the worth of several jobs. First, you could take an intuitive approach. You might decide that one job is more important than another and not dig any deeper into why in terms of specific job-related factors.

As an alternative, you could compare the jobs based on certain basic factors they have in common. In compensation management, these basic factors are called **compensable factors.** They are the factors that determine your definition of job content, establish how the jobs compare to each other, and set the compensation paid for each job. For example, the Equal Pay Act focuses on four compensable factors: skills, effort, responsibility, and working conditions.

Job Evaluation Methods   The simplest job evaluation method ranks each job relative to all other jobs, usually based on some overall compensable factor such as job difficulty. There are several steps in this job **ranking method,** as summarized in the *HR in Practice* box. *Job classification* is another simple, widely used method. Here the manager categorizes jobs into groups based on their similarity in terms of compensable factors such as skills and responsibility. The groups are called *classes* if they contain similar jobs, or *grades* if they contain jobs that are similar in difficulty but otherwise different. Thus, in the federal government's pay grade system, a press secretary and a fire chief might both be graded GS-10 (GS stands for General Schedule). The *point method* is a quantitative job evaluation technique. It involves identifying several compensable factors, each having several degrees, and then assigning points based on the number of degrees to come up with an actual number of points for each job.

Step 3: Group Similar Jobs into Pay Grades

Once a job evaluation method has been used to determine the relative worth of each job, the evaluation committee can start assigning pay rates to each job; it usually first groups jobs into pay grades. A *pay grade* comprises jobs of approximately equal difficulty or importance as determined by job evaluation. If the point method were used, the pay grade would consist of jobs falling within a range of points. If the ranking plan were used, the grade would consist of all jobs that fall within two or three ranks. If the classification system were used, then the jobs are already categorized into classes or grades. Ten to 16 grades per job cluster (or logical grouping such as factory jobs, clerical jobs, etc.) are common.

1. *Obtain job information.* Job analysis is the first step in the ranking method. Job descriptions for each job are prepared and these are usually the basis on which the rankings are made. (Sometimes job specifications also are prepared, but the job ranking method usually ranks jobs according to the whole job rather than a number of compensable factors. Therefore, job specifications—which provide an indication of the demands of the job in terms of problem solving, decision making, and skills, for instance—are not as necessary with this method as they are for other job evaluation methods.)

2. *Select raters and jobs to be rated.* It is often not practical to make a single ranking of all jobs in an organization. The more usual procedure is to rank jobs by department or in clusters (such as factory workers and clerical workers). This eliminates the need for having to compare directly, say, factory jobs and clerical jobs.

3. *Select compensable factors.* In the ranking method, it is common to use just one factor (such as job difficulty) and to rank jobs on the basis of the whole job. Regardless of the number of factors you choose, it's advisable to explain the definition of the factor(s) to the evaluators carefully so that they evaluate the jobs consistently.

4. *Rank jobs.* Next the jobs are ranked. The simplest way is to give each rater a set of index cards, each of which contains a brief description of a job. These cards are then ranked from lowest to highest. Some managers use an alternation ranking method for making the procedure more accurate; they use the cards to first choose the highest and the lowest, and then the next highest and next lowest, and so forth until all the cards have been ranked. Because it is usually easier to choose extremes, this approach facilitates the ranking procedure.

A job ranking is illustrated in Table 7.1. Jobs in this small health facility are ranked from maid up to office manager. The corresponding pay scales are shown on the right.

5. *Combine ratings.* Usually several raters rank the jobs independently. Then the rating committee (or employer) can average the rankings.

Table 7.1   Job Ranking by Olympia Health Care

RANKING ORDER	ANNUAL PAY SCALE
1. Office manager	$28,000
2. Chief nurse	27,500
3. Bookkeeper	19,000
4. Nurse	17,500
5. Cook	16,000
6. Nurse's aide	13,500
7. Maid	10,500

After ranking, it becomes possible to slot additional jobs between those already ranked and to assign an appropriate wage rate.

Step 4: Price Each Pay Grade: Wage Curves

The next step is to assign average pay rates to each of the pay grades. (Of course, if you choose not to slot jobs into pay grades, an individual pay rate has to be assigned to each individual job.) Assigning pay rates to each pay grade (or to each job) is usually accomplished with the help of a **wage curve,** which shows the average pay rates

How Employers Establish Pay Rates

229

Figure 7.3
Plotting a Wage
Curve

Note: The average pay
rate for jobs in each
grade (Grade I, Grade II,
Grade III, etc.) are plotted, and the wage curve
is fitted to the resulting
points.

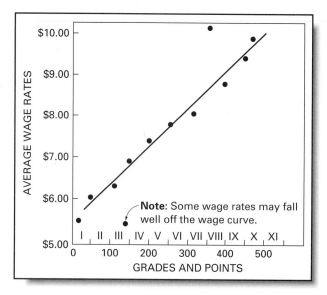

currently being paid for jobs in each pay grade, relative to the points or rankings
assigned to each job or grade by the job evaluation. An example of a wage curve is
presented in Figure 7.3. The purpose of the wage curve is to show the relationship
between (1) the value of the job as determined by one of the job evaluation methods
and (2) the current average pay rates for the grades. The wage line then becomes the
target for wages or salary rates for the jobs in each pay grade.

Step 5: Develop Rate Ranges

Finally, most employers do not just pay one rate for all jobs in a particular pay grade.
Instead, they develop rate ranges for each grade. So, there might be 10 levels or steps
and 10 corresponding pay rates within each pay grade. They may then fine-tune pay
rates to account for any unique circumstances.

Pricing Managerial and Professional Jobs

For managerial and professional jobs, job evaluation provides only a partial answer
to the question of how to pay these employees. Managerial and professional jobs
tend to emphasize nonquantifiable factors such as judgment and problem solving
more than do production and clerical jobs. There is also more of a tendency to pay
managers and professionals based on their performance, on what competitors are
paying, or on what they can do, rather than on intrinsic job demands such as working conditions.

For a company's top executives, the compensation plan generally consists of four
main components; base salary, short-term incentives, long-term incentives, and executive benefits and perks.[18] Base salary includes the obvious fixed compensation paid
regularly as well as, often, guaranteed bonuses such as "10% of pay at the end of
the fourth fiscal quarter, regardless of whether the company makes a profit." Short-
term incentives are usually paid in cash or stock for achieving short-term goals,

such as year-to-year increases in sales revenue. Long-term incentives include such things as stock options, which generally give the executive the right to purchase stock at a specific price for a specific period of time and are aimed at encouraging the executive to take actions that will drive up the price of the company's stock. Finally, special executive benefits and perks might include supplemental executive retirement plans, supplemental life insurance, and health insurance without a deductible or coinsurance.

Supplemental retirement plans head a list of executive perks, with about 60% of the companies offering them in one survey. Other popular executive perks include leased automobiles (57%), automobile allowance (45%), free medical examinations (44%), financial counseling (39%), country club membership (33%), and first-class airline seating (30%).[19]

CURRENT TRENDS IN COMPENSATION

The basic concern with job evaluation is that jobs defined in terms of a narrow range of duties and points may discourage employees from seeking broader responsibilities. (For example, an employee who is, say, a mechanic IV might be unwilling to move for a day to a mechanic V job, without extra pay.) Some therefore question whether job evaluation's tendency to slot jobs into narrow cubbyholes might not actually be counterproductive in today's high-performance work systems. Systems like these depend on flexible, multi-skilled job assignments and on high-involvement techniques like teamwork and participative decision making, so there's no place for employees who say, "That's not my job."

In fact, the evidence suggests that trying to combine a high-performance workplace with the more structured job evaluation approach may actually limit a firm's ability to perform better than its peers. The trend is therefore toward flexible pay approaches, like those we address next.[20] However, works for one company won't necessarily work for another, so it's important to take the company's needs into account. As one compensation experts says, "Each employer [must] define its own [compensation plan] needs and develop a system that meets those needs."[21]

Competency- and Skill-Based Pay

With competency- or skill-based pay, an employee is paid for the range, depth, and types of skills and knowledge he or she is capable of using rather than for the job currently held.[22] Competencies are "demonstrable characteristics of the person, including knowledge, skills, and behaviors, that enable performance."[23]

Why pay employees based on the skill levels they achieve, rather than based on the jobs they're assigned to? For example, why pay an accounting clerk II who has achieved a certain mastery of accounting techniques the same as (or more than) someone who is an accounting clerk IV? The answer is, to encourage the person to become more multi-skilled. With more companies organizing around project teams, employers expect employees to be able to rotate among jobs. Doing so requires having more skills.

More than 50% of *Fortune* 1000 firms use some form of skill-based pay.[24] One major aerospace firm uses skill-based pay by having all exempt employees negotiate "learning contracts" with their supervisors. The employees then receive pay increases for meeting learning (skills-improvement) objectives.[25]

Skill-based pay programs generally contain four main elements. The employer defines specific skills, and has a method for tying the person's pay to his or her skill competencies. A training system lets employees seek and acquire skills. There is a formal competency testing system. And, the work is designed in such a way that employees can easily move among jobs. A study of one such skill-based pay program concluded that it had resulted in 58% greater productivity, 16% lower labor cost per part, and an 82% reduction in scrap, versus a comparison facility.[26]

Broadbanding

Most firms end up with pay plans that slot jobs into classes or grades, each with its own vertical pay rate range. For example, the U.S. government's pay plan consists of 18 main grades (GS-1 to GS-18), each with its own pay range. For an employee whose

Figure 7.4
Broadbanded
Structure and How
It Relates to
Traditional Pay
Grades and Ranges

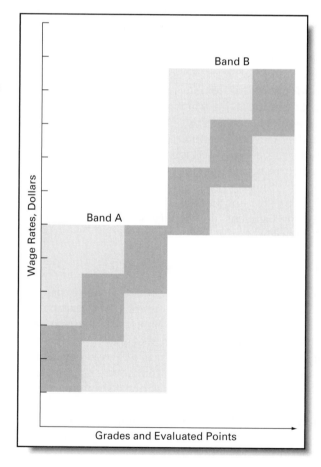

The annual cost of sending a U.S. expatriate manager from the United States to Europe varies widely according to the host country. For example, it is estimated that the annual cost of keeping a U.S. expatriate in France might average $193,000, whereas in neighboring Germany the cost would be $246,000.[27] Such wide discrepancies raise the issue of how multinational firms should compensate overseas employees. The issue is particularly important because of the growing need to staff overseas operations and because of the frequency with which managers and professionals are moved from country to country. Two basic international compensation policies are popular: home-based and host-based policies.[28]

Under a home-based salary plan, an international transferee's base salary reflects his or her home country's salary structure. Additional allowances are then tacked on for cost-of-living differences and housing and schooling costs, for instance. This is a reasonable approach for short-term assignments and avoids the problem of having to change the employee's base salary every time he or she moves. However, it can result in some difficulty at the host office if, say, employees from several different countries assigned to the same host office are all being paid different base salaries for performing essentially the same tasks. However, this still tends to be the prevailing approach.

In the host-based plan, the base salary for the international transferee is tied to the host country's salary structure. In other words, the manager from New York who is sent to France would have his or her base salary changed to the prevailing base salary for that position in France rather than keep his or her New York base salary. Of course, cost-of-living, housing, schooling, and other allowances are tacked on here as well. This approach can keep all employees in a host country office paid similarly, but might cause some consternation to the New York manager, who might, for instance, see his or her base salary plummet with a transfer to Bangladesh.

job falls in one of these grades, the pay range for that grade dictates his or her minimum and maximum salary.

The question is, How wide should the salary grades be, in terms of the number of job evaluation points they include? There is a downside to having narrow grades. For instance, if you want someone whose job is in grade 2 to fill in for a time in a job that happens to be in grade 1, it's difficult to reassign that person without lowering his or her salary. Similarly, if you want the person to learn about a job that happens to be in grade 3, the employee might object to the reassignment without a corresponding raise to grade 3 pay. Traditional grade pay plans thus breed inflexibility.

That is why some firms are broadbanding their pay plans. Broadbanding means collapsing salary grades and ranges into just a few wide levels, or bands, each of which contains a relatively wide range of jobs and salary levels. Figure 7.4 illustrates this. In Figure 7.4, the company's previous six pay grades are consolidated into two broad bands.

A company may create broadbands for all its jobs, or for specific groups such as managers or professionals. The pay rate range of each broadband is relatively large, since it ranges from the minimum pay of the lowest grade the firm merged into the broadband up to the maximum pay of the highest merged grade. Thus, for example, instead of having 10 salary grades, each of which contains a salary range of $15,000, the firm might collapse the 10 grades into 3 broadbands, each with a set of jobs such that the difference between the lowest- and highest-paid jobs might be $40,000 or more. For the jobs that fall in this broadband, there is therefore a much wider range of pay rates. You can move employees from job to job within the broadband more easily, without worrying about the employees moving outside the relatively narrow rate range associated with a traditional narrow pay grade. Broadbanding therefore breeds flexibility. The preceding *Global Issues* box (page 233) explains some issues in paying expatriate employees.

The "New Pay"

Skill-based pay and broadbanding are two examples of the newer approaches to pay that are popular today. The basic idea of what some call the "new pay" is to use the firm's pay plan to help the firm better achieve its performance objectives and implement its strategies.[29] For example, skill-based pay focuses employees' attention on raising skill levels. It thereby makes it easier to move employees from project to project, as demand warrants.

In general, three trends characterize pay plans today. First, as we've seen, there is more emphasis on rewarding individuals for their skills and competencies, and to defining salary grades much more broadly. Second, there is more emphasis on performance-based incentive pay. Third, there is more emphasis on giving individuals a choice in the rewards they receive.[30] We turn to performance-based pay, and flexible benefits in the following sections.

INCENTIVE PLANS

Many—perhaps most—employees don't just earn a salary or hourly wage. They also earn some type of incentive. This section addresses some popular **incentive plans**.[31] *Individual incentive programs* give performance-based pay to individual employees who meet their individual performance standards.[32] *Variable pay* refers to group pay plans that tie payments to productivity or to some other measure of the firm's profitability. Several incentive plan examples follow.

Piecework Plans

Piecework is the oldest incentive plan and still the most commonly used. Pay is tied directly to what the worker produces: The person is paid a "piece rate" for each unit he or she produces. Thus, if Tom Smith gets $0.40 apiece for finding addresses on the Web, then he would make $40 for finding 100 a day and $80 for 200.

Team or Group Incentive Plans

Companies often want to pay groups (rather than individuals) on an incentive basis, such as when they want to encourage teamwork. There are several ways to do so.[33] One involves tying team performance to the company's strategic goals. One company, for instance, set up a pool of money such that if the company reached 100% of its overall goal, the employees would share in about 5% of this. That 5% pool was then divided by the number of employees, to arrive at the value of a share. Each work team then received two goals. If the team achieved both of its goals, each employee would earn one share (in addition to his or her base pay). Employees on teams that reached only one goal would earn a half share. Those on teams reaching neither goal earned no shares. The results of this new plan—in terms of changing employee attitudes and focusing teams on strategic goals—was reportedly excellent.[34]

There are several reasons to use team or group incentive plans. Sometimes several jobs are interrelated, as they are on project teams, where one worker's performance reflects not just his or her own effort but that of co-workers as well. Here team incentives make sense.

A group incentive plan's main disadvantage is that each worker's rewards are not based just on his or her own efforts. If the person does not see his or her effort translating directly into proportional rewards, a group plan may be less effective than an individual plan.

Incentives for Managers and Executives

Most employers offer their managers incentives because of the role managers play in determining divisional and corporate profitability.[35] Surveys indicate, for instance, that over 90% of large companies pay managers and executives annual ("short-term") bonuses,[36] whereas about 70% of small firms have such plans.[37] Similarly, long-term incentive plans (such as stock options), which are intended to motivate and reward management for the corporation's long-term growth and prosperity, are used by most U.S. firms.[38] About 69% of companies in one survey had short-term incentives, although nearly a third of those said they didn't consider them effective in boosting employee performance.[39]

The size of the bonus is usually greater for top-level executives. Thus, an executive earning $250,000 in salary may be able to earn another 80% of his or her salary as a bonus, whereas a manager in the same firm earning $80,000 can earn only another 30%. Similarly, a supervisor might be able to earn up to 15% of his or her base salary in bonuses.

The stock option is one incentive companies use for managerial (and other) employees. A **stock option** is the right to purchase a specific number of shares of company stock at a specific price during a period of time. The executive hopes to profit by exercising his or her option to buy the shares in the future but at today's price. Stock price is affected by the firm's profitability and growth, and because the executive can affect these factors, the stock option can be an incentive.

Firms have begun de-emphasizing stock option plans, for several reasons. Many blame stock options for contributing to the numerous corporate scandals in the early 2000s, by providing too much incentive for questionable managerial decisions. Furthermore, until recently, most companies did not treat stock options as an expense. This could distort a company's reported financial performance, by making expenses look less than they really were. More companies are trying to emphasize accuracy and transparency in financial statements, so more are now expensing stock options. But, having to show the options as expense reduces, to some degree, the attractiveness to the companies of awarding the options. As one compensation consultant puts it, "The fact that this is now 'costing' them something will mean that they will have to do more of the cost/benefit analysis to see which design will give them the best return for their dollar."[40]

Incentives for Salespeople

Most companies pay their salespeople a combination of salary and commissions, usually with a sizable salary component. One compensation expert suggests a 70% base salary/30% incentive mix as an example that both cushioned the downside risk from the salesperson's point of view and limited the risk that the upside rewards would get out of hand from the firm's point of view.[41]

Setting effective quotas is an art. Questions to ask include: Are quotas communicated to the sales force within one month of the start of the period? Does the sales force know explicitly how their quotas are set? Do you combine bottom-up information (like account forecasts) with top-down requirements (like the company business plan)? Are quotas stable through the performance period? Are returns and debookings reasonably low? And, has your firm generally avoided compensation-related lawsuits?[42] One expert suggests the following as a rule of thumb as to whether the sales incentive plan is effective: 75% or more of the sales force achieving quota or better; 10% of the sales force achieving higher performance level (than previously); 5% to 10% of the sales force achieving below quota performance and receiving performance development coaching.[43]

Experts have traditionally suggested "locking in" quotas and incentive plans, on the assumption that frequent changes undermine salesperson motivation and morale. But in today's fast-changing industrial scene, such inflexibility is usually not advisable. One expert says, "Now that the product life cycles are often in the six-month to six-week range, the traditional approaches to most sales plans cannot accommodate the pace. . . . The sales organization and its emphasis must become more flexible than it's been."[44] The sales compensation plan and its quotas therefore tend to be reviewed more often today.

Merit Pay as an Incentive

Merit pay, or a **merit raise,** is any salary increase awarded to an employee based on his or her individual performance. It is different from a bonus in that it becomes part of the employee's base salary, whereas a bonus is a one-time payment. Although the term *merit pay* can apply to the incentive raises given to any employees—exempt or nonexempt, office or factory, management or nonmanagement—the term is more often used with respect to white-collar employees and particularly professional, office, and clerical employees. Merit increases historically average about 4%, depending on inflation and the state of the economy.[45]

Merit pay has both advocates and detractors and is the subject of much debate.[46] Advocates argue that only rewards such as these that are tied directly to performance can motivate improved performance. On the other hand, merit pay detractors present good reasons why merit pay can backfire. One is that it undermines just the sort of teamwork that most companies want to cultivate today. Another is that the value of merit pay depends on the performance appraisal system. If (as is often the case) the appraisals are viewed as unfair, so too will be the merit pay.[47] Another problem is that almost every employee thinks he or she is an above-average performer; being paid a below-average merit increase can thus be demoralizing.[48]

Profit-Sharing Plans

In a **profit-sharing plan,** most employees receive a share of the company's annual profits. Research on the effectiveness of such plans is sketchy. In one survey, about half of the companies believed that their profit-sharing plans had been beneficial,[49] but the benefits were not necessarily just higher performance or motivation. Instead, the plans may increase each worker's sense of commitment, participation, and part- nership. They may thus reduce turnover and encourage employee thrift. Although there are many such plans, cash plans are the most popular. Here, employees receive a percentage of profits (usually 15% to 20%) as profit shares at regular intervals.

Employee Stock Ownership Plan

About 35% of 400 U.S.-based companies provide stock options to both exempt and nonexempt employees.[50] One way to do this is through employee stock ownership plans. Under the most basic form of **employee stock ownership plan (ESOP),** a cor- poration contributes shares of its own stock—or cash to be used to purchase such stock—to a trust established to purchase shares of the firm's stock for employees.[51] These contributions are generally made annually in proportion to total employee compensation, with a limit of 15% of compensation. The trust holds the stock in indi- vidual employee accounts. It then distributes it to employees upon retirement or other separation from service (assuming that the employee has worked long enough to earn ownership of the stock).

ESOPs have several advantages. The corporation receives a tax deduction equal to the fair market value of the shares that are transferred to the trustee. Corporations can also claim an income tax deduction for dividends paid on ESOP-owned stock.[52] Employees are not taxed until they receive a distribution from the trust, usually at retirement, when their tax rate is reduced. And the **Employee Retirement Income Security Act (ERISA)** allows a firm to borrow against employee stock held in trust. The employer can then repay the loan in pretax rather than after-tax dollars, which is another tax incentive for using such plans.[53] Research also suggests that ESOPs encourage employees to develop a sense of ownership in and commitment to the firm and are related to improved firm performance.[54]

Scanlon Plan

The **Scanlon plan** is an incentive plan developed in 1937 by Joseph Scanlon, a United Steel Workers Union official,[55] and is remarkably progressive considering that it was developed long ago. It is one of many **gain-sharing plans,** the aim of which are to encourage improved employee productivity by sharing resulting financial gains with employees. Other popular types of gain-sharing plans include the Rucker and Improshare plans.

Scanlon plans today have five basic features.[56] The first is the *philosophy of cooperation* on which it is based. This philosophy assumes that managers and workers should rid themselves of the "us" and "them" attitudes that normally inhibit employees from developing a sense of ownership in the company. It substitutes instead a climate in which everyone cooperates because he or she understands that economic rewards are contingent on honest cooperation.

A second feature of a Scanlon plan is *identity.* This means that to focus employee efforts, the company's mission or purpose must be clearly articulated, and employees must understand how the business operates in terms of customers, prices, and costs, for instance. *Competence* is a third basic feature. The plan, say three experts, "explicitly recognizes that a Scanlon plan demands a high level of competence from employees at all levels."[57]

The fourth feature is the *involvement system.*[58] This takes the form of two levels of committees—the departmental level and the executive level. Employees present productivity-improving suggestions to the appropriate departmental-level committees, which transmit the valuable ones to the executive-level committee. The latter then decides whether to implement the suggestions.

The fifth element of the plan is the *sharing of benefits formula*. The Scanlon plan assumes that employees should share directly in any extra profits resulting from their cost-cutting suggestions. For example, if a suggestion is implemented and successful, all employees might share in 75% of the savings.

Earnings-At-Risk Pay Plans

The basic characteristic of an earnings-at-risk pay plan is that some portion of the employee's base salary is at risk. In the DuPont Company's plan, for instance, an employees' at-risk pay is a maximum of 6%. This means that each employee's base pay will be 94% of his or her counterpart's salary in other (not-at-risk) DuPont departments.[59] If the department achieves its goals, the employees get their full pay; if it exceeds its goals, they receive a bonus exceeding the 6%.

Three researchers studied the effects of one such earnings-at-risk incentive plan. They concluded that the employees were dissatisfied with their lower base salary, but that this dissatisfaction seemed to motivate them to work harder to earn the incentive and thereby raise their total pay.[60]

An Example: Incentives at Nucor Corporation

In today's performance-oriented environment, employers increasingly pay all or most employees an incentive. For example, Nucor Corp. is the largest steel producer in the United States; it also has the highest productivity, highest wages, and lowest labor cost per ton in the American steel industry.[61] Nucor employees earn bonuses of 100% or more of base salary. All participate in one of four performance-based incentive plans. With the *production incentive plan,* plant operating and maintenance employees and supervisors get weekly bonuses based on their workgroup's productivity. The *department manager incentive plan* pays department managers annual incentive bonuses based mostly on the ratio of net income to dollars of assets employed for their division. With the *professional and clerical bonus plan* employees who are not in one of the two previous plans get bonuses based on their division's net income return on assets. Finally, under the *senior officers incentive plan* Nucor senior managers (whose base salaries are lower than those of executives in comparable firms) get bonuses based on Nucor's annual overall percentage of net income to stockholder's equity.[62]

Technology and Incentives

Incentives are becoming ever more complicated. For one thing, as we've seen, more employees—not just salespeople—now get incentives. Furthermore, the range of behaviors for which employers pay incentives is now quite broad, from better service to cutting costs to answering more calls per hour.[63]

Tracking performance of dozens or hundreds of measures like these and then computing individual employees' incentives can be very time consuming. Several companies such as Incentives Systems Inc. therefore provide sophisticated software known as Enterprise Incentive Management (EIM) systems to automate the planning and management of plans like these. As one expert says, "EIM software automates the planning, calculation, modeling and management of incentive compensation plans, enabling companies to align their employees with corporate strategy and goals."[64]

Employers also increasingly use the Web to support their sales and other incentive programs. For example, SalesDriver, in Maynard, Massachusetts, runs Web-based sales-performance-based incentive programs. Firms like these specialize in creating online sales incentive programs. SalesDriver can help a company launch a campaign Web template in a day or less. Using the template, the sales manager can select from a catalog of 1,500 reward items, and award these to sales and marketing reps for meeting quotas for things like lead generation and total sales.[65]

EMPLOYEE BENEFITS

Benefits represent an important part of just about every employee's pay. They can be defined as all the indirect financial payments an employee receives for continuing his or her employment with the company.[66] Benefits include such things as time off with pay, health and life insurance, and child care facilities.

Providing and administering benefits is an increasingly expensive task.[67] Employee benefits account for over one-third of the total cost of company payrolls, with health insurance the most expensive single benefit cost.[68] Employees do seem to understand the value of health benefits. One study concluded that employees whose employers provided them with health insurance accepted wages about 20% lower than what they would have received working in jobs without such benefits.[69]

There are many benefits and various ways to classify them. In the remainder of this section we will classify benefits as pay for time not worked, insurance benefits, retirement benefits, and employee services benefits.

Pay for Time Not Worked

Supplemental Pay Benefits   Supplemental pay benefits, or pay for time not worked, are typically one of an employer's most expensive benefits because of all the time off that employees receive. Common time-off-with-pay periods include holidays, vacations, jury duty, bereavement leave, military duty, sick leave, sabbatical leave, maternity leave, and unemployment insurance payments for laid-off or terminated employees.

Unemployment Insurance   All states have unemployment insurance or compensation acts, which provide for weekly benefits if a person is unable to work through some fault other than his or her own. The benefits derive from an unemployment tax on employers that can range from 0.1% to 5% of taxable payroll in most states. States each have their own unemployment laws, which follow federal guidelines. An organization's unemployment tax reflects its experience with personnel terminations.

Unemployment benefits are not meant for all dismissed employees, only those terminated through no fault of their own. Thus, strictly speaking, a worker fired for chronic lateness has no legitimate claim to benefits. But in practice, many managers take a lackadaisical attitude toward protecting their employers against unwarranted claims. Therefore, employers spend thousands of dollars more per year on unemployment taxes than would be necessary if they protected themselves—for instance, by keeping careful records of lateness and absences, and by warning employees whose performance is inadequate.

Vacations and Holidays   The average number of annual vacation days varies around the world. For example, compared with the average 10-day U.S. vacation, vacation allowances vary from 6 days in Mexico to 10 days in Japan, 25 in Sweden, 25 in France, and 33 in Denmark. (On the other hand, Denmark, France, and several other European countries also have a six-day workweek![70])

In the United States, the number of paid holidays similarly varies considerably from employer to employer, from a minimum of about five to 13 or more. The most common paid holidays include New Year's Day, Memorial Day, Independence Day, Labor Day, Thanksgiving Day, and Christmas Day. Other common holidays include Martin Luther King Jr. Day, Good Friday, President's Day, Veteran's Day, the Friday after Thanksgiving, the day before Christmas, and the day before New Year's Day.[71]

Sick Leave   Sick leave provides pay to employees when they are out of work because of illness. Most sick leave policies grant full pay for a specified number of permissible sick days, usually up to about 12 per year. The sick days often accumulate at the rate of approximately one day per month of service.

Sick leave pay causes consternation for many employers. The problem is that although many employees use their sick days only when they are legitimately sick, others (in the eyes of some employers) take advantage of sick leave by using it as if it's extra vacation time, whether they are sick or not.

Employers utilize several tactics to eliminate or reduce this problem. Many use *pooled paid leave plans*. These plans—which lump together sick leave, vacation, and holidays into a single leave pool—have grown from 21% of firms surveyed five years ago to 66% today.[72] Other firms buy back unused sick leave at the end of the year by paying their employees a daily equivalent pay for each sick leave day not used. The drawback is that the policy can encourage legitimately sick employees to come to work despite their illness.[73] Others hold monthly lotteries in which only employees with perfect attendance are able to participate; those who participate are eligible to win a cash prize. Still others aggressively investigate all unplanned absences, for instance, by calling the absent employees at their homes when they are taking sick days.

Sick leave policy depends to some extent on the Family and Medical Leave Act of 1993. Among its provisions, the law stipulates that:

1. Private employers of 50 or more employees must provide eligible employees up to 12 weeks of unpaid leave for their own serious illness, the birth or adoption of a child, or the care of a seriously ill child, spouse, or parent.
2. Employers may require employees to take any unused paid sick leave or annual leave as part of the 12-week leave provided in the law.
3. Employees taking leave are entitled to receive health benefits while they are on unpaid leave under the same terms and conditions as when they were on the job.
4. Employers must guarantee employees the right to return to their previous or equivalent position with no loss of benefits at the end of the leave; however, the law provides a limited exception from this provision to certain highly paid employees.

One survey suggests that the act is working as planned. It found that most employees do take leave for family or medical reasons; fewer than in the past report they need leave but are unable to take it; many employers offer leave in excess of that which the act requires; and most employers report little or no adverse effects of the act on their businesses.[74] Note that seven states (California, Illinois, Louisiana, Massachusetts, Minnesota, North Carolina, and Vermont) and the District of Columbia have expanded upon the family medical and leave act. They have instituted "small necessities leave" laws. These provide leave for things like visiting physicians and attending school activities.[75]

Severance Pay   Some employers provide **severance pay**—a one-time separation payment—when terminating an employee. The payment may range from three or four days' wages to one or more years' salary. Other firms provide "bridge" severance pay by keeping employees (especially managers) on the payroll for several months, until they have found new jobs.

Such payments make sense on several grounds. It is a humanitarian gesture as well as good public relations. In addition, most managers expect employees to give them at least one or two weeks' notice if they plan to quit; it is therefore appropriate (and in some states mandatory) to provide at least one pay period's severance pay if an employee is terminated. Such payments can also reduce the possibility that a terminated employee will retaliate, for instance, by suing.

Plant closings and downsizings have put thousands of employees out of work, often with little or no notice or severance pay. Many states have been attempting to fight such closings, and a Supreme Court ruling (*Fort Halifax Packing Co.* v. *Coyne*) paved the way for states to cushion the economic impact of such closings. The Court ruled that states may force employers to provide severance pay to workers who lose their jobs because of plant closings. The Worker Adjustment and Retraining ("plant closing") Act of 1989 requires covered employers to give employees 60 days' written notice of plant closures or mass layoffs.

Insurance Benefits

Workers' Compensation   Workers' compensation laws[76] are aimed at providing sure, prompt income and medical benefits to work-related accident victims or their dependents, regardless of fault.[77] Every state has its own workers' compensation law, and some states even offer their own insurance programs. However, most require employers to purchase workers' compensation insurance through private state-approved insurance companies. The trend is toward improved workers' compensation benefits. For example, about half of all U.S. states recently changed their workers' compensation laws, and most increased benefits for disability and death.[78]

Workers' compensation benefits can be either monetary or medical. In the event of a worker's death or disablement, the person or his or her beneficiary is paid a cash benefit based on prior earnings—usually one-half to two-thirds of the worker's average weekly wage, per week of employment. In most states there is a set time limit—such as 500 weeks—for which benefits can be paid. If the injury causes a specific loss (such as loss of an arm), the employee may receive additional benefits based on a statutory list of losses, even though he or she may return to work. In addition to these cash benefits, employers must furnish medical, surgical, and hospital services needed by the employee.

For an injury or illness to be covered by workers' compensation, the employee need only prove that it arose while he or she was on the job. It does not matter that the employee may have been at fault or disregarded instructions. If he or she was on the job when the injury occurred, he or she is entitled to workers' compensation.

Many, or most, workers' compensation claims are legitimate, but some are not. Supervisors should be aware of typical red flags of fraudulent claims, including vague accident details, minor accidents resulting in major injuries, lack of witnesses, injuries occurring late Friday or very early Monday, and late reporting.[79]

Hospitalization, Medical, and Disability Insurance   Most employers—about 77% of medium and large firms—make available to their employees some type of hospitalization, medical, and disability insurance; along with life insurance, these benefits form the cornerstone of almost all benefit programs.[80] Many offer membership in a health maintenance organization (HMO) as a hospital/medical option. The HMO is a medical organization consisting of numerous specialists (surgeons, psychiatrists, etc.) operating out of a community-based health care center.[81]

Preferred provider organizations (PPOs) are a cross between HMOs and the traditional physician/patient arrangement.[82] Unlike an HMO, with its relatively limited list of health care providers often concentrated in one health care center, PPOs let employees select providers (such as participating physicians) who agree to provide price discounts and submit to certain utilization controls, such as on the number of diagnostic tests that can be ordered.[83]

The Pregnancy Discrimination Act   The Pregnancy Discrimination Act (PDA) is aimed at prohibiting sex discrimination based on "pregnancy, childbirth, or related medical conditions."[84] Before enactment of this law in 1978, employers generally paid temporary disability benefits for pregnancies in the form of either sick leave or disability insurance, if at all. However, although most employers provide temporary disability income to their employees for up to 26 weeks for most illnesses, those that provided benefits for pregnancy usually limited benefits to only six weeks for normal pregnancies. Many believed that the shorter duration of pregnancy benefits constituted discrimination based on sex.

The act requires employers to treat women affected by pregnancy, childbirth, or related medical conditions the same as any employee not able to work, with respect to all benefits, including sick leave and disability benefits, and health and medical insurance. Thus, it is illegal for most employers to discriminate against women by providing benefits of lower amount or duration for pregnancy, childbirth, or related medical conditions. For example, if an employer provides up to 26 weeks of temporary disability income to employees for all illnesses, it is also required to provide up to 26 weeks for pregnancy and childbirth.

COBRA Requirements   The ominously titled COBRA—Comprehensive Omnibus Budget Reconciliation Act—requires most private employers to make available to terminated or retired employees and their families continued health benefits for a period of time, generally 18 months. If the former employee chooses to continue these benefits, he or she must pay for them, as well as a small fee for administrative costs.

Take care in administering COBRA, especially with respect to informing employees of their COBRA rights. For example, you don't want a separated employee to be injured and come back and claim she didn't know her insurance coverage could have been continued. Therefore, when a new employee first becomes eligible for your company's insurance plan, the employee should receive and acknowledge having received an explanation of COBRA rights. More important, all employees separated from the company for any reason should sign a form acknowledging that they have received and understand their COBRA rights.

Long-Term Care   Today, there are several types of long-term care—care to support older persons in their old age—for which employers can provide insurance benefits for their employees.[85] For example, adult day care facilities offer structured programs including social and recreational activities. Assisted-living facilities offer shared housing and supervision for those who cannot function independently. Custodial care is assistance given by people who have no medical skills to help individuals perform daily living activities such as bathing. Home care is care received at home from a nurse, an aide, or another specialist. Hospice care includes health care and support services for terminally ill patients. An informal care provider is a nonlicensed caregiver, such as a relative or friend, who provides care at home. Respite care is care provided by a temporary caregiver; this allows the primary caregiver (such as a son or spouse) to take some time off. Nursing homes offer all levels of care, from custodial to skilled.[86]

Retirement Benefits

Social Security   Many people assume that Social Security provides income only when they are old, but it actually provides three types of benefits. First are the familiar retirement benefits, which provide an income if the employee retires at age 62 or thereafter and is insured under the Social Security Act. Second, survivor's or death benefits provide monthly payments to dependents regardless of the employee's age at death, again assuming that the employee was insured under the Social Security

Act. Finally, disability payments provide monthly payments to an employee and his or her dependents if the employee becomes totally disabled for work and meets certain specified work requirements.[87] The Medicare program, which provides a wide range of health services to people 65 and over, is also administered through the Social Security system.

Pension Plans[88]   Pension plans may be classified as defined benefit pension plans or as defined contribution benefit plans.[89] A **defined benefit pension plan** contains a formula for determining retirement benefits so that the actual benefits to be received are defined ahead of time. For example, the plan might include a formula that designates a dollar amount or a percentage of the last five years' annual salary as the basis for the person's eventual pension. A **defined contribution plan** specifies what contribution the employer will make to a retirement or savings fund set up for the employee. The defined contribution plan does not define the eventual benefit amount, only the periodic contribution to the plan. In a defined benefit plan, the employee knows ahead of time what his or her retirement benefits will be upon retirement. With a defined contribution plan, the employee cannot be sure of his or her retirement benefits. Those benefits depend on both the amounts contributed to the fund and the retirement fund's investment earnings. Changes in federal laws have made defined contribution plans more popular among employers.

For example, under the 401(k) plan, (based on Section 401(k) of the Internal Revenue Code), employees can have the employer place a portion of their compensation, which would otherwise be paid in cash, into a company profit-sharing or stock bonus plan. This results in a pretax reduction in salary, so the employee isn't taxed on those set-aside dollars until after he or she retires (or removes the money from the pension fund). Some employers also match a portion of what the employee contributes to the 401(k) plan. One attraction of 401(k) is that employees may have a range of investment options for the 401(k) funds, including mutual stock funds and bond funds. The Economic Growth and Tax Relief Reconciliation Act of 2001 (EGTRRA) boosts the attractiveness of retirement benefits like 401(k) plans by raising what employees can contribute from $10,500 per year in 2001 to $15,000 in 2006.[90]

The Employee Retirement Income Security Act (ERISA) is aimed at protecting the pensions of workers and in stimulating the growth of pension plans.[91] Before enactment of ERISA, pension plans often failed to deliver expected benefits to employees. Any number of reasons, such as business failure and inadequate funding, could result in employees losing their expected pensions and facing the prospect of being unable to retire.

Under ERISA, pension rights had to be **vested**—guaranteed to the employee—under one of three formulas, such as 100% vesting after 10 years of service (often referred to as cliff vesting).[92] However, the Tax Reform Act of 1986 further tightened these vesting rules. Today, participants in a pension plan must have a nonforfeitable right to 100% of their accrued benefits after five years of service. As an alternative, the employer may choose to phase in vesting over a period of three to seven years.

Among other things, the Pension Benefits Guarantee Corporation (PBGC) was established under ERISA to ensure that pensions meet vesting obligations; PBGC also insures pensions should a plan terminate without sufficient funds to meet its vested obligations.[93]

Employee Services Benefits

Although an employer's time off, insurance, and retirement benefits account for the main part of its benefits costs, most employees also provide a range of services, including personal services (such as legal and personal counseling), job-related services (such as subsidized child care facilities), educational subsidies, and executive perquisites (such as company cars and planes for its executives). Companies today are also offering more workplace benefits aimed at "easing family conflicts and time pressures."[94] These include flexible work hours, compressed workweeks, telecommuting, sabbatical leave, on-site fitness centers, employee discounts for health centers, athletic teams, discounts for social events, wellness programs, on-site ATM or check cashing, direct paycheck deposit, cafeteria on premises, on-site gift store, on-site dry cleaning, on-site postal service, on-site medical care, time off for children's school activities, child care referral, elder care referral (for the employee's parents), paternity leaves, and coffee carts.[95] Software giant SAS Institute offers preschool child care centers, a 36,000-square-foot gym, meditation rooms, a full-time in-house elder care consultant, high chairs in the cafeterias (where employees are allowed to bring their children for lunch), three weeks' paid vacation, a flexible work schedule, and a standard 35-hour workweek.[96]

Employee Assistance Programs (EAPs)   An EAP is a formal employer program for providing employees with counseling and/or treatment programs for problems such as alcoholism, gambling, and stress. It is estimated that 50% to 75% of employers with 3,000 or more employees offer EAPs,[97] often by contracting for services through large "one-stop shops."

The Cafeteria Approach

Employees tend to differ in what benefits they want and need. The trend today is thus toward providing flexibility and choice.

Flexible benefits plans were initially called cafeteria plans because (as in a cafeteria) employees could spend their benefits allowances on a choice of benefits options. Over the years, *flexible* has replaced *cafeteria*, although under the Internal Revenue Code regulations, the term *cafeteria* continues to be used.[98] The idea is to allow the employee to put together his or her own benefit package, subject to two constraints. First, the employer must carefully limit total cost for each benefit package. Second, each benefit plan must include certain nonoptional items, including, for example, Social Security, workers' compensation, and unemployment insurance.

Although most employees favor flexible benefits, many don't like to spend time choosing among available options, and many choose the wrong ones. The administrative costs can be reduced with packaged flexible benefit programs such as FlexSelect, from Towers, Perrin, Forster, and Crosby of New York. This is a user-friendly interactive program for personal computers that helps employees make flexible benefits choices.[99]

Benefits and Employee Leasing

Employee leasing firms arrange to have all the employer's employees transferred to the employee leasing firm's payroll. *Employee leasing* means the employee leasing firm becomes the legal employer and handles all employee-related paperwork. This usually includes recruiting, hiring, paying tax liabilities (Social Security payments, unemployment insurance, etc.), and handling day-to-day details such as performance appraisals (with the assistance of the on-site supervisor). However, it is with respect to benefits management that employee leasing is often most advantageous.

Getting insurance is often the most serious personnel problem smaller employers face. Even group rates for life or health insurance can be high when only 20 or 30 employees are involved. This is where employee leasing comes in. Remember that the leasing firm is the legal employer of the other company's employees. Therefore, the employees are absorbed into a much larger insurable group (along with other employers' former employees). The employee leasing company can therefore often offer benefits smaller companies can't obtain at such a low cost. A small business may thereby be able to get insurance for its employees that it couldn't otherwise afford. In some instances, the leasing firm's fee may be more than outweighed by the reduced benefits cost to the employer, plus the in-house labor cost savings gained by letting the leasing company handle human resource management.[100]

Employee leasing may sound too good to be true, and it sometimes is. Many employers are uncomfortable letting a third party become the legal employer of their employees (who are actually terminated by the employer and rehired by the leasing firm). Some employee leasing firms have a somewhat erratic history, and a number have gone out of business after apparently growing successfully for several years. Such a business failure means that the original employer has to hire back all its employees and find new insurance carriers to insure these "new" employees. Furthermore, Congress is continually tinkering with the tax code in such a way as to reduce the attractiveness of employee leasing.

Strategy and HR   By the 1990s, IBM was failing to exploit new technologies and losing touch with its customers.[101] Its board hired Louis Gerstner. His first strategy was to transform IBM from a sluggish giant to a lean winner. His new strategy meant reformulating the company's compensation plan. He instituted four basic compensation policies:

1. The marketplace rules. The company switched from its previous single salary structure (for nonsales employees) to different salary structures and merit budgets for different job families. This enabled IBM to take different compensation actions for different job families (for instance, for accountants, engineers, programmers, and so on).[102]
2. Fewer jobs, evaluated differently, in broadbands. Second, IBM scrapped its point job evaluation system and its traditional salary grades. The new system has no points. The old system contained 10 different compensable factors; the new one slots jobs into 10 bands based on just three (skills, leadership requirements, and scope/impact). In the United States, the number of separate job titles dropped from over 5,000 to less than 1,200.[103] Twenty-four salary grades dropped to 10 broadbands.
3. Managers manage. The previous compensation plan based raises on a complex system of rules. The new system is streamlined. Managers get a budget and some coaching, the essence of which is: "Either differentiate the pay you give to stars versus acceptable performers or the stars won't be around too long."[104]

4. Big stakes for stakeholders. Soon, most IBMers around the world "had 10% or more of their total cash compensation tied to performance."[105] In the new system, there are only three performance appraisal ratings. "A top-rated employee receives two-and-one-half times the award of an employee with the lowest ranking."[106]

IBM used its compensation plan to support its strategic aims. The new pay plan refocused employees' attention on the values of winning, execution, speed, and being market oriented.

REVIEW

Summary

1. Establishing pay rates involves five steps: conduct salary survey, evaluate jobs, develop pay grades, use wage curves, and develop pay ranges.

2. Job evaluation is aimed at determining the relative worth of a job. It compares jobs to one another based on their content, which is usually defined in terms of compensable factors such as skills, effort, responsibility, and working conditions.

3. Most managers group similar jobs into wage or pay grades for pay purposes. These grades are composed of jobs of approximately equal difficulty or importance as determined by job evaluation.

4. Developing a compensation plan for executive, managerial, and professional personnel is complicated by the fact that factors such as performance and creativity must take precedence over static factors such as working conditions. Market rates, performance, and incentives and benefits thus play a much greater role than does job evaluation for these employees.

5. Broadbanding means collapsing salary grades and ranges into just a few wide levels or bands, each of which then contains a relatively wide range of jobs and salary levels.

6. Piecework is the oldest type of incentive plan; a worker is paid a piece rate for each unit he or she produces. With a straight piecework plan, workers are paid on the basis of the number of units produced. With a guaranteed piecework plan, each worker receives his or her base rate (such as the minimum wage) regardless of how many units he or she produces.

7. Profit sharing and the Scanlon plan are examples of organizationwide incentive plans. The problem with such plans is that the link between a person's efforts and rewards is sometimes unclear. On the other hand, such plans may contribute to developing a sense of commitment among employees. Merit plans are other popular incentive plans.

8. Supplemental pay benefits provide pay for time not worked. They include unemployment insurance, vacation and holiday pay, severance pay, and supplemental unemployment benefits.

9. Insurance benefits are another type of employee benefit. Workers' compensation, for example, is aimed at ensuring prompt income and medical benefits to work accident victims or their dependents, regardless of fault. Most employers also provide group life insurance and group hospitalization, accident, and disability insurance.

10. Two types of retirement benefits are Social Security and pensions. Social Security does not just cover retirement

benefits but survivors and disability benefits as well. One of the critical issues in pension planning is vesting the money that employer and employee have placed in the latter's pension fund, which cannot be forfeited for any reason. ERISA ensures that pension rights become vested and protected after a reasonable amount of time.

KEY TERMS

- Fair Labor Standards Act
- Equal Pay Act
- Civil Rights Act
- salary survey
- job evaluation
- compensable factors
- ranking method
- wage curve
- incentive plan
- piecework

- stock option
- merit pay (merit raise)
- profit-sharing plan
- employee stock ownership plan (ESOP)
- Employee Retirement Income Security Act (ERISA)
- Scanlon plan
- gain-sharing plan

- benefits
- severance pay
- workers' compensation
- defined benefit pension plan
- defined contribution plan
- vested
- flexible benefits plan

DISCUSSION QUESTIONS AND EXERCISES

1. What is the difference between exempt and nonexempt jobs?
2. What is the relationship between compensable factors and job specifications?
3. Working individually or in groups, conduct salary surveys for the following positions: entry-level accountant and entry-level chemical engineer. What sources did you use, and what conclusions did you reach? If you were the HR manager for a local engineering firm, what would you recommend that you pay for each job?
4. Working individually or in groups, use published wage surveys to determine local area earnings for the following positions: file clerk I, accounting clerk II, and secretary V. How do the published figures compare with comparable jobs listed in your Sunday newspaper? What do you think accounts for any discrepancy?
5. Working individually or in groups, use the ranking method to evaluate the relative worth of the jobs listed in question 4. (You may use the U.S. Government's *Dictionary of Occupational Titles* or The Department of Labors O*NET as an aid.) To what extent do the local area earnings for these jobs correspond to your evaluations of the jobs?
6. Working individually or in groups, develop an incentive plan for the following positions: chemical engineer, plant manager, and used-car salesperson. What factors did you have to consider in reaching your conclusions?
7. A state university system in the Southeast recently instituted a Teacher Incentive Program for its faculty. Faculty committees within each university's college were told to award $5,000 raises (not bonuses) to about 40% of their faculty members based on how good a job they did teaching undergraduates and how many they taught per year. What are the potential advantages and pitfalls of such an incentive program? How well do you think it was accepted by the faculty? Do you think it had the desired effect?

8. What is merit pay? Do you think it's a good idea to award employees merit raises? Why or why not?

9. Working individually or in groups, compile a list of the perks available to the following individuals: the head of your local airport, the president of your college or university, and the president of a large company in your area. Do they all have certain perks in common? What do you think accounts for any differences?

10. You are the HR consultant to a small business with about 40 employees. At the present time the business offers five days of vacation, five paid holidays, and legally mandated benefits such as unemployment insurance payments. Develop a list of other benefits you believe the firm should offer, along with your reasons for suggesting them.

APPLICATION EXERCISES

Case Incident   *Salary Inequities at Acme Manufacturing*

Joe Black was trying to figure out what to do about a problem salary situation he had in his plant. Black recently took over as president of Acme Manufacturing. The founder, Bill George, had been president for 35 years. The company was family owned and located in a small eastern Arkansas town. It had approximately 250 employees and was the largest employer in the community. Black was a member of the family that owned Acme, but he had never worked for the company prior to becoming president. He had an MBA and a law degree, plus 15 years of management experience with a large manufacturing organization, where he was senior vice president for human resources when he made his move to Acme.

A short time after joining Acme, Black started to notice that there was considerable inequity in the pay structure for salaried employees. A discussion with the human resources director led him to believe that salaried employees' pay was very much a matter of individual bargaining with the past president. Hourly paid factory employees were not part of the problem because they were unionized and their wages were set by collective bargaining. An examination of the salaried payroll showed that there were 25 employees, ranging in pay from that of the president to that of the receptionist. A closer examination showed that 14 of the salaried employees were female. Three of these were front-line factory supervisors and one was the personnel director. The other 10 were nonmanagement.

This examination also showed that the human resources director appeared to be underpaid, and that the three female supervisors were paid somewhat less than any of the male super-

visors. However, there were no similar supervisory jobs in which there were both male and female job incumbents. When asked, the HR director said she thought the female supervisors may have been paid at a lower rate mainly because they were women, and perhaps Bill George did not think that women needed as much money because they had working husbands. However, she added that they may have been paid less because they supervised less-skilled employees than did male supervisors. Black was not sure that this was true.

The company from which Black had moved had a good job evaluation system. Although he was thoroughly familiar and capable with this compensation tool, Black did not have time to make a job evaluation study at Acme. Therefore, he decided to hire a compensation consultant from a nearby university to help him. Together they decided that all 25 salaried jobs should be in the job evaluation cluster, that a modified ranking method of job evaluation should be used, and that the job descriptions recently completed by the personnel director were current, accurate, and usable in the study.

The job evaluation showed that there was no evidence of serious inequities or discrimination in the nonmanagement jobs, but that the HR director and the three female supervisors were being underpaid relative to comparable male salaried employees.

Black was not sure what to do. He knew that if the underpaid female supervisors took the case to the local EEOC office, the company could be found guilty of sex discrimination and then have to pay considerable back wages. He was afraid that if he gave these women an immediate salary increase large enough to bring them up to where they should be, the male supervisors would be upset and the female supervisors might comprehend the total situation and want back pay. The HR director told Black that the female supervisors had never complained about pay differences, and they probably did not know the law to any extent.

The HR director agreed to take a sizable salary increase with no back pay, so this part of the problem was solved. Black believed he had four choices relative to the female supervisors:

1. To do nothing
2. To gradually increase the female supervisors' salaries
3. To increase their salaries immediately
4. To call the three supervisors into his office, discuss the situation with them, and jointly decide what to do ■

QUESTIONS

1. What would you do if you were Black? Why?
2. How do you think the company got into a situation like this in the first place?
3. Why would you suggest Black pursue the alternative you suggested?

Source: This case was prepared by Professor James C. Hodgetts of the Fogelman College of Business and Economics of the University of Memphis. All names are disguised. Used by permission.

Continuing Case

LearnInMotion.com: The Incentive Plan

Of all its HR programs, those relating to pay for performance and incentives are LearnInMotion.com's most fully developed. For one thing, the venture capital firm that funded it was very explicit about reserving at least 10% of the company's stock for employee incentives.

The agreement with the venture capital firm also included very explicit terms and conditions regarding LearnInMotion's stock option plan. The venture fund agreement included among its 500 or so pages a specific written agreement that LearnInMotion.com would have to send to each of its employees, laying out the details of the company's stock option plan. While there was some flexibility, the stock option plan details came down, in a nutshell, to this: (1) Employees would get stock options (the right to buy shares of LearnInMotion.com stock) at a price equal to 15% less than the venture capital fund paid for those shares when it funded LearnInMotion.com; (2) the shares will have a vesting schedule of 36 months, with one-third of the shares vesting once the employee has completed 12 full months of employment with the company, and one-third vesting upon successful completion of each of the following two full 12 months of employment; (3) if an employee leaves the company for any reason prior to his or her first full 12 months with the firm, the person is eligible for no stock options; (4) if the person has stock options and leaves the firm for any reason, he or she must exercise the options within 90 days of the date of leaving the firm, or lose the right to exercise them.

The actual number of options an employee gets depends on the person's bargaining power and on how much Jennifer and Mel think the person brings to the company: The options granted generally range from options to buy 10,000 shares for some employees up to 50,000 shares for other employees, but this has not raised any questions to date. When a new employee signs on, he or she receives a letter of offer. This provides minimal details regarding the option plan; after the person has completed the 90-day introductory period, he or she receives the five-page document describing the stock option plan, which Jennifer or Mel, as well as the employee, signs.

Beyond that, the only company incentive plan is the one for the two salespeople. In addition to their respective salaries, both salespeople receive about 20% of any sales they bring in, whether those sales are from advertising banners or course listing fees. It's not clear to Jennifer and Mel whether this incentive is effective. Each salesperson gets a base salary regardless of what he or she sells (one gets about $50,000, the other about $35,000). However, sales have simply not come up to the levels anticipated. Jennifer and Mel are not sure why. It could be that Internet advertising dried up after March 2000. It could be that their own business model is no good, and there's not enough demand for their company's services. They may be charging too much or too little. It could be that the salespeople can't do the job due to inadequate skills or inadequate training.

Or, of course, it could be the incentive plan. ("Or it could be all of the above," as Mel somewhat dejectedly said late one Friday evening.) They want to try to figure out what the problem is. They want you, their management consultants, to help them figure out what to do. Here's what they want you to do for them. ■

QUESTIONS AND ASSIGNMENTS

1. Up to this point we've awarded only a tiny fraction of the total stock options available for distribution. Should we give anyone or everyone additional options? Why or why not?
2. Should we put other employees on a pay-for-performance plan that somehow links their monthly or yearly pay to company sales? Why or why not? If so, how should we do it?
3. Is there another incentive plan you think would work better for the salespeople? What is it?
4. On the whole, what do you think the sales problem is?

Experiential Exercise

Purpose: The purpose of this exercise is to give you experience in performing a job evaluation using the ranking method.

Required Understanding: You should be thoroughly familiar with the ranking method of job evaluation and obtain (or write) job descriptions for your college's dean, department chairperson, and your professor.

How to Set Up the Exercise/Instructions: Divide the class into groups of four or five students. The groups will perform a job evaluation of the positions of dean, department chairperson, and professor using the ranking method.

1. Perform a job evaluation by ranking the jobs. You may use one or more compensable factors.
2. If time permits, a spokesperson from each group can put his or her group's ratings on the board. Did the groups end up with about the same results? How did they differ? Why do you think they differed?

TAKE IT TO THE WEB

For Internet exercises, updates to chapter material, and more, visit the Dessler Web site at

www.prenhall.com/dessler

ENDNOTES

1. For another example, see Parbudyal Singh, "Strategic Reward Systems at Southwest Airlines," *Compensation and Benefits Review* (March–April 2002): 28–32.

2. Thomas Patten Jr., *Pay: Employee Compensation and Incentive Plans* (New York: The Free Press, 1977), p. 1. See also "Aligning Work and Rewards: A Round Table Discussion," *Compensation and Benefits Review* 26, no. 4 (July–August 1994): 47–63; Marlene Morganstern, "Compensation and the New Employment Relationship," *Compensation and Benefits Review* 27, no. 2 (March 1995): 37–44; Joseph Martocchio, *Strategic Compensation* (Upper Saddle River, NJ: Prentice Hall, 2001); Richard Henderson, *Compensation Management in a Knowledge-Based World* (Upper Saddle River, NJ: Prentice Hall, 2000).

3. Based on Richard Henderson, *Compensation Management* (Reston, VA: Reston, 1980); Kenneth Sovereign, *Personnel Law* (Upper Saddle River, NJ: Prentice Hall, 1994): pp. 130–36, 202–29.

4. "State Minimum Wage Rates," *BNA Bulletin to Management* (September 26, 1996): 308–9.

5. Jeffrey Friedman, "The Fair Labor Standards Act Today: A Primer," *Compensation and Benefits Review* (January–February 2002): 53.

6. "The Evolution of Compensation," *Workplace Visions,* The Society for Human Resource Management, 2002.

7. A complete description of exemption requirements as found in U.S. Department of Labor, *Executive, Administrative, Professional and Outside Salesmen Exempted from the Fair Labor Standards Act* (Washington, DC: U.S. Government Printing Office, 1973).

8. Friedman, "Fair Labor Standards Act Today," 53.

9. "Employer Ordered to Pay $2 Million in Overtime," *BNA Bulletin to Management* (December 5, 1996): 391.

10. Michael Wolfe, "That's Not an Employee, That's an Independent Contractor," *Compensation and Benefits Review* (July/August 1996): 61.

11. Robert Nobile, "How Discrimination Laws Affect Compensation," *Compensation and Benefits Review* (July/August 1996): 38–42.

12. Henderson, *Compensation Management,* 101–27.

13. Joseph Famularo, *Handbook of Modern Personnel Administration* (New York: McGraw-Hill, 1972), pp. 27–29. See also Bruce Ellig, "Strategic Pay Planning," *Compensation and Benefits Review* 19, no. 9 (July/August 1987): 28–43; Thomas Robertson, "Fundamental Strategies for Wage and Salary Administration," *Personnel Journal* 65, no. 11 (November 1986): 120–32. One expert cautions against conducting salary surveys based on job title alone. He recommends job-content salary surveys that examine the content of jobs according to the size of each job so that, for instance, the work of the president of IBM and that of a small computer manufacturer would not be inadvertently compared. See Robert Sahl, "Job Content Salary Surveys: Survey Design and Selection Features," *Compensation and Benefits Review* (May/June 1991): 14–21.

14. "Annual Pay Levels and Growth in Pay by State," *BNA Bulletin to Management* (October 30, 1997): 350.

15. See, for example, "Who Needs Midpoints? On-line Pay Forums Are Convincing Workers of Their Net Worth," *BNA Bulletin to Management* (March 9, 2000): 73.

16. "Use of Wage Surveys," in *BNA Policy and Practice Services* (Washington, DC: Bureau of National Affairs, 1976), pp. 313–14. A survey of compensation professionals reported use of salary survey data. The surveys were used most often to adjust the salary structure and ranges. Other uses included determining the merit budget, adjusting individual job rates, and maintaining pay leadership. D. W. Belcher, N. Bruce Ferris, and John O'Neill, "How Wage Surveys Are Being Used," *Compensation and Benefits Review*

(September/October 1985): 34–51. For further discussion, see, for example, John Yurkutat, "Is 'The End of Jobs' the End of Surveys Too?" *Compensation and Benefits Review* (July/August 1997): 24–29; Nona Tobin, "Can Technology Ease the Pain of Salary Surveys?" *Public Personnel Management* 31, no. 1 (spring 2002): 65–78.

17. Allison Wellner, "Salaries in Site," *HR Magazine* (May 2001): 89–96.

18. Mark Meltzer and Howard Goldsmith, "Executive Compensation for Growth Companies," *Compensation and Benefits Review* (November/December 1997): 41–50. See also Bruce Ellig, "Executive Pay: A Primer," *Compensation and Benefits Review* (January/February 2003): 44–50.

19. "Supplemental Executive Retirement Plans Lead of Top Executive Perks," *Compensation and Benefits Review* (September/October 1998): 13.

20. Robert McNabb and Keith Whitfield, "Job Evaluation and High-Performance Practices: Compatible or Conflictual?" *Journal of Management Studies* 38, no. 2 (March 2001): 293–312.

21. Howard Risher, "Planning a Next Generation Salary System," *Compensation and Benefits Review* (December 2002): 22.

22. Gerald Ledford Jr., "Three Case Studies on Skill-Based Pay: An Overview," *Compensation and Benefits Review* (March/April 1991): 11–23.

23. Gerald Ledford Jr., "Paying for the Skills, Knowledge, and Competencies of Knowledge Workers," *Compensation and Benefits Review* (July/August 1995): 56.

24. Ledford, "Paying for Skills, Knowledge, and Competencies of Knowledge Workers," 55.

25. Ibid., 58. See also Melvyn Stark, Warren Luther, and Steve Valvano, "Jaguar Cars Drives Toward Competency-Based Pay," *Compensation and Benefits Review* (November/December 1996): 34–40. See also Bryan Murray and Barry Gerhart, "Skill Based Pay and Skill Seeking," *Human Resource Management Review* (fall 2000): 271–87.

26. Brian Murray and Barry Gerhard, "An Empirical Analysis of a Skill-Based Pay Program and Plant Performance and Outcomes," *Academy of Management Journal* 41, no. 1 (1998): 68–78.

27. Jack Anderson, "Compensating Your Overseas Executives, Part II: Europe in 1992," *Compensation and Benefits Review* (July/August 1990): 28. See also Marc Baranski, "Think Globally, Pay Locally: Finding the Right Mix," *Compensation and Benefits Review* (July/August 1999): 15–24.

28. Based on Anderson, "Compensating Your Overseas Executives," 29–31.

29. Patricia Zingheim and Jay Schuster, "Introduction: How Are the New Pay Tools Being Deployed?" *Compensation and Benefits Review* (July/August 1995): 10–14.

30. Edward Lawler III, "Pay Strategy: New Thinking for the New Millennium," *Compensation and Benefits Review* (January/February 2000): 7–12.

31. Except as noted, this section is based on Bureau of National Affairs, "Non-Traditional Incentive Pay Programs," *Personnel Policies Forum Survey*, no. 148 (May 1991).

32. Ibid., 3.

33. Henderson, *Compensation Management*, p. 363. See also A. J. Vogl, "Carrots, Sticks and Self-Deception," *Across the Board*, no. 1 (January 1994): 39–44.

34. Richard Seaman, "Rejuvenating an Organization with Team Pay," *Compensation and Benefits Review* (September/October 1997): 25–30.

35. James Thompson, L. Murphy Smith, and Alicia Murray, "Management Performance Incentives: Three Critical Issues," *Compensation and Benefits Review* 18, no. 5 (September/October 1986): 41–47; Baron Gerhart and Charlie Trevour, "Employment Variability Under Different Managerial Compensation Systems," *Academy of Management Journal* 39, no. 6 (1996): 1692–712; Ira Sager, "Stock Options: Lou Takes a Cue from Silicon Valley," *Business Week* (March 30, 1998): 34.

36. Bureau of National Affairs, *BNA Bulletin to Management* (January 6, 1983): 1; Christopher Young, "Trends in Executive Compensation," *Journal of Business*

Strategy 19, no. 2 (March/April, 1998): 21–25.

37. James Brinks, "Executive Compensation: Crossroads of the 80s," *Personnel Administrator* 26 (December 1981): 24.

38. "Long-Term Incentives: Trends and Approaches," *Personnel* 57 (July/August 1982): 60–61; Pearl Meyer, "Stock is No Longer Optional," *Journal of Business Strategy* 19, no. 2 (March/April 1998): 28–31.

39. "Short-Term Incentives Considered Ineffective, Survey Reveals," *Society for Human Resource Management* (January 2000): 5.

40. Elaine Denby, "Weighing Your Options," *HR Magazine* (November 2002): 46.

41. Bill O'Connell, "Dead Solid Perfect: Achieving Sales Compensation Alignment," *Compensation and Benefits Review* (March/April 1996): 46–47.

42. S. Scott Sands, "Ineffective Quotas: The Hidden Threat to Sales Compensation Plans," *Compensation and Benefits Review* (March/April 2000): 35–42. See also Sonjun Luo, "Does Your Sales Incentive Plan Pay for Performance?" *Compensation and Benefits Review* (January/February 2003): 18–24.

43. Peter Gundy, "Sales Compensation Programs: Built to Last," *Compensation and Benefits Review* (September/October 2002): 21–28.

44. Bill Weeks, "Setting Sells Force Compensation in the Internet Age," *Compensation and Benefits Review* (March/April 2000): 25–34.

45. Fay Hanson, "Currents in Compensation and Benefits," *Compensation and Benefits Review* (November/December 1998): 6.

46. See, for example, Herbert Meyer, "The Pay for Performance Dilemma," *Organizational Dynamics* (winter 1975): 39–50; Thomas Patten Jr., "Pay for Performance or Placation?" *Personnel Administrator* 24 (September 1977): 26–29; William Kearney, "Pay for Performance? Not Always," *MSU Business Topics* (spring 1979): 5–16. See also Hoyt Doyel and Janet Johnson, "Pay Increase Guidelines with Merit," *Personnel Journal* 64 (June 1985): 46–50; Jeffrey

Pfeffer, "Six Dangerous Myths About Pay," *Harvard Business Review* (May/June, 1998): 109–19.

47. Alfie Kohn, "Challenging Behaviorist Dogma: Myths About Money and Motivation," *Compensation and Benefits Review* (March/April 1998): 27–32.

48. James Brinks, "Is There Merit in Merit Increases?" *Personnel Administrator* 25 (May 1980): 60. See also Dan Gilbert and Glenn Bassett, "Merit Pay Increases Are a Mistake," *Compensation and Benefits Review* 26, no. 2 (March/April 1994): 20–25.

49. Bert Metzger and Jerome Colletti, "Does Profit Sharing Pay?" quoted in David Belcher, *Compensation Administration* (Upper Saddle River, NJ: Prentice Hall, 1973), p. 353. See also Edward Shepard, "Profit Sharing and Productivity: Further Evidence from the Chemicals Industry," *Industrial Relations* 33, no. 4 (October 1994): 452–66.

50. "Employers Expanding Stock Options to All," *HR Magazine* (October 1999): 30.

51. Based on Randy Swad, "Stock Ownership Plans: A New Employee Benefit," *Personnel Journal* 60 (June 1981): 453–55; Sager, "Stock Options," 34.

52. See James Brockardt and Robert Reilly, "Employee Stock Ownership Plans After the 1989 Tax Law: Valuation Issues," *Compensation and Benefits Review* (September/October 1990): 29–36.

53. Donald Sullivan, "ESOPs," *California Management Review* 20, no. 1 (fall 1979): 55–56. For a discussion of the effects of employee stock ownership on employee attitudes, see Katherine Klein, "Employee-Stock Ownership and Employee Attitudes: A Test of Three Models," *Journal of Applied Psychology* 72, no. 2 (May 1987): 319–31.

54. Everett Allen Jr., Joseph Melone, and Jerry Rosenbloom, *Pension Planning* (Homewood, IL: Irwin, 1981), p. 316; John Gamble, "ESOPs: Financial Performance and Federal Tax Incentives," *Journal of Labor Research* 9, no. 3 (summer 1998): 529–42.

55. Brian Moore and Timothy Ross, *The Scanlon Way to Improved Productivity: A Practical Guide* (New York: Wiley, 1978), p. 2. See also Woodruff Imberman, "Is Gainsharing the Wave of the Future?" *Management Accounting* (November 1995): 35–38.

56. Based in part on Steven Markham, K. Dow Scott, and Walter Cox Jr., "The Evolutionary Development of a Scanlon Plan," *Compensation and Benefits Review* (March/April 1992): 50–56.

57. Ibid., 51.

58. Moore and Ross, *Scanlon Way to Improved Productivity*, pp. 1–2.

59. Robert McNutt, "Sharing Across the Board: DuPont's Achievement Sharing Program," *Compensation and Benefits Review* (July/August 1990): 17–24.

60. Robert Renn et al., "Earnings and Risk Incentive Plans: A Performance, Satisfaction and Turnover Dilemma," *Compensation and Benefits Review* (July/August 2001): 68–72.

61. Janet Wiscombe, "Can Pay for Performance Really Work?" *Workforce* (August 2001): 30.

62. Susan Marks, "Incentives That Really Reward and Motivate," *Workforce* (June 2001): 108–14.

63. William Bulkeley, "Incentives System Fine-Tunes Pay/Bonus Plans," *Wall Street Journal* (August 16, 2001): B4.

64. Nina McIntyre, "EIM Technology to Successfully Motivate Employees," *Compensation and Benefits Review* (July/August 2001): 57–60.

65. Kathleen Cholewka, "Tech Tools," *Sales and Marketing Management* 153, no. 7 (July 2001): 24. See also Andrew Perlmutter, "Taking Motivation and Recognition Online," *Compensation and Benefits Review* (March–April 2002): 70–74.

66. Based on Frederick Hills, Thomas Bergmann, and Vida Scarpello, *Compensation Decision Making* (Fort Worth, TX: Dryden Press, 1994), p. 424. See also L. Kate Beatty, "Pay and Benefits Break Away from Tradition," *HR Magazine* 39, no. 11 (November 1994): 63–68.

67. "Benefit Costs Posted Biggest Jump Since 1992, B.L.S. Says," *BNA Bulletin to Management* (February 10, 2000): 45.

68. "Benefits Averaged One-Third of Company Payrolls in 2000," *BNA Bulletin to Management* (April 4, 2002): 108.

69. Craig Olson, "Will Workers Accept Lower Wages in Exchange for Health Benefits?" *Journal of Labor Economics* 20, no. 2 (April 2002): S.91–S.114.

70. "Vacation Allowances Are Far More General Abroad," *Compensation and Benefits Review* (September/October 1998): 15.

71. Henderson, *Compensation Management*, 555.

72. "SHRM Benefits Survey Finds Growth in Employer Use of Paid Leave Pools," *BNA Bulletin to Management* (March 21, 2002): 89.

73. Miriam Rothman, "Can Alternatives to Sick Pay Plans Reduce Absenteeism?" *Personnel Journal* 60 (October 1981): 788–91; Richard Bunning, "A Prescription for Sick Leave," *Personnel Journal* 67, no. 8 (August 1988): 44–49; Carl Quintanilla, "A Sick Leave Policy Backfires at Cincinnati's Public Schools," *Wall Street Journal* (July 14, 1998): A1.

74. Jane Waldfogel, "Family and Medical Leave: Evidence from the 2000 Survey," *Monthly Labor Review* 124, no. 9 (September 2001): 17–23.

75. "Review of State Law Reveals Six Trends Expected to Put Employers on the Hook," *BNA Bulletin to Management* (March 28, 2002): 97.

76. Famularo, *Handbook of Modern Personnel Administration,* 51–62; Sovereign, *Personnel Law,* 231–47.

77. Henderson, *Compensation Management,* 250. For an explanation of how to reduce workers' compensation costs, see Betty Strigel Bialk, "Cutting Workers' Compensation Costs," *Personnel Journal* 66, no. 7 (July 1987): 95–97; "Workers' Compensation Outlook: Cost Control Persists," *BNA Bulletin to Management* (January 30, 1997): 33.

78. Glenn Whittington, "Changes in Workers Compensation Laws During 2000,"

Monthly Labor Review 124, no. 1 (January 2001): 25–28.

79. "Workers Comp Claims Rise with Layoffs, but Employers Can Identify, Prevent Fraud," *BNA Bulletin to Management* (October 4, 2001): 313.

80. "Employee Benefits in Medium and Large Firms," *BNA Bulletin to Management* (September 4, 1997): 284–85.

81. Ibid.

82. Hills, Bergmann, and Scarpello, *Compensation Decision Making,* p. 137.

83. George Milkovich and Jerry Newman, *Compensation* (Burr Ridge, IL: Irwin, 1993), p. 445.

84. Based on Paul Greenlaw and Diana Foderaro, "Some Practical Implications of the Pregnancy Discrimination Act," *Personnel Journal* 58 (October 1979): 677–81. See also Commerce Clearing House, "Supreme Court Says Giving Women Pregnancy Leave Is Lawful Even in the Case Where Men Receive No Disability Leave Whatsoever," *Ideas and Trends in Personnel* (January 23, 1987): 9–10.

85. James Weil, "Baby Boomer Needs Will Spur Growth of Long-Term Care Plans," *Compensation and Benefits Review* (March/April 1996): 49.

86. Ibid., 51.

87. Jerome B. Cohen and Arthur Hanson, *Personal Finance* (Homewood, IL: Irwin, 1964), pp. 312–20. See also *BNA Bulletin to Management* (January 14, 1988): 12–13.

88. For examples of pension plans, see Henderson, *Compensation Management,* 289–90; Famularo, *Handbook of Modern Personnel Administration,* 37.1–37.9.

89. Avy Graham, "How Has Vesting Changed Since Passage of Employee Retirement Income Security Act?" *Monthly Labor Review* (August 1988): 20–25.

90. Ronald Grossman, "Reshaping the Retirement Benefit Bucket, EGTRRA-Style," *Society for Human Resource Management Legal Report* (September–October 2001): 1.

91. Robert Paul, "The Impact of Pension Reform on American Business," *Sloan Management Review* 18 (fall 1976): 59–71. See also John M. Walbridge Jr., "The Next Hurdle for Benefits Manager: Section 89," *Compensation and Benefits Review* 20, no. 6 (November/December 1988): 22–35.

92. Henderson, *Compensation Management,* 292. ERISA applies not just to pensions but also to various other benefits including retiree medical benefits. For a discussion, see Michael Langan, "ERISA After Twenty Years: Past, Present, and Future," *Benefits Law Journal* 7, no. 3 (autumn 1994): 225–70.

93. James Benson and Barbara Suzaki, "After Tax Reform, Part III: Planning Executive Benefits," *Compensation and Benefits Review* 20, no. 2 (March/April 1988): 45–57; "Post-Retirement Benefits Impact of FASB New Accounting Rule" (February 23, 1989): 57.

94. Don Bohl, "Mini Survey: Companies That Tend to Create the 'Convenient Work Place,'" *Compensation and Benefits Review* (May/June 1996): 23–26.

95. Ibid., 24–25.

96. Charles Fishman, "Moving Toward a Balanced Work Life," *Workforce* (March 2000): 38–42.

97. Richard T. Hellan, "Employee Assistance: An EAP Update: A Perspective for the '80s," *Personnel Journal* 65, no. 6 (1986): 51; Michael Prince, "EAPs Becoming Part of Larger Programs," *Business Insurance* 32, no. 24 (June 15, 1998): 14–16.

98. Henderson, *Compensation Management,* 568. See also "Couples Want Flexible Leave, Benefits," *BNA Bulletin to Management* (February 19, 1998): 53.

99. For information about this program, contact Towers, Perrin, Forster, and Crosby, 245 Park Avenue, New York, NY 10167. Hewitt Associates similarly has a program called FlexSystem (New York: Hewitt Associates). See also Michael Sturman, John Hannon, and George Milkovich, "Computerized Decision Aids for Flexible Benefits Decisions: The Effects of an Expert System and Decision Support System on Employee Intentions and Satisfaction with Benefits," *Personnel Psychology* 49 (1996): 883–908.

100. For a discussion, see, for example, Marvin Selter, "On the Plus Side of Employee Leasing," *Personnel Journal* (April 1986): 87–91; "Employee Leasing Raises Questions," *BNA Bulletin to Management* (August 22, 1996): 272.
101. Andrew Richter, "Paying the People in Black at Big Blue," *Compensation and Benefits Review* (May–June 1998): 51. See also Robert McNabb and Keith Whitfield, "Job Evaluation and High-Performance Work Practices: Compatible or Conflictful?" *Journal of Management Studies* 38 (March 2001): 293–313.
102. Richter, "Paying the People in Black," 54.
103. Ibid.
104. Ibid., 55.
105. Ibid., 56.
106. Ibid.

Chapter

8

Managing Labor Relations and Collective Bargaining

- The Labor Movement
- Unions and the Law
- The Union Drive and Election
- The Collective Bargaining Process
- What's Next for Unions?

When you finish studying this chapter, you should be able to:

■ Discuss *the nature of the major federal labor relations laws.*

■ Describe *the process of a union drive and election.*

■ Discuss *the main steps in the collective bargaining process.*

INTRODUCTION

*A*fter years of losses, Jeff Bezos knew that Amazon required a new strategy. He'd started his firm as an online seller of books, with independent wholesalers handling distribution. As Amazon grew, Bezos added new product lines, like CDs. He also opened company-owned call centers and distribution centers, staffed with Amazon employees. By 2001, facing huge losses, Bezos knew he had to de-emphasize growth and start cutting costs and boosting profits. But, Amazon now faced a dilemma. Fifty customer service representatives in its Seattle call center were trying to organize a union. If they were successful, and the union effort spread through Amazon, it might hinder the firm's new strategic emphasis on cutting costs and boosting profits.

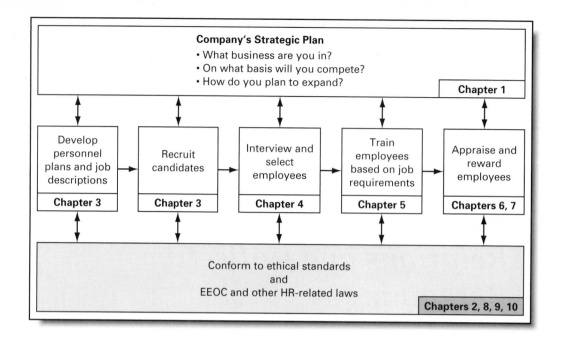

Company's Strategic Plan
- What business are you in?
- On what basis will you compete?
- How do you plan to expand?

Chapter 1

Develop personnel plans and job descriptions	Recruit candidates	Interview and select employees	Train employees based on job requirements	Appraise and reward employees
Chapter 3	Chapter 3	Chapter 4	Chapter 5	Chapters 6, 7

Conform to ethical standards
and
EEOC and other HR-related laws

Chapters 2, 8, 9, 10

THE LABOR MOVEMENT

Today, about 15 million U.S. workers—around 13.5% of the total number of men and women working in the United States—belong to unions.[1] Many are still traditionally blue-collar workers, but unions increasingly appeal to white-collar workers, too. For instance, federal, state, and local governments employ almost seven million union members, or about 37% of total government employees.

However, such figures mask the dramatic changes taking place in unions today: U.S. union membership peaked at about 34% in 1955. It has consistently fallen since then due to factors such as the shift from manufacturing to service jobs, and new legislation (such as occupational safety laws) that provide the sorts of protections that workers could once only obtain from their unions. Indeed, hundreds of local, state, and federal laws and regulations now address the sorts of concerns that helped drive the early union movement.[2]

Even with such declines, however, we cannot write off unions.[3] In the United States, for instance, a growing number of government and white-collar employees are turning to unions. In some industries (such as transportation and public utilities, where over 26% of employees belong to unions) it's still not easy to get a job without joining a union.[4] Union membership also varies widely by state, from a high of 26.8% in New York to a low of 3.7% in South Carolina.[5] Furthermore, although union membership around the world is also declining, union membership is still high in most countries: 37% in Canada, 43% in Mexico, 44% in Brazil, 29% in Germany, 33% in the United Kingdom, 44% in Italy, and 24% in Japan.[6] Even in the United States, membership may be stabilizing, with a wide range of workers including doctors, psychologists, graduate teaching assistants, and even fashion models forming or joining unions.[7]

Why Do Workers Organize?

People have spent much time analyzing why workers unionize, and many theories have been proposed. Yet, there is no simple answer, partly because each worker probably joins for his or her own reasons.

It does seem clear that workers don't unionize just to get more pay, although the pay issue is important. In fact, (for whatever reason) union members' weekly earnings are higher than nonunion workers'. They are about $50 per week more in service jobs, $60 in manufacturing, $130 in government, and as much as $300 per week more in construction jobs, for instance.[8] On the other hand, as an example, the UAW recently restarted efforts to organize workers at Nissan Motors' Smyrna, Tennessee, auto plant. The issue here isn't pay, since Nissan plant employees earn about the same per hour as UAW workers at other plants. Of greater concern "are increasing workloads, mounting injuries and what union officials described as inadequate retirement benefits at the Smyrna plant."[9]

Often, the urge to unionize seems to boil down to the workers' belief that it is only through unity that they can get their fair share of the pie and also protect themselves from arbitrary managerial whims.[10] In practice, this often means that low morale, fear of job loss, and poor communication foster unionization.

In one case, for example, a butcher hired by Wal-Mart said he was told he would be able to start management training and possibly move up to supervisor. He started work and bought a new car for the commute. However, he said his supervisor never mentioned the promotion again after the employee hurt his back at work and was out for five weeks. Faced with high car payments and feeling cheated, the butcher went to the Grocery Workers Union, which quickly sent an organizer to speak with the employee near the Wal-Mart store. The store's meat cutters eventually voted to unionize, but didn't celebrate for long. A week later Wal-Mart announced it would switch to completely prepackaged meat. Henceforth, the meat suppliers would do all the cutting at their factories, and the stores' meat cutters would no longer be required.[11]

What Do Unions Want? What Are Their Aims?

We can generalize by saying that unions have two sets of aims, one for *union security* and one for *improved wages, hours, working conditions,* and *benefits* for their members.

Union Security   First and probably foremost, unions seek to establish security for themselves. They fight hard for the right to represent a firm's workers and to be the *exclusive* bargaining agent for all employees in the unit. (As such, they negotiate contracts for all employees, including those who are not members of the union.) Five types of union security are possible:

1. *Closed shop.*[12] The company can hire only union members. This was outlawed in 1947 but still exists in some industries (such as printing).
2. *Union shop.* The company can hire nonunion people, but they must join the union after a prescribed period of time and pay dues. (If not, they can be fired.)
3. *Agency shop.* Employees who do not belong to the union still must pay union dues on the assumption that the union's efforts benefit *all* the workers.

4. *Open shop.* It is up to the workers whether they join the union—those who do not pay dues.
5. *Maintenance of membership arrangement.* Employees do not have to belong to the union. However, union members employed by the firm must maintain membership in the union for the contract period.

Not all states give unions the right to require union membership as a condition of employment. **Right-to-work** "is a term used to describe state statutory or constitutional provisions banning the requirement of union membership as a condition of employment."[13] Section 14(b) of the Taft–Hartley Act (an early labor relations act that we'll later discuss in more detail) permits states to forbid the negotiation of compulsory union membership provisions, not just for firms engaged in intrastate commerce, but for those in interstate commerce, too. Right-to-work laws don't outlaw unions. They do outlaw (within those states) any of the forms of union security. This understandably inhibits union formation in those states. Twenty-one "right-to-work states," from Florida to Mississippi to Wyoming, ban all forms of union security.

Improved Wages, Hours, Working Conditions, and Benefits for Members   Once their security is assured, unions fight to better the lot of other members—to improve their wages, hours, and working conditions, for example. The typical labor agreement also gives the union a role in other HR activities, including recruiting, selecting, compensating, promoting, training, and discharging employees.

The AFL-CIO

The American Federation of Labor and Congress of Industrial Organizations **(AFL-CIO)** is a voluntary federation of about 100 national and international labor unions in the United States. It resulted from the merger of the AFL and CIO in 1955, with the AFL's George Meany as its first president. For many people, it has become synonymous with the word *union* in the United States. However, about 2.5 million workers belong to unions that are not affiliated with the AFL-CIO. Of these workers, about half belong to the largest independent union, the United Auto Workers (about one million members).[14]

UNIONS AND THE LAW

Until about 1930, there were no special labor laws. Employers didn't have to engage in collective bargaining with employees and were virtually unrestrained in their behavior toward unions: The use of spies, blacklists, and the firing of agitators was widespread. "Yellow dog" contracts, whereby management could require nonunion membership as a condition for employment, were widely enforced. Most union weapons—even strikes—were illegal.

This one-sided situation lasted in the United States from the Revolution to the Great Depression (around 1930). Since then, in response to changing public attitudes, values, and economic conditions, labor law has gone through three clear changes: from "strong encouragement" of unions, to "modified encouragement coupled with regulation," to "detailed regulation of internal union affairs."[15]

Period of Strong Encouragement: The Norris-LaGuardia Act (1932) and the National Labor Relations Act (1935)

The **Norris-LaGuardia Act** set the stage for an era in which government encouraged union activity. The act guaranteed to each employee the right to bargain collectively "free from interference, restraint, or coercion." It declared yellow dog contracts unenforceable. It limited the courts' abilities to issue injunctions for activities such as peaceful picketing and payment of strike benefits.[16]

Yet this act did little to restrain employers from fighting labor organizations by whatever means they could muster. Therefore, the National Labor Relations Act (or **Wagner Act**) was passed in 1935 to add teeth to the Norris-LaGuardia Act. It did this by banning certain unfair labor practices, providing for secret-ballot elections and majority rule for determining whether a firm's employees were to unionize, and creating the **National Labor Relations Board (NLRB)** for enforcing these two provisions.

In addition to activities like overseeing union elections, the NLRB periodically issues interpretive rulings. For example, about six million employees fall under the "contingent" or "alternative" employee umbrella today. The NLRB therefore recently ruled that temporary employees could join the unions of permanent employees in the companies where their employment agencies assign them to work.[17]

Unfair Employer Labor Practices   The Wagner Act deemed as "statutory wrongs" (but not crimes) five unfair labor practices used by employers:

1. It is unfair for employers to "interfere with, restrain, or coerce employees" in exercising their legally sanctioned right of self-organization.
2. It is an unfair practice for company representatives to dominate or interfere with either the formation or the administration of labor unions. Among other management actions found to be unfair under practices 1 and 2 are bribing employees, using company spy systems, moving a business to avoid unionization, and blacklisting union sympathizers.
3. Employers are prohibited from discriminating in any way against employees for their legal union activities.
4. Employers are forbidden to discharge or discriminate against employees simply because the latter file unfair practice charges against the company.
5. Finally, it is an unfair labor practice for employers to refuse to bargain collectively with their employees' duly chosen representatives.

An unfair labor practice charge may be filed (see Figure 8.1) with the NLRB. The board then investigates the charge and determines whether it should take formal action. Possible actions include dismissal of the complaint, request for an injunction against the employer, and an order that the employer cease and desist.

From 1935 to 1947   Union membership increased quickly after passage of the Wagner Act in 1935. Other factors such as an improving economy and aggressive union leadership contributed to this as well. But by the mid-1940s, the tide had

Figure 8.1 NLRB Form 501: Filing an Unfair Labor Practice Charge

FORM NLRB 501
(2 81)

FORM EXEMPT UNDER
44 U.S.C. 3512

UNITED STATES OF AMERICA
NATIONAL LABOR RELATIONS BOARD
CHARGE AGAINST EMPLOYER

INSTRUCTIONS: File an original and 4 copies of this charge with NLRB Regional Director for the region in which the alleged unfair labor practice occurred or is occurring.	DO NOT WRITE IN THIS SPACE	
	CASE NO.	DATE FILED

1. EMPLOYER AGAINST WHOM CHARGE IS BROUGHT

a. NAME OF EMPLOYER	b. NUMBER OF WORKERS EMPLOYED	
c. ADDRESS OF ESTABLISHMENT *(street and number, city, State, and ZIP code)*	d. EMPLOYER REPRESENTATIVE TO CONTACT	e. PHONE NO.
f. TYPE OF ESTABLISHMENT *(factory, mine, wholesaler, etc.)*	g. IDENTIFY PRINCIPAL PRODUCT OR SERVICE	

h. THE ABOVE-NAMED EMPLOYER HAS ENGAGED IN AND IS ENGAGING IN UNFAIR LABOR PRACTICES WITHIN THE MEANING OF SECTION 8(a), SUBSECTIONS (1) AND _____ OF THE NATIONAL
(list subsections)
LABOR RELATIONS ACT, AND THESE UNFAIR LABOR PRACTICES ARE UNFAIR LABOR PRACTICES AFFECTING COMMERCE WITHIN THE MEANING OF THE ACT.

2. BASIS OF THE CHARGE *(be specific as to facts, names, addresses, plants involved, dates, places, etc.)*

BY THE ABOVE AND OTHER ACTS, THE ABOVE-NAMED EMPLOYER HAS INTERFERED WITH, RESTRAINED, AND COERCED EMPLOYEES IN THE EXERCISE OF THE RIGHTS GUARANTEED IN SECTION 7 OF THE ACT.

3. FULL NAME OF PARTY FILING CHARGE   *(if labor organization, give full name, including local name and number)*

4a. ADDRESS *(street and number, city, State, and ZIP code)*	4b. TELEPHONE NO.

5. FULL NAME OF NATIONAL OR INTERNATIONAL LABOR ORGANIZATION OF WHICH IT IS AN AFFILIATE OR CONSTITUENT UNIT *(to be filled in when charge is filed by a labor organization)*

6. DECLARATION

I declare that I have read the above charge and that the statements therein are true to the best of my knowledge and belief.

By _____   _____
   (signature of representative or person filing charge)   *(title, if any)*

Address _____ _____ _____
                                        (telephone number)   *(date)*

WILLFULLY FALSE STATEMENTS ON THIS CHARGE CAN BE PUNISHED BY FINE AND IMPRISONMENT
(U.S. CODE, TITLE 18, SECTION 1001)

begun to turn. Largely because of a series of massive postwar strikes, public policy began to shift against what many viewed as the union excesses of the times. The stage was set for passage of the Taft-Hartley Act of 1947.

Period of Modified Encouragement Coupled with Regulation: The Taft-Hartley Act (1947)

The **Taft-Hartley** (or Labor Management Relations) **Act** reflected the public's less-enthusiastic attitudes toward unions. It amended the Wagner Act with provisions aimed at limiting unions in four ways: by prohibiting unfair union labor practices; by enumerating the rights of employees as union members; by enumerating the rights of employers; and by allowing the president of the United States to temporarily bar national emergency strikes.

Unfair Union Labor Practices   The Taft-Hartley Act enumerated several labor practices that unions were prohibited from engaging in:

1. Unions were banned from restraining or coercing employees from exercising their guaranteed bargaining rights.
2. It is an unfair labor practice for a union to cause an employer to discriminate in any way against an employee in order to encourage or discourage his or her membership in a union.
3. It is an unfair labor practice for a union to refuse to bargain in good faith with the employer about wages, hours, and other employment conditions.

Rights of Employees   The Taft-Hartley Act also protected the rights of employees against their unions. For example, many people felt that compulsory unionism violated the basic U.S. right of freedom of association. New *right-to-work laws* sprang up in 19 states (mainly in the South and Southwest); these outlawed labor contracts that made union membership a condition for keeping one's job. (Recall that even today, union membership varies widely by state.[18])

Rights of Employers   The Taft-Hartley Act also explicitly gave employers certain rights. For example, it gave them full freedom to express their views concerning union organization. Thus, a manager can tell his or her employees that in his or her opinion unions are worthless, dangerous to the economy, and immoral. A manager can even, generally speaking, hint that unionization and subsequent high-wage demands might result in the permanent closing of the plant but not its relocation. Employers can set forth the union's record in regard to violence and corruption, if appropriate, and can play on the racial prejudices of workers by describing the union's philosophy toward integration. In fact, the only major restraint is that there can be no threat of reprisal or force or promise of benefit.[19]

The employer also cannot meet with employees on company time within 24 hours of an election or suggest to employees that they vote against the union while they are at home or in the employer's office, although he or she can do so while in their work area or where they normally gather.

National Emergency Strikes   The Taft-Hartley Act also allows the U.S. president to intervene in **national emergency strikes,** which are strikes (for example, on the part of steel firm employees) that might imperil national health and safety. The president may appoint a board of inquiry and, based on its report, apply for an injunction restraining the strike for 60 days. If no settlement is reached during that time, the injunction can be extended for another 20 days. During this period, employees are polled in a secret ballot to ascertain their willingness to accept the employer's last offer.

Period of Detailed Regulation of Internal Union Affairs: The Landrum-Griffin Act (1959)

In the 1950s, senate investigations revealed unsavory practices on the part of some unions, and the result was the **Landrum-Griffin Act** (officially, the Labor Management Reporting and Disclosure Act). An overriding aim of this act was to protect union members from possible wrongdoing on the part of their unions. It was also an amendment to the Wagner Act.

The Landrum-Griffin Act contains a bill of rights for union members. Among other things, this provides for certain rights in the nomination of candidates for union office. It also affirms a member's right to sue his or her union and ensures that no member can be fined or suspended without due process, which includes a list of specific charges, time to prepare defense, and a fair hearing.

The act also laid out rules regarding union elections. For example, national and international unions must elect officers at least once every five years, using some type of secret-ballot mechanism.

The senate investigators also discovered flagrant examples of employer wrongdoing. The Landrum-Griffin Act therefore also greatly expanded the list of unlawful employer actions. For example, companies can no longer pay their own employees to entice them not to join the union.

THE UNION DRIVE AND ELECTION

It is through the union drive and election that a union tries to be recognized to represent employees.[20] This process has five basic steps: initial contact, authorization cards, hearing, campaign, and the election.

Step 1: Initial Contact

During the initial contact stage, the union determines the employees' interest in organizing, and establishes an organizing committee.

The initiative for the first contact between the employees and the union may come from the employees, from a union already representing other employees of the firm, or from a union representing workers elsewhere. Sometimes, a union effort starts with a disgruntled employee's contacting the local union to learn how to organize his or her place of work (as at Wal-Mart). Sometimes, though, the campaign starts when a union decides it wants to expand to representing other employees in the firm or when the company looks like an easy one to organize. (For instance, the Teamsters Union—already firmly in place at UPS—began an intensive organizing campaign at FedEx.) In any case, there is an initial contact between a union representative and a few employees.

When an employer becomes a target, a union official usually assigns a representative to assess employee interest. The representative visits the firm to determine whether enough employees are interested to make a union campaign worthwhile. He or she also identifies employees who would make good leaders in the organizing campaign and calls them together to create an organizing committee. The objective is to "educate the committee about the benefits of forming a union, the law and procedures involved in forming a local union, and the issues management is likely to raise during a campaign."[21]

The union must follow certain guidelines when it starts contacting employees. The law allows union organizers to solicit employees for membership as long as it doesn't endanger the performance or safety of the employees. Therefore, much of the contact takes place off the job, perhaps at home or at eating places near work. Organizers can also safely contact employees on company grounds during off hours (such as lunch or break time). Under some conditions, union representatives may solicit employees at their workstations, but this is rare. In practice, there will be much informal organizing going on at the workplace as employees debate the merits of organizing. In any case, this initial contact stage may be deceptively quiet. In some instances the first inkling management has of a union campaign is the distribution or posting of a handbill soliciting union membership.

Technology, in the form of e-mail, is of course affecting the union organizing process. However, preventing union employees from sending pro-union e-mail messages on company e-mail systems can be a tricky matter. Prohibiting only union e-mail has been found to violate NLRB decisions, for instance. And instituting a rule barring workers from using e-mail for all non–work-related topics may similarly be ineffective if the company actually does little to stop e-mail other than pro-union messages.[22] The Web is another potent union tool. For example, when the Hotel Employees and Restaurant Employees Union, Local 2, wanted to turn up the heat on the San Francisco Marriott, it launched a new Web site. The site explains the union's eight-month boycott and provides a helpful list of other, union-backed hotels where prospective guests can stay. It also lists organizations that decided to stay elsewhere in response to the boycott.[23]

One expert says an employer's main goal shouldn't be to win representation elections, but to avoid them altogether. He says doing so means taking fast action when the first signs of union activity appear. His advice in a nutshell: Don't just ignore the union's efforts while it spreads pro-union rumors, such as "If we had a union, we wouldn't have to work so much overtime." Retain an attorney and react at once.[24]

Labor relations consultants are increasingly influencing the unionization process, with both management and unions using outside advisors. The use by management of consultants (who are often referred to disparagingly by unions as *union busters*) has apparently grown tremendously. A study by the AFL-CIO's Department of Organization and Field Services concluded, for example, that management consultants were involved in 85% of the elections they surveyed.[25]

Unions are not without creative ways to win elections, one of which is called union salting. **Union salting** refers to a union organizing tactic by which workers who are in fact employed full time by a union as undercover union organizers are hired by unwitting employers. A 1995 U.S. Supreme Court decision, *NLRB v. Town and Country Electric*, held the tactic to be legal.[26]

Step 2: Authorization Cards

For the union to petition the NLRB for the right to hold an election, it must show that a sizable number of employees may be interested in being organized. The next step is thus for union organizers to try to get the employees to sign **authorization cards** (see Figure 8.2). Before an election can be petitioned, 30% of the eligible employees in an appropriate bargaining unit must sign.

During this stage, both union and management typically use various forms of propaganda. The union claims it can improve working conditions, raise wages, increase benefits, and generally get the workers better deals. Management need not be silent; it can attack the union on ethical and moral grounds and cite the cost of union membership, for example. Management can also explain its record, express facts and opinions, and explain to its employees the law applicable to organizing campaigns and the meaning of the duty to bargain in good faith (if the union should win the election). However, neither side can threaten, bribe, or coerce employees. Further, an employer may not make promises of benefit to employees or make unilateral changes in terms and conditions of employment that were not planned to be implemented prior to the onset of union organizing activity. Managers also should not look through signed authorization cards if confronted with them by union representatives. Doing so could be construed as an unfair labor practice by the NLRB, which could view it as spying on those who signed.

During this stage, unions can picket the company, subject to three constraints: the union must file a petition for an election within 30 days after the start of picketing, the firm cannot already be lawfully recognizing another union, and there cannot already have been a valid NLRB election during the past 12 months.

Figure 8.2 Sample Authorization Card

**UNITED GLASS AND CERAMIC WORKERS
OF NORTH AMERICA, AFL-CIO, CLC**

OFFICIAL MEMBERSHIP APPLICATION AND AUTHORIZATION

I, hereby apply for membership in the United Glass and Ceramic Workers of North America, AFL-CIO, CLC. I hereby designate and authorize the United Glass and Ceramic Workers of North America, AFL-CIO, CLC, as my collective bargaining representative in all matters pertaining to wages, rates of pay, and other conditions of employment. I also authorize the United Glass and Ceramic Workers of North America, AFL-CIO, CLC, to request recognition from my employer as my bargaining agent.

SIGNATURE OF APPLICANT _____

EMPLOYED BY _____

APPLICATION RECEIVED BY _____

DATE _____

Source: © 1982 by CCH Incorporated. All rights reserved. Reprinted with permission from *Human Resources Management Ideas and Trends Newsletter.*

Step 3: The Hearing

After the authorization cards have been collected, one of three things can occur. The employer may choose not to contest union recognition, in which case no hearing is needed and a *consent election* is held immediately. The employer may choose not to contest the union's *right to an election* (and/or the scope of the bargaining unit, or which employees are eligible to vote in the election), in which case no hearing is needed and the parties can stipulate an election. Or, the employer may contest the union's right, in which case it can insist on a hearing to determine those issues. An employer's decision about whether to insist on a hearing is a strategic one based on the facts of each case and whether it feels it needs additional time to develop a campaign to try to persuade a majority of its employees not to elect a union to represent them.

Most companies contest the union's right to represent their employees, and thus decline to voluntarily recognize the union: They claim that a significant number of their employees do not really want the union. It is at this point that the U.S. Labor Department's NLRB gets involved. The NLRB is usually contacted by the union, which requests a hearing. Based on this, the regional director of the NLRB sends a hearing officer to investigate. (For example, did 30% or more of the employees in an appropriate bargaining unit sign the authorization cards?) The examiner sends both management and the union a notice of representation hearing that states the time and place of the hearing.

The **bargaining unit** is one decision to come out of the hearing; it is the group of employees that the union will be authorized to represent and bargain for collectively.

Finally, if the results of the hearing are favorable for the union, the NLRB directs that an election be held. It issues a Decision and Direction of Election notice to that effect, and sends NLRB Form 666 (see Figure 8.3) to the employer to post.

Step 4: The Campaign

During the campaign that precedes the election, the union and employer appeal to employees for their votes. The union emphasizes that it will prevent unfairness, set up a grievance/seniority system, and improve unsatisfactory wages. Union strength, they'll say, will give employees a voice in determining wages and working conditions. Management emphasizes that improvements such as those the union promises don't require unionization, and that wages are equal to or better than they would be with a union contract. Management also emphasizes the financial cost of union dues; the fact that the union is an "outsider"; and that if the union wins, a strike may follow.[27] It can even attack the union on ethical and moral grounds, while insisting that employees will not be as well off and may lose freedom. But neither side can threaten, bribe, or coerce employees.

The Supervisor's Role

Supervisors must be knowledgeable about what they can and can't do to legally hamper organizing activities, lest they commit unfair labor practices. Such practices could cause a new election to be held after the company has won a previous election or cause the company to forfeit the second election and go directly to contract negotiation. In one case, a plant superintendent reacted to a union's initial organizing

Figure 8.3 NLRB Form 666: Notice to Employees

Form NLRB 666
(7–72)

★NOTICE TO EMPLOYEES

FROM THE

National Labor Relations Board

A PETITION has been filed with this Federal agency seeking an election to determine whether certain employees want to be represented by a union.

The case is being investigated and NO DETERMINATION HAS BEEN MADE AT THIS TIME by the National Labor Relations Board.   IF an election is held Notices of Election will be posted giving complete details for voting.

It was suggested that your employer post this notice so the National Labor Relations Board could inform you of your basic rights under the National Labor Relations Act.

YOU HAVE THE RIGHT under Federal Law

- To self-organization
- To form, join, or assist labor organizations
- To bargain collectively through representatives of your own choosing
- To act together for the purposes of collective bargaining or other mutual aid or protection
- To refuse to do any or all of these things unless the union and employer, in a state where such agreements are permitted, enter into a lawful union security clause requiring employees to join the union.

It is possible that some of you will be voting in an employee representation election as a result of the request for an election having been filed.   While NO DETERMINATION HAS BEEN MADE AT THIS TIME, in the event an election is held, the NATIONAL LABOR RELATIONS BOARD wants all eligible voters to be familiar with their rights under the law IF it holds an election.

The Board applies rules which are intended to keep its elections fair and honest and which result in a free choice. If agents of either Unions or Employers act in such a way as to interfere with your right to a free election, the election can be set aside by the Board.   Where appropriate the Board provides other remedies, such as reinstatement for employees fired for exercising their rights, including backpay from the party responsible for their discharge.

(Continued)

NOTE:

The following are examples of conduct which interfere with the rights of employees and may result in the setting aside of the election.

- Threatening loss of jobs or benefits by an Employer or a Union

- Misstating important facts by a Union or an Employer where the other party does not have a fair chance to reply

- Promising or granting promotions, pay raises, or other benefits, to influence an employee's vote by a party capable of carrying out such promises

- An Employer firing employees to discourage or encourage union activity or a Union causing them to be fired to encourage union activity

- Making campaign speeches to assembled groups of employees on company time within the 24-hour period before the election

- Incitement by either an Employer or a Union of racial or religious prejudice by inflammatory appeals

- Threatening physical force or violence to employees by a Union or an Employer to influence their votes

Please be assured that IF AN ELECTION IS HELD every effort will be made to protect your right to a free choice under the law. Improper conduct will not be permitted. All parties are expected to cooperate fully with this agency in maintaining basic principles of a fair election as required by law. The National Labor Relations Board as an agency of the United States Government does not endorse any choice in the election.

NATIONAL LABOR RELATIONS BOARD
an agency of the
UNITED STATES GOVERNMENT

THIS IS AN OFFICIAL GOVERNMENT NOTICE AND MUST NOT BE DEFACED BY ANYONE

attempt by prohibiting distribution of union literature in the plant's lunchroom. Because solicitation of off-duty workers in non-work areas is generally legal, the company subsequently allowed the union to post union literature on the company's bulletin board and to distribute union literature in non-working areas inside the plant. However, the NLRB still ruled that the initial act of prohibiting distribution of the literature was an unfair labor practice, one that was not "made right" by the company's subsequent efforts. The NLRB used the superintendent's action as one reason for invalidating an election that the company won.[28] To avoid such problems, employers should have rules governing distribution of literature and solicitation of workers and train supervisors in how to apply them.[29]

Rules Regarding Literature and Solicitation   An employer can take a number of steps to legally restrict union organizing activity.[30] For example:

- Nonemployees can always be barred from soliciting employees during their work time—that is, when the employee is on duty and not on a break.
- Employers can usually stop employees from soliciting other employees for any purpose if one or both employees are on paid-duty time and not on a break.

- Most employers (not including retail stores, shopping centers, and certain other employers) can bar nonemployees from the building's interiors and work areas as a right of private property owners. In certain cases, nonemployees can also be barred from exterior private property such as parking lots—if there is a business reason (such as safety) and the reason is not just to interfere with union organizers.
- Whether or not employers must allow union representatives permission to organize on employer-owned property at shopping malls is a matter of legal debate. In 1992, the U.S. Supreme Court ruled in *Lechmere, Inc.* v. *National Labor Relations Board* that nonemployees may be barred from an employer's property if they have reasonable alternative means of communicating their message to the intended audience. On the other hand, if the employer permits other organizations such as the Salvation Army to set up at their workplaces, discriminating against the union organizers may be viewed as an unfair labor practice.[31]

Such restrictions are valid only if the employer does not impose them in a discriminatory manner. For example, if employees are permitted by company policy to collect money for a wedding shower and baby gifts, to sell Avon-type products or Tupperware, or to engage in other solicitation during their working time, the employer will not be able to lawfully prohibit them from union soliciting during work time.

Finally, remember that there are many more ways to commit unfair labor practices than just keeping union organizers off your private property. For example, one employer decided to have a cookout and paid day off two days before a union representation election. The NLRB held that this was too much of a coincidence and represented coercive conduct. The union had lost the first vote but won the second vote as a result.[32]

Step 5: The Election

Finally, the election can be held within 30 to 60 days after the NLRB issues its Decision and Direction of Election. The election is by secret ballot. The NLRB provides the ballots (see Figure 8.4), as well as the voting booth and ballot box. It also counts the votes and certifies the results of the election. Historically, the more workers that vote, the less likely a union victory. This is probably because more workers who are not strong supporters end up voting. The union is important, too: The Teamsters union is less likely to win a representation election than other unions.[33]

The union becomes the employees' representative if it wins the election, and winning means getting a majority of the votes *cast*, not a majority of the workers in the bargaining unit. (It is also important to keep in mind that when an employer commits an unfair labor practice, a "no union" election may be reversed. As representatives of their employer, supervisors must therefore be very careful not to commit such unfair practices.) Unions won about 53.6% of all representation elections held recently.[34]

Decertification Elections: When Employees Want to Oust Their Union

Winning an election and signing an agreement do not necessarily mean that the union is in the company to stay—quite the opposite. The same law that grants

Figure 8.4 Sample NLRB Ballot

UNITED STATES OF AMERICA

National Labor Relations Board

OFFICIAL SECRET BALLOT

FOR CERTAIN EMPLOYEES OF

Do you wish to be represented for purposes of collective bargaining by —

MARK AN "S" IN THE SQUARE OF YOUR CHOICE

YES

NO

DO NOT SIGN THIS BALLOT. Fold and drop in ballot box.
If you spoil this ballot return it to the Board Agent for a new one.

employees the right to unionize also gives them a way to legally terminate the union's right to represent them. The process is *decertification.* Around 450 to 500 decertification elections are typically held each year, of which the unions win 30%.[35] That's actually a more favorable rate for management than the rate for the original, representation elections.

Decertification campaigns don't differ much from certification campaigns (those leading up to the initial election).[36] The union organizes membership meetings and house-to-house visits, mails literature to homes, and uses phone calls, NLRB appeals, and (sometimes) threats and harassment to win the election.[37] Managers use meetings—including one-on-one meetings, small-group meetings, and meetings with entire units—as well as legal or expert assistance, letters, improved working conditions, and subtle or not-so-subtle threats in its attempts to win a decertification vote. Employers are also increasingly turning to consultants.

Strategy and HR   As it turned out, Amazon's strategy of expanding its network of company-owned call centers and distribution centers probably helped prompt efforts by the union to organize Amazon's workers. Call centers and distribution centers had the sorts of employees—customer service representatives and package handlers—who typically find unions attractive. But the union's efforts ran headlong into Amazon's new strategy of cutting costs and boosting profitability. Barely three months after the union began its organizing attempt in Seattle, Amazon fired over 300 customer service reps, including many union advocates, and closed its Seattle center. Some call center operations now take place in less-expensive locales—for instance, at the firm's call center outside New Delhi, India. Jeff Bezos was quoted as saying to Wall Street analysts that closing the Seattle call center "was clearly the right business decision for us as we pursue making this into a profitable company."

The company's position is that the closing had nothing to do with union organizing attempts there. Given Amazon's need to start showing a profit after more than five years of losing money, its argument is more than a little plausible. In any case, Amazon is doing its part to try to keep workers from talking about the events surrounding the closings. For example, it asked departing workers to sign a release that basically affirms they won't file any complaints, lawsuits, and so forth against the company. Even one of the union organizers at the Seattle center decided to sign: "They are holding out a pretty large carrot," he says.[38]

THE COLLECTIVE BARGAINING PROCESS

What Is Collective Bargaining?

When and if the union is recognized as a company's employees' representative, a day is set for meeting at the bargaining table. Representatives of management and the union meet to negotiate a labor agreement that contains agreements on specific provisions covering wages, hours, and working conditions.

What exactly is **collective bargaining**? According to the National Labor Relations Act:

> For the purpose of (this act) to bargain collectively is the performance of the mutual obligation of the employer and the representative of the employees to meet at reasonable times and confer in good faith with respect to wages, hours, and terms and conditions of employment, or the negotiation of an agreement, or any question arising thereunder, and the execution of a written contract incorporating any agreement reached if requested by either party, but such obligation does not compel either party to agree to a proposal or require the making of a concession.

In plain language, this means that both management and labor are required by law to negotiate wages, hours, and terms and conditions of employment "in good faith." In a moment we will see that the specific terms that are negotiable (because wages, hours, and conditions of employment are too broad to be useful in practice) have been clarified by a series of court decisions.

What Is Good Faith Bargaining?

Good faith bargaining is the cornerstone of effective labor management relations. It means that both parties communicate and negotiate. It means that proposals are matched with counterproposals and that both parties make every reasonable effort to arrive at an agreement.[39] It does not mean that either party is compelled to agree to a proposal. Nor does it require that either party make any specific concessions (although as a practical matter, some may be necessary).

When Is Bargaining Not in Good Faith?   As interpreted by the NLRB and the courts, examples of a violation of the requirements for good faith bargaining may include:

1. *Surface bargaining.* This involves going through the motions of bargaining without any real intention of completing a formal agreement.
2. *Concession.* Although no one is required to make a concession, the courts' and NLRB's definitions of *good faith* suggest that a willingness to compromise is an essential ingredient in good faith bargaining.
3. *Proposals and demands.* The NLRB considers the advancement of proposals as a positive factor in determining overall good faith.
4. *Dilatory tactics.* The law requires that the parties meet and "confer at reasonable times and intervals." Obviously, refusal to meet at all with the union does not satisfy the positive duty imposed on the employer.
5. *Imposing conditions.* Attempts to impose conditions that are so onerous or unreasonable as to indicate bad faith are scrutinized by the board.
6. *Unilateral changes in conditions.* This is viewed as a strong indication that the employer is not bargaining with the required intent of reaching an agreement.
7. *Bypassing the representative.* An employer violates its duty to bargain when it refuses to negotiate with the union representative.

The Negotiating Team

Both union and management send a negotiating team to the bargaining table, and both teams usually go into the bargaining sessions having done their homework. Union representatives have sounded out union members on their desires and conferred with union representatives of related unions.

Similarly, management uses several techniques to prepare for bargaining. For example, it compiles pay and benefit data, including comparisons to local pay rates and rates paid for similar jobs in the industry. Management also "costs" the current labor contract and determines the increased cost—total, per employee, and per hour—of the union's demands. It also tries to identify probable union demands. It uses information from grievances and feedback from supervisors to determine ahead of time what the union's demands might be and thus prepare counteroffers and arguments ahead of time.[40]

Bargaining Items

Labor law sets out categories of items that are subject to bargaining: These are *mandatory, voluntary,* and *illegal items.*

Voluntary (or permissible) **bargaining items** are neither mandatory nor illegal; they become a part of negotiations only through the joint agreement of both management and union. Neither party can be compelled against its wishes to negotiate over voluntary items. An employee cannot hold up signing a contract because the other party refuses to bargain on a voluntary item.

Figure 8.5 Bargaining Items

MANDATORY	PERMISSIBLE	ILLEGAL
Rates of pay	Indemnity bonds	Closed shop
Wages	Management rights as	Separation of employees
Hours of employment	to union affairs	based on race
Overtime pay	Pension benefits of	Discriminatory
Shift differentials	retired employees	treatment
Holidays	Scope of the bargaining unit	
Vacations	Including supervisors	
Severance pay	in the contract	
Pensions	Additional parties to	
Insurance benefits	the contract such as	
Profit-sharing plans	the international	
Christmas bonuses	union	
Company housing,	Use of union label	
meals, and discounts	Settlement of unfair	
Employee security	labor charges	
Job performance	Prices in cafeteria	
Union security	Continuance of past	
Management–union	contract	
relationship	Membership of bargaining	
Drug testing	team	
of employees	Employment of strikebreakers	

Source: From *Collective Bargaining and Labor Relations: Cases, Practice, and Law,* by Michael R. Carrell and Christina Heavrin, p. 127. Reprinted with permission of Prentice Hall, Upper Saddle River, New Jersey.

Illegal bargaining items are forbidden by law. The clause agreeing to hire "union members exclusively" would be illegal in a right-to-work state, for example.

About 70 **mandatory bargaining items** exist, some of which are in Figure 8.5. They include wages, hours, rest periods, layoffs, transfers, benefits, and severance pay. Others are added as the law evolves. For instance, drug testing evolved into a mandatory item as a result of court decisions in the 1980s.[41]

Bargaining Stages[42]

Bargaining typically goes through several stages.[43] First, each side presents its demands. At this stage, both parties are usually quite far apart on some issues. Second, there is a reduction of demands. At this stage, each side trades off some of its demands to gain others. Third come the subcommittee studies: the parties form joint subcommittees to try to work out reasonable alternatives. Fourth, the parties reach an informal settlement, and each group goes back to its sponsor. Union representatives check informally with their superiors and the union members; management representatives check with top management. Finally, when everything is in order, the

1. Be sure you have *set clear objectives* for every bargaining item and you understand on what grounds the objectives are established.[44]

2. *Do not hurry.*

3. When in doubt, *caucus* with your associates.

4. Be *well prepared* with firm data supporting your position.

5. Always strive to keep some *flexibility* in your position. Don't get yourself out on a limb.

6. Don't just concern yourself with what the other party says and does; *find out why*. Remember that economic motivation is not the only explanation for the other party's actions.

7. Respect the importance of *face saving* for the other party.

8. Constantly be alert to the *real intentions* of the other party with respect not only to goals but also to priorities.

9. Be a good *listener*.

10. Build a reputation for *being fair but firm*.

11. Learn to *control your emotions*; don't panic. Use emotions as a tool, not an obstacle.

12. Be sure as you make each bargaining move that you know its *relationship* to all other moves.

13. Measure each move against your *objectives*.

14. Pay close attention to the *wording* of every clause renegotiated; words and phrases are often sources of grievances.

15. Remember that collective bargaining negotiations are, by nature, part of a *compromise* process. There is no such thing as having all the pie.

16. Consider the impact of present negotiations on those in *future years*.

parties fine-tune and sign a formal agreement. The *HR in Practice* box summarizes negotiating guidelines.

Impasses, Mediation, and Strikes[45]

Impasses   In collective bargaining, an impasse occurs when the parties are unable to move further toward settlement. An impasse usually occurs because one party demands more than the other offers. Sometimes an impasse can be resolved through a third party, a disinterested person such as a mediator or arbitrator. If the impasse is not resolved in this way, a work stoppage, or *strike*, may be called by the union to pressure management.[46]

Third-Party Involvement   Three types of third-party interventions are used to overcome an impasse: mediation, fact-finding, and arbitration. With **mediation,** a neutral third party tries to assist the principals in reaching agreement. The mediator usually holds meetings with each party to determine where each stands regarding its position. He or she then uses this information to find common ground for further bargaining. The mediator is always a go-between. As such, he or she communicates assessments of the likelihood of a strike, the possible settlement packages available, and the like. The mediator does not have the authority to insist on a position or make a concession.

In certain situations, (as in a national emergency dispute in which the president of the United States determines that it would be a national emergency for a strike to occur), a fact-finder may be appointed. A **fact-finder** is a neutral party who studies the issues in a dispute and makes a public recommendation of what a reasonable settlement ought to be.[47] For example, presidential emergency fact-finding boards have successfully resolved impasses in certain critical transportation disputes.

Arbitration is the most definitive type of third-party intervention because the arbitrator may have the power to decide and dictate settlement terms. Unlike mediation and fact-finding, arbitration can guarantee a solution to an impasse. With *binding arbitration,* both parties are committed to accepting the arbitrator's award. With *nonbinding arbitration*, they are not. Arbitration may also be voluntary or compulsory (in other words, imposed by a government agency). In the United States, voluntary binding arbitration is the most prevalent.

Strikes   A strike is a withdrawal of labor; there are four main types of strikes. An *economic strike* results from a failure to agree on the terms of a contract—from an impasse, in other words. *Unfair labor practice strikes* protest illegal conduct by the employer. A **wildcat strike** is an unauthorized strike occurring during the term of a contract. A **sympathy strike** occurs when one union strikes in support of the strike of another. For example, in sympathy with employees of three papers—the *Detroit News, Detroit Free Press,* and *USA Today*—the United Auto Workers enforced a nearly six-year boycott that prevented the papers from being sold at Detroit-area auto plants, cutting sales by about 20,000 to 30,000 copies a day.[48]

Strikes needn't be an inevitable result of the bargaining process. Instead, studies show that they are often avoidable, but occur as a result of mistakes made during the bargaining process. Mistakes include discrepancies between union leaders' and rank-and-file members' expectations, and misperceptions regarding each side's bargaining goals.[49]

Picketing is one of the first activities occurring during a strike. The purpose of picketing is to inform the public about the existence of the labor dispute and often to encourage others to refrain from doing business with the employer against whom the employees are striking.

Employers can make several responses when they become the object of a strike. One is to shut down the affected area and thus halt their operations until the strike is over. A second alternative is to contract out work during the duration of the strike in order to blunt the effects of the strike on the employer. A third alternative is for the employer to continue operations, perhaps using supervisors and other nonstriking workers to fill in for the striking workers. A fourth alternative is the hiring of replacements for the strikers. In an economic strike, such replacements can be deemed permanent and would not have to be let go to make room for strikers who decided to return to work. If the strike were an unfair labor practice strike, the strikers would be entitled to return to their jobs if the employer makes an unconditional offer for them to do so.

Other Alternatives   Management and labor may both use other methods to try to break an impasse and achieve their aims. The union, for example, may resort to a *corporate campaign*. This is an organized effort by the union that exerts pressure on the corporation by pressuring the company's other unions, shareholders, directors, customers, creditors, and government agencies, often directly. Thus, individual members of the board of directors might be shocked by picketing of their homes, political figures might be pressured to agree to union demands, and the company's banks might become targets of a union member **boycott,** a removal of patronage.[50]

Inside games are another union tactic, one often used in conjunction with corporate campaigns. *Inside games* are union efforts to convince employees to impede or to disrupt production. They might do this, for example, by slowing the work pace, refusing to work overtime, filing mass charges with governmental agencies, or refusing to do work without receiving detailed instructions from supervisors (even though such instruction has not previously been required). Other inside games include scolding management and holding sick outs.[51] Inside games can thus be viewed as essentially de facto strikes, albeit "strikes" in which the employees are being supported by the company, which continues to pay them. In one inside game at Caterpillar's Aurora, Illinois, plant, United Auto Workers' grievances in the final stage before arbitration rose from 22 to 336. The effect, of course, was to clog the grievance procedure and tie up workers and management in unproductive endeavors on company time.[52]

Employers can try to break an impasse with lockouts. A **lockout** is a refusal by the employer to provide opportunities to work. The company (often literally) locks out employees, and prohibits them from doing their jobs (and thus from getting paid).

The NLRB does not generally view a lockout as an unfair labor practice. For example, if your product is a perishable one (such as vegetables), then a lockout may be a legitimate tactic to neutralize or decrease union power. A lockout *is* viewed as an unfair labor practice by the NLRB only when the employer acts for a prohibited purpose. It is not a prohibited purpose to try to bring about a settlement of negotiations on terms favorable to the employer. Lockouts are not widely used today, though. Employers are usually reluctant to cease operations when employees are willing to continue working (even though there may be an impasse at the bargaining table).[53]

During the impasse, both employers and unions can seek injunctive relief if they believe the other side is taking actions that could irreparably harm the other party. To obtain such relief, the NLRB must show the district court that an unfair labor practice—such as interfering with the union organizing campaign—if left unremedied, will irreparably harm the other party's statutory rights. (For example, if the employer is unfairly interfering with the union's organization campaign, or if the union is retaliating against employees for trying to gain access to the NLRB, the other side might press the NLRB for 10[j] injunctive relief.) Such relief is requested after the NLRB issues an unfair labor practices complaint. The injunctive relief is a court order compelling a party or parties either to resume or to desist a certain action.[54]

The Contract Agreement

The contract agreement may be 20 or 30 pages long or longer. It may contain just general declarations of policy or a detailed specification of rules and procedures. The tendency today is toward the longer, more detailed contract. This is largely a result of the increased number of items the agreements cover. The main sections of a typical contract cover subjects such as:

1. Management rights
2. Union security and automatic payroll dues deduction
3. Grievance procedures
4. Arbitration of grievances
5. Disciplinary procedures
6. Compensation rates
7. Hours of work and overtime
8. Benefits such as vacation, holidays, insurance, and pension
9. Health and safety provisions
10. Employee security seniority provisions
11. Contract expiration date

Handling Grievances

Signing the labor agreement is not the end of the process, because questions will always arise about what various clauses really mean. The *grievance process* addresses these issues. It is the process or steps that the employer and union have agreed to follow to ascertain if some action violated the agreement. The grievance process is not supposed to renegotiate contract points. Instead, the aim is to clarify what those points really mean, in the context of addressing grievances regarding things like time off, disciplinary action, and pay.

The potential for grievances and discontent is always present at work. Employees will use just about any issue involving wages, hours, or conditions of employment as the basis of a grievance. Discipline cases and seniority problems (including promotions, transfers, and layoffs) would probably top the list. Others would include grievances growing out of job evaluations and work assignments, overtime, vacations, incentive plans, and holidays.

Sometimes the grievance process gets out of hand. For example, members of American Postal Workers Union, Local 482, filed 1,800 grievances at the Postal Service's Roanoke, Virginia, mail processing facility (the usual rate is about 800 grievances per year). The employees apparently were responding to job changes, including transfers triggered by the Postal Service's efforts to further automate its processes.[55]

Whatever the source of the grievances, many firms today (and virtually all unionized ones) do (or should) give employees some means through which to air and settle their grievances. Grievance procedures are invariably a part of the labor agreement. But, even in nonunion firms, such procedures can help ensure that labor–management peace prevails.

In unionized companies, grievance handling is often called *contract administration*, since no labor contract can ever be so complete that it covers all contingencies and answers all questions. For example, suppose the contract says you can discharge an employee only for "just cause." You subsequently discharge someone for speaking back to you in harsh terms. Was it within your rights to discharge this person? Was speaking back to you harshly "just cause"?

The grievance procedure would handle and settle disagreements like these. The procedure provides an orderly system whereby employer and union determine whether the contract has been violated.[56] It is the vehicle for administering the contract on a day-to-day basis. This day-to-day collective bargaining should involve

DO
- Investigate and handle each and every case as though it may eventually result in an arbitration hearing.
- Talk with the employee about his or her grievance; give the person a good and full hearing.
- Require the union to identify specific contractual provisions allegedly violated.
- Comply with the contractual time limits of the company for handling the grievance.
- Visit the work area of the grievance.
- Determine whether there were any witnesses.
- Examine the grievant's personnel record.
- Fully examine prior grievance records.
- Treat the union representative as your equal.
- Hold your grievance discussion privately.
- Fully inform your own supervisor of grievance matters.

DON'T
- Discuss the case with the union steward alone—the grievant should definitely be there.
- Make arrangements with individual employees that are inconsistent with the labor agreement.
- Hold back the remedy if the company is wrong.
- Admit to the binding effect of a past practice.
- Relinquish to the union your rights as a manager.
- Settle grievances on the basis of what is "fair." Instead, stick to the labor agreement, which should be your only standard.
- Bargain over items not covered by the contract.
- Treat as subject to arbitration claims demanding the discipline or discharge of managers.
- Give long, written grievance answers.
- Trade a grievance settlement for a grievance withdrawal (or try to make up for a bad decision in one grievance by bending over backward in another).
- Deny grievances on the premise that your "hands have been tied by management."
- Agree to informal amendments in the contract.

interpretation only; it usually does not involve negotiating new terms or altering existing ones.[58]

Grievance procedures are typically multi-step processes. For example, step one might require the grievant to try and work out an agreement with his or her supervisor, perhaps with a union officer or colleague present. Appeals may then be taken successively to the supervisor's boss, then that person's boss, and perhaps finally to a special arbitrator.

Guidelines for Handling Grievances   The best way to handle a grievance is to develop a work environment in which grievances don't occur in the first place:[59] Doing so depends first on your ability to recognize, diagnose, and correct the causes of potential employee dissatisfaction before they become formal grievances. Typical causes include unfair appraisals, inequitable wages, or poor communications. The *HR in Practice* box presents some guidelines for handling a grievance should one occur.

What's Next for Unions?

Why the Union Decline?

Several factors contributed to the decline in union membership over the past 20 or so years. Unions traditionally appealed mostly to blue-collar workers, and the proportion of blue-collar jobs has been decreasing as service-sector and white-collar service jobs have increased. Furthermore, several economic factors, including intense international competition (see the *Global Issues in HR* box), outdated equipment and factories, mismanagement, new technology, and government regulation, have hit those industries (such as mining and manufacturing) that have traditionally been unionized. The effect of all this has been the permanent layoff of hundreds of thousands of union members, the permanent closing of company plants, the relocation of companies to nonunion settings (either in the United States or overseas), and mergers and acquisitions that have eliminated union jobs and affected collective bargaining agreements. Other changes, including the deregulation of trucking, airlines, and communications, have helped to erode union membership as well.[60] And (as noted earlier) various laws now provide protections that in earlier times only unions could provide.

How Unions Are Changing

Of course, unions are not sitting idly by and just watching their numbers dwindle. For example, unions are increasingly going after a "piece of the pie" in terms of ownership and control of corporations. As a United Steelworkers Union president put it, "We are not going to sit around and allow management to louse things up like they did in the past."[61] Today, more than eight million workers own a piece of their employers through employee stock ownership plans (ESOPs). Recall that these ESOPs are components of pension plans, through which a company's employees accumulate shares of their company's stock. Because of them, nonmanagement employees now sit on boards of directors at more than 300 firms in their role as representatives of the firm's employee stock ownership plans.

Unions are also becoming both more aggressive and more sophisticated in the way they present themselves to the public. The AFL-CIO has a program to train 1,000 unionists in the fundamentals of how to come across well on television, for instance.

And, unions are changing their recruitment targets. For example, one major union effort has been aimed at organizing white-collar workers. They are also targeting service industries such as insurance, banking, retail trade, and government. More than 10% of white-collar workers have already become unionized. The number is increasing rapidly, particularly among professionals, many of whom work in the public sector.[62] The AFL-CIO is also urging local unions to reach out more to minorities, youth, and women, and suggesting that they put more emphasis on educating their members about the drawbacks (in terms of job losses) of easing global trade too quickly.[63]

Cooperative Arrangements   Another, somewhat more risky (for the unions) approach is to agree to enter into more cooperative pacts with employers—for instance, working with them in developing team-based employee participation

Firms opening subsidiaries abroad find substantial differences in labor relations practices among the world's countries and regions. The following synopsis illustrates some of these differences by focusing on Europe. However, keep in mind that similarly significant differences exist in, say, South and Central America and Asia. Some important differences between labor relations practices in Europe and the United States include:[64]

- *Centralization.* In general, collective bargaining in Western Europe is likely to be industrywide or regionally oriented, whereas U.S. collective bargaining generally occurs at the enterprise or plant level.
- *Union structure.* Because collective bargaining is relatively centralized in most European countries, local unions in Europe tend to have much less autonomy and decision-making power than in the United States, and they basically concentrate on administrative and service functions.
- *Employer organization.* Due to the prevalence of industrywide bargaining, the employer's collective bargaining role tends to be performed primarily by employer associations in Europe; individual employees in the United States generally (but not always) represent their own interests in bargaining collectively with unions.
- *Union recognition.* Union recognition for collective bargaining in Western Europe is much less formal than in the United States. For example, in Europe there is no legal mechanism requiring an employer to recognize a particular union; even if a union claims to represent 80% of an employer's workers, another union can try to organize and bargain for the other 20%.

- *Union security.* Union security in the form of a formal closed-shop agreement is largely absent in continental Western Europe.
- *Labor–management contracts.* As in the United States, most European labor–management agreements are legally binding documents, except in Great Britain, where such collective agreements are viewed as "gentlemen's agreements" existing outside the law.
- *Content and scope of bargaining.* U.S. labor–management agreements tend to focus on wages, hours, and working conditions. European agreements, on the other hand, tend to be brief and simple and to specify minimum wages and employment conditions, with employers free to institute more favorable terms. The relative brevity of the European agreements is a function of two things: Industrywide bargaining makes it difficult to write detailed contracts applicable to individual enterprises, and in Europe government is much more heavily involved in setting terms of employment such as vacations and working conditions.
- *Grievance handling.* In Western Europe grievances occur much less frequently than in the United States; when raised, they are usually handled by a legislated machinery outside the union's formal control.
- *Strikes.* Generally speaking, strikes occur less frequently in Europe than in the United States. This is probably due to industrywide bargaining, which generally elicits less management resistance than in the United States, where demands "cut deeper into the individual enterprise's revenues."[65]

(Continued)

What's Next for Unions?

- *Government's role.* In Europe governments generally do not regulate the bargaining process but are much more interested in directly setting the actual terms of employment than is the case in the United States.
- *Worker participation.* Worker participation has a long and relatively extensive history in Western Europe, where it tends to go far beyond matters such as pay and working conditions. The aim is to create a system by which workers can participate in a meaningful way in the direct management of the enterprise. Determining wages, hours, and working conditions is not enough; employees should participate in formulating all management decisions. In many countries in Western Europe works councils are required; a *works council* is a committee in which plant workers consult with management about certain issues or share in the governance of the workplace.[66] Codetermination is a second form of worker participation in Europe; *codetermination* means that there is mandatory worker representation on an enterprise's board of directors. It is especially prevalent in Germany.

programs. About half the collective bargaining agreements signed recently encouraged cooperative labor–management relationships. *Cooperative clauses* cover things like joint committees to review drug problem, health care, and safety issues.[67]

Such programs can be good for all concerned. For many years, for example, Scott Paper Company "was the most struck company in the primary mill segment of the paper industry." With poor labor–management relations hurting the firm's competitiveness, management approached the United Paperworkers International Union to try to build a more cooperative relationship. Management and labor established joint labor–management committees at each site. The committees shared information regarding the company's performance and competition. The workers themselves gradually became heavily involved in redesigning their jobs. The teams were soon leading cost improvement projects, and helping to set budgets. By then, the company was producing more products with 22% fewer hourly paid employees. And, the employees were among the best paid in the industry and were working in participative, self-directed teams.[68]

Are Employee Participation Programs Unfair Labor Practices?

However, many unions still view programs like these with great skepticism. Committees like these sometimes give employees a voice in improving the way they do their jobs. Some unions fear the committees might therefore substitute for and make irrelevant the union. That fear has grown more urgent with the recent proliferation of employee participation programs such as team-based quality improvement programs. For example, a program giving employees more input in how they perform their jobs at UPS faced strong opposition from the Teamsters Union. Under this program, hourly employees work together in self-directed teams establishing priority on how work is done. UPS argues that the program recognizes that such employee involvement and teamwork can translate into higher productivity. For its part, the Teamsters Union (which represents the company's drivers and other hourly workers) is suspicious that the program is merely a tactic for subverting the union's influence on its members.[69]

Those in labor relations have actually debated this issue for many years. They have asked, Are employee participation programs like these "sham unions" and therefore illegal under the National Labor Relations Act? This is because, after passage of the early labor laws, some employers tried to circumvent the laws by establishing what were, in effect, company-led (and therefore "sham") unions.

Whether an employer's participation program is an impermissible labor organization revolves around two main things. One is, "does the company dominate the (sham) union?" The other is, "are the employees who participate in the program involved in traditionally union-type matters such as negotiating wages and working conditions?" If the answers are "yes," then the courts and NLRB might interpret it as a sham union.[70]

Recent decisions by the National Labor Relations Board make it somewhat easier (and safer) for companies to organize employer–employee management committees without violating the National Labor Relations Act. Employers can also take several steps to avoid conflicts with the act:[71] Integrate the committees (which often perform certain supervisory-type duties, such as hiring co-workers) into the actual management structure. Let the committees exercise clearly articulated managerial functions comparable to what an individual manager would have at that level. Ensure that (employer) veto power is used sparingly, and provide objective guidelines for its exercise. And, avoid mandatory committee reviews that involve a pattern of sharing proposals, responses, and compromises with the employer.

REVIEW

Summary

1. In addition to improved wages and working conditions, unions seek security when organizing. There are five possible arrangements, including the closed shop, the union shop, the agency shop, the open shop, and maintenance of membership.

2. The AFL-CIO is a national federation comprising 109 national and international unions. It can exercise only the power it is allowed to exercise by its constituent national unions.

3. During the period of strong encouragement of unions, the Norris-LaGuardia Act and the NLRA were passed; these marked a shift in labor law from repression to strong encouragement of union activity. They did this by banning certain types of unfair labor practices, by providing for secret-ballot elections, and by creating the NLRB.

4. The Taft-Hartley Act reflected the period of modified encouragement coupled with regulation. It enumerated the rights of employees with respect to their unions, enumerated the rights of employers, and allowed the U.S. president to temporarily bar national emergency strikes. Among other things, it also enumerated certain union unfair labor practices. For example, it banned unions from restraining or coercing employees from exercising their guaranteed bargaining rights. And employers were explicitly given the right to express their views concerning union organization.

5. The Landrum-Griffin Act reflected the period of detailed regulation of internal union affairs. It grew out of discoveries of wrongdoing on the part of both management and union leadership and contained a bill of rights for union members. (For example, it affirms a member's right to sue his or her union.)

6. There are four steps in a union drive and election: the initial contact, obtaining authorization cards, holding a hearing with the NLRB, and the election itself. Remember that the union need only win a majority of the votes cast, *not* a majority of the workers in the bargaining unit.

7. Bargaining collectively in good faith is the next step if and when the union wins the election. Good faith means that both parties communicate and negotiate, and that proposals are matched with counterproposals. Some hints on bargaining include do not hurry, be prepared, find out why, and be a good listener.

8. An impasse occurs when the parties aren't able to move further toward settlement. Third-party involvement—namely, arbitration, fact-finding, or mediation—is one alternative. Sometimes, though, a strike occurs. Responding to the strike involves such steps as shutting the facility, contracting out work, or possibly replacing the workers. Boycotts and lockouts are two other anti-impasse weapons sometimes used by labor and management.

KEY TERMS

- closed shop
- union shop
- agency shop
- open shop
- right to work
- AFL-CIO
- Norris-LaGuardia Act
- Wagner Act
- National Labor Relations Board (NLRB)
- Taft-Hartley Act
- national emergency strikes
- Landrum-Griffin Act
- union salting
- authorization cards
- bargaining unit
- collective bargaining
- good faith bargaining
- voluntary bargaining items
- illegal bargaining items
- mandatory bargaining items
- mediation
- fact-finding
- arbitration
- wildcat strike
- sympathy strike
- boycott
- lockout

DISCUSSION QUESTIONS AND EXERCISES

1. Discuss the steps in an NLRB election.
2. Describe important tactics you would expect the union to use during the union drive and election.
3. Briefly explain why labor law has gone through a cycle of repression and encouragement.
4. What is good faith bargaining? When is bargaining not in good faith?
5. Define *impasse, mediation,* and *strike,* and explain the techniques that are used to overcome an impasse.
6. In terms of 5–6 students, choose an organization (such as this university, or a company in which one student works) and list the areas in which the union has had an impact.

APPLICATION EXERCISES

Case Incident   *Disciplinary Action*

The employee, a union shop steward, was on her regularly scheduled day off at home. She was called by her supervisor and told to talk to three union members and instruct them to attend a work function called a "Quest for Quality Interaction Committee" meeting. The Quest for Quality program was a high priority with the employer for improving patient care at the hospital facility and was part of a corporate program. The union had objected to the implementation of the Quest for Quality program and had taken the position that employees could attend the program if their jobs were threatened, but they should do so under protest and then file a grievance afterward.

On the day in question, the union shop steward, in a conference call with the three employees, said she would not order them to attend the Quest for Quality meeting, although her supervisor had asked her to. The supervisor who had called the union shop steward had herself refused to order the employees to attend the meeting, but relied on the union shop steward to issue the order to the employees. When the shop steward failed to order the employees to attend the meeting, the employer suspended her for two weeks. She grieved the two-week suspension.

The union position was that the company had no authority to discipline the union shop steward on her day off for failure to give what it termed "a management direction to perform the specific job function of attending a mandatory corporate meeting." The union pointed out that it was unfair that the employer refused to order the employees directly to attend the meeting but then expected the union shop steward to do so. The union argued that while it is not unusual to call a union shop steward for assistance in problem solving, the company had no right to demand that he or she replace supervisors or management in giving orders and

then discipline the union official for refusing to do so.

The company position was that the opposition of the union to the Quest for Quality meetings put the employees in a position of being unable to attend the meetings without direction from the union shop steward; that the union shop steward was given a job assignment of directing the employees to attend the meeting; and that failure to follow that job assignment was insubordination and just cause for her suspension.

Nonetheless, the union contended that the arbitrator must examine the nature of the order when deciding whether the insubordination was grounds for discipline. As to the nature of the order in this case, the employer had to demonstrate that the order was directly related to the job classification and work assignment of the employee disciplined. The refusal to obey such an order must be shown to pose a real challenge to supervisory authority. The employee did not dispute the fact that she failed to follow the orders given to her by her supervisor, but pointed out that she was not on duty at the time and that the task being given to her was not because of her job with the company but because of her status as a union shop steward. ■

QUESTIONS

1. As the arbitrator, do you think the employer had just cause to discipline the employee? Why or why not?
2. If the union's opposition to the Quest for Quality program encouraged the employees not to participate, why shouldn't the union be held responsible for directing the employees to attend?

Source: Adapted from Cheltenham Nursing Rehabilitation Center 89 LA 361 (1987); discussion in Michael Carrell and Christina Heavrin, *Labor Relations and Collective Bargaining* (Upper Saddle River, NJ: Prentice Hall, 1995), pp. 100–101.

Continuing Case

LearnInMotion.com: Keeping a Watchful Eye Out for the Union

The employees at firms like LearnInMotion.com are young, well paid, and technologically sophisticated, and they're doing interesting, creative work with flexible hours. They are, in other words, exactly the sort of employees you might assume would have no interest in joining a union.

Jennifer, however, was surprised to find that unions are actively attempting to organize several dot-coms. For example, one article she happened to come across read, "Union activity at U.S. Internet companies is on the increase and is illustrated by the Washington alliance of technology workers attempting to unionize Amazon.com. [The union] claims to be receiving inquiries on a daily basis regarding union membership, as workers at Amazon complain of low pay and long hours."[72] "That's all we'd need is to have some disgruntled current or former employee call a union in on us," said Mel.

The fact that LearnInMotion.com is in New York (which has a relatively high proportion of union workers) and that several employees have left under less-than-pleasant circumstances suggest to Jennifer that perhaps she should be vigilant, and take steps now to prevent a problem later. The question is, what should she and Mel do? Now, they want you, their management consultants, to help them decide what to do. Here's what they want you to do for them. ■

QUESTIONS AND ASSIGNMENTS

1. Use the Internet to determine if the union mentioned (or any other union) organized or tried to organize a dot-com in the New York area in the past two years.
2. Produce a one-page position paper for us explaining concrete steps we can take today to avoid being unionized tomorrow.
3. How can we tell we're in the first, early stages of an organizing campaign? How can we find out for sure?

Experiential Exercise

Purpose: The purpose of this exercise is to give you practice in dealing with some of the elements of a union organizing campaign.

Required Understanding: You should be familiar with the material covered in this chapter, as well as the following incident, "An Organizing Question on Campus."

How to Set Up the Exercise/Instructions: Divide the class into groups of four or five students. Assume that you are labor relations consultants retained by the college to identify the problems and issues involved and to advise Art Tipton about what to do next. Each group will spend

about 45 minutes discussing the issues and outlining those issues as well as an action plan for Tipton. What should he do now?

If time permits, a spokesperson from each group should list on the board the issues involved and the group's recommendations.

An Organizing Question on Campus[73]

Art Tipton is a human resources director of Pierce University, a private university located in a large urban city. Ruth Ann Zimmer, a supervisor in the maintenance and housekeeping services division of the university, has just come into his office to discuss her situation. Zimmer's division of the university is responsible for maintaining and cleaning physical facilities of the university. Zimmer is one of the department supervisors who supervises employees who maintain and clean on-campus dormitories.

In the next several minutes, Zimmer proceeds to express her concerns about a union organizing campaign that has begun among her employees. According to Zimmer, a representative of the Service Workers Union has met with a number of the employees, urging them to sign union authorization cards. She has observed several of her employees "cornering" other employees to talk to them about joining the union and urge them to sign union authorization (or representation) cards. Zimmer even observed this during the working hours as employees were going about their normal duties in the dormitories. Zimmer reports that a number of her employees have come to her asking for her opinions about the union. They reported to her that several other supervisors in the department had told their employees not to sign

any union authorization cards and not to talk about the union at any time while they were on campus. Zimmer also reports that one of her fellow supervisors told his employees in a meeting that anyone who was caught talking about the union or signing a union authorization card would be disciplined and perhaps terminated.

Zimmer says that the employees are very dissatisfied with their wages and many of the conditions that they have endured from students, supervisors, and other staff people. She says that several employees told her that they had signed union cards because they believed that the only way university administration would pay attention to their concerns was if the employees had a union to represent them. Zimmer says that she made a list of employees whom she felt had joined or were interested in the union, and she could share these with Tipton if he wanted to deal with them personally. Zimmer closes her presentation with the comment that she and other department supervisors need to know what they should do in order to stomp out the threat of unionization in their department.

ENDNOTES

1. Yochi Dreazen, "Percentage of U.S. Workers in a Union Sank to Record Low of 13.5 Percent Last Year," *Wall Street Journal* (Jan. 19, 2001): A2.
2. James Bennett and Jason Taylor, "Labor Unions: Victims of Their Political Success?" *Journal of Labor Research* 22, no. 2 (spring): 261–73.
3. "Union Membership Falls Again in 1997," *BNA Bulletin to Management* (February 26, 1998): 61; see also Sharon Leonard, "Unions Could be Staging a Comeback," *HR Magazine* (December 1999): 207.
4. "Union Membership Falls Again," 61.
5. "Union Membership by State and Industry," *BNA Bulletin to Management* (May 29, 1997): 172–73.
6. "Union Membership Around the World," *BNA Bulletin to Management* (November 13, 1997): 364–65.
7. Stephen Greenhouse, "Labor, Revitalized with New Recruiting, Has Regained Power and Prestige," *New York Times* (October 9, 1999): A10.
8. "Union Membership and Earnings," *BNA Bulletin to Management* (February 13, 1997): 52–53.
9. Jeffrey Ball, "United Auto Workers Asks for a Vote on Unionization at This Factory," *Wall Street Journal* (August 15, 2001): A4; see also Jerry Fuller Jr. and Kim Hester, "A Closer Look at the Relationship Between Justice Perceptions and Union Participation," *Journal of Applied Psychology* 86, no. 6 (2001): 1096–105.
10. Michael E. Gordon and Angelo DeNis, "An Examination of the Relationship Between Union Membership and Job Satisfaction," *Industrial and Labor Relations Review* 48, no. 2 (January 1995): 222–36.

11. Ann Zimmerman, "Pro-Union Butchers at Wal-Mart Win a Union Battle but Lose War," *Wall Street Journal* (April 11, 2000): A14.

12. Based on Richard Hodgetts, *Introduction to Business* (Reading, MA: Addison-Wesley, 1977), pp. 213–14. See also Benjamin Taylor and Fred Witney, *Labor Relations Law* (Upper Saddle River, NJ: Prentice Hall, 1992), pp. 157–84.

13. Taylor and Whitney, *Labor Relations Law,* 170–71.

14. "Boardroom Reports," *The Conference Board* (December 15, 1976): 6. See also "Perspectives on Employment," *Research Bulletin 194, The Conference Board* (1986).

15. The following material is based on Arthur Sloane and Fred Witney, *Labor Relations* (Upper Saddle River, NJ: Prentice Hall, 2001), pp. 63–120.

16. Ibid., 106.

17. Karen Robinson, "Temp Workers Gain Union Access," *HR News,* Society for Human Resource Management 19, no. 10 (October 2000): 1.

18. "Union Membership by State and Industry," *BNA Bulletin to Management* (May 29, 1997): 172–73.

19. Sloane and Witney, *Labor Relations,* 102–6.

20. See William J. Glueck, "Labor Relations and the Supervisor," in M. Jean Newport, *Supervisory Management: Tools and Techniques* (St. Paul, MN: West Publishing, 1976), pp. 207–34. See also "Big Labor Tries the Soft Sell," *Business Week* (October 13, 1986): 126.

21. William Fulmer, "Step by Step Through a Union Election," *Harvard Business Review* 60 (July/August 1981): 94–102. For an interesting description of contract negotiations, see Peter Cramton and Joseph Tracy, "The Determinants of U.S. Labor Disputes," *Journal of Labor Economics* 12, no. 2 (April 1994): 180–209.

22. "Desktop Organizers: Unions Gained Access to Workers Via Employers' E-Mail Systems," *BNA Bulletin to Management* (September 30, 1999): 305.

23. Jessica Materna, "Union Launches Web Site to Air Grievances Against San Francisco Marriott," *San Francisco Business Times* 15, no. 39 (May 4, 2001): 15.

24. Jonathan Segal, "Expose the Unions Underbelly," *HR Magazine* (June 1999): 166–76.

25. *Labor Relations Consultants: Issues, Trends, Controversies* (Rockville, MD: Bureau of National Affairs, 1985), p. 7.

26. For a discussion, see Cory Fine, "Beware the Trojan Horse," *Workforce* (May 1998): 45–51.

27. Fulmer, "Step by Step Through a Union Election," 94. See also "An Employer May Rebut Union Misrepresentations," *BNA Bulletin to Management* (January 16, 1986): 17.

28. Frederick Sullivan, "Limiting Union Organizing Activity Through Supervisors," *Personnel* 55 (July/August 1978): 55–65. Richard Peterson, Thomas Lee, and Barbara Finnegan, "Strategies and Tactics in Union Organizing Campaigns," *Industrial Relations* 31, no. 2 (spring 1992): 370–81. See also Alan Story, "Employer Speech, Union Representation Elections, and the First Amendment," *Berkeley Journal of Employment and Labor Law* 16, no. 2 (1995): 356–457.

29. Sullivan, "Limiting Union Organizing Activity Through Supervisors," 60.

30. Ibid., 62–65.

31. "Union Access to Employer's Customers Restricted," *BNA Bulletin to Management* (February 15, 1996): 49; "Workplace Access for Unions Hinges on Legal Issues," *BNA Bulletin to Management* (April 11, 1996): 113.

32. B&D Plastics, Inc. 302 NLRB No. 33, 1971, 137 LRRM 1039; discussed in "No Such Thing as a Free Lunch," *BNA Bulletin to Management* (May 23, 1991): 153–54.

33. Edwin Arnold et al., "Determinants of Certification Election Outcomes in the Service Sector," *Labor Studies Journal* 25, no. 3 (fall 2000): 51.

34. "Unions Won Greater Share of Fewer Elections in 2001," *BNA Bulletin to Management* (June 27, 2002): 205.

35. "Unions Decertifications up in First Half of 1998," *BNA Bulletin to Management* (December 24, 1998): 406.

36. William Fulmer, "When Employees Want to Oust Their Union," *Harvard Business Review* 56 (March/April 1978): 163–70; Francis T. Coleman, "Once a Union, Not Always a Union," *Personnel Journal* 64, no. 3 (March 1985): 42–45. See also

"Decertification: Fulfilling Unions Destiny?" *Personnel Journal* 66 (June 1987): 144–48.

37. Fulmer, "When Employees Want to Oust Their Union," 167. See also David Meyer and Trevor Bain, "Union Decertification Election Outcomes: Bargaining Unit Characteristics and Union Resources," *Journal of Labor Research* 15, no. 2 (spring 1994): 117–36.

38. Mark Leon, "A Union of Their Own," *InfoWorld* 23 (March 12, 2001): 41–42. See also Tim Race, "The Updated Context Notwithstanding, the Issues Behind Unionization Drives at Dot-Coms Have a Familiar Ring," *New York Times* (January 22, 2001): C4.

39. Dale Yoder, *Personnel Management* (Upper Saddle River, NJ: Prentice Hall, 1972), p. 486. See also Michael Ballot, *Labor-Management Relations in a Changing Environment* (New York: Wiley, 1992), pp. 169–425.

40. "Boulwareism" is the name given to a strategy, now generally held in disfavor, by which the company, based on an exhaustive study of what it thought its employees wanted, made about one offer at the bargaining table and then refused to bargain any further unless convinced by the union on the basis of new facts that its original position was wrong. The NLRB subsequently found that the practice of offering the same settlement to all units, insisting that certain parts of the package could not differ among agreements, and communicating to the employees about how negotiations were going amounted to an illegal pattern. John Fossum, *Labor Relations* (Dallas, TX: Business Publications, 1982), p. 267. See also William Cooke, Aneil Mishra, Gretchen Spreitzer, and Mary Tschirhart, "The Determinants of NLRB Decision-Making Revisited," *Industrial and Labor Relations Review* 48, no. 2 (January 1995): 237–57.

41. Commerce Clearing House, "Drug Testing/Court Rulings," (January 25, 1988): 16.

42. Bargaining items based on Reed-Richardson, *Collective Bargaining by Objectives* (Upper Saddle River, NJ: Prentice Hall, 1997), pp. 113–15; bargaining stages based on William Glueck, "Labor Relations and the Supervisor," in M. Gene Newport, *Supervisory Management* (St. Paul, MN: West Publishing, 1976), pp. 200–234; Sloane and Witney, *Labor Relations*, pp. 214–56.

43. Yoder, *Personnel Management*, 517–18.

44. Richardson, *Collective Bargaining*, 150.

45. Fossum, *Labor Relations*, 298–322.

46. Although considerable research has been done on the subject, it's not clear what sorts of situations precipitate impasses. At times, however, it seems that the prospect of having the impasse taken to an arbitrator actually "chills" the negotiation process. Specifically, if neither the union nor the management negotiators want to make the tough choices, they might consciously or unconsciously opt to declare an impasse, knowing that the arbitrator will then have to take the heat. See Linda Babcock and Craig Olson, "The Causes of Impasses in Labor Disputes," *Industrial Relations* 31, no. 2 (spring 1992): 348–60.

47. Fossum, *Labor Relations*, 312. See also Thomas Watkins, "Assessing Arbitrator Competence," *Arbitration Journal* 47, no. 2 (June 1992): 43–48.

48. Gregg LeBar, "Awards and Incentives in Action," *Occupational Hazards* 59, no. 1 (January 1997): 91–92.

49. Jonathan Kramer and Thomas Hyclak, "Why Strikes Occur: Evidence from the Capital Markets," *Industrial Relations* 41, no. 1 (January 2002): 80–93.

50. For a discussion, see Herbert Northrup, "Union Corporate Campaigns and Inside Games as a Strike Form," *Employee Relations Law Journal* 19, no. 4 (spring 1994): 507–49.

51. Ibid., 513.

52. Ibid., 518.

53. For a discussion of the cost of a strike, see Woodruff Imberman, "Strikes Cost More Than You Think," *Harvard Business Review* 57 (May/June 1979): 133–38. The NLRB held in 1986 in Charter Equipment, Inc. 280 NLRB No. 71, that an employer could lawfully hire temporary replacements during the course of a lockout, in the absence of proof of specific antiunion motivation, in order to bring economic pressure to bear upon a union to support a legitimate bargaining position.

54. Clifford Koen Jr., Sondra Hartmen, and Dinah Payne, "The NLRB Wields a Rejuvenated Weapon," *Personnel Journal* (December 1996): 85–87.

55. Duncan Adams, "Worker Grievances Consume Roanoke, VA Mail Distribution Center," *Knight-Ridder/Tribune Business News* (March 27, 2001), item 1086009.

56. Sloane and Witney, *Labor Relations*, 229–31.

57. Walter Baer, *Grievance Handling: 101 Guides for Supervisors* (New York: American Management Association, 1970).

58. Reed Richardson, *Collective Bargaining* (Upper Saddle River, NJ: Prentice Hall, 1977), p. 184.

59. See, for example, Clyde Summers, "Protecting All Employees Against Unjust Dismissal," *Harvard Business Review* 58 (January/February 1980): 132–39; George Bohlander and Harold White, "Building Bridges: Non-Union Employee Grievance Systems," *Personnel* (July 1988): 62–66.

60. "AFL-CIO Launching New Strategy to Win Over Nonunion Workers," *Compensation and Benefits Review* 18, no. 5 (September/October 1986): 8; Shane R. Premeaux, R. Wayne Moody, and Art Bethke, "Decertification: Fulfilling Unions' 'Destiny'?" *Personnel Journal* 66, no. 6 (June 1987): 144.

61. "The Battle for Corporate Control," *Business Week* (May 18, 1987): 107.

62. Sar Levitan and Frank Gallo, "Collective Bargaining and Private Sector Employment," *Monthly Labor Review* (September 1989): 24–33; Charles Craver, "The American Labor Movement in the Year 2000," *Business Horizons* (November/December 1993): 64–69; Barbara Ettoree, "Will Unions Survive?" *Management Review* (August 1993): 9–15; Bill Leonard, "The New Fact of Organized Labor," *HR Magazine* (July 1999): 56.

63. J. A. Silja Talvi, "Labor's New Front Lines Promising You Should Know the Fruits of Economic Growth, for a Broader Base," *Christian Science Monitor* (January 29, 2001): 11.

64. Robert Sauer and Keith Voelker, *Labor Relations: Structure and Process* (New York: Macmillan, 1993), pp. 510–25.

65. Ibid., 516. See also Marino Regini, "Human Resource Management and Industrial Relations in European Companies," *International Journal of Human Resource Management* 4, no. 3 (September 1993): 555–68.

66. Quoted from Regini, "Human Resource Management," 559.

67. "Contracts Call for Greater Labor Management Teamwork," *BNA Bulletin to Management* (April 29, 1999): 133.

68. John Nee, Pamela Kennedy, and Donald Langham, "Increasing Manufacturing Effectiveness Through Joint Union/Management Cooperation," *Human Resource Management* 38, no. 1 (spring 1999): 77–85.

69. "Union Fights Team Program at UPS," *BNA Bulletin to Management* (March 14, 1996): 88.

70. Kenneth Jenero and Christopher Lyons, "Employee Participation Programs: Prudent or Prohibited?" *Employee Relations Law Journal* 17, no. 4 (spring 1997): 539.

71. These are from G. Roger King, "New Guidelines From the NLRB on Participative Management Initiatives and Employee Committees," *Society for Human Resource Management Legal Report* (November–December 2001): 3–4.

72. "U.S.: Rise in Union Activity at Dot.com Firms," *Guardian* (December 13, 2000): 18.

73. Raymond L. Hilgert and Cyril C. Ling, *Cases and Experiential Exercises in Human Resource Management* (Upper Saddle River, NJ: Prentice Hall, 1996), pp. 291–92.

Chapter 9

Ethics and Fair Treatment in Human Resource Management

- Ethics and Fair Treatment at Work
- What Shapes Ethical Behavior at Work?
- Ethics, Fair Treatment, and the Role of HR Management
- Employee Discipline and Privacy
- Managing Dismissals

When you finish studying this chapter, you should be able to:

- Explain *what is meant by ethical behavior.*

- Discuss *important factors that shape ethical behavior at work.*

- Discuss *at least four specific ways in which HR management can influence ethical behavior at work.*

- Exercise *fair disciplinary practices.*

- Discuss *at least four important factors in managing dismissals effectively.*

INTRODUCTION

The New York physician faced an ethical dilemma. She was not in private practice, but worked as a corporate physician for a large New York newspaper. As a physician, she felt she had to follow the medical code of ethics requiring her to fully divulge to her patients what their medical conditions were. But she says that the vice president for human resources at her company told her that she should instead avoid suggesting to the employees who came to see her that their injuries were work-related, thus reducing the potential for workers' compensation claims against the employer. What should the doctor do?

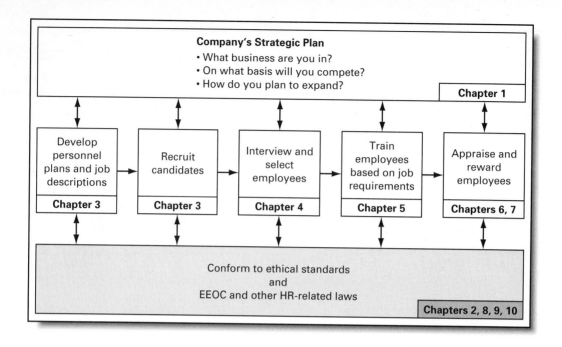

Company's Strategic Plan
- What business are you in?
- On what basis will you compete?
- How do you plan to expand?

Chapter 1

Develop personnel plans and job descriptions	Recruit candidates	Interview and select employees	Train employees based on job requirements	Appraise and reward employees
Chapter 3	Chapter 3	Chapter 4	Chapter 5	Chapters 6, 7

Conform to ethical standards
and
EEOC and other HR-related laws

Chapters 2, 8, 9, 10

ETHICS AND FAIR TREATMENT AT WORK

People face ethical choices every day. For example, is it wrong to use company e-mail for personal reasons? Is a $50 gift to a boss unacceptable? Compare your answers to those of other Americans by answering the quiz in Figure 9.1.

While headlines tend to focus on Enron-type financial misdeeds, many ethical blunders actually stem from HR-related tasks. One survey of 747 HR professionals found that 54% had observed misconduct ranging from violations of Title VII, to violations of the occupational safety and health act, to employees using drugs or alcohol or falsifying work records.[1] Another found that six of the 10 most serious ethical issues—workplace safety, security of employee records, employee theft, affirmative action, comparable work, and employee privacy rights—were HR related.[2]

Of course, HR activities need not just be a potential hotbed of ethical misdeeds. Instead, HR activities can drive positive ethical change, and can play a central role in the company's ethics efforts.[3] We'll focus on how in this and the following sections. Let's look first at what *ethics* means.

The Meaning of *Ethics*

Ethics refers to "the principles of conduct governing an individual or a group,"[4] and specifically to the standards you use to decide what your conduct should be. Ethical decisions are always characterized by two things. First, ethical decisions always involve *normative judgments*.[5] A normative judgment implies that "something is good or bad, right or wrong, better or worse."[6] "You are wearing a skirt and blouse" is a non-normative statement; "That's a great outfit!" is a normative one.

Figure 9.1 The Wall Street Journal Workplace-Ethics Quiz

The spread of technology into the workplace has raised a variety of new ethical questions, and many old ones still linger. Compare your answers with those of other Americans surveyed, on page 322.

Office Technology

1. Is it wrong to use company e-mail for personal reasons?
   ☐ Yes ☐ No

2. Is it wrong to use office equipment to help your children or spouse do schoolwork?
   ☐ Yes ☐ No

3. Is it wrong to play computer games on office equipment during the workday?
   ☐ Yes ☐ No

4. Is it wrong to use office equipment to do Internet shopping?
   ☐ Yes ☐ No

5. Is it unethical to blame an error you made on a technological glitch?
   ☐ Yes ☐ No

6. Is it unethical to visit pornographic Web sites using office equipment?
   ☐ Yes ☐ No

Gifts and Entertainment

7. What's the value at which a gift from a supplier or client becomes troubling?
   ☐ $25 ☐ $50 ☐ $100

8. Is a $50 gift to a boss unacceptable?
   ☐ Yes ☐ No

9. Is a $50 gift *from* the boss unacceptable?
   ☐ Yes ☐ No

10. Of gifts from suppliers: Is it OK to take a $200 pair of football tickets?
    ☐ Yes ☐ No

11. Is it OK to take a $120 pair of theater tickets?
    ☐ Yes ☐ No

12. Is it OK to take a $100 holiday food basket?
    ☐ Yes ☐ No

13. Is it OK to take a $25 gift certificate?
    ☐ Yes ☐ No

14. Can you accept a $75 prize won at a raffle at a supplier's conference?
    ☐ Yes ☐ No

Truth and Lies

15. Due to on-the-job pressure, have you ever abused or lied about sick days?
    ☐ Yes ☐ No

16. Due to on-the-job pressure, have you ever taken credit for someone else's work or idea?
    ☐ Yes ☐ No

Source: Wall Street Journal (21 October 1999): B1–B4. Ethics Officer Association, Belmont, Mass.; Ethics Leadership Group, Wilmette, IL; surveys sampled a cross-section of workers at large companies and nationwide.

Ethical decisions also always involve *morality,* which is society's accepted standards of behavior. Moral standards differ from other standards in several ways.[7] They address matters of serious consequence to society's well-being, such as murder, lying, and slander. They cannot be established or changed by decisions of authoritative bodies like legislatures,[8] and they should override self-interest. Many people (though not all) believe that moral judgments are never situational. They would argue that something that is morally right (or wrong) in one situation is right (or wrong) in another. Moral judgments tend to trigger strong emotions. Violating moral standards may make you feel ashamed or remorseful.[9]

It would simplify things if it was always clear which decisions were ethical and which were not. Unfortunately, it is not. Ethics—principles of conduct—are rooted in morality, so in many cases it's true that what is ethical is clear. (For example, if the decision makes the person feel ashamed or remorseful, or involves a matter of serious consequence such as murder, then chances are it's probably unethical.) On the other hand, perhaps in Albania bribing is so widely ingrained that many there don't view it as wrong. "Everyone is doing it" is no excuse. However, the fact that a society doesn't view bribery as wrong may suggest that someone making a bribe there may not be doing something wrong, at least in terms of his or her frame of reference.

Ethics and the Law

Furthermore, the law is not the best of guides about what is ethical, because something may be legal but not right, and something may be right but not legal. You can make a decision that involves ethics (such as firing an employee) based on what is legal. However, that doesn't mean the decision will be ethical, since a legal decision can be unethical (and an ethical one illegal). Firing a 38-year-old employee with 20 years' tenure without notice may be unethical, but still legal, for instance. Patrick Gnazzo, vice president for business practices at United Technologies Corp. (and a former trial lawyer) put it this way: "Don't lie, don't cheat, don't steal. We were all raised with essentially the same values. Ethics means making decisions that represent what you stand for, not just what the laws are."[10]

Ethics, Fair Treatment, and Justice

Companies where fairness and justice prevail also tend to be ethical companies. One study focused on how employees reacted to fair treatment. It concluded that, "to the extent that survey respondents believed that employees were treated fairly . . . [they] reported less unethical behavior in their organizations. They also reported that employees and their organizations were more aware of ethical issues [and] more likely to ask for ethical advice."[11] Similarly, "[H]iring, performance evaluation, discipline, and terminations can be ethical issues because they all involve honesty, fairness, and the dignity of the individual."[12] In practice, fair treatment reflects concrete actions such as "employees are trusted," "employees are treated with respect," and "employees are treated fairly" (see Figure 9.2).[13]

Workplace unfairness can be blatant. For example, some supervisors are "workplace bullies," yelling at or ridiculing subordinates, humiliating them, and sometimes even making threats. The employer should of course always prohibit such behavior, and many firms do have anti-harassment policies. For example, the policy at the Oregon Department of Transportation is that "it is the policy of the department that all employees, customers, contractors and visitors to the work site are entitled to a positive, respectful and productive work environment, free from behavior, actions, [and] language constituting workplace harassment."[14] Not surprisingly, employees of abusive supervisors are more likely to quit their jobs, and to report lower job and life satisfaction and higher stress if they remain in those jobs.[15]

Why Treat Employees Fairly?

There are many reasons that managers should be fair and just, and some are more obvious than others. The golden rule is one obvious rationale: As management guru Peter Drucker recently said, "[t]hey're not employees, they're people" and the manager should treat people with dignity and respect. An increasingly litigious

Figure 9.2 Perceptions of Fair Interpersonal Treatment Scale

What is your organization like most of the time? Circle YES if the item describes your organization, NO if it does not describe your organization, and ? if you cannot decide.

IN THIS ORGANIZATION . . .

1.	Employees are praised for good work	Yes	?	No
2.	Supervisors yell at employees (R)	Yes	?	No
3.	Supervisors play favorites (R)	Yes	?	No
4.	Employees are trusted	Yes	?	No
5.	Employees' complaints are dealt with effectively	Yes	?	No
6.	Employees are treated like children (R)	Yes	?	No
7.	Employees are treated with respect	Yes	?	No
8.	Employees' questions and problems are responded to quickly	Yes	?	No
9.	Employees are lied to (R)	Yes	?	No
10.	Employees' suggestions are ignored (R)	Yes	?	No
11.	Supervisors swear at employees (R)	Yes	?	No
12.	Employees' hard work is appreciated	Yes	?	No
13.	Supervisors threaten to fire or lay off employees (R)	Yes	?	No
14.	Employees are treated fairly	Yes	?	No
15.	Co-workers help each other out	Yes	?	No
16.	Co-workers argue with each other (R)	Yes	?	No
17.	Co-workers put each other down (R)	Yes	?	No
18.	Co-workers treat each other with respect	Yes	?	No

Note: R = the item is reverse scored.

Source: Michelle A. Donovan et al., "The Perceptions of Their Interpersonal Treatment Scale: Development and Validation of a Measure of Interpersonal Treatment in the Workplace," *Journal of Applied Psychology* 83, no. 5 (1998): 692. Copyright © 1997 by Michelle A. Donovan, Fritz Drasgow, and Liberty J. Munson at the University of Illinois at Urbana-Champaign. All rights reserved.

workforce is another obvious rationale. The manager wants to be sure to institute disciplinary and discharge procedures that will survive the scrutiny of arbitrators and the courts.

What may not be quite so obvious is that employees' perceptions of fairness also have important organizational ramifications. For example, perceptions of fairness relate to enhanced employee commitment; enhanced satisfaction with the organization, jobs, and leaders; and enhanced organizational citizenship behaviors.[16]

A recent study provides a vivid and appropriate illustration. College instructors completed surveys regarding the extent to which they saw their colleges as treating them with procedural and distributive justice. (Researchers generally distinguish between *procedural justice* and *distributive justice*. The former refers to fair processes, while the latter refers to fair outcomes.) The procedural justice questions included, for example "In general, the department/college's procedures allow for requests for clarification for additional information about a decision." The distributive justice questions included, "I am fairly rewarded considering the responsibilities I have." These instructors also completed organizational commitment questionnaires. These included questions such as "I am proud to tell others that I am part of this department/college." Their students then completed surveys. These contained items such as "the instructor put a lot of effort into planning the content of this course," "the instructor was sympathetic to my needs," and "the instructor treated me fairly."

The results were telling. Instructors who perceived high distributive and procedural justice reported higher organizational commitment. Furthermore, their students reported higher levels of instructor effort, pro-social behaviors, and fairness, as well as more positive reactions to their instructors. "Overall," as the researcher says, "the results imply that fair treatment of employees has important organizational consequences. . . ."[17]

WHAT SHAPES ETHICAL BEHAVIOR AT WORK?

Whether or not a person acts ethically at work is usually not a result of any one thing. For example, it's not just the employee's *ethical tendencies,* since even "ethical" employees can have their actions influenced by *organizational* factors.[18] Thus, unethical behavior is more prevalent in competitive settings, and in ones in which the company rewards such behavior.[19] The presence or absence of ethics codes and compliance mechanisms, or an unethical boss are some other elements in the equation. The manager's task is to first understand what shapes ethical behavior, and then to take concrete steps to ensure that ethical choices prevail. Let's look first at the factors that shape ethical behavior, and then, in the following section, turn to the steps the manager can take to help ensure that ethics prevails.

Individual Factors

Because people bring to their jobs their own ideas of what is morally right and wrong, the individual must shoulder much of the credit (or blame) for the ethical choices he or she makes. A survey of CEOs of manufacturing firms was conducted to explain the CEOs' intentions to engage (or to not engage) in two questionable business practices: soliciting a competitor's technological secrets and making payments to foreign government officials to secure business. The researchers concluded that the CEOs' personal predispositions more strongly affected their decisions than did environmental pressures or organizational characteristics.[20]

In terms of traits, it's hard to generalize about the characteristics of ethical or unethical people, but age is a factor. One study surveyed 421 employees to measure the degree to which age, gender, marital status, education, dependent children, region of the country, and years in business influenced responses to ethical decisions. (Decisions included "doing personal business on company time," "not reporting others' violations of company rules and policies," and "calling in sick to take a day off for personal use.") Older workers in general had stricter interpretations of ethical standards and made more ethical decisions than younger employees. This "age factor" is compounded by this: Most people tend to have a distorted view of how ethical they really are.[21] It's therefore easy to be lulled into a false sense of security regarding the ethics of one's actions.

In any case, honesty testing (as discussed in Chapter 4) shows that some people are more inclined toward making the wrong ethical choice. How would you rate your own ethics? Figure 9.3 presents a short self-assessment survey for helping you answer that question.

Figure 9.3   How Do My Ethics Rate?

Instrument

Indicate your level of agreement with these 15 statements using the following scale:

  1 = Strongly disagree
  2 = Disagree
  3 = Neither agree nor disagree
  4 = Agree
  5 = Strongly agree

	1	2	3	4	5
1. The only moral of business is making money.	1	2	3	4	5
2. A person who is doing well in business does not have to worry about moral problems.	1	2	3	4	5
3. Act according to the law, and you can't go wrong morally.	1	2	3	4	5
4. Ethics in business is basically an adjustment between expectations and the ways people behave.	1	2	3	4	5
5. Business decisions involve a realistic economic attitude and not a moral philosophy.	1	2	3	4	5
6. "Business ethics" is a concept for public relations only.	1	2	3	4	5
7. Competitiveness and profitability are important values.	1	2	3	4	5
8. Conditions of a free economy will best serve the needs of society. Limiting competition can only hurt society and actually violates basic natural laws.	1	2	3	4	5
9. As a consumer, when making an auto insurance claim, I try to get as much as possible regardless of the extent of the damage.	1	2	3	4	5
10. While shopping at the supermarket, it is appropriate to switch price tags on packages.	1	2	3	4	5
11. As an employee, I can take home office supplies; it doesn't hurt anyone.	1	2	3	4	5
12. I view sick days as vacation days that I deserve.	1	2	3	4	5
13. Employees' wages should be determined according to the laws of supply and demand.	1	2	3	4	5
14. The business world has its own rules.	1	2	3	4	5
15. A good businessperson is a successful businessperson.	1	2	3	4	5

ANALYSIS AND INTERPRETATION

Rather than specify "right" answers, this instrument works best when you compare your answer to those of others. With that in mind, here are mean responses from a group of 243 management students. How did your responses compare?

1. 3.09	6. 2.88	11. 1.58
2. 1.88	7. 3.62	12. 2.31
3. 2.54	8. 3.79	13. 3.36
4. 3.41	9. 3.44	14. 3.79
5. 3.88	10. 1.33	15. 3.38

Source: Adapted from A. Reichel and Y. Neumann, *Journal of Instructional Psychology* (March 1988): 25–53. With permission of the authors.

What Shapes Ethical Behavior at Work?

Organizational Factors

If people did unethical things at work solely for personal gain, it perhaps would be understandable (though inexcusable). The scary thing about unethical behavior at work is that it's usually not driven by personal interests. Table 9.1 summarizes the results of one survey of the principal causes of ethical compromises, as reported by six levels of employees and managers.

As you can see, being under the gun to meet scheduling pressures was the number-one factor in causing ethical lapses. For most of these employees, "meeting overly aggressive financial or business objectives," and "helping the company survive" were the two other top causes. "Advancing my own career or financial interests" ranked toward the bottom of the list of principal causes of ethical compromises. Thus (at least in this case) most ethical lapses occurred because employees were under the gun to do what they thought was best to help their companies. Several years ago, three former CUC International executives pleaded guilty to federal charges. Authorities then called it "the largest and longest" accounting fraud in history. The former executives said they had done so to keep the price of the company stock high.[22]

Having rules on the books forbidding this sort of thing does not, by itself, seem to work. For example, in 2002, New York's attorney general filed charges against Merrill Lynch, alleging that several of its analysts had issued optimistic ratings on stocks, while privately expressing concerns about those same stocks. The allegation was that they did so to aid and support Merrill Lynch's investment banking relationships with these companies. In making his case, the attorney general released

Table 9.1   Principal Causes of Ethical Compromises

	SENIOR MGMT.	MIDDLE MGMT.	FRONT LINE SUPV.	PROF. NON-MGMT.	ADMIN. SALARIED	HOURLY
Meeting schedule pressure	1	1	1	1	1	1
Meeting overly aggressive financial or business objectives	3	2	2	2	2	2
Helping the company survive	2	3	4	4	3	4
Advancing the career interests of my boss	5	4	3	3	4	5
Feeling peer pressure	7	7	5	6	5	3
Resisting competitive threats	4	5	6	5	6	7
Saving jobs	9	6	7	7	7	6
Advancing my own career or financial interests	8	9	9	8	9	8
Other	6	8	8	9	8	9

Note: 1 is high, 9 is low.

Source: O. C. Ferrell and John Fraedrich, *Business Ethics,* 3d ed. (New York: Houghton Mifflin, 1997), p. 28. Adapted from Rebecca Goodell, *Ethics in American Business: Policies, Programs, and Perceptions* (1994), p. 54. Permission provided courtesy of the Ethics Resource Center, 1120 6th Street, NW, Washington, DC, 20005.

numerous e-mails and other documents written by Merrill analysts. One, for instance, read:

> "Some of the communication with the goto people and the bankers prior to the initiation may have been a technical violation of the firm's written policies and procedures (which, I have now learned, say the company's bankers should not be told what the proposed rating is or will be, even if the company isn't currently under coverage), so my guess is the lawyers will want to offer this in detail. From what they've told me, however, even if there was a violation, this is not a big deal."[23]

The Boss's Influence

Another essential element seems to be the extent to which employees can model their ethical behavior on the ethical behavior of their supervisors. According to one report, for instance, "the level of misconduct at work dropped dramatically when employees said their supervisors exhibited ethical behavior." Only 25% of employees who agreed that their supervisors "set a good example of ethical business behavior" said they had observed misconduct in the last year, compared with 72% of those who did not feel that their supervisors set good ethical examples.[24]

In fact, the leader's actions may be "the single most important factor in fostering corporate behavior of a high ethical standard."[25] The boss sets the tone, and by his or her actions sends signals about what is right or wrong. A study by the American Society of Chartered Life Underwriters found that 56% of all workers felt some pressure to act unethically or illegally, and that the problem seems to be getting worse.[26] One writer gives these examples of how supervisors knowingly (or unknowingly) lead subordinates astray ethically:

- Tell staffers to do whatever is necessary to achieve results.
- Overload top performers to ensure that work gets done.
- Look the other way when wrongdoing occurs.
- Take credit for others' work or shift blame.[27]

Ethics Policies and Codes

An ethics policy and code is one way to signal that the firm is serious about ethics.[28] For example, IBM's code of ethics has this to say about tips, gifts, and entertainment:

> "No IBM employee, or any member of his or her immediate family, can accept gratuities or gifts of money from a supplier, customer, or anyone in a business relationship. Nor can they accept a gift or consideration that could be perceived as having been offered because of the business relationship. 'Perceived' simply means this: if you read about it in the local newspaper, would you wonder whether the gift just might have had something to do with a business relationship? No IBM employee can give money or a gift of significant value to a customer, supplier, or anyone if it could reasonably be viewed as being done to gain a business advantage."[29]

Sometimes ethics codes work, and sometimes they don't. Enron's ethical principles were widely available on the company's Web site. They stated, among other things that "as a partner in the communities in which we operate, Enron believes it has a responsibility to conduct itself according to certain basic principles." Those include, "respect, integrity, communication and excellence."[30]

Some firms urge employees to apply a quick "ethics test" to evaluate whether what they're about to do fits the company's code of conduct. For example, the Raytheon Co. asks employees who are faced with ethical dilemmas to ask:

Is the action legal?
Is it right?
Who will be affected?
Does it fit Raytheon's values?
How will it "feel" afterwards?
How will it look in the newspaper?
Will it reflect poorly on the company?[31]

The Organization's Culture

It is clear that ethics codes cannot themselves head off unethical behavior. About three-fourths of U.S. firms have formal ethics codes, and most offer ethics training. (About 95% of the largest, Fortune 50 firms, provide such training.) Yet about four of every 10 employees in the United States say they have witnessed serious legal or ethical problems where they work. Over 50% of all workers in the financial services and insurance industries said they felt under pressure to act illegally or unethically. Just under half reported participating in such activities.[32] What accounts for these anomalies?

One, as noted above, is that it's usually not just one or two things that create the environment in which unethical behavior can flourish; several things—the individual, the boss, the ethics code, and the degree of competition, for instance—interact. Another problem is that when it comes to ethical behavior, it's not what you say that's important; it's what you do. Parents can talk about being ethical, but if their children see them always cutting ethical corners—bringing home "free" office supplies from where they work, for instance—the children may assume that being unethical is really OK.

The same is true at work. Whether it's in regard to ethics or some other matter, the manager sets values and creates a culture through what he or she says and does. Employees then take their signals from that behavior and from that culture, and it influences what they do. It's therefore important that the firm's culture send clear signals about what is and isn't acceptable behavior.

What Is Organizational Culture? Organizational culture is the characteristic values, traditions, and behaviors a company's employees share. A value is a basic belief about what is right or wrong, or about what you should or shouldn't do. ("Honesty is the best policy" would be a value.) Values are important because they guide and channel behavior. Managing people and shaping their ethical (and other) behavior therefore depends on shaping the values they use as behavioral guides.

To an outside observer, a company's culture reflects itself in several ways. You can sense it from the employees' *patterns of behavior,* such as ceremonial events and written and spoken comments. For example, managers and employees may engage in behaviors such as hiding information, politicking, or expressing honest concern when a colleague requires assistance. You can also sense it from *physical manifestations* of the company's behavior, such as written rules, office layouts, organizational structure, and dress codes.[33]

In turn, these cultural symbols and behaviors tend to reflect the firm's shared *values*, such as "the customer is always right" or "don't be bureaucratic." If management and employees really believe in the value "honesty is the best policy," the written rules they follow and the things they do will hopefully reflect this value. Of course, these guiding standards—these values and beliefs—lay out what ought to be, not what is.[34] Like the parent in the example above, if management's stated values differ from what the managers actually value, it will show up in the managers' behavior. You have to "walk the talk" to set the right culture. Culture, then, reflects the firm's values and patterns of behavior, and its physical manifestations (such as written rules, rewards systems, and dress codes). The question is, of course, What does our culture say about the ethical values that our company holds dear?

Culture and the Manager   When it comes to creating a corporate culture, the manager does not have to leave the matter to chance; quite the opposite. Organizational culture means the characteristic values, traditions, and behaviors a company's employees share. The important thing to remember is that (as the anecdote about the parent shows) things like these don't just reflect what the manager says. They reflect what he or she actually does. Managers therefore have to think through how they're going to send the right signals to their employees. They do so in the following ways:

Clarify Expectations   First, make it clear what your expectations are with respect to the values you want subordinates to follow. Publishing a corporate ethics code is one way to do this. For example, Johnson & Johnson says, "We believe our first responsibility is to the doctors, nurses and patients, to mothers and fathers and all others who use our products and services."[35]

Use Signs and Symbols   "Walk the talk." *Symbolism*—what the manager actually does and thus the signals he or she sends—ultimately does the most to create and sustain the company's culture. For example, Southwest Airlines is known for its fun (some say zany) work attitude.[36] However, the company doesn't talk about fun or humor in its mission statement. Instead, it sets the tone by what it does from the first day a person is hired. For example, new employees "are welcomed with balloons, games, toys, and gifts. New hires, even pilots, learn company songs or cheers during orientation."[37]

Provide Physical Support   The physical manifestations of the manager's values—the firm's incentive plan, appraisal system, and disciplinary procedures, for instance—send strong signals regarding what employees should and should not do. Does the firm reward ethical behavior or penalize it?

Use Stories   Managers use stories to illustrate important company values. For example, IBM has stories, such as how IBM salespeople took dramatic steps (like driving all night through storms) to get parts to customers.

Organize Rites and Ceremonies   For example, at JC Penney, new management employees are inducted at ritualistic conferences into the "Penney Partnership."

Here they commit to the firm's ideology as embodied in its statement of core values. Each inductee solemnly swears allegiance to these values and then receives his or her "HCSC lapel pin." These letters symbolize JC Penney's core values of honor, confidence, service, and cooperation.

ETHICS, FAIR TREATMENT, AND THE ROLE OF HR MANAGEMENT

We've seen that there's no single cause of unethical behavior at work, so it is not surprising that there's no one "silver bullet" to prevent it. Creating a culture that encourages employees to do the right thing is not so simple. Instead, managers must take several steps to ensure ethical behavior by their employees. Many of these actions are clearly within the realm of HR. Let's consider specific examples.

Staffing and Selection

As one writer says, "the simplest way to tune up an organization, ethically speaking, is to hire more ethical people."[38] Indeed, dissuading ethically undesirable applicants can actually start before the applicant even applies, if the HR department creates recruitment materials containing explicit references to the company's stress on integrity and ethics. Employers can then use tools such as honesty tests and meticulous background checks (discussed in Chapter 4) to screen out those who may not fit their ethical standards.[39]

The selection process also operates more subtly, by sending signals about what the company's values really are—and thus what the company's culture is, in terms of ethical and fair treatment. For example, "if prospective employees perceive that the hiring process does not treat people fairly, they may assume that ethical behavior is not important in the company, and that 'official' pronouncements about the importance of ethics can be discounted."[40]

Training

Ethics training typically plays a big role in corporate ethics programs. Such training usually includes showing employees how to recognize ethical dilemmas, how to use ethical frameworks (such as codes of conduct) to resolve problems, and how to use HR functions (such as interviews and disciplinary practices) in ethical ways.[41] The problem is that this sort of emphasis on the mechanics of ethics compliance may not be enough. Instead, the training should also emphasize the moral underpinnings of the ethical choice and the company's deep commitment to integrity and ethics, and include the participation of top managers to underscore that commitment.[42]

Consider an example. Findings regarding sexual harassment training programs indicate that trainees who don't view sexual harassment as an ethical/moral matter may be more inclined to engage in such behavior than those who do. The problem is that "many sexual harassment training sessions are developed around the desire to avoid legal liability. The ethics perspective [to harassment training] recognizes legal standards but moves beyond what is legal to the question of what is right. . . . Sexual harassment training programs that overemphasize legal requirements may encourage organization members to reason at lower levels of cognitive moral development when considering issues of sexual harassment."[43] They should instead emphasize the ethical/moral aspects of such behavior.

Some ethics training may simply be futile. To some extent, the program's results depend on the ethical inclinations of the trainees. As two writers put it, "we suggest that high integrity employees represent a more highly ethical trainee pool than do low integrity employees. Those with a history of honesty (in terms of their attitudes toward theft, for instance) may be more amenable to ethics training than those who are not."[44]

Much ethics training is Internet-based. For example, Lockheed Martin Corp. uses its intranet to let its 160,000 employees take ethics and legal compliance training online. Lockheed's ethics software also keeps track of how well the company and its employees are doing in terms of maintaining high ethical standards.[45] For example, the program helped top management see that in one recent year, 4.8% of the company's ethics allegations involved conflicts of interest, and that it takes about 30 days to complete an ethics violation internal investigation.[46] Figure 9.4 shows how employers use training as part of their ethics programs.

Performance Appraisal

The firm's performance appraisal processes provide another opportunity to emphasize its commitment to ethics and fairness. The appraisal provides an occasion to make it clear that the company not only professes to adhere to high ethical standards but also actually measures (and then rewards) employees based upon their adherence to those ethical standards.

How the supervisors do the appraisals is important. Studies confirm that, in practice, some managers ignore accuracy and honesty in performance appraisals and instead use the process for political purposes (such as encouraging employees with whom they don't get along to leave the firm).[47] To send the signal that fairness and ethics are paramount, the employees' standards should be clear, employees should understand the basis upon which they're going to be appraised, and the appraisals themselves should be performed objectively and fairly.[48]

Reward and Disciplinary Systems

To the extent that behavior is a function of its consequences, it is the company's (and HR's) responsibility to ensure that the firm rewards ethical behavior and penalizes unethical behavior. In fact, "research suggests that employees expect the organization to dole out relatively harsh punishment for unethical conduct."[49] Where the company does not deal swiftly with unethical behavior, it's often the ethical employees (not the unethical ones) who feel punished.

Workplace Aggression and Violence

We will see in the next chapter that workplace aggression and violence are increasingly serious problems, as well as problems that often stem from real or perceived inequities. Thus, employees who see themselves as unfairly underpaid may take

Figure 9.4 The Role of Training in Ethics

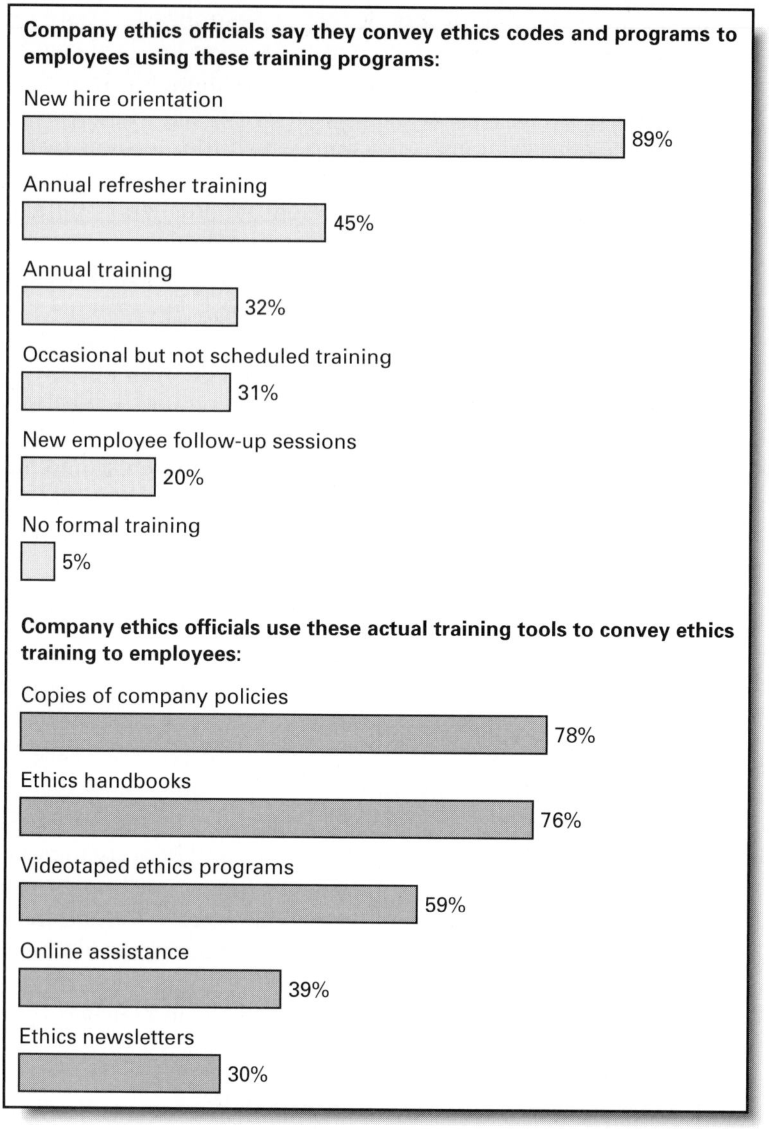

Company ethics officials say they convey ethics codes and programs to employees using these training programs:

New hire orientation

89%

Annual refresher training

45%

Annual training

32%

Occasional but not scheduled training

31%

New employee follow-up sessions

20%

No formal training

5%

Company ethics officials use these actual training tools to convey ethics training to employees:

Copies of company policies

78%

Ethics handbooks

76%

Videotaped ethics programs

59%

Online assistance

39%

Ethics newsletters

30%

Source: Susan Wells, "Turn Employees into Saints," *HR Magazine* (December 1999): 52.

negative actions ranging from employee theft to destruction of company property. Similarly, many HR actions including layoffs, being passed over for promotion, terminations, and discipline can prompt perceptions of unfair treatment that translate into dysfunctional behavior.[50]

Building Two-Way Communication

The opportunity for two-way communication plays an important role in our perceptions of how fairly we're being treated. Studies support this common-sense observation. One study concluded that three actions contributed to perceived fairness in business settings. These included *engagement* (involving individuals in the decisions that affect them by asking for their input and allowing them to refute the merits of one another's ideas and assumptions); *explanation* (ensuring that everyone involved and affected should understand why final decisions are made as they are and of the thinking that underlies the decisions); and *expectation clarity* (making sure everyone knows up front by what standards they will be judged and the penalties for failure).[51]

Given this, many employers take steps to facilitate two-way communication. For example, at Toyota Motor Manufacturing in Lexington, Kentucky, a *hotline* gives employees an anonymous method of bringing questions or problems to management's attention. The hotline is available 24 hours per day. Employees can pick up any phone, dial the hotline extension (the number is posted on the plant bulletin boards), and deliver their messages to the recorder. The HR manager reviews and answers all messages. Other firms administer periodic **opinion surveys.** For example, the FedEx Survey Feedback Action (SFA) program includes an anonymous survey. This lets employees express feelings about the company and their managers, and to some extent about service, pay, and benefits. Each manager then has an opportunity to discuss the anonymous department results with his or her subordinates, an action plan for improving work group commitment. Sample questions include:

"I can tell my manager what I think."
"My manager tells me what is expected."
"My manager listens to my concerns."
"My manager keeps me informed."

Other Illustrative HR Ethics Activities

HR supports the employer's ethics programs in other ways. For example, it is usually either HR or the firm's legal department that heads up its ethical compliance efforts. One study of Fortune 500 companies concluded that an HR officer was responsible for the program in 28% of responding firms. Another 28% gave the firm's legal officers responsibility, and 16% established separate ethics or compliance departments. The rest of the firms spread the responsibility among auditing departments, or positions such as public affairs and corporate communications.[52] Every two years Lockheed Martin surveys its employees regarding their adherence to the Lockheed's ethics code. It then institutes new ethics training programs based on the feedback it receives. (Johnson & Johnson uses its famous "credo" [its set of core ethical principles] as part of its management development programs.[53])

Strategy and HR   Like many companies in the cutthroat newspaper business, the physician's employer needed to reduce costs wherever it could. Workers' compensation claims are a significant part of most employers' human resource management expenses, and they therefore work hard to find legitimate ways to minimize these claims. The physician argued that the vice president for human resources told her to misinform the employees about whether their injuries or illnesses were work related. In doing so, the physician said, the company went too far. She felt that it required her to violate her medical code of ethics, and she therefore refused to comply. The company then fired her. She subsequently sued her employer, and so far there is no final ruling. The trial court decided that in offering physician care to its employees, the employer did imply that its physician's advice would meet basic professional ethics standards. An appeals court overturned that decision, and supported the employer's position. The case is now before a higher appeals court.

EMPLOYEE DISCIPLINE AND PRIVACY

The purpose of **discipline** is to encourage employees to behave sensibly at work (where *sensible* is defined as adhering to rules and regulations). In an organization, rules and regulations serve about the same purpose that laws do in society; discipline is called for when one of these rules or regulations is violated.[54] A fair and just discipline process is based on three pillars: rules and regulations, a system of progressive penalties, and an appeals process.

A set of clear rules and regulations is the first pillar. These rules address issues such as theft, destruction of company property, drinking on the job, and insubordination. Examples of rules include:

Poor performance is not acceptable. Each employee is expected to perform his or her work properly and efficiently and to meet established standards of quality.

Alcohol and drugs do not mix with work. The use of either during working hours and reporting for work under the influence of either are both strictly prohibited.

The vending of anything in the plant without authorization is not allowed; nor is gambling in any form permitted.

The purpose of these rules is to inform employees ahead of time what is and is not acceptable behavior. Employees must be told, preferably in writing, what is not permitted. This usually occurs during the employee's orientation. The employee orientation handbook usually contains the rules and regulations.

A system of progressive penalties is a second pillar of effective discipline. Penalties may range from oral warnings to written warnings to suspension from the job to discharge. The severity of the penalty is usually a function of the type of offense and the number of times the offense has occurred. For example, most companies issue warnings for the first unexcused lateness. However, for a fourth offense, discharge is the usual disciplinary action.

Finally, an appeals process should be part of the disciplinary process; this helps to ensure that supervisors mete out discipline fairly and equitably. The *HR in Practice* box summarizes discipline guidelines.

Formal Disciplinary Appeals Processes

Grievance-type disciplinary appeal procedures aren't limited to unionized firms. Consider FedEx's **guaranteed fair treatment** multi-step program. In *step 1, management review,* the complainant submits a written complaint to a member of

- *Make sure the evidence supports the charge of employee wrongdoing.* In one study, "the employer's evidence did not support the charge of employee wrongdoing" was the most frequent reason arbitrators gave for reinstating discharged employees or for reducing disciplinary suspensions.[55]
- *Ensure that the employees' due process rights are protected.* Arbitrators normally reverse discharges and suspensions that are imposed in a manner that violates basic notions of fairness or employee due process procedures.[56] For example, follow established progressive discipline procedures, and don't deny the employee an opportunity to tell his or her side of the story.[57]
- *The discipline should be in line with the way management usually responds to similar incidents.*[58]
- *Adequately warn the employee of the disciplinary consequences of his or her alleged misconduct.*
- *The rule that allegedly was violated should be "reasonably related" to the efficient and safe operation of the particular work environment.*

- *Management must fairly and adequately investigate the matter before administering discipline.*
- *The investigation should produce substantial evidence of misconduct.*
- *Applicable rules, orders, or penalties should be applied evenhandedly and without discrimination.*
- *The penalty should be reasonably related to the misconduct and to the employee's past work history.*
- *Maintain the employee's right to counsel.* All union employees have the right to bring help when they are called in for an interview that they reasonably believe might result in disciplinary action.[59]
- *Don't rob your subordinate of his or her dignity.*[60] Discipline your subordinate in private (unless he or she requests counsel).
- *Remember that the burden of proof is on you.* In U.S. society, a person is always considered innocent until proven guilty.
- *Get the facts.* Don't base your decision on hearsay evidence or on your general impression.
- *Don't act while angry.* Very few people can be objective and sensible when they are angry.

management (manager, senior manager, or managing director) within seven calendar days of the occurrence of the eligible issue. Then the manager, senior manager, and managing director of the employee's group review all relevant information; hold a telephone conference and/or meeting with the complainant; make a decision to either uphold, modify, or overturn management's action; and communicate their decision in writing to the complainant and the department's personnel representative.

If not satisfied, then in *step 2, officer complaint,* the complainant submits a written appeal to the vice president or senior vice president of the division within seven calendar days of the step 1 decision. Finally, in *step 3, executive appeals review,* the complainant may submit a written complaint within seven calendar days of the step 2 decision to the employee relations department. This department then investigates and prepares a case file for the executive review appeals board. The appeals board— the CEO, the COO, the chief personnel officer, and three senior vice presidents—then reviews all relevant information and makes a decision to uphold, overturn, or initiate a board of review or to take other appropriate action.

Discipline without Punishment

Traditional discipline has two potential flaws. First, no one feels good about being punished (although fairness guidelines like those previously mentioned can take the edge off this). A second shortcoming is that forcing your rules on employees may gain their short-term compliance, but not their cooperation when you are not around to enforce the rules.

Discipline without punishment (or nonpunitive discipline) aims to avoid these disciplinary problems. It does this by gaining the employees' acceptance of your rules and by reducing the punitive nature of the discipline itself. In summary:[61]

1. *Issue an oral reminder.* As a supervisor, your goal is to get the employee to agree to solve the disciplinary problem.
2. *Should another incident arise within six weeks, issue the employee a formal written reminder, a copy of which is placed in the personnel file.* In addition, privately hold a second discussion with the employee, again without any threats.
3. *Give a paid one-day "decision-making leave."* If another incident occurs after the written warning in the next six weeks or so, the employee is told to take a one-day leave with pay to stay home and consider whether the job is right for him or her and whether he or she wants to abide by the company's rules. When the employee returns to work, he or she meets with you and gives you a decision regarding whether he or she will follow the rules.
4. *If no further incidents occur in the next year or so, the one-day paid suspension is purged from the person's file.* If the behavior is repeated, dismissal (see later discussion) is required.[62]

The process would not apply to exceptional circumstances. Criminal behavior or in-plant fighting might be grounds for immediate dismissal, for instance. And if several incidents occurred at very close intervals, the supervisor might skip step 2—the written warning.

Electronic Employee Privacy

Employee surveillance is widespread. About 57% of U.S. companies monitor employees' e-mail and Internet use. Seventy percent of firms with 1,000 or more employees do so. Employers say they do so mostly to improve productivity and protect themselves from computer viruses, leaks of confidential information, and harassment suits.[63] New software can "secretly record everything your spouse, children and employees do online" on a particular computer. Other software lets the user "find out everything your spouse, children and employees do online via e-mail." "This program works so well it's scary" says someone who has used it.[64] When Turner Broadcasting System Inc. noticed that employees at its CNN London business bureau were piling up overtime claims, they installed new software to monitor every Web page every worker used. As the firm's network security specialist puts it, "If we see people were surfing the Web all day, then they don't have to be paid for that overtime."[65]

Electronic eavesdropping is legal—at least to a point. For example, federal law and most states' laws allow employers to monitor their employees' phone calls "in the ordinary course of business," says one legal expert. However, they must stop listening once they see the conversation is personal, not business related.[66] E-mail service may also be intercepted under federal law when it is to protect the property rights of the provider.[67] However, to be safe, more employers today are issuing e-mail and online services usage policies to, for instance, forewarn employees that those systems are intended to be used for business purposes only. They are having employees sign e-mail monitoring and telephone monitoring acknowledgment statements. One reason for explicit policy statements is the risk that employers may be held liable for illegal acts committed by their employees via e-mail. For example, messages sent by supervisors that contain sexual innuendo or ones defaming an employee can cause problems for the employer if the employer hasn't taken steps to prohibit such e-mail system misuse.[68]

Videotaping in the workplace seems to call for more legal caution. In one case, one U.S. Court of Appeals ruled that an employer's continuous video surveillance of employees in an office setting did not constitute an unconstitutional invasion of privacy.[69] Yet, a Boston employer had to pay over $200,000 to five workers it secretly videotaped in an employee locker room, after they sued in state court.[70]

Managing Dismissals

Dismissal is the most drastic disciplinary step and one that must be taken with deliberate care.[71] Specifically, the dismissal should be *just* in that sufficient cause exists for it. Furthermore, the dismissal should occur only after all reasonable steps to rehabilitate or salvage the employee have failed. However, there are undoubtedly times when dismissal is required, perhaps at once, and in these instances the employer should carry it out forthrightly.[72]

Of course, the best way to "handle" a dismissal is to avoid it in the first place, when possible. Many dismissals start with bad hiring decisions. Using sound selection practices including assessment tests, reference and background checks, drug testing, and clearly defined jobs can reduce the need for many dismissals.[73]

For more than 100 years, the prevailing rule in the United States has been that without an employment contract, either the employer or the employee can **terminate at will** the employment relationship. In other words, the employee could resign for any reason, at will, and the employer could similarly dismiss an employee for any reason, at will. Today, however, dismissed employees are increasingly taking their cases to court, and in many cases employers are finding that they no longer have a blanket right to fire. Instead, federal equal employment opportunity and other laws and various state laws and court rulings increasingly limit management's right to dismiss employees at will.

Grounds for Dismissal

There are four bases for dismissal: unsatisfactory performance, misconduct, lack of qualifications for the job, and changed requirements of (or elimination of) the job. *Unsatisfactory performance* may be defined as a persistent failure to perform assigned duties or to meet prescribed standards on the job.[74] Specific reasons include excessive absenteeism, tardiness, a persistent failure to meet normal job requirements, or an adverse attitude toward the company, supervisor, or fellow employees. *Misconduct* is deliberate and willful violation of the employer's rules and may include stealing, rowdy behavior, and insubordination. *Lack of qualifications* for the job is an employee's inability to do the assigned work although he or she is diligent. Because in this case the employee may be trying to do the job, it is reasonable for the employer to do what's possible to salvage him or her—perhaps by assigning the employee to another job, or retraining the person. *Changed requirements of the job* is an employee's incapability of doing the work assigned, after the nature of the job has been changed. Similarly, you may have to dismiss an employee when his or her job is eliminated. Again, the employee may be industrious, so it is reasonable to retrain or transfer this person, if possible.

Insubordination, a form of misconduct, is sometimes the grounds for dismissal. Stealing, chronic tardiness, and poor-quality work are concrete grounds for dismissal, but insubordination is sometimes harder to translate into words. To that end, it may be useful to remember that some acts are or should be deemed insubordinate whenever and wherever they occur. These include, for instance, direct disregard of the boss's authority, and disobedience of, or refusal to obey, the boss's orders—particularly in front of others.

Dismissing employees is never easy, but at least the employer can try to ensure the employee views the process as fair and just. Communication is important here. One study found, for instance, that "individuals who reported that they were given full explanations of why and how termination decisions were made were more likely to (1) perceive their layoff as fair, (2) endorse the terminating organization, and (3) indicate that they did not wish to take the past employer to court."[75]

Avoiding Wrongful Discharge Suits

Wrongful discharge occurs when an employee's dismissal does not comply with the law or with the contractual arrangement stated or implied by the firm via its employment application forms, employee manuals, or other promises. (In a *constructive discharge* claim, the plaintiff argues that he or she quit, but had no choice because the employer made the situation so intolerable at work.[76]) The time to protect against such suits is before the manager has erred and suits are filed.

Avoiding wrongful discharge suits requires at least a two-prong strategy. First is to follow employment policies and dispute resolution procedures (such as those outlined in this chapter) that make employees feel that they are treated fairly.[77] People who are fired and who walk away with the feeling that they've been embarrassed, stripped of their dignity, or treated unfairly financially (for instance, in terms of severance pay) are more likely to seek retribution in the courts. To some extent, employers can use severance pay to blunt a dismissal's sting. Figure 9.5 summarizes typical severance policies in manufacturing, and service industries. There is no way to make a termination pleasant, but an employer's first line of defense is to handle the dismissal with fairness and justice.

The second way to avoid wrongful discharge suits is to lay the groundwork— starting with the employment application—that will help avoid such suits before

Figure 9.5 Typical Severance Pay

MANUFACTURING INDUSTRIES

Percentage of companies paying indicated amount of severance:

	Key Execs	Senior Execs	Dept. Heads, Managers	Other Exempt	Nonexempt	Hourly
Less than 1 week per year:	8%	7%	7%	7%	8%	12%
1 week per year:	56	59	65	66	66	61
2 weeks per year:	19	20	19	19	19	23
3 weeks per year:	1	2	2	2	2	0
1 month per year:	9	8	6	3	2	1
Over one month:	6	4	2	2	2	3

SERVICE INDUSTRIES

Percentage of companies paying indicated amount of severance:

	Key Execs	Senior Execs	Dept. Heads, Managers	Other Exempt	Nonexempt	Hourly
Less than 1 week per year:	13%	12%	17%	19%	25%	24%
1 week per year:	46	45	56	58	58	56
2 weeks per year:	13	17	14	9	7	11
3 weeks per year:	0	0	2	0	0	0
1 month per year:	16	17	8	10	5	4
Over one month:	11	7	3	3	4	4

Column percentages in both charts may not equal 100 due to rounding.

Source: Right Management Consultants.

they get started. Steps to take include the following:

- Have applicants sign the employment application and make sure it contains a clearly worded statement that employment is for no fixed term and that the employer can terminate at any time. In addition, the statement should inform the job candidate that "nothing on this application can be changed."
- Review your employee manual to look for and delete statements that could prejudice your defense in a wrongful discharge case. For example, delete any reference to the fact that "employees can be terminated only for just cause" (unless you really mean that).
- Have clear written rules listing infractions that may require discipline and discharge, and then make sure to follow the rules.
- If a rule is broken, get the worker's side of the story in front of witnesses, and preferably get it signed. Then make sure to check out the story, getting both sides of the issue.
- Be sure that employees are appraised at least annually. If an employee shows evidence of incompetence, give that person a warning and provide an opportunity

to improve. All evaluations should be put in writing and signed by the employee.[78]

- Keep careful confidential records of all actions such as employee appraisals, warnings or notices, memos outlining how improvement should be accomplished, and so on.
- A final 10-step checklist to reduce exposure to wrongful discharge litigation would include: (1) Is employee covered by any type of written agreement, including a collective bargaining agreement? (2) Have written or oral representations been made to form a contract? (3) Is a defamation claim likely? (4) Is there a possible discrimination allegation? (5) Is there any workers' compensation involvement? (6) Have reasonable rules and regulations been communicated and enforced? (7) Has employee been given an opportunity to explain any rule violations or to correct poor performance? (8) Have all monies been paid within 24 hours after separation? (9) Has employee been advised of his or her rights under COBRA? (10) Has employee been advised of what the employee will tell a prospective employer in response to a reference inquiry?[79]

If humanitarianism and wrongful discharge suits aren't enough to encourage you to be fair in dismissing, consider this. One study found that managers run double their usual risk of suffering a heart attack during the week after they fire an employee.[80] During one five-year period, physicians interviewed 791 working people who had just undergone heart attacks to find out what might have triggered them. The researchers concluded that the stress associated with firing someone doubled the usual risk of a heart attack for the person doing the firing, during the week following the dismissal.

Personal Supervisory Liability

Managers should understand that courts sometimes hold them personally liable for their supervisory actions, particularly with respect to actions covered by the Fair Labor Standards Act and the Family and Medical Leave Act.[81] The Fair Labor Standards Act defines *employer* to include "any person acting directly or indirectly in the interest of an employer in relation to any employee . . . ," and this can mean the individual supervisor.

There are several ways to avoid creating situations in which personal liability becomes an issue. Managers should be fully familiar with applicable federal, state, and local *statutes* and know how to uphold their requirements. *Follow company policies and procedures,* since an employee may initiate a claim against an individual supervisor who he or she alleges did not follow company policies and procedures. The essence of many charges is that the plaintiff was treated differently than others, so *consistent application* of the rule or regulation is important. Administer the discipline in a manner that does not add to the *emotional hardship* on the employee (as would dismissing them in the middle of the workday when they have to publicly collect their belongings and leave the office). Most employees will try to present "their side of the story," and allowing them to do so can provide some measure of satisfaction to the employee that you treated the person fairly. *Do not act in anger,* since doing so personalizes the situation and undermines any appearance of objectivity. Finally, *utilize the HR department* for advice regarding how to handle difficult disciplinary matters.

The Termination Interview

Dismissing an employee is one of the most difficult tasks you can face at work.[82] The dismissed employee, even if warned many times in the past, may still react with disbelief or even violence. Guidelines for the **termination interview** itself are as follows:

1. *Plan the interview carefully.* According to experts at Hay Associates, this includes:
   - Make sure the employee keeps the appointment time.
   - Never inform an employee over the phone.
   - Allow 10 minutes as sufficient time for the interview.
   - Use a neutral site, never your own office.
   - Have employee agreements, the human resource file, and a release announcement (internal and external) prepared in advance.
   - Be available at a time after the interview in case questions or problems arise.
   - Have phone numbers ready for medical or security emergencies.

2. *Get to the point.* Do not beat around the bush by talking about the weather or making other small talk. As soon as the employee enters your office, give the person a moment to get comfortable and then inform him or her of your decision.

3. *Describe the situation.* Briefly, in three or four sentences, explain why the person is being let go. For instance, "Production in your area is down 4%, and we are continuing to have quality problems. We have talked about these problems several times in the past three months, and the solutions are not being followed through. We have to make a change."[83] Remember to describe the situation rather than attack the employee personally by saying things like, "Your production is just not up to par." Also emphasize that the decision is final and irrevocable.

4. *Listen.* Continue the interview until the person appears to be talking freely and reasonably calmly about the reasons for his or her termination and the support package (including severance pay).

5. *Review all elements of the severance package.* Describe severance payments, benefits, access to office support people, and the way references will be handled. However, under no conditions should any promises or benefits beyond those already in the support package be implied.

6. *Identify the next step.* The terminated employee may be disoriented and unsure what to do next. Explain where the employee should go next, upon leaving the interview.

Outplacement Counseling[84]   **Outplacement counseling** is a systematic process which provides terminated employees with career self-appraisal and job search skills.[85] Outplacement firms such as Drake Beam Morin, Inc. or Right Associates, Inc. usually provide the actual outplacement services. Managers who are let go typically have office space and secretarial services they can use at local offices of such firms, in addition to the counseling services. The outplacement counseling is part of the terminated employee's support or severance package.

Exit Interviews   Many employers conduct final **exit interviews** with employees who are leaving the firm. The HR department usually conducts the interview. The aim is to elicit information that might give the employer a better insight into what is right—or wrong—about the company. Exit interview questions to ask include: How were you recruited? Why did you join the company? Was the job presented correctly and honestly? Were your expectations met? What was the workplace environment like? What was your supervisor's management style like? What did you like most/least about the company? Were there any special problems areas? Why did you decide to leave, and how was the departure handled?[86]

The assumption, of course, is that because the employee is leaving, he or she will be candid. Based on one survey, though, the quality of information you can expect to get from exit interviews is questionable. The researchers found that at the time of separation, 38% of those leaving blamed salary and benefits, and only 4% blamed supervision. Followed up 18 months later, however, 24% blamed supervision and only 12% blamed salary and benefits. Getting to the real problem during the exit interview may thus require some digging.[87]

Layoffs and the Plant Closing Law

Nondisciplinary separations are a fact of life, and may be initiated by either employer or employee. For the employer, reduced sales or profits or the desire for more productivity may require layoffs. Employees may leave to retire or to seek better jobs. The Worker Adjustment and Retraining Notification Act (WARN Act, or the plant closing law) requires employers of 100 or more employees to give 60 days' notice before closing a facility or starting a layoff of 50 or more people.

A **layoff,** in which the employer sends workers home for a time, is usually not a permanent dismissal (although it may turn out to be). Instead, it is a situation in which three conditions are present: there is no work available for the employees, management expects the no-work situation to be temporary and probably short term, and management intends to recall the employees when work is again available.[88] However, some employers use the term *layoff* as a euphemism for discharge or termination. Layoffs are often subject to additional constraints abroad, as the *Global Issues* box illustrates.

Adjusting to Downsizings and Mergers

Downsizing—reducing, usually dramatically, the number of people employed by the firm—is being done by more and more employers.[89] The basic idea is to cut costs and raise profitability, although in one survey only 43% of the surveyed downsized firms saw operating earnings rise.[90]

Downsizings require careful planning, and consideration of several matters. One is compliance with all applicable laws, including WARN. Second is ensuring that the employer executes the dismissals in a manner that is just and fair. Third is the practical consideration of security, for instance with respect to retrieving keys and ensuring that those leaving do not take any prohibited items with them. Fourth is to take additional steps to reduce the remaining employees' uncertainty and to address their concerns. This typically involves a post-downsizing announcement, and an activities program including meetings at which senior managers field questions from the

Businesses expanding abroad soon discover that hiring, disciplining or discharging employees in Europe requires much more stringent communication than they do in the United States. For example, the European Union (EU) has a directive (law) that requires employers to provide employees with very explicit contracts of employment, usually within two months of their starting work.

How employers must comply with this law varies by country. For example, in the United Kingdom the employee must be given a written contract specifying, among other things, name of employer, grievance procedure, job title, rate of pay, disciplinary rules, pension plan, hours of work, vacation and sick-leave policies, pay periods, and date when employment began. In Germany, the contracts need not be in writing, although they customarily are, given the amount of detail they must cover, including minimum notice prior to layoff, wages, vacations, maternity/paternity rights, equal pay, invention rights, noncompetition clause, and sickness pay. The contract need not be in writing in Italy, but again, it usually is. Items covered include start date, probationary period, working hours, job description, place of work, basic salary, and a noncompetition clause. In France, the contract must be in writing, and specify information such as the identity of the parties, place of work, type of job or job descriptions, notice period, dates of payment, and work hours.

Although employment contract requirements differ from one European country to another, one thing can be said with certainty. When it comes to outlining the nature of the employment relationship, employers can't take fair treatment lightly, but instead must be very explicit about what the nature of the employer–employee relationship is to be.

remaining employees. It is usually also advisable for supervisors to meet with their employees informally to encourage an open discussion of any concerns. However, it's neither wise nor fair to make any assertions about "no more layoffs" unless they are true.

REVIEW

Summary

1. Ethics refers to the principles of conduct governing an individual or a group, and specifically to the standards you used to decide what your conduct should be.

2. Ethical decisions are always characterized by two things. First, ethical decisions always involve normative judgments. Second, ethical decisions also always involve morality, which is society's accepted standards of behavior.

3. Numerous factors shape ethical behavior at work. These include individual factors, organizational factors, the boss's influence, ethics policies and codes, and the organization's culture.

4. HR management can influence ethics and fair treatment at work in numerous ways. For example, having a fair and open selection process that emphasizes the company's stress on integrity and ethics, establishing special ethics

training programs, measuring employees' adherence to high ethical standards during performance appraisals, and rewarding (or disciplining) ethical (or unethical) work-related behavior are some examples.

5. Firms give employees vehicles through which to express opinions and concerns. For example, Toyota's hotline provides employees with an anonymous channel through which they can express concerns to top management. Firms such as IBM and FedEx engage in periodic anonymous opinion surveys.

6. Guaranteed fair treatment programs, such as the one at FedEx, help to ensure that grievances are handled fairly and openly. Steps include management review, officer complaint, and executive appeals review.

7. A fair and just discipline process is based on three prerequisites: rules and regulations, a system of progressive penalties, and an appeals process. A number of discipline guidelines are important, including that discipline should be in line with the way management usually responds to similar incidents; that management must adequately investigate the matter before administering discipline; and that managers should not rob a subordinate of his or her dignity.

8. The basic aim of discipline without punishment is to gain an employee's acceptance of the rules by reducing the punitive nature of the discipline itself. In particular, an employee is given a paid day off to consider his or her infraction before more punitive disciplinary steps are taken.

9. Managing dismissals is an important part of any supervisor's job. Among the reasons for dismissal are unsatisfactory performance, misconduct, lack of qualifications, changed job requirements, and insubordination. In dismissing one or more employees, however, remember that termination at will as a policy has been weakened by exceptions in many states. Furthermore, great care should be taken to avoid wrongful discharge suits.

10. Dismissing an employee is always difficult, and the termination interview should be handled properly. Specifically, plan the interview carefully (for instance, early in the week), get to the point, describe the situation, and then listen until the person has expressed his or her feelings. Then discuss the severance package and identify the next step.

11. Nondisciplinary separations such as layoffs and retirement occur all the time. The plant closing law (the Worker Adjustment and Retraining Notification Act) outlines requirements to be followed with regard to official notice before operations with 50 or more people are to be closed down.

12. Disciplinary actions are a big source of grievances. Discipline should be based on rules and adhere to a system of progressive penalties, and it should permit an appeals process.

KEY TERMS

- ethics
- opinion surveys
- discipline
- guaranteed fair treatment
- dismissal
- insubordination
- wrongful discharge
- termination interview
- outplacement counseling
- exit interviews
- layoff
- downsizing

DISCUSSION QUESTIONS AND EXERCISES

1. Describe the similarities and differences between a program such as FedEx's guaranteed fair treatment program and a typical union grievance procedure.

2. Explain how you would ensure fairness in disciplining, discussing particularly the prerequisites to disciplining, disciplining guidelines, and the discipline without punishment approach.

3. Why is it important in our highly litigious society to manage dismissals properly?

4. What techniques would you use as alternatives to traditional discipline? What do such alternatives have to do with "organizational justice"? Why do you think alternatives like these are important, given industry's need today for highly committed employees?

5. Working individually or in groups, interview managers or administrators at your employer or college in order to determine the extent to which the employer or college builds two-way communication, and the specific types of programs that are used. Do the managers think they are effective? What do the employees (or faculty members) think of the programs if they are in use at the employer or college?

6. Working individually or in groups, obtain copies of the student handbook for your college and determine to what extent there is a formal process through which students can air grievances. Do you think the process should be an effective one? Based on your contacts with other students, has it been an effective grievance process?

7. Working individually or in groups, determine the nature of the academic discipline process in your college. Do you think it is an effective one? Based on what you read in this chapter, would you recommend any modification of the student discipline process?

APPLICATION EXERCISES

Case Incident   *Allstate's Disappearing Agents*

Like many companies, Allstate faces pressure both to be cost competitive and to provide new services to its customers. It also faces pressure for continuous improvement in its financial performance from its shareholders. Assuming that for Allstate to survive and prosper it needs to respond both to customers and shareholders, what ethical responsibilities does it have toward another important group of stakeholders, its employees?

Here's the situation. Several years ago, the Allstate Corporation announced a series of strategic initiatives to (1) expand its selling service capabilities, (2) buy back company shares to raise its stock price, and (3) cut expenses by reducing the workforce. As part of its restructuring, Allstate would transfer its existing agents to an exclusive independent contractor program, whereby Allstate agents would become basically self-employed "independent contractors." This would markedly reduce the need for Allstate to provide agency support staff. In its press release on this initiative, Allstate management also announced it would soon eliminate 4,000 non-agent positions, or approximately 10% of the company's non-agents' workforce.

Said Allstate's CEO, "Now, many of our customers and potential customers are telling us they want our products to be easier to buy, easier to service, and more competitively priced. We will combine the power of our agency distribution system with the growth potential of direct selling and electronic commerce."

Proponents of restructurings like these might argue that Allstate is simply taking the steps needed to be competitive. They might even say that if Allstate did not cut jobs to create the cash flow required to fund new competitive initiatives, it might ultimately fail as a business, putting all 54,000 of its employees at risk.

Yet Allstate's program raises concerns. One analyst noted that by encouraging customers to purchase insurance products directly via the Internet, they threaten the commissions of its more than 15,000 agents. The announcement of cost cutting came one day after Allstate announced it would meet its regular quarterly dividend of 15 cents per share. The company has raised its dividend annually since the mid-1990s. ∎

DISCUSSION QUESTIONS

1. Is reducing the number of employees in a company in and of itself unethical? Why or why not?
2. If you decided it was generally ethical, what would the company have to do to make the employee dismissals unethical?
3. What responsibilities does a company like Allstate have toward its employees?
4. Is there a moral dimension to the question of marketing Allstate insurance via the Internet? If so, what is it?

Continuing Case

LearnInMotion.com: Are Our Ethics Out of Control?

It's probably safe to say that in creating LearnInMotion.com, Jennifer and Mel gave absolutely no thought to ethical behavior in their company. They did of course put endless hours into developing their business plan, raising money, installing computers and broadband lines, and trying to generate sales. But as far as taking specific concrete steps toward ensuring that everything that they and their employees did was aboveboard and ethical, they were batting zero, not because they were unethical people, but simply because the matter simply never entered their minds.

However, several ethics-related issues have recently come up, and they're causing concern for both Jennifer and Mel. Yesterday they received word from one of the main Internet service providers that someone in their company was using spamming techniques to send unsolicited LearnInMotion.com advertising information to tens of thousands of its subscribers, and threatening legal action if the spamming did not cease. A large customer called last week to complain that they'd recently learned that LearnInMotion.com was not reaching even half the number of potential users that LearnInMotion's sales brochures said it did, and

the customer therefore wanted a rebate. The CEO of LearnInMotion's largest competitor called Mel to say that their own internal tracking systems had noticed that someone at LearnInMotion.com had been methodically downloading its customers' names and files, and that if the electronic monitoring did not cease his company would file a lawsuit. All this, and more, led Jennifer and Mel to believe that they have to do something to ratchet up the ethical level in their company. Now, they want you, their management consultants, to help them actually do it. Here's what they want you to do for them. ∎

QUESTIONS AND ASSIGNMENTS

1. Are the sorts of issues raised in the case ethical ones? Why or why not?
2. Tell us: what are the sorts of factors that shape ethical behavior in a company like LearnInMotion.com?
3. In terms of human resource management, list at least six concrete staffing and selection, training, performance appraisal, and reward/disciplinary actions we can take right now to institute a greater appreciation for the high ethical standards we think our company should have.

Experiential Exercise

Purpose: The purpose of this exercise is to provide you with some experience in analyzing and handling an actual disciplinary action.

Required Understanding: Students should be thoroughly familiar with the following case, titled "Botched Batch." However, *do not read the "Award" or "Discussion" sections*

until after the groups have completed their deliberations.

How to Set Up the Exercise/Instructions: Divide the class into groups of four or five students. Each group should take the arbitrator's point of view and assume that they are to analyze the case and make the arbitrator's decision. Review the case again at this point, but please do not read the award and discussion.

Each group should answer the following questions:

1. What would your decision be if you were the arbitrator? Why?
2. Do you think that following their experience in this arbitration the parties will be more or less inclined to settle grievances by themselves without resorting to arbitration?

Botched Batch

Facts: A computer department employee made an entry error that botched an entire run of computer reports. Efforts to rectify the situation produced a second set of improperly run reports. As a result of the series of errors, the employer incurred extra costs of $2,400, plus a weekend of overtime work by other computer department staffers. Management suspended the employee for three days for negligence, and also revoked a promotion for which the employee had previously been approved.

Protesting the discipline, the employee stressed that she had attempted to correct her error in the early stages of the run by notifying the manager of computer operations of her mistake. Maintaining that the resulting string of errors could have been avoided if the manager had followed up on her report and stopped the initial run, the employee argued that she had been treated unfairly because the manager had not been disciplined even though he compounded the problem, whereas she was severely punished. Moreover, citing her "impeccable" work record and management's acknowledgment that she had always been a

"model employee," the employee insisted that the denial of her previously approved promotion was "unconscionable."

*(Please do **not** read beyond this point until after you have completed the experiential exercise.)*

Award: The arbitrator upholds the three-day suspension, but decides that the promotion should be restored.

Discussion: "There is no question," the arbitrator notes, that the employee's negligent act "set in motion the train of events that resulted in running two complete sets of reports reflecting improper information." Stressing that the employer incurred substantial cost because of the error, the arbitrator cites "unchallenged" testimony that management had commonly issued three-day suspensions for similar infractions in the past. Thus, the arbitrator decides, the employer acted with just cause in meting out an "evenhanded" punishment for the negligence.

Turning to the denial of the already approved promotion, the arbitrator says that this action should be viewed "in the same light as a demotion for disciplinary reasons." In such cases, the arbitrator notes, management's decision normally is based on a pattern of unsatisfactory behavior, an employee's inability to perform, or similar grounds. Observing that management had never before reversed a promotion as part of a disciplinary action, the arbitrator says that by tacking on the denial of the promotion in this case, the employer substantially varied its disciplinary policy from its past practice. Because this action on management's part was not "evenhanded," the arbitrator rules, the promotion should be restored.

Ethics Quiz Answers

Quiz is on page 295

1. 34% said personal e-mail on company computers is wrong.
2. 37% said using office equipment for schoolwork is wrong.
3. 49% said playing computer games at work is wrong.
4. 54% said Internet shopping at work is wrong.
5. 61% said it's unethical to blame your error on technology.
6. 87% said it's unethical to visit pornographic sites at work.
7. 33% said $25 is the amount at which a gift from a supplier or client becomes

troubling, while 33% said $50, and 33% said $100.

8. 35% said a $50 gift to the boss is unacceptable.

9. 12% said a $50 gift *from* the boss is unacceptable.

10. 70% said it's unacceptable to take the $200 football tickets.

11. 70% said it's unacceptable to take the $120 theater tickets.

12. 35% said it's unacceptable to take the $100 food basket.

13. 45% said it's unacceptable to take the $25 gift certificate.

14. 40% said it's unacceptable to take the $75 raffle prize.

15. 11% reported they lie about sick days.

16. 4% reported they take credit for the work or ideas of others.

ENDNOTES

1. Paul Schumann, "A Moral Principal's Framework for Human Resource Management Ethics," *Human Resource Management Review* 11 (2001): 94.

2. Kevin Wooten, "Ethical Dilemmas in Human Resource Management: An Application of a Multidimensional Framework, A Unifying Taxonomy, and Applicable Codes," *Human Resource Management Review* 11 (2001): 161.

3. For one thing "Hiring, performance evaluation, discipline, and terminations can be ethical issues because they all involve honesty, fairness, and the dignity of the individual"; Linda Trevino and Katherine Nelson, *Managing Business Ethics* (New York: John Wiley & Sons, 1999), p. 134.

4. Manuel Velasquez, *Business Ethics: Concepts and Cases* (Upper Saddle River, NJ: Prentice Hall, 1992), p. 9. See also Kate Walter, "Ethics Hot Lines Tap Into More Than Wrongdoing," *HR Magazine* (September 1995): 79–85; Skip Kaltenheuser, "Bribery is Being Outlawed Virtually Worldwide," *Business Ethics* (May 1998): 11.

5. The following discussion, except as noted, is based on Manuel Velasquez, *Business Ethics*, 9–12.

6. Ibid., 9.

7. This discussion is based on ibid., 12–14.

8. Ibid., 12. For further discussion, see Kurt Baier, *Moral Points of View,* abbr. ed. (New York: Random House, 1965), p. 88. See also Milton Bordwin, "The 3 R's of Ethics," *Management Review* (June 1998): 59–61.

9. For further discussion of ethics and morality, see Tom Beauchamp and Norman Bowie, *Ethical Theory and Business* (Upper Saddle River, NJ: Prentice Hall, 2001), pp. 1–19.

10. Richard Osborne, "A Matter of Ethics," *Industry Week* 49, no. 14 (September 4, 2000): 41–42.

11. Gary Weaver and Linda Trevino, "The Role of Human Resources in Ethics/Compliance Management: A Fairness Perspective," *Human Resource Management Review* 11 (2001): 115.

12. Trevino and Nelson, *Managing Business Ethics*, 134.

13. Michelle Donovan et al., "The Perceptions of Their Interpersonal Treatment Scale: Development and Validation of a Measure of Interpersonal Treatment in the Workplace," *Journal of Applied Psychology* 83, no. 5 (1998): 683–92.

14. Rudy Yandrick, "Lurking in the Shadows," *HR Magazine* (October 1999): 61–68.

15. Bennett Tepper, "Consequences of Abusive Supervision," *Academy of Management Journal* 43, no. 2 (2000): 178–90.

16. Weaver and Trevino, "Role of Human Resources," 117.

17. Suzanne Masterson, "A Trickle-Down Model of Organizational Justice: Relating Employees' and Customers' Perceptions of and Reactions to Fairness," *Journal of Applied Psychology* 86, no. 4 (2001): 594–601.

18. J. Fraedrich et al., "Assessing the Application of Cognitive Moral Development Theory to Business Ethics," *Journal of Business Ethics* 13 (1994): 829–38.

19. M. T. Hegarty and H. P. Sims Jr., "Organizational Philosophy, Policies, and Objectives Related to Unethical Decision

Behavior: A Laboratory Experiment," *Journal of Applied Psychology* 64 (1979): 331–38.

20. Sara Morris et al., "A Test of Environmental, Situational, and Personal Influences on the Ethical Intentions of CEOs," *Business and Society* (August 1995): 119–47.

21. Thomas Tyson, "Does Believing That Everyone Else is Less Ethical Have an Impact on Work Behavior?" *Journal of Business Ethics* 11 (1992): 707–17. See also Basil Orsini and Diane McDougall, "Fraud Busting Ethics," *CMA 1973* (June 1999): 18–21.

22. Floyd Norris and Diana Henriques, "Three Admit Guilty and Falsifying CUC's Books," *New York Times* (June 15, 2000): C1.

23. Gretchen Morgenson, "Requiem for an Honorable Profession," *New York Times* (May 5, 2002): Business 1.

24. "Ethics Policies are Big with Employers, but Workers see Small Impact on the Workplace," *BNA Bulletin to Management* (June 29, 2000): 201.

25. For a discussion, see Robert Jackyll, "Moral Mazes: Bureaucracy and Managerial Work," *Harvard Business Review* (September–October 1983): 118–30; Ishmael P. Akaah, "The Influence of Organizational Rank and Role of Marketing Professionals' Ethical Judgments," *Journal of Business Ethics* (June 1996): 605–14.

26. Discussed in Samuel Greengard, "Cheating and Stealing," *Workforce* (October 1997): 45–53.

27. From Guy Brumback, "Managing Above the Bottom Line of Ethics," *Supervisory Management* (December 1993): 12.

28. Deon Nel, Leyland Pitt, and Richard Watson, "Business Ethics: Defining the Twilight Zone," *Journal of Business Ethics* 8 (1989): 781. See also Brenner and Molander, *Is the Ethics of Business Changing?*; Daniel Glasner, "Past Mistakes Present Future Challenges," *Workforce* (May 1998): 117.

29. Quoted in Beauchamp and Bowie, *Ethical Theory and Business*, 109.

30. James Kunen, "Enron Division (and Values) Thing," *New York Times* (January 19, 2002): A19.

31. Dayton Fandray, "The Ethical Company," *Workforce* 79, no. 12 (December 2000): 74–77.

32. S. Greengard, "50 Percent of Your Employees are Lying, Cheating, and Stealing," *Workforce* 76 (October 1997): 44–53; Deborah Wells and Marshall Schminke, "Ethical Development and Human Resources Training: An Integrator Framework," *Human Resource Management Review* 11 (2001): 135–38.

33. James G. Hunt, *Leadership* (Newbury Park, CA: Sage Publications, 1991), pp. 220–24. One writer describes organizational culture as a sort of "organizational DNA," since "it's the stuff, mostly intangible, that determines the basic character of a business." See James Moore, "How Companies Have Sex," *Fast Company* (October–November 1997): 66–68.

34. Hunt, *Leadership*, 221. For a recent discussion of types of cultures, see, for example, "A Quadrant of Corporate Cultures," *Management Decision* (September 1996): 37–40.

35. Richard Osborne, "Core Value Statements: The Corporate Compass," *Business Horizons* (September–October 1991): 29.

36. "Promoting Workplace Fun Draws Serious Attention," *BNA Bulletin to Management* (August 8, 1999): 215.

37. Ibid.

38. J. Krohe Jr., "The Big Business of Business Ethics," *Across the Board* 34 (May 1997): 23–29, in Deborah Wells and Marshall Schminke, "Ethical Development and Human Resources Training, 135–58.

39. Editorial: "Ethical Issues in the Management of Human Resources," *Human Resource Management Review* 11 (2001): 6.

40. Weaver and Trevino, "Role of Human Resources," 123.

41. Editorial: "Ethical Issues in the Management of Human Resources," 6.

42. Weaver and Trevino, "Role of Human Resources," 123.

43. Anne O'Leary and Lynn Bowes-Sperry, "Sexual Harassment as Unethical Behavior: The Role of Moral Intensity," *Human Resource Management Review* 11 (2001): 73–92.

44. Wells and Schminke, "Ethical Development and Human Resources Training," 135–58.

45. Michael J. McCarthy, "How One Firm Attracts Ethics Electronically," *Wall Street Journal* (October 21, 1999): B1, B4.

46. Ibid., B1.

47. M. Ronald Buckley et al., "Ethical Issues in Human Resources Systems," *Human Resource Management Review* 11 (2001): 11, 29.

48. Weaver and Trevino, "Role of Human Resources," 113–34.

49. Ibid., 125.

50. Buckley et al., "Ethical Issues in Human Resources Systems," 11, 29.

51. Kim and Mauborgne, "Fair Process: Managing in the Knowledge Economy," pp. 65–75.

52. Weaver and Trevino, "Role of Human Resources," 114.

53. "Corporations' Drive to Embrace Ethics Gives HR Leaders Chance to Take Reins," *BNA Bulletin to Management* (November 7, 2002): 353.

54. Lester Bittel, *What Every Supervisor Should Know* (New York: McGraw-Hill, 1974), p. 308; see also Paul Falcone, "The Fundamentals of Progressive Discipline," *HR Magazine* (February 1997): 90–92.

55. For an example of a peer review appeals process see, for example, Dawn Anfuso, "Coors Taps Employee Judgement," *Personnel Journal* (February 1994): 50–59.

56. George Bohlander, "Why Arbitrators Overturn Managers in Employee Suspension and Discharge Cases," *Journal of Collective Negotiations* 23, no. 1 (1994): 76–77.

57. Ibid., 82.

58. Ibid. See also Ahman Karim, "Arbitration Considerations in Modifying Discharge Decisions in the Public Sector," *Journal of Collective Negotiations* 22, no. 3 (1993): 245–51; Joseph Martocchio and Timothy Judge, "When We Don't See Eye to Eye: Discrepancies Between Supervisors and Subordinates in Absence Disciplinary Decisions," *Journal of Management* 21, no. 2 (1995): 251–78.

59. Commerce Clearing House, "One Thing Unions Offer Is Fair Discipline—But Management Can Offer That Too," *Ideas and Trends in Personnel* (September 3, 1982):

168. See also Brian Klass and Daniel Feldman, "The Impact of Appeal System Structure on Disciplinary Decisions," *Personnel Psychology* 47, no. 1 (spring 1994): 91–108.

60. Commerce Clearing House, "Non-Union Employees, NLRB Rules, Have the Right to Help During Questioning by Management," *Ideas and Trends in Personnel* (August 6, 1982): 151.

61. Based on George Odiorne, *How Managers Make Things Happen* (Englewood Cliffs, NJ: Prentice Hall, 1961), pp. 132–43; see also Bittel, *What Every Supervisor Should Know,* 285–98; Cynthia Fukami and David Hopkins, "The Role of Situational Factors in Disciplinary Judgments," *Journal of Organizational Behavior* 14, no. 7 (December 1993): 665–76.

62. Nonpunitive discipline discussions based on David Campbell et al., "Discipline Without Punishment—At Last," *Harvard Business Review* (July/August 1995): 162–78; Gene Milbourne Jr., "The Case Against Employee Punishment," *Management Solutions* (November 1986): 40–45; Mark Sherman and Al Lucia, "Positive Discipline and Labor Arbitration," *Arbitration Journal* 47, no. 2 (June 1992): 56–58; Michael Moore, Victor Nichol, and Patrick McHugh, "No-Fault Programs: A Way to Cut Absenteeism," *Employment Relations Today* (winter 1992/1993): 425–32; "'Positive Discipline' Replaces Punishment," *BNA Bulletin to Management* (April 27, 1995): 136.

63. Eileen Zimmerman, "HR Must Know When Employee Surveillance Crosses the Line," *Workforce* (February 2002): 38–44.

64. Cynthia Kemper, "Big Brother," *Communication World* 18, no. 1 (December 2000/January 2001): 8–12.

65. Michael McCarthy, "Now the Boss Knows Where You're Clicking," *Wall Street Journal* (October 21, 1999): B1.

66. "Surveillance of Employees," *BNA Bulletin to Management* (April 25, 1996) p. 136.

67. "Telephone and Electronic Monitoring: A Special Report on the Issues and the Law," *BNA Bulletin to Management* (April 3, 1997): 2.

68. "Curbing the Risks of E-mail Use," *BNA Bulletin to Management* (April 10, 1997): 120.

69. *Vega-Rodriguez v. Puerto Rico Telephone Company,* CAL 962061, 4/8/97; discussed in "Video Surveillance Withstands Privacy Challenge," *BNA Bulletin to Management* (April 17, 1998): 121.

70. "Secret Videotaping Leads to $200,000 Settlement," *BNA Bulletin to Management* (January 22, 1998): 17.

71. Joseph Famularo, *Handbook of Modern Personnel Administration* (New York: McGraw-Hill, 1982), pp. 65.3–65.5.

72. Ibid., 65.3.

73. Andrea Poe, "Make Foresight 20/20," *HR Magazine* (February 20, 2000): 74–80.

74. Famularo, *Handbook,* 65.4.

75. Connie Wanderg et al., "Perceived Fairness of Layoffs Among Individuals Who Have Been Laid Off: A Longitudinal Study," *Personnel Psychology* 52 (1999): 59–84.

76. Paul Falcon, "Give Employees the (Gentle) Hook," *HR Magazine* (April 2001): 121–28.

77. "Fairness to Employees Can Stave Off Litigation," *BNA Bulletin to Management* (November 27, 1997): 377.

78. Note, however, that under court rulings at least one U.S. court of appeals (for the Seventh Circuit) has held that employee handbooks distributed to long-term employees before employers began amending their handbooks to contain "no contract," and "at-will employment" disclaimers may still be viewed by the court as contracts with these employees. The case was *Robinson v. Ada S. McKinley Community Services, Inc.* 19F.3d 359 (7th Cir. 1994); see Kenneth Jenero, "Employers Beware: You May Be Bound By the Terms of Your Old Employee Handbooks," *Employee Relations Law Journal* 20, no. 2 (autumn 1994): 299–312.

79. Kenneth Sovereign, *Personnel Law* (Upper Saddle River, NJ: Prentice Hall, 1999), p. 185.

80. "One More Heart Risk: Firing Employees," *The Miami Herald* (March 20, 1998): C1, C7.

81. Edward Isler et al., "Personal Liability and Employee Discipline," *Society for Human Resource Management Legal Report* (September–October 2000): 1–4.

82. Based on James Coil III and Charles Rice, "Three Steps to Creating Effective Employee Releases," *Employment Relations Today* (spring 1994): 91–94.

83. William J. Morin and Lyle York, *Outplacement Techniques* (New York: AMACOM, 1982), pp. 101–31; F. Leigh Branham, "How to Evaluate Executive Outplacement Services," *Personnel Journal* 62 (April 1983): 323–26; Sylvia Milne, "The Termination Interview," *Canadian Manager* (spring 1994): 15–16. There is debate regarding what is the "best day of the week" on which to terminate an employee. Some say Friday to give the employee a few days to "cool off"; others suggest midweek, in order to allow employees "who remain in the department or in the immediate work group some time to process the change and to talk with each other to sort it out." See Jeffrey Connor, "Disarming Terminated Employees," *HR Magazine* (January 2000): 113–14.

84. Morin and York, *Outplacement Techniques,* 117. See also Sonny Weide, "When You Terminate an Employee," *Employment Relations Today* (August 1994): 287–93.

85. Commerce Clearing House, *Ideas and Trends in Personnel* (July 9, 1982): 132–46.

86. Paul Brada, "Before You Go . . . ," *HR Magazine* (December 1998): 89–102.

87. Joseph Zarandona and Michael Camuso, "A Study of Exit Interviews: Does the Last Word Count?" *Personnel* 62, no. 3 (March 1981): 47–48.

88. Quoted from Commerce Clearing House, *Ideas and Trends* (August 9, 1988): 133. See also "Plant Closing Notification Rules: A Compliance Guide," *BNA Bulletin to Management* (May 18, 1989); Nancy Ryan, "Complying with the Worker Adjustment and Retraining Notification Act (WARN-ACT)," *Employee Relations Law Journal* 18, no. 1 (summer 1993): 169–76.

89. See, for example, "Cushioning the Blow of Layoffs," *BNA Bulletin to Management* (July 3, 1997): 216; "Levi Strauss Cushions Blow of Plant Closings," *BNA Bulletin to Management* (November 20, 1997): 370.

90. Eric Greenberg, "Upswing in Downsizings to Continue," *Management Review* (February 1993): 5.

Chapter 10

Protecting Safety and Health

- Employee Safety and Health: An Introduction
- What Causes Accidents?
- How to Prevent Accidents
- Employee Health: Problems and Remedies

When you finish studying this chapter, you should be able to:

- Discuss *OSHA and how it operates.*
- Describe *the supervisor's role in safety.*
- Explain *in detail three basic causes of accidents.*
- Explain *how to prevent accidents at work.*
- Discuss *major health problems at work and how to remedy them.*

INTRODUCTION

*C*on Edison delivers electric, gas, and steam to more than three million New York homes and businesses, and reliability has always been its top priority. It's therefore not surprising that for over 180 years, its basic strategy was to "Get the lights back on fast." Con Ed's employees had a "can do" attitude. Unfortunately, they sometimes ignored safety for the sake of getting outages fixed fast.

All that changed a few years ago. An explosion near New York City's Gramercy Park killed two Con Ed employees and a neighborhood resident. The explosion contaminated an apartment building with asbestos. Con Ed accepted the blame, and adopted a new strategy, "Get the lights back on fast—but, first do it safely." Now it had to implement that new safety-concious strategy throughout the firm.[1]

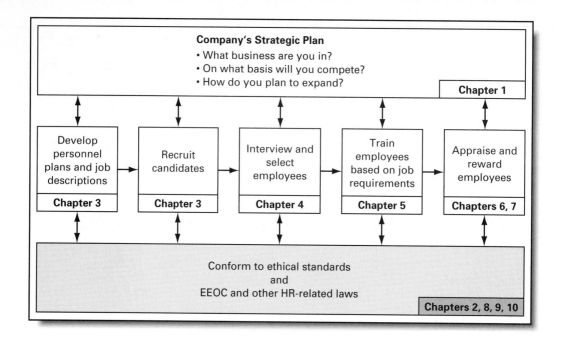

Company's Strategic Plan
- What business are you in?
- On what basis will you compete?
- How do you plan to expand?

Chapter 1

Develop personnel plans and job descriptions	Recruit candidates	Interview and select employees	Train employees based on job requirements	Appraise and reward employees
Chapter 3	**Chapter 3**	**Chapter 4**	**Chapter 5**	**Chapters 6, 7**

Conform to ethical standards
and
EEOC and other HR-related laws

Chapters 2, 8, 9, 10

EMPLOYEE SAFETY AND HEALTH: AN INTRODUCTION

Why Employee Safety and Health Are Important

Providing a safe work environment is important for several reasons, one of which is the staggering number of work-related accidents. For example, 6,026 U.S. workers recently died in workplace incidents. There were also over 6.2 million nonfatal injuries and illnesses resulting from accidents at work—roughly 6.3 cases per 100 full-time workers in the United States per year.[2] Technology is exacerbating the problem. Even new computers contribute to "sick building syndrome"—symptoms like headaches and sniffles, which some experts blame on poor ventilation and dust and fumes from on-site irritants.[3] Two engineers found that new computers emit chemical fumes (which, however, diminish after running constantly for a week[4]). And "safe" office work is actually susceptible to many other health and safety problems, including "repetitive trauma injuries related to computer use, respiratory illnesses stemming from indoor air quality, and high levels of stress, which are associated with a variety of factors, including task design."[5]

But even figures and comments like these don't tell the full story. They don't reveal the human suffering that injured workers and their families endure.[6] They don't reflect the fact that incident rates vary from industry to industry, from a high of 9.7 in manufacturing to a low of 1.9 in finance, insurance, and real estate.[7] And they don't reflect the legal implications of not providing a safe workplace, under the Occupational Safety and Health Act and other laws.

A Manager's Briefing on Occupational Law

The **Occupational Safety and Health Act**[8] was passed by Congress in 1970 "to assure so far as possible every working man and woman in the nation safe and healthful working conditions and to preserve our human resources." The only employers not covered by the act are self-employed persons, farms in which only immediate members of the employer's family are employed, and certain workplaces that are already protected by other federal agencies or under other statutes. Federal agencies are covered by the act, although provisions of the act usually don't apply to state and local governments in their role as employers.

The act created the **Occupational Safety and Health Administration (OSHA)** within the Department of Labor. OSHA's basic purpose is to administer the act and to set and enforce the safety and health standards that apply to almost all workers in the United States. OSHA has inspectors working out of branch offices throughout the country to ensure compliance.

OSHA Standards   OSHA operates under the general standard that each employer:

> shall furnish to each of his [or her] employees employment and a place of employment which are free from recognized hazards that are causing or are likely to cause death or serious physical harm to his [or her] employees.

To carry out this basic mission, OSHA is responsible for promulgating legally enforceable standards. These are contained in five volumes covering general industry standards, maritime standards, construction standards, other regulations and procedures, and a field operations manual. The standards are very complete and cover just about every conceivable hazard, in detail. Figure 10.1 shows a small part of the standard governing handrails for scaffolds.

OSHA Record-Keeping Procedures   Employers with 11 or more employees must maintain records of occupational injuries and illnesses, and report both occupational injuries and occupational illnesses. All occupational illnesses must be reported.[9] Similarly, most occupational injuries also must be reported, specifically those injuries that result in medical treatment (other than first aid), loss of consciousness, restriction of work (one or more lost workdays), restriction of motion, or transfer to another job.[10] A form used to report occupational injuries or illness is shown in Figure 10.2.

Figure 10.1   OSHA Standards Example

Guardrails not less than 2″ × 4″ or the equivalent and not less than 36″ or more than 42″ high, with a midrail, when required, of a 1″ × 4″ lumber or equivalent, and toeboards, shall be installed at all open sides on all scaffolds more than 10 feet above the ground or floor. Toeboards shall be a minimum of 4″ in height. Wire mesh shall be installed in accordance with paragraph (a)(17) of this section.

Source: General Industry Standards and Interpretations, U.S. Department of Labor, OSHA (Volume 1: Revised 1989, Section 1910.28(b)(15)), p. 67.

Figure 10.2 Form Used to Record Occupational Injuries and Illnesses

OSHA No. 101
Case or File No._____

Form approved
OMB No. 44R 1453

Supplementary Record of Occupational Injuries and Illnesses

EMPLOYER

1. Name _____
2. Mail address _____
   (No. and street)   (City or town)   (State)
3. Location, if different from mail address _____

INJURED OR ILL EMPLOYEE

4. Name _____ Social Security No. _____
   (First name)   (Middle name)   (Last name)
5. Home address _____
   (No. and street)   (City or town)   (State)
6. Age _____   7. Sex: Male _____ Female _____ (Check one)
8. Occupation _____
   (Enter regular job title, *not* the specific activity he/she was performing at time of injury.)
9. Department _____
   (Enter name of department or division in which the injured person is regularly employed, even
   though he/she may have been temporarily working in another department at the time of injury.)

THE ACCIDENT OR EXPOSURE TO OCCUPATIONAL ILLNESS

10. Place of accident or exposure _____
    (No. and street)   (City or town)   (State)
    If accident or exposure occurred on employer's premises, give address of plant or establishment in
    which it occurred. Do not indicate department or division within the plant or establishment. If accident
    occurred outside employer's premises at an identifiable address, give that address. If it occurred on a
    public highway or at any other place which cannot be identified by number and street, please provide
    place references locating the place of injury as accurately as possible.
11. Was place of accident or exposure on employer's premises? _____ (Yes or No)
12. What was the employee doing when injured? _____
    (Be specific. If he/she was using tools or equipment or handling
    material, name them and tell what he/she was doing with them.)

13. How did the accident occur? _____
    (Describe fully the events which resulted in the injury or occupational illness. Tell what
    happend and how it happened. Name any objects or substances involved and tell how they were involved. Give
    full details on all factors which led or contributed to the accident. Use separate sheet for additional space.)

OCCUPATIONAL INJURY OR OCCUPATIONAL ILLNESS

14. Describe the injury or illness in detail and indicate the part of body affected. _____
    (e.g.: amputation of right index finger
    at second joint; fracture of ribs; lead poisoning; dermatitis of left hand, etc.)
15. Name the object or substance which directly injured the employee. (For example, the machine or thing
    he/she struck against or which struck him/her; the vapor or poison inhaled or swallowed; the chemical or
    radiation which irritated the skin; or in cases of strains, hernias, etc., the thing he/she was lifting, pulling,
    etc.)

16. Date of injury or initial diagnosis of occupational illness _____
    (Date)
17. Did employee die? _____ (Yes or No)

OTHER

18. Name and address of physician _____
19. If hospitalized, name and address of hospital _____

Date of report _____   Prepared by _____
Official position _____

Inspections and Citations   OSHA standards are enforced through inspections and (if necessary) citations. However, OSHA may not conduct warrantless inspections without an employer's consent. It may, however, inspect after acquiring a judicially authorized search warrant or its equivalent.[11]

Like many government agencies, OSHA has wide-ranging compliance responsibilities but relatively limited funds for accomplishing its aims. As a result, over the past few years OSHA has tried to encourage cooperative safety programs rather than rely only on inspections and citations.[12] For example, its Cooperative Compliance Program targets a limited number of employers in a state. It then sends them notices asking that they work with OSHA to develop voluntary plans for addressing workplace safety and health problems.[13]

Such efforts notwithstanding, OSHA does of course still make extensive use of inspections and has a list of inspection priorities. *Imminent danger* situations get top priority. These are conditions in which a danger likely exists that can immediately cause death or serious physical harm. Second priority is given to catastrophes, fatalities, and accidents that have already occurred. (Employers must report these to OSHA within 48 hours.) Third priority is given to valid employee complaints of alleged violation of standards. Next in priority are periodic, special-emphasis inspections aimed at high-hazard industries, occupations, or substances. Finally, random inspections and reinspections generally have last priority. Most inspections result from employee complaints.

OSHA inspectors look for violations of all types, but some potential problem areas—such as scaffolding and fall protection—seem to grab more of their attention. Figure 10.3 summarizes the 10 most frequent OSHA inspection violation areas.[14]

OSHA no longer follows up every employee complaint with an inspection.[15] Under its priority system, OSHA conducts an inspection within 24 hours when a complaint indicates an immediate danger, and within three working days when a serious hazard exists. For a nonserious complaint filed in writing by a worker or a union, OSHA responds within 20 working days. It handles other, nonserious complaints, by writing to the employer and requesting corrective action.

After the inspection report has been submitted to the local OSHA office, the area director determines what citations, if any, will be issued. The **citations** inform the employer and employees of the regulations and standards that have been violated and of the time set for rectifying the problem.

OSHA can also impose penalties. In general, OSHA calculates these based on the gravity of the violation and usually takes into consideration such factors as the size of the business, the firm's compliance history, and the employer's good faith. Penalties generally range from $5,000 to up to $70,000 for willful or repeat serious violations, although in practice the penalties can be far higher. (In one settlement, willful and serious violations of OSHA rules that resulted in one death and two serious injuries prompted OSHA to propose a $1 million penalty for a steel plant in Middletown, Ohio).[16] In fact, many cases are settled with OSHA before litigation in what attorneys call *precitation settlements*. The citation and agreed-on penalties are issued simultaneously, after the employers initiate negotiation settlements with OSHA.[17]

In practice, OSHA must have a final order from the independent Occupational Safety and Health Review Commission (OSHRC) to enforce a penalty. Although that

Figure 10.3 The
OSHA Inspection Hit List

Source: Occupational Safety and
Health Administration.

Inspectors are expected to look for violations of all types, but violations OSHA deems serious are the ones inspectors are likeliest to target. In fiscal 1998, the 10 most frequently found serious violations related to problems with the following areas:

Rank	Area of Concern	No. of Serious Violations
1	Scaffolding	5,539
2	Fall protection	3,862
3	Hazard communication	3,274
4	Lockout/tagout	3,532
5	Machine guarding	2,266
6	Power presses	2,230
7	Mechanical power	2,151
8	Electrical	1,902
9	Excavation (construction)	1,399
10	Machine guarding (abrasive wheels)	1,338

"Lockout/tagout" refers to electrical repairs, during which switches for power must be shut off, locked, and tagged so power cannot be turned on while someone is repairing an electrical system. "Hazard communication" means proper use of material data safety sheets for chemical products at a worksite.

appeals process is quicker now than in the past, an employer who files a notice of contest can still drag out an appeal for years.[18]

Today inspectors and their superiors don't look just for specific hazards but also for evidence of a comprehensive safety approach. For example, factors contributing to a firm's OSHA liability include lack of a systematic safety approach; sporadic or irregular safety meetings; a lack of responsiveness to safety audit recommendations; not following up on employee safety complaints; and failure to regularly inspect the workplace, for instance, through employer walk-throughs and self-inspections.[19]

While some employers understandably view OSHA inspections with some trepidation, the inspection tips summarized in Figure 10.4—such as "check the inspector's credentials," and "accompany the inspector and take detailed notes"—can help ensure the inspection goes smoothly.[20]

Responsibilities and Rights of Employers and Employees   Both employers and employees have responsibilities and rights under the Occupational Safety and Health Act. For example, employers are responsible for providing "a workplace free from recognized hazards," for being familiar with mandatory OSHA standards, and for examining workplace conditions to make sure they conform with applicable standards.

Employees also have rights and responsibilities but cannot be cited for violations of their responsibilities. They are responsible, for example, for complying with all applicable OSHA standards, for following all employer safety and health rules and regulations, and for reporting hazardous conditions to the supervisor. Employees have a right to demand safety and health on the job without fear of punishment.

Figure 10.4 OSHA Inspection Tips

Initial Contact

- Refer the inspector to your OSHA coordinator.
- Check the inspector's credentials.
- Ask the inspector why he or she is inspecting your workplace. Is it a complaint? Programmed visit? Fatality or accident follow-up? Imminent danger investigation?
- If the inspection is the result of a complaint, the inspector won't identify the complainant, but you are entitled to know whether the person is a current employee.
- Notify your OSHA counsel, who should review all requests from the inspector for documents and information. Your counsel also should review the documents and information you provide to the inspector.

Opening Conference

- Establish the focus and scope of the planned inspection: Does the inspector want to inspect the premises or simply study your records?
- Discuss the procedures for protecting trade-secret areas, conducting employee interviews, and producing documents.
- Show the inspector that you have safety programs in place. He or she may not go to the work floor if paperwork is complete and up-to-date.

Walk-Around Inspection

- Accompany the inspector and take detailed notes.
- If the inspector takes a photo or video, you should too.
- Ask the inspector for duplicates of all physical samples and copies of all test results.
- Be helpful and cooperative, but don't volunteer information.
- To the extent possible, immediately correct any violation the inspector identifies.

Employers are forbidden to punish or discriminate against workers who complain to OSHA about job safety and health hazards. OSHA recently beefed up its rules, now requiring even greater employee involvement in OSHA's on-site consultations and that employees be informed of the inspection results.[21]

WHAT CAUSES ACCIDENTS?

Accidents occur for three main reasons: chance occurrences, unsafe working conditions, and unsafe acts by employees. Chance occurrences (such as walking past a window just as someone hits a ball through it) contribute to accidents but are more or less beyond management's control; we will therefore focus on unsafe conditions and unsafe acts.

Unsafe Conditions

Unsafe conditions are one main cause of accidents. These include such obvious factors as:

- Improperly guarded equipment
- Defective equipment

- Unsafe storage, such as congestion or overloading
- Improper illumination, such as glare or insufficient light
- Improper ventilation, such as insufficient air change or impure air source[22]

The basic remedy here is to eliminate or minimize the unsafe conditions. OSHA standards address the mechanical and physical working conditions that cause accidents. The manager can use a checklist of unsafe conditions for spotting problems; one checklist is in the *HR in Practice* box. The new *Occupational Hazards* magazine Web site (occupationalhazards.com) is a good source for safety, health, and industrial hygiene information.

Although accidents can occur anywhere, there are some high-danger zones. About one-third of industrial accidents occur around forklift trucks, wheelbarrows, and other handling and lifting areas. The most serious accidents usually occur near metal and woodworking machines and saws, or around transmission machinery such as gears, pulleys, and flywheels.[23]

Other Working Condition–Related Causes of Accidents Some working condition–related causes of accidents are less obvious because they involve the psychology of the workplace. For example, one researcher observed the official hearings regarding fatal accidents suffered by offshore oil workers in the British sector of the North Sea.[24] From this and similar studies, it's apparent that several basically psychological aspects of the work environment can set the stage for subsequent unsafe acts. A strong pressure to complete the work as quickly as possible, employees who are under stress, and a poor safety climate—for instance, supervisors who never mention safety—are some of the not-so-obvious working conditions that can set the stage for accidents.

Work schedules and fatigue also affect accident rates. Accident rates usually don't increase too noticeably during the first five or six hours of the workday, but after six hours the accident rate accelerates. This is due partly to fatigue and partly to the fact that accidents occur more often during night shifts.

Accidents also occur more frequently in plants with a high seasonal layoff rate and where there is hostility among employees, garnished wages, and blighted living conditions. Temporary stress factors such as high workplace temperature, poor illumination, and a congested workplace are also related to accident rates. Workers who work under stress and time pressure, or who feel their jobs are threatened or insecure, have more accidents than those who do not.[25]

Unsafe Acts

Most safety experts and managers know that it's impossible to eliminate accidents just by reducing unsafe conditions. People cause accidents, and no one has found a sure-fire way to eliminate **unsafe acts** such as:

- Throwing materials
- Operating or working at unsafe speeds—either too fast or too slow
- Making safety devices inoperative by removing, adjusting, or disconnecting them
- Lifting improperly[26]

I. GENERAL HOUSEKEEPING

Adequate and wide aisles—no materials protruding into aisles

Parts and tools stored safely after use—not left in hazardous positions that could cause them to fall

Even and solid flooring—no defective floors or ramps that could cause falling or tripping accidents

Waste and trash cans—safely located and not overfilled

Material piled in safe manner—not too high or too close to sprinkler heads

All work areas clean and dry

All exit doors and aisles clean of obstructions

Aisles kept clear and properly marked; no air lines or electric cords across aisles

II. MATERIAL HANDLING EQUIPMENT AND CONVEYANCES

On all conveyances, electric or hand, check to see that the following items are all in sound working condition:

Brakes—properly adjusted

Not too much play in steering wheel

Warning device—in place and working

Wheels—securely in place; properly inflated

Fuel and oil—enough and right kind

No loose parts

Cables, hooks or chains—not worn or otherwise defective

Suspended chains or hooks

Safety loaded

Properly stored

III. LADDERS, SCAFFOLD, BENCHES, STAIRWAYS, ETC.

The following items of major interest to be checked:

Safety feet on straight ladders

Guardrails or handrails

Treads, not slippery

No splintered, cracked, or rickety stairs

Ladders properly stored

Extension ladder ropes in good condition

Toeboards

IV. POWER TOOLS (STATIONARY)

Point of operation guarded

Guards in proper adjustment

Gears, belts, shafting, counterweights guarded

Foot pedals guarded

Brushes provided for cleaning machines

Adequate lighting

Properly grounded

Tool or material rests properly adjusted

Adequate work space around machines

Control switch easily accessible

Safety glasses worn

Gloves worn by persons handling rough or sharp materials

No gloves or loose clothing worn by persons operating machines

V. HAND TOOLS AND MISCELLANEOUS

In good condition—not cracked, worn, or otherwise defective

Properly stored

Correct for job

Goggles, respirators, and other personal protective equipment worn where necessary

(Continued)

Source: Courtesy of the Insurance Services Office, Inc., from "A Safety Committee Man's Guide," (1977): 1–64.

There is no one explanation for why an employee may behave in an unsafe manner. Sometimes, (as noted above) the working conditions may set the stage for unsafe
acts. For instance, employees who are under stress may behave in an unsafe manner
even if they know better.[27] Sometimes, employees aren't adequately trained in safe
work methods; some companies don't provide employees with the correct safe procedures to use, and employees may simply develop their own (often bad) work
habits. However, it's often the employee's attitudes, personality, or skills that
account for the bad behavior.

What Traits Characterize "Accident-Prone" People?   It may seem intuitively
obvious that some people are accident prone, but years of research have failed to
unearth any set of traits that accident repeaters have in common.[28] Today, most
experts doubt that there are some people who will have many accidents no matter
what situation they are put in (although some do suspect that accident
proneness is a type of deviant behavior characterized by impulsiveness).[29] Instead,
the consensus is that the person who is accident prone on one job may not be on a
different job.

Various human traits do relate to accident proneness in specific situations. For
example, accident-prone drivers performed worse on a test of motor skills than did
drivers with fewer accidents, and older adults with impaired vision were at a
higher risk for falls and motor vehicle crashes.[30] In fact, many human traits have
been found to be related to accident repetition in specific situations, as explained in
a moment.[31]

HOW TO PREVENT ACCIDENTS

The thing to remember about preventing accidents is that it's not always the employees who are causing them: "Although it is clear that individual behavior influences
accidents, starting and ending one's investigation at this level ignores the broader
contextual influence on behavior in organizations."[32] Certainly, screening out or
firing impulsive employees may reduce the incidence of unsafe behaviors. However,
so will mopping up oil spills and placing guardrails around machines; psychological

factors such as reducing stress and pressure are important, too. In practice, accident causes tend to be multifaceted, so the manager has to take a multifaceted approach to preventing them.[33]

Reduce Unsafe Conditions

Reducing unsafe conditions is an employer's first line of defense. Sometimes the solution for eliminating an unsafe condition is obvious. For example, slips and falls are often caused by debris or a slippery floor.[34] Employers work with safety engineers to "engineer out" potentially hazardous conditions, for instance by placing guardrails around moving machines.

Use Screening to Reduce Unsafe Acts

Accidents are similar to other types of poor performance, and psychologists have had success in screening out individuals who might be accident prone for some specific job. The basic technique is to identify the human trait (such as visual skill) that might relate to accidents on the specific job. Then determine whether scores on this trait predict accidents on the job.[35] Several examples follow. Again, however, whether using screening or some other method such as training or safety posters, the manager should keep in mind that relying solely on reducing unsafe acts isn't the only option. Programs like these should not take the place of eliminating hazards, providing personal protective equipment, and using training and warnings to reduce safety misbehaviors.[36]

Emotional stability and personality tests. Psychological tests—especially tests of emotional stability—have been used to screen out accident-prone taxi drivers. In this case, researchers found that taxi drivers who made five or more errors on such tests averaged three accidents, whereas those who made fewer than five errors averaged only 1.3 accidents.[37]

Tests of visual skills. Good vision plays a part in preventing accidents in many occupations, including driving and operating machines. In a study in a paper mill, 52 accident-free employees were compared with 52 accident-prone employees. The researcher found that 63% of the no-accident group passed a vision test, whereas only 3.3% of the accident group passed it.[38]

Employee selection. Experts suggest at least asking several safety-related questions during the selection interview—for instance, "What would you do if you saw a fellow employee working in an unsafe way?" "What would you do if your supervisor gave you a task, but didn't provide any training on how to safely perform it?"[39]

Use Posters and Other Propaganda

Propaganda such as safety posters can also help reduce unsafe acts. In one study, their use apparently increased safe behavior by more than 20%.[40] However, posters need to be combined with other techniques such as screening and training to reduce unsafe conditions and acts.

Provide Safety Training

Safety training can also reduce accidents. Such training is especially appropriate with new employees. It is important to instruct them in safe practices and procedures, warn them of potential hazards, and work on developing their predisposition toward safety.

Use Incentives and Positive Reinforcement

Some firms award incentives (such as cash bonuses) if particular safety goals are met. However, some contend that programs like these are misguided. OSHA has argued, for instance, that such plans don't actually cut down on injuries or illnesses but only on injury and illness *reporting.*

One option is to emphasize nontraditional reinforcement, for instance by giving employees recognition awards for attending safety meetings, for identifying hazards, or for demonstrating their safety and health proficiency.[41] One reinforcement program was instituted in a wholesale bakery that bakes, wraps, and transports pastry products to retail outlets nationwide.[42] The program stressed positive reinforcement and training. A reasonable goal (in terms of observed behaviors performed safely) was set and communicated to workers to ensure that they knew what was expected of them in terms of good performance. Employees were then presented with safety information and examples of safety dos and don'ts during a 30-minute training session.

At the conclusion of training, the employees were shown a graph plotting their pretraining safety record (in terms of observed incidents performed safely). They were encouraged to increase their performance to the new safety goal for their own protection, to decrease costs for the company, and to help the plant get out of last place in the safety ranking of the parent company. Then the graph and a list of safety dos and don'ts were posted in a conspicuous place in the work area. Workers could thus compare their current safety performance with both their previous performance and their assigned goal. Supervisors also praised employees when they performed selected incidents safely. Safety in the plant subsequently improved markedly.[43]

Safety incentives needn't be complicated. One organization uses a suggestion box. Employees make suggestions for improvements regarding unsafe acts or conditions. The employer follows up on all suggestions, the best of which result in gift certificates for their authors.[44]

Emphasize Top-Management Commitment

Safety programs require a strong and obvious management commitment to safety.[45] Here's an example:

> One of the best examples I know of in setting the highest possible priority for safety takes place at a DuPont Plant in Germany. Each morning at the DuPont Polyester and Nylon Plant the director and his assistants meet at 8:45 to review the past 24 hours. The first matter they discuss is not production, but safety. Only after they have examined reports of accidents and near misses and satisfied themselves that corrective action has been taken do they move on to look at output, quality, and cost matters.[46]

Foster a Culture of Safety

When it comes to creating a safety-oriented workplace, what the supervisor does is as, or more, important than what he or she says.[47] In other words, it's crucial to show by word and deed that safety is very important. One study assessed safety culture in terms of items such as "my supervisor says a good word whenever he sees the job done according to the safety rules," and "my supervisor approaches workers during work to discuss safety issues." The study found that (1) employees did develop consistent perceptions concerning supervisory safety practices, and (2) these safety climate perceptions predicted safety records in the months following the survey.[48]

Establish a Safety Policy

A safety policy should emphasize that the firm will do everything practical to eliminate or reduce accidents and injuries. It should also emphasize the fact that accident and injury prevention is not just important but of the utmost importance at your firm.

Set Specific Loss Control Goals

Analyze the number of accidents and safety incidents, then set specific safety goals to be achieved. For example, safety goals can be set in terms of frequency of lost-time injuries per number of full-time employees.[49]

Conduct Safety and Health Inspections Regularly

Routinely inspect all premises for possible safety and health problems using checklists such as those in the *HR in Practice* box (on pages 335–36) as aids. Similarly, investigate all accidents and "near misses" and have a system in place for letting employees notify management about hazardous conditions.[50] *Safety audits* measure several things, such as injury and illnesses statistics, workers' compensation costs, and vehicle accident statistics.[51]

Similarly, employee safety committees can improve workplace safety. Typical committee activities include evaluating safety adequacy, monitoring safety audit findings, and suggesting strategies for improving health and safety performance.[52] These and other safety steps are summarized in Figure 10.5.

Figure 10.5 Steps to Take to Reduce Workplace Accidents

- Reduce unsafe conditions.
- Reduce unsafe acts.
- Use posters and other propaganda.
- Provide safety training.
- Use positive reinforcement.
- Emphasize top-management commitment.
- Emphasize safety.
- Establish a safety policy.
- Set specific loss control goals.
- Conduct safety and health inspections regularly.
- Monitor work overload and stress.

Strategy and HR   Safety is particularly a problem in a large, complex utility like Con Ed, many of whose facilities go back 50 years or more. Back then, people didn't understand the risks of using products like asbestos, so today Con Ed employees find themselves working with hazardous materials on a daily basis. The Gramercy Park explosion forced management to redefine Con Ed's strategy. Today, "get the lights back on fast—but, first do it safely" sums up the firm's basic corporate approach, and that new approach has triggered big changes in how the company does things.

Injecting a "safety first" mentality into all the firm's operations involved many HR activities. Con Ed recruited and carefully trained over 80 new people for its environmental health and safety staff. The firm's health and safety staff no longer operates from a centralized, isolated department; instead, the unit's 126 members are spread out throughout Con Ed's local operating units, where they can monitor safety on a real-time basis. Con Ed also created thousands of pages of new policies and procedures that translate federal, state, and local environmental regulations into operating procedures its employees can actually use. The environmental health and safety staff produces a monthly video called *The eXcellence Files;* one of its regular features is "Close Calls," in which employees describe narrow escapes and lessons they can share with other workers. In one, an electrical worker describes how he heard a telltale clicking or "arcing" sound and fled just before flames shot out the end of the pipe. Now all employees instinctively put safety first. Con Ed's experience shows how top management can translate its strategy into specific HR strategies and practices.

EMPLOYEE HEALTH: PROBLEMS AND REMEDIES[53]

Various health-related substances and problems can undermine employee performance at work. These include alcoholism, stress, asbestos, computer monitors, AIDS, and workplace violence.

Alcoholism and Substance Abuse

Alcoholism and substance abuse are serious and widespread workplace problems.[54] Some experts estimate that as many as 50% of all "problem employees" in industry are actually alcoholics. In one auto assembly plant, 48.6% of the grievances filed over the course of a year were alcohol related.[55] One estimate places the cost of a substance abuser's damage to a company at $7,000 per abuser per year.[56]

Recognizing the alcoholic on the job isn't easy. Early symptoms such as tardiness can be similar to those of other problems and thus difficult to classify. The supervisor is not a psychiatrist, and without specialized training, identifying and dealing with the alcoholic is difficult. For many employers, dealing with alcohol and substance abuse begins with substance abuse testing. For example, more than one-third of businesses recently reported testing applicants and/or employees for alcohol.[57]

Table 10.1 shows observable behavior patterns that indicate alcohol-related problems. As you can see, alcohol-related problems range from tardiness in the earliest stages of alcohol abuse to prolonged, unpredictable absences in its later stages.[58]

Drug tests may not have the desired effect on reducing workplace accidents. One study, conducted in three hotels, concluded that preemployment drug testing

Table 10.1   Observable Alcohol-Related Behavior Patterns

STAGE	ABSENTEEISM	GENERAL BEHAVIOR	JOB PERFORMANCE ACTION

I
Early
	Tardiness
	Quits early
	Absence from work
	  situations
		Complaints from fellow
		  employees for not doing
		  his or her share
		Overreaction
		Complaints of not "feeling
		  well"
			Misses deadlines
			Commits errors
			  (frequently)
			Lower job efficiency

II
Middle
	("I drink to relieve
	  tension")
	Frequent days off for
	  vague or implausible
	  reasons
	("I feel guilty about
	  sneaking drinks";
	  "I have tremors")
		Makes untrue statements
		Marked changes
		Undependable statements
		Avoids fellow employees
		Borrows money from fellow
		  employees
		Exaggerates work
		  accomplishments
		Frequent hospitalization
		Minor injuries on the job
		  (repeatedly)
			Criticism from the boss
			General deterioration
			Cannot concentrate
			Occasional lapse of
			  memory
			Warning from boss

III
Late
Middle
	Frequent days off; several
	  days at a time
	Does not return from
	  lunch
	("I don't feel like eating";
	  "I don't want to talk
	  about it"; "I like to drink
	  alone")
		Aggressive and belligerent
		  behavior
		Domestic problems interfere
		  with work
		Financial difficulties
		  (garnishments, etc.)
		More frequent hospitalization
		Resignation: does not want to
		  discuss problems
		Problems with the laws in the
		  community
			Far below expectation
			Punitive disciplinary
			  action

IV
Approaching
Terminal
	Prolonged unpredictable
	  absences
	("My job interferes with
	  my drinking")
		Drinking on the job (probably)
		Completely undependable
		Repeated hospitalization
		Serious financial problems
		Serious family problems:
		  divorce
			Uneven
			Generally incompetent
			Faces termination or
			  hospitalization

Note: Based on content analysis of files of recovering alcoholics in five organizations. From *Managing and Employing the Handicapped: The Untapped Potential,* by Gopal C. Pati and John I. Adkins Jr., with Glenn Morrison (Lake Forest, IL: Brace-Park, Human Resource Press, 1981).

Source: From "The Employer's Role in Alcoholism Assistance," by Gopal C. Pati and John I. Adkins Jr., copyright July 1983. Used by permission of ACC Communications Inc./*Personnel Journal* (now known as *Workforce*), Costa Mesa, CA. All rights reserved.

seemed to have little or no effect on workplace accidents. However, a combination of preemployment and random ongoing testing was associated with a significant reduction in workplace accidents.[59]

The Problems of Job Stress and Burnout

Problems such as alcoholism and drug abuse sometimes stem from stress, especially *job stress.* Eighty-eight percent of managers in one survey reported elevated stress levels, with most reporting feeling under more stress than they could ever remember.[60]

A variety of external—environmental—factors can trigger stress.[61] These include work schedule, pace of work, job security, route to and from work, workplace noise, and the number and nature of customers or clients.[62] However, no two people react the same because personal factors also influence stress. For example, those with Type A personalities—people who are workaholics and who feel driven to always be on time and meet deadlines—normally place themselves under greater stress than do others.

Job stress has serious consequences for both the employee and the organization. The human consequences of job stress include anxiety, depression, anger, and various physical consequences, such as cardiovascular disease, headaches, and accidents. Stress also has serious consequences for the organization. These include diminished performance, and increased absenteeism, turnover, grievances, and health care costs.[63] A study of 46,000 employees concluded that health care costs of the high-stress workers were 46% higher than those of their less-stressed co-workers.[64] Yet stress is not necessarily dysfunctional. Some people, for example, find that they are more productive as a deadline approaches.

Reducing Your Own Job Stress   A person can do several things to alleviate stress. These range from commonsense remedies like getting more sleep and eating better to more exotic remedies such as biofeedback and meditation. Finding a more suitable job, getting counseling, and planning and organizing each day's activities are other sensible responses.[65] In his book *Stress and the Manager,* Dr. Karl Albrecht suggests the following to reduce job stress:[66]

- Build rewarding, pleasant, cooperative relationships with as many of your colleagues and employees as you can.
- Don't bite off more than you can chew.
- Build an especially effective and supportive relationship with your boss.
- Understand the boss's problems and help him or her to understand yours.
- Negotiate with your boss for realistic deadlines on important projects. Be prepared to propose deadlines yourself, instead of having them imposed on you.
- Find time every day for detachment and relaxation.
- Get away from your office from time to time for a change of scene and a change of mind.
- Don't put off dealing with distasteful problems.
- Make a constructive "worry list." Write down the problems that concern you, and beside each write down what you're going to do about it.

What the Employer Can Do   The employer and its HR specialists and supervisors can also play a role in identifying and reducing job stress:

- Monitor each employee's performance to identify symptoms of stress.
- Use attitude surveys to identify organizational sources of stress, and selection and placement procedures to ensure effective person–job match.
- Reduce personal conflicts on the job.
- Reduce the amount of red tape for employees.
- Provide employee assistance programs including professional counseling help.[67]

Giving employees more control over their jobs can also mediate the effects of job stress, as illustrated by one study.[68] Here researchers reduced the psychological strain caused by job stress by giving workers more control over their jobs. The jobs perceived as less stressful actually had high demands in terms of workload and pressure. However, the jobs apparently *felt* less stressful because they also ranked high in task clarity, job control, supervisory support, and employee skill utilization.[69]

Burnout is a phenomenon closely associated with job stress, and has been defined as the total depletion of physical and mental resources caused by excessive striving to reach an unrealistic work-related goal.[70] Burnout manifests itself in emotional exhaustion, depersonalization (a feeling that you can't get close to others), and feelings of diminished personal accomplishment.[71] Burnout's emotional symptoms include feelings of helplessness, resentment, and irritability.[72] Basically, a person burns out when the stress of trying to attain unattainable work-related goals becomes too great.

The burnout victim is usually a **workaholic**—a person for whom the constant stress of seeking an unattainable goal to the exclusion of other activities can lead to physical and perhaps mental collapse. This needn't be limited to upwardly mobile executives. For instance, social-work counselors caught up in their clients' problems are often burnout victims. Some signs of possible impending burnout include:[73]

- You are unable to relax.
- You identify so closely with your activities that when they fall apart, you do too.
- Your need for a particular crutch such as smoking, alcohol, or tranquilizers is increasing.
- You are constantly irritable, and family and friends are often commenting that you don't look well.
- You would describe yourself as a workaholic and constantly strive to obtain your work-related goals to the exclusion of almost all outside interests.

What can a burnout candidate do? Here are some suggestions:

Break patterns. First, survey how you spend your time. The more well rounded your life is, the better protected you are against burnout.

  Get away from it all periodically. Schedule occasional periods of introspection during which you can get away from your usual routine, perhaps alone, to seek a perspective on where you are and where you are going.

Reassess your goals in terms of their intrinsic worth. Are the goals you've set for yourself attainable? Are they really worth the sacrifices you'll have to make?

Think about your work. Could you do as good a job without being so intense or by also pursuing outside interests?

Reduce stress. Organize your time more effectively, build a better relationship with your boss, negotiate realistic deadlines, find time during the day for detachment and relaxation, reduce unnecessary noise around your office, and limit interruption.

Asbestos Exposure at Work

There are four major sources of occupational respiratory diseases: asbestos, silica, lead, and carbon dioxide. Of these, asbestos has become a major concern, in part because of publicity surrounding numerous huge lawsuits alleging asbestos-related diseases.

OSHA standards require several actions with respect to asbestos. They require that companies monitor the air whenever an employer expects the level of asbestos to rise to one-half the allowable limit (0.1 fibers per cubic centimeters). Engineering controls—walls, special filters, and so forth—are required to maintain an asbestos level that complies with OSHA standards. Respirators can only be used if additional efforts are then still required to achieve compliance.

Computer Monitor Health Problems and How to Avoid Them

Even with advances in computer screen technology (such as flat panel screens, and color) there's still a risk of monitor-related health problems at work. Problems include short-term eye burning, itching, and tearing, as well as eyestrain and eye soreness. Backaches and neckaches are also widespread. These often occur because employees try to compensate for monitor problems (such as glare) by maneuvering into awkward body positions. There may also be a tendency for computer users to suffer from cumulative motion disorders, such as carpal tunnel syndrome, caused by repetitive use of the hands and arms at uncomfortable angles.[74]

The National Institute of Occupational Health (NIOSH) provides general recommendations regarding computer monitors. These include:

1. *Give employees rest breaks.* NIOSH recommends a 15-minute rest break after two hours of continuous work for operators under moderate workloads and 15-minute breaks every hour for those with heavy workloads.
2. *Design the maximum flexibility into the workstation so that it can be adapted to the individual operator.* For example, use movable keyboards, adjustable chairs with midback supports, and a video display in which screen height and position are independently adjustable.
3. *Reduce glare with devices such as shades over windows, terminal screen hoods properly positioned, antiglare screen filters, and recessed or indirect lighting.* Special "personal glare screen" eyeglasses can also lower the effect of glare.[75]
4. *Give workers a complete preplacement vision exam to ensure properly corrected vision for reduced visual strain.*

Other suggestions include:

1. The height of the table or chair should allow wrists to be positioned at the same level as the elbow.[76]
2. The wrists should be able to rest lightly on a pad for support.
3. The feet should be flat on the floor, or on a footrest.[77]

AIDS in the Workplace

Some of the most crucial AIDS-related issues employers must address concern their legal responsibilities in dealing with AIDS sufferers. Although case law is still evolving, several conclusions are warranted. First, you cannot single out an employee to be tested for AIDS, because to do so would be to subject the person to discriminatory treatment under the Americans with Disabilities Act (ADA). Similarly, although you can probably require a physical exam that includes an AIDS test as a condition of employment, refusing to hire the person because of positive test results could put you at risk of a disability discrimination suit. Mandatory leave cannot be required of a person with AIDS unless work performance has deteriorated. Preemployment inquiries about AIDS (as with inquiries about any illnesses or disabilities) would not be advisable given the prohibitions of the ADA. Providing sympathy and support and making reasonable accommodations to persons with AIDS, and using education and counseling to deal with the fears of the person's co-workers seem to be among the best prescriptions for dealing with the concerns this disease elicits at work.[78]

Workplace Smoking

Smoking is a serious problem for employees and employers. For instance, the congressional Office of Technology Assessment estimates that each employee smoker costs an employer between $2,000 and $5,000 yearly.[79] These costs derive from higher health and fire insurance, as well as increased absenteeism and reduced productivity (which occurs when, for instance, a smoker takes a 10-minute break to smoke a cigarette down the hall).

What You Can and Cannot Do   In general, you can deny a job to a smoker as long as you do not use smoking as a surrogate for some other kind of discrimination. The EEOC, in other words, says that a policy of not hiring smokers is legal as long as the rules apply to all applicants and employees.[80] A "no-smokers hired" policy does not, according to one expert, violate the ADA. Smoking is not considered a disability, and, in general, "employers' adoption of a 'no-smokers-hired' policy is not illegal under federal law."[81] Therefore, you can probably institute a policy against hiring people who smoke.

Smoking Policies   State, city, and employer smoking bans are on the rise, and many employers now forbid smoking on their premises. In one survey of 283 employers, one-quarter of the organizations polled prohibited smoking anywhere on company premises—up from 14% the previous year.[82]

Dealing with Violence at Work

Violence against employees is a huge problem at work. Homicide is the second-biggest cause of fatal workplace injuries. Based on the national crime victimization survey for 1992–1996, there were an average of 1,000 workplace murders and 1.5 million workplace assaults each year.[83] However, like U.S. crime in general, workplace murders actually fell almost 40% (to 645) between 1995 and 1999, while violence-related injuries fell 27%.[84]

While robbery was the primary motive for homicide at work, a co-worker or personal associate committed roughly one of seven workplace homicides.[85] And these numbers are just the tip of the iceberg. For example, 29 U.S. Postal Service supervisors and colleagues were slain by disgruntled postal workers in one 10-year period, but there were also 350 assaults by postal workers in one year alone.[86]

By one estimate, workplace violence costs employers about $4 billion a year.[87] One report refers to bullying as the "silent epidemic" of the workplace, "where abusive behavior, threats, and intimidation often go unreported."[88] And, workplace violence isn't always aimed just at people. It can also manifest itself in sabotaging the firm's property, software, or information databases.[89]

Reducing Workplace Violence   HR managers can take several steps to reduce the incidence of workplace violence. They include:

Heighten Security Measures   Heightened security measures are an employer's first line of defense against workplace violence, whether that violence derives from co-workers, customers, or outsiders. These measures include[90] improve external lighting; use drop safes to minimize cash on hand and post signs noting that only a limited amount of cash is on hand; install silent alarms and surveillance cameras; increase the number of staff on duty; provide staff training in conflict resolution and nonviolent response; close establishments during high-risk hours late at night and early in the morning;[91] and issue a weapons policy that states, for instance, that regardless of their legality, firearms or other dangerous or deadly weapons cannot be brought onto the facility either openly or concealed.[92]

Improve Employee Screening   With about 30% of workplace attacks committed by co-workers, screening out potentially explosive internal and external applicants is the employer's next line of defense. Obtain a detailed employment application and solicit an applicant's employment history, educational background, and references.[93] Sample interview questions to ask might include, for instance, "What frustrates you?" and "Who was your worst supervisor and why?"[94] Certain background circumstances, such as the following, may provide a red flag indicating the need for a more in-depth background investigation of the applicant:[95]

- An unexplained gap in employment
- Incomplete or false information on the résumé or application
- A negative, unfavorable, or false reference
- Prior insubordinate or violent behavior on the job
- A criminal history involving harassing or violent behavior
- A prior termination for cause with a suspicious (or no) explanation
- History of drug or alcohol abuse

- Strong indications of instability in the individual's work or personal life as indicated, for example, by frequent job changes or geographic moves
- Lost licenses or accreditations[96]

Use Workplace Violence Training   Supervisors can be trained to identify the clues that typically precede violent incidents. Common clues include:[97]

> *Verbal threats.* Individuals often talk about what they may do. An employee might say, "Bad things are going to happen to so-and-so."
> *Physical actions.* Troubled employees may try to intimidate others, gain access to places where they do not belong, or flash a concealed weapon in the workplace to test reactions.
> *Frustration.* Most cases do not involve a panicked individual; a more likely scenario would involve an employee who has a frustrated sense of entitlement to a promotion, for example.
> *Obsession.* An employee may hold a grudge against a co-worker or supervisor, and some cases stem from romantic interest.[98]

The following are telltale signs of a potentially violent employee:[99]

- An act of violence on or off the job
- Erratic behavior evidencing a loss of perception or awareness of actions
- Overly confrontational or antisocial behavior
- Sexually aggressive behavior
- Isolationist or loner tendencies
- Insubordinate behavior with a suggestion of violence
- Tendency to overreact to criticism
- Exaggerated interest in war, guns, violence, mass murders, catastrophes, and so on
- Commission of a serious breach of security
- Possession of weapons, guns, knives, or like items in the workplace
- Violation of privacy rights of others, such as searching desks or stalking
- Chronic complaining and the raising of frequent, unreasonable grievances
- A retributory or get-even attitude

The U.S. Postal Service took steps to reduce workplace threats and assaults. The steps include more background checks, drug testing, a 90-day probationary period for new hires, more stringent security (including a hotline that allows employees to report threatening situations), a zero tolerance policy for reporting and recording potentially violent incidents, and training managers to create a healthier workplace culture.[100]

Violence Toward Women at Work   While men have more fatal occupational injuries than do women, the proportion of women who are victims of assault is much higher. Of all women who die on the job, 39% are the victims of assault, whereas only 18% of males who died at work were murdered.[101] The Gender-Motivated Violence Act, part of the comprehensive Violence Against Women Act passed by Congress in 1994, imposes significant liabilities on employers whose women employees become violence victims.[102]

Maintaining a healthy and safe environment for expatriates—employees who are posted overseas—presents some unique concerns.[103] For example, international terrorists sometimes target the facilities and executives of multinational enterprises, and the incidence of such attacks—although still low—has increased markedly.

The September 11 attacks and the ongoing need to protect overseas executives (and their families) has therefore fostered a thriving anti-terrorist securities industry. For example, security consultants provide advice (such as fortify executives' homes, and don't use the same schedule and route to work every day) as well as trained chauffeurs, guards, and armored vehicles.

Crime and imprisonment are safety issues while you're abroad as well. Theft and pickpocketing are always potential problems for travelers from abroad, for instance, but it's not always others' criminal behavior the traveler must watch out for. For example, "Travelers have been thrown in jail for exceeding a credit card limit, buying artifacts from an unlicensed dealer, entering an Islamic country with alcohol, or failing to meet a contract deadline," so that knowingly or innocently breaking local laws can be a major concern, too.[104]

Particularly when traveling in areas where medical facilities may not meet developed-country standards, dramatic events—sudden illnesses or serious accidents, for instance—can also be particularly serious abroad. Language difficulties, cultural misunderstandings, lack of normal support and infrastructure systems (such as telephones) can all combine to make an accident or illness that may be manageable in one country a disaster in another. As a result, many multinationals brief their business travelers and expatriates about what to expect and how to react when confronted with a health or safety problem abroad. Others also make use of insurance programs (such as that of the MEDEX Assistance Corporation) to help their overseas travelers and their families if assistance is required.

Fatal workplace violence against women has three main sources. Of all females murdered at work, more than three-fourths are victims of random criminal violence carried out by an assailant unknown to the victim, as might occur during a robbery. The remaining criminal acts are carried out either by co-workers, family members, or previous friends or acquaintances.

There's nothing typical about workplace violence, but research sheds some light on the typical female victim. The typical female assault victim is a white female (79%) in her early 30s (mean age approximately 31). She is working as a salesperson (31%) in a convenience store (46%) and is shot by an unknown assailant (88%) at about 11 p.m.[105] Tangible security improvements including better lighting, cash drop boxes, and similar steps are especially pertinent in reducing such violent acts against women. The *Global Issues in HR* box provides a global perspective.

Terrorism

Particularly in the current environment, the employer can take several steps to protect its employees and physical assets from terrorist attack. Steps to take include: institute policies to check mail carefully; identify ahead of time a lean "crisis organization" that can run the company on an interim basis after a terrorist threat; identify in advance under what conditions you will close the company down, as well as what the shutdown process will be and who can order it; institute a process to put the crisis management team together; prepare evacuation plans and make sure exits are well marked and unblocked; designate an employee who will communicate with families and off-site employees; identify an upwind, uphill off-site location near your facility to use as a staging area for all evacuated personnel; and designate in advance several employees who will do headcounts at the evacuation staging area.[106]

REVIEW

Summary

1. The area of safety and accident prevention is of concern to managers partly because of the staggering number of deaths and accidents occurring at work. There are three main reasons for safety programs: moral, legal, and economic.

2. The purpose of OSHA is to ensure every working person a safe and healthful workplace. OSHA standards are complete and detailed, and are enforced through a system of workplace inspections. OSHA inspectors can issue citations and recommend penalties to their area directors.

3. There are three basic causes of accidents: chance occurrences, unsafe conditions, and unsafe acts on the part of employees. In addition, three other work-related factors—the job itself, the work schedule, and the psychological climate—also contribute to accidents.

4. Unsafe acts on the part of employees are a main cause of accidents. Such acts are to some extent the result of certain behavior tendencies on the part of employees, and these tendencies are possibly the result of certain personal characteristics.

5. Most experts doubt that there are accident-prone people who have accidents regardless of the job. Instead, the consensus seems to be that the person who is accident prone in one job may not be on a different job. For example, vision is related to accident frequency for drivers and machine operators, but might not be for other workers, such as accountants.

6. There are several approaches to preventing accidents. One is to reduce unsafe conditions. The other approach is to reduce unsafe acts—for example, through selection and placement, training, positive reinforcement, propaganda, and top-management commitment.

7. Alcoholism, drug addiction, stress, and emotional illness are four important and growing health problems among employees. Alcoholism is a particularly serious problem that can drastically lower the effectiveness of your organization. Techniques including disciplining, discharge, in-house counseling, and referrals to an outside agency are used to deal with these problems.

8. Stress and burnout are other potential health problems at work. An employee can reduce job stress by getting away from work for a while each day, delegating, and developing a worry list.

9. Violence against employees is an enormous problem at work. Steps that can reduce workplace violence include improved security arrangements, better employee screening, and violence-reduction training.

KEY TERMS

- Occupational Safety and Health Act
- Occupational Safety and Health Administration (OSHA)

- citations
- burnout

- workaholic

DISCUSSION QUESTIONS AND EXERCISES

1. How would you go about providing a safer work environment for your employees?
2. Discuss how you would go about minimizing the occurrence of unsafe acts on the part of your employees.
3. Discuss the basic facts about OSHA—its purpose, standards, inspection, and rights and responsibilities.
4. Explain the supervisor's role in safety.
5. Explain what causes unsafe acts.
6. Answer the question, Is there such a thing as an accident-prone person?
7. Describe at least five techniques for reducing accidents.
8. Explain how an employee could reduce stress at work.

APPLICATION EXERCISES

Case Incident — *The New Safety Program*

Employees' safety and health are very important matters in the laundry and cleaning business. Each facility is a small production plant in which machines, powered by high-pressure steam and compressed air, work at high temperatures washing, cleaning, and pressing garments often under very hot, slippery conditions. Chemical vapors are continually produced, and caustic chemicals are used in the cleaning process. High-temperature stills are almost continually "cooking down" cleaning solvents in order to remove impurities so that the solvents can be reused. If a mistake is made in this process—such as injecting too much steam into the still—a boilover occurs, in which boiling chemical solvent erupts out of the still, onto the floor, and onto anyone who happens to be standing in its way.

As a result of these hazards and the fact that chemically hazardous waste is continually produced in these stores, several government agencies (including OSHA and the Environmental Protection Agency) have instituted strict guidelines regarding the management of these plants. For example, posters have to be placed in each store notifying employees of their right to be told what hazardous chemicals they are dealing with and what is the proper method for handling each chemical. Special waste-management firms must be used to pick up and properly dispose of the hazardous waste.

A chronic problem the owners have is the unwillingness on the part of the cleaning-spotting workers to wear safety goggles. Not all the chemicals they use require safety goggles, but some—like the hydrofluorous acid used to remove rust stains from garments—are very dangerous. The latter is kept in special plastic containers because it dissolves glass. Some of the employees feel that wearing safety goggles can be troublesome; they are somewhat uncomfortable, and they also become smudged easily and thus cut down on visibility. As a result, it is sometimes almost impossible to get employees to wear their goggles. ■

QUESTIONS

1. How should a dry cleaner go about identifying hazardous conditions that should be rectified? Name four probable hazardous conditions or areas in such a store, based on dry cleaning stores that you have seen.
2. Would it be advisable for such a firm to set up a procedure for screening out accident-prone individuals?
3. How would you suggest that owners get all employees to behave more safely at work? Also, how would you advise them to get those who should be wearing goggles to do so?

Continuing Case

LearnInMotion.com: The New Safety and Health Program

At first glance, a dot-com is one of the last places you'd expect to find potential safety and health hazards—or so Jennifer and Mel thought. There's no danger of moving machinery, no high-pressure lines, no cutting or heavy lifting, and certainly no forklift trucks. However, there are safety and health problems.

In terms of accident-causing conditions, for instance, the one thing dot-com companies have are lots of cables and wires. There are cables connecting the computers to each other and to the servers, and in many cases separate cables running from some computers to separate printers. There are 10 telephones in the office, all on 15-foot phone lines that always seem to be snaking around chairs and tables. There is, in fact, an astonishing amount of cable considering this is an office with less than 10 employees.

When the installation specialists wired the office (for electricity, high-speed DSL, phone lines, burglar alarms, and computers), they estimated they used well over 5 miles of cables of one sort or another. Most of these are hidden in the walls or ceilings, but many of them snake their way from desk to desk, and under and over doorways. Several employees have tried to reduce the nuisance of having to trip over wires whenever they get up by putting their plastic chair pads over the wires closest to them. However, that still leaves many wires unprotected. In other cases, they brought in their own packing tape, and tried to tape down the wires in those spaces where they're particularly troublesome, such as across doorways.

The cables and wires are only one of the more obvious potential accident-causing conditions. The firm's programmer, before he left the firm, had tried to repair the main server while the unit was still electrically alive. To this day, they're not sure exactly where he stuck the screwdriver, but the result was that he was "blown across the room," as Mel puts it. He was all right, but it was still a scare. And while they haven't yet received any claims, every employee spends hours at his or her computer, so carpal tunnel syndrome is a risk, as are a variety of other problems such as eyestrain and strained backs.

One recent accident particularly scared them. The firm uses independent contractors to deliver the firm's book- and CD-ROM–based courses in New York and two other cities. A delivery person was riding his bike at the intersection of Second Avenue and East 64th Street in New York when he was struck by a car. Luckily he was not hurt, but the bike's front wheel was wrecked, and the close call got Mel and Jennifer thinking about their lack of a safety program.

It's not just the physical conditions that concern the company's two owners. They also have some concerns about potential health problems such as job stress and burnout. While the business may be (relatively) safe with respect to physical conditions, it is also relatively stressful in terms of the demands it makes in hours and deadlines. It is not at all unusual for employees to get to work by 7:30 or 8:00 in the morning and to work through until 11:00 or 12:00 at night, at least five and sometimes six or seven days per week. Just getting the company's new calendar fine-tuned and operational required 70-hour workweeks for three weeks of five of LearnInMotion.com's employees.

The bottom line is that both Jennifer and Mel feel quite strongly that they need to do something about implementing a health and safety plan. Now, they want you, their management consultants, to help them actually do it. Here's what they want you to do for them. ■

QUESTIONS AND ASSIGNMENTS

1. Based upon your knowledge of health and safety matters and your actual observations of operations that are similar to ours, make a list of the potential hazardous conditions employees and others face at LearnInMotion.com. What should we do to reduce the potential severity of the top five hazards?

2. Would it be advisable for us to set up a procedure for screening out stress-prone or accident-prone individuals? Why or why not? If so, how should we screen them?

3. Write a short position paper on what we should do to get all our employees to behave more safely at work.

4. Based on what you know and on what other dot-coms are doing, write a short position paper on what we can do to reduce the potential problems of stress and burnout in our company.

Experiential Exercise

Purpose: The purpose of this exercise is to give you practice in identifying unsafe conditions.

Required Understanding: You should be familiar with material covered in this chapter, particularly that on unsafe conditions and the checklist in the *HR in Practice* box.

How to Set Up the Exercise/Instructions: Divide the class into groups of four or five students.

Assume that you are a safety committee retained by your school to identify and report on any possible unsafe conditions in and around the school building.

Each group will spend about 45 minutes in and around the building you are now in for the purpose of identifying and listing possible unsafe conditions. (*Hint:* Make use of the *HR in Practice* checklist.)

Return to the class in about 45 minutes, and a spokesperson for each group should list on the board the unsafe conditions you think you have identified. How many were there? Do you think these also violate OSHA standards? How would you go about checking?

ENDNOTES

1. Minda Zetlin, "Clean Slate: Here's How Con Edison, New York City's Utility Company, Transformed Itself from Environmental Wrongdoer to Environmental Leader," *Management Review* (February 2000): 26–27.

2. "Occupational Injuries and Illnesses," *BNA Bulletin to Management* (January 15, 1998): 13; "Workplace Deaths Unchanged: Homicides at Six Year Low," *BNA Bulletin to Management* (August 27, 1998): 269; "Workplace Injury, Illness Rates Fall," *Occupational Hazards* (February 2001): 33.

3. "Blame New Computers for Sick Buildings," *USA Today* 129, no. 2672 (May 2001): 53–55.

4. Michael Pinto, "Why Are Indoor Air Quality Problems so Prevalent Today?" *Occupational Hazards* (January 2001): 37–39.

5. Sandy Moretz, "Safe Havens?" *Occupational Hazards* (November 2000): 45–46.

6. *Workers' Compensation Manual for Managers and Supervisors* (Chicago: Commerce Clearing House, Inc., 1992), p. 12. See also Guy Toscano and Janice Windau,

"The Changing Character of Fatal Work Injuries," *Monthly Labor Review* 117, no. 10 (October, 1994): 17–28.

7. "On the Job Injuries, Illnesses Continue Steady Decline," *BNA Bulletin to Management* (January 20, 2000): 21.

8. Occupational Safety and Health Administration; much of this is based on *All About OSHA*, rev. ed. (Washington, DC: U.S. Department of Labor, 1980).

9. "OSHA Hazard Communication Standard Enforcement," *BNA Bulletin to Management* (February 23, 1989): 13.

10. Bureau of Labor Statistics, *What Every Employer Needs to Know About OSHA Record Keeping* (Washington, DC: U.S. Department of Labor, 1978), p. 3; "Is It a Recordable Injury? Depends on the Treatment," *BNA Bulletin to Management* (September 29, 1999): 284.

11. W. Scott Railton, "OSHA Gets Tough on Business," *Management Review* 80, no. 12 (December 1991): 28–29.

12. "Safety Program Rule Called Top OSHA Priority," *BNA Bulletin to Management* (October 31, 1996): 345.

13. "OSHA Seeks 'Cooperative Compliance,'" *BNA Bulletin to Management* (September 4, 1997): 288; "OSHA's Cooperative Program Shoves Off," *BNA Bulletin to Management* (December 25, 1997): 416.

14. William Atkinson, "When OSHA Comes Knocking," *HR Magazine* (October 1999): 35–38.

15. Michael Verespej, "OSHA Revamps Its Inspection Policies," *Industry Week* (September 17, 1979): 19–20. See also Horace E. Johns, "OSHA's Impact," *Personnel Journal* 67, no. 11 (November 1988): 102–7.

16. "Employers Hit with Megafines for OSHA Violations," *BNA Bulletin to Management* (May 9, 1996): 146.

17. "Settling Safety Violations Has Benefits," *BNA Bulletin to Management* (July 31, 1997): 248.

18. "OSHA Instruction on Penalties," *BNA Bulletin to Management* (February 7, 1991): 33; Commerce Clearing House, "OSHA Will Begin Higher Fines March 1st," *Ideas and Trends in Personnel* (January 23, 1991):

14; John Bruening, "OSHRC on the Comeback Trail," *Occupational Hazards* (January 1991): 33–36. OSHA is also stressing record-keeping violations. See, for example, Brian Jackson and Jeffrey Myers, "Just When You Thought You Were Safe: OSHA Record-Keeping Violations," *Management Review* 83, no. 5 (May 1994): 63.

19. Jim Lastowka, "Ten Keys to Avoiding OSHA Liability," *Occupational Hazards* (October 1999): 163–70.

20. Robert Grossman, "Handling Inspections: Tips from Insiders," *HR Magazine* (October 1999): 41–50.

21. Diane Hatch and James Hall, "A Flurry of New Federal Regulations," *Workforce* 80, no. 2 (February 2001): 98.

22. "A Safety Committee Man's Guide," Aetna Life and Casualty Insurance Company, Catalog 872684. See also Todd Nighswonger, "Get a Grip on Slips," *Occupational Hazards* (September 2000): 47–50.

23. Ibid.; see also "Workplace Fatalities," *BNA Bulletin to Management* (August 28, 1997): 276–77.

24. For a discussion of this, see David Hofmann and Adam Stetzer, "A Cross-Level Investigation of Factors Influencing Unsafe Behaviors and Accidents," *Personnel Psychology* 49 (1996): 307–8.

25. Willard Kerr, "Complementary Theories of Safety Psychology," in Edwin Fleishman and Alan Bass, *Industrial Psychology* (Homewood, IL: Dorsey Press, 1974), pp. 493–500; Alan Fowler, "How to Make the Workplace Safer," *People Management* 1, no. 2 (January 1995): 38–39. See also Hofmann and Stetzer, "Cross-Level Investigation," 307–10.

26. List of unsafe acts from "A Safety Committee Man's Guide," Aetna Life and Casualty Insurance Company.

27. See, for example, Hofmann and Stetzer, "Cross-Level Investigation," 307–8; C. Wright, "Routine Deaths: Fatal Accidents in the Oil Industry," *Sociological Review* 4 (1986): 265–89; D. E. Embrey, "Incorporating Management and Organizational Factors into Probabilistic Safety Assessment," *Reliability Engineering and System Safety* 38 (1992): 199–208.

28. A. G. Arbous and J. E. Kerrich, "The Phenomenon of Accident Proneness," *Industrial Medicine and Surgery* 2 (1953): 141–48, reprinted in Fleishman and Bass, *Industrial Psychology,* 485.

29. John Miner and J. Frank Brewer, "Management of Ineffective Performance," in Marvin Dunnette (ed.), *Handbook of Industrial and Organizational Psychology* (Chicago: Rand McNally, 1976), pp. 1004–5.

30. Cynthia Owsley et al., "Visual Processing Impairment and Risk of Motor Vehicle Crash Among Older Adults," *Journal of the American Medical Association* 279, no. 14 (April 18, 1998): 1083–89; Hosam Kamel et al., "The Activities of Daily Vision Scale: A Useful Tool to Assess for Risk in Older Adults with Vision Impairment," *Journal of the American Geriatrics Society* 48, no. 11 (November 2000): 1474–78; Hiroshi Matsuoka, "Development of a Short Test for Accident Proneness," *Perceptual and Motor Skills* 85, no. 3 (December 1997): 903–7; Janice Marra, "Profiling Employees and Assessing the Potential for Violence," *Public Management* 82, no. 2 (February 2000): 25–26.

31. Ernest McCormick and Joseph Tiffin, *Industrial Psychology* (Upper Saddle River, NJ: Prentice Hall, 1974), pp. 522–23; Norman Maier, *Psychology and Industrial Organization* (Boston: Houghton-Mifflin, 1965), pp. 458–62. For an example, see David DeJoy, "Attributional Processes and Hazard Control Management in Industry," *Journal of Safety Research* 16 (summer 1985): 61–71.

32. R. House, D. M. Rousseau, and M. Thomas-Hunt, "The Meso Paradigm: A Framework for the Integration of Micro and Macro Organizational Behavior," in L. L. Cummings and B. M. Staw (eds.), *Research in Organizational Behavior* 17 (Greenwich, CT: JAI Press, 1995), pp. 71–114.

33. Michael Frone, "Predictors of Work Injuries Among Employed Adolescents," *Journal of Applied Psychology* 83, no. 4 (1998): 565–76.

34. Susanna Figura, "Don't Slip Up on Safety," *Occupational Hazards* 58, no. 11 (November 1996): 29–31. See also Russ Wood, "Defining the Boundaries of Safety," *Occupational Hazards* (January 2001): 41–43.

35. Maier, *Psychology and Industrial Organization,* 463–67; McCormick and Tiffin, *Industrial Psychology,* 533–36; Blum and Nayler, *Industrial Psychology,* 525–27.

36. Gerald Wagner, "The Hierarchy of Controls: An Alternative to Behavior Based Safety," *Occupational Hazards* (May 1999): 95–97; John Grubbs, "Exploring Your Behavior Based Safety Options," *Occupational Hazards* (July 1999): 36–40.

37. D. Weschler, "Test for Taxicab Drivers," *Journal of Personnel Research* 5 (1926): 24–30, quoted in Maier, *Psychology and Industrial Organization,* 64. See also Leo DeBobes, "Psychological Factors in Accident Prevention," *Personnel Journal* 65 (January 1986); Curtiss Hansen, "A Causal Model of the Relationship Among Accidents, Biodata Personality, and Cognitive Factors," *Journal of Applied Psychology* 74, no. 1 (February 1989): 81–90.

38. Quoted in Maier, *Psychology and Industrial Organization,* 466.

39. Dan Hartshorn, "The Safety Interview," *Occupational Hazards* (October 1999): 107–11.

40. S. Laner and R. J. Sell, "An Experiment on the Effect of Specially Designed Safety Posters," *Occupational Psychology* 34 (1960): 153–69, in McCormick and Tiffin, *Industrial Psychology,* 536.

41. James Nash, "Rewarding the Safety Process," *Occupational Hazards* (March 2000): 29–34.

42. See Judi Komaki, Kenneth Barwick, and Lawrence Scott, "A Behavioral Approach to Occupational Safety: Pinpointing and Reinforcing Safe Performance in a Food Manufacturing Plant," *Journal of Applied Psychology* 63 (August 1978): 434–45. See also Peter Makin and Valerie Sutherland, "Reducing Accidents Using a Behavioral Approach," *Leadership and Organizational Development Journal,* no. 5 (1994): 5–10.

43. Judi Komaki, Arlene Heinzmann, and Lorealie Lawson, "Effect of Training and Feedback: Component Analysis of a Behavioral Safety Program," *Journal of Applied Psychology* 65 (June 1980): 261–70. See also Jorma Sari, "When Does Behavior Modification Prevent Accidents?" *Leadership and Organizational Development Journal*, no. 5 (1994): 11–15.

44. J. Nigel Ellis and Susan Warner, "Using Safety Awards to Promote Fall Prevention," *Occupational Hazards* (June 1999): 59–62.

45. Dov Zohar, "Safety Climate in Industrial Organizations: Theoretical and Implied Implications," *Journal of Applied Psychology* 65 (February 1980): 97. For a discussion of the importance of getting employees involved in managing their own safety program, see John Lutness, "Self-Managed Safety Program Gets Workers Involved," *Safety and Health* 135, no. 4 (April 1987): 42–45. See also Frederick Streff, Michael Kalsher, and E. Scott, "Developing Efficient Workplace Safety Programs: Observations of Response Co-Variations," *Journal of Organizational Behavior Management* 13, no. 2 (1993).

46. Willie Hammer, *Occupational Safety Management and Engineering* (Upper Saddle River, NJ: Prentice Hall, 1985), pp. 62–63.

47. Lester Bittel, *What Every Supervisor Should Know* (New York: McGraw-Hill, 1974), p. 25. For an example of an effective safety training program, see Michael Pennacchia, "Interactive Training Sets the Pace," *Safety and Health*, no. 1 (January 1987): 24–27. Appointing a safety committee can also be useful. See, for example, Neville Tompkins, "Getting the Best Help from Your Safety Committee," *HR Magazine*, no. 4 (April 1995): 76.

48. Dov Zohar, "A Group Level Model of Safety Climate: Testing the Effect of a Group Climate on Students in Manufacturing Jobs," *Journal of Applied Psychology* 85, no. 4 (2000): 587–96. See also Judith Erickson, "Corporate Culture: The Key to Safety Performance," *Occupational Hazards* (April 2000): 45–50.

49. *Workers' Compensation Manual for Managers and Supervisors,* 24; James Frierson, "An Analysis of ADA Provisions on Denying Employment Because of a Risk of Future Injury," *Employee Relations Law Journal,* no. 4 (spring 1992): 603–22.

50. "Workplace Safety: Improving Management Practices," *BNA Bulletin to Management* (February 9, 1989): 42, 47. See also Linda Johnson, "Preventing Injuries: The Big Payoff," *Personnel Journal* (April 1994): 61–64; David Webb, "The Bathtub Effect: Why Safety Programs Fail," *Management Review* (February 1994): 51–54.

51. Howard Street, "Getting Full Value From Auditing and Metrics," *Occupational Hazards* (August 2000): 33–36.

52. Lisa Cullen, "Safety Committees: A Smart Business Decision," *Occupational Hazards* (May 1999): 99–104.

53. This section based largely on Miner and Brewer, "Management of Ineffective Performance," 1005.

54. "Drug Use Among Employees," *BNA Bulletin to Management* (May 2, 1996): 140–41.

55. Gopal Pati and John Adkins Jr., "The Employer's Role in Alcoholism Assistance," *Personnel Journal* 62, no. 7 (July 1983): 568–72. For a discussion of how the work environment can encourage drug dealing, see Richard Lyles, "Should the Next Drug Bust Be in Your Company?" *Personnel Journal* 63 (October 1994): 46–49.

56. "Facing Facts About Workplace Substance Abuse," *Rough Notes* 144, no. 5 (May 2001): 114–18.

57. "Employee Alcohol Testing on the Rise," *BNA Bulletin to Management* (August 20, 1998): 261.

58. Pati and Adkins, "Employer's Role," 568–72. See also Commerce Clearing House, "How Should Employers Respond to Indications an Employee May Have an Alcohol or Drug Problem?" *Ideas and Trends* (April 6, 1989): 53–57.

59. Frank Lockwood et al., "Drug Testing Programs and Their Impact on Workplace Accidents: A Time Series Analysis,"

Journal of Individual Employment Rights 8, no. 4 (2000): 295–306.

60. Marice Cavanaugh et al., "An Empirical Examination of Self-Reported Work Stress Among U.S. Managers," *Journal of Applied Psychology* 85, no. 1 (2000): 65–74.

61. This is based on Terry Beehr and John Newman, "Organizational Stress, Employer Health, and Organizational Effectiveness: A Factor Analysis, Model, and Literature Review," *Personnel Psychology* 31 (winter 1978): 665–99. See also Shailendra Singh, "Managing Stress Through Empowerment: A Brief Literature Survey," *Management and Labor Studies* 22, no. 1 (January 1997): 26–32.

62. Eric Sundstrom et al., "Office Noise, Satisfaction, and Performance," *Environment and Behavior,* no. 2 (March 1994): 195–222.

63. Michael Manning, Conrad Jackson, and Marcelline Fusilier, "Occupational Stress, Social Support, and the Costs of Health Care," *Academy of Management Journal* 39, no. 3 (1996): 738–50.

64. "Stress, Depression Cost Employers," *Occupational Hazards* (December 1998): 24.

65. John Newman and Terry Beehr, "Personnel and Organizational Strategies for Handling Job Stress: A Review of Research and Opinion," *Personnel Psychology* (spring 1979): 1–43. See also "Work Place Stress: How to Curb Claims," *BNA Bulletin to Management* (April 14, 1988): 120.

66. Karl Albrecht, *Stress and the Manager* (Upper Saddle River, NJ: Prentice Hall, 1979), pp. 253–55. Reprinted by permission. For a discussion of the related symptoms of depression, see James Krohe Jr., "An Epidemic of Depression?" *Across the Board* (September 1994): 23–27.

67. "Managing Stress in the Workplace," *BNA Bulletin to Management* (January 18, 1996): 24. Reprinted with permission from *Bulletin to Management (BNA Policy and Practice Series)* (January 18, 1996): 24. Copyright 1996 by The Bureau of National Affairs, Inc. (800–372–1033), http://www.bna.com.

68. Pascale Carayon, "Stressful Jobs and Non-Stressful Jobs: A Cluster Analysis of Office Jobs," *Ergonomics,* no. 2 (1994): 311–23.

69. Ibid., 319–20.

70. Harvey Freudenberger, *Burn-out* (Toronto: Bantam Books, 1980).

71. Raymond Lee and Blake Ashforth, "A Meta-Analytic Examination of the Correlates of the Three Dimensions of Job Burnout," *Journal of Applied Psychology* 81, no. 2 (1996): 123–33.

72. Madan Tripathy, "Burnout Stress Syndrome and Managers," *Management and Labor Studies* 27, no. 2 (April 2002): 89–111.

73. Freudenberger, *Burn-out,* 16–18. See also Raymond Lee and Blake Ashforth, "A Further Examination of Managerial Burnout: Toward an Integrated Model," *Journal of Organizational Behavior* 14 (1993): 3–20.

74. J. A Savage, "Are Computer Terminals Zapping Workers' Health?" *Business and Society Review* (1994).

75. Anne Chambers, "Computervision Syndrome: Relief is in Sight," *Occupational Hazards* (October 1999): 179–84.

76. These are based on "Inexpensive Ergonomic Innovations," *BNA Bulletin to Management* (February 1, 1996): 40.

77. Sondra Lotz Fisher, "Are Your Employees Working Ergosmart?" *Personnel Journal* (December 1996): 91–92. See also William Kincaid, "Office Ergonomics for Maximum Performance," *Occupational Hazards* (May 1999): 85–88.

78. "AIDS and the Workplace: Issues, Advice, and Answers," *BNA Bulletin to Management* (November 14, 1985): 1–6. See also David Ritter and Ronald Turner, "AIDS: Employer Concerns and Options," *Labor Law Journal,* no. 2 (February 1987): 67–83; Bureau of National Affairs, "How Employers Are Responding to AIDS in the Workplace," *Fair Employment Practices* (February 18, 1988): 21–22. For a complete guide to services and information regarding "The Work Place and AIDS," see *Personnel Journal,* no. 10 (October 1987): 65–80. See also William H. Wager, "AIDS: Setting Policy, Educating Employees at

Bank of America," *Personnel,* no. 8 (August 1988): 4–10; Maureen Minehan, "New AIDS Survival Rates Mean Patients Returning to Work," *HR Magazine* 42, no. 10 (October 1997): 208.

79. Marco Colossi, "Do Employees Have the Right to Smoke?" *Personnel Journal* (April 1988): 72–79.

80. Daniel Warner, "We Do Not Hire Smokers: May Employers Discriminate Against Smokers?" *Employee Responsibilities and Rights,* no. 2 (June 1994): 129–40.

81. Ibid., 138.

82. "Smoking Bans on the Rise," *BNA Bulletin to Management* (March 16, 1989): 82.

83. Dean Boerger, "Rigorous Workplace Policies Help in Preventing Violence," *Business First—Columbus* 17, no. 41 (June 1, 2002): 25; Jane McDonald, "Murder at Work," *Risk Management* 48, no. 3 (March 2001): 7.

84. Carlos Tejada, "Danger on the Job: A Special News Report About Life on the Job—and Trends Taking Shape There," *Wall Street Journal* (June 26, 2001): A1.

85. Gus Toscano and Janice Windau, "The Changing Character of Fatal Work Injuries," *Monthly Labor Review* (October 1994): 17.

86. Based on Louis DiLorenzo and Darren Carroll, "The Growing Menace: Violence in the Workplace," *New York State Bar Journal* (January 1995): 24.

87. "Violence in Workplace Soaring, New Study Says," *Baltimore Business Journal* 18, no. 34 (January 5, 2001): 24.

88. "Bullies Trigger 'Silent Epidemic' at Work, but Legal Cures Remain Hard to Come By," *BNA Bulletin to Management* (February 24, 2000): 57.

89. Jennifer Laabs, "Employees Sabotage," *Workforce* (July 1999): 33–42.

90. "Workplace Violence: Sources and Solutions," *BNA Bulletin to Management* (November 4, 1993): 345.

91. Ibid.

92. "Weapons in the Workplace: A Review of Employer Policies," *BNA Bulletin to Management* (June 5, 1996): 1–7; Lloyd

Nigro and William Waugh Jr., "Violence in the American Workplace: Challenges to the Public Employer," *Public Administration Review* (July/August 1996): 326–33; "OSHA Addresses Top Homicide Risk," *BNA Bulletin to Management* (May 14, 1998): 148.

93. Alfred Feliu, "Workplace Violence and the Duty of Care: The Scope of an Employer's Obligation to Protect Against the Violent Employee," *Employee Relations Law Journal* 20, no. 3 (winter 1994/95): 395.

94. Dawn Anfuso, "Workplace Violence," *Personnel Journal* (October 1994): 66–77.

95. Feliu, "Workplace Violence and the Duty of Care," 395.

96. Quoted from ibid.

97. "Preventing Workplace Violence," *BNA Bulletin to Management* (June 10, 1993): 177. See also Jenny McCune, "Companies Grapple with Workplace Violence," *Management Review,* no. 3 (March 1994): 52–57.

98. Quoted or paraphrased from ibid., 177, and based on recommendations from Chris Hatcher.

99. Feliu, "Workplace Violence and the Duty of Care," 401–2.

100. "Employers Battling Workplace Violence Might Consider Postal Service Plan," *BNA Bulletin to Management* (August 5, 1999): 241.

101. This is based on Beverly Younger, "Violence Against Women in the Workplace," *Employee Assistance Quarterly* 9, no. 3-4 (1994): 113–33.

102. Kenneth Diamond, "The Gender-Motivated Violence Act: What Employers Should Know," *Employee Relations Law Journal* 25, no. 4 (spring 2000): 29–41.

103. This is based on Dennis Briscoe, *International Human Resource Management* (Upper Saddle River, NJ: Prentice Hall, 1995), pp. 167–69.

104. Ibid., 168.

105. Younger, "Violence Against Women," 120.

106. Lloyd Newman, "Terrorism: Is Your Company Prepared?" *Business and Economic Review* 48, no. 2 (February 2002): 7–10.

Module A

Managing HR Globally

- HR and the Internationalization of Business
- Improving International Assignments Through Selection
- Training and Maintaining International Employees

*U*ntil recently, Siemens, a 150-year-old German company, focused on making electrical products. As its CEO says, "Only a few years ago, business at Siemens used to be dominated by production. Today, [diversification into] software, engineering, and services are the backbone of our business—and the key to success." Siemens today is also global— "one of the few true global players in this new world," with over 400,000 employees working in 190 countries. In other words, Siemens became a world leader by pursuing a corporate strategy that emphasized diversifying into high-tech products and services, and doing so on a global basis.

With a corporate strategy like that, global HR plays a big role at Siemens: Sophisticated engineering and services require more focus on employee selection, training, and compensation than in the average firm, and globalization requires delivering these services globally.[1] HR has to be a strategic partner in the formulation and execution of this global firm's strategies.

HR AND THE INTERNATIONALIZATION OF BUSINESS

Companies are increasingly doing business abroad. Firms like Procter & Gamble, IBM, and Citicorp have long had extensive overseas operations, of course. But with the European market unification, the introduction of the euro currency, and the rapid development of demand in Asia and other parts of the world, even small firms are finding that success depends on their ability to market and manage overseas.

This confronts firms with some interesting management challenges. Market, product, and production plans must be coordinated on a worldwide basis. Organization structures capable of balancing centralized home-office control with adequate local autonomy must be created. And, of course, the firm must extend its HR policies and systems abroad. For example: Should we staff the local offices with local or U.S. managers? How should we appraise and pay our local employees? How should we deal with the unions in our offices abroad? We'll address these global HR topics in this module.

The HR Challenges of International Business

When researchers asked senior international HR managers in eight large companies, "What are the key global pressures affecting human resource management practices in your firm currently and for the projected future?" the three that emerged were:[2]

- Deployment. Easily getting the right skills to where we need them, regardless of geographic location.
- Knowledge and innovation dissemination. Spreading state-of-the-art knowledge and practices throughout the organization regardless of where they originate.
- Identifying and developing talent on a global basis. Identifying who can function effectively in a global organization and developing his or her abilities.[3]

Dealing with global staffing pressures like these is quite complex. For example, it involves addressing, on a global basis, activities including candidate selection, assignment terms and documentation, relocation processing and vendor management, immigration processing, cultural and language orientation and training, compensation administration and payroll processing, tax administration, career planning and development, and handling of spouse and dependent matters.[4]

At firms like Ford Motor Company, having a global HR perspective "requires understanding different cultures, what motivates people from different societies, and how that's reflected in the structure of international assignments."[5] In China, for instance, special insurance should cover emergency evacuations for serious health problems; telephone communication can be a "severe handicap" in Russia; and medical facilities in Russia may not meet international standards.[6] So the challenge of conducting HR activities abroad comes not just from the vast distances involved (though this is important) but also from the cultural, political, legal, and economic differences among countries and their peoples. Let's look at this.

How Intercountry Differences Affect Human Resource Management

Companies operating only within the borders of the United States generally have the luxury of dealing with a relatively limited set of economic, cultural, and legal variables. The United States is a capitalist, competitive society. And while the U.S. workforce reflects a multitude of cultural and ethnic backgrounds, shared values (such as an appreciation for democracy) help to blur potentially sharp cultural differences. Although the different states and municipalities certainly have their own laws affecting HR, a basic federal framework helps produce a fairly predictable set of legal guidelines regarding matters such as employment discrimination, labor relations, and safety and health.

A company operating multiple units abroad isn't blessed with such homogeneity. For example, minimum legally mandated holidays range from none in the United Kingdom to five weeks per year in Luxembourg. And while Italy has no formal requirements for employee representatives on boards of directors, they're required in Denmark for companies with more than 30 employees. The point is that the need to adapt personnel policies and procedures to the differences among countries complicates HR management in multinational companies. For example, consider the following.[7]

Cultural Factors   Countries differ widely in their cultures—in other words, in the basic values their citizens adhere to, and in the ways these values manifest themselves in the nation's arts, social programs, politics, and ways of doing things.

Cultural differences from country to country necessitate corresponding differences in management practices among a company's subsidiaries. For example, in a study of about 330 managers from Hong Kong, the People's Republic of China, and the United States, the U.S. managers tended to be most concerned with getting the job done. Chinese managers were most concerned with maintaining a harmonious environment, and Hong Kong managers fell between these extremes.[8] A classic study by Professor Geert Hofstede identified other international cultural differences. For example, Hofstede says societies differ in power distance—in other words, the extent to which the less-powerful members of institutions accept and expect an unequal distribution of power.[9] He concluded that acceptance of such inequality was higher in some countries (such as Mexico) than in others (such as Sweden).

Studies show how such cultural differences can influence HR policies.[10] For example, compared to U.S. employees, "Mexican workers expect managers to keep their distance rather than to be close, and to be formal rather than informal."[11]

In fact, the list of cultural differences is endless. In Germany, you should never arrive even a few minutes late and should always address senior people formally, with their titles.[12] Such cultural differences are a two-way street, and employees from abroad need orientation to avoid the culture shock of coming to work in the United States.[13] For example, in the Intel Corporation booklet "Things You Need to Know About Working in the U.S.A.," topics covered include sexual harassment, recognition of gay and lesbian rights, and Intel's expectations about behavior.[14]

Economic Systems   Differences in economic systems also translate into differences in HR practices. For one thing, some countries are more wedded to the ideals of free enterprise than are others. For instance, France—though a capitalist society—imposed tight restrictions on employers' rights to discharge workers, and limited the number of hours an employee could legally work each week.

Differences in labor costs are also substantial. Hourly compensation costs in U.S. dollars for production workers range from $2.46 in Mexico to $5.98 in Taiwan, $15.88 in the United Kingdom, $19.86 in the United States, and $24.01 in Germany, for instance.[15]

There are other labor costs to consider. For example, there are wide gaps in hours worked. Portuguese workers average about 1,980 hours of work annually, while

German workers average 1,648 hours. Several European countries, including the United Kingdom and Germany, require substantial severance pay to departing employees, usually equal to at least two years' service in the United Kingdom and one year's in Germany.[16] Compared to the usual two or three weeks of U.S. vacation, workers in France can expect two and half days of paid holiday per full month of service per year. Italians usually get between four and six weeks off per year, and Germans get 18 working days per year after six months of service.[17]

Legal and Industrial Relations Factors   Legal as well as industrial relations (the relationships among the worker, the union, and the employer) factors vary from country to country. For example, the U.S. practice of employment at will does not exist in Europe, where firing and laying off workers is usually time consuming and expensive. And in many European countries, **works councils** replace the informal or union-based worker-to-management mediations typical in U.S. firms. Works councils are formal, employee-elected groups of worker representatives that meet monthly with managers to discuss topics ranging from no-smoking policies to layoffs.[18]

Codetermination is the rule in Germany and several other countries. **Codetermination** means employees have the legal right to a voice in setting company policies. Workers elect their own representatives to the supervisory board of the employer, and there is a vice president for labor at the top-management level.[19] In the United States, HR policies on most matters such as wages and benefits are set by the employer, or by the employer in negotiations with its labor unions. The codetermination laws, including the Works Constitution Act, largely determine the nature of HR policies in many German firms.

The European Union[20]   In the 1990s, the separate countries of the former European Community (EC) were unified into a common market for goods, services, capital, and even labor called the European Union (EU). Tariffs for goods moving across borders from one EU country to another generally disappeared, and employees (with some exceptions) now find it easy to move freely between jobs in the EU countries. The introduction of a single currency—the euro—has further blurred many of these differences. The euro replaced the local currencies of most member countries in early 2002.

In addition to the participative processes (like codetermination) found in some EU countries, European Union law currently requires large firms to consult workers about certain corporate actions such as mass layoffs. However, a new EU directive will greatly expand this requirement. By 2008, more companies—including all those with 50 or more employees in the EU—must "inform and consult" employees about employee-related actions, even if the firms don't operate outside their own borders. And the consultation will then be "ongoing" rather than just for major, strategic decisions.[21]

However, intra-EU differences remain. Many countries have minimum wages while others don't, and workweek hours permitted vary from no maximum in the United Kingdom to 48 per week in Greece and Italy. Other differences exist in minimum number of annual holidays, and minimum advance notice of termination. Employment contracts are another big difference. For most U.S. positions, written correspondence is normally limited to a short letter listing the date, job title, and initial compensation for the new hire.[22] In most European countries, employers are usually required to provide a detailed statement of the job. The European Union, for instance, has a directive requiring employers to provide such a statement (including details of terms and conditions of work) within two months of the employee's starting work.[23]

The EU's increasing internal coordination will gradually reduce these differences. However, cultural differences will remain, and will translate into differences in management styles and practices. Such differences "may strain relations between headquarters and subsidiary personnel or make a manager less effective when working abroad than at home."[24] Firms therefore risk operational problems abroad unless they take special steps to select, train, and compensate their international employees and assignees. We'll turn to how to do this next.

IMPROVING INTERNATIONAL ASSIGNMENTS THROUGH SELECTION

International assignments are the heart of international HR, and it's therefore disconcerting to see how often such assignments fail. U.S. expatriates' assignments that end early (the failure rate) range from 16% to 50%, and the direct costs of each such failure can reach hundreds of thousands of dollars or more.[25] (In another survey, European and Japanese multinationals reported lower failure rates, with only about one-sixth of Japanese multinationals and 3% of European multinationals reporting more than a 10% expatriate recall rate.[26])

The exact number of failures is hard to quantify, in part because "failure" means different things to different people. An early return rate is perhaps the most obvious indicator. However, some expatriates may fail less conspicuously, quietly running up the hidden costs of reduced productivity and poisoned customer and staff relations.[27]

Why International Assignments Fail

Discovering why such assignments fail is therefore an important research task, and experts have made considerable progress. Personality is one factor. For example, in a study of 143 expatriate employees, extroverted, agreeable, and emotionally stable individuals were less likely to want to leave early.[28] And the person's intentions are important: For example, people who want expatriate careers try harder to adjust to such a life.[29] Nonwork factors like family pressures usually loom large in expatriate failures. In one study, U.S. managers listed, in descending order of importance for leaving early: inability of spouse to adjust, managers' inability to adjust, other family problems, managers' personal or emotional immaturity, and inability to cope with larger overseas responsibility.[30] Managers of European firms emphasized only the inability of the manager's spouse to adjust as an explanation for the expatriate's failed assignment. Other studies similarly emphasize dissatisfied spouses' effects on the international assignment.[31]

These findings underscore a truism regarding international assignee selection: It's usually not incompetence, but family and personal problems that undermine the international assignee. As one expert puts it:

> The selection process is fundamentally flawed. . . . Expatriate assignments rarely fail because the person cannot accommodate to the technical

demands of the job. The expatriate selections are made by line managers based on technical competence. They fail because of family and personal issues and lack of cultural skills that haven't been part of the [selection] process.[32]

Yet while nonwork aspects of foreign assignments (like living conditions in general, housing conditions, health care, and the adjustment of the spouse or significant other) can prompt assignees to leave early, that result certainly isn't inevitable. Providing realistic previews of what to expect, careful screening, improved orientation, and improved benefits packages are some obvious solutions. One way to reduce assignment problems is simply to shorten the length of the assignment, something employers are doing. A recent survey reports that 23% of the employers' overseas assignments lasted over three years, down from 32% in 1996.[33]

International Staffing: Home or Local?

Multinational companies (MNCs) employ several types of international managers. **Locals** are citizens of the countries where they are working. **Expatriates** are noncitizens of the countries in which they are working.[34] **Home-country nationals** are citizens of the country in which the multinational company has its headquarters.[35] **Third-country nationals** are citizens of a country other than the parent or the host country—for example, a British executive working in the Tokyo branch of a U.S. multinational bank.[36] Expatriates still represent a minority of multinationals' managers. Thus, "most managerial positions are filled by locals rather than expatriates in both headquarters or foreign subsidiary operations."[37]

There are several reasons to rely on local managers to fill your foreign subsidiary's management ranks. Many people don't want to work in a foreign country, and the cost of using expatriates is usually far greater than the cost of using local workers.[38] Locals may view the multinational as a "better citizen" if it uses local management talent, and some governments even press for the "nativization" of local management.[39] There may also be a fear that expatriates, knowing they're posted to the foreign subsidiary for only a few years, may overemphasize short-term projects rather than more necessary long-term tasks.[40]

Yet there are also reasons for using expatriates—either home-country or third-county nationals—for staffing subsidiaries. The major reason is usually technical competence. In other words, employers often can't find local candidates with the required technical qualifications.[41] Multinationals also view a successful stint abroad as a required step in developing top managers. (For instance, after a term abroad, the head of General Electric's Asia-Pacific region was transferred back to a top executive position as vice chairman at GE.) Control is another important reason to use expatriates. The assumption is that home-office managers are already steeped in the firm's policies and culture, and thus more likely to implement headquarters' instructions and ways of doing things.

Values and International Staffing Policy

Experts sometimes classify top executives' values as **ethnocentric, polycentric,** or **geocentric,** and these values translate into corresponding corporate behaviors and policies.[42] In an ethnocentrically run corporation, "the prevailing attitude is that home country attitudes, management style, knowledge, evaluation criteria, and managers are superior to anything the host country might have to offer."[43] In the polycentric corporation, "there is a conscious belief that only host country managers can ever really understand the culture and behavior of the host country market; therefore, the foreign subsidiary should be managed by local people."[44] Geocentric executives believe they must scour the firm's whole management staff on a global basis, on the assumption that the best candidate for a specific position anywhere may be in any of the countries in which the firm operates.

These values translate into three broad international staffing policies. With an ethnocentric staffing policy, the firm fills key management jobs with parent-country nationals.[45] At Royal Dutch Shell, for instance, most financial officers around the world are Dutch nationals. Reasons given for ethnocentric staffing policies include lack of qualified host-country senior-management talent, a desire to maintain a unified corporate culture and tighter control, and the desire to transfer the parent firm's core competencies (for instance, a specialized manufacturing skill) to a foreign subsidiary more expeditiously.[46]

A polycentric-oriented firm would staff its foreign subsidiaries with host-country nationals, and its home office with parent-country nationals. This may reduce the local cultural misunderstandings that might occur if it used expatriate managers. It will also almost undoubtedly be less expensive.

One expert estimates that an expatriate executive can cost a firm up to three times as much as a domestic executive. This is because of relocation expenses and other expenses such as schooling for children, annual home leave, and the need to pay income taxes in two countries.[47]

A geocentric staffing policy "seeks the best people for key jobs throughout the organization, regardless of nationality"—similar to what Ford Motor Company does.[48] This may let the global firm use its human resources more efficiently by transferring the best person to the open job, wherever he or she may be. It can also help build a stronger and more consistent culture and set of values among the entire global management team.

Values like these translate into other behaviors. For example, the ethnocentric ("we're the best") behaviors of host-country employees had a negative effect on workers' abilities to adjust in one study of 250 international assignees.[49]

Selecting International Managers

The processes firms use to select managers for their domestic and foreign operations obviously have many similarities. For either assignment, the candidate should have the technical knowledge and skills to do the job, and the intelligence and people skills to be a successful manager.[50]

However, we've seen that foreign assignments are different. There is the need to cope with colleagues whose culture may be different from one's own, and the stress that being alone in a foreign land can put on the single manager. And if spouse and children will share the assignment, there are the complexities and pressures that the family will have to confront, from learning a new language to finding new friends and attending new schools.

Selecting managers for these assignments therefore sometimes means testing them for traits that predict success in adapting to new environments. One study asked 338 international assignees from various countries and organizations to specify which traits were important for the success of managers on foreign assignment. The researchers identified five factors that contribute to success in such assignments: job knowledge and motivation, relational skills, flexibility/adaptability, extracultural openness, and family situation (spouse's positive opinion, willingness of spouse to live abroad, and so on; Figure M.1 shows some of the specific items that make up each of the five factors).[51] The five factors were not equally important in the foreign assignee's success, according to the assignees. "Family situation was generally found to be the most important factor, a finding consistent with other research on international assignments and transfers."[52]

With flexibility and adaptability often appearing high on results in studies like these, adaptability screening is sometimes part of the expatriate screening process. Often conducted by a psychologist or psychiatrist, adaptability screening aims to

Figure M.1 Five Factors and Specific Items Important to International Assignees' Success

I) Job Knowledge and Motivation
Managerial ability
Organizational ability
Imagination
Creativity
Administrative skills
Alertness
Responsibility
Industriousness
Initiative and energy
High motivation
Frankness
Belief in mission and job
Perseverance

II) Relational Skills
Respect
Courtesy and fact
Display of respect
Kindness
Empathy
Nonjudgmentalness
Integrity
Confidence

III) Flexibility/Adaptability
Resourcefulness
Ability to deal with stress
Flexibility
Emotional stability
Willingness to change
Tolerance for ambiguity
Adaptability
Independence
Dependability
Political sensitivity
Positive self-image

IV) Extracultural Openness
Variety of outside interests
Interest in foreign cultures
Openness
Knowledge of local language(s)
Outgoingness and extroversion
Overseas experience

V) Family Situation
Adaptability of spouse and family
Spouse's positive opinion
Willingness of spouse to live abroad
Stable marriage

Source: Adapted from Arthur Winfred Jr., and Winston Bennett Jr., "The International Assignee: The Relative Importance of Factors Perceived to Contribute to Success," *Personnel Psychology* 48 (1995): 106–7.

assess the assignee's (and spouse's) probable success in handling the foreign transfer, and to alert them to issues (such as the impact on children) the move may involve.[53] Here, experience is often the best predictor of future success. Companies like Colgate-Palmolive therefore look for overseas candidates whose work and nonwork experience, education, and language skills already demonstrate a commitment to and facility for living and working with different cultures.[54] Even several successful summers spent traveling overseas or participating in foreign student programs might provide some basis to believe that the potential transferee can adjust when he or she arrives overseas.

Many firms also use paper-and-pencil tests such as the Overseas Assignment Inventory. Based on research with more than 7,000 candidates, the test reportedly measures the characteristics and attitudes international assignment candidates should have.[55] Realistic previews about the problems to expect in the new job (such as mandatory private schooling for the children) as well as about the cultural benefits, problems, and idiosyncrasies of the country are another important part of the screening process. The rule, say some experts, should always be to "spell it all out" ahead of time, as many multinationals do for their international transferees.[56]

Unfortunately theory doesn't always translate into practice. The importance of adaptability screening notwithstanding, 70% of respondents in one survey listed "skills or competencies" as the most important selection criteria when choosing candidates for international assignments. They ranked "job performance" second. The ability to adapt to new cultural conditions—as measured by items like "prior international living experience or assignment," and "familiarity with assignment country"—were rarely ranked as most important or second most important.[57] One study found that selection for positions abroad is so informal that the researchers called it "the coffee machine system": Two colleagues meet at the office coffee machine, strike up a conversation about the possibility of a position abroad, and based on that and little more, a selection decision is made.[58] Perhaps this helps explain the high failure rate of foreign assignees.

General selection procedures also differ from country to country. One study surveyed 959 organizations in 20 countries. Those using structured interviews ranged from 10.3% in Italy to 12.1% in Sweden, 17.1% in Germany, 22.9% in France, 29.2% in Spain, 33% in the United Kingdom, 34.6% in the United States, 37.5% in Hong Kong, 54.8% in Canada, and 59.1% in Australia. On the other hand, some staffing practices (such as using educational qualifications in screening) exhibited little variability across countries.[59]

TRAINING AND MAINTAINING INTERNATIONAL EMPLOYEES

Careful screening is just the first step in ensuring the foreign assignee's success. The employee may then require special training. And, the firm will need special international HR policies for compensating the firm's overseas employees and for maintaining healthy labor relations.

Orienting and Training Employees on International Assignment

When it comes to providing the orientation and training required for success overseas, the practices of most U.S. firms reflect more form than substance. One consultant says that despite many companies' claims, there is generally little or no systematic selection and training for assignments overseas. In one survey, a sample of company executives agreed that international business required that employees be firmly grounded in the economics and practices of foreign countries. However, few of their companies actually provide such training to their employees.[60] A survey of U.S. companies that assign employees abroad found that only 42% have a "formal program for briefing employees regarding conditions in the host country."[61]

What sort of special training do overseas candidates need? One firm specializing in such programs prescribes a four-step approach.[62] Level 1 training focuses on the impact of cultural differences, and on raising trainees' awareness of such differences and their impact on business outcomes. Level 2 aims at getting participants to understand how attitudes (both negative and positive) are formed and how they influence behavior. (For example, unfavorable stereotypes may subconsciously influence how a new manager responds to and treats his or her new foreign subordinates.) Level 3 training provides factual knowledge about the target country, while Level 4 provides skill building in areas like language and adjustment and adaptation skills.

Beyond these special training needs, managers abroad continue to need traditional training and development. At IBM, for instance, such development includes rotating assignments that permit overseas managers to grow professionally. IBM and other firms also have management development centers around the world where executives can hone their skills. And classroom programs (such as those at the London Business School, or at INSEAD in France) provide overseas executives the sorts of educational opportunities (to acquire MBAs, for instance) that similar stateside programs do for their U.S.-based colleagues.

There are several trends in expatriate training and development. First, rather than providing only predeparture cross-cultural training, more firms are providing continuing, in-country cross-cultural training during the early stages of an overseas assignment. Second, employers are using returning managers as resources to cultivate the "global mind-sets" of their home-office staff. For example, automotive equipment producer Bosch holds regular seminars in which newly arrived returnees pass on their knowledge and experience to relocating managers and their families.

There's also increased use of software and the Internet for cross-cultural training. For example, Bridging Cultures is a self-training multimedia package for people who will be traveling and/or living overseas. It uses short video clips to introduce case study intercultural problems, and then guides users to selecting the strategy to best handle the situation. Cross-cultural training firms' Web sites include www.bennettinc.com/indexie.htm; www.livingabroad.com; www.worldwise-inc.com; and www.globaldynamics.com.[63]

International Compensation

The whole area of international compensation presents some tricky problems. On the one hand, there is logic in maintaining companywide pay scales and policies so that, for instance, divisional marketing directors throughout the world are paid within the same narrow range. This reduces the risk of perceived inequities, and dramatically simplifies the job of keeping track of disparate country-by-country wage rates.

Yet not adapting pay scales to local markets can produce more problems than it solves. The fact is, it can be enormously more expensive to live in some countries (like Japan) than others (like Greece); if these cost-of-living differences aren't considered, it may be almost impossible to get managers to take "high-cost" assignments. However, the answer is usually not just to pay, say, marketing directors more in one country than in another. For one thing, you could get resistance when you tell a marketing director in Tokyo who's earning $3,000 per week to move to your division in Spain, where his or her pay for the same job will drop by half (cost of living notwithstanding). One way to handle the problem is to pay a similar base salary companywide, and then add on various allowances according to individual market conditions.[64]

Yet determining equitable wage rates in many countries is no simple matter. There is a wealth of "packaged" compensation survey data available in the United States, but such data are not so easy to come by overseas. As a result, "one of the greatest difficulties in managing total compensation on a multinational level is establishing a consistent compensation measure between countries that builds credibility both at home and abroad."[65]

Some multinational companies conduct their own local annual compensation surveys. For example, Kraft conducts an annual study of total compensation in Belgium, Germany, Italy, Spain, and the United Kingdom. It focuses on the total compensation paid to each of 10 senior-management positions held by local nationals in these firms. The survey covers all forms of compensation including cash, short- and long-term incentives, retirement plans, medical benefits, and perquisites.[66] This information becomes the basis for annual salary increases and proposed changes in the benefits package.

The Balance Sheet Approach   The most common approach to formulating expatriate pay is to equalize purchasing power across countries, a technique known as the "balance sheet" approach.[67] More than 85% of North American companies reportedly use this approach.

The basic idea is that each expatriate should enjoy the same standard of living he or she would have had at home. With the balance sheet approach, four main home-country groups of expenses—income taxes, housing, goods and services, and discretionary expenses (child support, car payments, and the like)—are the focus of attention. The employer estimates what each of these four expenses is in the expatriate's home country, and what each will be in the host country. The employer then pays any differences—such as additional income taxes or housing expenses.

In practice, this usually boils down to building the expatriate's total compensation around five or six separate components. For example, base salary will normally be in the same range as the manager's home-country salary. In addition, however, there might be an overseas or foreign service premium. The executive receives this as a percentage of his or her base salary, in part to compensate for the cultural and physical adjustments he or she will have to make.[68] There may also be several allowances, including a housing allowance and an education allowance for the expatriate's children. Income taxes represent another area of concern. A U.S. manager posted abroad must often pay not just U.S. taxes but also income taxes in the host country.

Table M.1   The Balance Sheet Approach (Assumes Base Salary of $80,000)

ANNUAL EXPENSE	CHICAGO, USA	BRUSSELS, BELGIUM (U.S.$ EQUIVALENT)	REQUIRED ALLOWANCE
Housing & utilities	$35,000	$ 67,600	$32,600
Goods & services	6,000	9,500	3,500
Taxes	22,400	56,000	33,600
Discretionary income	10,000	10,000	0
Total	$73,400	$143,100	$69,700

Source: Joseph Martocchio, *Strategic Compensation* (Upper Saddle River, NJ: Prentice Hall, 2001), Table 12–15, p. 294.

Table M.1 illustrates the balance sheet approach. In this case, the manager's annual earnings are $80,000, and she faces a U.S. income tax rate of 28%, and a Belgium income tax rate of 70%. The other costs are based on the index of living costs abroad published in the "U.S. Department of State Indexes of Living Costs Abroad, Quarters Allowances, and Hardship Differentials," available at http://www.state.gov.

Incentives   Performance-based incentives tend to be less prevalent abroad. In Europe, firms traditionally emphasize a guaranteed annual salary and companywide bonus.[69] Based on one survey, European compensation directors do want to see more performance-based pay. However, they first have to overcome several problems—including the public relations aspects of such a move (such as selling the idea of more emphasis on performance-based pay). A survey several years ago suggests that U.S. firms that offer overseas managers long-term incentives (80% in this survey) use overall corporate performance criteria (like worldwide profits) when awarding incentive pay—although, ironically, a manager's local performance may have little or no effect on how the company as a whole performs.[70]

What U.S. companies do offer are various incentives to get expatriates to accept and stay on international assignment. Foreign service premiums are financial payments over and above regular base pay, and typically range between 10% and 30% of base pay. Note, though, that since managers tend to get these premiums in small increments with their base pay, it's easy to misconstrue these as regular "pay raises," and then to become disillusioned when the premium stops upon the expatriates' return. Hardship allowances compensate expatriates for exceptionally hard living and working conditions at certain foreign locations. Differentials recently ranged from 5% in Mexico and Greece to 15% in Bombay, 20% in Belarus, and 25% in Sierra Leone.[71] Employers also usually pay these incrementally (with each paycheck), so it's important to make it clear that this is not a permanent raise. Mobility premiums are typically lump-sum payments to reward employees for moving from one assignment to another.

Performance Appraisal of International Managers

Several things complicate the task of appraising an expatriate's performance.[72] For one thing, the question of who actually appraises the expatriate is crucial. Obviously, local management must have some input, but cultural differences here may distort the appraisals. Thus, host-country bosses might evaluate a U.S. expatriate manager in India somewhat negatively if they find his or her use of participative decision making culturally inappropriate. On the other hand, home-office managers may be so out of touch that they can't provide valid appraisals, since they're not fully aware of the situation the manager faces locally. Similarly, the procedure may require measuring the expatriate by objective criteria such as profits and market share, but local events (such as political instability) may affect the manager's performance while remaining "invisible" to home-office staff.

Two experts make these suggestions for improving the expatriate appraisal process:[73]

1. **Stipulate the assignment's difficulty level.** Most would view being an expatriate manager in China as more difficult than working in England; the appraisal should take into account such difficulty-level differences.
2. **Weigh the evaluation more toward the on-site manager's appraisal** than toward the home-site manager's distant perceptions of the employee's performance.
3. If (as is usually the case) the home-office manager does the actual written appraisal, have him or her use a former expatriate from the same overseas location for advice. This helps ensure consideration of unique local issues during the appraisal.
4. **Modify the normal performance criteria** used for that particular position to fit the overseas position. For example, "maintaining positive labor relations" might be more important in Chile, where labor instability is more common, than in the United States.[74]

International Labor Relations

Firms opening subsidiaries abroad will find substantial differences in labor relations practices among the world's countries and regions. This is important; remember that while union membership as a percentage of wage and salary earners is dropping in the United States, it is still relatively high in most countries compared with the United States' 14%: for example, Brazil, 44%; Argentina, 39%; Germany, 29%; Denmark, 80%; Japan, 24%; Egypt, 39%; and Israel, 23%.[75]

The following synopsis illustrates some of these labor relations differences by focusing on Europe. However, similarly significant differences would exist as we move, say, to South and Central America, and to Asia.[76]

- **Centralization.** In general, collective bargaining in Western Europe is likely to be industrywide or regionally oriented, whereas in the United States it generally occurs at the enterprise or plant level.
- **Union structure.** European collective bargaining is more centralized, and local unions tend to have less autonomy and decision-making power than in the United States.
- **Employer organization.** Due to the prevalence of industrywide bargaining in Europe, employer associations (rather than individual employers) tend to perform the employer's collective bargaining role.
- **Union recognition.** Union recognition for collective bargaining in Western Europe is much less formal than in the United States. For example, in Europe

there is no legal mechanism requiring an employer to recognize a particular union; even if a union claims to represent 80% of an employer's workers, another union can try to organize and bargain for the other 20%.

- Union security. Union security in the form of formal closed-shop agreements is largely absent in continental Western Europe.
- Content and scope of bargaining. U.S. labor-management agreements tend to focus on wages, hours, and working conditions. European agreements tend to be brief and to specify minimum wages and employment conditions, leaving individual employers free to institute more generous terms. As noted earlier, industrywide bargaining makes it difficult to write detailed contracts applicable to individual enterprises. And in Europe the government is heavily involved in setting terms of employment (such as vacations and working conditions).
- Grievance handling. In Western Europe grievances occur much less often than in the United States; when raised, legislated machinery outside the union's formal control usually handles them.
- Strikes. With some exceptions, strikes generally occur less frequently in Europe. This is probably due to industrywide bargaining, which generally elicits less management resistance than in the United States, where union demands "cut deeper into the individual enterprise's revenues."[77]
- Worker participation. Worker participation has a long history in Western Europe, where it tends to go far beyond matters such as pay and working conditions. The aim is to create a system by which workers can participate directly in the management of the enterprise. Works councils and codetermination are two examples.[78]

Safety and Fair Treatment Abroad

Making provisions to ensure employee safety and fair treatment doesn't stop at a country's borders. While the U.S. has often taken the lead with respect to matters such as occupational safety, other countries are also quickly adopting such laws. In any event, it's hard to make a legitimate case for being less safety conscious or fair with workers abroad than you are with those at home.

High-profile companies including Nike, Inc., have received bad publicity for—and taken steps to improve—the working conditions, long hours, and low pay rates for factory workers in countries such as Indonesia.[79] Also under discussion is a plan to create the Fair Labor Association. This would be a private entity controlled by both corporate and human rights or labor representatives. It would take steps such as accrediting auditors to certify whether or not companies comply with their code of conduct.[80]

Having employees abroad does raise some unique safety and fair treatment issues, however. For example, kidnapping has become a way of life in some countries south of the U.S. border, and in many places—"Brazil, Nigeria, the Philippines, Russia, and New Guinea, to name a few—street crime is common, although tourists and business people are rarely kidnapped or assassinated."[81] As one security executive at an oil company put it, "It's crucial for a company to understand the local environment, local conditions and what threat exists."[82] Keeping business travelers out of crime and terror's way is a specialty all its own, but suggestions here include:[83]

- Provide expatriates with general training about traveling, living abroad, and the place they're going to, so they're more oriented when they get there.
- Tell them not to draw attention to the fact they're Americans—by wearing flag emblems or T-shirts with American names, or by using American cars, for instance.
- Have travelers arrive at airports as close to departure time as possible and wait in areas away from the main flow of traffic where they're not as easily observed.
- Equip the expatriate's car and home with adequate security systems.
- Tell employees to vary their departure and arrival times and take different routes to and from work.
- Keep employees current on crime and other problems by regularly checking, for example, the State Department's travel advisory service and consular information sheets (http://travel.state.gov/travelwarnings.html). These provide up-to-date information on possible threats in almost every country of the world.
- Advise employees to remain confident at all times: Body language can attract perpetrators, and those who look like victims often become victimized.[84]

Repatriation: Problems and Solutions

Effectively repatriating returning employees is important. Particularly after companies spend hundreds of thousands of dollars helping the person develop international expertise, it's disconcerting to know that perhaps 50% of returnees leave their companies within two years of coming home. In one survey, 76% of employers said providing returnees with opportunities to use their foreign experiences (advising future expatriates, managing projects that involve the former host country, and so on) is the best way to avoid having them leave the firm prematurely.[85] However, that's only part of the solution.[86]

For one thing, expatriates often fear they're "out of sight, out of mind" during an extended foreign stay, and such fears are often well founded. Many firms hurriedly assign returning expatriates to mediocre or makeshift jobs.[87] Perhaps more exasperating is discovering that the firm has promoted the expatriate's former colleagues while he or she was overseas. Even the expatriate's family may undergo a sort of reverse culture shock, as they face the task of picking up old friendships and starting new schools, and giving up the perks of the overseas job, like a company car and driver. Consider Scott Fedje's experience. As an executive with a Fortune 500 apparel manufacturer, he'd spent five years in Hong Kong, and came home to a promotion and pay raise. But "I felt lost," he says. "Most of us who returned went from a position of high responsibility and a dynamic environment to a cubicle, a project, and a whole month to make a single decision." People he had worked with at the home office five years before had moved on, and his new position lacked the intellectual stimulation he got during five years in Hong Kong. He resigned a few months later.[88]

Progressive multinationals anticipate and avoid these problems by taking several sensible steps:[89]

- Have written repatriation agreements. These guarantee in writing that the international assignee will not be kept abroad longer than some period (such as three years), and that on return he or she will be given a mutually acceptable job. Many firms, including Dow Chemical and Union Carbide, use such repatriation agreements.

- Assign a sponsor. The employee should get a sponsor (such as a senior manager at the parent firm's home office) whose role is to look after the expatriate while he or she is away. This includes keeping the person apprised of significant company events and changes back home, monitoring his or her career progress and interests, and nominating the person for key openings when he or she is due to come home.
- Provide career counseling. Formal career counseling sessions can ensure that the returnee's new job assignments meet his or her needs.[90]
- Keep communications open. Keep the expatriate "plugged in" to home-office business affairs by providing management meetings around the world, frequent home leave combined with stays at headquarters for specific projects, and regularly scheduled meetings at headquarters.[91]
- Develop reorientation programs. Provide the repatriate and his or her family with a reorientation program to facilitate their adjustment back into the home culture.

Strategy and HR   When Siemens celebrated its 150th anniversary recently, it was, according to its CEO, "a perfect occasion to analyze the enduring qualities that helped us survive so long—and identify what we must have to succeed in the future." As part of this review, one of the central questions was, Which human resource strategies will ensure that Siemens's people—and the company—can succeed in tomorrow's challenging global environment? The answers help illustrate why the concepts and techniques we've discussed in this book are important in supporting a firm's strategy. And, they illustrate how managers apply HR concepts and techniques in global firms. Siemens sums up its basic HR strategy in five points. These show how HR supports Siemens's strategy.

1. A living company is a learning company. The markets in which Siemens does business are changing fast, and the firm's HR processes therefore have to help employees learn on a continuing basis. Siemens uses its system of combined classroom and hands-on apprenticeship training around the world. The firm also provides its technical trainees with backgrounds in management, and its management trainees with schooling in technology. It offers its employees extensive continuing education and management development, "so they always keep up with market needs, wherever they work. . . ."

2. Global teamwork is the key to developing and using all the potential of the firm's human resources. At Siemens, teamwork "means breaking down all the traditional barriers within the corporate world"—employees must be able to work across divisions, across disciplines, and across regions. This means employees have to understand the whole process, not just bits and pieces. This in turn means Siemens employees have to assume more responsibility, which in turn means the firm must provide extensive training and development so its employees can handle added responsibilities. Optimizing global teamwork also means taking steps to ensure that all employees feel they're part of a strong, unifying corporate identity. Siemens accomplishes this in part by bringing together managers from around the world for various management development activities.

3. Redefine management to meet the challenges of globalization. To help it do this, Siemens instituted regular strategic performance assessments that encourage each employee to develop his or her potential. The firm's "management dialogue process" provides regular feedback from the bottom to the top to let Siemens managers know how they are doing—and how they can improve.

4. Long-term growth and profitability depend on achieving a balance of interests. Building shareholder value is important, but "we can be profitable only with creative, satisfied, and highly motivated people." Providing challenging growth opportunities and a supportive work environment are therefore cornerstones on which the firm builds its HR practices.

5. A climate of mutual respect is the basis of all relationships—within the company and with society. At Siemens (and at other firms), "the wealth of nationalities, cultures, languages, and outlooks represented by our people is one of our most valuable assets. This great diversity demands openness, transparency, and fairness in the way we deal with one another."[92]

REVIEW

Summary

1. International business is important to almost every business today. This confronts managers with many new challenges, including coordinating production, sales, and financial operations on a worldwide basis. As a result, companies today have pressing international HR needs with respect to selecting, training, paying, and repatriating global employees.

2. Intercountry differences affect a company's HR management processes. Cultural factors suggest differences in values, attitudes, and therefore behaviors and reactions of people from country to country. Economic and labor cost factors help determine whether HR's emphasis should be on efficiency, commitment building, or some other approach. Industrial relations and specifically the relationship between the worker, the union, and the employer influence the nature of a company's specific HR policies from country to country.

3. A large percentage of expatriate assignments fail, but the batting average can be improved through careful selection. There are various sources HR can use to staff domestic and foreign subsidiaries. Often managerial positions are filled by locals rather than expatriates, but this is not always the case.

4. Selecting managers for expatriate assignments means screening them for traits that predict success in adapting to dramatically new environments. Such traits include adaptability and flexibility, cultural toughness, self-orientation, job knowledge and motivation, relational skills, extracultural openness, and family situation. Adaptability screening focusing on the family's probable success in handling the foreign assignment can be an especially important step in the selection process.

5. Training for overseas managers typically focuses on cultural differences, on how attitudes influence behavior, and on factual knowledge about the target country. The most common approach to formulating expatriate pay is to equalize purchasing power across countries, a technique known as the balance sheet approach. The employer

estimates expenses for income taxes, housing, goods and services, and reserve, and pays supplements to the expatriate in such a way as to maintain the same standard of living he or she would have had at home.

6. The expatriate appraisal process can be complicated by the need to have both local and home-office supervisors provide input into the performance review. Suggestions for improving the process include stipulating difficulty level, weighing the on-site manager's appraisal more heavily, and having the home-site manager get background advice from managers familiar with the location abroad before completing the expatriate's appraisal.

7. Repatriation problems are common, but you can minimize them. They include the often well-founded fear that the expatriate is "out of sight, out of mind" and difficulties in reassimilating the expatriate's family back into the home-country culture. Suggestions for avoiding these problems include using repatriation agreements, assigning a sponsor, offering career counseling, and keeping the expatriate plugged in to home-office business.

KEY TERMS

- works councils
- codetermination
- locals

- expatriates
- home-country nationals
- third-country nationals

- ethnocentric
- polycentric
- geocentric

DISCUSSION QUESTIONS AND EXERCISES

1. What intercountry differences affect HR manager? Give several examples of how each may specifically affect HR manager.
2. You are the HR manager of a firm that is about to send its first employees overseas to staff a new subsidiary. Your boss, the president, asks you why such assignments often fail, and what you plan to do to avoid such failures. How do you respond?
3. What special training do overseas candidates need? In what ways is such training similar to and different from traditional diversity training?
4. How does appraising an expatriate's performance differ from appraising that of a home-office manager? How would you avoid some of the unique problems of appraising the expatriate's performance?
5. Working individually or in groups, write an expatriation and repatriation plan for your professor, whom your school is sending to Bulgaria to teach HR for the next three years.
6. Give three specific examples of multinational corporations in your area. Check in the library or on the Internet or with each firm to determine in what countries these firms have operations, and explain the nature of some of their operations, and whatever you can find out about their international HR policies.
7. Choose three traits useful for selecting international assignees, and create a straightforward test to screen candidates for these traits.
8. Use a library or Internet source to determine the relative cost of living in five countries as of this year, and explain the implications of such differences for drafting a pay plan for managers being sent to each country.

APPLICATION EXERCISES

Case Incident — "Boss, I Think We Have a Problem"

Central Steel Door Corporation has been in business for about 20 years, successfully selling a line of steel industrial-grade doors, as well as the hardware and fittings required for them. Focusing mostly in the United States and Canada, the company had gradually increased its presence from the New York City area, first into New England and then down the Atlantic Coast, then through the Midwest and West, and finally into Canada. The company's basic expansion strategy was always the same: Choose an area, open a distribution center, hire a regional sales manager, then let that regional sales manager help staff the distribution center and hire local sales reps.

Unfortunately, the company's traditional success in finding sales help has not extended to its overseas operations. With the introduction of the new European currency, Mel Fisher, president of Central Steel Door, decided to expand his company abroad, into Europe. However, the expansion has not gone smoothly at all. He tried for three weeks to find a sales manager by advertising in the *International Herald Tribune,* which is read by businesspeople in Europe and by American expatriates living and working in Europe. Although the ads placed in the *Tribune* also run for about a month on the *Tribune's* Internet Web site, Mr. Fisher so far has received only five applications. One came from a possibly viable candidate, whereas four came from candidates to whom Mr. Fisher refers as "lost souls"— people who seem to have spent most of their time traveling restlessly from country to country sipping espresso in sidewalk cafés. When asked what he had done for the last three years, one told Mr. Fisher he'd been on a "walkabout."

Other aspects of his international HR activities have been equally problematic. Fisher alienated two of his U.S. sales managers by sending them to Europe to temporarily run the European operations, but neglected to work out a compensation package that would cover their relatively high living expenses in Germany and Belgium. One ended up staying the better part of the year, and Mr. Fisher was rudely surprised to be informed by the Belgian government that his sales manager owed thousands of dollars in local taxes. The managers had hired about 10 local people to staff each of the two distribution centers. However, without full-time local European sales managers, the level of sales was disappointing, so Fisher decided to fire about half the distribution center employees. That's when he got an emergency phone call from his temporary sales manager in Germany: "I've just been told that all these employees should have had written employment agreements and that in any case we can't fire anyone without at least one year's notice, and the local authorities here are really up in arms. Boss, I think we have a problem." ■

QUESTIONS

1. Based on the chapter and the case incident, compile a list of 10 international HR mistakes Mr. Fisher has made so far.
2. How would you have gone about hiring a European sales manager? Why?
3. What would you do now if you were Mr. Fisher?

1. Heinrich Pierer, "Managing a Global Player in the Age of Information," *Management International Review* (October 15, 1999): 9–12.

2. Karen Roberts, Ellen Kossek, and Cynthia Ozeki, "Managing the Global Workforce: Challenges and Strategies," *Academy of Management Executive* 12, no. 4 (1998): 93–106. See also Mary Ann Von Glinow, Ellen A. Drost, and Mary B. Teagarden, "Best Practices in International HRM: Lessons Learned from a Globally Distributed Consortium on Theory and Practice," *Asia Pacific Journal of HRM* 40, no. 1 (2002): 146–66.

3. Ibid., 94.

4. Nancy Wong, "Mark Your Calendar! Important Task for International HR," *Workforce* (April 2000): 72–74.

5. Charlene Solomon, "Today's Global Mobility," *Global Workforce* (July 1998): 16.

6. "Fifteen Top Emerging Markets," *Global Workforce* (January 1998): 18–21.

7. These are based on Eduard Gaugler, "HR Management: An International Comparison," *Personnel* (August 1988): 24–30. See also Yasuol Kuwahara, "New Developments in Human Resources Management in Japan," *Asia Pacific Journal of Human Resources* 31, no. 2 (1993): 3–11; Charlene Solomon, "How Does Your Global Talent Measure Up?" *Personnel Journal* (October 1994): 96–108.

8. David Ralston, Priscilla Elsass, David Gustafson, Fannie Cheung, and Robert Terpstra, "Eastern Values: A Comparison of Managers in the United States, Hong Kong, and the People's Republic of China," *Journal of Applied Psychology* 71, no. 5 (1992): 664–71.

9. Geert Hofstede, "Cultural Dimensions in People Management," in Vladimir Pucik, Noel Tishy, and Carole Barnett (eds.), *Globalizing Management* (New York: John Wiley & Sons, 1992), p. 143.

10. Randall Schuler, Susan Jackson, Ellen Jackofsky, and John Slocum Jr., "Managing Human Resources in Mexico: A Cultural Understanding," *Business Horizons* (May–June 1996): 55–61.

11. Ibid.

12. Valerie Frazee, "Establishing Relations in Germany," *Global Workforce* (April 1997): 17.

13. Charlene Solomon, "Destination U.S.A.," *Global Workforce* (April 1997): 19–23.

14. Ibid., 21.

15. Annual 2000 figures. www.bls.gov/news.release/ichcc.hr0.htm.

16. "Comparing Employment Practice," *BNA Bulletin to Management* (April 22, 1993): 1.

17. "Vacation Policies Around the Globe," *Global Workforce* (October 1996): 9.

18. Carolyn Hirschman, "When Operating Abroad, Companies Must Adopt European Style HR Plan," *HR News* 20, no. 3 (March 2001): 1, 6.

19. This is discussed in Gaugler, "HR Management," 28. See also Carlos Castillo, "Collective Labor Rights in Latin America and Mexico," *Relations Industrielles/Industrial Relations* 55, no. 1 (winter 2000): 59.

20. See Rae Sedel, "Europe 1992: HR Implications of the European Unification," *Personnel* (October 1989): 19–24; Chris Brewster and Ariane Hegewish, "A Continent of Diversity," *Personnel Management* (January 1993): 36–39; http://europa.eu.int/indexen.htm.

21. "Inform, Consult, Impose: Workers' Rights in the EU," *Economist* (June 16, 2001): 3.

22. Alan Chesters, "Employment Contracts—In Writing or Not?" *Global Workforce* (April 1997): 12.

23. Ibid.

24. John Daniels and Lee Radebaugh, *International Business* (Upper Saddle River, NJ: Prentice Hall, 2001), p. 764.

25. For a discussion, see Margaret Shaffer and David Harrison, "Expatriates' Psychological Withdrawal from International Assignments: Work, Nonwork, and Family Influences," *Personnel Psychology* 51 (1998): 87–118.

26. R. L. Tung, "Selection and Training Procedures of U.S., European, and Japanese Multinationals," *California Management Review* 25 (1982): 51–71; see also Jennifer Laabs, "Like Finding a Needle in a

Haystack: Recruiting in the Global Village," *Workforce* 77, no. 4 (April 1998): 30–33.

27. Tung, "Selection and Training Procedures," 88. See also Jan Selmer, "Expatriate Selection: Back to Basics?" *International Journal of Human Resource Management* 12, no. 8 (December 2001): 1219–33.

28. Paula Caliguri, "The Big Five Personality Characteristics as Predictors of Expatriates' Desire to Terminate the Assignment and Supervisor-Rated Performance," *Personnel Psychology* 53, no. 1 (spring 2000): 67–88.

29. Jan Selmer, "Expatriation: Corporate Policy, Personal Intentions and International Adjustment," *International Journal of Human Resource Management* 9, no. 6 (December 1998): 997–1007.

30. Discussed in Charles Hill, *International Business* (Burr Ridge, IL: Irwin, 1994), pp. 511–15.

31. Charlene Solomon, "One Assignment, Two Lives," *Personnel Journal* (May 1996): 36–47; Michael Harvey, "Dual-Career Couples During International Relocation: The Trailing Spouse," *International Journal of Human Resource Management* 9, no. 2 (April 1998): 309–30.

32. Michael Schell, quoted in Charlene Solomon, "Success Abroad Depends on More Than Job Skills," 52.

33. Carla Joinson, "Cutting Down the Days," *HR Magazine* (April 2000): 90–97; "Employers Shortened Assignments of Workers Abroad," *BNA Bulletin to Management* (January 4, 2001): 7.

34. Daniels and Radebaugh, *International Business*, 767. See also Castillo, "Collective Labor Rights," 59.

35. Arvind Phatak, *International Dimensions of Management* (Boston: PWS Kent, 1989), pp. 106–7. See also Johngseok Bae and Chris Rowley, "The Impact of Globalization on HRM: The Case of South Korea," *Journal of World Business* 36, no. 4 (winter 2001): 402–28.

36. Ibid., 106.

37. Daniels and Radebaugh, *International Business*, 767.

38. Ibid., 769; Phatak, *International Dimensions*, 106.

39. Phatak, *International Dimensions*, 108.

40. Daniels and Radebaugh, *International Business*, 769.

41. Ibid. Phatak, *International Dimensions*, 106.

42. Howard Perlmutter, "The Torturous Evolution of the Multinational Corporation," *Columbia Journal of World Business* 3, no. 1 (January–February 1969): 11–14, discussed in Phatak, *International Dimensions*, 129; Carol Leininger and Rue Yuan, "Aligning International Editing Efforts with Global Business Strategies," *IEEE Transactions on Professional Communication* 41, no. 1 (March 1998): 16–24.

43. Phatak, *International Dimensions*, 129.

44. Ibid.

45. Hill, *International Business*, 507.

46. Ibid., 507–10.

47. Ibid., 509.

48. Ibid. See also Michael Harvey et al., "An Innovative Global Management Staffing System: A Competency-Based Perspective," *Human Resource Management* 39, no. 4 (winter 2000): 381–94.

49. Gary Florkowski and Daniel Fogel, "Expatriate Adjustments and Commitment: The Role of Host Unit Treatment," *International Journal of Human Resource Management* 10, no. 5 (October 1999): 783–807.

50. Phatak, *International Dimensions*, 113; Charlene Solomon, "Staff Selection Impacts Global Success," *Personnel Journal* (January 1994): 88–101. For another view, see Anne Harzing, "The Persistent Myth of High Expatriate Failure Rates," *International Journal of Human Resource Management* 6, no. 2 (May 1995): 457–74; Mason Carpenter et al., "International Assignment Experience at the Top Can Make a Bottom-Line Difference," *Human Resource Management* 30, no. 2–3 (summer–fall 2000): 277–85.

51. Arthur Winfred Jr. and Winston Bennett Jr., "The International Assignee: The Relative Importance of Factors Perceived to Contribute to Success," *Personnel Psychology* 48 (1995): 99–114; table on

pp. 106–7. See also Edwin Davison and Betty Punnett, "International Assignments: Is There a Role for Gender and Race in Decisions?" *International Journal of Human Resource Management* 6, no. 2 (May 1995): 411–41.

52. Arthur and Bennett, "The International Assignee," 110; Gretchen Spreitzer, Morgan McCall Jr., and Joan Mahoney, "Early Identification of International Executive Potential," *Journal of Applied Psychology* 82, no. 1 (1997): 6–29.

53. Phatak, *International Dimensions*, 119.

54. See, for example, Blocklyn, "Developing the International Executive," 45.

55. Discussed in Madelyn Callahan, "Preparing the New Global Manager," *Training and Development Journal* (March 1989): 30. The publisher of the inventory is the New York consulting firm Moran, Stahl & Boyer. For a discussion of how firms such as Coca-Cola recruit and develop international managers, see Jennifer Laabs, "The Global Talent Search," *Personnel Journal* (August 1991): 38–44; T. S. Cahn, "Developing International Managers: A Partnership Approach," *Journal of Management Development* 13, no. 3 (1994): 38–46.

56. Blocklyn, "Developing the International Executive," 45.

57. "International Assignment Policies and Practices," *BNA Bulletin to Management* (May 1, 1997): 140–41, based on a survey by Organization Resources Counselors, Inc., New York City.

58. Hilary Harris and Chris Brewster, "The Coffee Machine System: How International Selection Really Works," *International Journal of Human Resource Management* 10, no. 3 (June 1999): 488–500.

59. Anne Marie Ryan et al., "An International Look at Selection Practices: Nation and Culture as Explanations for Variability in Practice," *Personnel Psychology* 52 (1999): 359–91.

60. Callahan, "Preparing the New Global Manager," 29–30. See also Charlene Solomon, "Global Operations Demand That HR Rethink Diversity," *Personnel Journal* (July 1994): 40–50.

61. Valerie Frazee, "Expats Are Expected to Dive Right In," *Personnel Journal* (December 1996): 31.

62. This is based on ibid., 30. See also Rita Bennett et al., "Cross-Cultural Training: A Critical Step in Ensuring the Success of National Assignments," *Human Resource Management* 39, no. 2–3 (summer–fall 2000): 239–50.

63. Mark Mendenhall and Gunther Stahl, "Expatriate Training and Development: Where Do We Go from Here?" *Human Resource Management* 39, no. 2–3 (summer–fall 2000): 251–65.

64. James Stoner and R. Edward Freeman, *Management*, 4th ed. (Upper Saddle River, NJ: Prentice Hall, 1989), p. 783. See also John Cartland, "Reward Policies in a Global Corporation," *Business Quarterly* (autumn 1993): 93–96; Laura Mazur, "Europay," *Across the Board* (January 1995): 40–43; Joseph Martocchio, *Strategic Compensation* (Upper Saddle River, NJ: Prentice Hall, 2001).

65. Hewitt Associates, "On Compensation," (May 1989): 1 (Hewitt Associates, 86–87 East Via De Ventura, Scottsdale, AZ 85258). See also Carolyn Gould, "Expat Pay Plans to Suffer Cutback," *Workforce* (September 1999): 40–46.

66. Hewitt Associates, "On Compensation," 2. See also Stephenie Overman, "Check the Vitality of Health Care Abroad," *HR Magazine* (March 2000): 77–84.

67. Hill, *International Business*, 519–20; Valerie Frazee, "Is the Balance Sheet Right for Your Expats?" *Global Workforce* (September 1998): 19–26; Stephenie Overman, "Focus on International HR," *HR Magazine* (March 2000): 87–92.

68. Phatak, *International Dimensions*, 134.

69. Except as noted, this section is based on Martocchio, *Strategic Compensation*, 280–83.

70. This is based on Brian Brooks, "Long-Term Incentives: International Executives Need Them, Too," *Personnel* (August 1988): 40–42. See also James Ward and Mark Blumenthal, "Localization: A Study in Cost Containment," *Innovations in International Compensation* 17, no. 4 (November 1991): 324; Mazur, "Europay," 40–43.

71. U.S. Department of State, "U.S. Department of State Indexes of Living Costs Abroad, Quarters Allowances, and Hardship Differentials" (Washington, DC: U.S. Government Printing Office, October 1999). Available online at http://www.state.gov

72. Except as noted, this is based on Gary Addou and Mark Mendenhall, "Expatriate Performance Appraisal: Problems and Solutions," in Mark Mendenhall and Gary Addou, *International Human Resource Management* (Boston: PWS Kent Publishing, 1991), pp. 364–74.

73. Ibid., 366. See also Maddy Janssens, "Evaluating International Managers' Performance: Parent Company Standards as Control Mechanism," *International Journal of Human Resource Management* 5, no. 4 (December 1994): 853–73.

74. Addou and Mendenhall, "Expatriate Appraisal," 370.

75. "Union Membership Around the World," *BNA Bulletin to Management* (November 13, 1997): 364–65.

76. Robert Sauer and Keith Voelker, *Labor Relations: Structure and Process* (New York: Macmillan, 1993), pp. 510–25.

77. Ibid., 516. See also Marino Regini, "Human Resource Management and Industrial Relations in European Companies," *International Journal of Human Resource Management* 4, no. 3 (September 1993): 555–68.

78. Quoted from ibid., 519.

79. Aaron Bernstein, "A Floor Under Foreign Factories?" *Business Week* (November 2, 1998): 126–28.

80. Ibid., 126.

81. Samuel Greengard, "Mission Possible: Protecting Employees Abroad," *Workforce* (August 1997): 30–32.

82. Ibid., 32.

83. These are based on or quoted from ibid., 32.

84. Ibid., 32.

85. Andrea Poe, "Welcome Back," *HR Magazine* (March 2000): 94–105.

86. Ibid. See also Linda Stroh, "Predicting Turnover Among Repatriates: Can Organizations Affect Retention Rates?" *International Journal of Human Resource Management* 6, no. 2 (May 1995): 443–56; J. Stewart Black and Hal Gregerson, "The Right Way to Manage Expats," *Harvard Business Review* (March–April 1999): 52–62.

87. Phatak, *International Dimensions*, 124. See also Reyer Swaak, "Today's Expatriate Families: Dual Careers and Other Obstacles," *Compensation and Benefits Review* 27, no. 3 (May 1995): 21–26; Michael Harvey et al., "Strategic Global Human Resource Management: The Role of Inpatriate Managers," *Human Resource Management Review* 10, no. 2 (2000): 153–75; Marja Tahvanainen, "Expatriate Performance Management: The Case of Nokia Telecommunications," *Human Resource Management* 39, nos. 2, 3, (summer–fall 2000): 267–75.

88. Jobert Abueva, "Many Repatriations Fail, at Huge Cost to Companies," *New York Times* (May 17, 2000): E1.

89. These are based on Briscoe, *International Human Resource Management*, 66; Phatak, *International Dimensions*, 124; Daniels and Radebaugh, *International Business*, 772; Valerie Frazee, "Welcome Your Repatriates Home," *Global Workforce* (April 1997): 24–28.

90. Briscoe, *International Human Resource Management*, 66. See also Yehuda Baruch and Yochanan Altman, "Expatriation and Repatriation in MNCs: A Taxonomy," *Human Resource Management* 41, no. 2 (summer 2002): 239–59.

91. Phatak, *International Dimensions*, 126; Hal Gregersen and Linda Stroh, "Coming Home to the Arctic Cold: Antecedents to Finnish Expatriate and Spouse Repatriation Adjustment," *Personnel Psychology* 50 (1997): 651.

92. Heinrich Pierer, "Managing a Global Player in the Age of Information," *Management International Review* (October 15, 1999): 9–12.

GLOSSARY

A

action learning A training technique by which management trainees are allowed to work full time analyzing and solving problems in other departments. [170]

adverse impact The overall impact of employer practices that result in significantly higher percentages of members of minorities and other protected groups being rejected for employment, placement, or promotion. [41]

affirmative action Steps that are taken for the purpose of eliminating the present effects of past discrimination. [29]

AFL-CIO A voluntary federation in the United States of about 100 national and international (i.e., with branches in Canada) unions. [262]

Age Discrimination in Employment Act of 1967 The act prohibiting arbitrary age discrimination and specifically protecting individuals over 40 years old. [29]

agency shop A form of union security in which employees who do not belong to the union must still pay union dues on the assumption that union efforts benefit all workers. [261]

Albemarle Paper Company v. Moody Supreme Court case in which it was ruled that the validity of job tests must be documented and that employee performance standards must be unambiguous. [36]

alternation ranking method An appraisal process in which the employee who is highest on a trait being measured and also the one who is lowest is identified, alternating between highest and lowest until all employees to be rated have been addressed. [198]

Americans with Disabilities Act (ADA) The act requiring employers to make reasonable accommodations for disabled employees; it prohibits discrimination against disabled persons. [38]

application form The form that provides information on education, prior work record, and skills. [94]

appraisal interview The culmination of an appraisal, in which the supervisor and subordinate review the appraisal and make plans to remedy deficiencies and reinforce strengths. [205]

arbitration The most definitive type of third-party intervention, in which the arbitrator usually has the power to determine and dictate the settlement terms. [278]

authority The right to make decisions, direct others' work, and give orders. [3]

authorization cards In order to petition for a union election, the union must show that at least 30% of employees may be interested in being unionized. Employees indicate this interest by signing authorization cards. [268]

B

bargaining unit The group of employees the union will be authorized to represent. [269]

behavior modeling A training technique in which trainees are first shown good management techniques in a film, are then asked to play roles in a simulated situation, and are then given feedback and praise by their supervisor. [173]

benefits Indirect financial payments given to employees. They may include health and life insurance, vacation, pension, education plans, and discounts on company products, for instance. [239]

bona fide occupational qualification (BFOQ) Requirement that an employee be of a certain religion, sex, or national origin where that is reasonably necessary to the organization's normal operation. Specified by the 1964 Civil Rights Act. [42]

boycott The combined refusal by employees and other interested parties to buy or use the employer's products. [279]

burnout The total depletion of physical and mental resources caused by excessive striving to reach an unrealistic work-related goal. [343]

business necessity Justification for an otherwise discriminatory employment practice, provided there is an overriding legitimate business purpose. [43]

C

career management A process for enabling the employees to better understand and develop their career skills and interests, and he used the skills and interests most effectively both within the company and, if necessary, after they leave the firm. [210]

case study method A development method in which the manager is presented with a written description of an organizational problem to diagnose and solve. [171]

central tendency The tendency to rate all employees about average. [207]

citations Summons informing employers and employees of the regulations and standards that have been violated in the workplace. [331]

Civil Rights Act of 1964, Title VII Rights guaranteed by the Constitution of the United States that makes it unlawful practice for an employer to discriminate against any individual with respect to hiring, compensation, terms, conditions, or privileges of employment because of race, color, religion, sex, or nation. [224]

Civil Rights Act of 1991 (CRA 1991) This act places burden of proof back on employers and permits compensatory and punitive damages. [36]

closed shop A form of union security in which the company can hire only union members. This was outlawed in 1947 but still exists in some industries (such as printing). [261]

codetermination The right to a voice in setting company policies; workers generally elect representatives to the superadvisory board. [362]

collective bargaining The process through which representatives of management and the union meet to negotiate a labor agreement. [274]

compensable factor A fundamental, compensable element of a job, such as skills, effort, responsibility, and working conditions. [228]

competitive advantage The basis for superiority over competitors and thus for hoping to claim certain customers. [10]

content validity A test that is *content valid* is one in which the test contains a fair sample of the tasks and skills actually needed for the job in question. [119]

controlled experimentation Formal methods for testing the effectiveness of a training program, preferably with before-and-after tests and a control group. [179]

criterion validity A type of validity based on showing that scores on the test (*predictors*) are related to job performance (*criterion*). [119]

critical incident method Keeping a record of uncommonly good or undesirable examples of an employee's work-related behavior and reviewing it with the employee at predetermined times. [202]

D

defined benefit pension plan A plan that contains a formula for determining retirement benefits. [244]

defined contribution plan A plan in which the employer's contribution to employees' retirement or savings funds is specified. [244]

discipline A procedure that corrects or punishes a subordinate for violating a rule or procedure. [308]

dismissal Involuntary termination of an employee's employment with the firm. [311]

disparate impact An unintentional disparity between the proportion of a protected group applying for a position and the proportion getting the job. [42]

disparate treatment An intentional disparity between the proportion of a protected group and the proportion getting the job. [42]

downsizing Refers to the process of reducing, usually dramatically, the number of people employed by the firm. [316]

E

employee orientation A procedure for providing new employees with basic background information about the firm. [158]

Employee Retirement Income Security Act (ERISA) Signed into law by President Ford in 1974 to require that pension rights be vested, and protected by a government agency, Pension Benefits Guarantee Corporation. [237]

employee stock ownership plan (ESOP) A corporation contributes shares of its own stock to a trust in which additional contributions are made annually. The trust distributes the stock to employees upon retirement or separation from service. [237]

Equal Employment Opportunity Commission (EEOC) The commission, created by Title VII, empowered to investigate job discrimination complaints and sue on behalf of complainants. [28,224]

Equal Pay Act of 1963 An amendment to the Fair Labor Standards Act designed to require equal pay for women doing the same work as men. [28]

ethics The study of standards of conduct and moral judgment; also the standards of right conduct. [294]

ethnocentric A management philosophy that leads to the creation of home market–oriented firms. [364]

exit interviews Interviews conducted by the employer immediately prior to the employee leaving the firm with the aim of better understanding what the employee thinks about the company. [316]

expatriates Non-citizens of the country in which they are working. [364]

F

fact finder In labor relations, a neutral party who studies the issues in a dispute and makes a public recommendation for a reasonable settlement. [278]

Fair Labor Standards Act Congress passed this act in 1936 to provide for minimum wages, maximum hours, overtime pay, and child labor protection. The law has been amended many times and covers most employees. [223]

federal agency guidelines Guidelines issued by federal agencies charged with ensuring compliance with equal employment federal legislation explaining recommended employer procedures in detail. [30]

flexible benefits plan Individualized plans allowed by employers to accommodate employee preferences for benefits. [245]

forced distribution method An appraisal method by which the manager places predetermined percentages of subordinate in performance categories. [200]

G

gain-sharing plan An incentive plan that engages employees in a common effort to achieve productivity objectives and share the gains. [237]

geocentric A staffing policy that seeks the best people for key jobs throughout the organization, regardless of nationality. [364]

good faith bargaining A term that means both parties are communicating and negotiating and that proposals are being matched with counterproposals, with both parties making every reasonable effort to arrive at agreements. It does not mean that either party is compelled to agree to a proposal. [274]

good faith effort strategy Employment strategy aimed at changing practices that have contributed in the past to excluding or underutilizing protected groups. [52]

graphic rating scale A scale that lists a number of traits and a range of performance for each. The employee is then rated by identifying the score that best describes his or her level of performance for each trait. [198]

***Griggs* v. *Duke Power Company* Case** heard by the Supreme Court in which the plaintiff argued that his employer's requirement that coal handlers be high school graduates was unfairly discriminatory. In finding for the plaintiff, the Court ruled that discrimination need not be overt to be illegal, that employment practices must be related to job performance, and that the burden of proof is on the employer to show that hiring standards are job related. [35]

guaranteed fair treatment Employer programs aimed at ensuring that all employees are treated fairly, generally by providing formalized, well-documented, and highly publicized vehicles through which employees can appeal any eligible issues. [308]

H

halo effect A common appraisal problem in which the rating of a subordinate on one trait influences the way the person is rated on other traits. [207]

home-country nationals Citizens of the country in which the multinational company has its headquarters. [364]

human resource management The policies and practices one needs to carry out the "people" or human resource aspects of a management position, including recruiting, screening, training, rewarding, and appraising. [2]

I

illegal bargaining items Items in collective bargaining that are forbidden by law; for example, the clause agreeing to hire "union members exclusively" would be illegal in a right-to-work state. [276]

incentive plan A plan in which a production standard is set for a specific work group, and its members are paid incentives if the group exceeds the production standard. [234]

in-house development centers A company-based method for exposing prospective managers to realistic exercises to develop improved management skills. [175]

insubordination Willful disregard or disobedience of the boss's authority or legitimate orders; criticizing the boss in public. [312]

interview A procedure designed to solicit information from a person's oral responses to oral inquiries. [127]

J

job analysis The procedure for determining the duties and skill requirements of a job and the kind of person who should be hired for it. [66]

job description A list of a job's duties, responsibilities, reporting relationships, working conditions, and supervisory responsibilities—one product of a job analysis. [66]

job evaluation A formal and systematic comparison of jobs to determine the worth of one job relative to another. [128]

job posting Posting notices of job openings on company bulletin boards is an effective recruiting method. [79]

job rotation A management training technique that involves moving a trainee from department to department to broaden his or her experience and identify strong and weak points. [170]

job specification A list of job's "human requirements," that is, the requisite education, skills, personality, and so on—another product of a job analysis. [66]

L

Landrum-Griffin Act The law aimed at protecting union members from possible wrongdoing on the part of their unions. [266]

layoff A situation in which there is a temporary shortage of work and employees are told there is no work for them but that management intends to recall them when work is again available. [316]

learning organization An organization "skilled at creating, acquiring, and transferring knowledge and at modifying its behavior to reflect new knowledge and insights." [176]

line manager A manager who is authorized to direct the work of subordinates and responsible for accomplishing the organization's goals. [3]

lockout A refusal by the employer to provide opportunities to work. [279]

M

management assessment centers A situation in which management candidates are asked to make decisions in hypothetical situations and are scored on their performance. It usually also involves testing and the use of management games. [125]

management by objectives (MBO) A performance management method through which the manager set specific measurable goals with each employee and then periodically discusses the latter is progress toward these goals, usually in an organization wide effort. [202]

management development Any attempt to improve current or future management performance by imparting knowledge, changing attitudes, or increasing skills. [170]

mandatory bargaining items Items in collective bargaining that a party must bargain over if they are introduced by the other party—for example, pay. [276]

mediation Intervention in which a neutral third party tries to assist the principals in reaching agreement. [277]

mentoring Having a senior person to assist and help guide the proteges career. [212]

merit pay (merit raise) Any salary increase awarded to an employee based on his or her individual performance. [236]

N

national emergency strikes Strikes that might "imperil the national health and safety." [265]

National Labor Relations Board (NLRB) The agency created by the Wagner Act to investigate unfair labor practice charges and to provide for secret-ballot elections and majority rule in determining whether or not a firm's employees want a union. [263]

Norris-LaGuardia Act This law marked the beginning of the era of strong encouragement of unions and guaranteed to each employee the right to bargain collectively "free from interference, restraint, or coercion." [263]

O

Occupational Safety and Health Act The law passed by Congress in 1970 "to assure so far as possible every working man and woman in the nation safe and healthful working conditions and to preserve our human resources." [329]

Occupational Safety and Health Administration (OSHA) The agency created within the Department of Labor to set safety and health standards for almost all workers in the United States. [329]

Office of Federal Contract Compliance Programs (OFCCP) The office responsible for implementing executive orders and ensuring compliance of federal contractors. [29]

on-the-job training (OJT) Training a person to learn a job while working at it. [163]

open shop Perhaps the least attractive type of union security from the union's point of view; the workers decide whether or not to join the union, and those who join must pay dues. [262]

opinion surveys Questionnaires that regularly ask employees their opinions about the company, management, and work life. [307]

organizational development (OD) A method aimed at changing the attitudes, values, and beliefs of employees so that employees can improve the organization. [175]

outplacement counseling A systematic process by which a terminated person is trained and counseled in the techniques of self-appraisal and securing a new position. [315]

P

paired comparison method An appraisal method in which he every subordinate to be rated his paired with and compared to every other subordinate on each trait. [200]

peer appraisal Appraisal of an employee by his or her peers. [196]

performance analysis Verifying that there is a performance deficiency and determining whether that deficiency should be rectified through training or through some other means (such as transferring the employee). [161]

performance management The process through which companies ensure that employees are working toward organizational goals. It includes practices through which the manager defines the employees's goals and work, develops the employee's skills and capabilities, evaluates the person's goal directed behavior, and then rewards him or her in a fashion consistent with the companies and the person's needs. [192]

personnel replacement charts Company records showing present performance and promotability of inside candidates for the most important positions. [76]

piecework A system of pay based on the number of items processed by each individual worker in a unit of time, such as items per hour or items per day. [234]

plant closing law The Worker Adjustment and Retraining Notification Act, which requires notifying employees in the event an employer decides to close its facility. [247]

polycentric A management philosophy oriented toward pursuing a limited number of individual foreign markets. [364]

Pregnancy Discrimination Act (PDA) An amendment to Title VII of the Civil Rights Act that prohibits sex discrimination based on "pregnancy, childbirth, or related medical conditions." [29]

Preretirement counseling Employer-sponsored counseling aimed at providing information to ease the passage of employees into retirement. [214]

profit-sharing plan A plan whereby most employees share in the company's profits. [237]

protected class Persons such as minorities and women protected by equal opportunity laws including Title VII. [35]

Q

qualifications inventories Manual or computerized systematic records listing employees' education, career and development interests, languages, special skills, and so on to be used in forecasting inside candidates for promotion. [76]

quota strategy Employment strategy aimed at mandating the same results as the good faith effort strategy through specific hiring and promotion restrictions. [50]

R

ranking method The simplest method of job evaluation that involves ranking each job relative to all other jobs, usually based on overall difficulty. [228]

ratio analysis A forecasting technique for determining future staff needs by using ratios between sales volume and number of employees needed. [75]

reliability The characteristic that refers to the consistency of scores obtained by the same person when retested with the identical or equivalent tests. [119]

retirement The point at which a person gives up work, usually between the ages of 60 to 65, but increasingly earlier today due to firms' early retirement incentive plans. [214]

Right to work The public policy in a number of states that prohibits union security of any kind. [262]

S

salary survey A survey aimed at determining prevailing wage rates. A good salary survey provides specific wage rates for specific jobs. Formal written questionnaire surveys are the most comprehensive, but telephone surveys and newspaper ads are also sources of information. [227]

Scanlon plan An incentive plan developed in 1937 by Joseph Scanlon and designed to encourage cooperation, involvement, and sharing of benefits. [237]

sensitivity training A method for increasing employees' insights into their own behavior by candid discussions in groups led by special trainers. [176]

severance pay A one-time payment some employers provide when terminating an employee. [241]

sexual harassment Harassment on the basis of sex that has the purpose or effect of substantially interfering with a person's work performance or creating an intimidating, hostile, or offensive work environment. [30]

staff manager A manager who assists and advises line managers. [3]

stock option The right to purchase a stated number of shares of company stock at today's price at some time in the future. [235]

strategic human resource management The "linking of HRM with strategic goals and objectives in order to improve business performance and develop organizational cultures." [12]

survey feedback A method that involves surveying employees' attitudes and providing feedback to department managers so that problems can be solved by the managers and employees. [175]

sympathy strike A strike that takes place when one union strikes in support of another's strike. [278]

T

Taft-Hartley Act (Labor Management Relations Act) A law prohibiting union unfair labor practices and enumerating the rights of employees as union members. It also enumerates the rights of employers. [265]

task analysis A detailed study of a job to identify the skills required so that an appropriate training program may be instituted. [169]

team building Improving the effectiveness of teams such as corporate officers and division directors through the use of consultants, interviews, and team-building meetings. [176]

terminate at will The idea, based in law, that the employment relationship can be terminated at will by either the employer or the employee for any reason. [311]

termination interview The interview in which an employee is informed of the fact that he or she has been dismissed. [315]

test validity The accuracy with which a test, interview, and so on measures what it purports to measure or fulfills the function it was designed to fill. [119]

third-country nationals Citizens of a country other than the parent or host country. [364]

Title VII of the 1964 Civil Rights Act The section of the act that says an employer cannot discriminate on the basis of race, color, religion, sex, or national origin with respect to employment. [28]

training The process of teaching new employees the basic skills they need to perform their jobs. [159]

trend analysis Study of a firm's past employment needs over a period of years to predict future needs. [75]

U

union salting A union organizing tactic by which workers who are in fact employed full time by a union as undercover union organizers are hired by unwitting employers. [267]

union shop A form of union security in which the company can hire nonunion people but they must join the union after a prescribed period of time and pay dues. (If they do not, they can be fired.) [261]

unsafe acts Behavior tendencies and undesirable attitudes that cause accidents. [334]

unsafe conditions The mechanical and physical conditions that cause accidents. [333]

upward feedback Having subordinate evaluate their supervisors performance. [197]

V

vestibule/simulated training A method in which trainees learn on the job or on simulated equipment they would use on the job, but are actually trained off the job. [164]

Vietnam Era Veterans' Readjustment Act of 1974 An act requiring that employers with government contracts take affirmative action to hire disabled veterans. [40]

Vocational Rehabilitation Act of 1973 The act requiring certain federal contractors to take affirmative action for disabled persons. [29]

voluntary bargaining items Items in collective bargaining over which bargaining is neither illegal nor mandatory—neither party can be compelled against its wishes to negotiate over those items. [275]

W

wage curve Shows the relationship between the value of the job and the average wage paid for this job. [229]

Wagner Act A law that banned certain types of unfair labor practices and provided for secret-ballot elections and majority rule for determining whether or not a firm's employees want to unionize. [263]

Wards Cove* v. *Atonio U.S. Supreme Court decision that makes it difficult to prove a case of unlawful discrimination against an employer. [35]

wildcat strike An unauthorized strike occurring during the term of a contract. [278]

worker involvement programs Programs that aim to boost organizational effectiveness by getting employees to participate in planning, organizing, and managing their jobs. [169]

workers' compensation Provides income and medical benefits to work-related accident victims or their dependents regardless of fault. [242]

works councils Formal, employee-elected groups of worker representatives that meet monthly with managers to discuss topics ranging from no-smoking policies to layoffs. [362]

wrongful discharge An employee dismissal that does not comply with the law or does not comply with the contractual arrangement stated or implied by the firm via its employment application forms, employee manuals, or other promises. [312]

INDEX

Index